Software Constr
and Data Structures
with
Ada 95

Software Construction and Data Structures with Ada 95

MICHAEL B. FELDMAN
The George Washington University

Addison-Wesley Publishing Company

Reading, Massachusetts • Menlo Park, California • New York
Don Mills, Ontario • Harlow, United Kingdom • Amsterdam • Bonn
Sydney • Singapore • Tokyo • Madrid • San Juan • Milan • Paris

Executive Editor: Lynne Doran Cote
Associate Editor: Katherine Harutunian
Senior Marketing Manager: Tom Ziolkowski
Managing Editor: Jim Rigney
Production Supervisor: Patsy DuMoulin
Prepress Services Buyer: Caroline Fell
Senior Manufacturing Coordinator: Judy Sullivan
Cover Designer: Barbara T. Atkinson
Production Services: Diane Freed
Compositor: Innodata
Illustrator: PD&PS

Library of Congress Cataloging-in-Publication Data

Feldman, Michael B.
    Software construction and data structures with Ada 95 / Michael B.
Feldman
        p.   cm.
    ISBN 0-201-88795-9
    1. Ada (Computer program language)   I. Title
QA76.73.A16F444   1996
005.7´3—dc20   95-51754
                                                                   CIP

Access the latest information about Addison-Wesley books from our World Wide Web page:

http://www.aw.com/cseng/

1 2 3 4 5 6 7 8 9 10 — MA — 99989796

Preface

This text is the first in its field to use Ada 95 throughout as the language of instruction. It is intended for use in a second or third course at the undergraduate level; it is also suitable for self-study. I assume a basic knowledge of Ada—equivalent to the first eight chapters of Feldman/Koffman, *Ada 95: Problem Solving and Program Design, Second Edition*, © Addison-Wesley 1996. I also present a summary of the Ada type system in Chapter 1, and a synopsis of other features, oriented to readers with Pascal experience, in Appendix I. Because many readers may have experience with Ada 83 but not with Ada 95, I point out new features wherever appropriate.

BASIC PRINCIPLES

As the title indicates, this book is about software construction and data structures. It presents most of the classical data structures, together with many algorithms, in a framework based on software construction using the encapsulation principle. Attention is paid to "object thinking" through heavy emphasis on the state and behavior of objects, on the use of private types to achieve encapsulation and tight control over operations, and on the use of generic templates to achieve flexibility and reusability.

Performance prediction ("big O" notation) is introduced early in Chapter 3 and pervades the remaining chapters; the notion of trade-offs—for example, time versus space and speed versus abstraction—is emphasized throughout. The presentation of "big O" is correct but rather informal, avoiding heavy mathematical notation that might intimidate some readers.

Inheritance and dynamic dispatching are introduced in the middle of the book. However, these important techniques are kept under rather tight control, because overuse of inheritance is now seen by industry as potentially creating large and unmanageable hierarchies of classes. Indeed, the growing popularity of the Standard Template Library in the C++ community indicates that generic templates are at least as important as inheritance structures in building understandable and maintainable software. I have tried for balance, with a preference for generics but with due regard for the role of inheritance.

Packages and application programs—about 200 in all—are presented in complete and compilable form; I have an aversion to program fragments. However, for teaching purposes, which are described below, not all programs are fully functional:

- Sometimes only a package interface is given, so that the student can write the implementation as an exercise.
- Sometimes the implementation is provided, but some or all of the operations are "stubbed out" so as to be compilable but nonfunctional. The intention is to direct the student to fill in the code for the stubs.

In developing the packages and application programs, I have chosen a well-balanced mixture of examples from the computer science, data management, and mathematical software domains.

GENERAL ORGANIZATION

Each chapter introduces some data structures concepts, a few ADTs, and one or more applications thereof, all in the context of an integrated approach to Ada 95.

The first chapter is a general introduction to abstraction, with a brief survey of the Ada type system and the way it is described in the Ada standard. Also presented are a few basic Ada 95 topics, describing the changes to the names of standard packages, generalized declaration order, and removal of the write-only restriction on OUT parameters.

The second chapter introduces five simple but very useful ADTs:

- Rational numbers
- Currency (dollars and cents)
- Calendar dates
- Simple video-screen control using ANSI escape sequences
- Simple window management

These ADTs are then used in later chapters.

Chapter 3 discusses recursion and "big O," with emphasis on informal estimation of the performance of an algorithm. "Big O" comparison is done using a keyed-table example, with the table implemented first as an unordered array and then as an ordered one. This example lays the groundwork for the recurring generic keyed table introduced in Chapter 5 and reimplemented in later chapters as appropriate data structures (linked lists, binary search trees, hash tables) are brought into play.

A discussion of the relationship between performance *prediction* and performance *measurement* is given in Section 3.6, along with a package for measuring elapsed CPU time and some suggestions for implementing it on time-shared computers. Ada's standard time services provide only time of day, which is fine for personal computers but useless for measuring CPU time on a shared system. Therefore one must resort to using operating-system services. The example in this section suggests how to do this and some code is given in an appendix for implementing it under UNIX.

Chapter 4 introduces multidimensional and unconstrained arrays, with examples from vectors and matrices, as well a general discussion of storage mappings for multi-dimensional arrays.

Chapter 5 introduces generics, including a generic sort and a generic binary search, and generic ADTs for bit-mapped sets, vectors, and keyed tables.

Chapter 6 introduces variant records, with examples taken from personnel records, geometric shapes, variable-length strings, and metric (dimensioned) quantities. Also introduced here are Ada 95 tagged types, with a revision of the personnel example to show type extension as a much more dynamic kind of variant record.

Chapter 7 introduces queues and stacks, with different implementations—all as generic ADTs, of course. Stacks are used to implement several simple expression-to-RPN translators; queues are applied in a discrete simulation of a supermarket.

Chapters 8 and 9 present dynamic linear linked structures. Chapter 8 introduces the basics. Chapter 9 presents some interesting generic applications—including a reimplementation of the keyed table—as well as introducing Ada 95 unbounded strings, general access types and heterogeneous lists.

Chapter 10 introduces directed graphs, with an application to state graphs.

Chapter 11 presents the basics of binary trees, using expression trees and binary search trees as the main examples. The chapter concludes with an extended example of a cross-referencer, including an example of Ada 95 subprogram pointers to implement finite state machines and other table-driven programming.

Chapter 12 presents some "advanced" examples of trees: threaded binary trees, heaps, AVL trees, and general (nonbinary) trees. The heap is presented as a data structure in its own right, with operations provided in a generic package. An example is given of using this heap package to implement priority queues; the same generic heap package is reused in Chapter 14 to implement heap sort.

Chapter 13 gives a brief introduction to hash tables; Chapter 14 presents a collection of sorting algorithms, classified by their "big Os."

Finally, Chapter 15 gives a brief introduction to concurrent programming. Ada task types and protected types are presented through a series of small examples, followed by two major applications: a bank simulation and the famous Dining Philosophers.

PROGRAM LIBRARY

The packages and programs in this book make up an integrated and coherent program library. The book can be used most effectively by making actual use of the program files, completing the intentionally incomplete ones, building on or modifying them, and so on. To facilitate this approach, students and teachers should have easy access to the roughly 200 program files in electronic form so that no time is wasted in keying them in. To this end, the programs are archived on various Ada-related Internet servers and CD-ROMs.

From Addison-Wesley, via ftp in the directory:

```
ftp://ftp.aw.com/cseng/authors/feldman/cs2-ada
```

From the World Wide Web, which will also include any future support and announcements:

```
http://www.aw.com/cseng/authors/feldman/cs2-ada
```

From the author's ftp site at The George Washington University:

```
ftp://ftp.gwu.edu/pub/ada/courses
```

At all sites, three compressed archives are provided:

- `cs2code.zip` (DOS/Windows)
- `cs2code.tar.Z` (UNIX)
- `cs2code.sit.hqx` (Macintosh)

ACKNOWLEDGMENTS

The programs in this book have been tested with the GNAT compiler running on a Sun SPARC server under Solaris; I acknowledge the School of Engineering and Applied Science Computing Facility (SEASCF) at The George Washington University for providing the computer resources. I have also tested the programs under DOS on an IBM-PC compatible.

I am indebted to Peter Hermann and Mark Weiss for some algorithms and bits of code. Thanks are due to the following formal reviewers: Martin D. Fraser, Lisa Levy-Kortright, Akhtar Lodgher, Don Meredith, M. Susan Richman, and Debora Weber-Wulff.

I am also grateful for the patience and the sometimes tough reviews of the hundreds of students in CSci 131 at The George Washington University, who have dealt with 5 years of draft versions without complaining too much, and for the active participation of students and faculty at Richard Stockton College, Nicholls State University, New York University, and Washington University at St. Louis.

The editorial and production staff, including Lynne Doran Cote, Katherine Harutunian, Patsy DuMoulin, Bob Woodbury, Diane Freed, and Judith Abrahms, deserve hearty thanks for their expert and always good-natured assistance.

Finally, a rousing cheer for the Home Team: Ruth, Ben, and Keith Feldman, for their love and patience through the years of seemingly unending textbook projects.

Michael B. Feldman
Bethesda, Maryland

Contents

CHAPTER 1

Abstraction and the Ada Type System

This is a book about algorithms and data structures, using an approach very much oriented toward the important concepts of *abstraction* and *abstract data types (ADTs)*.

The dictionary defines *abstraction* as the act or process of separating the inherent qualities or properties of a thing from the actual physical object to which they belong. Abstraction in programming is the process of separating the essential properties of a thing from the actual details of the way it is implemented or stored.

In computing, an *abstract data type* is a program unit whose specification provides a type and a set of operations on that type. In Ada, ADTs are implemented using packages and private types. In this chapter, you will see how Ada's standard package `Ada.Calendar` should be viewed as an ADT, and you will use a number of its operations for the first time in an application program. The Ada predefined type `String` is also treated as an ADT in this chapter.

In the next chapter, you will learn how to write ADTs and how to design a test plan to demonstrate that an ADT works as it should.

1.1   YOUR ADA STARTING POINTS

This book does not teach the rudiments of Ada from the beginning. Here are some of the things you should know about Ada before attempting the material in this book:

- The basics—the form of a program, the declaration of constants and variables, the way to use the standard `Text_IO` library for input and output

- Control structures—assignment, `IF`, `CASE`, `FOR` and `WHILE` loop statements

- Data structures—the predefined types `Integer`, `Float`, `Character`, and `Boolean`, and the way to define subtypes of these; simple record and one-dimensional array types

- System structures—procedures, functions, exception handling, and a bit about packages

You should also know how to edit, compile, link, and execute a program using a validated Ada compiler on a computer that is available to you.

These are the major Ada topics you will study in this book:

- Multidimensional and unconstrained array types

- Variant records

- Access types and dynamic storage allocation

- Generic units

- Tagged types and other object-oriented features

- Concurrent programming structures

Ada 95

This book uses Ada 95 as its "official" programming language. Ada 95 is the revised version of Ada whose standard became official when it was adopted by the International Standards Organization (ISO) in February 1995 and by the American National Standards Institute (ANSI) in April 1995. The original Ada is widely referred to as Ada 83, to distinguish it from the revised version, and we will do the same wherever a distinction is necessary.

Ada 95 is a nearly 100% "upward compatible" revision of Ada 83, so if you learned Ada 83 before reading this book, all your knowledge is still useful. Almost every Ada 83 program you have seen or written can be compiled and run correctly with an Ada 95 compiler.

Ada 95 corrects a few troublesome features of Ada 83 and introduces some interesting extensions. In this book, we will point these changes out, as appropriate, either in the text or in footnotes. Section 1.2 introduces a few Ada 95 features you should know about from the beginning.

1.2 SOME ADA 95 CHANGES

In this section, we describe some changes to the basic structure of an Ada program. These changes concern *names of standard packages*, *declaration order*, and *OUT parameters*.

Names of Standard Packages

Ada 95 has many more standard packages than Ada 83, including standard packages for powerful string operations, elementary mathematical functions such as square root and cosine, and random number generators. These packages are not required in Ada 83; they are often provided as compiler-dependent packages. Ada 95 also provides a feature called *hierarchical packages*, which allows a package to be declared a "child" of a parent package.

We will see some examples of the new packages, and will introduce our own child packages, in later chapters. For now, you should note that Ada 95 compilers supply a package called `Ada`, under which most of the standard packages are grouped as children. Thus, `Calendar` is now officially called `Ada.Calendar`, `Text_IO` is now called `Ada.Text_IO`, and so on. In order that existing Ada 83 programs be compatible with Ada 95, the Ada 83 package names can still be used and are treated as *renamings* of, (or "nicknames" for) the new official names. In this book, we use the new names consistently.

There are two new standard packages that you will find immediately useful. These provide for input/output operations on values of the predefined `Integer` and `Float` types; they are called, respectively, `Ada.Integer_Text_IO` and `Ada.Float_Text_IO`. All the familiar `Get` and `Put` procedures are available, including the formatting parameters `Width (Integer)`, `Fore`, `Aft`, and `Exp (Float)`. As usual, a program using these packages must be preceded by the appropriate context clause (`WITH` clause)—for example,

```
WITH Ada.Integer_Text_IO;
```

The examples in this book use the new packages wherever appropriate.

Declaration Order

Ada 83 allows a fairly flexible order of declarations of types, variables, constants, and subprograms within a given subprogram's declarative section. Generally, these can be intermixed as long as nothing is referenced before it has been declared. However, students of Ada 83 are often unpleasantly surprised to discover that subprogram bodies must come at the end of the declarations. In the most frequently arising case, attempting to declare a variable or a constant after the declaration of a procedure or function body results in a compilation error message something like "illegal declaration of basic declarative item."

This seemingly strange rule was imposed in Ada 83 in an attempt to improve the readability of programs by ensuring that variable and constant declarations, which are short, were not "buried" between long subprogram bodies. The rule caused more inconvenience than it eliminated, so it has been eliminated in Ada 95. Declarations of any kind can be freely intermixed as long as the sensible rule is followed that nothing can be referenced before it has been declared.

OUT Parameters

Procedures in Ada can take parameters of IN, OUT, and IN OUT modes. Within the procedure body, an IN parameter may not appear on the left side of an assignment; it is treated as a constant within the procedure body, and therefore may not be changed there. In Ada 83, an OUT parameter may not appear on the *right* side of an assignment; the resulting compilation error message is something like "illegal reading of an OUT parameter."

As a result of this rule, an OUT parameter cannot be computed in stages, in statements of the form

```
OutParam := OutParam + 1;
```

or otherwise used in the procedure. The standard solution is to use a temporary variable for the computation and copy its value into the OUT parameter just before the procedure returns to its caller. This is an annoying requirement; the rule is eliminated in Ada 95. OUT parameters can be used freely within the procedure. Program 1.1 illustrates the changes just described. If you have an Ada 95 compiler and the program source file available, you should compile, link, and execute it to test your familiarity with the compiler and observe the program's behavior.

PROGRAM 1.1 Illustrating Some Ada 95 Changes

```
WITH Ada.Text_IO;
WITH Ada.Integer_Text_IO;
PROCEDURE Ada95_Changes IS
------------------------------------------------------------------------
--| This program shows four small changes in Ada 95:
--|
--| (1) new names for standard packages (e.g., Ada.Text_IO)
--| (2) new standard packages for numeric input/output
--| (3) variables can legally be declared after procedure bodies
--| (4) OUT parameters can be legally used within the procedure
--|
--| Author: Michael B. Feldman, The George Washington University
--| Last Modified: October 1995
------------------------------------------------------------------------
```

```
   PROCEDURE ShowOutParameter (Result: OUT Integer) IS
   BEGIN
     Result := 2;
     Result := Result + 1; -- Result on the right is illegal in Ada 83!
   END ShowOutParameter;

   Y: Integer;   -- declaring Y after a procedure body
                 -- is illegal in Ada 83!

BEGIN -- Ada95_Changes

   ShowOutParameter(Result => Y);
   Ada.Text_IO.Put(Item => "Y's value is now");
   Ada.Integer_Text_IO.Put(Item => Y, Width => 1);
   Ada.Text_IO.New_Line;

END Ada95_Changes;
```

1.3   THE LIFE CYCLE OF SOFTWARE DEVELOPMENT

Developing software in classes is somewhat different from doing it in the real world. In a class, you are generally given the problem specification by an instructor. Sometimes the problem specification is ambiguous or incomplete, so interaction between the instructor and the students is necessary for the students to determine the details.

In the real world, the initial specification for a software product (a large program system) may also be incomplete. The specification is clarified through extensive interaction between the prospective users of the software and its designers. Through this interaction, the software designers determine precisely what the users want the proposed software to do and the users determine what to expect from the software product. Although it may seem like common sense to proceed in this manner, very often a supposedly final version of a software product does not perform as expected. The reason is usually a communication gap between those responsible for the product's design and its eventual users; generally, when the software fails to meet expectations, both parties are at fault.

One cause of the communication gap is that software users are often not familiar enough with computers and their capabilities to know whether their requests are reasonable or how to specify what they want. Software designers, on the other hand, often assume that they are the best judges of what the user really wants; they are quick to interpret a user's incomplete or unclear specification as a "blank check," allowing them to do what they think best. To avoid this communication gap and produce software that performs correctly and efficiently, truly meeting the needs of its user community, we must recognize that software is not just coded, but developed and maintained in a systematic fashion. Classically, the process of developing software is called the *software life cycle*, which consists of these phases:

1. *Requirements specification*. State the problem and gain a clear understanding of what is required for its solution. This sounds easy, but it can be the most critical

part of problem solving. A good problem solver must be able to recognize and define the problem precisely. If the problem is not totally defined, you must study it carefully, eliminating the unimportant aspects and focusing on the root problem. The solution may require an interactive program, to be operated by a human user, or a set of types and subprograms to be used not by an end user but by another developer, or both. It is, in any case, very important to understand just who the "customer" is.

2. *Analysis*. Identify problem inputs, desired outputs, and any additional requirements for or constraints on the solution. Identify the information that is supplied as problem data and the results that should be computed and displayed. Also identify how input is to be obtained. Will an interactive user interface be used? What about external disk files? Finally, determine the required form, and the units, in which the results should be displayed (for example, as a table with specific column headings).

3. *Design*. Historically, most software has been developed as a set of functions. First the functions were identified, and then the data upon which the functions acted. A more modern view is that software is best when it is a faithful model of some aspect of the real world. In this view, the world is best seen as a collection of things, or *objects*, that carry out actions or have actions performed upon them. The objects are the data types and variables necessary for the system to produce the desired outputs from the desired inputs.

   Having identified the objects (the "nouns" of the system) identify the operations (the "verbs") to be performed on each kind of object. Generally, each type and its operations are grouped into a module, or package; the interface, or "contract," between the module and its human users or its "client" programs is specified. A program often consists of a relatively small main procedure that makes use of a number of modules; to an increasing degree, these modules are already available in software libraries. It is important at this stage to identify those parts of the system that do *not* have to be written because someone else has already written them.

   Once the basic module structure is determined, develop the individual algorithms for the various operations and the main algorithm to solve the overall problem.

   The modern technique of beginning a design from the system's objects, rather than from its functions or operations, is commonly called *object-oriented design*.

   It is very important to document your design in written form. This can take any of a number of forms, including structure charts, high-level pseudocode, block diagrams, and so on. Your instructor will generally specify his or her preferred form of documentation; you will find it much easier to develop it before you start programming, or at least while programming, instead of rushing it through just before the project is due. At that point, it will be too late for you to get the benefit of understanding your own design by carefully writing it down.

4. *Developing a Test Plan*. It is important to specify, in as much detail as possible, just how the correctness of the various module operations, and of the overall

program, will be tested. In college programming, you often design, code, debug, and test your programs yourself, or perhaps with a colleague or two. It is tempting to test the programs using just a few arbitrarily chosen test data. Once you believe that the program is correct, you simply hand it in to the instructor and go on to other work. Because you are the programmer and also do the testing and are responsible for correcting any bugs, the testing process often is not as complete as it should be.

Unfortunately, even for simple programs, this is insufficient. A single test case, or a set of arbitrarily or randomly chosen ones, is usually not enough. You must consider special cases, endpoints of the data ranges, responses of the program to "bad" input, and so on. It is more effective to write your test plan *before* you actually code the program, so that you can specify tests based on the desired inputs and outputs. In this way, you will avoid being biased by an intimate knowledge of your own code.

In the "real world," testing is a rigorous process that is usually performed by a group other than the programmers; the users of the software product are often involved in the testing phase. It is important to identify bugs early, because the software that controls a rocket or processes payroll checks must be absolutely free of errors before its first use.

On the other hand, a maxim in computing, attributed to Dr. Edsger Dijkstra in the early 1970s, states that "testing shows only the *presence* of bugs, not the *absence* of bugs." Complex programs require complex and rigorous testing to find as many bugs as possible, but unfortunately it is impossible to test every possible state of a complex program. Therefore, it is important to develop a testing strategy that is as effective as possible, but also to have a well-managed process for correcting any errors that arise after the formal testing phase is over.

We could have included developing the test plan as a part of the design stage; we chose instead to present it as a separate phase of the life cycle, to emphasize the great importance of developing a testing strategy *before* the program is coded.

5. *Implementation or coding*. Implement the various modules, and the overall program, in a specific programming language. Test modules as they are developed; it is neither necessary nor desirable to implement the entire system before beginning to test its parts.

6. *Testing*. Carry out your test plan systematically. If you need to correct errors, be sure to rerun *all* your tests, so that you are sure that fixing one error did not introduce another. Rerunning a series of tests after correcting an error is generally called *regression testing*.

7. *Operation* (sometimes called *production*).

8. *Maintenance*. A software product usually must continue to perform effectively over a long period, sometimes in a changing environment. This requirement may necessitate periodic updating of the program. If the purpose of the update is to correct newly discovered errors, the update process is usually called

maintenance; if the purpose is to incorporate changes—for example, revised tax laws or new features desired by the users—the update process is called *enhancement*.

The software life cycle is iterative. During the design phase, problems may arise that make it necessary to modify the requirements specification. Any such changes require the approval of the users. Similarly, during coding it may become necessary to reconsider decisions made in the design phase. Again, any changes must be approved both by the system designers and by the users.

Estimates vary as to the percentage of life-cycle time spent in each phase. For example, a typical system may require a year to proceed through the first three phases, 3 months of testing, then 4 years of operation and maintenance. Because the lifetime of a software product often far exceeds its initial development time, you can see why it is important to design and document software in such a way that it can be easily understood and maintained by a variety of users.

In this section, we have described a systematic approach to the development of software. The "sizes"—number of pages of documentation, the number of person-hours expended, and so on—of the various steps of the life cycle should be proportional to the scale of the problem: relatively small for simple problems and relatively large for complex problems. It is important to learn that the same steps are always present.

1.4   THE GOALS OF SOFTWARE ENGINEERING

The disciplined, systematic development of software, following well-defined methods such as the one we have described here, is often called *software engineering*, to stress its similarity to the systematic methods used in traditional engineering. However, one need not be an actual engineer or even an engineering student to develop good software, and "software engineering" is therefore less exclusive than it sounds. To emphasize that excellent software is often developed by many kinds of people, whether or not they are engineers, we use the terms *software development* and *software developer* in this book.

Whether we describe ourselves as software engineers or as software developers, it is important to recognize that our main goal is to develop effective and useful software. In this book, we study modern software development methods that are intended to produce software that has these six important properties:

1. *Correctness*. The software meets its specifications; that is, for each set of correct inputs, it produces correct output. Our emphasis on developing a test plan helps to ensure correctness.

2. *Predictability*. The software behaves in a predictable, understandable manner even when it is presented with incorrect inputs. This is a very important property: To the extent that software possesses it, it does not fail, produce "garbage"

output, or "crash." Predictability is sometimes known as *robustness*. We achieve predictability by developing robust exception handling, and by designing test cases that present "bad" inputs to show that our exception handling is working as it should. Software that is correct and predictable is usually described as *reliable*.

3. *Understandability*. Software is developed, used, and maintained by humans, and therefore must be designed so that humans can understand it. At the coding level, this means that a proper coding style must be used and proper comments provided. Furthermore, the overall structure of a system should be clear. It should be possible to isolate the various objects and their operations easily, and to see without difficulty how the program objects and operations are related to the objects and operations in the domain of the problem. Understandability is fostered by careful object-oriented design and by careful documentation of the design and implementation.

4. *Modifiability*. From our discussion of the software life cycle, we know that software is rarely put into use once for all time. In practice, errors must be identified and repaired, even if they become apparent long after the software has been released, and software often must be enhanced to accommodate changing user requirements. We must therefore try to design software not just for today, but for tomorrow. Changes should "scale up" properly: a small change in the requirements should require only a small change in the design and implementation. The simplest example of design for modifiability is the use of subtypes with range constraints, and named constants, instead of "magic numbers" scattered throughout the code. We will introduce many techniques for improving the modifiability of programs.

5. *Reusability*. A software module is reusable if it can immediately, or at least easily, be adapted for use in a larger system other than the one for which it was originally designed. Not all good software is reusable; some is developed for, and very specifically tailored to, a single application. However, it is possible to develop large libraries of reusable software components, built with no specific application in mind but instead providing very general capabilities for a large range of applications. The availability of such libraries makes each application smaller and simpler, because many of its parts have already been designed, coded, and tested. Much of this book focuses on producing just such components, in the form of Ada generic packages.

6. *Efficiency*. A software product is efficient if it makes optimal use of the computer resources—time, memory, I/O devices—available to it. History has shown us that excessive or premature concentration on efficiency can cause a program to be very difficult to debug or modify. It is said that "it is easier to make a correct program fast than a fast program correct." In this book, we emphasize algorithm performance prediction—analysis of the space and time requirements of an algorithm as a function of the number of data points— because the most important aspect of developing an efficient *program* is choosing an *algorithm* with good time and space performance.

1.5 USING ABSTRACTION TO MANAGE COMPLEXITY

Beginning programmers often find it difficult to get started on a problem. They are often reluctant to start writing the code for a program until they have worked out the solution for every detail. Of course, preplanning and concern for detail are commendable, but these normally positive work habits can be overdone to the extent that they block the problem-solving process. To make problem solving flow as smoothly as possible, use the strategy of "divide and conquer" to decompose a problem into more manageable subproblems.

As mentioned in the introduction to this chapter, abstraction is a very important concept in this book. Although we are concerned mainly with abstraction as a technique for solving problems on a computer, you should understand that you are aided by abstraction every time you use a system of any complexity without having to consider the inner structure or workings of that system. Here are a few examples:

- You use the controls on a microwave oven to heat a meal without thinking about how the microwave process actually works. In fact, the high-frequency waves cause the molecules in the food to move about rapidly, generating heat, but you need not know this to cook your food.

- You set the wall control on your central heating system, to keep your home at a given temperature, without thinking about how a thermostat works. In fact, typically, a spiral strip, consisting of two different metals bonded together, expands and contracts with the temperature in the room, making or breaking an electrical contact that switches your furnace on or off. Ignorance of this fact does not hinder you from setting the temperature.

- You monitor the speed of your car by watching the speedometer; you need not know that a typical speedometer works by counting the number of wheel revolutions per minute to compute your speed in miles (or kilometers) per hour.

- You press buttons on your telephone, or spin an old-fashioned phone dial, and are connected to a friend, without thinking about either how the telephone system actually makes the connection between your phone and your friend's, or how your voice is transformed into an electrical signal that travels through the wires or through the air.

What do these examples have in common? In each case, you are using a system that has an *interface*—buttons, dials, gauges, and so forth—that is designed to be relatively simple to use. The user does not need any knowledge of the internal structure of the system—its *implementation*in order to use the system effectively. Developing interfaces and implementations is one of the key themes of this book.

Abstraction Versus Implementation

With these real-life examples in mind, let's proceed to take a look at some examples of abstraction from the world of programming.

Integer and Floating-Point Representations

Your ability to use things called *integers* and *real numbers* in programming depends on abstraction, since, in reality, nothing exists in the computer but sequences of bits, operated on by instructions that "understand" the connection between that which you perceive as an integer—written in your source program as a base-10 number—and that group of 8 or 16 or 32 bits in the computer's memory.

Usually, integer arithmetic is carried out by hardware instructions. To understand the kind of software-level abstraction we will be performing in this book, consider arithmetic on real numbers. In many computers, no real or floating-point instructions are available in the hardware instruction set. Sometimes—as in the case of the "math coprocessor" chips used in some models of the Apple Macintosh and IBM-PC families—the hardware instructions are an option the purchaser may choose not to buy.

When you declare two `Float` variables X and Y, and then write, say, an assignment statement X := X*Y + 3.0;, the compiler not only allocates memory locations to be used to store the variables X and Y, but may also have to generate calls to *subroutines* to do the addition and multiplication operations. The point is that through the use of the abstraction *variable name* and the abstraction *real number*, both provided in any reasonable high-level language, you are relieved of worrying about the details of the internal storage or actual instructions used to implement the calculation you specify when you write an assignment. Abstraction is the way we arrive at a situation called *information hiding*, in which details of a data representation or a procedure are hidden from those who have no need (or desire) to see them.

We shall frequently contrast *abstraction* and *implementation*. The abstraction is essentially that which is made visible to the user (in this case, the high-level-language (HLL) programmer); the implementation comprises all the "messy details" that have been hidden away. In this example, we have used an abstraction we might call *RealNumbers*, including the operations of *addition*, *multiplication*, and *assignment* or *storage* of reals. There is also an operation of *creation*, which we used by declaring X and Y to be of the type `Float`. The implementation of a real number as an area of memory divided into mantissa and exponent parts, and the operations as subroutines to be called by your machine-language program, have been taken care of by the compiler designer.

Figure 1.1 shows this relationship for what an HLL programmer sees as an integer quantity. The exact bit pattern used by the hardware is generally of little or no concern to the programmer, although in this case the internal value occupies 16 bits, but the programmer generally does not have to know even this.

Figure 1.2 shows an example of the same value, this time when declared as floating-point by the programmer and stored in 32-bit form in an Intel 80486-based computer. The two values appear to the programmer to be nearly the same, but they have clearly different internal representations.

Two-Dimensional Arrays

Perhaps you have used two-dimensional arrays at some time during your programming experience. You may be aware that the computer's memory is not two-dimensional, but is addressed simply as a sequence of bytes or words. It is clear, then, that there must be

```
x: Integer
      ⋮

x: = 735;--stores value
      ⋮
```

x │ 00000010 │ 11011111 │

(a) Abstraction of integer assignment
as seen by the programmer

(b) Sixteen-bit location (two bytes)
with binary equivalent of 735
stored

Figure 1.1 Abstraction and Implementation of Integer Assignment

something located between your high-level-language program and that linear memory, that can interpret a statement like A(3,4):=B(4,7)+1.0; correctly. As in the previous example, this "something" is the compiler; abstraction has been used to give you expressive power that is not present in the machine itself.

The abstraction you have used might be called *RectangularArrays*, including the operations of *retrieval* (the subscripted reference B(4,7) to the right of a := sign), *storage* (the reference A(3,4) to the left of a := sign), and *creation* (the declaration of the arrays and their sizes at the beginning of your program). The compiler designer has seen to the implementation of the rectangular arrays as areas of linear memory, and of the assignment and retrieval operations as formulas, generated into your machine-language program, that express the correspondence.

If you declared your array to hold elements of type Float, then, without thinking about it in so many words, you've also used the abstraction *Real Numbers,* since the values stored in the rectangular array are reals. An important aspect of the power of abstraction is the ability to "nest" abstractions many levels deep.

Figure 1.3 shows the abstraction and one common implementation of a 3×4 array of floats.

```
x: Float
     ⋮
x: = 735.0;
```

(a) Abstraction of float assignment

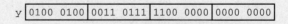

y │ 0100 0100 │ 0011 0111 │ 1100 0000 │ 0000 0000 │

(b) 32-bit location on Intel-80486 (4 bytes) with
binary float equivalent of 735.0

Figure 1.2 Abstraction and Implementation of Float Assignment

```
W: Array (1..3,1..4) of float
```

(a) Ada declaration

```
          1    2    3    4
      ┌─────────────────────────
    1 │  0.0 -1.0  4.1  5.2
      │
    2 │  1.8  2.2  0.0 -3.1
      │
    3 │ -5.1  1.2  2.3  0.7
```

```
┌──────┐
│ 0.0  │
├──────┤
│ -1.0 │
├──────┤
│ 4.1  │
├──────┤
│ 5.2  │
├──────┤
│ 1.8  │
├──────┤
│ 2.2  │
├──────┤
│ 0.0  │
├──────┤
│ -3.1 │
├──────┤
│ -5.1 │
├──────┤
│ 1.2  │
├──────┤
│ 2.3  │
├──────┤
│ 0.7  │
└──────┘
```

(b) Programmer's view of filled-in array

(c) Filled-in array as stored by compiler

Figure 1.3 Abstraction and Implementation of Two-Dimensional Array

Storage of Information on Magnetic Tape

Magnetic tapes are used in large computer centers to store very large files very economically; they are also used in the personal computer world to *back up* disk files. Let us assume that useful information on tape is recorded at a density of 1600 characters per running inch of tape (the density is usually much higher). A gap of about $\frac{3}{4}$ inch is left between groups of useful characters, to allow the tape motors space to accelerate and decelerate before and after reading. Thus a file of, say, personnel records, of 200 characters each, would waste much more tape than it uses if each record were stored on its own section of tape, since a record would occupy only $\frac{1}{8}$ inch of tape followed by a $\frac{3}{4}$ inch gap.

This is one reason why records are *blocked* on tape or disk files. A number of actual records are grouped together on one section of tape between gaps. If the blocking factor were, for example, 10, then a block would occupy $1\frac{1}{4}$ inch of tape, with the same $\frac{3}{4}$ inch gap.

However, tape is inexpensive, so economical use of storage is a secondary reason for blocking. A more important reason is that a fair amount of overhead is associated with each tape read or write operation: The time it takes to set up the operation and to start and stop the tape-drive motor is significant by comparison with the time it takes to transfer the information on the tape to and from main storage. Thus time and motor wear and tear are saved if more information can be read or written in a single operation once the drive motor is up to speed.

Let us suppose that you write a program in a high-level language to process this file. Your program is written to process one record at a time, yet actually a number of records—a block—are being read from your tape file in one I/O operation. You need not be worried about this "mismatch"; in fact, the operating system or compiler designers have applied abstraction to hide these "messy details" from you, and your program ends up processing exactly the record it requires. The abstraction *LogicalRecord* is implemented as a block of records written as one physical tape record; you use the operations of reading and writing records, which are implemented so that even though your program executes many "write" operations, an actual write to tape is executed only when a block of records has been assembled in an area of main storage, usually called a *buffer*.

In the terminology of operating systems, we refer to *logical* as opposed to *physical* records, files, devices, and so on. The terms *logical* and *physical* bear a close correspondence to the terms *abstraction* and *implementation*. The tape example is illustrated in Figure 1.4.

Sequential Files on Disk

Perhaps you have written a program that uses a series of Ada Get operations, or the equivalent in another language, to read information from a sequential disk file. Your program treated the disk file as though it were one continuous sequence of records, one after the other, terminated by a file marker.

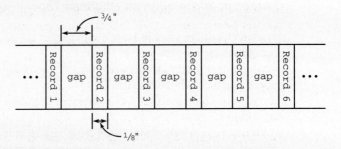

(a) Magnetic tape with 1600-character/inch storage density, showing storage of unblocked 200-character records. Each input operation reads one physical record and thus one logical record

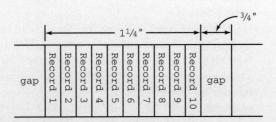

(a) Magnetic tape with same density and record size, but with 10-record blocking factor. Each input operation reads one physical record but 10 logical records

Figure 1.4 Abstraction and Implementation of Magnetic Tape File

However, in a modern disk system, the file itself is actually stored quite differently. The operating system's disk-management services are programmed so as to minimize the time it takes to get a given amount of information from the disk, and it happens that this optimization is done by organizing the file into blocks that are scattered all over the disk. Yet, when you write a `Get` call, you assume that the next value to be read is adjacent to the preceding one. You are not at all concerned about the physical structure of the disk file, which is complicated and full of messy detail.

Procedural Abstraction and Incremental Development

Procedural abstraction is an approach that maintains that procedure development should separate the concern of *what* is to be achieved by a procedure from the details of *how* it is to be achieved. In other words, you can specify what you expect a procedure to do, then use that procedure in the design of a problem solution before you know how to implement the procedure.

It is also advisable to develop and test your program *incrementally*—that is, a bit at a time. There are two strategies for doing this in a systematic way: *top-down* and *bottom-up*.

In top-down development, having worked out a preliminary design and refinement of your program into procedures, you code at least a substantial part of the main program (which is often little more than a series of procedure calls), then test the overall program flow using miniature, limited-function versions of your procedures, called *stubs*. You then implement the full procedures one at a time, testing them as you go. This is called top-down programming because you fill in detail, then test, starting with the main program and moving downward into lower and lower levels of procedures.

In bottom-up development, you start again from your preliminary design, but this time you write the procedures one at a time and test each one using a very simple main, or "test driver," program whose only function is to help you test and debug the procedure. This is called bottom-up programming because you start with the lower-level procedures and work your way back up to the main program. Generally, programmers perform a combination of top-down and bottom-up development.

Data Abstraction and Software Components

The above discussion is centered on the idea of developing *one* program, *one* time, to solve *one* problem. Refinement is used to break the problem down into smaller pieces and to develop procedures that will aid in solving it.

The experience of the last two decades has shown us that we should also focus on developing reusable software components, analogous to the hardware components in our computers, that are so generally useful that they can simply be "plugged in" to aid in the solution of many problems, not just one. The Calendar and Input/Output packages supplied with Ada compilers are examples of reusable components. Indeed, one of the most important themes of this book is a systematic presentation of the development of a kind of software component, *abstract data types (ADTs)*. Abstract data types are produced using *data abstraction*.

Data abstraction is a powerful programming tool that takes procedural abstraction a step further. It is the conceptual approach of combining a set of values with a set of operations on those values. Furthermore, data abstraction assumes that we can use such data types without knowing the details of their representation in the underlying computer system. Just as procedural abstraction enables us to focus on *what* a procedure does without worrying about *how* it does it, data abstraction enables us to consider the data objects needed, and the operations that must be performed on those objects, without thinking about unnecessary details. An ADT is an abstract description of the values and operations of a type—that is, a description that does not make reference to the implementation of the type.

Each chapter of this book presents one or more ADT components and one or more application programs that illustrate how the components are used.

1.6   A QUICK TOUR OF THE ADA TYPE SYSTEM

Before we proceed with our study of ADTs, we must consider just what a type is. Further, because building good ADTs will require detailed knowledge of the way Ada's type system works, we need to review the general structure of that type system.

Types and Strong Typing

The most important principle for you to remember about types in general, and Ada types in particular, is this:

A type always consists of a *set of values* and a *set of operations* that are appropriately applied to those values.

For example, an integer type, in any programming language for digital computers, consists of a finite set of integer values together with a set of operations, such as addition, subtraction, multiplication, division, and comparison. It is meaningless to think of a type only as a set of values; the operations are an inherent part of the type.

Many programming languages, including Ada, employ a related concept called *strong typing* or *static typing*. Strong typing means that

- Every object (variable) in the language has a unique type that does not change during the life of that object.

- Each object's type is defined (by a declaration) at compilation time so that the compiler can determine whether that object is being used correctly—that is, whether all operations on it are appropriate.

Strong typing is a relative term; it is possible for one language to be more strongly typed than another, and no useful language has perfectly strong typing. Later in the book we will see some desirable "loopholes" in Ada's strong type system.

To understand the idea of *appropriate* operations, consider kinds of operations that might be *inappropriate*. For example, adding together the values of two character variables is not appropriate; characters—alphabetical letters, for example—are not numerical quantities for which arithmetic operations make sense. Similarly, attempting to multiply two external files is inappropriate. Because each variable has a unique type that is known to the compiler, the compiler can check the appropriateness of all operations applied to a variable, generally flagging an inappropriate operation with a "type clash" or "type inconsistency" diagnostic message.

On the other hand, not all errors can be caught at compilation time; some cannot be detected until the program is running and computes a new value or reads data from the outside. Strong typing facilitates execution-time error detection: Because the compiler knows the set of values and the appropriate operations for each variable, it can generate executable instructions that will, for example, check to make sure that a value to be stored in a given variable is in range for that variable's type.

Suppose the data requirements for a program specify that a certain integer variable must acquire only positive values. If the variable has been declared positive, the compiler can ensure that no nonpositive value can be stored in it, *raising an exception* (Constraint_Error in Ada) if this requirement is violated during execution. Assigning a negative value to a positive variable is another inappropriate operation.

In summary, many computer scientists and user organizations believe that using languages with strong typing leads to more reliable programs, because

- More errors can be located at compilation time.

- Even those errors that cannot be detected at compilation time can usually be reported more reliably and gracefully at execution time.

Types in Ada

Types are essentially divided into *scalar* (sometimes called *simple*) types and *composite* (sometimes called *structured*) types. A *scalar* type is one for which each value has a single component. In other words, a scalar value cannot be decomposed directly by a program. In contrast, a *composite* type—a record or array type—consists of components: Records have fields; arrays have elements.

Ada's type system provides three very useful operations that are automatically applicable to *all* types, both scalar and composite, with the exception of LIMITED PRIVATE types, which we will introduce in Chapter 5. These three operations are:

- *Assignment or copying*—the familiar ":=" operation,

- *Equality test* —the familiar "=" operation

- *Inequality test*—the familiar "/=" operation

The assignment operation allows one value of a type to be copied into a variable of the same type; the entire value—even if it is a large composite—is copied. The equality test and the inequality test cause one value of a type to be compared with another value of the same type. As in assignment, the values, no matter how large, are compared in their entirety; they are equal if and only if all the bits of one agree with the corresponding bits of the other.

Scalar Types

Ada's scalar types comprise

- Integer types

- Floating-point types

- Fixed-point types

- Enumeration types

- Access (or pointer) types

The first three categories are collectively called *numeric* types. We will examine these, and enumeration types, in this section, deferring the last category until Chapter 8. Notice that in the list above, all the types are given in the plural. This is because an important aspect of Ada is the ability to create user-defined scalar types. Although you may be accustomed to defining your own enumeration types, you might find the idea of defining your own integer-valued or floating point–valued types to be unusual; many students do. Indeed, most languages do not provide this ability. As we shall see in Section 1.7, the presence of this ability in Ada makes it easier to develop portable programs—programs that can be compiled using any Ada compiler and executed on any kind of computer.

Predefined Numeric Types

An integer type is declared in the following form:

```
TYPE SomeIntegerType IS RANGE MinimumValue..MaximumValue;
```

Every integer type consists of a finite and ordered set of integer values. Because the set is finite, and because its integer values are ordered, it has a minimum and a maximum value. These values can be accessed using the attribute functions `SomeIntegerType'First` and `SomeIntegerType'Last`.

A floating-point type is declared as follows:

```
TYPE SomeFloatType IS
  DIGITS NumberOfDigits RANGE MinimumValue..MaximumValue;
```

A floating-point type consists of a finite and ordered set of numerical values. Because the set is finite, and because its values are ordered, it has a minimum and maximum value. As in the case of integer types, given a type `SomeFloatType`, these two

values can be accessed using the attribute functions `SomeFloatType'First` and
`SomeFloatType'Last`. Floating-point types are just an approximate way to represent the real numbers. Because a floating-point value in a computer must occupy a
finite amount of memory (say, 32 bits), most values are inexact and are represented
only to a certain precision, or number of significant figures. For example, the value $\frac{1}{3}$
cannot be represented exactly. We can write it as 0.333, but of course this is not exactly
$\frac{1}{3}$. The number of significant decimal digits in a floating-point type `SomeFloatType`
can be accessed as `SomeFloatType'Digits`.

Figures 1.5 and 1.6 show how the *Ada 95 Reference Manual* describes the predefined integer and floating-point types. These descriptions are part of Ada's package
`Standard`, in which the predefined types and operations are all given. This is not a
true package, in the sense that it must be `WITH`-ed; rather, it is automatically available
to every Ada program unit. The full package `Standard` is presented as Appendix C.

In the figures, note that the operations are all specified, but that in the type declarations, the details—the ranges, and the number of digits in the type `Float`—are given
as "implementation-defined." This is very important: It tells us that the language standard does *not* predefine the minimum and maximum values of the predefined types, nor

```
-- This is the section of the package Standard that describes
-- the predefined type Integer and its operations.
-- Excerpted and reformatted from the 95 Reference Manual, Annex A.

  TYPE Integer IS RANGE implementation_defined;

  -- "Implementation_Defined" means that the Standard does
  -- not specify the range of values, instead leaving this
  -- up to the compiler writer, who usually bases it on the
  -- word size and arithmetic system of the hardware.

-- The predefined operators for this type are as follows:
  FUNCTION "="    (Left, Right : Integer) RETURN Boolean;
  FUNCTION "/="   (Left, Right : Integer) RETURN Boolean;
  FUNCTION "<"    (Left, Right : Integer) RETURN Boolean;
  FUNCTION "<="   (Left, Right : Integer) RETURN Boolean;
  FUNCTION ">"    (Left, Right : Integer) RETURN Boolean;
  FUNCTION ">="   (Left, Right : Integer) RETURN Boolean;

  FUNCTION "+"    (Right : Integer) RETURN Integer;
  FUNCTION "-"    (Right : Integer) RETURN Integer;
  FUNCTION "ABS"  (Right : Integer) RETURN Integer;

  FUNCTION "+"    (Left, Right : Integer) RETURN Integer;
  FUNCTION "-"    (Left, Right : Integer) RETURN Integer;
  FUNCTION "*"    (Left, Right : Integer) RETURN Integer;
  FUNCTION "/"    (Left, Right : Integer) RETURN Integer;
  FUNCTION "REM"  (Left, Right : Integer) RETURN Integer;
  FUNCTION "MOD"  (Left, Right : Integer) RETURN Integer;

  FUNCTION "**"   (Left : Integer; Right : Integer) RETURN Integer;

  -- Predefined subtypes:

  SUBTYPE Natural  IS Integer RANGE 0 .. Integer'Last;
  SUBTYPE Positive IS Integer RANGE 1 .. Integer'Last;
```

Figure 1.5 Section of Package Standard Describing Integer

```
-- Section of package Standard that defines the type Float and its
-- operations.
-- Excerpted and reformatted from the Ada 95 Reference Manual, Annex A.

 TYPE Float IS DIGITS Implementation_Defined;

-- Neither the range of values nor the precision (number of
-- significant digits) is specified; this is up to the compiler
-- writer.

-- The predefined operators for this type are as follows:
FUNCTION "="  (Left, Right : Float) RETURN Boolean;
FUNCTION "/=" (Left, Right : Float) RETURN Boolean;
FUNCTION "<"  (Left, Right : Float) RETURN Boolean;
FUNCTION "<=" (Left, Right : Float) RETURN Boolean;
FUNCTION ">"  (Left, Right : Float) RETURN Boolean;
FUNCTION ">=" (Left, Right : Float) RETURN Boolean;

FUNCTION "+"  (Right : Float) RETURN Float;
FUNCTION "-"  (Right : Float) RETURN Float;
FUNCTION "ABS"(Right : Float) RETURN Float;

FUNCTION "+"  (Left, Right : Float) RETURN Float;
FUNCTION "-"  (Left, Right : Float) RETURN Float;
FUNCTION "*"  (Left, Right : Float) RETURN Float;
FUNCTION "/"  (Left, Right : Float) RETURN Float;

FUNCTION "**" (Left : Float; Right : Integer) RETURN Float;
```

Figure 1.6 Section of Package Standard Describing Float

the number of significant digits in `Float`. We will return to this point shortly; it is important enough to merit its own section. For now, note only that the familiar arithmetic and comparison operators are given as function specifications. We will frequently use this form for describing operators.

We shall ignore fixed-point types, which are used only rarely. The only exception is the predefined fixed-point type `Duration`, which measures elapsed time. We shall use this type occasionally.

Predefined Enumeration Types

An enumeration type is one whose finite set of values is listed, or *enumerated*, in the type declaration, in the form

```
TYPE SomeEnumerationType IS (value_1, value_2, . . ., value_n);
```

Because the values are finite and ordered, `SomeEnumerationType'First` and `SomeEnumerationType'Last` are appropriate for enumeration types, as are the comparison operations `"<"`, `"<="`, `">"`, and `"<="`. Naturally, assignment, equality, and inequality are also available for enumeration types, but arithmetic operations are not.

Package `Standard` provides two predefined enumeration types, `Boolean` and `Character`, shown in Figures 1.7 and 1.8. `Boolean` has predefined logical operators.

```
-- The declaration of type Character is based on the standard ISO
-- 8859-1 character set.
-- There are no character literals corresponding to the positions
-- for control characters.
-- They are indicated in italics in this definition.

TYPE Character IS

    (nul,    soh,    stx,    etx,    eot,    enq,    ack,    bel,
     bs,     ht,     lf,     vt,     ff,     cr,     so,     si,

     dle,    dc1,    dc2,    dc3,    dc4,    nak,    syn,    etb,
     can,    em,     sub,    esc,    fs,     gs,     rs,     us,

     ' ',    '!',    '"',    '#',    '$',    '%',    '&',    ''',
     '(',    ')',    '*',    '+',    ',',    '-',    '.',    '/',

     '0',    '1',    '2',    '3',    '4',    '5',    '6',    '7',
     '8',    '9',    ':',    ';',    '<',    '=',    '>',    '?',

     '@',    'A',    'B',    'C',    'D',    'E',    'F',    'G',
     'H',    'I',    'J',    'K',    'L',    'M',    'N',    'O',

     'P',    'Q',    'R',    'S',    'T',    'U',    'V',    'W',
     'X',    'Y',    'Z',    '[',    '\',    ']',    '^',    '_',

     '`',    'a',    'b',    'c',    'd',    'e',    'f',    'g',
     'h',    'i',    'j',    'k',    'l',    'm',    'n',    'o',

     'p',    'q',    'r',    's',    't',    'u',    'v',    'w',
     'x',    'y',    'z',    '{',    '|',    '}',    '~',    del,

     reserved_128, reserved_129, bph, nbh,
     reserved_132, nel, ssa, esa,

     hts, htj, vts, pld, plu, ri, ss2, ss3,

     dcs, pu1, pu2, sts, cch, mw, spa, epa,

     sos, reserved_153, sci, csi,
     st, osc, pm, apc,
     . . . );

-- The predefined operators for the type Character are the same as
-- for any enumeration type.
```

Figure 1.7 Section of Package `Standard` Describing `Character`

Attributes of Scalar Types

An important aspect of Ada's type system is the notion of *attributes*. These are characteristics of a type or variable that can be used by a program. Scalar types all have these three attributes:

- `First`, which gives the first or lowest value in the type

- `Last`, which gives the last or highest value

- `Range`, which gives the range of the type

In addition, discrete scalar types—that is, integer and enumeration types—have these important attributes:

```
TYPE Boolean IS (False, True);

-- The predefined relational operators for this type are as follows:

FUNCTION "="   (Left, Right : Boolean) RETURN Boolean;
FUNCTION "/="  (Left, Right : Boolean) RETURN Boolean;
FUNCTION "<"   (Left, Right : Boolean) RETURN Boolean;
FUNCTION "<="  (Left, Right : Boolean) RETURN Boolean;
FUNCTION ">"   (Left, Right : Boolean) RETURN Boolean;
FUNCTION ">="  (Left, Right : Boolean) RETURN Boolean;

-- The predefined logical operators and the predefined logical
-- negation operator are as follows:

FUNCTION "AND" (Left, Right : Boolean) RETURN Boolean;
FUNCTION "OR"  (Left, Right : Boolean) RETURN Boolean;
FUNCTION "XOR" (Left, Right : Boolean) RETURN Boolean;

FUNCTION "NOT" (Right : Boolean) RETURN Boolean;
```

Figure 1.8 Section of Package `Standard` Describing `Boolean`

- `Pos`, which, given a value in a type, gives its position in the type

- `Val`, which, given a position in a type, gives the value in that position

- `Pred`, which, given a value in a type, gives the value that precedes it in the type

- `Succ`, which, given a value in a type, gives the value that follows

As an example, consider the enumeration type `Days`:

```
TYPE Days IS
   (Monday, Tuesday, Wednesday, Thursday, Friday, Saturday, Sunday);
```

and the variables

```
Today, Tomorrow: Days;
```

Now assuming the assignment:

```
Today := Friday;
```

we have

```
Days'First is Monday
Days'Last is Sunday
Days'Pos(Monday) is 0
Days'Val(0) is Monday
Days'Pos(Sunday) is 6
Days'Val(6) is Sunday
Days'Pred(Wednesday) is Tuesday
Days'Pred(Today) is Thursday
Days'Succ(Tuesday) is Wednesday
Days'Succ(Today) is Saturday
```

Because integer and enumeration types are not cyclical (that is, they do not "wrap around"), the queries `Days'Pred(Monday)` and `Days'Succ(Sunday)` are undefined and would cause an execution-time exception—namely the raising of `Constraint_Error`—if attempted. Similarly, if `Today` had the value `Sunday`, then `Days'Succ(Today)` would cause an exception. Whether the assignment statement

```
Tomorrow := Day'Succ(Today);
```

would cause an exception depends on the value of `Today`; it cannot cause a compilation error because the value of `Today` is usually unknown at compilation time. We chose an enumeration type for the example, but the same attributes would work in the same way if we had used an integer type instead.

Subtypes

A subtype of a given type defines a subset of the base type's set of values. The operations of the base type are passed on to the subtype; sometimes we say that the subtype *inherits* the operations of the base type. It is important to realize that a subtype does *not* create an entire new type. Because a subtype merely selects a subset of the base type's values, any value in the subtype will necessarily also be in the base type. Consider the subtype

```
SUBTYPE Small IS Integer RANGE -10..10;
```

and assume that `I` is of type `Integer` and `S` is of type `Small`. The two assignment statements

```
I := S;
S := I;
```

are both legal at compilation time. However, the first statement requires no check to be done at execution time, because any value that `S` could hold will also be in range for `I`. The second statement requires a check to be made at execution time; the compiler will generate the checking instructions as part of the object program.

Why is the check necessary? Suppose the value of `I` is to be read in from the terminal; it is therefore not known at compilation time. Suppose the user enters `20` in response to a prompt for a value for `I`. This value is quite legal for `I`, but is out of range for `S`, so `Constraint_Error` should be raised for the attempted assignment. The subset relationship also shows the need for the check: Any value in the subset will be in range for the full set, but a value in the full set does not necessarily belong in the subset.

We say that the variables `I` and `S` are *compatible*; each variable's value can be copied into the other, provided only that it is in the proper range of the other variable.

Subtypes are very useful in programming; they allow the programmer to "fine-tune" the ranges of variables, according to the data requirements of the program. Because the ranges are specified explicitly, the compiler can ensure that assignments are always appropriate, at compilation time if possible, or with execution-time checks if necessary. We will use subtypes frequently in this book.

Assignment Compatibility

An expression involving floating-point operands can be assigned to a variable only of type `Float` (or a subtype thereof). An expression involving integer operands can be assigned to a variable only of type `Integer` (or a subtype thereof). An attempt to assign a value of the wrong type to a variable will result in a compilation error; an attempt to assign an out-of-range value to a variable (e.g., a negative expression result to a `Positive` variable) will cause `Constraint_Error` to be raised.

Conversions Among Numeric Types

Ada does not usually allow the mixing of types in an expression. However, it does provide a means for performing *explicit conversion* of a value of one type into a value of another. Specifically, Ada allows explicit conversion among integer, fixed-point, and float values. This is done using a function-call syntax, in which the name of the new type is used as the function. The result of this "function call" is of the new type, unless the result is out of range, in which case `Constraint_Error` is raised as usual.

An integer value always has an exact equivalent in floating-point form, but a floating-point value does not always have an exact integer equivalent. Ada therefore *rounds* such a conversion to the nearest integer value. Suppose we have the following declarations:

```
SUBTYPE NonNegFloat IS Float RANGE 0.0..Float'Last;

F: Float;
N: NonNegFloat;
I: Integer;
P: Positive;
T: Natural;
```

Here are some conversions that can be done:

```
F := Float(I);          -- always possible
N := Float(P);          -- always possible
I := Integer(F);        -- always possible; result is rounded
I := Integer(N);        -- always possible, result is rounded

N := NonNegFloat(I);    -- raises Constraint_Error if I is negative
T := Natural(F);        -- raises Constraint_Error if F is negative

I := Integer(5.49);     -- result is 5
I := Integer(5.51);     -- result is 6
I := Integer(5.5);      -- result is 6, depending on compiler
```

Conversion between two subtypes of `Integer` or two subtypes of `Float` is always possible and will succeed if and only if the result is in range. If I happens to be −57, for example,

```
T := Natural(I);
```

will cause `Constraint_Error` to be raised.

Record Types

A record type is declared in the following way:

```
TYPE SomeRecordType IS RECORD
    Field1 : Type1;
    Field2 : Type2;
      .
      .
      .
Fieldn : Typen;
END RECORD;
```

Each field is given with its type. An object or variable of type `SomeRecordType` is declared as usual:

```
FirstRecord: SomeRecordType;
```

In addition to the always-available assignment, the equality test, and the inequality test, record types permit the operations of field storage and field retrieval, both using "dot" notation to select the desired field. If `FirstRecord` and `SecondRecord` are both of type `SomeRecordType`, we can write

```
FirstRecord.Field1 := SecondRecord.Field1;
```

Also available for records is *aggregate assignment*, for example:

```
FirstRecord :=
  (Field1 => Value1, Field2 > Value2, . . . , Fieldn => Valuen);
```

It is also legal to omit the field names and write

```
FirstRecord :=
  (Value1, Value2, . . . , Valuen);
```

as long as all the `Value`s are supplied, in the proper order.

Finally, parameters to subprograms, and function return type, are allowed to be record types.

Array Types

An array type is declared in the following form:

```
TYPE SomeArrayType IS ARRAY SubscriptType OF ElementType;
```

The subscript can be of integer or enumeration type. For example,

```
TYPE HoursWorked IS ARRAY(Days) OF NonNegFloat;
TYPE Vector IS ARRAY(Small) OF Integer;
TYPE List IS ARRAY(1..5) OF Character;
```

are all permissible. In general, good programming style encourages the use of a subscript type that is a named type or subtype (as in the first two cases), rather than an explicit range (as in the last case).

Array element storage and retrieval is analogous to record field storage and retrieval. Syntactically, parentheses are used. Suppose `Array1` and `Array2` are of type `SomeArrayType` and `S1` and `S2` are of type `SubscriptType`:

```
Array1(S1) := Array2(S2);
```

copies an element of `Array2` into the given element of `Array1`.

Of course, array assignment, equality test, and inequality test are available, and arrays can be passed as parameters to subprograms and returned as function results.

Aggregate Array Assignment

As in the case of records, an entire array can be filled with values using three methods:

- Assignment to each element with an individual assignment statement, either randomly or sequentially

- Copying one entire array to another with an array assignment statement, as discussed just above

- Storing values in an entire array using an aggregate, similar to that used in records

It is the third method that concerns us now. Given an array `A` of type `Vector`, the 21 `Integer` values could, if they were all known in advance, be stored in `A` with a single statement such as

```
A := (1, 27, 35, -4, 15, . . .);
```

where the ellipsis must be replaced completely with the other 16 values. This is surely tedious, but it is better than writing 21 separate assignment statements. As in the case of records, named association can also be used:

```
A := (-10 => 1, -9 => 27, . . .);
```

where the remaining 19 values also need to be supplied. Although in record aggregates we prefer named association, in array aggregates it can be cumbersome, because an array can have a large number of elements. In using array aggregates, we will generally use positional association unless there is a good reason not to do so.

A common and useful application of array aggregates is to initialize most or all elements of an array with the *same* value. Suppose that our array `A` were to be "cleared" so that all values were 0. This could be done in a loop:

```
FOR I IN Small LOOP
    A(I) := 0;
END LOOP;
```

or with a single aggregate assignment:

```
A := (-10..10 => 0);
```

or, better,

```
A := (Small => 0);
```

The aggregate assignment is certainly more concise, expresses the will of the programmer clearly, and also may possibly execute faster. Suppose now that A were to be initialized such that its first 5 elements were as above, but the other 16 were to be 0. The assignment

```
A := (1, 27, 35, -4, 15, OTHERS => 0);
```

does the trick. The OTHERS clause instructs the compiler to store 0s in all those elements not expressly listed in the aggregate. If, say, only the first, third, and fifth elements were nonzero, named association could be used:

```
A := (1 => 1, 3 => 27, 5 => 35, OTHERS => 0);
```

Finally, the assignment

```
A := (OTHERS => 0);
```

fills the entire array with 0s even more concisely: Because no other elements were explicitly filled, the OTHERS applies to all elements. If A were a large array, for example, if the range of Small were −100. .100 instead of −10. .10, the OTHERS notation would be very convenient indeed!

In using an aggregate, it is important to remember that *all* elements of the array must be initialized by the aggregate; otherwise a compilation error results. OTHERS initializes all elements not otherwise given.

Multidimensional Arrays

Arrays need not be limited to a single dimension. We will discuss multidimensional arrays in depth in Chapter 4; for now, let us be content with a type declaration,

```
TYPE FunnyTable IS ARRAY (Days, Small) OF Integer;
```

a variable declaration,

```
TodaysTable: FunnyTable;
```

an element assignment

```
TodaysTable(Sunday, -5) := 13;
```

and an aggregate assignment

```
TodaysTable := (OTHERS => (OTHERS => 2));
```

which stores the value 2 in each of the 147 (7×21) elements of the array.

Strings

The only predefined composite type in Ada is the string, which we will consider in some depth in Section 1.12.

Type Composition

Types give the programmer much power and flexibility for creating complex data structures. In Ada, a record field or array element can be of any type, including another composite type. This lets the programmer compose, or nest, structures in other structures to create ever larger ones. It is quite common to see arrays of records, arrays of arrays, records with arrays as fields, records with records as fields, and so on.

Derived Types

It is possible in Ada to *derive* a type from another type. Derivation creates a new type, not just a subset relationship. Values of derived types cannot be directly combined or assigned to variables of other derived types. Consider

```
TYPE Small  IS NEW Integer RANGE -100..100;
TYPE Little IS NEW Integer RANGE -100..100;
```

Each of these types has its own set of values and inherits the operations of `Integer`. However, objects of one type are *incompatible* not only with objects of the other type, but also with `Integer`. That the types share the same range of values is coincidental. If `I` is of type `Integer`, `L` is of type `Little`, and `S` is of type `Small`, then all of these assignments are illegal and will give rise to compilation errors:

```
I := L;
I := S;
L := I;
S := I;
S := L;
L := S;
```

You might well ask why the types should be incompatible even though they seem to have the same set of values. The answer is that sometimes we wish to separate one group of variables from another and allow the compiler to help us refrain from *accidentally* mixing them together, because they represent, say, different physical quantities that should not be intermixed.

In fact, Ada does allow us to intermix values of different derived types, but only if we do it *intentionally*, through explicit conversion. Thus `Little(S)`, `Small(L)`, `Integer(S)`, and so on, are legal conversions.

We will not use derived types much in this book—we prefer to use subtypes, as discussed above, and new types, as discussed below—but you should know that derived types exist; they appear in other books and in "real" programs you might encounter.

New Types

If you have ever written a type declaration for an enumeration, record, or array type in Ada, you have created a *new type*. For example, consider the two enumeration types

```
TYPE USFlagColors     IS (Red, White, Blue);
TYPE FrenchFlagColors IS (Red, White, Blue);
```

These are distinct types, even though they seem to have the same structure and the same set of values. A value of type `USFlagColors` cannot be assigned to a variable of type `FrenchFlagColors`. The variable and the value are *incompatible*. Similar incompatibilities exist between record or array types that appear to have the same structure but have different type names.

Interestingly, Ada allows us to create new numeric types, of the integer, float, or fixed variety. This is the subject of Section 1.6.

Private Types

An Ada package specification can provide a type declaration labeled `PRIVATE`, in the following form:

```
TYPE T IS PRIVATE;
```

The actual type declaration appears at the end of the specification, in a special section called the `PRIVATE` section. Whether the actual structure of the type is scalar or composite, the set of predefined operations available to a client of the package is limited to the always-present assignment, equality test, and inequality test. This means that even if the type happens to be an integer type, no arithmetic is predefined, and if the type happens to be a record type, no field selection is available to client programs. Private types allow their authors complete control over the set of operations. This book uses private types frequently, beginning in Chapter 2.

1.7   A SET OF NUMERIC TYPES FOR THIS BOOK

In the preceding section, we mentioned that it is possible to create new numeric types in Ada, but we did not go into detail as to why we would wish to do so. In fact, from time to time in this book we will indeed create our own numeric types.

Why would we bother to create our own types? After all, Ada provides some predefined numeric types that would seem capable of serving us well. The answer is that new numeric types aid us in developing portable programs—that is, programs that will compile correctly using any Ada compiler and will execute correctly on any computer for which a compiler exists.

Let's look again at the predefined numeric types. The *Ada 95 Reference Manual* predefines `Integer` and `Float`, but does not specify what their ranges are to be! Each compiler writer is free to set a range for each predefined type used by that compiler. Some compilers use the range $-32767..32767$ for `Integer`, because that is the range that can be accommodated in a 16-bit memory location. Some computers provide an extra negative value in the hardware; in those computers compilers might use the range $-32768..32767$. Other compilers use the range $-214748348..2147483647$ for `Integer`, because that range can be accommodated in a 32-bit location.

Now suppose we defined a subtype

```
SUBTYPE MyBigInteger IS Integer RANGE -100_000..100_000;
```

This definition would compile correctly using any compiler that used the 32-bit integer range. Making `MyBigInteger` a subtype of `Integer` is dangerous, though: We could use `MyBigInteger` values freely in many programs, then switch to a different compiler and be unpleasantly surprised to discover that these values will not compile or work if the new compiler happens to use the 16-bit range for `Integer`.

Most computers have either 16-bit or 32-bit words, but some have words of unusual size, such as 24 or 60 bits. Because Ada does not specify precisions and ranges for the predefined types, this variety of word sizes can be accommodated, but this causes a problem for us: How do we ever specify numerical values that we are sure will work with all compilers on all computers? Our solution is one that is commonly used in industry for Ada projects: We define our own numeric types. Changing the declaration above to

```
TYPE MyBigInteger IS RANGE -100_000..100_000;
```

does the trick: The RM obliges every compiler to store values of this type using *some* hardware storage method supported by the computer for which it is generating code. In the unusual case where the hardware simply cannot accommodate a given range—because it is absurdly large, for example—the compiler will just issue an error message. In practice, this rarely happens, because reasonable integer ranges can almost always be accommodated.

In this book we shall take advantage of the fact that in practical compilers the range of predefined `Integer` is at least –32767. .32767. We can therefore safely and portably use subtypes of the predefined `Integer` type wherever the subtype range will lie within –32767. .32767. To handle a larger range—for example, the 100,000 situation mentioned above—we will resort to declaring a new integer type to accommodate just the range we need.

For this book's purposes, we can use predefined `Float` with confidence, because practical compilers give a precision of at least six decimal digits and six significant figures are the most we will need here.

This handling of numeric types is a workable compromise between the naive extreme of using *only* the predefined types—which, as we have seen, can lead to portability problems—and the "industrial-strength" extreme of *never* using the predefined types, which, in our view, leads to unnecessary complexity in our programs.

1.8 ABSTRACT DATA TYPES (ADTs)

An abstract data type, or ADT, is just what its name suggests: an *abstract description* of a *data type*—that is, a description of the values of the type, and the operations on those values, in an abstract manner independent of any particular implementation.

For example, we could specify the type `Integer` as follows:

- *Values*—all integers in the range `MinInteger` through `MaxInteger`, inclusive

- *Arithmetic Operations*—addition, subtraction, multiplication, division, and remainder

- *Comparison Operations*— <, <=, =, /=, >, and >=

Mathematically, there is no reason to limit the set of integers to a finite range; we do so only because in this book we are interested in solving problems on digital computers, and, generally, in digital computers the set of integers is a finite set. Note that no reference is made to the way in which integers are implemented—for example, that they are stored in the computer in 32-bit binary form. This implementation detail is not relevant to the ADT specification.

A program that uses an ADT is called a *client program*. A client program should be designed before it is coded, written as an abstract algorithm that manipulates objects of the type and uses the type's operations abstractly. Later, when the abstract algorithm is transformed into statements in a programming language, these manipulations can be written without the programmer's knowing the details of the internal representation of the data type or the implementation of its operators. In this way, we separate the *use* of the data and the operators (by the client program) from the *representation* of the type and the *implementation* of the operators (by the abstract data type).

Using ADTs provides several advantages. It allows us to implement the client program and the abstract data type independently of each other. If we decide to change the implementation of an operator (function or procedure) in the abstract data type, we can do so without affecting the client program. Finally, because the internal representation of a data type is hidden from its client program, we can even change the internal representation at a later time without modifying the client.

An ADT is an important kind of *reusable software component*. ADTs are written to be usable by a variety of client programs. An ADT generally has no knowledge of the client programs that will use it; the client programs need have no knowledge of the internal details of the ADT. Ideally, as we have pointed out, ADTs are thought of as analogous to the various integrated electronic components used in modern computers and other devices: One needs to understand only the interface to an ADT to "plug it into" a program, as electronic components are plugged into a circuit board.

ADTs and their use by abstract client programs could be studied theoretically, without ever writing a concrete program. We could, for example, introduce all our ADTs in the structured English form shown above and write all our client algorithms in pseudocode. However, in order to use ADTs in actual programs solving actual problems, we must have a concrete notation in which to specify and implement ADTs. Ada packages happen to be a very convenient concrete form for this work. The specification of the predefined Ada types, extracted from `PACKAGE  Standard` and shown in Figures 1.5 through 1.8, is a good approximation to the ADT form we desire: In each of those figures, the type is named and its values described, and a list of operations is given.

To emphasize that ADTs are independent of specific programming languages, we will sometimes introduce them in the structured-English form. Often, however, we will find it convenient to skip the structured English and use Ada notation directly, using comments to fill in descriptive material that the Ada syntax cannot express. We will construct the specification of an ADT—the abstract part—using an Ada package specification, and the implementation of the ADT using a package body.

ADTs facilitate programming in the large because they reside in ever larger libraries of program resources. The availability of large libraries of general resources makes the client programs much simpler, because their writers do not have to "reinvent the wheel." The modern software industry is devoting much time and effort to the development of component libraries; your study of ADTs will give you a taste of the way this development is done.

The Structure of an ADT

Abstract data types are a general concept in programming, independent of any particular programming language. An ADT consists of the specification of one or more data types and a set of operations applicable to the type or types. Generally, the type is a composite type, often a record of some kind. The operations can be grouped into several classes:

- *Constructor*. A constructor creates, or constructs, an object of the type by putting its component parts together into a unified whole.

- *Selector*. A selector selects a particular component of an object.

- *Inquiry*. An inquiry operation asks whether an object has a particular property—for example, whether it is empty.

- *Input/output*. As usual, an input/output operation is the communication link between the value of an object and the world outside the program, usually a human operator at the terminal or a disk file or printer.

Ada Features for ADTs

Ada provides many capabilities to help us develop ADTs. Here is a summary of the main data abstraction features we use in this book.

- Ada provides *subtypes, derived types,* and *new types*. This has been discussed above.

- Ada provides *record field initialization*. This allows us to define a record type in such a way that each field in each variable of that type is initialized to a predetermined value.

- Ada provides *packages*. As we will see throughout this book, a package is an ideal way of grouping together resources—types, functions, procedures, important constants, and so on—and making them available to client programs. A package specification acts as a "contract" between the writer of the package and the writer of the client program. Furthermore, the compiler checks to make sure that the contract is followed: Everything promised in the specification must be delivered in the package body, and client programs must use the package resources correctly, for example, by calling procedures only with the correct parameters.

- Ada provides *private types*. The private-type capability enables us to write a package that provides a new type to client programs, in such a way that the client program cannot accidentally misuse values of the type by referencing information that is most properly kept private—that is, restricted for the internal use of the package body only.

- Ada provides *operator overloading*. This allows us to write new arithmetic and comparison operators for new types and to use them just as we use the predefined operators.

- Ada provides *user-defined exceptions*. This enables the writer of a package to provide exceptions to client programs, in order to signal to a client when it has done something inappropriate with the package. The writer of the client program can write exception handlers for user-defined exceptions that work exactly the same way as the handlers we write for the predefined exceptions, such as `Constraint_Error`.

- Ada provides *attributes* such as `First` and `Last`. Attributes make it possible to write subprograms that manipulate data structures without knowing all their details. This is especially useful in the case of arrays, in which a subprogram that manipulates an array parameter can be written without knowing the array bounds: It need only inquire about the array bounds by asking for the `First` and `Last` attributes.

- Finally, Ada provides *generic definition*. Generic definition allows us to write subprograms and packages that are so general that they do not even have to know all the details of the types they manipulate; these types can be passed to the generic unit as parameters when the generic unit is instantiated. We have seen generic instantiation so far only with respect to the `Text_IO` libraries. Chapter 5 will introduce more information about generics and show you how to write generic units of your own.

1.9 OBJECT-ORIENTED PROGRAMMING

The term *object* seems to appear everywhere in current computer technology. Reading the literature, from textbooks to scholarly journals to trade magazines, one gets the impression that an "object-oriented" this-or-that seems to be the only acceptable kind of this-or-that. The pervasiveness of this terminology makes it essential that we try to put it in perspective.

To a certain extent, the term *object-oriented* is a marketing or advertising term: If one's product is object-oriented, it is likely to sell better than if it is not. However, we cannot dismiss the term as simply salesmanship. *Object-oriented* does have some technical meaning, even if its importance is sometimes exaggerated by advertising.

Object-oriented *design* (*OOD*) was mentioned in Section 1.3 as the development of software starting with consideration of its nouns or objects, rather than with its verbs or functions. This is a design methodology, and an object-oriented design can be implemented, as can all software designs, using any number of different coding techniques and languages. This book uses OOD as its general approach, although we purposely keep the approach somewhat informal.

Object-oriented *programming* (*OOP*) is a programming methodology, used for implementing object-oriented designs using a number of language features. These are:

- *Encapsulation*, provided very well by Ada's packages and especially by private types and introduced here starting in Chapter 2.

- *Genericity*, provided by Ada's generics capability and introduced in Chapter 5.

- *Inheritance*, through which a new type takes on some or all of the properties of an existing one. This is provided by Ada's derived types and is extended considerably in tagged types, which are introduced in Chapter 6.

- *Polymorphism*, partially supported by Ada's procedure and function name overloading, and extended significantly through the concept of *dynamic dispatching*, which is introduced in Chapter 9.

An *object-oriented language (OOL)* is one that possesses these features.
In current OOP terminology, an object has two important characteristics:

1. It has *state*—that is, it has a value that may change over time, and

2. it has *behavior*—that is, it has a set of operations that act on it, and these operations are the only ones that can change its state (value).

In working with this book, you will be using OOP concepts from the start. You are familiar with Ada variables; *object* is in many ways just a more modern name for *variable*. As you know, each variable has a type—either a predefined type or a programmer-defined one—and can take on values only from that type's set of values. An Ada variable, therefore, has state.

Each type also has a set of operations associated with it. The predefined types, such as `Integer` or `Ada.Calendar.Time`, all have predefined operations, and *only* the given operations are valid for values of the given type. Throughout the book, we emphasize Ada compilers' concern for the validity of operations; they give compilation errors where possible and compile runtime checks into your program where necessary. An Ada variable therefore has behavior.

Further, you will be using Ada packages throughout, starting with the input/output packages and other predefined packages such as `Ada.Calendar` and `Ada.Numerics`. If you've studied Ada previously, you've used other packages and have perhaps even written one or two yourself. Having reached this point, you are quite accustomed to encapsulation.

Section 1.8 explored the idea of writing new types and sets of operations and implementing these in ADT packages. Most of the ADTs in this book define new types as private record types; private types allow us to control precisely which predefined and programmer-defined operations are valid.

Finally, you will be writing your own generics beginning with Chapter 5 and studying inheritance and polymorphism beginning with Chapter 6. By then, you will have been introduced to most of what you need to do OOP.

Some writers use the term *object-based programming* to describe programming that uses "only" encapsulation and genericity but not inheritance and polymorphism. These writers believe that inheritance and polymorphism are of paramount importance, and that any program that doesn't take advantage of these two concepts is simply not object-oriented. By this definition, Ada 83 is an object-based language and Ada 95 is an object-oriented one.

We think this distinction is somewhat artificial; encapsulation and genericity are just as important as inheritance and polymorphism in developing good object-oriented designs. By the time you approach the end of this text, you will have been introduced to all these concepts in what we hope is a balanced way, and you'll be equipped to judge them for yourself.

1.10   A PREDEFINED ADT: THE `ADA.CALENDAR` PACKAGE

Before you learn to write ADTs, it is helpful to study an existing one in detail. Ada provides a predefined package `Ada.Calendar`, which serves as an excellent example of a well-thought-out ADT. `Ada.Calendar` is always provided with an Ada compiler (indeed, it *must* be provided) and our own ADTs will often be written in the style of `Ada.Calendar`. Systematic study of `Ada.Calendar` will teach you much about the design of ADTs and prepare you to start writing your own.

Resources Provided by `Ada.Calendar`

Package `Ada.Calendar` uses a type `Duration`, which is actually defined in package `Standard`. `Duration` is a measure of *elapsed* time: One duration unit is exactly equal to one elapsed second. Note that this is not the same as the time of day. Time of day, often called "wall clock time" in computing applications, gives a particular instant of time: 12:05 P.M. on January 25, 1980, for example. Duration measures the *passage* of time: Two minutes, or 120 seconds, elapse between 12:05 P.M. and 12:07 P.M. on the same day. Time of day is one of the resources provided by `Ada.Calendar`, in the form of a type `Time`.

The purpose of `Ada.Calendar` is to provide a useful number of operations on time-of-day values. Figure 1.9 shows the entire specification of package `Ada.Calendar`, which we have copied straight from the Ada standard, making changes only in the formatting and comments in the specification.

```
PACKAGE Ada.Calendar IS

  -- standard Ada package, must be supplied with compilers
  -- provides useful services for dates and times

  -- type definitions

  TYPE Time IS PRIVATE;

  SUBTYPE Year_Number  IS Integer RANGE 1901..2099;
  SUBTYPE Month_Number IS Integer RANGE 1..12;
  SUBTYPE Day_Number   IS Integer RANGE 1..31;
  SUBTYPE Day_Duration IS Duration RANGE 0.0..86_400;
  -- Duration is a predefined (standard) fixed-point type;
  -- Day_Duration range is the number of seconds in 24 hours

  -- constructor operation

  -- constructs a Time value from its components; note that the
  -- default for Seconds is 0.0, so if Seconds value isn't given,
  -- the time is assumed to be at midnight

  FUNCTION Time_Of (Year    : Year_Number;
                    Month   : Month_Number;
                    Day     : Day_Number;
                    Seconds : Day_Duration:=0.0) RETURN Time;

  -- selector operations

  FUNCTION Year    (Date : Time) RETURN Year_Number;
  FUNCTION Month   (Date : Time) RETURN Month_Number;
  FUNCTION Day     (Date : Time) RETURN Day_Number;
  FUNCTION Seconds (Date : Time) RETURN Day_Duration;

  -- splits a Time value into its component parts

  PROCEDURE Split  (Date : IN Time;
                    Year : OUT Year_Number;
                    Month : OUT Month_Number;
                    Day : OUT Day_Number;
                    Seconds : OUT Day_Duration);

  -- read the computer's clock to get the current time of day

  FUNCTION Clock RETURN Time;

  -- arithmetic and comparison operations

  -- note that only the "sensible" operations are defined.
  -- this is possible because Time is a private type with no
  -- predefined operations except := and =

  FUNCTION "<"  (Left, Right : Time)     RETURN Boolean;
  FUNCTION "<=" (Left, Right : Time)     RETURN Boolean;
  FUNCTION ">"  (Left, Right : Time)     RETURN Boolean;
  FUNCTION ">=" (Left, Right : Time)     RETURN Boolean;

  FUNCTION "+"  (Left : Time;     Right : Duration) RETURN Time;
  FUNCTION "+"  (Left : Duration; Right : Time)     RETURN Time;
  FUNCTION "-"  (Left : Time;     Right : Duration) RETURN Time;
  FUNCTION "-"  (Left : Time;     Right : Time)     RETURN Duration;

  -- exported exceptions

  -- Time_Error is raised by Time_Of if its actual parameters
  -- don't form a proper date, and also by "+" and "-" if they
  -- can't return a date whose year number is in range,
  -- or if "-" can't return a value that is in the
  -- range of the type Duration.

  Time_Error : EXCEPTION;
```

```
PRIVATE

   -- implementation-dependent (the details depend on the computer's
   -- internal clock structure, and are not important because Calendar
   -- provides all the operations we need)

END Calendar;
```

Figure 1.9 Full Specification of Package `Ada.Calendar`

The first line of code in `Ada.Calendar` is a partial type definition:

```
TYPE Time IS PRIVATE;
```

The definition is completed at the bottom of the figure, below the word `PRIVATE`. Ada provides certain rules for the use of private types. First, variables of the type may be declared; for example,

```
MyBirthDay : Ada.Calendar.Time;
LastWeek : Ada.Calendar.Time;
```

are permissible declarations. Second, one variable of a private type may be assigned the value of another variable of the same type, and two variables of a private type may be compared for equality or inequality. For example,

```
LastWeek := MyBirthday;
IF LastWeek /= MyBirthday THEN...
```

are both valid operations. *No other operations are predefined*. Indeed, one of the purposes of private types is to allow the writer of a package to define *exactly* those operations he or she deems appropriate.

Following the definition of `Time` are four subtype declarations. Three of these give the acceptable ranges for year, month, and day values; the fourth specifies the number of duration units, or seconds, in a 24-hour day: 86,400. The Ada standard specifies that any time value from midnight on January 1, 1901, to midnight on December 31, 2099, must be treated as a unique valid value by `Ada.Calendar`.

`Time` is treated as a private type for two reasons. First, the internal representation of a time value is dependent on the form used by the hardware clock for time values. Second, not all operations make sense for time values. If `Time` were treated as simply some sort of integer value, for example, we could multiply two times together; however, multiplying 3 P.M. by 4 P.M. is meaningless! Making `Time` a private type allowed the designers of Ada to control precisely the set of sensible operations on `Time` values. What are these operations?

To use time values well, the client program must be able to create time values—for example, by supplying a month, a day, and a year. `Ada.Calendar` provides a function `Time_Of` for this purpose. An operation such as `Time_Of`, which *constructs* a value of the new type from its component parts, is called a *constructor* operation. There are also five *selector* operations, `Year`, `Month`, `Day`, `Seconds`, and `Split`, which allow the client program to select various components of a time value in a useful form (integer and duration values). The first four of these operations are functions that return individual components; `Split` is a procedure that produces all four components in a single call. The next operation is `Clock`, which returns the current time of day as a `Time` value.

We know from the discussion above that each time value is unique; also, time values are *monotonically increasing*; that is, as time progresses, each new value is greater than the preceding one. This conforms to our "real-world" view of time and to the concepts of "earlier" and "later." Because time is monotonically increasing—*totally ordered* is another mathematical term with similar meaning—we can confidently compare two values. Just as for any private type, Ada already provides equality and inequality operators, so `Ada.Calendar` provides the others: `<`, `<=`, `>`, and `>=`. Notice that these are specified as functions; they can be used in function form, for example

```
IF Ada.Calendar."<="(RightNow, AnotherTime) THEN
```

or as normal infix operators, for example

```
IF RightNow <= AnotherTime THEN
```

(The latter form is permitted *only* if a `USE Ada.Calendar` appears at the top of the program.)

To perform computations with time values, Ada provides some arithmetic operations. Only those operations that make sense are provided by the package, as follows:

```
FUNCTION "+" (Left : Time; Right : Duration) RETURN Time;
FUNCTION "+" (Left : Duration; Right : Time) RETURN Time;
FUNCTION "-" (Left : Time; Right : Duration) RETURN Time;
FUNCTION "-" (Left : Time; Right : Time)     RETURN Duration;
```

For example, adding two times together makes no sense (what does it mean to add 3 P.M. to 4 P.M.?); it is therefore not possible to do so with `Ada.Calendar` operations. It does make sense to add a duration to a time; for example, 3 P.M. plus 1 hour is 4 P.M. The two `"+"` operations are provided to ensure that the time value can appear on the right or on the left. Finally, the subtraction operations are sensible ones: Subtracting 3 P.M. from 4 P.M. gives 1 elapsed hour; subtracting 2 hours from 7 A.M. gives 5 A.M. These operations serve as excellent examples of the usefulness of private types in ensuring that a client cannot perform meaningless operations or operations that do not make physical sense.

The final line of code in the specification defines an exception `Time_Error`. This exception is raised whenever a `Time_Of` call would return an invalid time value—for example, if 2 (February), 30, and 1990 were supplied as parameters, because February 30 does not exist. `Ada.Calendar` also understands leap years, so `Time_Error` would be raised if 2, 29, and 1995 were supplied to `Time_Of`, because 1995 is not a leap year. `Time_Error` is also raised if the subtraction operator is given two times that are so far apart that the computer cannot represent the number of elapsed seconds that separate them.

1.11 APPLICATION: TIME AROUND THE WORLD

As an example of the use of `Ada.Calendar`, consider the problem of determining the time in other time zones around the world.

Problem Specification

Write a program to allow the user to enter the abbreviation of one of a set of cities and display the current time in that city.

Analysis

Given a table of city codes and the number of time zones separating each from the user's home time zone, we can use `Ada.Calendar` to find the current local time, then add or subtract the appropriate number of seconds to find the time elsewhere.

Data Requirements

Problem inputs

```
City : Cities
```

Design

Algorithm

1. Read the value of `City` from the keyboard.

2. Find the current local time.

3. Find the time in `City` by using the time zone offset table.

4. Display the local time and the time in `City`.

Test Plan

Since you can easily look up the number of hours of offset, test the program for the different allowed cities and be certain that the time is computed properly. Also test, as usual, for invalid input—that is, a token that is not a city code.

Implementation

Program 1.2 gives the program for `World_Time`. Type `Cities` gives a list of city names or abbreviations; a procedure `ReadCity` reads a city name robustly, refusing to permit an invalid city to be entered; and a procedure `DisplayTime` is used to display a time value in a useful form.

PROGRAM 1.2 Time Around the World

```
WITH Ada.Text_IO;
WITH Ada.Integer_Text_IO;
```

```
WITH Ada.Calendar;
PROCEDURE World_Time IS
-------------------------------------------------------------------------
--|
--| Finds the current time in any of several time zones
--|
--| Author: Michael B. Feldman, The George Washington University
--| Last Modified: July 1995
--|
-------------------------------------------------------------------------

  TYPE Cities IS (Paris, London, Rio, Caracas, DC,
                  Chicago, Denver, Seattle, Honolulu);

  PACKAGE City_IO IS NEW Ada.Text_IO.Enumeration_IO(Cities);

  TYPE TimeDiffs IS ARRAY (Cities) OF Integer;

  -- table of time differences from DC; modify this table if you are
  -- not located in the Eastern U.S. time zone
  Offsets : CONSTANT TimeDiffs :=
    (Paris => +6, London => +5, Rio => +2, Caracas => -1, DC => 0,
     Chicago => -1, Denver => -2, Seattle => -3, Honolulu => -5);

  TimeHere  : Ada.Calendar.Time;
  TimeThere : Ada.Calendar.Time;
  There     : Cities;

  FUNCTION AdjustTime (T: Ada.Calendar.Time; City: Cities;
                       OffsetTable: TimeDiffs)
    RETURN Ada.Calendar.Time IS

  -- given a time value, finds the corresponding time
  -- in a given time zone

  BEGIN -- AdjustTime

    RETURN Ada.Calendar."+"(T, Duration(OffsetTable(City) * 3600));

  END AdjustTime;


  PROCEDURE ReadCity(City : OUT Cities) IS

  -- reads a city name from the terminal, robustly

  BEGIN -- ReadCity

    LOOP
      BEGIN -- exception handler block
        Ada.Text_IO.Put_Line
          (Item => "Please enter one of the following:");
        Ada.Text_IO.Put_Line
          (Item => "Paris, London, Rio, Caracas, DC,");
        Ada.Text_IO.Put
          (Item => "Chicago, Denver, Seattle, Honolulu >");

        City_IO.Get(Item => City);
        EXIT; -- good input data
      EXCEPTION -- bad input data
        WHEN Ada.Text_IO.Data_Error =>
          Ada.Text_IO.Skip_Line;
          Ada.Text_IO.Put
            (Item => "Invalid city name; please try again.");
          Ada.Text_IO.New_Line;
      END; -- exception handler block

    END LOOP;

  END ReadCity;
```

```
PROCEDURE DisplayTime(T: Ada.Calendar.Time) IS

-- displays a Ada.Calendar.Time value in hh:mm:ss form

  TYPE DayInteger IS RANGE 0..86400;

  SecsPastMidnight : DayInteger; -- could be larger than 32767
  MinsPastMidnight : Natural;
  Secs             : Natural;
  Mins             : Natural;
  Hrs              : Natural;

BEGIN -- DisplayTime

  SecsPastMidnight := DayInteger(Ada.Calendar.Seconds(T));
  MinsPastMidnight := Natural(SecsPastMidnight/60);
  Secs             := Natural(SecsPastMidnight REM 60);
  Mins             := MinsPastMidnight REM 60;
  Hrs              := MinsPastMidnight / 60;

  Ada.Integer_Text_IO.Put (Item => Hrs, Width => 1);
  Ada.Text_IO.Put (Item => ':');
  IF Mins < 10 THEN
    Ada.Text_IO.Put (Item => '0');
  END IF;
  Ada.Integer_Text_IO.Put (Item => Mins, Width => 1);
  Ada.Text_IO.Put (Item => ':');
  IF Secs < 10 THEN
    Ada.Text_IO.Put (Item => '0');
  END IF;
  Ada.Integer_Text_IO.Put (Item => Secs, Width => 1);

END DisplayTime;

BEGIN -- World_Time
  ReadCity(City => There);
  TimeHere := Ada.Calendar.Clock;
  TimeThere := AdjustTime
    (T=>TimeHere, City => There, OffsetTable => Offsets);

  Ada.Text_IO.Put(Item => "Current local time is");
  DisplayTime(T => TimeHere);
  Ada.Text_IO.New_Line;
  Ada.Text_IO.Put(Item => "Current time in");
  City_IO.Put(Item => There, Width => 1);
  Ada.Text_IO.Put(Item => "is");
  DisplayTime(T => TimeThere);
  Ada.Text_IO.New_Line;

END World_Time;
```

The function `AdjustTime` does the work of computing the new time. It contains a table of offsets, or numbers of time zones away from local time. `Ada.Calendar."+"` is used to add or subtract the appropriate number of seconds:

```
RETURN Ada.Calendar."+"(T, Duration(Offsets(City) * 3600));
```

The array `Offsets` gives the time-zone differences; the number of seconds is computed by multiplying the number of time zones by 3600 (the number of seconds in an hour), then converting to type `Duration`.

It is important to note that on most computers, `Ada.Calendar.Clock` gives the current *local* time, not some universal time value. The array `Offsets` is initialized to the offsets from the authors' home time zone, the Eastern zone; you will have to change the table values if you are running this program in another zone. Exercise 3 suggests an approach to solving this problem in a more robust manner.

As an example of the use of `Calendar`, consider the problem of determining the times in other time zones around the world. We describe this project using the life cycle steps introduced in Section 1.3.

1.12   A PREDEFINED ADT: STRINGS IN ADA

In this section, we will take a systematic look at the character string, an important data structure in many applications. Figure 1.10 shows the part of package `Standard` describing this type. It is interesting to note that the comparison operators are all defined for strings, even though a string is just an array of characters. The comparison is done following lexicographical, or dictionary, order, so that `"ABC"` is less than `"BC"` even though the first string is longer. This agrees with our intuition about the way strings should be compared.

Ada's predefined type `String` is a certain kind of array of characters. A variable of type `String` is called a *string variable*, or sometimes just a *string*. The basic ideas are as follows:

- A string variable is in fact an array of characters, with a subscript range that must be a subtype of `Positive`.

- String variables can be compared and assigned like other Ada variables, but their lengths must match exactly.

```
-- Predefined string type:

TYPE String IS ARRAY(Positive RANGE <>) OF Character;

PRAGMA Pack(String); -- pack characters into words if possible

-- The predefined operators for this type are as follows:

FUNCTION "="  (Left, Right : String) RETURN Boolean;
FUNCTION "/=" (Left, Right : String) RETURN Boolean;
FUNCTION "<"  (Left, Right : String) RETURN Boolean;
FUNCTION "<=" (Left, Right : String) RETURN Boolean;
FUNCTION ">"  (Left, Right : String) RETURN Boolean;
FUNCTION ">=" (Left, Right : String) RETURN Boolean;

-- These four operators provide string concatenation

FUNCTION "&"  (Left : String;    Right : String)    RETURN String;
FUNCTION "&"  (Left : Character; Right : String)    RETURN String;
FUNCTION "&"  (Left : String;    Right : Character) RETURN String;
FUNCTION "&"  (Left : Character; Right : Character) RETURN String;
```

Figure 1.10 Section of Package `Standard` Describing `String`

- It is possible to assign or refer to a part, or *slice*, of a string.

- Strings can be concatenated, or "pasted together," to form longer ones.

The type `String` is predefined in the language and is given in Fig. 1.9. The string operations are sufficiently systematic and powerful that it makes sense to treat the string facility as though it were a separate ADT. Later in this book, we will present ADTs for several alternative methods for representing strings of varying length, with operations even more powerful than the predefined ones.

Declaring a String Variable

The declarations

```
NameSize : CONSTANT Positive := 11;
FirstName : String(1..NameSize);
LastName : String(1..NameSize);
```

allocate storage for two string variables: `FirstName` and `LastName`. String variables `FirstName` and `LastName` can store 11 characters each (subscript range 1..11). In general, a string variable of type `String(1..N)` can be used to store a string of up to N characters.

Referencing Individual Characters in a String

We can manipulate individual characters in a string variable in the same way as we manipulate individual elements of an array. The program fragment below reads 11 characters into string variable `FirstName` and displays all characters stored in the string.

```
Text_IO.Put(Item => "Enter your first name and an initial,");
Text_IO.Put(Item => " exactly 11 characters > ");

FOR I IN 1..NameSize LOOP
   Text_IO.Get (Item => FirstName(I));
END LOOP;

Text_IO.Put (Item => "Hello ");
FOR I IN 1..NameSize LOOP
   Text_IO.Put (Item => FirstName(I));
END LOOP;

Text_IO.Put(Item => '!');
Text_IO.New_Line;
```

A sample run of this program segment is shown below.

```
Enter your first name and an initial, exactly 11 characters > Jonathan B.
Hello Jonathan B.!
```

Eleven data characters are read into string variable `FirstName` after the prompt in the first line is displayed. The string variable `FirstName` is

```
(1)  (2)  (3)  (4)  (5)  (6)  (7)  (8)  (9)  (10)  (11)
 J    o    n    a    t    h    a    n         B     .
```

A Character Is Not Compatible with a One-Character String

String variable `OneString`, declared below, is a string of length 1.

```
OneString : String(1..1);
NextCh : Character;
```

The assignment statements

```
OneString(1) := NextCh;
NextCh := OneString(1);
```

are valid; they store a copy of `NextCh` in string `OneString`. However, the assignment statements

```
OneString := NextCh;
NextCh := OneString;
```

are invalid; they cause a "type compatibility" compilation error. A string that happens to be only one character long is still of a different type from a character!

Assigning, Comparing, and Displaying Strings

Besides manipulating individual characters in a string variable, we can manipulate the string as a unit. The assignment statement

```
LastName := "Appleseed";
```

appears to store the string value `Appleseed` in the string variable `LastName` declared earlier. This is not true, however: String assignment is correct only if the lengths of the strings on both sides are exactly the same. Because `Appleseed` has only nine letters, the assignment above might cause a warning at compilation time but would always cause `Constraint_Error` to be raised at execution time. If we add two blanks, the assignment will take place as desired:

```
LastName := "Appleseed ";
```

The string variable `LastName` is defined as shown below:

```
(1)   (2)   (3)   (4)   (5)   (6)   (7)   (8)   (9)   (10)  (11)
 A     p     p     l     e     s     e     e     d     #     #
```

(the # characters are used here only to show the locations of the blanks.)
   The statements

```
Text_IO.Put(Item => LastName);
Text_IO.Put (Item => ', ');
Text_IO.Put (Item => FirstName);
Text_IO.New_Line;
```

display the output line

```
Appleseed   , Jonathan B.
```

Note the two blanks following the last name!

As with other array types, we can copy the contents of one string variable to another of the same length, and we can compare two strings of the same length. The statement

```
FirstName := LastName;
```

copies the string value stored in `LastName` to `FirstName`; the `Boolean` condition

```
FirstName = LastName
```

is `True` after the assignment, but would have been `False` before.

Reading Strings

Ada provides several `Get` procedures in `Ada.Text_IO` for entering a string value. The statement

```
Text_IO.Get(FirstName);
```

reads *exactly* 11 characters (including blanks, punctuation, and so on) into the string variable `FirstName`. The data entry operation is *not* terminated by pressing RETURN; if only five characters are entered before RETURN is pressed, the computer simply waits for the additional six characters! This is a common error made by many Ada beginners, who think their program is "stuck" when nothing seems to happen after RETURN is pressed. In fact, the program is doing just what it was told: Read *exactly* 11 characters. It is not possible to read more than 11 characters into `FirstName`; the additional characters just stay in the file, waiting for the next `Get` call.

This is an unsatisfying way to read strings, because it provides no way to read a string shorter than the maximum length of the string variable. A better way is to use the `Get_Line` procedure in `Ada.Text_IO`. Given a variable

```
NameLength : Natural;
```

the statement

```
Text_IO.Get_Line (Item => LastName, Last => NameLength);
```

tries to read 11 characters as before, but if RETURN is pressed before 11 characters are read, reading stops. `NameLength` is used as an `OUT` parameter corresponding to `Get_Line`'s formal parameter `Last`; after the `Get` operation, `NameLength` contains the actual number of characters read. If fewer characters are read than the string can accommodate, the remaining characters in the string are *undefined*.

Given the declarations

```
FirstNameLength : Natural;
LastNameLength  : Natural;
```

the statements

```
Text_IO.Put(Item => "Enter your first name followed by CR > ");
Text_IO.Get_Line(Item => FirstName, Last => FirstNameLength);
Text_IO.Put(Item => "Enter your last name followed by CR > ");
Text_IO.Get_Line(Item => LastName, Last => LastNameLength);
```

can be used to enter string values into the string variables `FirstName` and `LastName`. Up to 11 characters can be stored in `FirstName` and `LastName`. If the data characters `Johnny` are entered after the first prompt and the data characters `Appleseed` are entered after the second prompt, string `FirstName` is defined as

```
(1)  (2)  (3)  (4)  (5)  (6)  (7)  (8)  (9)  (10)  (11)
 J    o    h    n    n    y    ?    ?    ?     ?     ?
```

and string `LastName` is defined as

```
(1)  (2)  (3)  (4)  (5)  (6)  (7)  (8)  (9)  (10)  (11)
 A    p    p    l    e    s    e    e    d     ?     ?
```

The variables `FirstNameLength` and `LastNameLength` will contain 6 and 9, respectively. The statement

```
Text_IO.Put(Item => FirstName);
```

will display `Johnny`, followed by five characters of arbitrary ("garbage") value. The last five characters are unpredictable, because no values were placed in them by the `Get_Line` operation.

String Slicing

The flexibility of string handling in Ada is enhanced by *string slicing*. This is the ability to store into, or extract, a *slice*, or section, of a string variable just by specifying the bounds of the desired section.

Given the string variables `FirstName` and `LastName` as above, the slices

```
FirstName(1..4)
LastName (5..11)
```

refer to the first through fourth characters of `FirstName` and the fifth through eleventh characters of `LastName`, respectively. The statement

```
Text_IO.Put(Item => FirstName(1..FirstNameLength));
```

displays the string `Johnny` with no extra blanks. Given declarations

```
WholeNameLength : Natural;
WholeName : String(1..24);
```

the statements

```
WholeNameLength := FirstNameLength + LastNameLength + 2;
WholeName(1..LastNameLength) := LastName(1..LastNameLength);
WholeName(LastNameLength+1..LastNameLength+2) := ", ";
WholeName(LastNameLength+3..WholeNameLength) :=
  FirstName(1..FirstNameLength);
Text_IO.Put(Item => WholeName(1..WholeNameLength));
```

will store in `WholeName` and will display

```
Appleseed, Johnny
```

String Concatenation

One more string operation should be considered here. The *string concatenation* operator `&`, applied to two strings `S1` and `S2`, concatenates, or "pastes together," its two arguments. The statement

```
S3 := S1 & S2;
```

stores in `S3` the concatenation of `S1` and `S2`. For the assignment to be valid, the length of `S3` still must match the sum of the lengths of `S1` and `S2`; if it does not, `Constraint_Error` will be raised, as usual. Continuing with the name example above, `WholeName` can be created more simply using concatenation:

```
WholeNameLength := FirstNameLength + LastNameLength + 2;
WholeName(1..WholeNameLength) :=
  LastName(1..LastNameLength) & ", " & FirstName(1..FirstNameLength);
```

The result of a concatenation can also be passed directly as a parameter, for example to `Text_IO.Put`:

```
Text_IO.Put(Item =>
  LastName(1..LastNameLength) & ", " &
  FirstName(1..FirstNameLength));
```

String Attributes

Like most types in Ada, a string is provided with a set of attributes. These will be used quite a bit in this book, beginning with the next chapter.

Given a string `S`, the important attribute functions for `S` are

- `S'First`, which returns the value of the first *subscript* of `S`

- `S'Last`, which returns the value of the last subscript of `S`

- `S'Length`, which returns the length of `S`—that is, the number of characters in `S`

- `S'Range`, which returns the *range* `S'First..S'Last`

It important to keep in mind that these attributes refer more to the subscripts than to the actual values of the characters in the string. For example, if we wanted to refer to the value of the first character in `S`, we would write `S(S'First)`, rather than `S'First`, which refers to the value of the first subscript.

Now suppose we were interested in the value of the *second* character. Writing `S(2)` would not always be correct. Specifically, `S` might be only a formal parameter to a subprogram. Suppose we passed to this subprogram an actual parameter that was a slice `T(3..5)` of some other string `T`. In this case there would be no `S(2)`; `Constraint_Error` would be raised if we tried to refer to it.

The solution to this problem lies in remembering the `Succ` and `Pred` attributes. Assuming that the string contains at least two characters, we can get the second character by writing S(Positive'Succ(S'First)); under the same assumption, we can always get the next-to-last character by writing S(Positive'Pred(S'Last)).

SUMMARY

In this chapter, you have taken a quick trip through the Ada type system and learned about abstraction, data abstraction, and abstract data types, or ADTs. The ADT idea is a powerful one; it is an important approach to building reusable software components and is one of the essential topics in this book.

Ada was designed to facilitate constructing ADTs and provides many features for doing so. Subtypes, new and derived types, attributes, operator overloading, packages, private types, and exceptions all contribute to our ability to create effective and useful ADTs. You have seen how Ada's predefined types are given in ADT form by the package Standard, and examined the Ada.Calendar package and Ada's predesigned support for strings.

Armed with this basic introduction to abstraction and using ADTs, you are ready to proceed to Chapter 2, in which you will learn how to develop your own ADTs.

EXERCISES

1. Explain the various kinds of operations in an ADT.
2. Write a program that tests the operations in package Calendar. For example, try to add together two time values. Also investigate what happens when Time_Of is called with parameters that would lead to an invalid time value (February 30, for example, or February 29, 1991). Does Calendar behave correctly, as the specification suggests?
3. The World_Time program presented in Section 1.11 has a limitation: The array of time-zone offsets must be completely redefined if the program user is not in the Eastern U.S. time zone. In many applications, time-zone offsets are computed with respect to Greenwich Mean Time, often referred to as GMT or Zulu. This is the local time in Greenwich, England. Modify World_Time so that Zulu is used as the "zero point" for the offsets. (Encyclopedias and almanacs usually describe the various official time zones around the world; so do amateur radio guides.) Because a computer's clock normally reports only local time, your program will need to find out from the user in which time zone he or she is located before it can compute the time elsewhere.
4. Another limitation in World_Time is that the various time-zone offsets are given there as integers. In fact, there are actually time zones that are not an integral number of hours from GMT. When it's midnight in London (GMT), it's 5:30 A.M. in Delhi, India, 9:30 A.M. in Adelaide, Australia, and 8:30 P.M. in St. Johns, Newfoundland, Canada. Modify World_Time to accommodate nonintegral time-zone offsets.

CHAPTER 2

Writing Abstract Data Types

Chapter 1 presented some general background about abstraction, the Ada type system, and about the general ideas embodied in the abstract data type (ADT) concept. In this chapter, you will learn to write ADTs and you will see the details of several useful reusable components: rational numbers or fractions, monetary values, calendar dates, video screen controls, and simple display "windows." You'll also learn how to design a test plan to demonstrate that an ADT works as it should.

2.1   ADT DESIGN: RATIONAL NUMBERS

This section explains how to specify and implement an abstract data type for doing arithmetic with fractions or rational numbers. A *rational number* is a number with a *numerator* and a *denominator*. For example, the rational number $\frac{a}{b}$ has a numerator of a and a denominator of b; the rational number $\frac{2}{3}$ has a numerator of 2 and a denominator of 3.

Every integer is also equivalent to a rational number: The integer 4 is equivalent to the rational $\frac{4}{1}$. A rational number cannot have a denominator of 0, but a numerator of zero is fine. Fractions are useful in certain engineering applications—for example, where we want to represent the number $\frac{1}{3}$ exactly and not as the floating-point approximation 0.3333. . . . Although programming languages usually have built-in support for integers and floats, they rarely support rationals directly.

An *improper rational* is a rational number whose numerator is larger than its denominator—for example, $\frac{5}{3}$. The term *improper* is historical; there is nothing wrong with a rational that's "improper." Also, each rational is algebraically equivalent to many others. For example,

$$\frac{2}{3} = \frac{4}{6} = \frac{6}{9} = \ldots = \frac{24}{36} = \ldots$$

A rational whose numerator and denominator have no common divisors is referred to as *reduced*, or sometimes *in lowest terms*. An example of a rational in lowest terms is $\frac{2}{3}$; the others in the series can all be reduced to $\frac{2}{3}$.

Requirements

We require a facility to provide full support for creating and manipulating rationals. Operations include

- *Creating* a rational value
- *Comparing* rational values as is done with other numerical quantities, namely providing support for =, /=, <, <=, >, and >=
- *Doing arithmetic* with rationals—namely, providing support for +, −, *, and /
- *Inputting and outputting* rational values

Ideally, the user of this facility—a programmer writing other applications requiring rationals—should perceive little or no difference between working with rationals and working with floats or integers.

Analysis

Since we are developing a reusable component—a package of facilities for dealing with rationals—and not an application program designed for a single use, there are no specific initial problem inputs or final problem outputs. We will need to provide input/output capabilities for reading rational values from the keyboard or from a disk file, and for writing rational values to the screen or a file. The main constraint on the design is the requirement that users—in this case, programmers, not end users—be able to deal with rationals in a way consistent with their experience in dealing with other numerical quantities in their programs.

Design of the `Rationals` Package

For the basic operations on `Rational` values, we will construct an abstract data type package to represent the data structure for a rational number with operators for each of the tasks listed above. We will represent each rational quantity as a record with numerator and denominator fields, and we will make the rational type `PRIVATE` to prevent client programs from directly manipulating the fields.

We can use Ada's predefined assignment, equality, and inequality for rationals, but to do so is meaningful only if we store all rationals in lowest terms. To understand why, remember that Ada's predefined equality compares two records by determining whether each field of one record is equal to the corresponding field of the other. If each comparison yields a true result, the overall equality is true. If our design did not require rationals to be in lowest terms, the equality check would return incorrect results; for example, $\frac{2}{3} = \frac{6}{9}$ is true in the "real world," but would be false in our system. However, if $\frac{6}{9}$ were never actually stored in our system, but is replaced with its reduced equivalent, $\frac{2}{3}$, this problem cannot arise. We will consider detailed algorithms for reduction, as well as rational arithmetic, a bit later. First we need a structured specification of the ADT. The package specification for the abstract data type `Rationals` appears as Program 2.1.

Program 2.1 Specification for `Rationals` Package

```
PACKAGE Rationals IS

------------------------------------------------------------------------
--| Specification of the abstract data type for representing
--| and manipulating rational numbers.
--| All rational quantities in this package are initialized
--| to 0/1.
--| Author: Michael B. Feldman, The George Washington University
--| Last Modified: July 1995
------------------------------------------------------------------------

  TYPE Rational IS PRIVATE;

  ZeroDenominator: EXCEPTION;

  FUNCTION "/" (X : Integer; Y : Integer) RETURN Rational;
  -- constructor:
  -- Pre : X and Y are defined
  -- Post: returns a rational number
  --    If Y > 0, returns Reduce(X,Y)
  --    If Y < 0, returns Reduce(-X,-Y)
  -- Raises: ZeroDenominator if Y = 0

  FUNCTION Numer (R : Rational) RETURN Integer;
  FUNCTION Denom (R : Rational) RETURN Positive;
  -- selectors:
  -- Pre: R is defined
  -- Post: Numer returns the numerator of R; Denom returns the
  --     denominator

  FUNCTION "<" (R1 : Rational; R2 : Rational) RETURN Boolean;
  FUNCTION "<="(R1 : Rational; R2 : Rational) RETURN Boolean;
  FUNCTION ">" (R1 : Rational; R2 : Rational) RETURN Boolean;
```

```
FUNCTION ">="(R1 : Rational; R2 : Rational) RETURN Boolean;
-- inquiry operators: comparison of two rational numbers
-- Pre : R1 and R2 are defined
-- Post: return R1 < R2, R1 > R2, R1 <= R2, and R1 >= R2, respectively

FUNCTION "+"(R: Rational) RETURN Rational;
FUNCTION "-"(R: Rational) RETURN Rational;
FUNCTION "ABS"(R: Rational) RETURN Rational;
-- monadic arithmetic constructors:
-- Pre: R is defined
-- Post: return R, -R, and ABS R, respectively

FUNCTION "+"(R1 : Rational; R2 : Rational) RETURN Rational;
FUNCTION "-"(R1 : Rational; R2 : Rational) RETURN Rational;
FUNCTION "*"(R1 : Rational; R2 : Rational) RETURN Rational;
FUNCTION "/"(R1 : Rational; R2 : Rational) RETURN Rational;
-- dyadic arithmetic constructors:
-- Pre : R1 and R2 are defined
-- Post: return the rational sum, difference, product, and
--    quotient of R1 and R2, respectively

PRIVATE
-- A record of type Rational consists of a pair of Integer values
-- such that the first number represents the numerator of a rational
-- number and the second number represents the denominator.

TYPE Rational IS RECORD
   Numerator : Integer := 0;
   Denominator: Positive := 1;
END RECORD;
END Rationals;
```

Specifying an ADT: A Detailed Look at the `Rationals` Specification

The first declaration in Program 2.1 is that of the type being exported to the client program. The type `Rational` is declared to be `PRIVATE` so that client programs are prevented from directly referencing the internal details of a variable of type `Rational`.

The private type definition is completed at the bottom of the specification, in the `PRIVATE` section. A `Rational` quantity is a record with an `Integer` field, `Numerator`, and a `Positive` field, `Denominator`. We require the denominator to be positive so that it can never be zero. Note that both fields of the record are initialized, so that every object of type `Rational` automatically has the initial value $\frac{0}{1}$. This helps us to ensure that all `Rational` operations will be meaningful, by making it more difficult for a client program to pass uninitialized storage, containing unpredictable random or "garbage" values, to the operators.

Making the type `PRIVATE` is important because we require all `Rational` values to be in lowest terms. If we allowed the client program direct access to the fields of the record, the client could assign, say, 2 to the numerator field and 4 to the denominator field. This would be inconsistent with the lowest-terms assumption of all the operations, and would therefore lead to unpredictable and incorrect results. You can see how `PRIVATE` types help us ensure the correctness and consistency of our operations.

Specifying Operations with Preconditions and Postconditions

Returning to the beginning of the specification, the first operator given is a *constructor* "/".

```
FUNCTION "/" (X : Integer; Y : Integer) RETURN Rational;
-- Pre    : X and Y are defined
-- Post   : constructor: returns a rational number in lowest terms
--    If Y > 0, returns Reduce(X,Y)
--    If Y < 0, returns Reduce(-X,-Y)
-- Raises: ZeroDenominator if Y = 0
```

This function takes two `Integer` arguments X and Y and returns a reduced rational number equivalent to $\frac{X}{Y}$. Here we are taking advantage of the fact that Ada allows us to return a record as the result of a function. Note that the inputs to "/" can both be negative; the constructor will always return a positive denominator by multiplying numerator and demominator by –1 if necessary.

Note the form of the comments following the specification. The line

```
-- Pre: X and Y are defined.
```

describes the *precondition* for the function. This is the condition that we require to be true before the function is called; in this case, we require that the calling program has assigned definite values to X and Y. The next three comment lines describe the *postcondition* for the function. We are stating our assumptions about the parameters and promising that *if* the preconditions are true just before the function is called, *then* the postcondition will be true after the function execution is completed.

Preconditions and postconditions form an informal contract between the operation's designer and its user. The designer promises that the operation execution will cause the postcondition to be true if the user calls the operation *only* when the preconditions are true. If the operation is called when a precondition is not true—for example, if X and Y haven't been assigned definite values—then "all bets are off"; that is, we cannot be responsible for the outcome.

The contract is informal because Ada provides no automatic way to ensure that the preconditions are met or to guarantee that the operation's execution in fact makes the postcondition true. (In this case, Ada gives us no way to ensure that a variable has been defined.) Explicit preconditions and postconditions are therefore nothing more than documentation, but this documentation is valuable to the user of the operation. The use of preconditions and postconditions also aids in verifying the correctness of a program that calls this operation. In this book, we will generally document our procedures and functions with preconditions and postconditions.

The final comment line in the constructor specification indicates whether the operation can raise any exceptions, and under what circumstances. In this case, if Y happens to be 0, `ZeroDenominator`—an exception provided by our package—will be raised.

Will the exception be raised if the preconditions are not met—that is, if Y is not defined? We do not know, and cannot know, because even undefined memory contains some unknown pattern of bits. If the "garbage" value in Y happens to be 0, the exception will be raised; if it happens to be nonzero, the exception will not be raised and the result of the operation is unpredictable. In general, we will use preconditions to state assumptions about the user input that the operation *cannot* test, and exceptions to indicate a violation of an assumption that we *can* test.

Specifying Operations by Operator Overloading

A client of `Rationals` can create a rational number by calling " / ". Given the declaration

```
R: Rationals.Rational;
```

the assignment

```
R := Rationals."/"(2,-4)
```

creates a record with –1 in the numerator and 2 in the denominator (remember the lowest-terms postcondition).

The next two operators are *selector* functions `Numer` and `Denom`, which, given a rational, return the values stored in its numerator and denominator, respectively. The next four operators specify the comparison operators `"<"`, `">"`, `"<="`, and `">="`; the monadic or unary operators `"+"`, `"-"`, and `"ABS"` follow, and then the dyadic or binary operators `"+"`, `"-"`, `"*"`, and `"/"`. All these operators are specified by analogy with the corresponding operators for the predefined integer and float types you saw in package `Standard`.

Defining new operations as operator symbols is called *operator overloading*. Recall the similar group of operators in `Ada.Calendar`; it makes no difference whether the operators are provided by a predefined package such as `Ada.Calendar` or by a user-defined package such as `Rationals`. Operators are really nothing more than functions with a special syntax, appearing between their parameters instead of preceding them. Because function names can be overloaded, so can operator names. Operator overloading allows us to write operations that are mathematical in nature using the familiar mathematical symbols.

It is important to understand that Ada allows us to overload *only* those operator symbols already available in the language; we cannot, for example, define a new operator `"?"`, because `"?"` is not already an operator in Ada. Also bear in mind that, for reasons beyond the scope of this book, it is *not* possible under most circumstances to define our own operator `"="`. It is similarly prohibited (and will cause a compilation error) to overload `"/="`, the two membership operators `"IN"` and `"NOT IN"`, and the short-circuit logical operators `"AND THEN"` and `"OR ELSE"`. Note that overloading `"AND"` and `"OR"` is permitted.

Generally, ADTs can be written so that Ada's predefined `"="` and `"/="` work correctly. This is true of `Ada.Calendar` and also of `Rationals`, and will be so in many other ADT packages we develop in this book.

After the package specification is written and compiled into the Ada program library, programmers can implement and compile (but not link or execute) client programs that use the abstract data type `Rational`. The next step is to implement in the package body all the operations promised by the specification.

Detailed Design and Implementation of the Package Body

We first consider the important algorithms of the implementation. We have made an essential design decision to represent all rationals in reduced, or lowest-terms, form. We first find the greatest common divisor, or GCD, of the absolute values of the rational's numerator and denominator, then divide both numerator and denominator by this value. To find the GCD of two positive integers M and N, we use a classical algorithm published by the ancient Greek scientist Euclid about 2000 years ago.

Algorithm for GCD

1. Divide M by N and store the remainder in R.
2.  ```
    WHILE R /= 0 LOOP
    ```
    Set the value of M to that of N.
    Set the value of N to that of R.
    Divide M by N and store the remainder in R
```
END LOOP;
```
3. The result is in N.

Now we can find the sum and product of rationals. The sum of two rationals X and Y is the result of reducing

$$\frac{(\mathrm{Numer}(X) \times \mathrm{Denom}(Y)) + (\mathrm{Denom}(X) \times \mathrm{Numer}(Y))}{\mathrm{Denom}(X) \times \mathrm{Denom}(Y)}$$

to lowest terms. For example,

$$\frac{1}{6} + \frac{2}{3} = \frac{(1 \times 3) + (6 \times 2)}{6 \times 3} = \frac{15}{18} = \frac{5}{6}$$

The product of two rationals X and Y is the result of reducing

$$\frac{\mathrm{Numer}(X) \times \mathrm{Numer}(Y)}{\mathrm{Denom}(X) \times \mathrm{Denom}(Y)}$$

to lowest terms. Subtraction is like addition, except that the numerator is the difference instead of the sum of the cross-products; division is like multiplication, except that the numerator and denominator of the result are interchanged. If you're not sure you understand this, try some examples by hand.

In comparing two rationals, because the denominators are always positive, we can simply "cross-multiply" and compare the numerators and denominators. Thus X < Y is determined by the Boolean expression

```
(Numer(X) x Denom(Y)) < (Numer(Y) x Denom(X))
```
```

For example, $\frac{1}{6} < \frac{2}{3}$ because $(1 \times 3) < (6 \times 2)$.

The package body is shown as Program 2.2. Let us look at several of the operations in detail.

The Rational Constructor "/"

Here is the specification of this constructor operation, taken from the ADT specification in Program 2.1:

```
FUNCTION "/" (X : Integer; Y : Integer) RETURN Rational;
-- constructor: returns a rational number in lowest terms
-- Pre : X and Y are defined
-- Post: returns a rational number
--    If Y > 0, returns Reduce(X,Y)
--    If Y < 0, returns Reduce(-X,-Y)
-- Raises: ZeroDenominator if Y = 0
```

In implementing this specification, we assume the preconditions and implement the function so that the postconditions are met. Here is the body of this function, taken from Program 2.2:

```
FUNCTION "/" (X : Integer; Y : Integer) RETURN Rational IS

  G: Positive;

BEGIN -- "/"

  IF Y = 0 THEN
    RAISE ZeroDenominator;
  END IF;

  IF X = 0 THEN
    RETURN (Numerator => 0, Denominator => 1);
  END IF;

  G := GCD(ABS X, ABS Y);
  IF Y > 0 THEN
    RETURN (Numerator => X/G, Denominator => Y/G);
  ELSE
    RETURN (Numerator => (-X)/G, Denominator => (-Y)/G);
  END IF;

END "/";
```

First, if the desired denominator is 0, there is no point in proceeding further; we simply raise the required exception. The function will return immediately, raising the exception at the point in the client program at which it was called. It is then the client's responsibility to handle the exception; our package cannot correct invalid input, but can only report it to the client. Abstract data types generally follow this policy of "garbage in, exception out." An ADT cannot be held responsible for correcting invalid or meaningless input, but should be robust enough that it does not produce invalid or meaningless output either. For all inputs meeting the preconditions, our result must be predictable, and raising an exception is a predictable consequence.

We next consider the other possibilities: A numerator of 0 is a perfectly acceptable value, so we simply return the rational $\frac{0}{1}$; a negative denominator causes numerator and denominator to be multiplied by –1, to satisfy the postcondition that the denominator be positive.

Other Operations

Many of the other operations of Program 2.2 are written as straightforward implementations of the algorithms given above. Some are left as *stubs* for you to complete.

Using stubs allows the overall package to be partially tested without requiring that all operations be fully coded. A stub is simply a "framework" for an operation. All we require of a stub is that it be legally compilable and executable. Generally this means that a stub must either return its input unchanged or compute some meaningful part of its computation. For example, in Program 2.2, the "-" and ">" operations are shown as stubs. The first operation returns a known rational value as its result; the second always returns True.

```
FUNCTION "-"(R1 : Rational; R2 : Rational) RETURN Rational IS
BEGIN -- stub
  RETURN 1/1;
END "-";

FUNCTION ">" (R1 : Rational; R2 : Rational) RETURN Boolean IS
BEGIN -- stub
  RETURN True;
END ">";
```

If stubs are available for the operations, the client programs can be compiled and executed to test the overall flow of control, with the understanding that stubbed-out operations will return incorrect results. When all operations in the package body have been completed, the client programs can be executed in a meaningful way. Completing the operations in package Rationals, shown as Program 2.2, is left as an exercise.

Program 2.2 Body of Rationals Package

```
PACKAGE BODY Rationals IS
------------------------------------------------------------------------
--| Body of the abstract data type for representing
--| and manipulating rational numbers.
--| Author: Michael B. Feldman, The George Washington University
--| Last Modified: July 1995
------------------------------------------------------------------------
  -- local function GCD, not provided to clients

  FUNCTION GCD(M: Positive; N: Positive) RETURN Positive IS
  -- finds the greatest common divisor of M and N
  -- Pre: M and N are defined
  -- Post: returns the GCD of M and N, by Euclid's Algorithm

    R    : Natural;
    TempM: Positive;
    TempN: Positive;
```

```
BEGIN -- GCD

  TempM := M;
  TempN := N;

  R := TempM REM TempN;

  WHILE R /= 0 LOOP
    TempM := TempN;
    TempN := R;
    R := TempM REM TempN;
  END LOOP;

  RETURN TempN;

END GCD;

-- exported operations

FUNCTION "/" (X : Integer; Y : Integer) RETURN Rational IS
  G: Positive;
BEGIN -- "/"

  IF Y = 0 THEN
    RAISE ZeroDenominator;
  END IF;

  IF X = 0 THEN
    RETURN (Numerator => 0, Denominator => 1);
  END IF;

  G := GCD(ABS X, ABS Y);
  IF Y > 0 THEN
    RETURN (Numerator => X/G, Denominator => Y/G);
  ELSE
    RETURN (Numerator => (-X)/G, Denominator => (-Y)/G);
  END IF;

END "/";

-- selectors

FUNCTION Numer (R : Rational) RETURN Integer IS
BEGIN -- Numer
  RETURN R.Numerator;
END Numer;

FUNCTION Denom (R : Rational) RETURN Positive IS
BEGIN -- Denom
  RETURN R.Denominator;
END Denom;

-- inquiry operators

FUNCTION "<" (R1 : Rational; R2 : Rational) RETURN Boolean IS
BEGIN
  RETURN Numer(R1) * Denom(R2) < Numer(R2) * Denom(R1);
END "<";

FUNCTION ">" (R1 : Rational; R2 : Rational) RETURN Boolean IS
BEGIN -- stub
  RETURN True;
END ">";

FUNCTION "<=" (R1 : Rational; R2 : Rational) RETURN Boolean IS
BEGIN -- stub
  RETURN True;
END "<=";
```

```
FUNCTION ">=" (R1 : Rational; R2 : Rational) RETURN Boolean IS
BEGIN -- stub
  RETURN True;
END ">=";

-- monadic arithmetic operators

FUNCTION "+"(R : Rational) RETURN Rational IS
BEGIN -- "+"
  RETURN R;
END "+";

FUNCTION "-"(R : Rational) RETURN Rational IS
BEGIN -- "-"
  RETURN (-Numer(R)) / Denom(R);
END "-";

FUNCTION "ABS"(R : Rational) RETURN Rational IS
BEGIN -- "ABS"
  RETURN (ABS Numer(R)) / Denom(R);
END "ABS";

-- dyadic arithmetic operators

FUNCTION "+"(R1 : Rational; R2 : Rational) RETURN Rational IS
  N:  Integer;
  D: Positive;
BEGIN -- "+"
  N := Numer(R1) * Denom(R2) + Numer(R2) * Denom(R1);
  D := Denom(R1) * Denom(R2);
  RETURN N/D;  -- compiler will use Rational constructor here!
END "+";

FUNCTION "*"(R1 : Rational; R2 : Rational) RETURN Rational IS
  N: Integer;
  D: Positive;
BEGIN -- "*"
  N := Numer(R1) * Numer(R2);
  D := Denom(R1) * Denom(R2);
  RETURN N/D;  -- compiler will use Rational constructor here!
END "*";

FUNCTION "-"(R1 : Rational; R2 : Rational) RETURN Rational IS
BEGIN -- stub
  RETURN 1/1;
END "-";

FUNCTION "/"(R1 : Rational; R2 : Rational) RETURN Rational IS
BEGIN -- stub
  RETURN 1/1;
END "/";

END Rationals;
```

The Child Package `Rationals.IO`

The `Rationals` package cannot be used very meaningfully as it stands, because it provides no way to read or display rational values. We could build input/output operations into the package, but we choose instead to write a separate package for input/output. This is analogous to the input/output packages provided by `Ada.Text_IO`; we will use this style frequently in this book.

There is no inherent reason why we could not write a completely separate package for input/output, which would be structurally just like a client package. However, to indicate the close relationship between the rationals package and its associated input/output package, we construct the latter as an Ada 95 *child package*.[1] Just as the various standard libraries are given in Ada 95 as children of Ada, we write the rational input/output package as a child of Rationals and call it Rationals.IO. We will introduce a number of child packages in this book. Think of a child package as an extension of its parent package, adding (usually) operations to the parent. Child packages in Ada 95 provide a way of extending a package without modifying or recompiling the parent.

Programs 2.3 and 2.4 show, respectively, the specification and the body of Rationals.IO, which you should find easy to understand. We note only that the Get and Put operations—which read from the keyboard and write to the screen—are implemented as calls to the more general procedures, which use named files. Note that because this package is a child of Rationals, it does not have a WITH Rationals context clause. Rather, the very name of the child—Rationals.IO in this case— indicates the relationship.

Program 2.3 Specification for Rationals.IO Child Package

```
WITH Ada.Text_IO;
PACKAGE Rationals.IO IS
------------------------------------------------------------------------
--| Specification of the input/output child package for Rationals
--| Author: Michael B. Feldman, The George Washington University
--| Last Modified: July 1995
------------------------------------------------------------------------
  PROCEDURE Get (Item : OUT Rational);
  PROCEDURE Get (File: IN Ada.Text_IO.File_Type; Item : OUT Rational);
  -- Pre : File is open
  -- Post: The first integer number read is the numerator of Item;
  --       the second integer number is the denominator of Item.
  --       A "/" between the two numbers is optional.
  --       The Rational constructor "/" is called
  --       to produce a rational in reduced form.

  PROCEDURE Put (Item : IN Rational);
  PROCEDURE Put (File: IN Ada.Text_IO.File_Type; Item : IN Rational);
  -- Pre : Item is defined; File is open
  -- Post: displays or writes the numerator and denominator of Item.

END Rationals.IO;
```

Program 2.4 Body of Rationals.IO Child Package

```
WITH Ada.Text_IO;
WITH Ada.Integer_Text_IO;
PACKAGE BODY Rationals.IO IS
------------------------------------------------------------------------
--|
--| Body of the input/output child package for Rationals
--|
--| Author: Michael B. Feldman, The George Washington University
--| Last Modified: July 1995
--|
------------------------------------------------------------------------
```

---

[1]Child packages are new in Ada 95; they are not available in Ada 83.

```
-- input procedures

PROCEDURE Get (File: IN Ada.Text_IO.File_Type; Item : OUT Rational) IS

  N: Integer;
  D: Integer;
  Dummy: Character; --- dummy character to hold the "/"

BEGIN -- Get

  Ada.Integer_Text_IO.Get(File => File, Item => N);
  Ada.Text_IO.Get (File => File, Item => Dummy);
  Ada.Integer_Text_IO.Get(File => File, Item => D);
  Item := N/D;

END Get;

PROCEDURE Get (Item : OUT Rational) IS

BEGIN -- Get

  Get(File => Ada.Text_IO.Standard_Input, Item => Item);

END Get;

-- output procedures

PROCEDURE Put (File: IN Ada.Text_IO.File_Type; Item : IN Rational) IS

BEGIN -- Put

  Ada.Integer_Text_IO.Put
    (File => File, Item => Numer(Item), Width => 1);
  Ada.Text_IO.Put(File => File, Item => '/');
  Ada.Integer_Text_IO.Put
    (File => File, Item => Denom(Item), Width => 1);

END Put;

PROCEDURE Put (Item : IN Rational) IS

BEGIN -- Put

  Put(File => Ada.Text_IO.Standard_Output, Item => Item);

END Put;

END Rationals.IO;
```

Testing the `Rationals` Package

Once the package is completed, we can execute client programs that use the abstract data type for rational arithmetic. Program 2.5 shows a client program that uses abstract data type `Rationals`. This program, `Test_Rationals_1`, uses the data type `Rational` and five of its operators. The body of `Test_Rationals_1` begins by assigning values to the rational numbers A and B, then reading data into rational numbers C and D. Next, the sum A+B and the product C*D are saved in E and F, respectively, and displayed. Finally, the sum A+E*F is displayed, which shows that the result of one operation can be used as an input to another.

Program 2.5 Test of `Rationals` Package

```
WITH Ada.Text_IO;
WITH Rationals;
WITH Rationals.IO;
PROCEDURE Test_Rationals_1 IS
------------------------------------------------------------------------
--| Very rudimentary test of package Rationals and Rationals.IO
--| Author: Michael B. Feldman, The George Washington University
--| Last Modified: July 1995
------------------------------------------------------------------------
  A: Rationals.Rational;
  B: Rationals.Rational;
  C: Rationals.Rational;
  D: Rationals.Rational;
  E: Rationals.Rational;
  F: Rationals.Rational;

BEGIN -- Test_Rationals_1

  A := Rationals."/"(1, 3);
  B := Rationals."/"(2, -4);
  Ada.Text_IO.Put(Item => "A = ");
  Rationals.IO.Put(Item => A);
  Ada.Text_IO.New_Line;
  Ada.Text_IO.Put(Item => "B = ");
  Rationals.IO.Put(Item => B);
  Ada.Text_IO.New_Line;

  -- Read in rational numbers C and D.
  Ada.Text_IO.Put(Item => "Enter rational number C > ");
  Rationals.IO.Get(Item => C);
  Ada.Text_IO.Put(Item => "Enter rational number D > ");
  Rationals.IO.Get(Item => D);
  Ada.Text_IO.New_Line;

  E := Rationals."+"(A,B);                     -- form the sum
  Ada.Text_IO.Put(Item => "E = A + B is ");
  Rationals.IO.Put(Item => E);
  Ada.Text_IO.New_Line;

  F := Rationals."*"(C,D);                     -- form the product
  Ada.Text_IO.Put(Item => "F = C * D is ");
  Rationals.IO.Put(Item => F);
  Ada.Text_IO.New_Line;

  Ada.Text_IO.Put(Item => "A + E * F is ");
  Rationals.IO.Put(Item => Rationals."+"(A, Rationals."*"(E,F)));
  Ada.Text_IO.New_Line;

END Test_Rationals_1;
```

Exception Propagation

Suppose, in response to the prompt to enter C, the user enters 3 / 0. Let us trace the execution. The client calls `Rationals.IO.Get`. At what point is the zero denominator noticed, and what happens? `Rationals.IO.Get` reads an integer N, then a "dummy" character to skip past the user's /, then a second integer D. Both integers—including the zero—are read correctly from the keyboard. The `Get` procedure then tries to form the expression N/D, which calls our rational constructor "/". As we saw above, the constructor detects the zero denominator and raises the exception ZeroDenominator. Because the constructor only *raises* the exception but does not *handle* it, the exception is immediately *propagated* to the calling program, which is Rationals.IO.Get. This procedure has no exception handler either, so the exception is propagated to *its* calling program, namely Test_Rationals_1. Because Test_Rational_1 also has no handler, the exception is propagated all the way to the Ada runtime system, which terminates the program with its own exception report.

Program 2.6 shows a modification of our client program in which a ZeroDenominator handler is given for the main program block. In this case, entering a zero denominator will cause the program to terminate, but with our own message instead of the runtime system's message. Exercise 1 calls for changing the program so that it remains "alive" and gives the user a chance to reenter the input values.

Program 2.6 Test of Rationals Package with USE Clause and Exception Handler

```
WITH Ada.Text_IO;   USE Ada.Text_IO;
WITH Rationals;     USE Rationals;
WITH Rationals.IO;  USE Rationals.IO;
PROCEDURE Test_Rationals_2 IS
--------------------------------------------------------------------
--|Tests the package Rationals,
--|this time with USE clause and an exception handler
--|Author: Michael B. Feldman, The George Washington University
--|Last Modified: July 1995
--------------------------------------------------------------------

  A: Rational;
  B: Rational;
  C: Rational;
  D: Rational;
  E: Rationals.Rational;
  F: Rationals.Rational;

BEGIN -- Test_Rationals_2

  A := 1/3;
  B := 2/(-4);
  Put(Item => "A = ");
  Rationals.IO.Put(Item => A);
  New_Line;
  Put(Item => "B = ");
  Rationals.IO.Put(Item => B);
  New_Line;

  -- Read in rational numbers C and D.
  Put(Item => "Enter rational number C > ");
  Get(Item => C);
  Put(Item => "Enter rational number D > ");
  Get(Item => D);
  New_Line;

  E := A + B;                       -- form the sum
  Put(Item => "E = A + B is ");
  Put(Item => E);
  New_Line;
```

```
F := C * D;                           -- form the product
Put(Item => "F = C * D is ");
Put(Item => F);
New_Line;

Put(Item => "A + E * F is ");
Put(Item => A + E * F);
New_Line;

EXCEPTION

WHEN ZeroDenominator =>
  Ada.Text_IO.Put(Item =>
    "Zero not allowed in denominator; terminating program.");
  Ada.Text_IO.New_Line;

END Test_Rationals_2;
```

Using the USE Clause

Program 2.6 also shows the advantage of sometimes using the USE clause, which allows unqualified references to package capabilities. In Program 2.5, where there is no USE, the rational addition operation is written

```
E := Rationals."+"(A,B);
```

but in TestRational2 it is written

```
E := A + B;
```

One of the advantages of Ada's permitting operator symbols such as "+" to be defined as functions is that they can be used in expressions in infix form, as in the above line. When the expressions become more complex, this feature makes programs even more readable. Compare the line

```
Rational_IO.Put(Item => Rationals."+"(A, Rationals."*"(E,F)));
```

from Program 2.5 with the corresponding line in Program 2.6:

```
Rational_IO.Put(Item => A + E * F);
```

This practice is, however, possible only if a USE clause appears in the client program. Otherwise, the operator must not only be qualified (as in Rationals."+") but must also be used as a prefix function call like any other function call.

When reading Program 2.6, note that the USE clause would also have allowed us to write unqualified references to all the other operations in Rationals, but that we chose to leave some of the qualified references (for example, the Rationals.IO.Put statements) as they were. This shows that qualified references are still *permitted*, even though a USE appears.

This example contains a mixture of qualified and unqualified references, just to show the possibilities. This is not good programming style; it is important to be consistent. Most Ada experts advise that qualified references should be used wherever possible, because they clarify programs by always indicating the name of the package whose operation is being called. These same experts often advocate *never* writing a USE clause, because then qualified references are mandatory. In this book, we use the USE where appropriate—for example, to make infix ADT operators possible—but we also use qualified references in most cases, even where a USE is present and the qualification is optional.

The USE TYPE Clause

The USE clause enables us to make references to resources provided by a package without qualifying those references with the package name. To state it officially, the USE clause makes the exported resources *directly visible*. Programs 2.5 and 2.6 illustrated the difference for the Rationals case; the most important benefit of the USE was to allow the arithmetic and comparison operators to be written in infix form. Given a USE, we could write, for P, Q, and R of type Rational,

```
P := Q + R;
```

as in everyday arithmetic. Without the USE, we would have to write

```
P := Rationals."+"(Q,R);
```

which is not very natural.

On the other hand, many people in industry recommend against using the USE statement, because in a program that WITHs and USEs many packages, the USEs make so many types and operations directly visible that the reader can become confused. Ada 95 adds the USE TYPE statement as a compromise, so that USE can in general be avoided without losing the benefit of user-defined operators. Writing, for example,

```
USE TYPE Rationals.Rational;
```

gives direct visibility to the infix operators declared in the package, but to nothing else, and specifically not to functions and procedures such as Numer and Denom, or exceptions such as ZeroDenominator. Program 2.7 shows a modification of Program 2.5, in which USE TYPE appears. Notice that the operators can be now written in infix form, but the variables must be declared as Rationals.Rational and the function Numer and exception ZeroDenominator must be written Rationals.Numer and Rationals.ZeroDenominator, respectively; otherwise, a compilation error would result.

Advantages of PRIVATE Types

A client program that uses the ADT Rationals does not need to know the actual internal representation of data type Rational (i.e., a record with two fields). The client can call an operator function of ADT Rationals to perform an operation (e.g., rational addition) without having this knowledge. In fact, it is better to hide this information from the client program to prevent the client from directly manipulating the individual fields of a rational variable.

Program 2.7 Test of `Rationals` Package with `USE TYPE` Clause

```
WITH Ada.Text_IO;
WITH Ada.Integer_Text_IO;
WITH Rationals;
USE TYPE Rationals.Rational; -- Ada 95: USEs infix operators only
WITH Rationals.IO;
PROCEDURE Test_Rationals_3 IS
-------------------------------------------------------------------------
--|
--| Tests the package Rationals,
--| this time with Ada 95 USE TYPE clause and an exception handler
--|
--| Author: Michael B. Feldman, The George Washington University
--| Last Modified: July 1995
--|
-------------------------------------------------------------------------
-- Note: the Rational infix operators (+, <=, etc.) can be used
-- without qualification, but not the Rational type name itself,
-- or other subprograms like Numer, or the exported exception
-- ZeroDenominator, which must still be qualified.

  A: Rationals.Rational;
  B: Rationals.Rational;
  C: Rationals.Rational;
  D: Rationals.Rational;
  E: Rationals.Rational;

BEGIN -- Test_Rationals_3

  A := 1/3;
  B := 2/(-4);
  Ada.Text_IO.Put(Item => "A = ");
  Rationals.IO.Put(Item => A);
  Ada.Text_IO.New_Line;
  Ada.Text_IO.Put(Item => "B = ");
  Rationals.IO.Put(Item => B);
  Ada.Text_IO.New_Line;

  -- Read in rational numbers C and D.
  Ada.Text_IO.Put(Item => "Enter rational number C > ");
  Rationals.IO.Get(Item => C);
  Ada.Text_IO.Put(Item => "Enter rational number D > ");
  Rationals.IO.Get(Item => D);
  Ada.Text_IO.New_Line;

  E := A + B;                    -- form the sum
  Ada.Text_IO.Put(Item => "E = A + B is ");
  Rationals.IO.Put(Item => E);
  Ada.Text_IO.New_Line;

  Ada.Text_IO.Put(Item => "A + E * B is ");
  Rationals.IO.Put(Item => A + E * B);
  Ada.Text_IO.New_Line;

  Ada.Text_IO.Put(Item => "B's numerator is ");
  Ada.Integer_Text_IO.Put(Item => Rationals.Numer(B), Width => 1);
  Ada.Text_IO.New_Line;

EXCEPTION
  WHEN Rationals.ZeroDenominator =>
    Ada.Text_IO.Put(Item =>
      "Zero not allowed in denominator; terminating program.");
    Ada.Text_IO.New_Line;
END Test_Rationals_3;
```

It is best for a client program not to have direct access to the representation of a rational quantity for three reasons:

- It is easier to write and read a client program that treats a rational quantity just the same as a predefined one—that is, without being cluttered with direct reference to implementation details.

- The client program cannot directly store values in the fields of a rational variable. For example, storing 4 and 12, respectively, in these fields would violate the package's assumption that all rationals are stored in reduced form.

- If we change the representation—for example, to an array of two elements instead of a record—the client program does not have to be modified in any way, but simply recompiled.

A fourth advantage would apply if the type were not so simple but represented something more sophisticated—say, a database record of some kind. Each record might contain information "for internal use only," that is, for use only by the data management program itself, rather than for use by clients. Making the record `PRIVATE` ensures that not the entire record structure is made available to the client, but only the information that the ADT designer chooses to supply via the ADT operations. This is an important advantage for large, complicated, and secure applications.

2.2 DEVELOPING A TEST PLAN

The test programs shown in Programs 2.5 through 2.7 are only brief examples of client programs; they do not really constitute full tests of the ADT. Systematic and thorough testing, using a well-chosen set of test cases, is an essential part of effective software development; without a well-crafted set of tests we simply cannot persuade ourselves or others that our software performs "as advertised." Much of today's complex software is released to customers with errors in it that simply were not discovered even by thorough testing, but that fact does not relieve software developers of the obligation to test as best they can.

At intervals in this book, we will discuss testing strategies. We start here, with a discussion of how one might develop a test plan for a software component. Ideally, such a plan should be written *before* the component is even coded. A test plan really should be thought of as part of the detailed design, because it can and should be created based on knowledge of the input and output data requirements, which should be set down on paper long before coding begins.

The main question you should ask yourself in starting to develop a test plan is, "Suppose I were going to spend a lot of money to buy this component for use in a critical system. What would I need to know about the component in order to be certain that the results I get from it are reliably correct? How can I have confidence that I am getting my money's worth?"

In considering the `Rationals` ADT, we need to answer these questions:

1. Does the constructor in fact produce a correct rational value for any legal values of numerator and denominator? Is the exception `ZeroDenominator` raised when it ought to be raised?

2. Do the comparison operators work correctly?

3. Do the arithmetic operators work correctly?

4. Are the results of the operations *composable*? That is, can we always use the rational result of one operation as an input to another rational operation?

Putting this differently, we are testing to make sure that if the preconditions for each operation hold before we call the operation, then the postconditions hold after the operation is called.

Let's think about how to test the constructor `"/"`. The preconditions require only that the numerator and denominator be well-defined integers. The postconditions tell us that the resulting rational will be in reduced form and that if it is negative, the minus sign will be in the numerator. Also, a zero denominator should cause the exception to be raised.

Choosing tests completely at random will not necessarily test all these conditions. Table 1.1 is a table of test cases that will do so. In each case we indicate *what* the test values are, *why* we chose that particular test, and *what* we expect the result to be.

Table 1.2 shows some test cases for the addition operation. We need not use large numbers to test addition; we need only test the different combinations of positive, negative, and zero rationals.

Table 1.1 Test Cases for Rational Constructor Operation

Test Case No.	Values	Condition	Expected Result
1	1/2	Positive/Positive	1/2
2	(−1)/2	Negative/Positive	−1/2
3	1/(−2)	Positive/Negative	−1/2
4	(−1)/(−2)	Negative/Negative	1/2
5	1/0	ZeroDenominator	Exception raised
6	72/30	Reduction	12/5
7	123/125	Reduction	123/125

Table 1.2 Test Cases for Rational Addition Operation

Test Case No.	Values	Condition	Expected Result
1	2/3 + 3/2	Positive + Positive	13/6
2	2/3 + (−3/2)	Positive + Negative	−5/6
3	(−2/3) + 3/2	Negative + Positive	5/6
4	(−2/3) + (−3/2)	Negative + Negative	−13/6
5	0/1 + 3/2	Zero + Nonzero	3/2
6	3/2 + 0/2	Reduction	3/2

Exercise 2 requires you to complete the test plan for the rational operators. This might seem like a large number of test cases, but there are many operators in this package.

In summary, a test plan should be carefully designed, with just enough well-chosen test cases to make sure the operations behave correctly. It is a good idea to choose values such that, where possible, the expected result is either obvious or easily hand-calculated.

2.3 ADT DESIGN: AN ADT FOR DOLLARS AND CENTS

In this section, we develop an ADT for monetary quantities, which we will call `Currency`. What is important about this ADT is that in writing operations for `Currency` values, we discover that not all operations make sense. An advantage of the ADT approach is that we can control the set of operations to allow only meaningful ones to be performed.

Requirements

We require a way to represent monetary values that will ensure that calculations with these quantities make sense and are exact. Only sensible operations should be allowed. It is meaningful to compare, add, subtract, and divide monetary quantities, but not to multiply them: $4.00/$2.00 is a dimensionless ratio 2.0, but $2.00 $\times$ $3.00 has no meaning. On the other hand, it is certainly sensible to multiply a currency value by a "normal" dimensionless quantity—for example, to find 25% of $150.00.

To understand the exact-result requirement, you must realize that not every fractional decimal value can be represented exactly as a binary floating-point quantity, so that sometimes operations such as addition and subtraction cause the result to be rounded off. Although this approximation to the real numbers is often acceptable, it is unacceptable in monetary calculations: You would not be happy if the bank approximated your account balance.

Analysis

As was the case with rationals, we are asked to construct a software component providing a type and a set of operations. There are no specific problem inputs and outputs, but we will need to provide input and output operations so that our user—again, another programmer—can write client programs that read and display currency values.

To ensure exact operations, we cannot simply use floating-point values. Because integer arithmetic is exact, we will represent currency as a pair of two nonnegative integer values, `Dollars` and `Cents`, and a `Boolean` value to indicate whether the currency value is positive or not. We will then be able to write an ADT that provides exact operations.

Design: the Specification for `Currency`

Program 2.8 shows the specification for this ADT package. The type `Quantity` is declared to be `PRIVATE` so that we can control all operations on values of this type. Note that we are also providing a subtype `CentsType`, which has range 0..99.

Program 2.8 Specification for `Currency` Package

```
PACKAGE Currency IS
-------------------------------------------------------------------------
--| Specification of the abstract data type for representing
--| and manipulating Currency numbers.
--| All values of type Currency.Quantity are initialized to 0.0.
--|
--| Author: Michael B. Feldman, The George Washington University
--| Last Modified: July 1995

-------------------------------------------------------------------------

  SUBTYPE CentsType IS Integer RANGE 0..99;
  TYPE    Quantity  IS PRIVATE;

  -- Operations

  FUNCTION MakeCurrency (F : Float) RETURN Quantity;
  -- constructor:
  -- Pre : F is defined
  -- Post: returns a Currency Quantity

  FUNCTION MakeFloat    (Q : Quantity) RETURN Float;
  -- constructor:
  -- Pre: Q is defined
  -- Post: returns the value of Q in Float form

  FUNCTION Dollars   (Q : Quantity) RETURN Natural;
  FUNCTION Cents     (Q : Quantity) RETURN CentsType;
  FUNCTION IsPositive(Q : Quantity) RETURN Boolean;
  -- selectors:
  -- Pre:  Q is defined
  -- Post: Dollars returns the Dollars part of Q; Cents the Cents part

  FUNCTION "<" (Q1 : Quantity; Q2 : Quantity) RETURN Boolean;
  FUNCTION ">" (Q1 : Quantity; Q2 : Quantity) RETURN Boolean;
  FUNCTION "<="(Q1 : Quantity; Q2 : Quantity) RETURN Boolean;
  FUNCTION ">="(Q1 : Quantity; Q2 : Quantity) RETURN Boolean;
  -- inquiry operators:
  -- Pre : Q1 and Q2 are defined
  -- Post: return Q1 < Q2, Q1 > Q2, Q1 <= Q2, and Q1 >= Q2, respectively

  FUNCTION "+"  (Q : Quantity) RETURN Quantity;
  FUNCTION "-"  (Q : Quantity) RETURN Quantity;
  FUNCTION "ABS"(Q : Quantity) RETURN Quantity;
  -- monadic arithmetic constructors:
  -- Pre: Q is defined
  -- Post: return Q, -Q, ABS Q respectively

  FUNCTION "+" (Q1 : Quantity; Q2 : Quantity) RETURN Quantity;
  FUNCTION "-" (Q1 : Quantity; Q2 : Quantity) RETURN Quantity;
```

```
FUNCTION "*" (F  :  Float;    Q : Quantity)      RETURN Quantity;
FUNCTION "*" (Q  :  Quantity; F : Float )     RETURN Quantity;
FUNCTION "/" (Q1 : Quantity; Q2 : Quantity) RETURN Float;
FUNCTION "/" (Q  :  Quantity; F : Float )     RETURN Quantity;
-- dyadic arithmetic constructors:
-- Pre : Q1 and Q2 are defined
-- Post: these are the sensible arithmetic operators on Quantity.
--    Note that multiplying two monetary values is not sensible.

PRIVATE

-- A record of type Quantity consists of a pair of Natural values
-- such that the first number represents the Dollars part
-- and the second number represents the Cents part.
-- The sign of a Quantity value is indicated by a Boolean field
-- called Positive.

  TYPE Quantity IS RECORD
    Positive: Boolean := True;
    Dollars : Natural := 0;
    Cents :   CentsType := 0;
  END RECORD; -- Quantity

END Currency;
```

Looking at the operations on the `Currency` type, we see first that operators are provided to produce a `Currency` quantity from its `Dollars` and `Cents` components, and to convert in both directions between our `Currency` type and `Float` values. The next group of operations are selectors to return the `Dollars` and `Cents` parts, and an inquiry operator to determine whether or not a `Currency` value is positive.

The next four operators are the usual comparison operations we saw in `Ada.Calendar` and `Rationals`. Note that we can use predefined equality/inequality with no problem, because two `Currency` values are equal if and only if their `Dollars`, `Cents`, and signs are respectively equal. The comparison operators are followed by the three monadic arithmetic operators we saw in `Rationals`. Their meanings should be obvious.

The final six operators are interesting ones. Note that addition and subtraction are defined for `Currency` values, as one would expect. But multiplication is defined only for a `Currency` value and a `Float` value, not for two `Currency` values. This is because the product of two `Currency` values is meaningless, but finding, for example, 0.25 (which might represent 25%) of a `Currency` value is indeed meaningful. The two multiplication operations allow the mixed operands to be presented in either order. Similarly, the division operations are meaningful ones: Dividing one `Currency` value by another gives a normal `Float`; dividing a `Currency` value by a `Float` gives a `Currency` value.

The last part of the specification is, as usual, the PRIVATE part, in which the `Currency` type is defined in full. Note that it is just a record with three fields, and that all three fields are initialized as before.

Detailed Design and Implementation of the Body of the `Currency` ADT

As we did in the `Rationals` case, we now look at the important algorithms in `Currency` calculations. We are allowing both positive and negative values, and representing a `Currency` value as a pair of integers. Given a `Currency` quantity Q, denote its `Dollars` and `Cents` parts by `Q.Dollars` and `Q.Cents` respectively; we carry the sign separately as a flag Q.Positive. First let us see how to convert a `Float` value to a `Currency` value:

Algorithm for Converting a `Float F` to a `Currency` Quantity `Q`:

1. `Q.Dollars` is the integer part of `ABS(F)`; `ABS` means absolute value, as usual;

2. `Q.Cents` is $100 \times (\text{ABS}(F) - Q.\text{Dollars})$;

3. `Q.Positive` is `True` if and only if F >= 0.0.

Note that the `Cents` part of a `Currency` value is calculated as the fractional part of the `Float` value, multiplied by 100.

Now let us look at key algorithms for adding and subtracting two positive `Currency` values:

To add two positive `Currency` values `Q1` and `Q2` to produce `Result`:

1. Set `TempCents` to the sum of `Q1.Cents` and `Q2.Cents`.

2. `IF TempCents` > 99, `THEN` we have a carry:

3. `Result.Cents` is `TempCents` – 100.

4. `Result.Dollars` is `Q1.Dollars` + `Q2.Dollars` + 1

5. `ELSE` no carry:

6. `Result.Cents` is `TempCents`

7. `Result.Dollars` is `Q1.Dollars` + `Q2.Dollars`

   `END IF;`

To subtract Q2 from Q1 to produce Result:

1. `IF` Q1 < Q2 `THEN`

2. Result is negative:

3. Interchange Q1 and Q2

   `END IF;`

4.   IF Q1.Cents < Q2.Cents THEN we need a borrow:

    5.   Result.Cents is (100 + Q1.Cents) - Q2.Cents

    6.   Result.Dollars is (Q1.Dollars - 1) - Q2.Dollars

7.   ELSE no borrow:

    8.   Result.Cents is Q1.Cents - Q2.Cents

    9.   Result.Dollars is Q1.Dollars - Q2.Dollars

    END IF;

Make sure you understand these algorithms; try some examples by hand to test yourself.

Now Program 2.9 gives the body for Currency.

Program 2.9 Body of Currency Package

```
PACKAGE BODY Currency IS
-----------------------------------------------------------------------
--| Body of the abstract data type for representing
--| and manipulating Currency numbers.
--| All values of type Currency.Quantity are initialized to 0.0.
--| Author: Michael B. Feldman, The George Washington University
--| Last Modified: July 1995
-----------------------------------------------------------------------

-- internal operations, not exported to the client

  FUNCTION Add (Q1: Quantity; Q2: Quantity) RETURN Quantity IS
  -- Pre:  Q1 >= 0.0 and Q2 >= 0.0.
  -- Post: Returns the sum of Q1 and Q2.
  -- This is just an auxiliary routine used in "+" and "-" below.

    Result    : Quantity;
    TempCents : Natural;

  BEGIN -- Add

    TempCents := Q1.Cents + Q2.Cents;
    IF TempCents > 99 THEN -- we had a carry
      Result.Cents    : = TempCents - 100;
      Result.Dollars  : = Q1.Dollars + Q2.Dollars + 1;
    ELSE
      Result.Cents    : = TempCents;
      Result.Dollars: = Q1.Dollars + Q2.Dollars;
    END IF;
    RETURN Result;

  END Add;

  FUNCTION Subtract (Q1: Quantity; Q2: Quantity) RETURN Quantity IS
  -- Pre:  Q1 >= 0.0 and Q2 >= 0.0.
  -- Post: Returns the difference of Q1 and Q2.
  -- This is just an auxiliary routine used in "+" and "-" below.
```

```
      Result     : Quantity;
      TempCents : Natural;

   BEGIN -- Subtract

      IF Q1 > Q2 THEN -- Result is positive
        IF Q2.Cents > Q1.Cents THEN -- we need a borrow
          Result.Cents   := (100 + Q1.Cents) - Q2.Cents;
          Result.Dollars := (Q1.Dollars - 1) - Q2.Dollars;
        ELSE
          Result.Cents   := Q1.Cents   - Q2.Cents;
          Result.Dollars := Q1.Dollars - Q2.Dollars;
        END IF;
      ELSE              -- Result is negative
        Result.Positive := False;
        IF Q1.Cents > Q2.Cents THEN -- we need a borrow
          Result.Cents   := (100 + Q2.Cents) - Q1.Cents;
          Result.Dollars := (Q2.Dollars - 1) - Q1.Dollars;
        ELSE
          Result.Cents   := Q2.Cents   - Q1.Cents;
          Result.Dollars := Q2.Dollars - Q1.Dollars;
        END IF;
      END IF;
      RETURN Result;

   END Subtract;

   -- Exported Operators

   FUNCTION "+" (Q1 : Quantity; Q2 : Quantity) RETURN Quantity IS
   BEGIN
     IF Q1.Positive AND Q2.Positive THEN
       RETURN Add (Q1,Q2);
     ELSIF (NOT Q1.Positive) AND (NOT Q2.Positive) THEN
       RETURN -Add(-Q1, -Q2);
     ELSIF Q1.Positive AND (NOT Q2.Positive) THEN
       RETURN Subtract(Q1, -Q2);
     ELSE -- NOT Q1.Positive AND Q2.Positive;
       RETURN Subtract (Q2, -Q1);
     END IF;
   END "+";

   FUNCTION "-" (Q1 : Quantity; Q2 : Quantity) RETURN Quantity IS
   BEGIN
     RETURN Q1 + (-Q2);
   END "-";

   FUNCTION MakeCurrency (F : Float)    RETURN Quantity IS
     Result: Quantity;
     T: Float;
   BEGIN

     T := Float'Truncation(ABS F); -- get whole-number part
     Result := (Positive => True,
                Dollars => Natural (T),  -- just a type change
                Cents   => Natural(100.0 * (ABS F - T)));
     IF F < 0.0 THEN
       Result.Positive := False;
     END IF;

     RETURN Result;
   END MakeCurrency;
```

```
FUNCTION MakeFloat (Q : Quantity) RETURN Float IS
  Result: Float;
BEGIN
  Result := Float (100 * Q.Dollars + Q.Cents) / 100.0;
  IF Q.Positive THEN
    RETURN Result;
  ELSE
    RETURN -Result;
  END IF;
END MakeFloat;

FUNCTION Dollars (Q : Quantity) RETURN Natural IS
BEGIN
  RETURN Q.Dollars;
END Dollars;

FUNCTION Cents (Q : Quantity) RETURN CentsType IS
BEGIN
  RETURN Q.Cents;
END Cents;

FUNCTION IsPositive (Q : Quantity) RETURN Boolean IS
BEGIN
  RETURN Q.Positive;
END IsPositive;

FUNCTION ">" (Q1 : Quantity; Q2 : Quantity) RETURN Boolean IS
BEGIN
  RETURN MakeFloat(Q1) > MakeFloat (Q2);
END ">";

FUNCTION "<" (Q1 : Quantity; Q2 : Quantity) RETURN Boolean IS
BEGIN -- stub
  RETURN True;
END "<";

FUNCTION "<=" (Q1 : Quantity; Q2 : Quantity) RETURN Boolean IS
BEGIN -- stub
  RETURN True;
END "<=";

FUNCTION ">=" (Q1 : Quantity; Q2 : Quantity) RETURN Boolean IS
BEGIN -- stub
  RETURN True;
END ">=";

FUNCTION "+"(Q : Quantity) RETURN Quantity IS
BEGIN
  RETURN Q;
END "+";

FUNCTION "-"(Q : Quantity) RETURN Quantity IS
BEGIN
  RETURN (Positive => NOT Q.Positive,
          Dollars => Q.Dollars,
          Cents   => Q.Cents);
END "-";

FUNCTION "ABS" (Q : Quantity) RETURN Quantity IS
BEGIN -- stub
  RETURN Q;
END "ABS";
```

```
   FUNCTION "*"(F  : Float;    Q  : Quantity) RETURN Quantity IS
   BEGIN
     RETURN (MakeCurrency(F * MakeFloat(Q)));
   END "*";

   FUNCTION "*"(Q  : Quantity; F  : Float    ) RETURN Quantity IS
   BEGIN -- stub
     RETURN Q;
   END "*";

   FUNCTION "/"(Q1 : Quantity; Q2 : Quantity) RETURN Float IS
   BEGIN
     RETURN MakeFloat(Q1) / MakeFloat(Q2);
   END "/";

   FUNCTION "/"(Q  : Quantity; F  : Float    ) RETURN Quantity IS
   BEGIN -- stub
     RETURN Q;
   END "/";

END Currency;
```

The key to understanding the operations is the first four function bodies. The first two, Add, and Subtract, are not provided to client programs; they are there only to make writing the other operators more convenient for us.

Add and Subtract are implemented following the algorithms above. The exported addition operator "+", which can handle positive or negative values, uses Add or Subtract according to the signs of its operands; the exported operator "−" just adds a negated value.

MakeCurrency and MakeFloat are our constructors to convert to and from Currency values. Note that MakeCurrency uses the Ada 95 attribute Float' Truncation, which returns just the whole-number part of its argument. Finally, the remaining operators are given, mostly as stubs. You can complete the package, and develop a program to test it, as an exercise. Programs 2.10 and 2.11 give the specification and body for a child package Currency.IO, which you can use as part of your testing process. We do not show a test program; we leave its development as Exercise 4.

Program 2.10 Specification for Currency.IO Child Package

```
WITH Ada.Text_IO;
PACKAGE Currency.IO IS
-----------------------------------------------------------------------
--|
--| Specification of the input/output child package for Currency
--|
--| Author: Michael B. Feldman, The George Washington University
--| Last Modified: July 1995
--|
-----------------------------------------------------------------------

   -- input operations to read a Quantity from terminal or file

   PROCEDURE Get (Item: OUT Quantity);
   PROCEDURE Get (File: IN Ada.Text_IO.File_Type; Item : OUT Quantity);
```

```
-- Pre : File is open
-- Post: The currency quantity is read as a normal
--   floating point value.

-- output operations to display a Quantity on terminal or
-- write it to an external file

PROCEDURE Put (Item: IN Quantity; Width: IN Natural:=8);
PROCEDURE Put (File: IN Ada.Text_IO.File_Type;
              Item: IN Quantity; Width: IN Natural:=8);
-- Pre:  File is open, Item is defined
-- Post: Displays or writes the currency quantity.
--       Width is used by analogy with Integer_IO

END Currency.IO;
```

Program 2.11 Body of `Currency.IO` Child Package

```
WITH Ada.Text_IO;
WITH Ada.Integer_Text_IO;
WITH Ada.Float_Text_IO;
PACKAGE BODY Currency.IO IS
------------------------------------------------------------------------
--|
--| Body of the input/output child package for Currency
--|
--| Author: Michael B. Feldman, The George Washington University
--| Last Modified: July 1995
--|
------------------------------------------------------------------------
  --input procedures
  PROCEDURE Get (File: IN Ada.Text_IO.File_Type; Item : OUT Quantity) IS
    F: Float;
  BEGIN -- Get

    -- just read it as a Float quantity, then convert
    Ada.Float_Text_IO.Get(File => File, Item => F);
    Item := MakeCurrency(F);

  END Get;

  PROCEDURE Get (Item : OUT Quantity) IS
  BEGIN -- Get
    Get(File => Ada.Text_IO.Standard_Input, Item => Item);
  END Get;

  -- output procedures

  PROCEDURE Put (File : IN Ada.Text_IO.File_Type;
                 Item : IN Quantity; Width: IN Natural:=8) IS
  BEGIN -- Put

    -- dollars first
    IF IsPositive(Item) THEN
      Ada.Integer_Text_IO.Put
        (File=>File, Item=>Dollars (Item),Width=>1);
    ELSE
      Ada.Integer_Text_IO.Put
        (File=>File, Item=>-Dollars (Item),Width=>1);
    END IF;
```

```
       -- then decimal point and cents
     Ada.Text_IO.Put(File => File, Item => '.');
     IF Cents (Item) < 10 THEN
       Ada.Text_IO.Put(File => File, Item => '0');
     END IF;
     Ada.Integer_Text_IO.Put
         (File => File, Item => Cents (Item),Width => 1);

   END Put;

   PROCEDURE Put (Item : IN Quantity; Width: IN Natural:=8) IS
   BEGIN -- Put
     Put(File => Ada.Text_IO.Standard_Output,
         Item => Item, Width => Width);
   END Put;

END Currency.IO;
```

This example shows the advantage of using a `PRIVATE` type not just to encapsulate representation details, but also to give us complete control over the operations a client is permitted to perform. As part of developing your test program, you might wish to attempt some operations not provided in the package—for example, multiplying two `Currency` values. Attempting this will result in a compilation error; this tells you that the compiler is aiding you in controlling the client operations.

2.4   ADT DESIGN: CALENDAR DATES

As we saw in Chapter 1, `Ada.Calendar` provides a useful set of operations for dealing with time values, and a few operations such as `Month` and `Day` for selecting components of a value of type `Time`. However, `Ada.Calendar` does not really give us a good set of operations for manipulating dates in a convenient way.

For example, we might need to pay a bill 45 days from today. What will the date be then? Or we might need to know on which day of the week Christmas will fall next year. These are but two of many examples of date manipulation. In this section, we will examine an ADT called `Dates`, which provides a number of operations to facilitate working with dates. In writing `Dates`, we will build on our knowledge of `Ada.Calendar` and use its facilities where possible.

Design: Specification of the `Dates` ADT

How shall we represent a date? It turns out to be convenient for many applications to represent a date in a form that gives the calendar year and the sequential day within the year. This form is called *Julian*, named for the ancient Roman emperor Julius Caesar, who developed the 365/366-day calendar, a variant of which we still use. This date format is often used in data processing: The first two digits are the last two digits of the year; the last three digits are the sequential day in the year. January 1, 1993, is 93001; December 31, 1993, is 93365. Naturally, all sequential days after February 28 are different in leap years than in non-leap years, so that (for example) December 31, 1992 was 92366.

In this package, we use a variant of the Julian form—namely, a record whose two fields represent the calendar year (as in package `Ada.Calendar`) and the sequential day within the year. Program 2.12 gives the specification of the package. Note that the `Date` type is PRIVATE; why? If the client program could go directly to the `DayOfYear` field, it could store, say, 366 for a non-leap year. This would be incorrect, so we prevent this kind of abuse of our abstraction by making the type PRIVATE.

Program 2.12 Specification for `Dates` Package

```
WITH Ada.Calendar;
PACKAGE Dates IS
------------------------------------------------------------------------
--| specification for package to represent calendar dates
--| Author: Michael B. Feldman, The George Washington University
--| Last Modified: September 1995
------------------------------------------------------------------------

  SUBTYPE YearNumber   IS Ada.Calendar.Year_Number;
  SUBTYPE MonthNumber  IS Ada.Calendar.Month_Number;
  SUBTYPE DayNumber    IS Ada.Calendar.Day_Number;
  SUBTYPE JulianDay    IS Positive RANGE 1..366;
  SUBTYPE WeekDay      IS Positive RANGE 1..7;

  TYPE Date IS PRIVATE;

  -- exported exception
  Date_Error : EXCEPTION;

  -- constructors
  FUNCTION Today                       RETURN Date;
  -- Pre:  none
  -- Post: returns the current date

  FUNCTION MakeDate(Year  : YearNumber;
                    Month : MonthNumber;
                    Day   : DayNumber) RETURN Date;
  -- Pre:    Year, Month, and Day are defined
  -- Post:   returns a Date object
  -- Raises: Date_Error if Year, Month, and Day do not
  --    form a valid date (e.g. 6/31/93 or 2/29/93)

  -- selectors
  FUNCTION Year       (Right: Date) RETURN YearNumber;
  FUNCTION Month      (Right: Date) RETURN MonthNumber;
  FUNCTION DayOfMonth (Right: Date) RETURN DayNumber;
  FUNCTION DayOfYear  (Right: Date) RETURN JulianDay;
  FUNCTION DayOfWeek  (Right: Date) RETURN WeekDay;
  -- Pre: Right is defined
  -- Post: these return the corresponding parts of the Date object

  -- comparison operators
  FUNCTION "<"  (Left, Right: Date) RETURN Boolean;
  FUNCTION "<=" (Left, Right: Date) RETURN Boolean;
  FUNCTION ">"  (Left, Right: Date) RETURN Boolean;
  FUNCTION ">=" (Left, Right: Date) RETURN Boolean;
  -- Pre:  Left and Right are defined
  -- Post: these return the result of the corresponding comparison
```

```
   -- arithmetic operators
   FUNCTION "+"  (Left: Date; Right: JulianDay) RETURN Date;
   FUNCTION "+"  (Left: JulianDay; Right: Date) RETURN Date;
   FUNCTION "-"  (Left: Date; Right: JulianDay) RETURN Date;
   -- Pre:  the arguments are defined
   -- Post: return a Date in the near future or recent past

   PRIVATE
     TYPE Date IS RECORD
       Year:       YearNumber   := YearNumber'First;
       DayOfYear: JulianDay    := 1;
     END RECORD;
END Dates;
```

In addition to the Date type, the package provides subtypes YearNumber, MonthNumber, and DayNumber, by simply "nicknaming" the corresponding Ada.Calendar subtypes. Also provided are JulianDay, as discussed above, and WeekDay, with range 1..7, to provide a way of returning the day of the week to a client program. Also provided is an exception Date_Error, which will be discussed further below.

What about the operations on Date values? Most are defined by analogy with Ada.Calendar operations. For example, Today returns the current date and MakeDate creates a Date value from its components. Today is analogous to Ada.Calendar.Clock; MakeDate is analogous to Ada.Calendar.Time_ Of. The selector functions Year, Month, DayOfMonth, DayOfYear, and DayOfWeek are self-explanatory and are analogous to Ada.Calendar.Year, Ada.Calendar.Month, and Ada.Calendar.Day. As Exercise 6, you can write a procedure analogous to Ada.Calendar.Split.

In looking at the three arithmetic operators, we see that—again by analogy with Ada.Calendar—only sensible operations are provided. Adding two dates, for example, is meaningless. Dates does *not* provide an operation for subtracting one date from another. Such an operation would indeed be meaningful; you can develop it as suggested in Exercise 8.

The Body of the Dates ADT

The body of Dates is given as Program 2.13.

Program 2.13 Body of Dates Package

```
WITH Ada.Calendar;
PACKAGE BODY Dates IS
-------------------------------------------------------------------------
--|
--| body for package to represent calendar dates
--|
--| Author: Michael B. Feldman, The George Washington University
--| Last Modified: September 1995
--|
-------------------------------------------------------------------------

-- body for package to represent calendar dates
```

```
-- tables containing the Julian day of the last day of each month
NonLeapDayEndOfMonth: ARRAY(MonthNumber) OF JulianDay :=
-- Jan  Feb  Mar  Apr  May  Jun  Jul  Aug  Sep  Oct  Nov  Dec
   (31,  59,  90, 120, 151, 181, 212, 243, 273, 304, 334, 365);

LeapDayEndOfMonth: ARRAY(MonthNumber) OF JulianDay :=
-- Jan  Feb  Mar  Apr  May  Jun  Jul  Aug  Sep  Oct  Nov  Dec
   (31,  60,  91, 121, 152, 182, 213, 244, 274, 305, 335, 366);

FUNCTION IsLeap(Year: YearNumber) RETURN Boolean IS
-- Pre:  Year is defined
-- Post: returns True if and only if Year is a leap year
BEGIN
   RETURN (Year REM 4 = 0) AND
          ((Year REM 100 /= 0) OR (Year REM 400 = 0));
END IsLeap;

FUNCTION MakeDate(Year  : YearNumber;
                  Month : MonthNumber;
                  Day   : DayNumber) RETURN Date IS

   TempTime: Ada.Calendar.Time;
   Result:   Date;

BEGIN -- MakeDate

   TempTime := Ada.Calendar.Time_Of
               (Year=>Year, Month=>Month, Day=>Day);
   -- assert: date is valid if and only if Time_Error is not raised

   Result.Year := Year;

   -- If it's January, finding the day is easy. If not,
   -- look up days to end of previous month in table
   IF Month = MonthNumber'First THEN -- it's January
     Result.DayOfYear := Day;
   ELSIF IsLeap(Year) THEN          -- leap year
     Result.DayOfYear := LeapDayEndOfMonth(Month-1) + Day;
   ELSE                             -- not leap year
     Result.DayOfYear := NonLeapDayEndOfMonth(Month-1) + Day;
   END IF;

   RETURN Result;

EXCEPTION

   WHEN Ada.Calendar.Time_Error =>
     RAISE Date_Error;

END MakeDate;

FUNCTION Today RETURN Date IS
-- Finds today's date and returns it as a record of type Date
-- Today's date is gotten from PACKAGE Ada.Calendar

   RightNow  : Ada.Calendar.Time;   -- holds internal clock value

BEGIN -- Today

   -- Get the current time value from the computer's clock
   RightNow := Ada.Calendar.Clock;

   -- Extract the current month, day, and year from the time value
   -- and call date constructor to put it in our form
   RETURN MakeDate(Month => Ada.Calendar.Month(RightNow),
               Day    => Ada.Calendar.Day  (RightNow),
               Year   => Ada.Calendar.Year (RightNow));
```

```
      END Today;

      FUNCTION Year (Right: Date) RETURN YearNumber IS
      BEGIN
        RETURN Right.Year;
      END Year;

      FUNCTION DayOfYear (Right: Date) RETURN JulianDay IS
      BEGIN
        RETURN Right.DayOfYear;
      END DayOfYear;

      FUNCTION Month (Right: Date) RETURN MonthNumber IS

        DayOfYear: JulianDay;
        Result   : MonthNumber;

      BEGIN -- Month

        DayOfYear := Right.DayOfYear;

        -- search table until a quantity > Right.Day is found
        IF IsLeap(Right.Year) THEN           -- leap year
          FOR WhichMonth IN MonthNumber LOOP
            Result := WhichMonth;
            EXIT WHEN LeapDayEndOfMonth(WhichMonth) >= DayOfYear;
          END LOOP;
        ELSE                                 -- not leap year
          FOR WhichMonth IN MonthNumber LOOP
            Result := WhichMonth;
            EXIT WHEN NonLeapDayEndOfMonth(WhichMonth) >= DayOfYear;
          END LOOP;
        END IF;

        RETURN Result;

      END Month;

      FUNCTION DayOfMonth (Right: Date) RETURN DayNumber IS

        WhichMonth: MonthNumber;
        Result    : DayNumber;

      BEGIN -- DayOfMonth

        WhichMonth := Month(Right);              -- call routine above
        IF WhichMonth = MonthNumber'First THEN   -- it's January
          Result := Right.DayOfYear;
        ELSIF IsLeap(Right.Year) THEN            -- leap year
          Result := Right.DayOfYear - LeapDayEndOfMonth(WhichMonth - 1);
        ELSE
          Result := Right.DayOfYear - NonLeapDayEndOfMonth(WhichMonth - 1);
        END IF;

        RETURN Result;

      END DayOfMonth;

      FUNCTION DayOfWeek (Right: Date) RETURN WeekDay IS

        SUBTYPE Code IS Natural RANGE 0..6;

        Result    : WeekDay;
```

```
      MonthCode : Code;
      Century   : Code;
      ThisMonth : MonthNumber;
      ThisYear  : YearNumber;

BEGIN -- DayOfWeek

   ThisMonth := Month(Right);
   ThisYear  := Year(Right);

   CASE ThisMonth IS

      WHEN 1 =>  IF IsLeap(ThisYear) THEN
                    MonthCode := 5;
                 ELSE
                    MonthCode := 6;
                 END IF;
      WHEN 2 =>  IF IsLeap(ThisYear) THEN
                    MonthCode := 1;
                 ELSE
                    MonthCode := 2;
                 END IF;
      WHEN 3  => MonthCode := 2;
      WHEN 4  => MonthCode := 5;
      WHEN 5  => MonthCode := 0;
      WHEN 6  => MonthCode := 3;
      WHEN 7  => MonthCode := 5;
      WHEN 8  => MonthCode := 1;
      WHEN 9  => MonthCode := 4;
      WHEN 10 => MonthCode := 6;
      WHEN 11 => MonthCode := 2;
      WHEN 12 => MonthCode := 4;

   END CASE;

   IF ThisYear/100 = 19 THEN
      Century := 0;
   ELSE
      Century := 6;
   END IF;

   Result := (((ThisYear REM 100) + ((ThisYear REM 100) / 4)
               + DayOfMonth(Right) +    MonthCode +   Century)
               REM 7) + 1;
   RETURN Result;

END DayOfWeek;

-- comparison operators

FUNCTION "<" (Left, Right: Date) RETURN Boolean IS
BEGIN
   IF Left.Year = Right.Year THEN
      RETURN Left.DayOfYear < Right.DayOfYear;
   ELSE
      RETURN Left.Year < Right.Year;
   END IF;
END "<";

FUNCTION "<=" (Left, Right: Date) RETURN Boolean IS
BEGIN
   IF Left.Year = Right.Year THEN
      RETURN Left.DayOfYear <= Right.DayOfYear;
   ELSE
      RETURN Left.Year < Right.Year;
   END IF;
END "<=";
```

```
FUNCTION ">" (Left, Right: Date) RETURN Boolean IS
BEGIN
  IF Left.Year = Right.Year THEN
    RETURN Left.DayOfYear > Right.DayOfYear;
  ELSE
    RETURN Left.Year > Right.Year;
  END IF;
END ">";

FUNCTION ">=" (Left, Right: Date) RETURN Boolean IS
BEGIN
  IF Left.Year = Right.Year THEN
    RETURN Left.DayOfYear >= Right.DayOfYear;
  ELSE
    RETURN Left.Year > Right.Year;
  END IF;
END ">=";

-- arithmetic operators

FUNCTION "+" (Left: Date; Right: JulianDay)  RETURN Date IS

  Result : Date;
  Temp   : Positive;
  YearMax: JulianDay;

BEGIN

  IF IsLeap(Left.Year) THEN                 -- leap year
    YearMax := 366;
  ELSE
    YearMax := 365;
  END IF;

  IF (Right = 366) AND THEN              -- special case, adding
     (NOT IsLeap(Left.Year + 1)) AND THEN -- 366 to Dec 31 when
    Left.DayOfYear = YearMax THEN         -- next year not leap

    Result := (Left.Year + 2, DayOfYear => 1);

  ELSE                                      -- normal case

    Temp := Left.DayOfYear + Right;
    IF Temp > YearMax THEN                  -- into next year
      Result := (Year => Left.Year + 1, DayOfYear => Temp - YearMax);
    ELSE
      Result := (Year => Left.Year,     DayOfYear => Temp);
    END IF;

  END IF;

  RETURN Result;

EXCEPTION
  WHEN Constraint_Error =>                  -- next year out of range
    RAISE Date_Error;
END "+";

FUNCTION "+"  (Left: JulianDay; Right: Date) RETURN Date IS
BEGIN
  RETURN Right + Left; -- use the other "+" above
END "+";

FUNCTION "-"  (Left: Date; Right: JulianDay) RETURN Date IS

  Difference: Integer; -- to hold difference between day fields
  Result: Date;
```

```
    BEGIN

      IF (Right = 366) AND THEN              -- special case, subtracting
         (NOT IsLeap(Left.Year - 1)) AND THEN -- 366 from Jan 1 when
         Left.DayOfYear = 1 THEN             -- previous year not leap

        Result := MakeDate(Year => Left.Year - 2, Month => 12, Day => 31);

      ELSE

        Difference := Left.DayOfYear - Right;
        IF Difference > 0 THEN    -- result is in the same year
          Result := (Year => Left.Year, DayOfYear => Difference);
        ELSE                      -- result is in previous year
          IF IsLeap(Left.Year - 1) THEN
            Result :=
              (Year => Left.Year-1, DayOfYear => 366+Difference);
          ELSE
            Result :=
              (Year => Left.Year-1, DayOfYear => 365+Difference);
          END IF;
        END IF;

      END IF;

      RETURN Result;

    EXCEPTION
      WHEN Constraint_Error =>              -- previous year out of range
        RAISE Date_Error;
    END "-";

END Dates;
```

In this package body, we first declare two "tables" in the form of arrays. These arrays are indexed by MonthNumber, and each element contains the number of days from January 1 to the end of the month in question. There are two tables, one for leap years and one for non-leap years.

The various operations in the package body are almost all algorithmically straightforward; you can read them closely to understand the details. The only operation whose workings are less than obvious is DayOfWeek, which finds the day of the week on which a given date falls. The algorithm provided here is adapted from one that appears in a number of different sources. The original was apparently developed in 1917 by a German professor, W. Jacobstal.

Now consider how the way leap year is determined. We have used the very simple criterion everyone knows: If the year is divisible by 4, it is a leap year. In fact, astronomically the formula is more complicated: If a year is divisible by 4 and also by 100, it is not a leap year unless it is also divisible by 400. Because Ada.Calendar defines years only in the range 1901..2099, the only "century year" is 2000, which is divisible by 400. Therefore we can use the simple rule as long as we remain consistent with Ada.Calendar. We choose instead to implement the complete algorithm, in case you ever need to modify the package to represent dates that lie outside the Ada.Calendar range.

There are many calendars; many have changed over the centuries. Traditional Hebrew, Muslim, and Chinese calendars are only a few of the many ways humankind has invented for reckoning days, months, years, and centuries. The study of calendars is very interesting, but is far away from this book's topic. If you are interested, you can study another calendar and think about how to implement it in a Dates package.

Finally, Program 2.14 illustrates the use of some of the Dates operations. We have not provided a Dates.IO package, choosing instead to illustrate one form of date output by including a local procedure PutDate in the test program. Writing a Dates.IO package is left as Exercise 5.

Program 2.14 Demonstration of Dates Package

```
WITH Dates; USE Dates;
WITH Ada.Text_IO;
WITH Ada.Integer_Text_IO;
PROCEDURE Test_Dates IS
----------------------------------------------------------------------
--| Simple test of Dates package
--| Author: Michael B. Feldman, The George Washington University
--| Last Modified: October 1995
----------------------------------------------------------------------

  TYPE Days IS (Mon, Tue, Wed, Thu, Fri, Sat, Sun);
  PACKAGE Days_IO IS NEW Ada.Text_IO.Enumeration_IO(Enum => Days);

  ThatDay, ThisDay: Date;

  PROCEDURE PutDate(Item: IN Date) IS
  BEGIN

    -- DayOfWeek returns 1..7, but positions are 0..6.
    Days_IO.Put(Item => Days'Val(DayOfWeek(Item) - 1), Width => 4);

    Ada.Integer_Text_IO.Put(Item => Month(Item), Width => 1);
    Ada.Text_IO.Put('/');
    Ada.Integer_Text_IO.Put(Item => DayOfMonth(Item), Width => 1);
    Ada.Text_IO.Put('/');
    Ada.Integer_Text_IO.Put(Item => Year(Item) REM 100, Width => 1);

  END PutDate;

BEGIN -- Test_Dates

-- First, is today's date OK?
ThisDay := Today;
PutDate(Item => ThisDay);
Ada.Text_IO.New_Line(Spacing => 2);

-- Now make a table of dates for the current year.
Ada.Text_IO.Put("Today        Yesterday     31 days from today");
Ada.Text_IO.New_Line(Spacing => 2);

FOR WhichMonth IN MonthNumber LOOP
  ThisDay := MakeDate
    (Year => Year(ThisDay), Month => WhichMonth, Day=> 1);
  ThatDay := ThisDay - 1;
  PutDate(Item => ThisDay);
  Ada.Text_IO.Put(Item => "      ");
```

```
    PutDate(Item => ThatDay);
    Ada.Text_IO.Put(Item => "      ");
    PutDate(Item => ThisDay + 31);
    Ada.Text_IO.New_Line;
  END LOOP;

  -- Now make a table of dates for a leap year.
  Ada.Text_IO.New_Line;
  Ada.Text_IO.Put("Today          Yesterday     31 days from today");
  Ada.Text_IO.New_Line(Spacing => 2);

  FOR WhichMonth IN MonthNumber LOOP
    ThisDay := MakeDate
      (Year => 1992, Month => WhichMonth, Day => 1);
    ThatDay := ThisDay - 1;
    PutDate(Item => ThisDay);
    Ada.Text_IO.Put(Item => "     ");
    PutDate(Item => ThatDay);
    Ada.Text_IO.Put(Item => "      ");
    PutDate(Item => ThisDay + 31);
    Ada.Text_IO.New_Line;
  END LOOP;

  END Test_Dates;
```

2.5 ADT DESIGN: SIMPLE SCREEN HANDLER

Ada's `Text_IO` package provides operations for reading from the terminal keyboard and writing to the screen, but it provides no direct operations for controlling the screen in interesting ways, such as moving the cursor to a given row-column position before writing. Doing this requires an additional package that uses `Text_IO` to send *control characters* to the terminal; the control characters act as instructions to it rather than as data it should display.

The Specification and Body of the `Screen` Package

Program 2.15 shows the specification for `Screen`. This package provides two constants, `ScreenWidth` and `ScreenHeight`, corresponding to the number of columns (usually 80) and rows (usually 25, but for various technical reasons we will use 24) on the screen. There are also two subtypes, `Width` and `Height`, giving the ranges for valid cursor positions (`1..ScreenWidth` and `1..ScreenHeight`, respectively).

Program 2.15 Specification for `Screen` Package

```
PACKAGE Screen IS
-------------------------------------------------------------------------
--| Procedures for drawing pictures on ANSI Terminal Screen
--| Author: Michael B. Feldman, The George Washington University
--| Last Modified: October 1995
-------------------------------------------------------------------------

  ScreenHeight : CONSTANT Integer := 24;
  ScreenWidth  : CONSTANT Integer := 80;

  SUBTYPE Height IS Integer RANGE 1..ScreenHeight;
  SUBTYPE Width IS Integer RANGE 1..ScreenWidth;
```

```
TYPE Position IS RECORD
   Row    : Height := 1;
   Column: Width := 1;
END RECORD;

PROCEDURE Beep;
-- Pre : none
-- Post: the terminal beeps once

PROCEDURE ClearScreen;
-- Pre : none
-- Post: the terminal screen is cleared

PROCEDURE MoveCursor (To: IN Position);
-- Pre : To is defined
-- Post: the terminal cursor is moved to the given position

END Screen;
```

Screen provides a type Position, which groups in a record the horizontal and vertical coordinates. We choose not to make this a PRIVATE type, because client programs can do no harm by making direct references to the Row and Column values. Grouping the fields together allows us to deal with the position as a single value, which is convenient in client programs.

The package provides three procedures. The first two, Beep and ClearScreen, take no parameters: A procedure call statement

```
Screen.Beep;
```

causes the terminal to beep; a procedure call statement

```
Screen.ClearScreen;
```

causes the screen to go blank, erasing all previous information from it. The last procedure, MoveCursor, takes row and column parameters, so that, for example,

```
Screen.MoveCursor (To => (Row => 10, Column => 22));
Ada.Text_IO.Put (Item => '*');
```

has the effect of displaying an asterisk at row 10, column 22. Finally,

```
Screen.MoveCursor (To => (Row => 5, Column => 10));
Ada.Text_IO.Put (Item => "-----");
```

displays the string ----- in row 5, columns 10 through 14, inclusive.

Program 2.16 gives the body for this package. The strings that are being sent to the terminal are known as *escape sequences*. An escape sequence is preceded by the character ASCII.ESC, and is used to give an instruction to the terminal, rather than to give it data to display. These escape sequences are rather esoteric and can be learned in their entirety only by reading a manual describing the ANSI terminal controls. The two sequences used here are among the most common, and will suffice for the screen-control work needed in this book.

Program 2.16 Body of Screen Package

```
WITH Ada.Text_IO;
WITH Ada.Integer_Text_IO;
PACKAGE BODY Screen IS
------------------------------------------------------------------------
--|
--| Procedures for drawing pictures on ANSI Terminal Screen
--| These procedures will work correctly only if the actual
--| terminal is ANSI compatible. ANSI.SYS on a DOS machine
--| will suffice.
--|
--| Author: Michael B. Feldman, The George Washington University
--| Last Modified: September 1995
--|
------------------------------------------------------------------------

  PROCEDURE Beep IS
  BEGIN
    Ada.Text_IO.New_Line;
    Ada.Text_IO.Put (Item => ASCII.BEL);
  END Beep;

  PROCEDURE ClearScreen IS
  BEGIN
    Ada.Text_IO.New_Line;
    Ada.Text_IO.Put (Item => ASCII.ESC);
    Ada.Text_IO.Put (Item => "[2J");
  END ClearScreen;

  PROCEDURE MoveCursor (To: IN Position) IS
  BEGIN
    Ada.Text_IO.New_Line;
    Ada.Text_IO.Put (Item => ASCII.ESC);
    Ada.Text_IO.Put ("[");
    Ada.Integer_Text_IO.Put (Item => To.Row, Width => 1);
    Ada.Text_IO.Put (Item => ';');
    Ada.Integer_Text_IO.Put (Item => To.Column, Width => 1);
    Ada.Text_IO.Put (Item => 'f');
  END MoveCursor;

END Screen;
```

Using the `Screen` Package

Program 2.17 uses the `Screen` package to draw vertical and horizontal lines on the screen, dividing the screen into four quadrants. The loop

```
FOR Count IN Screen.Width LOOP
  Screen.MoveCursor (To => (Row => 12, Column => Count);
  Ada.Text_IO.Put (Item => '-');
  Screen.MoveCursor (To =>
        (Row => 13, Column => (Screen.Screen_Width - Count) + 1);
  Ada.Text_IO.Put (Item => '-'));
END LOOP;
```

draws a horizontal separator consisting of two lines of hyphen characters on rows 12 and 13 of the screen. The parameters to the first call of `Screen.`

MoveCursor move the cursor one position to the right in each loop iteration; just to make the program more interesting, the second call moves the cursor one position to the left each time.

Program 2.17 Dividing the Screen into Four Pieces

```
WITH Ada.Text_IO;
WITH Screen;
PROCEDURE Four_Pieces IS
------------------------------------------------------------------------
--| This program divides the screen into four pieces using
--| horizontal and vertical lines. Screen operations are used
--| to position the cursor.
--| Author: Michael B. Feldman, The George Washington University
--| Last Modified: October 1995
------------------------------------------------------------------------

BEGIN -- Four_Pieces

  Screen.ClearScreen;

  FOR Count IN Screen.Height LOOP
    Screen.MoveCursor (To => (Row => Count, Column => 41));
    Ada.Text_IO.Put (Item => '|');
    Screen.MoveCursor (To =>
      (Row => (Screen.ScreenHeight - Count) + 1, Column => 42));
    Ada.Text_IO.Put (Item => '|');
  END LOOP;

  FOR Count IN Screen.Width LOOP
    Screen.MoveCursor (To => (Row => 12, Column => Count));
    Ada.Text_IO.Put (Item => '-');
    Screen.MoveCursor (To =>
      (Row => 13, Column => (Screen.ScreenWidth - Count) + 1));
    Ada.Text_IO.Put (Item => '-');
  END LOOP;

  Screen.MoveCursor (To => (Row => 24, Column => 1));

END Four_Pieces;
```

ANSI-compatible terminals or emulator programs are probably the most common ones in use today. Even the most sophisticated windowed workstations usually have an ANSI or VT-100 "mode," which will allow output using Screen to appear correctly on the video device. Exercises 9 and 10 provide for writing a more sophisticated ANSI package and for writing a package for a non-ANSI terminal.

2.6 ADT DESIGN: SIMPLE WINDOW MANAGER

Windows are a very common scheme for handling interactive input/output on today's computers. A window is just a bounded area of the screen used for writing output and, sometimes, echoing input. Most current window systems (for example, Macintosh, Microsoft Windows, and X-windows) are very powerful and interesting to use. Such systems are, in general, specific to a particular computer family, operating system, or terminal type.

In this section, we introduce a very simple, even oversimplified windowing system as an example of an ADT. By studying this ADT, you will get some idea of how windows work, without being overwhelmed by details either of specific machines or of graphics algorithms, both of which are beyond the scope of this book. This simple system is, however, entirely portable and can be compiled and used with any Ada compiler. `Windows` uses the `Screen` package described in section 2.5, so it will produce meaningful output on any terminal that is ANSI- or VT-100-compatible, which includes most "dumb terminals" and also the ANSI.SYS mode of the IBM PC family.

What's a Window?

To get an idea of how windowing systems work, you can look at Figure 2.1, which shows some writing on a terminal screen assumed to have 24 rows and 80 columns.

This output was produced by Program 2.18, which makes a number of calls of operations in the `Windows` package. Before studying `Windows` in detail, let us examine this client program and its output.

Program 2.18 Demonstration of Windows Package

```
WITH Windows;
WITH Screen;
PROCEDURE Test_Windows IS
------------------------------------------------------------------------
--| Very simple test of Windows package
--| Author: Michael B. Feldman, The George Washington University
--| Last Modified: October 1995
------------------------------------------------------------------------

  W1: Windows.Window;
  W2: Windows.Window;
  W3: Windows.Window;

BEGIN -- Test_Windows

  Screen.ClearScreen;

  W1 := Windows.Open(UpperLeft => (Row => 2, Column => 5),
                     Height => 10, Width => 18);
  W2 := Windows.Open(UpperLeft => (Row => 15, Column => 20),
                     Height => 7, Width => 7);

  Windows.Borders(W => W1, Corner => '+',Down => '|', Across => '-');
  Windows.Title(W1, "Window One", '_');
  Windows.Put(W1, "This is the first string going in the window.");
  Windows.Put(W1, "And this is the second one.");

  Windows.Put(W2, "This is a window without a border or a title.");

  W3 := Windows.Open(UpperLeft => (Row => 5, Column => 35),
                     Height => 8, Width => 25);

  Windows.New_Line(W1);
  Windows.Put(W1, "Bye.");

  Windows.Borders(W => W3, Corner => '*',Down => '*', Across => '*');
  Windows.Title(W3, "Window Three", ';');
```

```
Windows.Put
   (W3, "This is the first string going in the third window.");
Windows.Put(W3, "And this is the second one.");
Windows.New_Line(W3);
Windows.Put(W3, "So long.");
Screen.MoveCursor(To => (Row => 23, Column => 1));

END Test_Windows;
```

The display in Figure 2.1 shows output in three areas of the screen. Each is a window; each was created by a call to `Windows.Open` as shown in Program 2.18. The three calls are scattered throughout the program a bit to indicate that windows do not all have to be opened at once. As you can see from the form of the `Windows.Open` calls, this operation specifies the coordinates of the upper left corner of the window, as well as its height and width.

Windows `W1` and `W3` have borders and titles; `W2` does not. The `Windows.Put` and `Windows.New_Line` operations used in this test program should be obvious, because they are closely related to their `Ada.Text_IO` counterparts. The main difference, of course, is that these operations work within the confines of a window specified by the first parameter. Note that the text in each window "wraps around" or flows onto the next line, if the window is too narrow to hold the full string. Also notice that a bordered window has a "writable area" two rows and two columns smaller than one without borders, and that putting a title in a window reduces its "writable" area further by two rows.

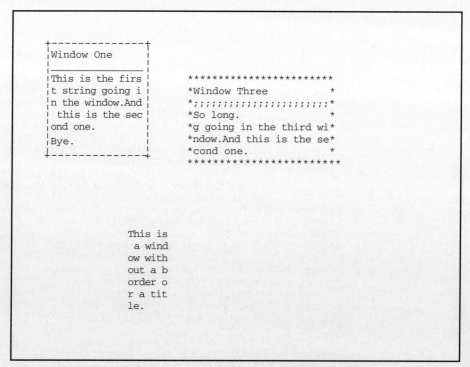

Figure 2.1 Windowed Output from a Windows Client Program

The Specification of the `Windows` Package

Program 2.19 shows the specification of `Windows`. Its operations are more like `Ada.Text_IO` operations than like the arithmetic ones we have seen in earlier ADTs. A `Window` object is defined as a record with three fields, each of type `Screen.Position`. Two of the fields contain the coordinates of the upper left and lower right corners; the third field gives the current location of the cursor within the window.

Program 2.19 Specification for Windows Package

```
WITH Screen;
PACKAGE Windows IS
-----------------------------------------------------------------------
--| Manager for simple, nonoverlapping screen windows
--| Author: Michael B. Feldman, The George Washington University
--| Last Modified: October 1995
-----------------------------------------------------------------------

  TYPE Window IS PRIVATE;

  FUNCTION Open (UpperLeft: Screen.Position;
                 Height    : Screen.Height;
                 Width     : Screen.Width) RETURN Window;
  -- Pre: UpperLeft, Height, and Width are defined
  -- Post: returns a Window with the given upper-left corner,
  --    height, and width

  PROCEDURE Title (W     : IN OUT Window;
                   Name  : IN String;
                   Under : IN Character);
  -- Pre:  W, Name, and Under are defined
  -- Post: Name is displayed at the top of the window W, underlined
  -- with the character Under.

  PROCEDURE Borders (W                     : IN OUT Window;
                     Corner, Down, Across : IN Character);
  -- Pre:  All parameters are defined
  -- Post: Draw border around current writable area in window with
  -- characters specified. Call this BEFORE Title.

  PROCEDURE MoveCursor (W : IN OUT Window;
                        P : IN Screen.Position);
  -- Pre:  W and P are defined, and P lies within the area of W
  -- Post: Cursor is moved to the specified position.
  --       Coordinates are relative to the
  --       upper left corner of W, which is (1, 1)

  PROCEDURE Put (W  : IN OUT Window;
                 Ch : IN Character);
  -- Pre:  W and Ch are defined.
  -- Post: Ch is displayed in the window at
  --    the next available position.
  --    If end of column, go to the next row.
  --    If end of window, go to the top of the window.

  PROCEDURE Put (W : IN OUT Window;
                 S : IN String);
  -- Pre:  W and S are defined
  -- Post: S is displayed in the window, "line-wrapped" if necessary
```

```
      PROCEDURE New_Line (W : IN OUT Window);
      -- Pre:  W is defined
      -- Post: Cursor moves to beginning of next line of W;
      --   line is not blanked until next character is written

   PRIVATE
      TYPE Window IS RECORD
         First  : Screen.Position; -- coordinates of upper left
         Last   : Screen.Position; -- coordinates of lower right
         Current: Screen.Position; -- current cursor position
      END RECORD;

   END Windows;
```

Consider how we would display a character within a window. Generally, the window operation calls in a client program "jump around" from window to window as the program progresses, first putting a bit of information in one window, then in another, and so on, perhaps returning later to the first window. You can see examples of this in Program 2.18. Interleaving window operations in this way requires that each window "remember" where the cursor must be to write a character in the next location relative to that window. This is the purpose of the Current field in the window record. Each time an operation seeks to display information in a window, the actual screen cursor must be moved to the proper location, namely the location given by the Current field of the window record.

In window W3 in Figure 2.1, notice that the line "So long" appears at the top of the window. This is because the window was full of previously displayed text; the Windows operations respond to this situation by starting again in the upper left corner of the window.

The Body of the **Windows** Package

The body of this package is given as Program 2.20.

Program 2.20 The Body of the Windows Package

```
WITH Ada.Text_IO;
WITH Screen;
PACKAGE BODY Windows IS
-----------------------------------------------------------------------
--|
--| Body of simple Windows package
--|
--| Author: Michael B. Feldman, The George Washington University
--| Last Modified: October 1995
--|
-----------------------------------------------------------------------
   FUNCTION Open (UpperLeft: Screen.Position;
                  Height    : Screen.Height;
                  Width     : Screen.Width) RETURN Window IS
      Result: Window;
   BEGIN
      Result.Current:= UpperLeft;
      Result.First  := UpperLeft;
      Result.Last   := (Row    => UpperLeft.Row + Height - 1,
                        Column => UpperLeft.Column + Width - 1);
      RETURN Result;
   END Open;
```

```
PROCEDURE EraseToEndOfLine (W : IN OUT Window) IS
BEGIN
  Screen.MoveCursor (W.Current);
  FOR Count IN W.Current.Column .. W.Last.Column LOOP
    Ada.Text_IO.Put (' ');
  END LOOP;
  Screen.MoveCursor (W.Current);
END EraseToEndOfLine;


PROCEDURE Put (W  : IN OUT Window;
              Ch : IN CHARACTER) IS
BEGIN

  -- If at end of current line, move to next line
  IF W.Current.Column > W.Last.Column THEN
    IF W.Current.Row = W.Last.Row THEN
      W.Current.Row := W.First.Row;
    ELSE
      W.Current.Row := W.Current.Row + 1;
    END IF;
    W.Current.Column := W.First.Column;
  END IF;


  -- If at First char, erase line
  IF W.Current.Column = W.First.Column THEN
    EraseToEndOfLine (W);
  END IF;

  Screen.MoveCursor (To => W.Current);

  -- here is where we actually write the character!
  Ada.Text_IO.Put (Ch);
  W.Current.Column := W.Current.Column + 1;

END Put;

PROCEDURE Put (W : IN OUT Window;
              S : IN String) IS
BEGIN
  FOR Count IN S'Range LOOP
    Put (W, S (Count));
  END LOOP;
END Put;

PROCEDURE New_Line (W : IN OUT Window) IS
BEGIN
  IF W.Current.Column = 1 THEN
    EraseToEndOfLine (W);
  END IF;
  IF W.Current.Row = W.Last.Row THEN
    W.Current.Row := W.First.Row;
  ELSE
    W.Current.Row := W.Current.Row + 1;
  END IF;
  W.Current.Column := W.First.Column;
END New_Line;

PROCEDURE Title (W     : IN OUT Window;
                 Name  : IN String;
                 Under : IN Character)IS
```

```
   BEGIN

      -- Put name on top line
      W.Current := W.First;
      Put (W, Name);
      New_Line (W);
      -- Underline name if desired, and reduce the writable area
      -- of the window by one line
      IF Under = ' ' THEN   -- no underlining
        W.First.Row := W.First.Row + 1;
      ELSE                  -- go across the row, underlining
        FOR Count IN W.First.Column..W.Last.Column LOOP
          Put (W, Under);
        END LOOP;
        New_Line (W);
        W.First.Row := W.First.Row + 2;  -- reduce writable area
      END IF;
   END Title;

   PROCEDURE Borders (W                     : IN OUT Window;
                      Corner, Down, Across : IN Character) IS
   BEGIN
      -- Put top line of border
      Screen.MoveCursor (W.First);
      Ada.Text_IO.Put (Corner);
      FOR Count IN W.First.Column + 1 .. W.Last.Column - 1 LOOP
        Ada.Text_IO.Put (Across);
      END LOOP;
      Ada.Text_IO.Put (Corner);

      -- Put the two side lines
      FOR Count IN W.First.Row + 1 .. W.Last.Row - 1 LOOP
        Screen.MoveCursor ((Row => Count, Column => W.First.Column));
        Ada.Text_IO.Put (Down);
        Screen.MoveCursor ((Row => Count, Column => W.Last.Column));
        Ada.Text_IO.Put (Down);
      END LOOP;

      -- Put the bottom line of the border
      Screen.MoveCursor ((Row => W.Last.Row, Column => W.First.Column));
      Ada.Text_IO.Put (corner);
      FOR Count IN W.First.Column + 1 .. W.Last.Column - 1 LOOP
        Ada.Text_IO.Put (Across);
      END LOOP;
      Ada.Text_IO.Put (Corner);

      -- Make the Window smaller by one character on each side
      W.First :=
        (Row => W.First.Row + 1, Column => W.First.Column + 1);
      W.Last  :=
        (Row => W.Last.Row - 1, Column => W.Last.Column - 1);
      W.Current := W.First;
   END Borders;

   PROCEDURE MoveCursor (W : IN OUT Window;
                         P : IN Screen.Position) IS
      -- Relative to writable Window boundaries, of course
   BEGIN
      W.Current.Row    := W.First.Row + P.Row;
      W.Current.Column := W.First.Column + P.Column;
   END MoveCursor;

END Windows;
```

Many of the operations are filled with detail, but they are really not difficult to understand. The first operation is `Open`, which simply stores the coordinates of the upper left corner in the `First` and `Current` fields, then computes and stores in the `Last` field the coordinates of the lower right corner, given the upper left, height, and width. The next operation is an internal one; we choose not to provide it to clients. This operation, `EraseToEndOfLine`, writes blank characters from the current cursor position to the end of the current line in the window.

The third operation is really the key one in the package. `Put` displays a character in the next available position in the window. If the preceding character was displayed at the end of a line (relative to the window, of course), the new character must be placed at the start of the next line, the rest of which is blanked out. If the preceding character was displayed in the bottom right corner of the window, the new one must go at the top left. (In a real windowing system, the text would "scroll up" in the window; this is beyond the scope of our discussion.)

Note the statement

```
Screen.MoveCursor(To => W.Current);
```

which is really the critical one. In this statement, the physical cursor is moved to the correct location in the window.

Following `Put` is another `Put`, which displays a string in the window. This is done by a series of single-character `Put` calls. We cannot simply use `Ada.Text_IO.Put` with a string argument, because the wraparound would not be done by `Ada.Text_IO`.

The remaining operations are straightforward; we leave it to you to study them in detail.

2.7 A FEW MORE ADA 95 TOPICS

In this section we introduce several Ada 95 topics. These are *the math functions package*, `Float`-*to*-`Integer` *type conversion, additions to* `Ada.Text_IO`, *and command line parameters.*

Mathematics Packages

Ada 83 provided no standard package for mathematical functions such square root, exponential, sine, and the like. Compiler suppliers typically provided these, but the package names, and occasionally the function names, differed from compiler to compiler. Ada 95 remedies this lack by providing some standard facilities for these often-needed operations. Specifically, a package `Ada.Numerics` and a package `Ada.Numerics.Elementary_Functions`, are required by the Ada 95 standard.

```
PACKAGE Ada.Numerics IS

  Argument_Error : EXCEPTION;
  Pi : CONSTANT :=
    3.14159_26535_89793_23846_26433_83279_50288_41971_69399_37511;
  e  : CONSTANT :=
    2.71828_18284_59045_23536_02874_71352_66249_77572_47093_69996;

END Ada.Numerics;
```

Figure 2.2 Package `Ada.Numerics`

Their specifications are shown in Figures 2.2 and 2.3, respectively. They are given as figures and not programs because, as in the case of the standard packages given in Chapter 1, they are supplied with the compiler in precompiled form.

```
PACKAGE Ada.Numerics.Elementary_Functions IS

  FUNCTION Sqrt(X : Float) RETURN Float;
  FUNCTION Log (X : Float) RETURN Float;
  FUNCTION Log (X, Base: Float) RETURN Float;
  FUNCTION Exp (X : Float) RETURN Float;
  FUNCTION "**" (Left, Right: Float) RETURN Float;

  FUNCTION Sin (X : Float) RETURN Float;
  FUNCTION Cos (X : Float) RETURN Float;
  FUNCTION Tan (X : Float) RETURN Float;
  FUNCTION Cot (X : Float) RETURN Float;

  FUNCTION Arcsin(X : Float) RETURN Float;
  FUNCTION Arccos(X : Float) RETURN Float;
  FUNCTION Arctan(Y : Float;
                  X : Float := 1.0) RETURN Float;
  FUNCTION Arccot(X : Float;
                  Y : Float := 1.0) RETURN Float;

  FUNCTION Sinh(X : Float) RETURN Float;
  FUNCTION Cosh(X : Float) RETURN Float;
  FUNCTION Tanh(X : Float) RETURN Float;
  FUNCTION Coth(X : Float) RETURN Float;
  FUNCTION Arcsinh (X : Float) RETURN Float;
  FUNCTION Arccosh (X : Float) RETURN Float;
  FUNCTION Arctanh (X : Float) RETURN Float;
  FUNCTION Arccoth (X : Float) RETURN Float;

  FUNCTION Sin (X, Cycle : Float) RETURN Float;
  FUNCTION Cos (X, Cycle : Float) RETURN Float;
  FUNCTION Tan (X, Cycle : Float) RETURN Float;
  FUNCTION Cot (X, Cycle : Float) RETURN Float;

  FUNCTION Arcsin(X, Cycle : Float) RETURN Float;
  FUNCTION Arccos(X, Cycle : Float) RETURN Float;
  FUNCTION Arctan(Y : Float;
                  X : Float := 1.0;
                  Cycle : Float) RETURN Float;
  FUNCTION Arccot(X : Float;
                  Y : Float := 1.0;
                  Cycle : Float) RETURN Float;

END Ada.Numerics.Elementary_Functions;
```

Figure 2.3 Ada 95 Elementary Functions Package

Programs 2.21 and 2.22 illustrate the use of the elementary functions library, displaying, respectively, a table of square roots and a sine curve. Note that Program 2.22 refers to Ada.Numerics.Pi as well as to Math.Sin. The output of Program 2.23 is shown in Figure 2.4.

Program 2.21 Table of Square Roots

```
WITH Ada.Text_IO;
WITH Ada.Integer_Text_IO;
WITH Ada.Float_Text_IO;
WITH Ada.Numerics.Elementary_Functions;
USE Ada.Numerics.Elementary_Functions;
PROCEDURE Square_Root_Table IS
------------------------------------------------------------------------
--| Displays a table of square roots; illustrates the USE clause
--| Author: Michael B. Feldman, The George Washington University
--| Last Modified: July 1995
------------------------------------------------------------------------

  MaxNumber : CONSTANT Positive := 20;

BEGIN -- Square_Root_Table

  Ada.Text_IO.Put (Item => "Number Square Root");
  Ada.Text_IO.New_Line;
  Ada.Text_IO.Put (Item => "------ -----------");
  Ada.Text_IO.New_Line;

  FOR Number IN 1..MaxNumber LOOP
    Ada.Integer_Text_IO.Put (Item => Number, Width => 3);
    Ada.Float_Text_IO.Put
      (Item => Sqrt (Float(Number)), Fore => 7, Aft => 5, Exp => 0);
    Ada.Text_IO.New_Line;
  END LOOP;

END Square_Root_Table;
```

Program 2.22 Plotting a Sine Curve

```
WITH Ada.Text_IO;
WITH Ada.Float_Text_IO;
WITH Ada.Numerics;
USE Ada.Numerics;
WITH Ada.Numerics.Elementary_Functions;
USE Ada.Numerics.Elementary_Functions;
PROCEDURE Sine_Curve IS
------------------------------------------------------------------------
--| Plots a sine curve.
--| Author: Michael B. Feldman, The George Washington University
--| Last Modified: July 1995
------------------------------------------------------------------------

  RadPerDegree : CONSTANT Float := Pi / 180.0;
                                             -- radians per degree
                                             -- Pi in Ada.Numerics
  MinAngle :   CONSTANT Float   := 0.0;      -- smallest angle
  MaxAngle :   CONSTANT Float   := 360.0;    -- largest angle
  PlotWidth :  CONSTANT Integer := 40;       -- width of plot
  PlotHeight : CONSTANT Integer := 20;       -- height of plot
```

```
    StepAngle :    CONSTANT Float :=
                              (MaxAngle-MinAngle) / Float(PlotHeight);
                                              -- change in angle
    Star :         CONSTANT Character := '*';    -- symbol being plotted
    Blank:         CONSTANT Character := ' ';    -- to "pad" the '*'

    SUBTYPE ColumnRange IS Integer RANGE 0..PlotWidth;

    Angle :        Float;                    -- angle in degrees
    Radian :       Float;                    -- angle in radians
    Scale :        Float;                    -- scale factor
    Pad :          ColumnRange;              -- size of blank padding
BEGIN -- Sine_Curve

    Ada.Text_IO.Put(Item => "                     Sine curve plot");
    Ada.Text_IO.New_Line(2);
    Scale := Float(PlotWidth / 2);
    Angle := MinAngle;

    WHILE Angle <= MaxAngle LOOP

      Radian := Angle * RadPerDegree;
      Pad := Natural(Scale * (1.0 + Sin(Radian)));

      Ada.Float_Text_IO.Put
        (Item =>Angle, Fore => 4, Aft => 0, Exp => 0);

      -- Display blank padding
      Ada.Text_IO.Put(Item => Blank);
      FOR BlankCount IN 1 .. Pad LOOP
        Ada.Text_IO.Put(Item => Blank);
      END LOOP;

      Ada.Text_IO.Put(Item => Star);          -- Plot * in next column
      Ada.Float_Text_IO.Put
        (Item =>Sin(Radian), Fore => 6, Aft => 6, Exp => 0);
      Ada.Text_IO.New_Line;
      Angle := Angle + StepAngle;

    END LOOP;

END Sine_Curve;
```

Ada 95 also provides standard packages for float and discrete (integer, enumeration) random number generators.

Float-to-Integer Type Conversion

A minor annoyance in Ada 83 appears when one converts a `Float` value to an `Integer` one. If `I` is an integer variable and `F` a float variable, we know that

```
I := Integer(F);
```

is a legal statement. This is a rounding operation; the `Float` value is converted to the nearest integer. Suppose the `Float` value is exactly halfway between two integers? The Ada 83 standard indicates that the rounding is compiler-dependent and can go in either direction. This uncertainty is resolved by Ada 95; a `Float` value halfway between two integers is rounded away from zero. `Integer(3.5)` will produce 4; `Integer(-3.5)` will produce −4.

```
                              Sine curve plot

      0.0                          *         0.000000
     18.0                            *          0.309017
     36.0                             *            0.587785
     54.0                               *            0.809017
     72.0                                *             0.951057
     90.0                                 *              1.000000
    108.0                                *             0.951057
    126.0                               *            0.809017
    144.0                             *            0.587785
    162.0                           *          0.309017
    180.0                         *       -0.000000
    198.0                      *         -0.309017
    216.0                 *          -0.587785
    234.0            *         -0.809017
    252.0        *         -0.951056
    270.0  *         -1.000000
    288.0        *         -0.951056
    306.0            *         -0.809017
    324.0                 *         -0.587785
    342.0                      *         -0.309017
    360.0                           *          0.000000
```

Figure 2.4 Output from Program 2.22

Additions to `Ada.Text_IO`

Here we present two useful additions to `Ada.Text_IO`. The first is related to external files: In Ada 83 there is no standard way to append new data to the end of an existing file. This capability is provided, in a nonstandard fashion, by many compiler suppliers. In Ada 95, appending to the end of a file is provided by the addition of a file mode `Append_File` to the existing `In_File` and `Out_File` modes. If `MyFile` is a variable of type `Ada.Text_IO.File_Type` and `project7.dat` is an existing file in the file system,

```
Ada.Text_IO.Open
  (File=>MyFile, Mode=>Ada.Text_IO.Append_File, Name=>"project7.dat");
```

opens the file for output and moves to the current end of it, so that any new `Put` operations append the written data to the end of the file.

The second welcome addition to `Ada.Text_IO` is a pair of one-character input procedures:

```
PROCEDURE Look_Ahead (Item: OUT Character; End_Of_Line: OUT Boolean);
PROCEDURE Get_Immediate(Item: OUT Character);
```

`Look_Ahead` sets `End_Of_Line` to `True` if the current input pointer is at end of line, including, at end of page, or at end of file; in each of these cases, the value of `Item` is not specified. Otherwise `End_Of_Line` is set to `False` and `Item` is set to the the next character (without consuming it) from the file. This lets us look one character ahead in the input stream without actually reading the character.

Get_Immediate reads the next character from the keyboard, without waiting for the ENTER key to be pressed. As in the case of the other Get operations, these two have counterparts for external files as well as for the standard input or keyboard file. Program 2.23 illustrates the use of Get_Immediate.

Program 2.23 Demonstrating Ada.Text_IO.Get_Immediate

```
WITH Ada.Text_IO;
PROCEDURE Immediate IS
-------------------------------------------------------------------------
--|
--| Demonstrate Ada 95 procedure Ada.Text_IO.Get_Immediate,
--| which allows reading a character without waiting for a <CR>
--|
--| Author: Michael B. Feldman, The George Washington University
--| Last Modified: October 1995
--|
-------------------------------------------------------------------------

  Command: Character;

BEGIN -- Immediate

  Command := 'a';
  LOOP
    EXIT WHEN (Command = 'q') OR (Command = 'Q');
    Ada.Text_IO.Put(Item =>
      "Enter q or Q to quit; any other character to continue.");
    Ada.Text_IO.Get_Immediate(Item => Command);
    Ada.Text_IO.New_Line;
    Ada.Text_IO.Put(Item => "You entered ");
    Ada.Text_IO.Put(Item => Command);
    Ada.Text_IO.New_Line;
  END LOOP;

END Immediate;
```

Command-Line Parameters

The final Ada 95 feature we will discuss in this section is the package Ada. Command_Line, which allows a program to retrieve the flags or parameters entered on the operating system command line when the program is invoked. This is another feature that is missing from Ada 83, that was provided by compiler suppliers in non-standard ways. The specification for this package is shown in Figure 2.5.

Argument_Count returns the number of arguments on the command line; Argument takes a positive parameter and returns a given command-line argument, so if Number is 2, Argument returns the second argument. Note that Argument always returns a string; if the program requires an integer or enumeration value, the 'Val attribute can be used, as always, to convert the string. Finally, the function Command_Name allows the program to find out its own name as known to the operating system—that is, the name by which it is invoked on the command line.

```
PACKAGE Ada.Command_Line IS

  FUNCTION Argument_Count RETURN Natural;

  FUNCTION Argument (Number : IN Positive) RETURN String;

  FUNCTION Command_Name RETURN String;

  TYPE Status IS RANGE implementation-defined;

  Success : CONSTANT Status;
  Failure : CONSTANT Status;

  PROCEDURE Set_Status (Code : IN Status);

END Ada.Command_Line;
```

Figure 2.5 Ada 95 Command-Line Package

Some operating systems allow a program, invoked by the command line, to return a value, usually a small nonnegative integer, to the command shell. The procedure Set_Status can be used to set this value if the operating system allows it.

Program 2.24 illustrates the use of these functions.

Program 2.24 Demonstrating Ada.Command_Arguments

```
WITH Ada.Text_IO;
WITH Ada.Command_Line;
PROCEDURE Command_Arguments IS
-------------------------------------------------------------------
--|
--| demonstrate Ada 95 command-line parameters
--|
--| Author: Michael B. Feldman, The George Washington University
--| Last Modified: September 1995
--|
-------------------------------------------------------------------

  HowMany: Natural; -- how many command-line arguments were there?

BEGIN -- Command_Arguments

  Ada.Text_IO.Put(Item => Ada.Command_Line.Command_Name);

  HowMany := Ada.Command_Line.Argument_Count;

  IF HowMany = 0 THEN
    Ada.Text_IO.Put_Line(Item => ": No command-line arguments today.");
  ELSE
    Ada.Text_IO.Put_Line(Item => ": The command-line arguments are: ');

    FOR Count IN 1..HowMany LOOP
      Ada.Text_IO.Put_Line
        (Item => Ada.Command_Line.Argument(Number => Count));
    END LOOP;
  END IF;

END Command_Arguments;
```

SUMMARY

In this chapter, you have been introduced to five ADTs: rational numbers, currency quantities, calendar dates, screen positions, and windows. By now, you should be getting the flavor of the kinds of operations commonly found in ADTs, and of a number of important Ada features—packages, private types, overloaded operators, and exceptions—that support the writing of ADTs.

The next chapter introduces two important and very fundamental computing concepts, namely recursion and algorithm performance prediction, and shows how ADTs and performance prediction are related.

EXERCISES

1. Modify Program 2.6 so that it does not terminate if the user enters a zero denominator. *Hint*: See the procedure `ReadCity` in Program 1.2 for an example showing how to build an exception-handling loop.

2. Complete the test plan begun in Section 2.2, then finish the body of `Rationals` by implementing those operations left as stubs. Implement your test plan as a program. You have three choices for entering the test data: "hard-wired" (coded directly into the program), entered interactively, or read from an external file you create with an editor.

3. Modify the child package `Rationals.IO` so that the interactive `Get` procedure does its own exception handling and does not return to its caller until the input is valid. *Hint*: See the procedure `ReadCity` in Program 1.2. Think about whether it is possible to make the file-oriented `Get` procedure equally robust.

4. Complete the package body, and develop a full test plan, for `Currency`.

5. Design, code, and test a child package `Dates.IO` that provides terminal and file operations for values of type `Dates.Date`. You have much flexibility here, because there are many commonly used external formats for dates. Choose one or more that suit you and design accordingly.

6. The `Ada.Calendar` package provides a procedure `Split`, which takes a value of type `Ada.Calendar.Time` and returns its components as `OUT` parameters. Develop and test a procedure `Dates.Split` that behaves analogously when it is given a value of type `Dates.Date`.

7. In the `Dates` package, the subtype `Dates.JulianDay` has range 1..366: the date-arithmetic operators use this type as an operand. This means that a date cannot be extended more than one year into the future or the past. We can always add several years' worth of days, one year at a time. This is cumbersome for each client program to do, so it makes sense to provide a package operation to do it.

    Suppose we defined a type that allowed one to add or subtract an arbitrary number of days. What would an appropriate range for this type be? (*Hint*: Package `Ada.Calendar` is defined only for a certain range of years.) Define such a type, then write the accompanying arithmetic operations to be added to the `Dates` package. In developing the addition algorithm, you will probably find it easiest to do the addition in a loop, one year at a time. Of course, the loop will be coded *inside* the addition operation.

8. `Dates` does not provide an operation that subtracts two `Date` values and returns the number of days between them. Develop such an operation. Would you use the `JulianDay` subtype as the result type, or the "larger" day type described in the preceding problem?

9. Obtain a copy of the documentation for the ANSI terminal control sequences and use this manual to develop a more complete and sophisticated terminal control package. Look especially at controls such as reverse video, blinking, and the like. Write an interesting client program to demonstrate your terminal controller's capabilities.

10. If your computer laboratory supports terminals that are not ANSI-compatible (for example, Zenith-mode terminals), obtain a manual for the terminals and modify `Screen` to handle them properly. You can probably do this by modifying only the body of `Screen` (Program 2.15) to handle the different escape sequences.

11. The window-manager package `Windows` does not provide a procedure to close a window (erase it from the screen). Extend the window manager to provide such a procedure, which would erase a window by writing blank characters over the window's entire area. Note that the "writable" area of the window is altered by borders and titles, so you will need to develop a way to know the window's original dimensions. One way to do this is to carry this information in the window record. Another way is to add flags to the record indicating whether or not the window is bordered or titled, and to use this information to expand the area that is erased.

12. Suppose that in using the `Windows` package, a client program contained the statement

    ```
    Windows.Put(Ch => ASCII.BS);
    ```

    where `ASCII.BS` is Ada's name for the backspace character. Would the `Put` operation handle this correctly? If not, modify it so that it will.

CHAPTER 3

Algorithms, Recursion, Performance Prediction, and Performance Measurement

In this chapter, you will study two important aspects of algorithms. The first is the use of *recursion* or *recursive algorithms* to solve certain computing problems. A recursive algorithm moves ahead by applying itself to a smaller part of the problem; in programming terms, the algorithm, written as a function or procedure, "calls itself." Several useful but easy-to-understand recursive algorithms will be presented, together with Ada programs implementing them.

The second area introduced in this chapter is *performance prediction*. You will learn techniques and rules of thumb to estimate the computation time of an algorithm, or, more specifically, the *variation* of the computation time as a function of the *size* of the problem being solved. An important bit of terminology in performance prediction is "big *O*" notation. This notation is a way of representing the "order of magnitude" or "growth rate" of an algorithm—in other words, the variation with problem size we have just mentioned. You'll be introduced to the most common variations or "big *O*'s" to be encountered later in the book. These are the *constant*, *logarithmic*, *linear*, *quadratic*, and *N log N* growth rates.

At the end of the chapter, you will be introduced to the idea of a *keyed table*, which is a simplified model of a data base. The operations on such a table will be presented, the "big O's" of two different implementations will be compared, and an application of the table handler will be given.

Finally, you will learn how to *measure* the execution time of a program or algorithm.

3.1 ALGORITHMS AND ALGORITHM DESIGN

Informally, an algorithm is a method used to solve a problem on a computer. Formally, an algorithm is

a *finite sequence of instructions*,

each of which has a *clear meaning* and

can be performed with a *finite amount of effort*

in a *finite length of time*

using a *finite amount of memory.*

The finiteness is important: A program is an algorithm if it eventually terminates and never goes into an infinite loop, no matter what input we give it.

The computation time and memory space required by data structures and the algorithms that work on them are important, and sometimes scarce, resources. Indeed, you will see in this book frequent references to trade-offs. A *trade-off* is a situation in which alternative solutions to a problem are considered in terms of their resource requirements. One solution may require more time but less space than another; a third might require more time *and* more space than either of the others, but the programs might be simpler and easier to maintain, making it more economical in human terms. We thus speak in terms of *trading off* space for time, or performance for clarity, or computer resources for human ones.

No book can give you a "right answer" that will serve in every case. When you are faced with a trade-off situation in deciding on a computer solution to a problem you have, you must base your decision on the specific circumstances at that time. What a book *can* supply is a set of tools for you to use in analyzing all the factors and trade-offs; the analysis itself, and the final decision, are up to you and your colleagues.

You can see that data structures and algorithms are interrelated and cannot be studied completely apart from one another. Since you already have some experience in writing algorithms, in this chapter we will not go back to first principles. Instead, we will focus your attention on two central concepts in the area of algorithms. One is the important and useful mathematical notion of recursion, a tool we will use frequently in this book. The other is performance prediction, a tool to "give us a handle" on the time requirements of a problem solution.

```
5! = 5 × 4!
   = 5 × (4 × 3!)
   = 5 × (4 × (3 × 2!))
   = 5 × (4 × (3 × (2 × 1!)))
   = 5 × (4 × (3 × (2 × 1)))
   = 5 × (4 × (3 × 2))
   = 5 × (4 × 6)
   = 5 × 24
   = 120
```

Figure 3.1 Recursive Calculation of 5!

3.2   RECURSIVE ALGORITHMS

In this section, we introduce a concept in algorithm design called *recursion*. A recursive algorithm—an algorithm that uses recursion—is defined in terms of itself; the solutions to many interesting programming problems are stated clearly and elegantly in recursive form. In this book, you will see many recursive algorithms.

Factorial

A classical simple example of recursion is the definition of the factorial of a positive integer N. Written $N!$ and read "N factorial," this is easily understood as the product $1 \times 2 \times \ldots \times N$. Thus, $3! = 6$, $4! = 24$, $5! = 120$, and so on. But we can write a definition without any "dot-dot-dot" as follows:

To find $N!$:

1.   If $N = 1$ then $N! = 1$;

2.   Otherwise $N! = N \times (N - 1)!$

We have defined the "!" operation in terms of "!". Notice that the definition is not circular, because the "!" is applied to a smaller and smaller number each time until it is applied to 1. Figure 3.1 shows the definition applied to calculate 5!.

Try the definition on some other numbers to make sure you understand how the recursion works. You will discover that $N!$ gets very large very quickly: Even an innocent-looking calculation, such as 10!, produces a rather large number (3,628,800). In fact, if you were to write a program to calculate $N!$ and run it on a computer using 16 bits to represent an integer, your program could not calculate factorials larger than 7!, because $8! > 32767$. On a computer with a 32-bit integer representation, your program would fail to compute 13!.

Program 3.1 shows a recursive Ada function to compute the factorial of a positive number.

Program 3.1 Recursive Factorial Function

```
FUNCTION Factorial (N : IN Positive) RETURN Positive IS

-- Computes the factorial of N (N!) recursively
-- Pre : N is defined
-- Post: returns N!
```

```
BEGIN  -- Factorial

  IF N = 1 THEN
    RETURN 1;                        -- stopping case
  ELSE
    RETURN N * Factorial(N-1);  -- recursion
  END IF;

END Factorial;
```

Program 3.2 declares the factorial function as a local function and attempts to compute and display factorials up to 20!. Compiling and executing Program 3.2 will give you an indication of how far your compiler's representation of Positive will let you go.

Program 3.2 A Test of the Factorial Function

```
WITH Ada.Text_IO;
WITH Ada.Integer_Text_IO;
PROCEDURE Test_Factorial IS
----------------------------------------------------------------------
--| Display the factorials of several natural numbers
--| Author: Michael B. Feldman, The George Washington University
--| Last Modified: October 1995
----------------------------------------------------------------------

  FUNCTION Factorial (N : IN Positive) RETURN Positive IS

  -- Computes the factorial of N (N!) recursively
  -- Pre : N is defined
  -- Post: returns N!

  BEGIN  -- Factorial

    IF N = 1 THEN
      RETURN 1;                        -- stopping case
    ELSE
      RETURN N * Factorial(N-1);  -- recursion
    END IF;

  END Factorial;

BEGIN -- Test_Factorial

  Ada.Text_IO.Put(Item => "  N           N!");
  Ada.Text_IO.New_Line;
  Ada.Text_IO.Put(Item => "---------------");
  Ada.Text_IO.New_Line;

  FOR Num IN 1..20 LOOP

    Ada.Integer_Text_IO.Put(Item => Num, Width => 3);
    Ada.Integer_Text_IO.Put(Item => Factorial(Num), Width => 11);
    Ada.Text_IO.New_Line;

  END LOOP;

END Test_Factorial;
```

It is very important to notice that a workable recursive algorithm must always reduce the size of the data set, or the number that it is working with, each time it is recursively called, and must always provide a *stopping case*, or *terminating condition*, such as the first line in our factorial algorithm. Otherwise, the algorithm may never terminate, getting itself stuck in an "infinite recursion."

Finding the factorial of a positive integer is only a simple example of what can be a very handy tool in developing algorithms. You will see this in the rest of this section, where attention will be focused on four other recursive solutions. Ada programs are given for three of the four; a program for the fourth will be shown later.

These algorithms are finding the *reversal of a string*, the *permutations of a set*, the *recursive binary search*, and the *recursive merge sort*.

Reversal of a String

In our natural languages, there is a certain type of phrase known as a *palindrome*. This is a phrase that reads the same forwards and backwards. Two examples of English palindromes are "radar" and "Able was I ere I saw Elba." The phrase "Madam, I'm Adam," supposedly spoken by the Biblical first man when he met his wife-to-be, Eve, is a palindrome if we neglect case, spaces, and punctuation. (Adam, in his first fit of anger, might also have said "Mad am I, Madam.")

One way to discover whether a phrase, or string of characters, is a palindrome, is to find the reverse of the string. The string is a palindrome if its reverse is identical to it.

We can find the reverse of a string very easily using the following algorithm:

To find the reverse of a string:

1. If the string contains only one character, its reverse is identical to it and we're finished.

2. Otherwise, save the first character.

3. *Find the reverse* of the remaining string, then concatenate the saved character onto the right-hand end.

Notice that we've found the reverse of a string by saving the first character and finding the reverse of what's left. This is a recursive algorithm: To carry it out on the whole set of data, we need to carry it out on a smaller set of data.

It is important to realize that step 1 and step 3 are very different in kind from one another. Step 1 is a terminating condition, sometimes called a *stopping case* or a *trivial case*. It is a step that can be carried out without making a further recursive call. Step 3, on the other hand, requires the recursive call "*find the reverse*." Every recursive algorithm must have at least one terminating condition, otherwise the algorithm has no way to stop and will, in theory, execute an infinte number of recursive calls. In practice, because every subprogram uses some memory when it is called, a recursive subprogram that never reaches a terminating condition will exhaust the memory available to it and terminate in that graceless fashion. In Ada, `Storage_Error` will be raised in this situation.

Program 3.3 shows an Ada function `Flip(S)`, which returns the reverse of a string (we have to call it `Flip` because `REVERSE` is a reserved word in Ada).

Program 3.3 Find the Reverse of a String

```
FUNCTION Flip(S: String) RETURN String IS
  -- Pre: S is defined
  -- Post: returns the reverse of S

  C : Character;  -- to save the first character of S

BEGIN -- Flip

  IF S'Length <= 1 THEN
    RETURN S;
  ELSE
    C := S(S'First);
    RETURN Flip(S(S'First + 1 .. S'Last)) & C;
  END IF;

END Flip;
```

Note the place in which `Flip` is called recursively by `Flip`. Also, we have used the Ada attributes `Succ`, `First`, and Last to advantage in working with the string argument to `Flip`. The expression `S(S'First)` gives us the first character of the string; the slice

```
S(S'First + 1 .. S'Last)
```

gives us the second through last characters of S. Using this slice as an argument to `Flip` is what is called for in step 3 of the algorithm.

Program 3.4 shows a function `Palindrome(S)`, which uses `Flip` to determine whether its string argument S is a palindrome. The `IF` statement on this function could be replaced by the simpler form

```
RETURN Flip(S) = S;
```

Program 3.4 Is a String a Palindrome?

```
FUNCTION Palindrome (S: String) RETURN Boolean IS
-- Pre:  S is defined
-- Post: returns True if and only if S is a palindrome

BEGIN

  IF S = Flip(S) THEN
    RETURN True;
  ELSE
    RETURN False;
  END IF;

END Palindrome;
```

Permutations of a Set

Consider a small company that owns four automobiles for its officials to use. Each official has a designated automobile; the office building has a four-car garage. Letting the cars be called A, B, C, and D, and the garage stalls 1, 2, 3, and 4, what are the different ways in which the cars can be parked in the garages?

Suppose A parks in stall 1. Then we can list all the possibilities remaining for B, C, and D. Suppose then that B parks in stall 2. Clearly C and D can park in two different ways: C in stall 3 and D in stall 4, or the other way around.

Now suppose C parks in stall 2. Then it is B and D that use stalls 3 and 4 in one of two ways. And if D parks in stall 2, then it is B and C sharing stalls 3 and 4.

Clearly, then, there are six possibilities once A has parked in stall 1. It's easy to see that another six possibilities arise if B parks in stall 1, and twelve more if C and D park there. There are a total of 24 possibilities, all shown in Figure 3.2.

This is an example of finding the *permutations* of the elements of a set, where here the set consists of the company's automobiles, and a permutation is an assignment to the stalls in the garage. If the set has N members, the number of permutations is $N!$.

Let's try to write an algorithm to print out the permutations of the members of a set. Letting the set be {A, B, C, D}, we can say:

To print all permutations of {A, B, C, D}:

1. Start with the set in the order {A, B, C, D}.

2. Print A, followed by all permutations of {B, C, D}.

3. Interchange A and B, then print B, followed by all permutations of {A, C, D}.

4. Interchange B and C, then print C, followed by all permutations of {B, A, D}.

5. Interchange C and D, then print D, followed by all permutations of {B, C, A}.

We have interchanged A with B, C, and D in turn (as though B, C, and D had parked, in turn, in stall 1).

To print out all permutations of {B, C, D}, we have a problem just like the larger one, but smaller! And printing out the permutations of {C, D} is just a smaller version of that problem! This sort of problem—one in which the same algorithm can be applied repeatedly to smaller and smaller sets—lends itself to a recursive solution.

Let's construct a recursive Ada subprogram—a procedure this time—to print the permutations of an ordered set S with members numbered 1 through N. Without concerning ourselves with how a set is implemented, assume we have a predefined procedure PrintSet(S), which prints the entire set S in order; a function CopySet(S), which returns an exact copy of S; a function SizeOf(S), which returns the number of members of S; and a procedure Interchange(S,k,i), which interchanges the ith and kth members of S. Our recursive procedure, which is called Print_Permutations(S,k,N), prints the permutations of the kth through Nth members of S. The detailed Ada source code is shown as Program 3.5. Make sure you understand how it works!

```
A B C D        B A C D        C A B D        D A B C
A B D C        B A D C        C A D B        D A C B
A C B D        B C A D        C B A D        D B A C
A C D B        B C D A        C B D A        D B C A
A D B C        B D A C        C D A B        D C A B
A D C B        B D C A        C D B A        D C B A
```

Figure 3.2 Permutations of {A, B, C, D}

Program 3.5 Printing Permutations of a Set

```
PROCEDURE PrintPermutations (S : IN Set;
                             K : IN Positive) IS
-- Pre:  S and K are defined
-- Post: displays all permutations of S with members
--    1..K-1 held constant and members K..N varying

  N  : Positive    := SizeOf(S);
  S1 : Set (1..N) := CopySet(S);
  -- The local variable is used here so the input set
  -- S doesn't get changed.

BEGIN

  IF K = N THEN              -- stopping case
    PrintSet (S1);
  ELSE
    FOR I IN K .. N LOOP    -- recursive case

      Interchange (S1, I, K);
      PrintPermutations (S1, K + 1);
      -- this recursive call prints all permutations of
      -- the Set with the 1st through k-th members held
      -- constant and the k+1st through N-th varying.

    END LOOP;
  END IF;

END PrintPermutations;
```

Recursive Binary Search

Imagine that you've written up a list of your friends, placing their names in alphabetical order, together with their telephone numbers. Because you're very popular, you have many friends and this list is quite long, running over a number of pages.

Let's consider a clever way to look up a friend's phone number in this long list. (Actually, it's way better suited to a computer than to a person, but that's because people often "look things up" intuitively instead of using algorithms!)

To look up a name:

1. Divide your list in half.

2. Find the name right in the middle of the list. (If the number of names is even, choose the one just below the middle.) If this name is the one whose number you're searching for, you're finished.

3. If your friend's name is *earlier* in the alphabet than the middle one, ignore all the names from this middle one to the end, and *look up the name* only in the first half. Divide this shorter list in half, then look at its middle element, and so on.

4. If your friend's name is *later* in the alphabet than the middle one, ignore the first half of the list and *look up the name* in the second half, as above.

Eventually, one of two things will happen: you'll find your friend in the list, or you'll divide the list in half so many times that only one name will remain and it won't be the one you wanted! (In case of an even number, no names at all will remain.) This will mean that the friend you were looking for isn't in your list.

Like the reversal and permutation algorithms, this method is recursive: the same method applied to the full list is applied to half the list, then to half of the half, etc. Let's construct an Ada function for this. We'll let the list be implemented as an array with subscripts 1..*N*. The function will be called `LookUpName(L, Name)`, which looks up `Name` in the array `L`. `LookUpName` will return the location of `Name` if it can find it, and zero if it can't.

Since our list is implemented as an array, we can use two interesting features of Ada: the *array slice* and *array attributes*. If `L` is an array, then the attribute `L'First` gives the value of its lowest subscript and `L'Last` gives the value of its highest subscript. Furthermore, the slice `L(k..m)` refers to the subarray `L(k)` through `L(m)`. Thus the function call `LookUpName(L(k..m), Name)` will search only in the subarray `L(k)` through `L(m)`; the call

```
LookUpName(L(L'First..L'Last),Name)
```

will search the entire array (as will just `LookUpName(L, Name)`, by the way).

The Ada source code for this function is given as Program 3.6. Try finding the locations of some names in the table given in Figure 3.3.

Program 3.6 Recursive Binary Search

```
FUNCTION LookUpName(L: List; Name: NameType) RETURN Natural IS
-- Pre:  L and Name are defined and L has at least one element
-- Post: returns location of Name in L, or 0 if Name not present

  Lower:  Positive;
  Upper:  Positive;
  Middle: Positive;

BEGIN

  Lower := L'First;
  Upper := L'Last;
  Middle := (Lower + Upper) / 2;
  -- integer division gives middle item if number of items
  -- is odd, item just below middle otherwise.

  IF Name = L(Middle) THEN      -- stopping case - we found it!
    RETURN Middle;

  ELSIF Lower = Upper THEN      -- stopping case - subarray has
    RETURN 0;                   -- only one name and it's not the one

  ELSIF Name < L(middle) THEN  -- recursion - look in first half
    RETURN LookUpName(L(Lower..Middle-1),Name);

  ELSE                          -- recursion - look in second half
    RETURN LookUpName(L(Middle+1..Upper),Name);

  END IF;

END LookUpName;
```

```
 1        Alan
 2        Alex
 3        Ben
 4        Bill
 5        Dileep
 6        Eugene
 7        Farhad
 8        Jessica
 9        Jorge
10        Justin
11        Keith
12        Kevin
13        Kristin
14        Nguyen
15        Sharon
16        Sherry
```

Figure 3.3 Table of Names in Alphabetical Sequence

We call this algorithm *recursive binary search*. It is an example of a whole class of algorithms known as *divide-and-conquer*, which work, as does this one, by dividing and subdividing the set of data into two parts.

Recursive Merge Sort

Our last example of recursion in this section involves sorting the elements of a list into ascending sequence. We will just sketch out an algorithm, *Recursive merge sort*, leaving the details until Chapter 14.

The algorithm depends on our knowing how to *merge* two sorted lists into a single sorted list. Informally, the two sorted lists {B, G, H, P} and {A, F, K, L, R, Z} can be merged into a single list {A, B, F, G, H, K, L, P, R, Z}, much as you might merge two sorted decks of 3″ × 5″ cards into a single deck.

Without being concerned about the details of the merge operation, consider how the two original sorted lists came to be sorted. Why not by the very same process? In other words, if we start with a single unsorted list, we can write an informal algorithm as follows:

To sort a list:

1. If the list contains only one element, it is already sorted.

2. If the list contains two elements, these elements are either in the correct order and the list is already sorted, or they are not, so interchange them.

3. Otherwise, divide the list in half, *sort* each of the two halves, and then merge them.

Aha! Another recursive algorithm! Our sorting method moves forward by dividing its problem in half, then applying itself to the two halves of the list. Recursive merge sort is thus another divide-and-conquer algorithm, with steps 1 and 2 as the stopping cases. An example of its use is shown in Figure 3.4.

```
Original     (Z A  C F  Q B  G K  P N  D E  M H  R T)
Divide       (Z A  C F  Q B  G K)(P N  D E  M H  R T)
Divide       (Z A  C F)(Q B  G K)(P N  D E)(M H  R T)
Divide       (Z A)(C F)(Q B)(G K)(P N)(D E)(M H)(R T)
Sort pairs   (A Z)(C F)(B Q)(G K)(N P)(D E)(H M)(R T)
Merge        (A C  F Z)(B G  K Q)(D E  N P)(H M  R T)
Merge        (A B  C F  G K  Q Z)(D E  H M  N P  R T)
Merge        (A B  C D  E F  G H  K M  N P  Q R  T Z)
Sorted!
```

Figure 3.4 Example of Recursive Merge Sort

You have seen four recursive algorithms in this section, and will see many more throughout this book. Recursion is not a mysterious or magical concept; it is just another tool in the algorithm designer's tool kit. It is time now to move to another important topic in algorithms—namely, performance prediction.

3.3 PERFORMANCE PREDICTION AND THE "BIG *O*" NOTATION

In considering the trade-offs among alternative problem solutions, an important factor is the expected computation time of each of the alternatives. It is difficult to predict the *actual* computation time of an algorithm without knowing the intimate details of the underlying computer, the object code generated by the compiler, and other related factors. The actual time must really be measured for a given algorithm, language, compiler, and computer system by means of some carefully designed performance tests, usually called *benchmarks*.

On the other hand, it is very helpful to know the way the running time will *vary* or *grow* as a function of the "problem size": the number of elements in an array, the number of records in a file, and so forth. Programmers sometimes discover that programs that have run in perfectly reasonable time, for the small test sets they have used, take extraordinarily long when run with "real world"-size data sets or files. These programmers were deceived by the "growth rate" of the computation.

To take an example, programs whose running time varies with the *square* of the problem size are not unusual. A program taking, say, 1 second to complete a file-handling problem with 10 records in the file, will require not 2 but 4 seconds for 20 records. Increasing the file size by a factor of 10, to 100 records, will multiply the original run time by 100, to 100 seconds. One thousand records will need 10,000 seconds, or about 3 hours, to complete! And 10,000 records (the number of accounts in a fair-sized bank, or students in a fair-sized university) will need almost 2 weeks! This is a long time by comparison to the 1 second taken by the 1-record test.

Suppose that this program is moved to a newer computer that is, say, twice as fast in every respect as the old one. All the running times will be halved, which means that the 2-week run will now take "only" 1 week. This is probably still much longer than the time that was desired. The difficulty lies not in the original computer being "too slow," but in the poor growth-rate performance of the algorithm, and only real improvement in the growth rate will yield significant performance speedup.

It is also futile to blame this sort of poor performance on a language or a compiler. A compiler only translates the high-level statements of an algorithm into machine instructions; it does not—cannot—change the algorithm in any significant way. A better compiler can effect the sort of incremental speedup expected from a faster computer, but it cannot compensate for a poorly chosen or poorly coded algorithm.

This example shows that it makes sense to know something about growth rates, lest program running time grow in unpleasantly surprising ways when problems grow to meaningful size. Sometimes there is no choice: There may be no alternative solution to that program running in "squared," or *quadratic*, time. But at least a programmer with some experience in performance estimation will not be surprised!

Algorithm Growth Rates

Getting a precise estimate of the computation time of an algorithm is often difficult, but as you have seen, it helps to "get a handle on it." We do this by trying to write a formula for the computation time in terms of the problem size N. By the problem size, generally we mean the number of data items that must be processed by the algorithm.

The computation time of an algorithm consists of two factors. One factor depends on the programming language, compiler, and speed and instruction set of the underlying computer. It is often a good assumption that this *system-dependent* factor is reasonably constant, not varying with the problem size, and so we can "factor it out." (Obviously it's nice to have a small system dependent-constant as well as a small growth rate, but reducing the size of the constant is hard to do in a general way precisely because it's system-dependent!)

We give the name *growth rate* to that part of the formula that does vary with problem size. In discussing the growth rates of algorithms, it is conventional to use the notation $O()$ (read "growth rate," "big O," or "order of magnitude"). The most common growth rates you will normally encounter are the following:

- $O(1)$, or *constant*

- $O(\log N)$, or *logarithmic* (the logarithm is usually taken to the base 2)

- $O(N)$, or *linear* (directly proportional to N)

- $O(N \log N)$, (usually just called $N \log N$)

- $O(N^2)$, or *quadratic* (proportional to the square of N)

To give you an idea of the computation time of typical file sizes, Figure 3.5 shows the values of each of these functions for a number of different values of N. The values happen to be powers of 2, but this is just to make the computation of logarithms convenient.

From this table you can see that as N grows, $\log N$ remains quite small with respect to N and $N \log N$ grows fairly large, but not nearly as large as N^2. In studying sorting in

N	1	$\log N$	$N \log N$	N^2
1	1	0	0	1
2	1	1	2	4
4	1	2	8	16
8	1	3	24	64
16	1	4	64	256
32	1	5	160	1024
64	1	6	384	4096
128	1	7	896	16384
256	1	8	2048	65536
512	1	9	4608	262144
1024	1	10	10240	1048576
2048	1	11	22528	4194304
4096	1	12	49152	16777216
8192	1	13	106496	67108864
16384	1	14	229376	268435456
32768	1	15	491520	1073741824

Figure 3.5 Table of Common Algorithm Growth Rates

Chapter 14, you'll discover that most sorting methods have growth rates of $N \log N$ or N^2. In the next section we will look at some common algorithmic structures and discuss ways to estimate their growth rates.

Estimating the Growth Rate of an Algorithm

While there are no absolute "cookbook" rules that will always work to estimate performance, we can "get a handle on it" by taking advantage of the fact that algorithms are developed in a *structured* way. Structured algorithms combine statements into usefully complex blocks in four ways:

- *Sequence*, or writing one statement below another

- *Decision*, or the well-known if-then or if-then-else

- *Loop*, including counting loops, while loops, until loops, and the general loop-exit-end loop structure

- *Subprogram call*

In Figure 3.6 you can see the Ada notation for a number of different variations on these structures. Now let's take a look at some typical algorithm structures and estimate their "big O's." We'll always use N to denote the "problem size."

Simple Statement

A simple statement is, for example, an assignment statement. If we assume that the statement contains no function calls (whose execution time may, of course, vary with problem size), the statement takes a fixed amount of time to execute. This we denote by $O(1)$, because if we factor out the constant execution time, we're left with 1.

```
      Temp := A;                         IF x > Max THEN
         A := B;                            Max := x;
         B := Temp;                      END IF;
```

(a). Sequence   (b). Decision

```
      IF x > y THEN                      IF x >= y AND x >= z THEN
         Max := x;                          Max := x;
      ELSE                               ELSIF y >= x AND y >= z THEN
         Max := y;                          Max := y;
      END IF;                            ELSE
                                            Max := z;
                                         END IF;
```

(c). If-then-else   (d). If-then-elsif-else

```
      FOR i IN p .. q LOOP               WHILE x > 0 LOOP
         x := x + i;                        y := y + 3;
      END;                                  x := x/2;
                                         END LOOP;
```

(e). Counting Loop   (f). While loop

```
      LOOP
         x := x + k;
         EXIT WHEN x >= 100;
         y := y - z;
      END LOOP;
```

(g). Loop-exit-end loop

Figure 3.6 Some Ada Control Structures

Sequence of Simple Statements

A sequence of simple statements takes time equal to the sum of the individual statement times. If the individual statements are $O(1)$, then so is the sum.

Decision

For purposes of estimating performance, we rely on the fact that both the THEN part and the ELSE part can be arbitrary structures in their own right. Whether the THEN path or the ELSE path will be executed depends, of course, on the data and other execution-time conditions. To estimate conservatively, then, we must take the larger of the two individual "big O's" as the "big O" of the decision.

There are variations of the decision structure. For example, the CASE structure is really a multiway IF-THEN-ELSE, so in estimating a CASE, we just take the largest "big O" of all of the CASE choices.

Similarly, Ada and many other languages provide a structure such as IF-THEN-ELSIF-ELSE, as was shown in Figure 3.6. This is also just a multiway decision.

Note that performance estimation can sometimes get complicated: The condition tested in a decision may involve a function call, and the timing of the function call may itself vary with problem size!

Counting Loop

A *counting loop* is a loop in which the loop counter is incremented or decremented each time the loop is executed. This is different from some loops we will consider a bit later, in which the counter is multiplied or divided by a value.

What is the performance of a simple counting loop? Suppose the body of the loop contains only a sequence of simple statements. Then the performance of the loop is just the number of times the loop executes. Let us use the term *trip count* to mean the number of times a loop executes. If the trip count is constant—independent of problem size—the the whole loop is $O(1)$. On the other hand, if the loop is something like

```
FOR Counter IN 1..N LOOP
```

the trip count does depend on N, so the performance is $O(N)$. These two loop structures, in which the body contains only simple statements, are shown in Figure 3.7.

Now suppose that the loop body is more complex. Real algorithms have this sort of complexity, so let's consider a number of possibilities. Remember that we cannot cover every case; we will look at some common ones that will be encountered in this book, so that you can recognize these when you see them.

Figure 3.8 shows a double counting loop. The outer loop's trip count is clearly N. However, the inner loop executes N times for each time the outer loop executes, so the body of the inner loop will be executed $N \times N$ times, and the performance of the entire structure is $O(N^2)$.

In Figure 3.9, a structure is shown that looks deceptively similar to the last one.

The outer loop surely has a trip count of N. But the trip count of the inner loop depends not only on N but also on the value of OuterCounter! If OuterCounter is 1, the inner loop has a trip count of 1. If OuterCounter is 2, the inner loop trip count is 2; if OuterCounter is 3, the inner loop trip count is 3. Finally, if OuterCounter is N, the inner loop trip count is N.

How many times will the body of the inner loop be executed? It will be the *sum*

$$1 + 2 + 3 + \ldots + N - 1 + N.$$

```
FOR Counter IN 1 .. 5 LOOP
  ...
  -- something with O(1) performance
  ...
END LOOP;
```

(a). Trip Count Is Constant

```
FOR Counter IN 1 .. N LOOP
  ...
  -- something with O(1) performance
  ...

END LOOP;
```

(b). Trip Count Depends on N

Figure 3.7 Two Simple Counting Loops

```
FOR OuterCounter IN 1 .. N LOOP
  FOR InnerCounter IN 1 .. N LOOP

  ...
    -- something with O(1) performance
           ...

  END LOOP;
END LOOP;
```

Figure 3.8 A Double Counting Loop

```
FOR OuterCounter IN 1 .. N LOOP
  FOR InnerCounter IN 1 .. OuterCounter LOOP

  ...
    -- something with O(1) performance
           ...

  END LOOP;
END LOOP;
```

Figure 3.9 Another Double Counting Loop.

This summation, as you have probably learned in an algebra course, is

$$N \times (N + 1)/2 = ((N^2) + N)/2.$$

We will say that the performance of this structure is $O(N^2)$, since for large N the contribution of the $N/2$ term is negligible. For example, if N is 100, including the $N/2$ term gives 5050; ignoring it gives 5000, a difference of only 1%.

It is interesting that making the inner loop trip count depend on OuterCounter does not alter the "big O," since we neglect the term in N.

The structure in Figure 3.10 is similar, but the trip count of the inner loop decreases rather than increasing as above. If OuterCounter is 1, the inner loop has a trip count of N. If OuterCounter is 2, the inner loop trip count is $N - 1$; if OuterCounter is 3, the inner loop trip count is $N - 2$. Finally, if OuterCounter is N, the inner loop trip count is 1.

The number of times the body of the inner loop is executed is the sum

$$N + N - 1 + N - 2 + \ldots + 1$$

which is really the same sum as before:

$$N \times (N + 1)/2 = ((N^2) + N)/2.$$

This structure also has performance $O(N^2)$.

Look at the loop structures in Fig. 3.11 and convince yourself that in all cases the performance is $O(N^3)$.

From these examples we can generalize as follows: a structure with k nested counting loops—loops in which the counter is just incremented or decremented by 1—has performance $O(N^k)$ if the trip count of each loop depends on the problem size. A growth rate of $O(N^k)$ is called *polynomial*.

```
FOR OuterCounter IN 1 .. N LOOP
   FOR InnerCounter IN OuterCounter .. N LOOP

   ...
      -- something with O(1) performance
   ...

   END LOOP;
END LOOP;
```

Figure 3.10 Yet Another Double Counting Loop

Multiplicatively Controlled Loop

By a *multiplicatively controlled loop*, we mean one in which the variable controlling the loop is multiplied or divided by a constant each time the loop is executed. Multiplicatively controlled loops arise often in the kinds of algorithms you will see in this book.

```
FOR OuterCounter IN 1 .. N LOOP
   FOR MiddleCounter IN 1 .. N LOOP
      FOR InnerCounter IN 1 .. N LOOP

      ...
      -- something with O(1) performance
      ...

      END LOOP;
   END LOOP;
END LOOP;

FOR OuterCounter IN 1 .. N LOOP
   FOR MiddleCounter IN 1 .. OuterCounter LOOP
      FOR InnerCounter IN 1 .. MiddleCounter LOOP

      ...
      -- something with O(1) performance
      ...

      END LOOP;
   END LOOP;
END LOOP;

FOR OuterCounter IN 1 .. N LOOP
   FOR MiddleCounter IN 1 .. OuterCounter LOOP
      FOR InnerCounter IN MiddleCounter .. N LOOP

      ...
      -- something with O(1) performance
      ...

      END LOOP;
   END LOOP;
END LOOP;
```

Figure 3.11 Some Triple Counting Loops

Although most programming languages have a special structure for counting loops, they usually have no structure designed specifically to accommodate multiplicative control; we just use a WHILE, UNTIL, or general loop.

Recall that whatever the specific structure used, every loop needs

- An *initialization* step, which gives the starting value(s) of the control variable(s)

- A *termination condition*, which is tested during each iteration and which indicates the circumstances under which the loop stops executing

- A *modification step*, indicating how the control variable(s) should be changed to move the loop along from its starting point to its ending point

The difference between a WHILE structure and an UNTIL structure is that in the former the termination condition is tested before each iteration, and in the latter the condition is tested at the end of each iteration.

Consider the structure in Figure 3.12.

In this loop, whose performance clearly depends on the problem size N, the variable Control is multiplied by the constant 2 until Control becomes larger than N. Since Control's starting value is 1, after k iterations,

$$\text{Control} = 2^k$$

The number of iterations k can be found just by taking logarithms of both sides so that we get

$$\log_2 \text{Control} = k$$

Since the loop stops when Control >= N, the performance of this algorithm is $O(\log N)$.

Looking at the structure a bit more generally, suppose we multiply Control by some other constant factor. Giving this constant the name Factor, we can see that after k iterations

$$\text{Control} = \text{Factor}^k$$

```
Control := 1;
WHILE Control <= N LOOP

   ...
   -- something with O(1)
   ...

   Control := 2 * Control;
END LOOP;
```

Figure 3.12 A Multiplicatively Controlled Loop

and so, by the argument above, the performance is $O(\log_k N)$ instead of $O(\log_2 N)$. However, in considering the "big O" of an algorithm, it doesn't matter what base we use for logarithms. This is because the logarithm of a number to one base is just a constant times the logarithm of the same number to a different base. Since constant factors are "factored out" of a "big O," the base doesn't matter and we usually just refer to $O(\log N)$ or $O(\log_2 N)$. In Exercise 6, you can fill in the details of a proof that the base really doesn't matter.

Now look at Figure 3.13, where the control variable is *divided* by a factor (2 in this case) instead of multiplied.

This is very similar to the previous example. There, `Control` was started at a small value and multiplied repetitively until it reached some maximum; here, `Control` is started at a large value and divided repetitively until it reaches a minimum.

What is the "big O" of this structure? Instead of repeating the analysis above, we just say that it is $O(\log N)$ and leave the details for Exercise 7.

Now look at the two structures in Figure 3.14. Here we have analogies to the nested counting loops we considered earlier. The performance of these structures is $O(N \log N)$; you can do the analysis as Exercise 8.

Subprogram Call

We can handle a subprogram call by realizing that the subprogram is also an algorithm with its own "big O," then imagining that this algorithm appears "in line" with the calling program.

In this way, we can deal with it as we have dealt with other complex algorithms above. If the subprogram call appears inside a decision statement, its "big O" is used in determining the maximum of the "big O's" of the different branches of the decision. If the subprogram call appears inside a loop, its "big O" is, essentially, multiplied by the trip count of the loop.

If the subprogram (call it A) in turn calls another subprogram (call it B), we use B's "big O" in calculating A's, and then A's in calculating the calling program's "big O," and so on for deeper nesting of subprograms.

Things get tricky if A and B are the same subprogram—that is, if a recursive call is involved. In calculating A's "big O," then, the depth of recursion—the number of times that A is called recursively—is usually itself a function of the problem size, so we need to do the same sort of analysis we have been doing with other structures, to get a handle on the depth of recursion.

```
Control := N;
WHILE Control >= 1 LOOP

  ...
  -- something with O(1)
  ...

  Control := Control / 2;
END LOOP;
```

Figure 3.13 Another Multiplicatively Controlled Loop

```
FOR Counter IN 1 .. N LOOP

  Control := 1;
  WHILE Control <= N LOOP
    ...
    -- something with O(1)
    ...

    Control := 2 * Control;
  END LOOP;

END LOOP;

Control := N;
WHILE Control >= 1 LOOP

  FOR Counter IN 1 .. N LOOP
    ...
    -- something with O(1)
    ...
  END LOOP;

  Control := Control / 2;
END LOOP;
```

Figure 3.14 Two N log N Loop Structures

The structures you have seen in this section show examples of the most common "big O" performances: constant, linear, quadratic, log N, and N log N. They also show how to think through the "big O" analysis for composite program control structures.

Some Examples of Performance Prediction

Let's return to the algorithms in Section 3.2 and estimate their performance. This experience will give you some ideas as to how to do a "big O" analysis on recursive programs.

Factorial

In calculating $N!$, 1 is subtracted from the argument of `Factorial` each time a recursive call is done. Since multiplying one number by another is $O(1)$, the result is very similar to a one-level counting loop: its performance is $O(N)$.

String Reversal

Each time `Flip` is called, its argument—the string—is shortened by one character. Thus, the number of recursive calls is determined by the length of the string—in fact, directly proportional to it—so the performance seems to be $O(N)$.

However, a subprogram call is involved: concatenation of a character to the end of a string. If that operation does not depend on the string length, the performance of `Flip` is indeed $O(N)$. On the other hand, if for some reason the concatenation operation had to "walk across" the whole string to add the new character onto the end—a linear operation—then we would have an overall result of $O(N^2)$ because a linear operation would be done a linear number of times. Without knowing more about concatenation, we cannot go any farther.

Permutations of a Set

Earlier when we introduced the idea of permutations, we calculated that a set of size N has $N!$ permutations. Therefore, the program `PrintPermutations` has growth rate $O(N!)$, much larger than any of the other growth rates we've seen. Since algorithms with factorial growth rate are almost impossibly slow for interestingly large values of N, we try to avoid them.

On the other hand, sometimes we cannot avoid factorial growth. Whichever algorithm we choose for printing all permutations, we cannot escape the mathematical fact that a set of size N has $N!$ permutations. Anyone claiming an algorithm which can print $N!$ values with performance better than $O(N!)$ is claiming something magic, not mathematical!

Recursive Binary Search

Recall that in `LookUpName` we divide our sorted list in half, then in half again, and so on, until we either find what we're looking for or are left with only one element which is not the one we want. This is just a recursive version of the loop structure shown in Figure 3.13, for which we have already discovered a performance of $O(\log N)$.

Recursive Merge Sort

Recursive merge sort, as we saw before, is another divide-and-conquer algorithm (involving repeated halving of the list to be sorted). The number of times we divide the list in half is $\log N$, so the performance seems to be $\log N$, but here again a lower-level subprogram is called, namely "merge," whose implementation is unknown to us.

Here is a hint: The merge operation is usually linear in performance, because all elements in each list are copied once. The topmost level will then merge two lists of length $N/2$, requiring the copying of N values; the second level will do two merges, but each list is of length $N/4$, and so on. Thus, if we add up all the merging done at a given level of recursion, we always get exactly N operations. But since there are $\log N$ levels of recursion, we arrive at a growth rate of $O(N \log N)$. This is a recursive version of a loop structure in Figure 3.14.

This discussion of performance prediction has been rather informal. It is often possible, for many algorithms you will see in this book, and for others you will write yourself, to do an approximate, rough prediction to "get a handle on it." However, it would be misleading if we implied that all performance prediction is easy, or that it can all be done informally. It is important to realize that for many algorithms, performance prediction is very difficult and requires rigorous mathematical proof techniques. As you continue in courses in the theory of algorithms, you will learn such techniques and they will serve you well. In the meantime, our informal approach will suffice; if you apply it to programs you that encounter or consider writing, you will find that the informal method generally serves you well too.

3.4 DESIGN: AN ADT FOR KEYED TABLES

To show how performance prediction can be done comparatively, let's take up a practical example. We'll consider a bit more fully the problem of maintaining a table such as the phone list discussed earlier. Let us assume that each element to be stored in the table is in the form of a record containing a *key field* and some other fields. We use the key field to look up elements in the table. In the phone list case, each record's key is the name of a friend and another field in the record contains that friend's phone number. For simplicity, we assume that at most one element with a given key can be stored.

Keyed tables are a very common structure in computing, with many applications. Let us therefore consider the table to be an ADT. The purpose of this section is first to specify the keyed table, then to present two alternative implementations of the table handler, estimating the performance of the various operations for the two implementations. The keyed-table ADT will reappear several times throughout the book, as we introduce interesting ways to implement it; each time we bring in a new implementation, we will revisit the performance estimations.

Specifying the Keyed Table

Consider the operations one must do to maintain a table of records. Even if you are maintaining a set of paper file cards, each of which contains the name and phone number of a friend, these are the important operations. Figure 3.15 sketches a package specification for a table handler. All the type declarations are omitted for the time being. The specification shows five operations, each with its preconditions and postconditions:

- `InitializeTable`, which creates an empty table, either "from scratch" or by emptying one that already contains some elements

- `Insert`, which adds a new element to the table, storing it by its key

- `Delete`, which deletes from the table the element with a given key

- `Retrieve`, which copies from the table the element containing a given key

- `Traverse`, which displays all elements of the table, in order by key

The last operation requires some discussion. Traversing a table means processing all table elements, "visiting" each element exactly once. To make the operation more useful to humans, we require that the elements be visited in the order of the keys. Traversal is a very general operation; we can imagine a number of different actions we

```
PACKAGE Tables IS

-- Specification of the abstract data type for a table of
-- element records, each element containing a key.

-- Data structures

   TYPE KeyType     IS ...; -- to be defined later
   TYPE ElementType IS ...; -- to be defined later
   TYPE TableType   IS ...; -- to be defined later

-- Operators

   PROCEDURE InitializeTable (T : IN OUT TableType);
   -- Pre : None
   -- Post: T is an initialized Table, that is, it behaves as though
   --    it were an empty table with no elements.

   PROCEDURE Insert (T       : IN OUT TableType;
                     E       : ElementType;
                     Success : OUT Boolean);
   -- Pre : T is initialized and E is defined
   -- Post: Inserts element E into table T
   --    Success is True if insertion is performed, and False
   --    if T already has an element with the same key as E.

   PROCEDURE Retrieve (T       : TableType;
                       Target  : KeyType;
                       E       : OUT ElementType;
                       Success : OUT Boolean);
   -- Pre : T is initialized and Target is defined
   -- Post: Copies into E the element of T whose key is Target.
   --    Success is True if the copy is performed, and False
   --    if T has no element whose key is Target.

   PROCEDURE Delete (T        : IN OUT TableType;
                     Target   : KeyType;
                     Success. : OUT Boolean);
   -- Pre : T is initialized and Target is defined
   -- Post: Deletes from T the element with key Target
   --    Success is True if deletion is performed, and False
   --    if T has no element whose key is Target.

   PROCEDURE Traverse (T : TableType);
   -- Pre : T is initialized.
   -- Post: The elements of T are displayed in order by key.

END Tables;
```

Figure 3.15 Sketch of Specification for Keyed Table Package

might take on each element as it is visited. To keep the discussion simple at this point, we assume that Traverse simply displays the contents of the table, in ascending sequence by key.

Let's discuss two possible implementations of this table, both of which use an array, and consider the performance of the various operations in each implementation. We won't bother to give detailed programs for them, since we're interested only in "reasoning out" the performance issues. We assume that the array can hold up to

`Capacity` elements, and that the actual number of elements in the array at a given moment is given by `CurrentSize`.

Given that the table variable has been declared, `InitializeTable` in both implementations simply involves setting `CurrentSize` to zero to indicate that the table is empty, a constant-time operation. Assuming that the client program cannot access the table except through these abstract operations, it does not matter whether the table elements are initialized to some default value or contain "garbage" or previously stored results. In either case, the client perceives an empty table; what is important to the client is how the operations behave, not the details of what they are doing. Therefore, even if the table has been partially filled, `InitializeTable` need not actually empty the table; it need only set `CurrentSize` to zero.

Implementation 1: Unordered Array

In Implementation 1 we leave the array unordered, updating it simply by keeping track of the number of positions currently occupied, then inserting a newly-arriving element in the next available position. The `Insert` operation thus has performance O(1) (constant), since the number of operations required to store an element in the next available position in an array doesn't depend on the size of the array or on the number of elements that are already there.

What about the `Retrieve` operation? Since the elements are not in any particular order in the table, we need to start at one end of the occupied portion of the table and check the key of every element, until either we find the one we wanted or we reach the other end of the occupied portion. Sometimes we find our element on the first attempt; sometimes we need to search the entire table; on the average, we check half the elements. When we locate the desired element, we copy a table element back to the output parameter, which takes constant time. Since both the worst and the average situations depend directly on the number of elements in the table, we can say that a `Retrieve` operation is linear or $O(N)$ (actually $O($`CurrentSize`$)$).

The `Delete` operation also has linear performance. We delete the element corresponding to a given key by searching for it as in a `Search`, then removing it by moving all elements below it up one position, as shown in Figure 3.16a. Since the number of operations for both the search and the move depend directly on `CurrentSize`, we have a linear operation.

We can speed up `Delete` by recognizing that because the elements in the table are not in order, we lose nothing by simply copying the latest element into the position occupied by the one to be deleted, as shown in Figure 3.16b, then recovering the vacated space by decrementing `ActualElements`. Although the average time for a `Delete` is surely reduced by this optimization, the growth rate is unchanged, because the search part of the operation is still linear. This is a very good example of the two parts of the actual performance of an algorithm: the average time per operation and the growth rate.

The `Traverse` operation involves sorting the table, since we want the elements to be visited and displayed in key order. The details of the sorting process are left for Chapter 14, where many sorting algorithms are presented and compared. For completeness here, we will simply mention that the growth rate of a sorting algorithm is, in

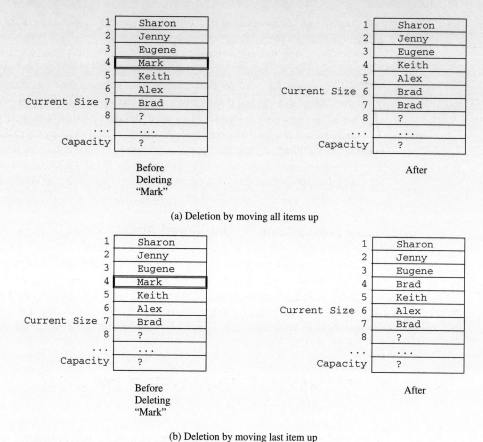

(a) Deletion by moving all items up

(b) Deletion by moving last item up

Figure 3.16 Deleting from an Unordered Table

most cases, either $O(N \log N)$ or $O(N2)$. Assuming we always choose an $N \log N$ sorting method, `Traverse` has an $N \log N$ component (sorting the array) and a linear component (movng through the array an element at a time). The overall "big O" is the larger of these two, or $N \log N$.

Implementation 2: Array Ordered by Key

This implementation corresponds to the kind of table discussed in the phone list example, where we discovered the Binary Search algorithm, which carries out a `Search` with $O(\log N)$ performance.

`Insert` and `Delete` turn out to have linear performance in this implementation. In an `Insert`, we need to insert the newly arriving element in its proper place in the array, to preserve the ordering. To do this, we find this place by using a modified `Search` operation: Because the element is not yet in the table, the search will always be unsuccessful, but instead of just reporting that fact, we will make the search report the last location it tested, which will tell us exactly where the new element needs to go. This will work correctly except where the new key is smaller than the previously smallest key or greater than the previously greatest one, so we can simply test those two possibilities as special cases before beginning the binary search.

Once the proper location has been found, we need to make room for the new element by moving those with larger keys forward one position. Thus, the performance has a logarithmic component and a linear one; as `CurrentSize` increases, it is so much greater than its logarithm that the logarithmic component can be ignored. Thus, `Insert` has linear performance.

`Delete` is really just like `Search` except that we remove the element to be deleted by moving all elements with greater keys back one position in the array. Since we cannot use the speedup from Implementation 1 (why?), the move is linear, so the whole `Delete` operation is linear.

`Retrieve` is a log N operation in this implementation, because after we find the element to be copied (a log N search), the actual copying is $O(1)$, so we can ignore it.

The last operation to consider is `Traverse`. Because the table is already ordered, `Traverse` can simply start at the beginning and step through the array, displaying each element as it encounters that element. Thus, `Traverse` is a linear operation.

Figure 3.17 gives a tabular summary of the growth rates of the operations in both implementations.

3.5 APPLICATION: A SIMPLE EMPLOYEE DATA BASE

This section presents an extended project. It is very important to read this section carefully, because it serves as the basis for a series of projects to be presented in later chapters.

As an example of the use of the table package described in Section 3.4, consider a simple system for maintaining employee records of a small company with a maximum workforce size of, say, 25. An employee record has six fields:

- An identifying number, which we use as the key

- The employee's name, a string of 30 characters filled with blanks at the end if necessary

	Implementation 1 Unordered	Implementation 2 Ordered
`InitializeTable`	$O(1)$	$O(1)$
`Insert`	$O(1)$	$O(N)$
`Retrieve`	$O(N)$	$O(\log N)$
`Delete`	$O(N)$	$O(N)$
`Traverse`	$O(N \log N)$	$O(N)$

Figure 3.17 Summary of Growth Rates for Implementations 1 and 2

- The employee's gender, an enumeration type

- The number of dependents (spouse, children, and so on) living with the employee (this is important for tax purposes)

- The employee's pay rate, a currency value, of course

- The employee's date of hiring, a date value

We develop the employee system in the following phases:

1. Develop the basic ADT package, `Employees`, providing constructor and selector operations similar to those of `Dates` and `Currency`.

2. Develop the basic input/output child package, `Employees.IO`, that provides the appropriate `Get` and `Put` operations.

3. Test the employee packages with a simple test program, `Test_Employees`.

   When phase 3 is completed, we know that we can create employee records, select their fields, read, and display them. This makes it much easier to debug the later stages.

4. Develop a package, `Tables`, capable of providing a keyed table of employees, following the model discussed in section 3.4. This table package will use the packages from phases 1 and 2.

5. Test this package using a simple test program, `Test_Employee_Tables`.

   When phases 4 and 5 are completed, we know that the entire employee system is working smoothly.

6. Finally, develop and test an interactive, menu-driven user interface (`Employee_UI`) to the employee system, allowing a terminal user to enter commands to create and maintain the employee database.

The package structure of the desired system is shown diagrammatically in Figure 3.18. The boxes represent packages and the main program; an arrow from package P to package or program Q means that Q is a client of P and, therefore, has a context clause `WITH P`.

The Basic `Employees` Package and `Employees.IO` Child Package

Let's proceed with the first two phases. Program 3.7 shows a specification for a simple employee ADT. We assume that the `Dates` and `Currency` packages from Chapter 2 are available. We leave it to you to write the body of `Employees`, which is easy, given your experience with the ADTs of Chapter 2.

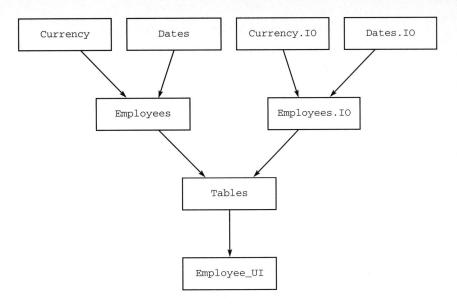

Figure 3.18 Package Structure for Employee System

Program 3.7 ADT Specification for Employees

```
WITH Currency;
WITH Dates;
PACKAGE Employees IS
----------------------------------------------------------------------
--| Specification for ADT package to handle Employee records
--| Author: Michael B. Feldman, The George Washington University
--| Last Modified: October 1995
----------------------------------------------------------------------

  -- constant and type definitions

  MaxName: CONSTANT Positive := 30;
  SUBTYPE NameType IS String(1..MaxName);

  SUBTYPE IDType IS Positive RANGE 1111..9999;
  TYPE    GenderType IS (Female, Male);

  TYPE Employee IS PRIVATE;

  -- operations

  -- constructor

  FUNCTION MakeEmployee (ID:       IDType;
                         Name:     NameType;
                         Gender:   GenderType;
                         NumDepend: Natural;
```

```
                        Salary:    Currency.Quantity;
                        StartDate: Dates.Date) RETURN Employee;
  -- Pre: all input parameters are defined
  -- Post: returns a value of type Employee


  -- selectors

  FUNCTION RetrieveID        (OneEmp: Employee) RETURN IDType;
  FUNCTION RetrieveName      (OneEmp: Employee) RETURN NameType;
  FUNCTION RetrieveGender    (OneEmp: Employee) RETURN GenderType;
  FUNCTION RetrieveNumDepend (OneEmp: Employee) RETURN Natural;
  FUNCTION RetrieveSalary    (OneEmp: Employee)
    RETURN Currency.Quantity;
  FUNCTION RetrieveDate      (OneEmp: Employee)
    RETURN Dates.Date;
  --Pre: OneEmp is defined
  --Post: each selector retrieves its desired field

PRIVATE

  TYPE Employee IS RECORD
    ID:        IDType := IDType'Last;
    Name:      NameType := (OTHERS => ' ');
    Gender:    GenderType := Female;
    NumDepend: Natural := 0;
    Salary:    Currency.Quantity := Currency.MakeCurrency(0.00);
    StartDate: Dates.Date := Dates.MakeDate(1980, 1, 1);
  END RECORD;

END Employees;
```

Program 3.8 gives the specification for `Employees.IO`; Program 3.9 shows the body. Note that the `Get` is not robust; it simply prompts the user for the required input. Also, no file operations are provided. Finally, the body of `Employees.IO` requires `Currency.IO`, which was given in Chapter 2, and `Dates.IO`, which was not given there. Therefore, you must complete `Dates.IO` before you can complete `Employees.IO`.

Program 3.8 Specification for `Employees.IO`

```
PACKAGE Employees.IO IS
-------------------------------------------------------------------------
--| Child Package for Employee Input/Output
--| Author: Michael B. Feldman, The George Washington University
--| Last Modified: July 1995
-------------------------------------------------------------------------

  PROCEDURE Get (Item: OUT Employee);
  --reads an Employee record from the terminal
  --Pre: none
  --Post: Item contains a record of type Employee

  PROCEDURE Put (Item: IN Employee);
  --displays an Employee record on the screen
  --Pre: Item is defined
  --Post: displays the fields of Item on the screen

END Employees.IO;
```

Program 3.9 Body of `Employees.IO`

```
WITH Ada.Text_IO;
WITH Ada.Float_Text_IO;
WITH Ada.Integer_Text_IO;
WITH Dates.IO;
WITH Currency.IO;
PACKAGE BODY Employees.IO IS
------------------------------------------------------------------------
--| Body of Child Package for Employee Input/Output
--| Author: Michael B. Feldman, The George Washington University
--| Last Modified: July 1995
------------------------------------------------------------------------

  PACKAGE GenderType_IO IS
    NEW Ada.Text_IO.Enumeration_IO(Enum => GenderType);

  PROCEDURE Get (Item: OUT Employee) IS

    S: String(1..MaxName);
    Count: Natural;

  BEGIN -- simple, non-robust Get

    Ada.Text_IO.Put(Item => "ID > ");
    Ada.Integer_Text_IO.Get(Item => Item.ID);
    Ada.Text_IO.Skip_Line;

    Ada.Text_IO.Put(Item => "Name > ");
    Ada.Text_IO.Get_Line(Item => S, Last => Count);
    Item.Name(1..Count) := S(1..Count);

    Ada.Text_IO.Put(Item => "Gender (Female or Male) > ");
    GenderType_IO.Get(Item => Item.Gender);

    Ada.Text_IO.Put(Item => "Number of dependents > ");
    Ada.Integer_Text_IO.Get(Item => Item.NumDepend);

    Ada.Text_IO.Put(Item => "Salary > ");
    Currency.IO.Get(Item => Item.Salary);

    Ada.Text_IO.Put(Item => "Starting Date, mmm dd yyyy > ");
    Dates.IO.Get(Item => Item.StartDate);

  END Get;

  PROCEDURE Put (Item: IN Employee) IS

  BEGIN -- simple Put

    Ada.Integer_Text_IO.Put(Item => Item.ID, Width => 1);
    Ada.Text_IO.New_Line;
    Ada.Text_IO.Put(Item => Item.Name);
    Ada.Text_IO.New_Line;
    GenderType_IO.Put(Item => Item.Gender);
    Ada.Text_IO.New_Line;
    Ada.Integer_Text_IO.Put(Item => Item.NumDepend, Width => 1);
    Ada.Text_IO.New_Line;
    Currency.IO.Put(Item => Item.Salary);
    Ada.Text_IO.New_Line;
```

```
      Dates.IO.Put(Item => Item.StartDate);
      Ada.Text_IO.New_Line;

   END Put;

END Employees.IO;
```

Testing `Employees` and `Employees.IO`

We can proceed to phase 3. Program 3.10 shows a simple test program that reads and displays three employee records.

Program 3.10 A Simple Test of `Employees` and `Employees.IO`

```
WITH Ada.Text_IO;
WITH Employees;
WITH Employees.IO;
PROCEDURE Test_Employees IS
-----------------------------------------------------------------------
--| Simple Test of Employee Table
--| Author: Michael B. Feldman, The George Washington University
--| Last Modified: July 1995
-----------------------------------------------------------------------

  OneEmployee: Employees.Employee;

BEGIN -- Test_Employees

  FOR Count IN 1..3 LOOP

    Employees.IO.Get(Item => OneEmployee);
    Ada.Text_IO.Put(Item => "--------------------");
    Ada.Text_IO.New_Line;
    Ada.Text_IO.Put(Item => "You entered ");
    Ada.Text_IO.New_Line;
    Employees.IO.Put(Item => OneEmployee);
    Ada.Text_IO.Put(Item => "--------------------");
    Ada.Text_IO.New_Line;

  END LOOP;

END Test_Employees;
```

A typical run of this program will produce the following output:

```
ID > 1234
Name > John Brown
Gender (Female or Male) > male
Number of dependents > 3
Salary > 50000
Starting Date, mmm dd yyyy > jan 1 1996
--------------------
You entered
1234
John Brown
MALE
3
50000.00
JAN 1 1996
--------------------
```

```
ID > 5678
Name > Virginia Dare
Gender (Female or Male) > female
Number of dependents > 1
Salary > 25000
Starting Date, mmm dd yyyy > feb 28 1980
-------------------
You entered
5678
Virginia Dare
FEMALE
1
25000.00
FEB 28 1980
-------------------
ID > 7777
Name > George Washington
Gender (Female or Male) > make

raised ADA.IO_EXCEPTIONS.DATA_ERROR
Trace Back Information
     Program Name                File Name                Line
     ------------                ---------                ----
     employees.io.get            employees-io.adb         32
     test_employee               test_employee.adb        17
```

The user entered `make` instead of `male` for the gender of the last employee; `Ada.Text_IO.Data_Error` was raised, giving the *trace back* shown. The precise form of the *trace back* varies from compiler to compiler, but the information in it allows to to find the line of your program that caused the exception to be raised.

Ideally, the exception should not be propagated to the main program, but should be handled in an exception-handling loop within `Employees.IO.Get`. Providing this robustness is left as an exercise.

Specification of the Employee Data Base Package `Tables`

Program 3.11 shows the specification for a table handler for records of type `Employees.Employee`.

Program 3.11 ADT Specification for Employee Table

```
WITH Employees;
PACKAGE Tables IS
-----------------------------------------------------------------------
--| ADT for simple employee table type
--| Author: Michael B. Feldman, The George Washington University
--| Last Modified: October 1995
-----------------------------------------------------------------------

  SUBTYPE KeyType IS Employees.IDType;
  SUBTYPE ElementType IS Employees.Employee;
  TYPE TableType IS LIMITED PRIVATE;
```

```
      PROCEDURE InitializeTable (T : IN OUT TableType);
      -- Pre : None
      -- Post: T is an initialized Table.

      PROCEDURE Insert (T       : IN OUT TableType;
                        E       : ElementType;
                        Success : OUT Boolean);
      -- Pre : T is initialized and Target is defined
      -- Post: Inserts element E into table T
      --    Success is True if insertion is performed, and False
      --    if T already has an element with the same key as E.

      PROCEDURE Retrieve (T       : TableType;
                          Target  : KeyType;
                          E       : OUT ElementType;
                          Success : OUT Boolean);
      -- Pre : T is initialized and Target is defined
      -- Post: Copies into E the element of T whose key is Target.
      --    Success is True if the copy is performed, and False
      --    if T has no element whose key is Target.

      PROCEDURE Delete (T       : IN OUT TableType;
                        Target  : KeyType;
                        Success : OUT Boolean);
      -- Pre : T is initialized and Target is defined
      -- Post: Deletes from T the element with key Target
      --    Success is True if deletion is performed, and False
      --    if T has no element whose key is Target.

      PROCEDURE Traverse (T : TableType);
      --  Pre : T is initialized.
      --  Post: The elements of T are displayed in order by key.

PRIVATE

   MaxElements: CONSTANT Positive := 25;
   SUBTYPE TableIndex IS Natural RANGE 1..MaxElements;
   SUBTYPE TableRange IS Natural RANGE 0..MaxElements;
   TYPE Elements IS ARRAY(TableIndex) OF ElementType;

   TYPE TableType IS RECORD
     ActualElements: Elements;
     CurrentSize:    TableRange := 0;
   END RECORD;

END Tables;
```

This more definite specification, based on the abstract sketch given in Figure 3.15, uses SUBTYPEs to define KeyType and ElementType as "nicknames" of the corresponding items of Employees. TableType is then declared as LIMITED PRIVATE. We will discuss this shortly.

The PRIVATE section gives the implementation details. Note the two subtypes:

- CompanyIndex, which is used to subscript the array that will hold the employee records,

- CompanyRange, which gives the range of the actual number—which could be zero—of elements in the array

Finally, we have the array type `Elements` and the record type `TableType`. The latter has two fields, the employee array and the actual number of elements in the table.

Using this specification, a client program could actually declare and use *several* employee tables, each with the same structure. This might be useful, for example, in keeping a table for each of several company offices in different cities.

The Table as a `LIMITED PRIVATE` Type

The definition of `TableType` as a `LIMITED PRIVATE` type warrants explanation. A `LIMITED PRIVATE` type not only excludes a client program from manipulating details of objects of the type, but removes the assignment and equality-testing operations as well. To give ourselves maximum flexibility in implementing the table package, we need to assure ourselves that a client program could not use the predefined symbols `":="` or `"="` in a meaningless or misleading way.

The table is represented as an array. Most of the time, this array will be only partially filled with data; the unfilled part of the array will contain unspecified "garbage." The various table operations deal with this fact by working only with the filled part of the array, which is the array slice from 1 to `CurrentSize`.

The writer of a client program, writing an equality-check operation on two table objects, will almost always get an incorrect result, because even if the two tables contain the same data, the "garbage" in the arrays will differ. Since equality simply compares all the bits in one array to the corresponding bits in the other, it will return `False` even if the arrays are logically equal. Therefore, our best policy is simply to prevent the use of `"="` by a client; we do this by making the table type `LIMITED PRIVATE`. This gives us the most flexibility in choosing a table implementation while allowing us to guarantee (as ADT writers must) that client operations will always be meaningful ones. As we will see in later chapters, it is also wise to prevent the client from using `":="` to copy one table to another.

A Reusable Package for Debugging Other Packages

Before proceeding to the body of `Tables`, we introduce a debugging package that can assist you in developing and debugging other packages. The purpose is to allow a package developer to *instrument* the package by placing, in each subprogram of the package, calls to tracing operations that will write a message when the subprogram is called, and another when the subprogram is ready to return to its caller.

However, we do not want these tracing operations to be called when the package is operating normally, only when it is being debugged. Accordingly, we will allow a client of the package to set a switch indicating whether the trace output is desired.

Program 3.12 shows the specification for this package. It provides an enumeration type giving the values `Off` and `On`, a procedure `SetDebug`, and procedures `Enter` and `Leave`. As can be seen from the comments, `Enter` and `Leave` are intended to be used by the writer of the package and `SetDebug` is intended to be used by the client.

`SetDebug` has two parameters: a required parameter `WhichWay`, indicating how to set the debug switch, and an optional parameter `FileName`, to specify a file to which the debugging output is to be written. A client calling

```
Debugging_Support.SetDebug(WhichWay => On, FileName => "trace.txt");
```

is specifying that trace output go to the given file.

Program 3.12 Specification for `Debugging_Support`

```
WITH Ada.Text_IO;
PACKAGE Debugging_Support IS
------------------------------------------------------------------------
--| Package Giving Operations Useful for Debugging Other Packages
--| WITH-ed by the body of a package to provide an easy way to
--| trace calls and returns from subprograms;
--| WITH-ed by a client of the package only to turn debugging on.
--| Author: Michael B. Feldman, The George Washington University
--| Last Modified: January 1996
------------------------------------------------------------------------

  TYPE Switch IS (Off, On);

  PROCEDURE SetDebug(WhichWay: IN Switch; FileName: String := "");
  -- Pre:  WhichWay is defined
  -- Post: Debugging support is turned On or Off, as the case may be;
  --       If FileName = "", debugging output goes to Standard_Output;
  --       otherwise, debugging output goes to the given file.

  PROCEDURE Enter(Subprogram: IN String; Message: IN String := "");
  -- Pre:  Subprogram is defined
  -- Post: Writes a message to Standard_Output or an external file
  --       Enter is not intended as a user operation, but should
  --       be called only from within a package being debugged.

  PROCEDURE Leave(Subprogram: IN String; Message: IN String := "");
  -- Pre:  Subprogram is defined
  -- Post: Writes a message to Standard_Output or an external file
  --       Leave is not intended as a user operation, but should
  --       be called only from within a package being debugged.

END Debugging_Support;
```

Now Program 3.13 shows the body of `Debugging_Support`. It is very straightforward and easy to understand. The procedures `Enter` and `Leave` are "silent" unless the package client has turned on the debugging switch, and write their output to the screen unless the client has specified an external file. We will use `Debugging_Support` in developing the body of our employee table package.

Program 3.13 Body for `Debugging_Support`

```
WITH Ada.Text_IO;
PACKAGE BODY Debugging_Support IS
------------------------------------------------------------------------
--| Body of Package for Debugging Other Packages
--| WITH-ed by the body of a package to provide an easy way to
--| trace calls and returns from subprograms;
```

```
--| WITH-ed by a client of the package only to turn debugging on.
--| Author: Michael B. Feldman, The George Washington University
--| Last Modified: January 1996
-------------------------------------------------------------------------

  DebuggingIsOn: Boolean := False;
  -- no debugging unless client calls SetDebug(WhichWay => On);

  DebugFile: Ada.Text_IO.File_Type;
  WritingToFile: Boolean := False;
  -- use standard output unless client gives a file name

  PROCEDURE SetDebug(WhichWay: IN Switch; FileName: String := "") IS
  BEGIN -- SetDebug
    IF WhichWay = Off THEN
      DebuggingIsOn := False;
    ELSE
      DebuggingIsOn := True;

      -- Open debugging file, if any
      IF FileName /= "" THEN
        WritingToFile := True;
        Ada.Text_IO.Create(File => DebugFile,
                           Mode => Ada.Text_IO.Out_File,
                           Name => FileName);
      END IF;
    END IF;
  END SetDebug;

  PROCEDURE Enter(Subprogram: IN String; Message: IN String := "") IS
  BEGIN -- Enter
    IF WritingToFile THEN
      Ada.Text_IO.Put
        (File => DebugFile, Item => ">>>>> Entering " & Subprogram);
      IF Message /= "" THEN
        Ada.Text_IO.Put(File => DebugFile, Item => "; " & Message);
      END IF;
      Ada.Text_IO.New_Line(File => DebugFile);
    ELSE -- standard output
      Ada.Text_IO.Put(Item => ">>>>> Entering " & Subprogram);
      IF Message /= "" THEN
        Ada.Text_IO.Put(Item => "; " & Message);
      END IF;
      Ada.Text_IO.New_Line;
    END IF;
  END Enter;

  PROCEDURE Leave(Subprogram: IN String; Message: IN String := "") IS
  BEGIN -- Leave
    IF WritingToFile THEN
      Ada.Text_IO.Put
        (File => DebugFile, Item => ">>>>> Leaving " & Subprogram);
      IF Message /= "" THEN
        Ada.Text_IO.Put(File => DebugFile, Item => "; " & Message);
      END IF;
      Ada.Text_IO.New_Line(File => DebugFile);
    ELSE -- standard output
      Ada.Text_IO.Put(Item => ">>>>> Leaving " & Subprogram);
      IF Message /= "" THEN
        Ada.Text_IO.Put(Item => "; " & Message);
      END IF;
      Ada.Text_IO.New_Line;
```

```
      END IF;
   END Leave;

END Debugging_Support;
```

Body of the Employee Data Base Package `Tables`

We return now to the employee table package, whose body is shown in Program 3.14. The operations `InitializeTable`, `Insert`, and `Traverse` are coded in full; the operations `Retrieve` and `Delete` are given as stubs. Note the way in which all the procedures use the services of `Debugging_Support`.

Program 3.14 Body of Employee Table ADT

```
WITH Employees.IO;
WITH Debugging_Support; USE Debugging_Support;
PACKAGE BODY Tables IS
-------------------------------------------------------------------------
--|
--| Body of the abstract data type for a table of
--| element records, each element containing a key.
--|
--| Author: Michael B. Feldman, The George Washington University
--| Last Modified: October 1995
--|
-------------------------------------------------------------------------

  PROCEDURE InitializeTable (T : IN OUT TableType) IS
  BEGIN -- InitializeTable

    Enter(Subprogram => "InitializeTable");

    T.CurrentSize := 0;

    Leave
      (Subprogram => "InitializeTable",
       Message => "table is initialized.");

  END InitializeTable;

  PROCEDURE Insert (T       : IN OUT TableType;
                    E       : ElementType;
                    Success : OUT Boolean) IS
  BEGIN -- Insert

    Enter(Subprogram => "Insert");

    Success := True;

    -- First search table for E's ID; set Success false if found
    FOR Which IN 1..T.CurrentSize LOOP
      IF Employees.RetrieveID(T.ActualElements(Which)) =
         Employees.RetrieveID(E) THEN
        Success := False;
        RETURN;
      END IF;
    END LOOP;
```

```
      -- we didn't find a matching record, so we can insert this one
      T.CurrentSize := T.CurrentSize + 1;
      T.ActualElements(T.CurrentSize) := E;

      Leave(Subprogram => "Insert");

   END Insert;

   PROCEDURE Traverse (T : TableType) IS
   BEGIN -- Traverse

      Enter(Subprogram => "Traverse");
      FOR Count IN 1..T.CurrentSize LOOP
        Employees.IO.Put(Item => T.ActualElements(Count));
        Ada.Text_IO.New_Line;
      END LOOP;

      Leave(Subprogram => "Traverse");

   END Traverse;

   PROCEDURE Retrieve (T       : TableType;
                       Target  : KeyType;
                       E       : OUT ElementType;
                       Success : OUT Boolean) IS
   BEGIN -- stub

      Enter(Subprogram => "Retrieve", Message => "under construction");
      Leave(Subprogram => "Retrieve");

   END Retrieve;

   PROCEDURE Delete (T       : IN OUT TableType;
                     Target  : KeyType;
                     Success : OUT Boolean) IS
   BEGIN -- stub

      Enter(Subprogram => "Delete", Message => "under construction");
      Leave(Subprogram => "Delete");

   END Delete;

END Tables;
```

InitializeTable simply sets the current size to zero. There is no need to do more, because the other operations depend on the current size and therefore ignore the "garbage" in the unfilled parts of the array. Insert implements the table as an unordered array; it just adds the new record to the end of the table. Traverse loops through the table, calling Employees.IO.Put to display each employee.

Program 3.15 is a brief program that tests some of the table operations. Notice that this program also uses Debugging_Support.

Program 3.15 A Test of the Employee Table ADT

```
WITH Ada.Text_IO;
WITH Employees;
WITH Employees.IO;
```

```
WITH Tables;
WITH Debugging_Support;
USE  Debugging_Support;
PROCEDURE Test_Employee_Table IS
-------------------------------------------------------------------------
--| Simple Test of Employee Table
--| Author: Michael B. Feldman, The George Washington University
--| Last Modified: July 1995
-------------------------------------------------------------------------

  OneEmployee: Employees.Employee;
  Success: Boolean;
  OneTable: Tables.TableType;
BEGIN -- Test_Employee_Table

  SetDebug(WhichWay => On);

  Tables.InitializeTable(T => OneTable);

  FOR Count IN 1..3 LOOP

    Ada.Text_IO.Put(Item => "--------------------");
    Ada.Text_IO.New_Line;

    Employees.IO.Get(Item => OneEmployee);

    Ada.Text_IO.Put(Item => "--------------------");
    Ada.Text_IO.New_Line;

    Tables.Insert(T => OneTable, E => OneEmployee, Success =>
    Success); Tables.Traverse(T => OneTable);

    Ada.Text_IO.Put(Item => "--------------------");
    Ada.Text_IO.New_Line;

  END LOOP;

END Test_Employee_Table;
```

Here is some typical output from the test program:

```
>>>>> Entering InitializeTable
>>>>> Leaving InitializeTable; table is initialized.
--------------------
ID > 1234
Name > John Smith
Gender (Female or Male) > male
Number of dependents > 3
Salary > 50000
Starting Date, mmm dd yyyy > jan 1 1996
--------------------
>>>>> Entering Insert
>>>>> Leaving Insert
>>>>> Entering Traverse
1234
John Smith
MALE
3
```

```
50000.00
JAN 1 1996

>>>>> Leaving Traverse
--------------------
--------------------
ID > 5678
Name > Virginia Dare
Gender (Female or Male) > female
Number of dependents > 1
Salary > 45000
Starting Date, mmm dd yyyy > feb 28 1990
--------------------->>>>> Entering Insert
>>>>> Leaving Insert
>>>>> Entering Traverse
1234
John Smith
MALE
3
50000.00
JAN 1 1996

5678
Virginia Dare
FEMALE
1
45000.00
FEB 28 1990

>>>>> Leaving Traverse
--------------------
--------------------
ID > 3456
Name > George Washington
Gender (Female or Male) > male
Number of dependents > 5
Salary > 75000
Starting Date, mmm dd yyyy > mar 15 1980
--------------------
>>>>> Entering Insert
>>>>> Leaving Insert
>>>>> Entering Traverse
1234
John Smith
MALE
3
50000.00
JAN 1 1996
5678
Virginia Dare
FEMALE
1
45000.00
FEB 28 1990
3456
George Washington
MALE
5
75000.00
MAR 15 1980
>>>>> Leaving Traverse
--------------------
```

Developing the Interactive User Interface

We have completed phases 1 through 5 of the development. Phase 6 calls for an menu-driven user interface, Employee_UI, so that users can enter table operations interactively. Program 3.16 shows the shell of this program. The interactive command input is provided, but the user interface is not yet "connected" to the operations in the table package. Completing this program is left as an exercise.

Program 3.16 Menu-Driven User Interface for Employee Database

```
WITH Ada.Text_IO;
WITH Screen;
WITH Tables;
PROCEDURE Employee_UI IS
------------------------------------------------------------------------
--| Shell of menu-driven user interface for Employee "data base"
--| when correct input is entered, a message is displayed
--| instead of actually executing the command .
--| Author: Michael B. Feldman, The George Washington University
--| Last Modified: October 1995
------------------------------------------------------------------------

   TYPE MenuValues IS (I,        -- Initialize data base
                       A,        -- Add a record
                       D,        -- Delete a record
                       F,        -- retrieve (Find) and display a record
                       R,        -- find and Replace a record
                       P,        -- Display all records
                       Q);       -- Quit the program

   PACKAGE Menu_IO IS
     NEW Ada.Text_IO.Enumeration_IO (Enum => MenuValues);

   MenuSelection : MenuValues;

BEGIN -- Employee_UI

   LOOP -- main program loop

     Screen.ClearScreen;
     Screen.MoveCursor (To=>(Row => 5, Column => 20));
     Ada.Text_IO.Put (Item => "Select one of the operations below.");
     Screen.MoveCursor (To=>(Row => 7, Column => 20));
     Ada.Text_IO.Put (Item => "I  Initialize the Employee Database");
     Screen.MoveCursor (To=>(Row => 8, Column => 20));
     Ada.Text_IO.Put (Item => "A  Add a New Employee to the Database");
     Screen.MoveCursor (To=>(Row => 9, Column => 20));
     Ada.Text_IO.Put (Item => "D  Delete an Employee from the
     Database");
     Screen.MoveCursor (To=>(Row => 10, Column => 20));
     Ada.Text_IO.Put (Item => "F  Find and Display One Employee");
     Screen.MoveCursor (To=>(Row => 11, Column => 20));
     Ada.Text_IO.Put (Item => "R  Replace Old Record with New One");
     Screen.MoveCursor (To=>(Row => 11, Column => 20));
     Ada.Text_IO.Put (Item => "P  Display All Records in the Database");
     Screen.MoveCursor (To=>(Row => 12, Column => 20));
     Ada.Text_IO.Put (Item => "Q  Exit the program");
```

```
LOOP
  BEGIN -- exception handler block

    Screen.MoveCursor (To=>(Row => 14, Column => 20));
    Ada.Text_IO.Put ("Please type a command, then press Enter > ");

    -- this statement will raise Data_Error if input is invalid
    Menu_IO.Get (Item => MenuSelection);

    -- these statements will be executed
    -- only if the input is correct;
    -- otherwise, control passes to exception handler
    Screen.MoveCursor (To=>(Row => 15, Column => 20));
    Ada.Text_IO.Put ("Thank you for correct input.");
    Ada.Text_IO.New_Line;
    EXIT;       -- valid data; go ahead to process it

  EXCEPTION    -- invalid data

    WHEN Ada.Text_IO.Data_Error =>
      Screen.Beep;
      Screen.MoveCursor (To=>(Row => 15, Column => 20));
      Ada.Text_IO.Put (Item => "Value entered is not a command.");
      Ada.Text_IO.New_Line;
      DELAY 1.0;
      Ada.Text_IO.Skip_Line;
      Screen.MoveCursor (To=>(Row => 15, Column => 20));
      Ada.Text_IO.Put (Item => "                            ");
    WHEN OTHERS =>
      Screen.Beep;
      Screen.MoveCursor (To=>(Row => 15, Column => 20));
      Ada.Text_IO.Put (Item => "Unknown error; try again,
      please.");
      Ada.Text_IO.New_Line;
      DELAY 1.0;
      Ada.Text_IO.Skip_Line;
      Screen.MoveCursor (To=>(Row => 15, Column => 20));
      Ada.Text_IO.Put (Item => "                            ");
  END;          -- of exception handler block

END LOOP;


Screen.MoveCursor (To=>(Row =>22, Column => 20));
CASE MenuSelection IS
  WHEN I =>
    Ada.Text_IO.Put (Item => "I entered; here we'd initialize");
  WHEN A =>
    Ada.Text_IO.Put (Item => "A entered; here we'd insert");
  WHEN D =>
    Ada.Text_IO.Put (Item => "D entered; here we'd delete");
  WHEN F =>
    Ada.Text_IO.Put (Item => "F entered; here we'd find");
  WHEN R =>
    Ada.Text_IO.Put (Item => "R entered; here we'd replace");
  WHEN P =>
    Ada.Text_IO.Put (Item => "P entered; here we'd display all");
  WHEN Q =>
    Ada.Text_IO.Put (Item => "Q entered; have a nice day.");
    EXIT;  -- the main loop and quit the program
END CASE;
```

```
    Ada.Text_IO.New_Line;
    DELAY 2.0;

  END LOOP;

END Employee_UI;
```

3.6   MEASURING PROGRAM PERFORMANCE

Much of this chapter has emphasized *predicting* the performance of an algorithm or a program. In this section, we will discuss approaches to *measuring* performance—that is, finding out the actual running time of a program or a section of program.

What Should Be Measured?

We know that several factors influence a program's running time. The specific computer, the compiler, the chosen algorithm, and the number of data values all play their roles. Although a single measurement—clocking the running time of a program one time, with one set of data, on one specific computer—is sometimes useful, in general we are interested less in a single measurement than in a set of measurements in which all factors but one are held constant, and in that remaining factor. Here are some examples of sets of measurements:

1. A single program, compiled by the same compiler and using the same set of data, executed on several similar but different computers—for example, on an Intel 80386 computer, running at 33 megahertz (MHz) nominal speed, and on an Intel 80486 computer, at 50 MHz speed

2. A single Ada source program, executed on the same computer with the same data, but compiled with two or more different Ada compilers

3. A case similar to case 2, but using a single compiler with different settings of its "optimization switch" used as compilation time

4. A sorting program, run on the same computer three times: once with a set of values already sorted, once with the same values in reverse order, and once with the same values in some random order

5. One program, run repeatedly on the same computer with systematically varying numbers of data values

6. A case similar to case 4, but comparing two different algorithms on the same varying sets of data

As you can see, there are many possibilities for comparison. It is most important to know just what you are measuring and to hold all factors constant except the one whose results you wish to compare. There is no substitute for a carefully designed set of measurements; a carelessly designed measurement experiment is likely to produce misleading or meaningless results.

Timing an Algorithm Using Ada on a Personal Computer

As you know, package `Ada.Calendar` provides the `Ada.Calendar.Clock` operation, which returns the time of day as a value of type `Ada.Calendar.Time`. In addition, one such value can be subtracted from another to give a `Duration` value.

You could use these operations directly to insert timing instructions into a program, or a section of a program, as follows;

1. In your code, before the first line you wish to time, insert a statement that calls `Ada.Calendar.Clock`, storing the result in a variable, say `StartTime`.

2. After the last line you wish to time, insert a statement to read the clock again and subtract `StartTime` from it. This will give, as a `Duration` value, the elapsed time in seconds.

As you will see in the next section, `Ada.Calendar` operations are not meaningful for this purpose on a time-sharing system. Therefore, instead of directly using `Ada.Calendar`, we show in Program 3.17 the specification for a package `CPUClock`, providing a subtype `CPUTime` as an ordinary nonnegative `Float` value. The operations provided are similar to those on a stopwatch: a procedure `ResetCPUTime`, which resets the "stopwatch" to zero, and a function `CPUTime`, which returns the elapsed CPU time, in seconds, since the "stopwatch" was last reset.

Program 3.17 Specification for CPU Timing Package

```
PACKAGE CPUClock IS
------------------------------------------------------------------------
--| Specification for a package to do CPU timing of algorithms
--| Author: Michael B. Feldman, The George Washington University
--| Last Modified: October 1995
------------------------------------------------------------------------

  SUBTYPE CPUSecond IS Float RANGE 0.0 .. Float'Last;
  -- We make CPUSecond a Float type so the usual operations are available

  PROCEDURE ResetCPUTime;
  -- Pre:  none
  -- Post: resets a CPU timer

  FUNCTION CPUTime RETURN CPUSecond;
  -- Pre:  none
  -- Post: returns the number of CPUSeconds since the last reset

END CPUClock;
```

Program 3.18 gives a body for this package, suitable for use on a personal computer such as an IBM PC-compatible or an Apple Macintosh. As you can see, the `ResetCPUTime` operation simply stores the current clock value in a variable internal to the package, and the `CPUTime` function returns the elapsed CPU time as discussed in the previous paragraph. This implementation, using `Ada.Calendar`, gives meaningful results on a PC because there is only one user at a time on a PC, and so the running time of a program is almost exactly the same thing as the elapsed clock time.

Program 3.18 Body of CPU Timing Package

```
WITH Ada.Calendar; USE Ada.Calendar;
PACKAGE BODY CPUClock IS
-----------------------------------------------------------------------
--| This body is compatible with Ada compilers whose output
--| runs on single-user IBM-PC-family and Apple Macintosh computers
--| Author: Michael B. Feldman, The George Washington University
--| Last Modified: October 1995
-----------------------------------------------------------------------

  SavedTime : Ada.Calendar.Time;

  PROCEDURE ResetCPUTime IS
  BEGIN
    SavedTime := Ada.Calendar.Clock;
  END ResetCPUTime;

  FUNCTION CPUTime RETURN CPUSecond IS
  BEGIN
    RETURN CPUSecond (Ada.Calendar."-"(Ada.Calendar.Clock,SavedTime));
  END CPUTime;

BEGIN -- initialization of package

  -- this statement is executed once, when the package is elaborated,
  -- i.e., just before its client program starts executing

  ResetCPUTime;

END CPUClock;
```

Program 3.19 shows an example of a timing experiment: A large two-dimensional array is filled with values, each of which is the product of the row and column subscripts. If the array is 50 by 50, 2,500 multiplications are required for execution of this algorithm.

Program 3.19 Test of CPU Timing Package

```
WITH Ada.Text_IO;
WITH CPUClock;
USE TYPE CPUClock.CPUSecond;
WITH Ada.Integer_Text_IO;
WITH Ada.Float_Text_IO;
PROCEDURE TestClok IS
-----------------------------------------------------------------------
--| An example program to show how the CPUClock operations
--| can be used
--| Author: Michael B. Feldman, The George Washington University
--| Last Modified: October 1995
-----------------------------------------------------------------------

  TrialTime      : CPUClock.CPUSecond;   -- CPU time for each trial
  TotalTime      : CPUClock.CPUSecond;   -- total time for all trials
  NumberOfTrials : CONSTANT Integer := 10;
  NumberOfCycles : CONSTANT Integer := 5;
```

```
Maxindex         : CONSTANT Integer := 50;
A                : ARRAY (1 .. Maxindex, 1 .. Maxindex) OF Integer;

BEGIN -- TestClok

   TotalTime := 0.0;

   FOR Trial IN 1 .. NumberOfTrials LOOP

      CPUClock.ResetCPUTime;

      -- this loop runs each trial a number of times before
      -- reading the clock, which allows the time to build up to
      -- a more easily measured value
      FOR Cycle IN 1 .. NumberOfCycles LOOP

         -- this pair of loops is really the algorithm being timed;
         -- for MaxIndex = 50 we are doing 2,500 multiplications
         FOR Row IN 1 .. Maxindex LOOP
           FOR Col IN 1 .. Maxindex LOOP
             A (Row, Col) := Row * Col;
           END LOOP;
         END LOOP;

      END LOOP;

      -- read clock; accumulate total time
      TrialTime := CPUClock.CPUTime;
      TotalTime := TotalTime + TrialTime;

      -- display results for this trial
      Ada.Text_IO.Put(Item => "Trial ");
      Ada.Integer_Text_IO.Put(Item => Trial, Width => 1);
      Ada.Text_IO.Put (Item => " time used ");
      Ada.Float_Text_IO.Put
         (Item => TrialTime, Fore => 1, Aft => 2, Exp => 0);
      Ada.Text_IO.Put (Item => " seconds; total time so far ");
      Ada.Float_Text_IO.Put
         (Item => TotalTime, Fore => 1, Aft => 2, Exp => 0);
      Ada.Text_IO.Put(Item => " seconds.");
      Ada.Text_IO.New_Line;
      Ada.Text_IO.New_Line;

   END LOOP;

END TestClok;
```

On a very fast computer, even 2,500 multiplications take only a very brief time to execute, often much less than a second, and the interval may be so small that the clock function cannot reliably measure it. Therefore, Program 3.19 has an extra loop around the algorithm, so that the entire algorithm is really executed five times before the clock is read. The actual time of the algorithm is, then, one fifth the reported time.

Sometimes there is even some random fluctuation in the CPU timer's reading. This too results from the relatively coarse "resolution" of some clock hardware. The example program therefore has yet another loop; this one causes the entire experiment to run 10 times. A reasonable measure of the actual time for each run of the algorithm is then one fifth of the *average* times of the ten cycles. Exercise 13 invites you to modify this program so that the results are reported in this fashion.

Exercise 14 depends on the fact that the algorithm is $O(N^2)$, because the number of multiplications is the product of the number of rows by the number of columns. In this exercise, you can modify the program to vary the number of rows and columns, reporting and plotting the results to see whether the actual timings reflect the "big O" estimate.

Finally, Exercise 15 asks you to run the program using different computers or different compilers and to compare the results.

Timing an Algorithm Using Ada on a Multiuser Computer

Ada provides the `Ada.Calendar` operations to produce the time of day, and we can compute elapsed time as the difference of two time measurements. However, these values measure the real time, often called the *wall-clock time*, because they represent the time of day as seen on a clock on the wall.

We have seen that wall-clock time measurements are meaningful on a PC. Are they meaningful on a time-sharing computer, such as a multiuser UNIX or VMS computer in the computer center? On such a computer, the operating system is juggling many simultaneous users, giving each running program a small amount of time before giving control to another running program. It is this "time-slicing" that gives you and your colleagues the illusion that each of you is alone on the computer—the computer can, usually, skip around rapidly enough that you seldom realize others are sharing the machine. Only when the load on the computer is very heavy do you notice that the computer is slow to respond to your keystrokes, or that a compilation is proceeding at what seems like a glacial pace.

This fast-versus-slow perceived behavior is exactly the problem with trying to use wall-clock measurements on a shared computer. A compilation, say, may appear to be taking 5 seconds now, but at "rush hour" in the lab—when all students are desperately trying to finish their projects—the same compilation may appear to be taking 30 seconds or more. In fact, the compilation is taking just about the same actual time in both cases; what is different is the level of *contention* or "competition" in the system. You and your colleagues are, literally, slowing each other down. If we could measure the actual CPU time for both compilations, we would find them very similar.

We would like to be able to use Ada directly to measure the actual CPU time taken by our program. Unfortunately, Ada does not provide standard facilities for this procedure; we need to use operating system services. This means that we must use an Ada facility called *interfacing*, which allows us to write a subprogram in another language (Fortran, Pascal, or C, for example) and call it, or perhaps call a subprogram in the system library, from an Ada program unit. The details of this process are beyond the scope of our discussion, and are highly system-dependent. Appendix J presents some ideas and sample code for interfacing to the operating-system timing services.

The interfacing code is enclosed in an alternative package body for `CPUClock`, so that you can use the same package spec and timing calls regardless of the computer you are running on. If you are working in a laboratory with a time-shared computer, ask your instructor or system manager to provide a version of the `CPUClock` package body that will provide meaningful results for that system.

SUMMARY

In this chapter, we have discussed algorithms and, in particular, the two important areas of recursion and performance prediction.

An algorithm is a method used to solve a problem in a systematic way; it consists of a finite number of steps that will complete its work, regardless of the input given to it, in a finite amount of time with a finite effort.

A recursive algorithm is one that "invokes itself"; its own name appears in its definition. Infinite recursion is avoided by making certain that the algorithm has in its definition a specific step indicating the conditions for stopping the recursion, and that each recursive call operates on a data set smaller than the previous one.

Five recursive algorithms were presented: factorial, string reversal, permutations, binary search, and merge sort. The Ada versions of these algorithms made clear that recursive programs can be written straightforwardly in the Ada language.

Performance prediction is the process of estimating how the computation or running time of an algorithm or program varies with the "problem size." The currently accepted way of expressing this variation, often called "growth rate," is the $O(. . .)$, or "big O," notation.

Although there is no easy, guaranteed way to calculate the performance, there are certain techniques and rules of thumb that are helpful in "getting a handle on it." Performance prediction is facilitated when programs are written according to structured coding conventions, because such programs have a well-defined loop and decision structure.

In the section on performance prediction, examples were given of various program structures and their "big O" formulas. The most common growth rates in our data-structures work are, in order of steepness: constant, or $O(1)$; logarithmic, or $O(\log N)$; linear, or $O(N)$; $O(N \log N)$; and quadratic, or $O(N^2)$.

The design section introduced you to two different implementations of a table as an array. Although few program details were given, the growth rates of the various operations were "reasoned out" and compared for both implementations.

Finally, we introduced some ideas for actually measuring the running time of a program, and discussed the difference between a measurement on a single-user personal computer and one on a time-sharing system.

This concludes the "preliminaries" part of the book. Equipped with an introduction to abstract data types, recursion, and performance prediction, you are ready to see how these concepts play important roles in the study of data structures.

EXERCISES

1. Give a recursive definition of the integer addition operation. Write and test a recursive function to produce the sum of two integers. (*Hint*: Use the built-in "+" operation only to add 1 to a number.)
2. Give a recursive definition of the integer multiplication operation. Write and test a recursive function to carry out the definition. (*Hint:* Multiplication is repeated addition.)

3. Give a recursive definition of the integer exponentiation operation. Write and test a recursive function to carry out the definition (*Hint:* Exponentiation is repeated multiplication).

4. The Fibonacci numbers of order 1 are a sequence of positive integers starting with 1, 2, 3, 5, 8, ... In other words, each number except the first two is the sum of the two previous numbers. Give a recursive definition of this sequence; write a recursive procedure to print out the first 25 numbers.

5. What is the "big *O*" of the usual algorithm to set to zero all the elements of a two-dimensional square array with N rows and N columns?

6. Show that in computing a "big *O*" that turns out to have a logarithmic component—that is, something of the form log(. . .)—the base we use to represent the logarithm does not matter.

7. Show that the growth rate of the algorithmic structure given in Figure 3.13 is $O(\log N)$.

8. Show that the growth rates of the structures in Figure 3.14 are $O(N \log N)$.

9. Complete the bodies of the packages `Employees`, `Employees.IO`, and `Tables` in Section 3.5, using either the unordered or the ordered implementation discussed in Section 3.4, and complete the interactive program `Employee_UI`, which allows the terminal user to input operations and data that maintain the employee data base.

10. A real data base program would not require that data be entered interactively each time the program is run. Instead, the records would be stored in a disk file and the client program would operate something like this:

    Step 1: Read all the employee records from a file created by the previous run.

    Step 2: Accept operations from the interactive user, until, say, a "quit" command is entered.

    Step 3: Write the records in the array back out into the disk file and terminate the program.

    Modify the package and your client program from exercise 10 to operate in this manner.

11. Consider the problem of searching for a key k in an unordered array where duplicate keys are permitted.

    Discuss the performance of each of the following cases:

    a. k does not appear in the array.

    b. k appears once in the array.

    c. k appears several times in the array (not necessarily in adjacent locations!) but only the location of the first appearance is desired.

    d. k appears several times in the array and the locations of all appearances are to be reported.

12. Repeat the preceding problem for an ordered array.

13. Modify Program 3.19 so that the timing results are reported more usefully, in terms of the average of the five cycles and the 10 trials.

14. Modify Program 3.19 so that a number of different array sizes are used. Vary the number of rows and columns in some systematic way (8, 16, 32, 64, 128, for example) so that you can determine easily whether the actual results follow the theoretical "big *O*." You might wish to plot the results on graph paper. If t is a

specific execution time, try plotting t/N^2 and see whether the result approximates a straight line.

15. Try compiling the timing package and Program 3.19 using several different compilers on the same personal computer, if you have access to several compilers. If not, try the timing experiment with one compiler on computers of differing speeds, or on a PC and a time-shared computer. How do the results compare? How does the variation compare with the "big O" in each case?

CHAPTER 4

Multidimensional and Unconstrained Array Types

4.1 Data Structures: Multidimensional Arrays

4.2 Data Structures: Unconstrained Array Types

4.3 Application: A General Sorting Program

4.4 ADT Design: Mathematical Vectors

4.5 ADT Design: Mathematical Matrices

4.6 Storage Mappings

So far, the arrays we have seen have been one-dimensional ones, and the array bounds have always been declared as part of the type declaration. In this chapter we look at more interesting array structures.

A *multidimensional array* has, as its name suggests, more than one dimension. Instead of being a linear collection of elements, it may have the "shape" of a rectangle (two-dimensional) or even of a rectangular solid or cube (three-dimensional). In fact, there is in theory no limit to the number of dimensions an array type can have, although it is rare to see an example with more than three. Multidimensional arrays give us the ability to structure information in useful tabular forms.

In this chapter, you will learn how to declare and use multidimensional arrays. You will also learn about *storage mapping functions*, which relate the abstraction of multidimensional arrays to their implementation in computer memory.

An *unconstrained array type* is one declared in such a way that the bounds of the array are not specified in the type declaration; rather, they are supplied only when a variable of the type is declared. Many arrays of the same number of dimensions but of differing sizes can be declared from the same type definition. Moreover, subprograms can be written that accept these arrays as parameters and work with them without knowing their sizes in advance. This is extremely helpful in writing general-purpose programs such as sorts and numerical algorithms.

As it happens, we have been using an unconstrained array type all along in this book. Ada's *String* type is one of these, predefined in *Standard*. In this chapter, you will learn how to define and use unconstrained array types of your own.

The chapter presents three design examples: general sorting, mathematical vectors, and mathematical matrices.

4.1 DATA STRUCTURES: MULTIDIMENSIONAL ARRAYS

Our first example of a multidimensional array is the multiplication table for the integers 1 through 15. Here are declarations for a subscript range, an array type, and a variable:

```
SUBTYPE OneToFifteen IS Integer RANGE 1..15;

TYPE FifteenByFifteen IS
  ARRAY(OneToFifteen, OneToFifteen) OF Positive;

MultiplicationTable: FifteenByFifteen;
```

A given element of this array can be referred to as

```
MultiplicationTable(Row, Column)
```

where `Row` and `Column` are of type `OneToFifteen`.

Each element of the array contains the product of its row and column subscripts. We can initialize this array using nested FOR loops:

```
FOR Row IN OneToFifteen LOOP
  FOR Column IN OneToFifteen LOOP
    MultiplicationTable(Row, Column) := Row * Column;
  END LOOP;
END LOOP;
```

and display the array in tabular form, as in Fig. 4.1, with a similar fragment:

```
-- display column titles
Ada.Text_IO.Put(Item => "       ");
FOR Column IN OneToFifteen LOOP
  Ada.Integer_Text_IO.Put(Item => Column, Width => 4);
END LOOP;
Ada.Text_IO.New_Line;

-- march across each row
FOR Row IN OneToFifteen LOOP
  Ada.Integer_Text_IO.Put(Item => Row, Width => 4); -- row title
  FOR Column IN OneToFifteen LOOP
    Ada.Integer_Text_IO.Put
      (Item=>MultiplicationTable(Row, Column), Width=>4);
  END LOOP;
  Ada.Text_IO.New_Line;
END LOOP;
```

Let us look at a more realistic example. Cloud Nine Airways (CNA), a new airline company, provides service to seven cities: Boston, Chicago (O'Hare Airport), Newark, Philadelphia, Seattle, and Washington, DC (National Airport). Let us represent these cities using an enumeration type containing the standard three-letter codes used by airlines and travel agents:

	1	2	3	4	5	6	7	8	9	10	11	12	13	14	15
1	1	2	3	4	5	6	7	8	9	10	11	12	13	14	15
2	2	4	6	8	10	12	14	16	18	20	22	24	26	28	30
3	3	6	9	12	15	18	21	24	27	30	33	36	39	42	45
4	4	8	12	16	20	24	28	32	36	40	44	48	52	56	60
5	5	10	15	20	25	30	35	40	45	50	55	60	65	70	75
6	6	12	18	24	30	36	42	48	54	60	66	72	78	84	90
7	7	14	21	28	35	42	49	56	63	70	77	84	91	98	105
8	8	16	24	32	40	48	56	64	72	80	88	96	104	112	120
9	9	18	27	36	45	54	63	72	81	90	99	108	117	126	135
10	10	20	30	40	50	60	70	80	90	100	110	120	130	140	150
11	11	22	33	44	55	66	77	88	99	110	121	132	143	154	165
12	12	24	36	48	60	72	84	96	108	120	132	144	156	168	180
13	13	26	39	52	65	78	91	104	117	130	143	156	169	182	195
14	14	28	42	56	70	84	98	112	126	140	154	168	182	196	210
15	15	30	45	60	75	90	105	120	135	150	165	180	195	210	225

Figure 4.1 Multiplication Table for Integers 1 Through 15

```
TYPE Cities IS (BOS, ORD, EWR, PHL, SEA, DCA);
```

It is not obvious that all these codes are related to city names, but that is what they are. We can tabulate the average daily number of CNA flights leaving each city in an array declared as

```
TYPE FlightTable IS ARRAY (Cities) OF Natural;
CNAFlightsLeaving: FlightTable;
```

but in this section we are interested in multidimensional arrays, not in one-dimensional ones. Let us tabulate the number of nonstop flights *from* each city *to* each city:

```
TYPE RouteMap IS ARRAY (Cities, Cities) OF Natural;
CNACityPairs: RouteMap;
```

Here the row and column subscript types are the same. We can indicate that two flights per day leave Boston for Chicago by writing

```
CNACityPairs (BOS, EWR) := 2;
```

With 36 such assignment statements, we can fill the array. Figure 4.2 shows this route map filled with values.

Note that some cities are not connected nonstop to all the others. Given city variables From and a city To, we can indicate that three flights leave From for To by writing

```
CNACityPairs (From, To) := 3;
```

We can store values in the entire array by using a two-dimensional aggregate:

```
CNACityPairs :=
 (BOS => (BOS=>0, ORD=>3, EWR=>2, PHL=>0, SEA=>0, DCA=>1),
  ORD => (BOS=>3, ORD=>0, EWR=>3, PHL=>1, SEA=>2, DCA=>2),
  EWR => (BOS=>1, ORD=>3, EWR=>0, PHL=>2, SEA=>0, DCA=>1),
  PHL => (BOS=>0, ORD=>0, EWR=>3, PHL=>0, SEA=>0, DCA=>2),
  SEA => (BOS=>0, ORD=>2, EWR=>0, PHL=>1, SEA=>0, DCA=>1),
  DCA => (BOS=>1, ORD=>3, EWR=>2, PHL=>1, SEA=>1, DCA=>0));
```

	Destination City					
	BOS	ORD	EWR	PHL	SEA	DCA
BOS	0	3	2	0	0	1
ORD	3	0	3	1	2	2
EWR	1	3	0	2	0	1
PHL	0	0	3	0	0	2
SEA	0	2	0	1	0	1
DCA	1	3	2	1	1	0

(Origin City labels the rows)

Figure 4.2 Cloud Nine Airways City-Pair Services

The row and column subscript types need not be the same; we could tabulate the number of flights leaving each city on each of the 7 days with the array type DailyFlights:

```
TYPE Days IS (Mon, Tue, Wed, Thu, Fri, Sat, Sun);
TYPE DailyFlights IS ARRAY (Cities, Days) OF Natural;
CNADailyFlights: DailyFlights;
```

Figure 4.3 shows this table filled with values; you can write the aggregate assignment.

Finally, we can use *three* dimensions to tabulate the fares for each city pair, by class of seat (1 = First Class, 2 = Coach):

```
SUBTYPE Classes IS Integer RANGE 1..2;
SUBTYPE FareRange IS Float RANGE 0.00 .. 2000.00;
TYPE FareTable IS ARRAY (Cities, Cities, Classes) OF FareRange;
CNAFareTable: FareTable;
```

Alternatively, we could have used an enumeration type for the classes. This would, in fact, have been better style in a real program; we used an integer subtype here just for variety.

	Mon	Tue	Wed	Thu	Fri	Sat	Sun
BOS	6	5	5	5	7	6	7
ORD	11	10	10	10	12	11	12
EWR	7	6	6	6	8	7	8
PHL	5	4	4	4	6	5	6
SEA	4	3	3	3	5	4	5
DCA	8	7	7	7	9	8	9

Figure 4.3 Cloud Nine Airways Departures by Day of the Week

Using Multidimensional Arrays

Given the Cloud Nine arrays as presented above, we now go through a set of examples. First, given a positive variable `TotalFlights`, we compute the average total number of flights leaving Boston:

```
TotalFlights := 0;
FOR Destination IN Cities LOOP
  TotalFlights := TotalFlights + CNACityPairs(BOS, Destination);
END LOOP;
```

Here we total across a row, by holding the row subscript constant and varying the column subscript. Next, we compute the average number of *arriving* flights at Chicago:

```
TotalFlights := 0;
FOR Origin IN Cities LOOP
  TotalFlights := TotalFlights + CNACityPairs(Origin, ORD);
END LOOP;
```

in which we are totaling down a column by holding the column subscript constant and varying the row subscript.

What is the total number of flight segments flown by CNA?

```
TotalSegments := 0;
FOR Origin IN Cities LOOP
  FOR Destination IN Cities LOOP
    TotalSegments :=
      TotalSegments + CNACityPairs(Origin, Destination);
  END LOOP;
END LOOP;
```

Here we sum all the elements of the array using nested loops.

In this introduction to multidimensional arrays, we have used integer and enumeration subscript types, and scalar element types. Naturally, array elements can be of arbitrary type, as in the case of one-dimensional arrays. As always in Ada, array assignment and equality/inequality tests are defined for multidimensional arrays; these can, of course, be passed as parameters or returned as function results.

4.2   DATA STRUCTURES: UNCONSTRAINED ARRAY TYPES

The purpose of unconstrained array types is to allow subprograms that operate on arrays to be written without prior knowledge of the bounds of the arrays. Let us start with a type definition:

```
TYPE ListType IS ARRAY (Integer RANGE <>) OF Float;
```

The construct `Integer RANGE <>` means that the subscript range, or bounds, of any variable of type `ListType` must form an integer subrange; the symbol `"<>"` (which is read "box") means "We'll fill in the missing values when we declare `ListType` variables."

The type `ListType` is said to be *unconstrained*. When variables are declared, the compiler must know how much storage to allocate, so variable declaration *must* carry a range constraint—for example,

```
L1 : ListType(1..50);    -- 50 elements
L2 : ListType(-10..10); -- 21 elements
L3 : ListType(0..20);    -- 21 elements
```

Operations on Unconstrained Array Types

The operations of assignment and equality testing are defined for unconstrained array types, but for either operation to proceed without raising `Constraint_Error`, both operands must be variables of the same unconstrained array type and both operands must have the same number of elements. Thus,

```
L1 := L2;
```

will raise `Constraint_Error`, but the following operations will all succeed:

```
L2 := L3;
L1 (20..40) := L2;
L2 (1..5) := L1 (6..10);
```

These slicing operations were introduced in Chapter 1, in the discussion of Ada strings. Ada's string type is actually defined in `Standard` as follows:

```
TYPE String IS ARRAY (Positive RANGE <>) OF Character;
```

making strings just a special case of unconstrained arrays. The slicing operations work for all one-dimensional arrays just as they do for strings.

Attribute Functions for Unconstrained Arrays

Ada defines a number of attribute functions that can be used to determine the bounds of array variables. Given the type `ListType` above and the variable `L2`,

> `L2'First` returns the low bound of `L2`, or –10 in this case.
>
> `L2'Last` returns the high bound of `L2`, or 10.
>
> `L2'Length` returns the number of elements in `L2`, or 21.
>
> `L2'Range` returns the range –10..10.

The last attribute is useful in controlling loops—for instance,

```
FOR WhichElement IN L2'Range LOOP
  Ada.Float_Text_IO.Put
    (Item=>L2(WhichElement), Fore=>1, Aft=>2, Exp=>0);
  Ada.Text_IO.New_Line;
END LOOP;
```

The construct `L2'Range` is a short way of writing `L2'First..L2'Last`, so the same fragment could be written

```
FOR WhichElement IN L2'First..L2'Last LOOP
  Ada.Float_Text_IO.Put
    (Item=>L2(WhichElement), Fore=>1, Aft=>2, Exp=>0);
  Ada.Text_IO.New_Line;
END LOOP;
```

To show the utility of unconstrained arrays, consider a function to find the maximum value stored in an array of floating-point numbers. For this function to be generally useful and reusable, it must be able to work for all kinds of floating-point arrays, no matter what their bounds. Using the type `ListType`, Program 4.1 shows such a function, contained in a test program. The program also contains a procedure `DisplayList`, which displays the contents of a `ListType` variable, whatever its bounds. The main program declares two lists of differing bounds, then displays the lists and tests the function `MaxValue`. From the output of the program, you can see that the maximum is found correctly even though the two lists have different sizes.

Program 4.1 Finding the Largest Value in an Array

```
WITH Ada.Text_IO;
WITH Ada.Float_Text_IO;
PROCEDURE Test_Max_Value IS
------------------------------------------------------------------------
--| Illustrates use of unconstrained array types
--| Author: Michael B. Feldman, The George Washington University
--| Last Modified: September 1995
------------------------------------------------------------------------

  TYPE ListType IS ARRAY(Integer RANGE <>) of Float;

  L1 : ListType(1..5);      -- 5 elements
  L2 : ListType(-4..3);     -- 8 elements

  -- local procedure to display the contents of a list

  PROCEDURE DisplayList(L: ListType) IS
  -- Pre: L is defined
  -- Post: display all values in the list

  BEGIN -- DisplayList

    FOR Count IN L'Range LOOP
      Ada.Float_Text_IO.Put(Item=>L(Count), Fore=>3, Aft=>1, Exp=>0);
    END LOOP;
    Ada.Text_IO.New_Line;

  END DisplayList;

  FUNCTION MaxValue(L: ListType) RETURN Float IS
  -- Pre: L is defined
  -- Post: returns the largest value stored in L

    CurrentMax : Float;

  BEGIN -- MaxValue

    CurrentMax := Float'First;      -- minimum value of Float

    FOR WhichElement IN L'Range LOOP
      IF L(WhichElement) > CurrentMax THEN
```

```
              CurrentMax := L(WhichElement);
          END IF;
      END LOOP;
      -- assert: CurrentMax contains the largest value in L

      RETURN CurrentMax;

  END MaxValue;

BEGIN -- Test_Max_Value

  L1 := (0.0, -5.7, 2.3, 5.9, 1.6);
  L2 := (3.1, -2.4, 0.0, -5.7, 8.0, 2.3, 5.9, 1.6);

  Ada.Text_IO.Put(Item=> "Testing MaxValue for float lists");
  Ada.Text_IO.New_Line;
  Ada.Text_IO.New_Line;
  Ada.Text_IO.Put(Item=> "Here is the list L1");
  Ada.Text_IO.New_Line;
  DisplayList(L => L1);

  Ada.Text_IO.Put(Item=> "The maximum value in this list is ");
  Ada.Float_Text_IO.Put(Item => MaxValue(L=>L1),
            Fore=>1, Aft=>2, Exp=>0);
  Ada.Text_IO.New_Line;
  Ada.Text_IO.New_Line;

  Ada.Text_IO.Put(Item=> "Here is the list L2");
  Ada.Text_IO.New_Line;
  DisplayList(L => L2);

  Ada.Text_IO.Put(Item=> "The maximum value in this list is ");
  Ada.Float_Text_IO.Put(Item => MaxValue(L=>L2),
            Fore=>1, Aft=>2, Exp=>0);
  Ada.Text_IO.New_Line;

END Test_Max_Value;
```

Slicing and Unconstrained Arrays

In Section 1.12, we studied array slicing in the context of strings. Slicing is actually
more general: It is available for *all* one-dimensional unconstrained arrays in Ada. For
example, given the function MaxValue from Program 4.1 and a float variable Y, it is
permissible to call MaxValue with a slice as its parameter, as in

```
Y := MaxValue(L => L2(0..2));
```

which would search only the given slice of the array for a maximum value. As an exercise, you can modify Program 4.1 to test this concept.

4.3 APPLICATION: A GENERAL SORTING PROGRAM

We have introduced the concept of sorting and sort algorithms in earlier chapters. The
utility of a sort procedure is greatly enhanced if it can be used with a wide variety of
arguments. In this section, we develop a sort that will work for arrays of the same

unconstrained type but differing bounds; in Chapter 5 we will exploit the full generality of Ada's generics to create a sort that will work with any unconstrained array type at all, regardless of its index type or element type.

Requirements

You are employed in the customer support department of a software company. The toll-free telephone system is open 7 days per week. Your supervisor is interested in knowing how many calls arrive each day, and also in seeing the data presented in ascending order. That is, the day with the fewest calls will appear first and the day with the most calls will appear last. Your supervisor might also wish to see only the data for weekdays or for weekend days.

Analysis and Design

Since you are experienced in data handling, you realize that this is basically a sorting problem, so you develop a sort program that will work with arrays of call records. The program should correctly handle arrays of one through seven elements, so that, for example, just the weekdays or just the weekend days can be sorted.

Here is a good application of unconstrained array types. Let us define the types.

```
TYPE Days IS (Mon, Tue, Wed, Thu, Fri, Sat, Sun);
SUBTYPE DayRange IS Natural RANGE 0..6;
TYPE CallRecord IS RECORD
  DayOfWeek    : Days;
  NumberOfCalls: Natural;
TYPE Callers IS ARRAY(DayRange RANGE <>) OF CallRecord;
```

and write a procedure `Exchange` that is capable of exchanging two elements of type `Natural`. The procedure `SelectSort` will implement a very simple sorting algorithm.

Algorithm

Fill each position in the array, starting from the beginning of the array, with the smallest element in the subarray from that position to the end. This can be refined to

```
FOR each position in the array LOOP
    Exchange the value at this position with the smallest value in the subarray from this
    position to the bottom.

END LOOP;
```

This can be further refined to

```
FOR each position PositionToFill in the array LOOP

    Set IndexOfMin to PositionToFill
```

FOR each position `ItemToCompare` from `PositionToFill` to bottom of array
`LOOP`

  `IF` value at `ItemToCompare` < value at `IndexOfMin` `THEN`

    Set `IndexOfMin` to `ItemToCompare`

   `END IF;`

 `END LOOP;`

 Exchange the values at `IndexOfMin` and `PositionToFill`.

`END LOOP;`

This is not a very efficient sorting method, but its simplicity makes it useful for this example, which is designed to show the array structure without concentrating on the sort method. What is its "big O"?

Coding

Program 4.2 shows the sort procedure `SelectSort`, together with auxiliary procedures `Exchange` and `DisplayCallers`. The main program declares three arrays of type `Callers` with differing bounds, and illustrates the sort procedure operating on the three arrays in turn. Note how the attributes are used in `SelectSort` to make the procedure independent of the bounds of the parameter.

Program 4.2 Sorting Arrays of Unconstrained Type

```
WITH Ada.Text_IO;
WITH Ada.Integer_Text_IO;
PROCEDURE Phone_Service IS
------------------------------------------------------------------------
--| Shows sorting of unconstrained arrays and slices
--| Author: Michael B. Feldman, The George Washington University
--| Last Modified: September 1995
------------------------------------------------------------------------
  SUBTYPE DayRange IS Natural  RANGE 0..6;
  SUBTYPE Weekdays IS DayRange RANGE 0..4;
  SUBTYPE Weekend  IS DayRange RANGE 5..6;

  TYPE Days IS (Mon, Tue, Wed, Thu, Fri, Sat, Sun);
  TYPE CallRecord IS RECORD
    DayOfWeek    : Days;
    NumberOfCalls: Natural;
  END RECORD;

  TYPE Callers IS ARRAY(DayRange RANGE <>) of CallRecord;

  PACKAGE Days_IO IS NEW Ada.Text_IO.Enumeration_IO(Enum => Days);

  ThisWeek:       Callers(DayRange);
  WeekdayCallers: Callers(Weekdays);
  WeekendCallers: Callers(Weekend);

  PROCEDURE DisplayCallers (List: Callers) IS
  -- Pre:  List is defined
  -- Post: display all elements in the vector
```

```
    BEGIN -- DisplayCallers
      FOR Count IN List'Range LOOP
        Days_IO.Put  (Item=>List(Count).DayOfWeek, Width=>3);
        Ada.Integer_Text_IO.Put
          (Item=>List(Count).NumberOfCalls, Width=>4);
        Ada.Text_IO.New_Line;
      END LOOP;
      Ada.Text_IO.New_Line;
    END DisplayCallers;

    PROCEDURE Exchange(Value1, Value2: IN OUT CallRecord) IS
    -- Pre:  Value1 and Value2 are defined
    -- Post: Value1 and Value2 are interchanged

      TempValue: CallRecord;

    BEGIN -- Exchange
      TempValue := Value1;
      Value1    := Value2;
      Value2    := TempValue;
    END Exchange;

    PROCEDURE SelectSort(List: IN OUT Callers) IS
    -- Pre:  List is defined
    -- Post: elements of List are arranged in ascending order

      IndexOfMin: DayRange;

    BEGIN

      FOR PositionToFill IN List'First..List'Last -- 1 LOOP

        -- Find the element in subarray 1..PositionToFill
        -- with smallest value
        IndexOfMin := PositionToFill;

        FOR ItemToCompare IN PositionToFill + 1..List'Last LOOP
          IF List(ItemToCompare).NumberOfCalls
           < List(IndexOfMin).NumberOfCalls THEN
            IndexOfMin := ItemToCompare;
          END IF;
        END LOOP;
        -- assert: element at List(PositionToFill) is
        -- smallest in subarray

        IF IndexOfMin /= PositionToFill THEN
          Exchange(List(PositionToFill),List(IndexOfMin));
        END IF;

      END LOOP;

    END SelectSort;

BEGIN -- Phone_Service

  ThisWeek := ((Mon, 12), (Tue, 23), (Wed, 100), (Thu, 40),
               (Fri, 52), (Sat, 17), (Sun,    2));
  WeekdayCallers := ThisWeek(Weekdays);
  WeekendCallers := ThisWeek(Weekend);

  Ada.Text_IO.Put(Item=> "Testing SelectSort for telephone callers ");
  Ada.Text_IO.New_Line;
  Ada.Text_IO.Put(Item=> "Here is ThisWeek before sorting.");
  Ada.Text_IO.New_Line;
  DisplayCallers(List => ThisWeek);
  Ada.Text_IO.New_Line;
```

```
      SelectSort(List => ThisWeek);
      Ada.Text_IO.Put(Item=> "Here is ThisWeek after upward sorting.");
      Ada.Text_IO.New_Line;
      DisplayCallers(List => ThisWeek);
      Ada.Text_IO.New_Line;

      Ada.Text_IO.Put(Item=> "Here is WeekdayCallers before sorting.");
      Ada.Text_IO.New_Line;
      DisplayCallers(List => WeekdayCallers);
      Ada.Text_IO.New_Line;

      SelectSort(List => WeekdayCallers);
      Ada.Text_IO.Put
        (Item=> "Here is WeekdayCallers after upward sorting.");
      Ada.Text_IO.New_Line;
      DisplayCallers(List => WeekdayCallers);
      Ada.Text_IO.New_Line;

      Ada.Text_IO.Put
        (Item=> "Here is WeekendCallers before sorting.");
      Ada.Text_IO.New_Line;
      DisplayCallers(List => WeekendCallers);
      Ada.Text_IO.New_Line;

      SelectSort(List => WeekendCallers);
      Ada.Text_IO.Put
        (Item=> "Here is WeekendCallers after upward sorting.");
      Ada.Text_IO.New_Line;
      DisplayCallers(List => WeekendCallers);
      Ada.Text_IO.New_Line;

END Phone_Service;
```

4.4   ADT DESIGN: MATHEMATICAL VECTORS

Many of the first computers, developed in the 1940s and 1950s, were intended chiefly for the solution of scientific and engineering—that is, mathematical—problems. Indeed, the first devices resembling what we would call digital computers—built in the mid-1940s—were designed mainly to perform calculations that led to the tables used for artillery control. Later it was realized that computers could be very powerful in data processing and in other less mathematical applications such as language translation, large-scale information systems, and so on.

In the mid-1950s, when an alternative was sought to coding mathematical problems in machine language, Fortran was developed by John Backus and his team at IBM. Given the predominance of vectors and matrices in mathematical problems, it is not surprising that the Formula Translator—Fortran—embodied support for these in the form of what were (and still are) called arrays. The single- and multidimensional arrays of Fortran are implementations of the mathematical abstractions of vectors, matrices, and tensors (three-dimensional matrices); they serve as the models for similar implementations in Fortran's successor languages: Algol, PL/I, Basic, Pascal, and, of course, Ada. We have seen many uses for arrays, but their origins were in mathematics.

A *vector* of N components is a set of N values that is ordered in the sense that each value is assigned a specific "position" in the set. For example, the vector $U = <3, 5, -1>$ is different from the vector $V = <5, -1, 3>$: They both have the same set of values, but the values appear in different orders. Generally, we implement vectors through the use of one-dimensional arrays.

It is important to realize that the type of a vector's elements need not be scalar or even numerical, although integers and floats are the types seen most frequently in engineering problems. In Ada, we could, of course, also have vectors of rational numbers.

Requirements

Develop a means of performing arithmetic on mathematical vectors.

Analysis

Mathematicians have defined a number of standard operations on vectors. Among these are several we will study here. In each case, we assume that U and V are vectors with the same element type and number of components; designate the element type as *ElementType* and the index range, or bounds, of the vectors by the range $R_{min}..R_{max}$.

The *vector sum* of U and V, written $U + V$, is a vector T with bounds $R_{min}..R_{max}$ such that, for each r in the range $R_{min}..R_{max}$

$$T_r = U_r + V_r$$

That is, the components of the two vectors are added pairwise.

The *inner product* of U and V, written $U \cdot V$ and sometimes called the *scalar product* or *dot product*, is a value of type `ElementType`, whose value is the sum of all the pairwise products

$$U_r \times V_r$$

taken over all the components. This operation is called the scalar product because the result is a scalar value—that is, a single value of type `ElementType`.

The *sum of V with a scalar K*, written $K + V$, is a vector T, with the same bounds as V, whose components have values

$$T_r = K + V_r$$

The *product of V by a scalar K*, written $K \times V$, is a vector T, with the same bounds as V, whose components have values

$$T_r = K \times V_r$$

Design of the Vector Package

We will develop `Vectors` as an ADT package, listing the operations above in the specification and implementing them in the package body. We can use an unconstrained array type for the vectors, so that our vector operations can deal with vectors of differing sizes at different times.

```
TYPE Vector IS ARRAY (Integer RANGE <>) OF Float;
```

Now we can declare `Vector` variables such as

```
V: Vector(1..5);
Q: Vector(-5..6);
```

and they'll have the proper dimensions.
Program 4.3 shows the package specification for `Vectors`.

Program 4.3 Specification for `Vectors` Package

```
PACKAGE Vectors IS
--------------------------------------------------------------------------
--| Specification for vector arithmetic package
--| Author: Michael B. Feldman, The George Washington University
--| Last Modified: October 1995
--------------------------------------------------------------------------

  TYPE Vector IS ARRAY(Integer RANGE <>) OF Float;

  -- exported exception, raised if two vectors are not conformable
  -- (i.e., have different bounds)

  Bounds_Error : EXCEPTION;

  FUNCTION "+" (K : Float; Right : Vector) RETURN Vector;
  -- Pre:  K and Right are defined
  -- Post: returns the sum of the vector and the scalar
  --    Result(i) := K + Right(i)

  FUNCTION "*" (K : Float; Right : Vector) RETURN Vector;
  -- Pre:  K and Right are defined
  -- Post: returns the product of the vector and the scalar
  --    Result(i) := K * Right(i)

  FUNCTION "*" (Left, Right : Vector) RETURN Float;
  -- Pre:    Left and Right are defined
  -- Post:   returns the inner product of Left and Right
  -- Raises: Bounds_Error if Left and Right have different bounds

  FUNCTION "+" (Left, Right : Vector) RETURN Vector;
  -- Pre:    Left and Right are defined
  -- Post:   returns the sum of Left and Right
  --    result(i) := Left(i) + Right(i)
  -- Raises: Bounds_Error if Left and Right have different bounds

END Vectors;
```

The `Vector` type is not defined as private because we wish to allow client programs access to the individual vector components in the usual array-referencing way. If the type were private, that access would be forbidden! The operations are specified as Ada operator symbols, which will allow a client program to write

```
V3 := V2 + V1;
```

for example, just as a mathematician would. An exception `Bounds_Error` is provided by the package, because the vector addition and inner-product operations make no sense if their vector operands do not have the same bounds. This precondition will have to be checked in the bodies of these operations; if it is not met, `Bounds_Error` is raised to the client program.

Coding the Body of `Vectors`

The body of `Vectors` is shown in Program 4.4. Notice in the scalar addition operation how a vector is created to hold the result: The construct `Right'Range` is another way to write the longer form `Right'First..Right'Last`. When the result vector is returned to the calling program, there must be a vector there of the proper size to hold it; otherwise, `Constraint_Error` is raised as usual.

Program 4.4 Body for `Vectors` Package

```
PACKAGE BODY Vectors IS
-------------------------------------------------------------------------
--| Body of Vectors package
--| Author: Michael B. Feldman, The George Washington University
--| Last Modified: October 1995
-------------------------------------------------------------------------

  FUNCTION "+" (K : Float; Right : Vector) RETURN Vector IS
    Result : Vector(Right'Range);
  BEGIN
    FOR R IN Right'Range LOOP
      Result(R) := K + Right(R);
    END LOOP;

    RETURN Result;
  END "+";

  FUNCTION "*" (K : Float; Right : Vector) RETURN Vector IS
  BEGIN -- stub
    RETURN Right;
  END "*";

  FUNCTION "+" (Left, Right : Vector) RETURN Vector IS
    Result : Vector(Left'Range);
  BEGIN
    -- First check for conformability
    IF Left'First = Right'First AND
       Left'Last  = Right'Last  THEN

    -- if conformable, go on to compute
      FOR R IN Left'Range LOOP
        Result(R) := Left(R) + Right(R);
      END LOOP;

      RETURN Result;
```

```
      ELSE
        RAISE Bounds_Error;
      END IF;
  END "+";

  FUNCTION "*" (Left, Right : Vector) RETURN Float IS
    Sum : Float;
  BEGIN -- stub
    RETURN 0.0;
  END "*";

END Vectors;
```

The scalar-multiplication and inner-product operations are left as stubs for you to complete as an exercise.

Program 4.5 shows a test program for the vector operations. The last test attempts to add two vectors with dissimilar bounds; the exception `Vectors.Bounds_Error` should be raised when this case is executed.

Program 4.5 Using the `Vectors` Package

```
WITH Ada.Text_IO;
WITH Ada.Float_Text_IO;
WITH Vectors;
USE TYPE Vectors.Vector;
PROCEDURE Test_Vectors IS
------------------------------------------------------------------------
--| Example of use of Vector operations
--| Author: Michael B. Feldman, The George Washington University
--| Last Modified: October 1995
------------------------------------------------------------------------

  V1: Vectors.Vector(1..4) := (1.0, 0.0, -2.0, 3.0);
  V2: Vectors.Vector(1..4) := (0.0, -5.0, 3.0, 1.0);
  V3: Vectors.Vector(1..3) := (1.0, 2.0, 3.0);
  V4: Vectors.Vector(1..4);

  PROCEDURE DisplayVector(V: Vectors.Vector) IS
  BEGIN
    FOR Component IN V'First..V'Last LOOP
      Ada.Float_Text_IO.Put
      (Item => V(Component), Fore=>5, Aft=>2, Exp=>0);
    END LOOP;
  END DisplayVector;

BEGIN -- Test_Vectors
  Ada.Text_IO.Put(Item => "V1      = ");
  DisplayVector(V => V1);
  Ada.Text_IO.New_Line;

  Ada.Text_IO.Put(Item => "V2      = ");
  DisplayVector(V => V2);
  Ada.Text_IO.New_Line;

  Ada.Text_IO.Put(Item => "V3      = ");
  DisplayVector(V => V3);
  Ada.Text_IO.New_Line;

  V4 := 3.0 + V1;
```

```
     Ada.Text_IO.Put(Item => "3.0 + V1 = ");
     DisplayVector(V => V4);
     Ada.Text_IO.New_Line;

     V4 := V1 + V2;

     Ada.Text_IO.Put(Item => "V1 + V2  = ");
     DisplayVector(V => V4);
     Ada.Text_IO.New_Line;

     Ada.Text_IO.Put(Item => "V1 * V2  = ");
     Ada.Float_Text_IO.Put(Item => V1 * V2, Fore=>1, Aft=>2, Exp=>0);
     Ada.Text_IO.New_Line;

     V4 := V1 + V3;    -- should raise exception!

END Test_Vectors;
```

The `Vectors` package is somewhat oversimplified. In ordinary mathematics, two vectors can be added if they have the same lengths but different bounds. Also, ordinarily the scalar-vector addition can be written with the scalar on either side of the addition operator. In Ada, since the compiler cannot understand the intention of an infix operator, if we wish the scalar to appear on either side we must provide two operators. As an exercise, you can modify our `Vectors` package to accommodate this mathematical realism.

4.5   ADT DESIGN: MATHEMATICAL MATRICES

So far, we have seen unconstrained array types with only one dimension. Now we will examine multidimensional unconstrained array types. These are useful in representing tables or mathematical matrices of varying size. As an example, we will consider matrices. Matrix operations can be written in a manner similar to that for vector ones, using a type definition such as

```
TYPE Matrix IS ARRAY (Integer RANGE <>, Integer RANGE <>) OF Float;
```

The two occurrences of the "box" symbol allow (and require) both sets of bounds to be specified when variables are declared. The specification for a package `Matrices` is shown as Program 4.6.

Program 4.6 Specification for Matrix Package

```
PACKAGE Matrices IS
-----------------------------------------------------------------------
--| Specification for package Matrices
--| Author: Michael B. Feldman, The George Washington University
--| Last Modified: October 1995
-----------------------------------------------------------------------

  TYPE Matrix IS ARRAY(Integer RANGE <>, Integer RANGE <>) OF Float;

  -- exported exception, raised if two matrices are not conformable
  Bounds_Error : EXCEPTION;

  FUNCTION "+" (K : IN Float; M : IN Matrix) RETURN Matrix;
  -- adds a scalar to a matrix
  -- Pre: K and M are defined
  -- Post: returns the sum of the scalar and the matrix
  --    Result(i,j) := K + M(i,j)
```

```
FUNCTION "*" (K : IN Float; M : IN Matrix) RETURN Matrix;
-- multiplies a matrix by a scalar
-- Pre: K and M are defined
-- Post: returns the product of the scalar and the matrix
--    Result(i,j) := K * M(i,j)

FUNCTION "+" (Left, Right : IN Matrix) RETURN Matrix;
-- finds the sum of two matrices
-- Pre: Left and Right are defined and have the same bounds
-- Post: returns the sum of Left and Right
--    Result(i,j) := Left(i,j) + Right(i,j)
--    Raises Bounds_Error if the matrices are not conformable

FUNCTION "*"(Left, Right : IN Matrix) RETURN Matrix;
-- finds the product of two matrices
-- Pre: Left and Right are defined
--    and Left's column bounds agree with Right's row bounds
-- Post: returns the product of Left and Right
--    Raises Bounds_Error if the matrices are not conformable

FUNCTION Transpose(M : IN Matrix) RETURN Matrix;
-- finds the transpose of a matrix
-- Pre: M is defined
-- Post: returns a matrix such that Result(i,j) = M(j,i)
--    Result has M's bounds, interchanged

END Matrices;
```

Assuming M and N are matrices with the same bounds and K is a scalar, the operators $M + N$, $K + M$ and $K \times M$ are similar to their counterparts in the vector case. In the case of matrix addition, the precondition that the matrices must have matching bounds must be checked by the operators.

Here is the code for the matrix sum operation:

```
FUNCTION "+" (K : ElementType; M : IN Matrix) RETURN Matrix IS

  Result : Matrix(M'Range(1), M'Range(2));

BEGIN

  FOR R IN M'Range(1) LOOP
    FOR C IN M'Range(2) LOOP
      Result(R, C) := K + Right(R, C);
    END LOOP;
  END LOOP;

  RETURN Result;

END "+";
```

Notice the attributes used to establish the bounds of the parameter and the result: `M'First(1)` means "the low bound of the first dimension"; `M'Last(2)` means "the high bound of the second dimension." The construct `M'Range(1)` is another way to write `M'First(1)..M'Last(1)`. For multidimensional arrays, the "dimension number" must be given; for one-dimensional arrays, no "dimension number" is required or permitted.

Mathematically, the *transpose* of a matrix, T, returns a matrix whose second dimension is the same as M's first dimension, and whose first dimension is the same as M's second dimension. For all row and column values r and c, $T_{rc} = M_{cr}$.

The definition of matrix multiplication $M \times N$, common in many applications, is not as obvious as the others. The precondition for multiplication is that the second bounds of M must be the same as the first bounds of N (M must have as many columns as N has rows). The product is a matrix P, with M's row bounds and N's column bounds. So if M has bounds (1..5, –3..0) and N has bounds (–3..0, 6..8) then $M \times N$ has bounds (1..5, 6..8). Each element of P, designated P_{rc}, is given by the formula

$$P_{rc} = \sum_k M_{rk} \times N_{kc}$$

where the index k ranges over the columns of M. Writing and testing the package body for `Matrices` is left as an exercise.

4.6   STORAGE MAPPINGS

An interesting study in abstraction versus implementation is provided by the *storage mappings* used for one-dimensional and multidimensional arrays. A storage mapping is a formula that maps the abstraction of an array onto the storage units of the underlying hardware.

In this section, we discuss storage mappings in a general way; there are a few Ada declarations here, but the discussion is intended to show you how languages in general handle the array question. Also, although for simplicity we use numerical array elements and integer subscripts in these examples, nearly everything we say in this section generalizes both to enumeration subscript types and to array elements of arbitrary type.

One-Dimensional Arrays

Consider the declaration

```
T: ARRAY(1..10) OF Integer;
```

This declaration indicates that the compiler is to set aside space for 10 integer values and that the valid range of subscripts into the resulting array is 1, 2, . . . , 10. (Declaring an array type, then declaring T to be a variable of that type, has the same effect and is usually considered better Ada style; in this section, we use the simpler form given above for brevity.)

Once the array declaration has been elaborated at execution time, we know that we can carry out two operations on array elements: We can store a value, as in the assignment `T(2) := 3`, or we can retrieve a previously stored value, as in the assignment `Y := T(2)`. We could just as well have stored or retrieved using a variable as the subscript, as in `T(I) := 3`, as long as we made certain that at the time the statement was executed I had a value in the range 1 thru 10.

These array element operations are familiar; why belabor them here? The point is that there are really two separate operations involved—a storage operation and a retrieval operation—even though Ada, like most programming languages, permits the same array-element-referencing syntax to be used on either side of the assignment operator. These two abstract operations have been implemented in a way that is syntactically convenient and intuitively comfortable.

What sort of machine instructions would a compiler have to produce in order to support subscripting in array element operations? When an array is declared, space is reserved for as many elements as are requested by the declaration. How much space is this? It depends, in fact, on the type of the array elements and the basic storage unit of the computer.

For example, some computers represent an integer as one 16-bit word and a floating-point number as two words, or 32 bits. In that sort of computer, an array of 100 floating-point numbers will require 200 16-bit words of memory. In other computers, space is allocated in 8-bit bytes rather than in 16-bit words; the same array requires 400 bytes, because floating-point numbers in that machine occupy 4 bytes each.

Similarly, an array of one hundred 200-character student records, including name, address, course grades, etc., would require a total of 20,000 bytes.

When the space has been allocated, the compiler must generate certain instructions that encode the relationship between a subscript reference such as `A(i)` and the internal storage in the particular computer involved. This relationship is called the *storage mapping*, or sometimes the *storage mapping function*.

Letting add(`T`) be the machine address of the first storage unit (byte, word, or other unit) of the array, and NUNITS be the number of storage units per array element, what is the storage mapping for an array such as `T`, above? We need a formula that tells us how many elements to "skip over" in order to reach the *i*-th one. Clearly we need to skip over $i - 1$ of them. So the address of `T(i)` is in fact

$$\text{add}(T) + (i - 1) \times \text{NUNITS}$$

Is this formula correct? Consider a 4-byte float in a computer in which addressing is done byte-by-byte, so NUNITS = 4. The address of `T(1)` is in fact simply add(`T`) because the second term drops out; the address of `T(2)` is add(`T`) + 4, and so on.

The array `T` is really a special case, since the lowest subscript value is 1. In the more general situation, the only restriction on the lowest value is that it cannot be greater than the highest subscript value. These two values are usually called the *range* of the subscripts.

Under the more general scheme, what should the storage mapping look like? Call the lowest subscript value `First`, and the highest `Last`. Then assuming we declare

```
T: ARRAY(First..Last) OF Float;
```

we will need (`Last` − `First` + 1) × NUNITS of space, such that `T(First)` maps to add(`T`). To get to an arbitrary `T(i)`, how many elements do we need to skip over? It is `i` − `First` elements.

To see this, suppose that `First` = 3 and `Last` = 10, as in

```
T: ARRAY(3..10) OF Float;
```

Clearly eight elements will be required, each NUNITS long; to get to `T(5)`, say, we need to skip elements 3 and 4, which is $5 - 3 = 2$ elements. To get to the first element `T(3)`, we skip no elements ($3 - 3 = 0$). So our storage mapping becomes

$$T(i) \text{ maps to add}(T) + (i - \text{First}) \text{ NUNITS}$$

Notice, by the way, that this is perfectly consistent with the special case used in Fortran-66: In that language, First = 1 always. It also works even if First and/or Last are negative. Let us try finding the storage mapping for NUNITS = 4 and the declaration

```
T: ARRAY(-5..7) OF Float;
```

This will require $7 - (-5) + 1$ 4-byte elements, or 52 bytes; T(i) maps to add(T) $+ (i - (-5)) \times 4$ or add(T) $+ (i + 5) \times 4$. Then T(-5) maps to add(T); T(0) maps to add(T) + 20 (we've skipped over five elements!) and so on. This arrangement is shown in Figure 4.4.

A brief aside: There is nothing sacred about mapping the lowest-subscripted element to add(T); indeed, in some computers, such as the Hewlett-Packard HP-3000, the hardware design is such that add(T) maps most conveniently to the zeroth element, so elements with negative and positive subscripts are said to lie below and above the zero point, respectively. Even if there is no zeroth element, add(T) is mapped to the place where it would be located if there were one. For uniformity in this book, we shall retain the convention that the lowest-subscripted element maps to add(T).

Another aside: Some earlier programming languages restricted the low bound of an array subscript. In Fortran-66, the low bound was required to be 1; in many versions of BASIC it was required to be 0, and, indeed, arrays in C are assumed to have a low bound of 0.

Two-Dimensional Arrays

An R × C array M is said to have R *rows* and C *columns*, and then refer to any particular element in the array by using two subscripts r and c in an expression M(r,c). Note that if we were to view M pictorially, as in Figure 4.5, the rows would be oriented horizontally, the columns vertically, and the subscript reference would give the row subscript first. (There is nothing sacred about this view; it is just a convention to help us visualize the array.)

As in the one-dimensional case, we have an abstraction *2-D Array*, implemented in most programming languages by the feature that allows us to declare two-dimensional arrays and to store and retrieve elements in them in the form M(r,c). How do compilers implement this abstraction?

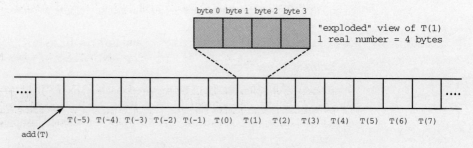

Figure 4.4 Storage Allocation in Linear Memory for T: ARRAY(-5..7) OF Float.

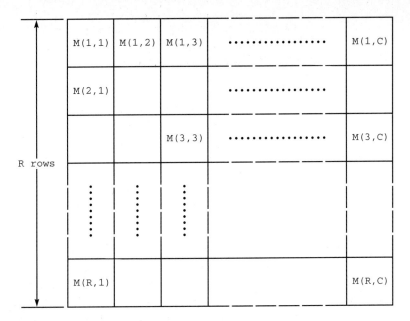

Figure 4.5 Abstract View of a Rectangular Array

Memory in most computers is organized logically in linear fashion, with the addresses of the storage units (words or bytes) running in a single increasing sequence. Therefore, a structure with two dimensions has to be mapped onto a structure with only one dimension. Programming languages often implement the abstraction *2-D Array* in a form called *row-major*, in which the two-dimensional array is stored row by row in linear memory, as shown in Figure 4.6.

That this is not the only way to do it is evidenced by the column-major scheme in Fortran, in which a two-dimensional array is stored column by column. This is shown for the same array in Figure 4.7.

What is the storage mapping function for a two-dimensional array stored in row-major form? As before, let us begin with the familiar case in which the rows and columns are numbered `1..R` and `1..C` respectively. Since the array is stored row by row, to reach any element in the `r`-th row we need to "skip over" `r - 1` rows; then to reach the c-th element in the `r`-th row, we need to "skip over" `c - 1` elements. Each row has `C` elements; each element requires NUNITS of storage. Thus, the mapping function is

$$\texttt{M(r,c)} \text{ maps to add(M)} + (\texttt{r} - 1)\texttt{C} \times \text{NUNITS} + (\texttt{c} - 1) \times \text{NUNITS}$$

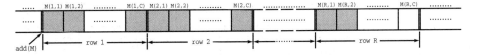

Figure 4.6 Row-Major Implementation of Rectangular Array in Linear Memory

Figure 4.7 Column-Major Implementation of Rectangular Array in Linear Memory

Letting NUNITS = 4 as above (for, say, a four-byte float), for the 5×6 array in Figure 4.8, 120 bytes of storage are needed.

M(1, 1) maps to add(M) + 0.

M(5, 6) maps to add(M) + $4 \times 6 \times 4 + 5 \times 4$ = add(M) + 116.

M(3, 2) maps to add(M) + $2 \times 6 \times 4 + 1 \times 4$ = add(M) + 52.

```
M: ARRAY (1..5,1..6) of float
```

(a) Declaration

1.0	-3.5	7.4	2.0	-4.5	0.0
-4.6	0.0	1.0	2.3	-1.5	1.0
-2.2	-1.0	2.0	0.0	-5.72	0.0
-5.0	1.0	-2.1	3.0	2.3	-4.0
0.0	4.35	3.6	1.0	0.0	1.0

(b) Abstract view

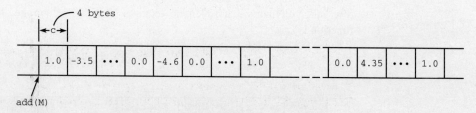

(c) Row-major implementation in linear memory (note real numbers are stored as 4-byte floating point)

Figure 4.8 Abstraction and Implementation of a 5×6 Array of Float Values

As in the one-dimensional case, we can generalize this idea to permit subscripts to have an arbitrary integer range, as in Pascal or Ada (or Fortran-77, for that matter). Consider, then, the declaration in Ada

```
M: ARRAY(FirstR..LastR, FirstC..LastC) OF Float;
```

The details of the row-major storage mapping function are left as an exercise, as is the question of developing a storage mapping for two-dimensional arrays implemented, as in Fortran, in column-major form.

Higher-Dimensional Arrays

There is often a need in programming problems to work with arrays of higher dimension than 2, and most programming languages support a feature to permit up to some fairly large number of subscripts.

How is this facility implemented? It is a generalization of the two-dimensional case. Considering three-dimensional arrays, for example, the third dimension is conventionally called a plane, and the new subscript is conventionally added before the one for a row. So the Ada declaration

```
A: ARRAY(1..4,1..5,1..6) OF Float;
```

would be interpreted as an array with four planes, each having five rows and six columns. A reference $A(p,r,c)$ would then be interpreted as that element at the intersection of the pth plane, rth row, and cth column.

As in the two-dimensional case, this abstract structure is then mapped onto linear storage in either row-major or column-major fashion. In row-major form, we reach the element $A(p,r,c)$ by skipping over $p-1$ planes to reach the pth plane, then $r-1$ rows to reach the rth row, then $c-1$ elements (each in a column) to reach the cth element. In column-major form, we imagine first skipping over $c-1$ columns to reach the cth column, then $r-1$ rows to reach the rth row, then $p-1$ elements (each in a plane) to reach the pth element. These schemes are illustrated in Figure 4.9, for the case of an array $A(-1..1,0..3,5..6)$.

Obtaining storage mapping functions for this case and for higher dimensionality is left as a set of exercises. The general idea is that in any row-major scheme, of whatever dimension, the leftmost subscript varies most slowly; in any column-major scheme, the rightmost subscript varies most slowly.

The Ada Standard Does Not Specify Storage Mappings

As mentioned above, programming-language reference manuals have generally specified a required storage mapping. Fortran (in all its versions) has specified a column-major mapping; PL/I, Pascal, and C all use row-major.

Alone among popular languages, Ada does not specify any particular array storage mapping. The Ada standard in general takes no position on the details of how storage is to be allocated, instead leaving this task to compiler implementers, who are most

```
M: ARRAY (-1..1,0..3,5..6)
```

(a) Declaration

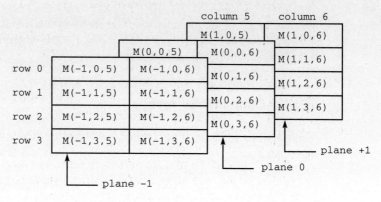

(b) Abstract view

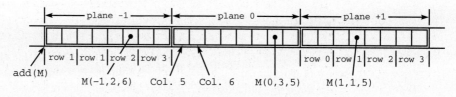

(c) Row-major implementation

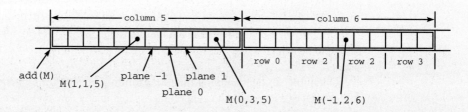

(d) Column-major implementation

Figure 4.9 Abstraction and Implementation of a Three-Dimensional Array in Linear Memory

familiar with the underlying hardware for which their products produce code. A programmer in a high-level language rarely needs to make explicit use of a storage mapping, so finding appropriate mappings is likely to be done closer to optimally when they are not overspecified in the standard.

To see how this can be a real advantage, consider an Ada program that must call a procedure written in another language, passing to the procedure a multidimensional array. If the two storage mappings agree, then the array will "make sense" both to the Ada caller and to the foreign-language procedure. Otherwise, the calling program must make a large effort to transpose the array.

Storage-mapping problems caused much difficulty in the 1960s, when PL/I proponents advocated writing new programs in PL/I to interface with older Fortran subprograms. Whenever multidimensional arrays were involved, there was trouble: PL/I required row-major mapping, whereas Fortran required column-major. Indeed, storage mapping-incompatibility is sometimes cited as a major factor in the failure of PL/I to replace Fortran as a science and engineering language.

In theory, this interfacing problem is relatively easy to solve with Ada: A compiler designed so that programs can interface easily with a row-major language is quite free to use a row-major mapping; to interface with Fortran, an Ada compiler is perfectly free to use a column-major mapping. Indeed, the same compiler is free to use different mappings for different array types.

In practice, this has not happened with Ada compilers, which almost universally use row-major mappings. Also, aggregate assignments to multidimensional arrays are written *as if* the mapping were row-major—for instance,

```
SomeArray := (OTHERS => (OTHERS => 0.0));
```

Although the Ada standard does not require *all* compilers to use the same storage mapping, or other storage allocations, you can always find out how a *specific* compiler handles these by consulting the programming guide supplied with that compiler.

It is interesting to note that the Ada 95 standard specifies, in Annex B, an interface to Fortran (along with others to Cobol and to C) allowing the programmer to specify that an array type be stored according to the Fortran conventions. The details of this are beyond the scope of this text; if you are interested in storage mappings or interfacing to other languages, you are invited to consult the Ada 95 LRM.

A consequence of the Ada standard's not specifying a storage mapping for multidimensional arrays is that although it is perfectly permissible to declare an Ada array type whose element type also happens to be an array type, such a type is *not* equivalent to a two-dimensional array type. Contrast this with the situation in Pascal, for example, in which a two-dimensional array is *by definition* the same as a one-dimensional array of one-dimensional arrays. This necessarily implies a row-major mapping. The situation in C is very similar to that in Pascal.

One final comment on array storage mappings: Row- and column-major mappings are not the only ones possible. Indeed, in Chapter 12, Exercise 6, you will find some discussion of an interesting tree-structured storage mapping.

SUMMARY

Multidimensional arrays have been introduced in this chapter. Nested loops are needed to manipulate the elements of a mutidimensional array in a systematic way. The correspondence between the loop-control variables and the array subscripts determines the order in which the array elements are processed.

Also introduced in this chapter were unconstrained array types, as illustrated by general sorting, mathematical vectors, and mathematical matrices.

Finally, array storage mappings were discussed, to illustrate how array abstractions are implemented in computer memory.

EXERCISES

1. A certain city has just held an election. The results from the mayor's race have been reported by each precinct (neighborhood) as follows:

Precinct	Candidate A	Candidate B	Candidate C	Candidate D
1	192	48	206	37
2	147	90	312	21
3	186	12	121	38
4	114	21	408	39
5	267	13	382	29

Write a program to do the following:
a. Display the table with appropriate headings for the rows and columns.
b. Compute and display the total number of votes, and the percentage of the total votes cast, received by each candidate.
c. If any one candidate received over 50% of the votes, the program should print a message declaring that candidate the winner.
d. If no candidate received 50% of the votes, the program should print a message declaring a runoff between the two candidates receiving the highest number of votes; the two candidates should be identified by their one-letter designations.
e. Run the program once with the data given in the table and once with Candidate C receiving only 108 votes in Precinct 4.

2. Write a program that reads the five cards representing a poker hand into a two-dimensional array (first dimension, suit; second dimension, rank). Evaluate the poker hand by determining whether the hand is a flush (all one suit), a straight (five cards with consecutive ranks), a straight flush (five consecutive cards of one suit), four of one rank, a full house (three of one rank, two of another), three of one rank, two pair, or one pair.

3. Do Problem 2, but represent a card as a record with two fields representing the suit and the rank, and a poker hand as a one-dimensional array of these records. Contrast the new solution with that of problem 2. Which representation of the poker hand do you find more natural?

4. Modify Program 4.4 to call MaxValue with parameters L1(2..4), L2(0..2), and L2(-4..-1). Ascertain that the program correctly finds the given maximum values.

5. Complete and test the body of the Vectors package given in Program 4.4.

6. Suppose that *V* is a vector and *X* is a scalar. Mathematically, the operations on a vector and a scalar are commutative; that is, $V + X$ and $X + V$ give the same result, as do $V \times X$ and $X \times V$. The `Vectors` package would be more useful if the corresponding operators were made commutative. This can be done in Ada using additional overloaded operators. Revise the `Vectors` package to allow these commutative operators.

7. A mathematician, looking at our `Vectors` package, would probably say that we have used an excessively strong requirement for conformability. In fact, it is not necessary that two vectors have the same *bounds* to be conformable; they need only have the same *lengths*. Revise and test `Vectors` to make it more satisfactory to mathematicians.

8. Complete and test the `Matrices` package of Section 4.5.

9. Obtain a detailed storage mapping function for a two-dimensional array stored in row-major form.

10. Obtain a detailed storage mapping function for a two-dimensional array stored in column-major form.

11. Obtain a detailed storage mapping function for a three-dimensional array stored in row-major form.

12. Obtain a detailed storage mapping function for a three-dimensional array stored in column-major form.

13. Obtain a general storage mapping function for an array of D dimensions stored in row-major form.

14. Obtain a general storage mapping function for an array of D dimensions stored in column-major form.

15. To understand the value of the Ada 95 interface to Fortran, suppose that it did not exist, and that a specific Ada compiler stores multi-dimensional arrays in row-major form. We know that Fortran stores them in column-major form. Suppose an Ada program creates a three-dimensional array, then needs to pass it to a subroutine written in Fortran. Assume that in both languages, subroutine linkage arrangements just pass the address of the array, thus the same physical copy of the array is used by both programs. A reference to, say `M(1,5,4)` in the Ada program refers to a *different* physical location from that referred to by the same reference in the Fortran program. What has to be done to make the two languages communicate better? Write whatever programs you need.

CHAPTER 5

Generic Subprograms and Packages

This chapter introduces you to an important feature of Ada that makes the language extremely useful for developing reusable software components: generics. A *generic component* (package or subprogram) is one that is parametrized at the level of the types it works with. There are generic formal and actual parameters, just like the "normal" ones we use with subprograms and variant records. A generic component can be instantiated or "tailored" to work with a specific type. This means that a very general program or package can be written whose code is independent of the type it manipulates. Versions of it can be created, using a single statement for each version, to handle many different types.

This chapter shows you how to create your own generics and tailor them for many interesting purposes; the remaining chapters of this book introduce many other generic units. Through the careful design of generic units, an entire industry of reusable, tailorable software components can be built up and used for a wide range of applications.

5.1 ADA STRUCTURES: GENERIC UNITS

Ada's system of types and procedures requires that the type of a procedure's actual parameter always match that of the formal parameter. This means that a procedure or function that needs to do the same thing to values of two different types must be written twice—once for each type. Consider the procedure `Exchange`:

```
PROCEDURE Exchange(Value1, Value2: IN OUT Natural) IS
  TempValue: Natural;
BEGIN
  TempValue := Value1;
  Value1    := Value2;
  Value2    := TempValue;
END Exchange;
```

A procedure to exchange two `Float` values would have the same sequence of statements, but the type references would be different:

```
PROCEDURE Exchange(Value1, Value2: IN OUT Float) IS
  TempValue: Float;
BEGIN
  TempValue := Value1;
  Value1    := Value2;
  Value2    := TempValue;
END Exchange;
```

Obviously, we could modify the first version to give the second version by using an editor. Because we are likely to need the `Natural` version again, we modify a copy of it. This gives two versions of a procedure that are almost the same; because of overloading, the two can both be called `Exchange`. Carrying this to its extreme, we could build up a large library of `Exchange` programs with our editor and be ready for any eventuality. `Exchange` could even be made to work with array or record structures, because Ada allows assignment for any type.

There is a problem with this approach: It clutters our file system with a large number of similar programs. Worse still, suppose that a bug turns up in the statements for `Exchange` or in another program with more complexity. The bug will have turned up in *one* of the versions; the same bug will probably be present in all of them, but we will probably forget to fix all the others! This is, in miniature, a problem long faced by industry: multiple versions of a program, all similar but not exactly alike, all requiring debugging and other maintenance.

Returning to our simple example, it would be nice if we could create *one* version of `Exchange`, test it, and then put it in the library. When we needed a version to work with a particular type, we could just tell the compiler to use our pretested `Exchange` but to change the type it accepts. The compiler would make the change automatically, and we would still have only a single copy of the procedure to maintain.

It happens that Ada allows us to do exactly this. The solution to this problem is *generics*. A generic unit is a *recipe*, or *template*, for a procedure, function, or package. Such a unit is declared with *formal parameters* that are *types*, and sometimes are *procedure* or *function names*. An analogy can be drawn with an unusual recipe for a layer cake: All the elements are there *except* that the following items are left as variables to be plugged in by the baker:

- The number of layers
- The kind of filling between the layers
- The flavor of the cake itself
- The flavor of the icing

This recipe was pretested by the cookbook author, but before we can use it for a three-layer yellow cake with marshmallow filling and chocolate icing, we need to (at least mentally) make all the changes necessary to the list of ingredients. Only after this *instance* of the recipe has been created does it make sense to try to make a cake using it.

Generic Type Parameters

Program 5.1 is a specification for a generic exchange program. This specification indicates to the compiler that we wish `ValueType` to be a formal parameter. The formal parameters are listed between the word `GENERIC` and the procedure heading. Writing

```
TYPE ValueType IS PRIVATE;
```

tells the compiler that *any* type, *including* a private one, can be plugged in as the kind of element to exchange. We will introduce more examples of type parameters below.

Program 5.1 Specification for Generic Exchange Procedure

```
GENERIC

  TYPE ValueType IS PRIVATE;  -- any type OK except LIMITED PRIVATE

PROCEDURE Swap_Generic(Value1, Value2: IN OUT ValueType);
-----------------------------------------------------------------------
--| Specification for generic exchange procedure
--| Author: Michael B. Feldman, The George Washington University
--| Last Modified: September 1995
-----------------------------------------------------------------------
```

The body of `Swap_Generic` is presented as Program 5.2. Notice that `Swap_Generic` looks essentially the same as the integer and float versions, except for the use of `ValueType` wherever a type is required. `ValueType` is a *formal type parameter*.

Program 5.2 Body of Generic Exchange Procedure

```
PROCEDURE Swap_Generic(Value1, Value2: IN OUT ValueType) IS
-----------------------------------------------------------------------
--| Body of generic exchange procedure
--| Author: Michael B. Feldman, The George Washington University
--| Last Modified: September 1995
-----------------------------------------------------------------------

  TempValue: ValueType;
```

```
BEGIN -- Swap_Generic

  TempValue := Value1;
  Value1    := Value2;
  Value2    := TempValue;

END Swap_Generic;
```

Compiling the specification and the body creates a version of the generic that is ready to be *instantiated*, or "tailored" by plugging in the desired type. Here are two instances:

```
PROCEDURE IntegerSwap IS NEW Swap_Generic (ValueType => Integer);
PROCEDURE CharSwap IS NEW Swap_Generic (ValueType => Character);
```

The notation is familiar; we have used it in creating instances of `Text_IO.Enumeration_IO`. Program 5.3 shows how `Swap_Generic` could be tested and used. The two instantiations shown above appear in the program.

Program 5.3 A Test of the Generic Swap Procedure

```
WITH Swap_Generic;
WITH Ada.Text_IO;
WITH Ada.Integer_Text_IO;
PROCEDURE Test_Swap_Generic IS
-----------------------------------------------------------------------
--| Test program for Swap_Generic
--| Author: Michael B. Feldman, The George Washington University
--| Last Modified: September 1995
-----------------------------------------------------------------------

  X : Integer;
  Y : Integer;

  A : Character;
  B : Character;

  PROCEDURE IntegerSwap IS NEW Swap_Generic (ValueType => Integer);
  PROCEDURE CharSwap IS NEW Swap_Generic (ValueType => Character);

BEGIN -- Test_Swap_Generic

  X := 3;
  Y := -5;
  A := 'x';
  B := 'q';

  Ada.Text_IO.Put("Before swapping, X and Y are, respectively ");
  Ada.Integer_Text_IO.Put(Item => X, Width => 4);
  Ada.Integer_Text_IO.Put(Item => Y, Width => 4);
  Ada.Text_IO.New_Line;

  IntegerSwap(Value1 => X,Value2 => Y);

  Ada.Text_IO.Put("After swapping, X and Y are, respectively ");
  Ada.Integer_Text_IO.Put(Item => X, Width => 4);
  Ada.Integer_Text_IO.Put(Item => Y, Width => 4);
  Ada.Text_IO.New_Line;
  Ada.Text_IO.New_Line;
```

```
Ada.Text_IO.Put("Before swapping, A and B are, respectively");
Ada.Text_IO.Put(Item => A);
Ada.Text_IO.Put(Item => B);
Ada.Text_IO.New_Line;

CharSwap(Value1 => A,Value2 => B);

Ada.Text_IO.Put("After  swapping, A and B are, respectively");
Ada.Text_IO.Put(Item => A);
Ada.Text_IO.Put(Item => B);
Ada.Text_IO.New_Line;

END Test_Swap_Generic;
```

Generic Subprogram Parameters

Sometimes a generic recipe needs to be instantiated with the names of functions or procedures. To continue the food analogy, a certain fish recipe can be prepared by either baking or broiling; the rest of the recipe is independent. Thus, the action "desired cooking method" would be a parameter of that recipe.

Consider the function `Maximum`, which returns the larger of its two `Integer` operands:

```
FUNCTION Maximum (Value1, Value2: Integer) RETURN Integer IS

  Result: Integer;

BEGIN

  IF Value1 > Value2 THEN
    Result := Value1;
  ELSE
    Result := Value2;
  END IF;

  RETURN Result;

END Maximum;
```

We would like to create a function that returns the larger of its two operands *regardless of the types of these operands*. As in the case of `Generic_Swap`, we can use a generic type parameter to indicate that an instance can be created for any type. This is not enough, however. The `IF` statement compares the two input values. Suppose the type we use to instantiate does not have an obvious, predefined "greater than" operation. Suppose the type is a user-defined record with a key field, for example. "Greater than" is not predefined for records! We can surely write such an operation, but we need to tell the compiler to use it; when writing a generic, we need to reassure the compiler that all the operations used in the body of the generic will exist at instantiation time. Let us indicate in the generic specification that a comparison function will exist.

Program 5.4 is the desired generic specification. The `WITH` syntax shown here takes getting used to, but it works.

Program 5.4 Specification for Generic Maximum Function

```
GENERIC

  TYPE ValueType IS PRIVATE;
  WITH FUNCTION Compare(L, R : ValueType) RETURN Boolean;
```

```
FUNCTION Maximum_Generic(L, R : ValueType) RETURN ValueType;
------------------------------------------------------------------------
--| Specification for generic maximum function
--| Author: Michael B. Feldman, The George Washington University
--| Last Modified: September 1995
------------------------------------------------------------------------
```

The body of the generic function, presented as Program 5.5, looks similar to the one just given for `Maximum`.

Program 5.5 Body of Generic Maximum Function

```
FUNCTION Maximum_Generic(L, R : ValueType) RETURN ValueType IS
------------------------------------------------------------------------
--|
--| Body of generic maximum function
--|
--| Author: Michael B. Feldman, The George Washington University
--| Last Modified: September 1995
--|
------------------------------------------------------------------------

BEGIN -- Maximum_Generic

  IF Compare(L, R) THEN
    RETURN L;
  ELSE
    RETURN R;
  END IF;

END Maximum_Generic;
```

An instantiation for `Float` values might be

```
FUNCTION FloatMax IS
  NEW Maximum_Generic (ValueType=>Float, Compare=> ">");
```

Notice how the "greater than" operator is supplied. It makes no difference that the generic expected a function and we gave it an operator; after all, an operator is a function. What is important is that the *structure* of the actual parameter matches the structure of the formal parameter. As long as a ">" is available for `Float` (of course there is, in `Standard`), the instantiation will succeed.

The Ada compiler has no idea what the function `Compare` will do when the generic is instantiated. It turns out, then, that if we just supply "<" as an actual parameter for `Compare`, the instantiation finds the minimum instead of the maximum! Program 5.6 shows a total of six instantiations, giving minimum and maximum functions for `Integer`, `Float`, and `Currency` values. All the minimums are called `Minimum`; all the maximums are called `Maximum`; this is just the normal Ada overloading principle in action.

Program 5.6 Test of Generic Maximum Function

```
With Ada.Text_IO;
WITH Ada.Float_Text_IO;
```

```
WITH Ada.Integer_Text_IO;
WITH Currency; USE Currency;
WITH Currency.IO;
WITH Maximum_Generic;
PROCEDURE Test_Maximum_Generic IS
-------------------------------------------------------------------------
--| Test program for Generic Maximum, using six instances
--| Author: Michael B. Feldman, The George Washington University
--| Last Modified: September 1995
-------------------------------------------------------------------------

   FUNCTION Maximum IS
     NEW Maximum_Generic (ValueType=>Quantity, Compare=> ">");
   FUNCTION Minimum IS
     NEW Maximum_Generic (ValueType=>Quantity, Compare=> "<");

   FUNCTION Maximum IS                  Integer
     NEW Maximum_Generic (ValueType=>Quantity, Compare=> ">");
   FUNCTION Minimum IS
     NEW Maximum_Generic (ValueType=>Integer,  Compare=> "<");

   FUNCTION Maximum IS                  Float
     NEW Maximum_Generic (ValueType=>Quantity, Compare=> ">");
   FUNCTION Minimum IS                  Float
     NEW Maximum_Generic (ValueType=>Quantity, Compare=> "<");

BEGIN -- Test_Maximum_Generic

   Ada.Text_IO.Put("Maximum of -3 and 7 is ");
   Ada.Integer_Text_IO.Put(Item => Maximum(-3, 7), Width=>1);
   Ada.Text_IO.New_Line;
   Ada.Text_IO.Put("Minimum of -3 and 7 is ");
   Ada.Integer_Text_IO.Put(Item => Minimum(-3, 7), Width=>1);
   Ada.Text_IO.New_Line(Spacing => 2);

   Ada.Text_IO.Put("Maximum of -3.29 and 7.84 is ");
   Ada.Float_Text_IO.Put
     (Item => Maximum(-3.29, 7.84), Fore=>1, Aft=>2, Exp=>0);
   Ada.Text_IO.New_Line;
   Ada.Text_IO.Put("Minimum of -3.29 and 7.84 is ");
   Ada.Float_Text_IO.Put
     (Item => Minimum(-3.29, 7.84), Fore=>1, Aft=>2, Exp=>0);
   Ada.Text_IO.New_Line(Spacing => 2);

   Ada.Text_IO.Put("Maximum of 23.65 and 37.49 is ");
   Currency.IO.Put
     (Item => Maximum(MakeCurrency(23.65), MakeCurrency(37.49)));
   Ada.Text_IO.New_Line;
   Ada.Text_IO.Put("Minimum of 23.65 and 37.49 is ");
   Currency.IO.Put
     (Item => Minimum(MakeCurrency(23.65), MakeCurrency(37.49)));
   Ada.Text_IO.New_Line(Spacing => 2);

END Test_Maximum_Generic;
```

Generic Array Parameters

An important use for generics, combined with unconstrained array types, is building very general subprograms to deal with arrays. For a generic to be instantiated for many different array types, we need to specify formal parameters for the index and array types.

Program 5.7 is a specification for a function `Maximum_Array_Generic` that returns the "largest" of all the elements in an array, regardless of the index or element type. We place "largest" in quotation marks because we already know that we can make it work as a minimum-finder as well.

Program 5.7 Specification for Generic Array Maximum Function

```
GENERIC
  TYPE ValueType IS PRIVATE;  -- any nonlimited type
  TYPE IndexType IS (<>);     -- any discrete type
  TYPE ArrayType IS ARRAY(IndexType RANGE <>) OF ValueType;
  WITH FUNCTION Compare(L, R : ValueType) RETURN Boolean;

FUNCTION Maximum_Array_Generic(List: ArrayType) RETURN ValueType;
----------------------------------------------------------------------
--| Specification for generic version of array maximum finder
--| Author: Michael B. Feldman, The George Washington University
--| Last Modified: September 1995
----------------------------------------------------------------------
```

The syntax of the specification for `IndexType` means "any discrete type is acceptable as an actual parameter." Recalling that discrete types are the integer and enumeration types and subtypes, this is exactly what we need for the index type of the array. The specification for `ArrayType` looks like a type declaration, but *it is not*. Rather, it is a description to the compiler of the *kind* of array type that is acceptable as an actual parameter. In this case, the array type must be indexed by `IndexType` (or a subtype thereof) and must have elements of type `Valuetype` (or a subtype thereof).

The body of `Maximum_Array_Generic` is shown in Program 5.8.

Program 5.8 Body of Generic Array Maximum Function

```
FUNCTION Maximum_Array_Generic(List: ArrayType) RETURN ValueType IS
----------------------------------------------------------------------
--| Body of generic array maximum finder
--| Author: Michael B. Feldman, The George Washington University
--| Last Modified: September 1995
----------------------------------------------------------------------

  Result: ValueType;

BEGIN -- Maximum_Array_Generic

  FOR WhichElement IN List'Range LOOP
    IF Compare(List(WhichElement), Result) THEN
      Result := List(WhichElement);
    END IF;
  END LOOP;

  RETURN Result;

END Maximum_Array_Generic;
```

You can write a test program for it as an exercise. As a hint, consider the following declarations:

```
TYPE FloatVector IS ARRAY(Integer RANGE <>) OF Float;
TYPE RationalVector IS ARRAY (Positive RANGE <>) OF Rational;
```

and instantiate the generic as follows:

```
FUNCTION Maximum IS
   NEW Maximum_Array_Generic(ValueType=>Float, IndexType=>Integer,
                        ArrayType=>FloatVector, Compare=>">");

FUNCTION Minimum IS
   NEW Maximum_Array_Generic(ValueType=>Rational, IndexType=>Positive,
                        ArrayType=>RationalVector, Compare=>"<";
```

5.2   APPLICATION: A GENERIC SORTING PROGRAM

Let us continue our study of generics with the development of a generic sort procedure that uses much of what we have done in this chapter. We develop a sort procedure that will work correctly for *any* variable of *any* unconstrained array type, regardless of its bounds, index type, or element type.

In Program 4.2 we developed SelectSort, which works for any array of a *particular* unconstrained array type. We need only to modify it to make it generic. We also have our procedure Swap_Generic, which we can instantiate and use to handle exchanges.

Program 5.9 is the specification for the generic sort routine. This is similar to Maximum_Array_Generic from Program 5.7.

Program 5.9 Specification for Generic Sort Procedure

```
GENERIC

   TYPE ElementType IS PRIVATE;   -- any nonlimited type will do
   TYPE IndexType   IS (<>);      -- any discrete type for index
   TYPE ListType    IS ARRAY (IndexType RANGE <>) OF ElementType;
   WITH FUNCTION Compare (Left, Right : ElementType) RETURN Boolean;

PROCEDURE Sort_Generic(List: IN OUT ListType);
-----------------------------------------------------------------------
--| Specification for Generic Exchange Sort - will sort input
--| array in order according to Compare
--| Author: Michael B. Feldman, The George Washington University
--| Last Modified: September 1995
-----------------------------------------------------------------------
```

With your current knowledge of generics, you can easily understand this specification. The body of the generic sort is presented as Program 5.10. Notice that the body begins with the context clause

```
WITH Swap_Generic;
```

and instantiates this procedure for whatever the element type turns out to be. We have here a case of one generic instantiating another; this is the kind of situation that demonstrates the power of generics to help write very general programs. The rest of the procedure body is very similar to `SelectSort` (Program 4.2), with the necessary modifications.

Program 5.10 Body of Generic Sort Procedure

```
WITH Swap_Generic;
PROCEDURE Sort_Generic(List: IN OUT ListType) IS
------------------------------------------------------------------------
--| Body of Generic Sort Procedure
--| Author: Michael B. Feldman, The George Washington University
--| Last Modified: September 1995
------------------------------------------------------------------------

  -- we need to make an instance of Swap_Generic for this case
  PROCEDURE Exchange IS NEW Swap_Generic (ValueType => ElementType);

  IndexOfMax: IndexType;

BEGIN -- Sort_Generic

  FOR PositionToFill IN List'First .. IndexType'Pred(List'Last) LOOP

    IndexOfMax := PositionToFill;

    FOR ItemToCompare IN IndexType'Succ(PositionToFill) .. List'Last
LOOP
      IF Compare(List(ItemToCompare), List(IndexOfMax)) THEN
        IndexOfMax := ItemToCompare;
      END IF;
    END LOOP;

    IF IndexOfMax /= PositionToFill  THEN
      Exchange(List(PositionToFill), List(IndexOfMax));
    END IF;

  END LOOP;

END Sort_Generic;
```

Using the Generic Sort to Order an Array of Records

`Sort_Generic` can be especially useful in sorting arrays of records. Consider the following declarations:

```
MaxSize : CONSTANT Positive := 250;
MaxScore : CONSTANT Positive := 100;

SUBTYPE StudentName IS String(1..20);
SUBTYPE ClassIndex  IS Positive RANGE 1..MaxSize;
SUBTYPE ClassRange  IS Natural RANGE 0..MaxSize;
SUBTYPE ScoreRange  IS Natural RANGE 0..MaxScore;

TYPE ScoreRecord IS RECORD
  Name:  StudentName;
  Score: ScoreRange;
END RECORD;

TYPE ScoreArray IS ARRAY (ClassIndex RANGE <>) OF ScoreRecord;
```

Here is a "compare" function that tells us whether one record is "less than" another (in the sense that one score is lower than the other):

```
FUNCTION ScoreLess(Score1, Score2 : ScoreRecord) RETURN Boolean IS
BEGIN
  RETURN Score1.Score < Score2.Score;
END ScoreLess;
```

This function compares the score fields of the two records, returning `True` if the first record is "less than" the second and `False` otherwise. We could have named this function `"<"`, of course, but chose not to do so in the interest of clarity. Given `Sort_Generic`, it takes only a single instantiation statement to create a sort that will order an array of score records in ascending order:

```
PROCEDURE SortUpScores IS NEW Sort_Generic
  (ElementType => ScoreRecord,
   IndexType   => ClassIndex,
   ListType    => ScoreArray,
   Compare     => ScoreLess);
```

Given variables `Scores` and `ClassSize` as follows:

```
Scores: ScoreArray(ClassIndex'First..ClassIndex'Last);
ClassSize: ClassRange;
```

we see that `Scores` can hold up to 250 records, and `ClassSize` can be used to determine the actual number of records read from a file into the array. The array can easily be put into ascending order by score, just by calling `SortUpScores` with the appropriate array slice:

```
SortUpScores(List => Scores(1..ClassSize));
```

Program 5.11 demonstrates the sort for two entirely different array types: an array of float values and an array of phone call records like the one we used in Section 4.3.

Program 5.11 Test of Generic Sort Procedure

```
WITH Ada.Text_IO;
WITH Ada.Integer_Text_IO;
WITH Ada.Float_Text_IO;
WITH Sort_Generic;
PROCEDURE Test_Sort_Generic IS
-------------------------------------------------------------------------
--| Demonstrates Sort_Generic using two unrelated kinds of lists;
--| this is not a realistic application, but rather just shows that
--| many instances of a generic can occur within one client program.
--| Author: Michael B. Feldman, The George Washington University
--| Last Modified: September 1995
-------------------------------------------------------------------------

  SUBTYPE Index IS Integer RANGE 1..10;
  TYPE    FloatVector IS ARRAY(Index RANGE <>) OF Float;

  V1 : FloatVector(1..10);

  SUBTYPE DayRange IS Natural  RANGE 0..6;
```

```
SUBTYPE Weekdays IS DayRange RANGE 0..4;
SUBTYPE Weekend  IS DayRange RANGE 5..6;

TYPE Days IS (Mon, Tue, Wed, Thu, Fri, Sat, Sun);
TYPE CallRecord IS RECORD
  DayOfWeek    : Days;
  NumberOfCalls: Natural;
END RECORD;

TYPE Callers IS ARRAY(DayRange RANGE <>) of CallRecord;

PACKAGE Days_IO IS NEW Ada.Text_IO.Enumeration_IO(Enum => Days);

ThisWeek:        Callers(DayRange);

-- if we are going to sort CallRecords,
-- we need to know how to compare them

FUNCTION "<" (L, R: CallRecord) RETURN Boolean IS
BEGIN
  RETURN L.NumberOfCalls < R.NumberOfCalls;
END "<";

FUNCTION ">" (L, R: CallRecord) RETURN Boolean IS
BEGIN
  RETURN L.NumberOfCalls > R.NumberOfCalls;
END ">";

-- local procedures to display the contents of two kinds of lists

PROCEDURE DisplayCallers (List: Callers) IS
BEGIN -- DisplayCallers
  FOR Count IN List'Range LOOP
    Days_IO.Put  (Item=>List(Count).DayOfWeek, Width=>3);
    Ada.Integer_Text_IO.Put
      (Item=>List(Count).NumberOfCalls, Width=>4);
    Ada.Text_IO.New_Line;
  END LOOP;
  Ada.Text_IO.New_Line;
END DisplayCallers;

PROCEDURE DisplayFloatVector (V: FloatVector) IS
BEGIN
  FOR Count IN V'First..V'Last LOOP
    Ada.Float_Text_IO.Put(Item=>V(Count), Fore=>4, Aft=>2, Exp=>0);
  END LOOP;
  Ada.Text_IO.New_Line;
END DisplayFloatVector;

-- two instances of Sort_Generic for Float vectors;
-- the first sorts in increasing order, the second in decreasing order

PROCEDURE SortUpFloat IS NEW Sort_Generic
  (ElementType => Float,
   IndexType   => Index,
   ListType    => FloatVector,
   Compare     => "<");

PROCEDURE SortDownFloat IS NEW Sort_Generic
  (ElementType => Float,
   IndexType   => Index,
   ListType    => FloatVector,
   Compare     => ">");
```

```
-- two instances of Sort_Generic for Callers;
-- the first sorts in increasing order, the second in decreasing order

PROCEDURE SortUpCallers IS NEW Sort_Generic
   (ElementType => CallRecord,
    IndexType   => DayRange,
    ListType    => Callers,
    Compare     => "<");

PROCEDURE SortDownCallers IS NEW Sort_Generic
   (ElementType => CallRecord,
    IndexType   => DayRange,
    ListType    => Callers,
    Compare     => ">");

BEGIN -- Test_Sort_Generic

  V1 := (0.7, 1.5, 6.9, -3.2, 0.0, 5.1, 2.0, 7.3, 2.2, -5.9);
  Ada.Text_IO.New_Line;
  Ada.Text_IO.Put(Item=> "Testing Sort_Generic for float vectors");
  Ada.Text_IO.New_Line;
  Ada.Text_IO.Put(Item=> "Here is the vector before sorting.");
  Ada.Text_IO.New_Line;
  DisplayFloatVector(V => V1);
  Ada.Text_IO.New_Line;

  SortUpFloat(List => V1);
  Ada.Text_IO.Put(Item=> "Here is the vector after upward sorting.");
  Ada.Text_IO.New_Line;
  DisplayFloatVector(V => V1);
  Ada.Text_IO.New_Line;

  SortDownFloat(List => V1);
  Ada.Text_IO.Put(Item=> "Here is the vector after downward sorting.");
  Ada.Text_IO.New_Line;
  DisplayFloatVector(V => V1);
  Ada.Text_IO.New_Line;

  ThisWeek := ((Mon, 12), (Tue, 23), (Wed, 100), (Thu, 40),
               (Fri, 52), (Sat, 17), (Sun,   2));

  Ada.Text_IO.Put(Item=> "Testing Sort_Generic for  telephone callers");
  Ada.Text_IO.New_Line;
  Ada.Text_IO.Put(Item=> "Here is ThisWeek before sorting.");
  Ada.Text_IO.New_Line;
  DisplayCallers(List => ThisWeek);
  Ada.Text_IO.New_Line;

  SortUpCallers(List => ThisWeek);
  Ada.Text_IO.Put(Item=> "Here is ThisWeek after upward sorting.");
  Ada.Text_IO.New_Line;
  DisplayCallers(List => ThisWeek);
  Ada.Text_IO.New_Line;

  SortDownCallers(List => ThisWeek);
  Ada.Text_IO.Put(Item=> "Here is ThisWeek after downward sorting.");
  Ada.Text_IO.New_Line;
  DisplayCallers(List => ThisWeek);
  Ada.Text_IO.New_Line;

END Test_Sort_Generic;
```

5.3 APPLICATION: A GENERIC BINARY SEARCH PROGRAM

Sorting and searching are both very important applications in computing. Having examined a simple generic sorting program, we will now look at a generic version of binary search, which was discussed in Section 3.2. Recall that it is meaningful to use binary search only on a table of *sorted* values, and that the "big O" of binary search is log *N*.

We choose to show an iterative version, rather than the recursive one given earlier, both for the sake of variety and also because the iterative version does not require *O*(log *N*) levels of recursion. For large *N*, this would be a large number of recursive calls; it is better to avoid these, especially because the iterative algorithm is as easy to understand as the recursive one.

Specification of the Generic Binary Search

Program 5.12 shows the generic specification for the generic binary search.

Program 5.12 Specification for Generic Binary Search Procedure

```
GENERIC

  TYPE KeyType IS PRIVATE;
  TYPE ElementType IS PRIVATE;
  TYPE IndexType IS (<>);
  TYPE ListType IS ARRAY (IndexType RANGE <>) OF ElementType;
  WITH FUNCTION "<"(Left, Right: KeyType) RETURN Boolean;
  WITH FUNCTION KeyOf  (Element: ElementType) RETURN KeyType;

PROCEDURE Binary_Search_Generic (List    : IN ListType;
                                 Target  : IN KeyType;
                                 Location: OUT IndexType;
                                 Found   : OUT Boolean);
----------------------------------------------------------------------
--| Performs an iterative binary search of an ordered array of
--| keys with bounds List'First..List'Last.
--| Pre :  Target and List are defined, and List is sorted upward
--| Post:  If Target is found in array List, returns True in Found
--|        and the location in Location; otherwise,
--|        returns False in Found and returns in Location
--|        the location in which to insert Target
--| Raises: Ada will raise Constraint_Error
--|        if List'Last = IndexType'Last and Target would be
--|        inserted beyond List'Last.
--| Author: Michael B. Feldman, The George Washington University
--| Last Modified: October 1995
----------------------------------------------------------------------
```

Let's discuss the six generic parameters. Here, we take a slightly different approach from that of the sort program. In general, we will be searching arrays of records, usng some field in the record as the search key. Let's call the key and record types `KeyType` and `ElementType`, respectively. As in the sort program, we also specify the index and the list types. The last two parameters are given by

```
WITH FUNCTION "<"(Left, Right: KeyType) RETURN Boolean;
WITH FUNCTION KeyOf  (Element: ElementType) RETURN KeyType;
```

The formal comparison parameter, shown here as `"<"`, compares *keys*, not *elements*. We therefore provide a sixth parameter, `KeyOf`, so that the client can specify exactly how to find the key field of an element.

This binary search is, in another way, more general than the simple one given in Section 3.2. That program returns 0 if the search is unsuccessful, whereas this one returns, in the `OUT` parameter `Location`, the location into which to insert this value. The client can then choose whether or not to actually perform the insertion. This generality will make it possible to use binary search in the generic table handler we present in Section 5.8.

Before we examine the body of the binary search procedure, let's see how it might be instantiated and used. Program 5.13 shows a test of the generic search procedure, instantiating for a record consisting of a name and a test score.

Program 5.13 A Test of Generic Binary Search

```
WITH Ada.Text_IO;
WITH Ada.Integer_Text_IO;
WITH Binary_Search_Generic;
PROCEDURE Test_Binary_Search IS
-------------------------------------------------------------------------
--| Test of generic binary search, array of records
--| Author: Michael B. Feldman, The George Washington University
--| Last Modified: October 1995
-------------------------------------------------------------------------

  Success: Boolean;
  WhereFound: Positive;

  SUBTYPE NameType IS String(1..10);
  SUBTYPE ScoreType IS Natural RANGE 0..100;

  TYPE ScoreRecord IS RECORD
    Name: NameType;
    Score: ScoreType := 0;
  END RECORD;

  TYPE ScoreArray IS ARRAY(Positive RANGE <>) OF ScoreRecord;
  Test1: ScoreArray(1..9);

  FUNCTION NameOf   (Item: ScoreRecord) RETURN NameType IS
  BEGIN
    RETURN Item.Name;
  END NameOf;

  PROCEDURE BinarySearch IS
    NEW Binary_Search_Generic(ElementType => ScoreRecord,
                      KeyType => NameType,
                      IndexType => Positive,
                      ListType  => ScoreArray,
                      "<" => "<",
                      KeyOf => NameOf);

  PROCEDURE DisplayArray(I: ScoreArray) IS
  BEGIN
    FOR Count IN I'Range LOOP
      Ada.Text_IO.Put(Item => I(Count).Name);
```

```
            Ada.Integer_Text_IO.Put(Item => I(Count).Score, Width => 4);
            Ada.Text_IO.New_Line;
        END LOOP;
        Ada.Text_IO.New_Line;
    END DisplayArray;

BEGIN -- Test_Binary_Search

    Test1 := (("Bill       ",29),
              ("Dave       ",69),
              ("Ernie      ",50),
              ("Jill       ",75),
              ("Katie      ",66),
              ("Marianne   ",66),
              ("Nora       ",82),
              ("Samuel     ",95),
              ("Yetta      ",95));
    DisplayArray(Test1);

    BinarySearch(Test1, "Dave       ", WhereFound, Success);
    IF Success THEN
        Ada.Text_IO.Put(Item => "Dave is at location ");
        Ada.Integer_Text_IO.Put(Item => WhereFound, Width => 1);
        Ada.Text_IO.New_Line;
    ELSE
        Ada.Text_IO.Put(Item => "Dave would be at location ");
        Ada.Integer_Text_IO.Put(Item => WhereFound, Width => 1);
        Ada.Text_IO.New_Line;
    END IF;

    BinarySearch(Test1, "Adam       ", WhereFound, Success);
    IF Success THEN
        Ada.Text_IO.Put(Item => "Adam is at location ");
        Ada.Integer_Text_IO.Put(Item => WhereFound, Width => 1);
        Ada.Text_IO.New_Line;
    ELSE
        Ada.Text_IO.Put(Item => "Adam would be at location ");
        Ada.Integer_Text_IO.Put(Item => WhereFound, Width => 1);
        Ada.Text_IO.New_Line;
    END IF;

    BinarySearch(Test1, "Bill       ", WhereFound, Success);
    IF Success THEN
        Ada.Text_IO.Put(Item => "Bill is at location ");
        Ada.Integer_Text_IO.Put(Item => WhereFound, Width => 1);
        Ada.Text_IO.New_Line;
    ELSE
        Ada.Text_IO.Put(Item => "Bill would be at location ");
        Ada.Integer_Text_IO.Put(Item => WhereFound, Width => 1);
        Ada.Text_IO.New_Line;
    END IF;

    BinarySearch(Test1, "Mary       ", WhereFound, Success);
    IF Success THEN
        Ada.Text_IO.Put(Item => "Mary is at location ");
        Ada.Integer_Text_IO.Put(Item => WhereFound, Width => 1);
        Ada.Text_IO.New_Line;
    ELSE
        Ada.Text_IO.Put(Item => "Mary would be at location ");
        Ada.Integer_Text_IO.Put(Item => WhereFound, Width => 1);
        Ada.Text_IO.New_Line;
    END IF;
```

```
BinarySearch(Test1, "Zachary    ", WhereFound, Success);
IF Success THEN
  Ada.Text_IO.Put(Item => "Zachary is at location ");
  Ada.Integer_Text_IO.Put(Item => WhereFound, Width => 1);
  Ada.Text_IO.New_Line;
ELSE
  Ada.Text_IO.Put(Item => "Zachary would be at location ");
  Ada.Integer_Text_IO.Put(Item => WhereFound, Width => 1);
  Ada.Text_IO.New_Line;
END IF;

END Test_Binary_Search;
```

To specify how to find the key part of a score record, we write

```
FUNCTION NameOf (Item: ScoreRecord) RETURN NameType IS
BEGIN
  RETURN Item.Name;
END NameOf;
```

and use this function as an actual parameter in the instantiating statement

```
PROCEDURE BinarySearch IS
  NEW Binary_Search_Generic(ElementType => ScoreRecord,
                            KeyType => NameType,
                            IndexType => Positive,
                            ListType => ScoreArray,
                            "<" => "<",
                            KeyOf => NameOf);
```

You should examine the various cases used in the test program and try to predict the response for each case.

Now suppose the array we are searching contains simple integer elements.

```
TYPE IntegerArray IS ARRAY(Positive RANGE <>) OF Integer;
```

In this case, there is no actual key, because there is no record whose field is the key. However, the binary search procedure requires a `KeyOf` function to fill that parameter. In this case, we can write a "dummy" function that simply returns the value of its integer input.

```
FUNCTION Identity (Value: Integer) RETURN Integer IS
BEGIN
  RETURN Value;
END Identity;
```

Now we can instantiate `Generic_Binary_Search`, as follows:

```
PROCEDURE BinarySearch IS
  NEW Binary_Search_Generic(ElementType => Integer,
                            KeyType => Integer,
                            IndexType => Positive,
                            ListType => IntegerArray,
                            "<" => "<",
                            KeyOf => Identity);
```

Modifying the test program to fit this case is left as an exercise.

Body of the Generic Binary Search

Look now at Program 5.14, the body of the search procedure.

Program 5.14 Body of Generic Binary Search Procedure

```
PROCEDURE Binary_Search_Generic (List    : IN ListType;
                                 Target  : IN KeyType;
                                 Location : OUT IndexType;
                                 Found   : OUT Boolean) IS
---------------------------------------------------------------------
--| Body of Generic Binary Search Procedure
--| Author: Michael B. Feldman, The George Washington University
--| Last Modified: October 1995
---------------------------------------------------------------------

  Middle : IndexType;       -- the subscript of the middle element
  Success: Boolean;
  Left   : IndexType;
  Right  : IndexType;

BEGIN -- Binary_Search_Generic

  Left := List'First;
  Right := List'Last;
  Success:= False;

  IF Target = KeyOf(List(Left)) THEN
    Found := True;
    Location := Left;
  ELSIF Target < KeyOf(List(Left)) THEN -- Target goes in pos. 1
    Found := False;
    Location := Left;
  ELSIF Target = KeyOf(List(Right)) THEN
    Found := True;
    Location := Right;
  ELSIF NOT (Target < KeyOf(List(Right))) THEN -- Target beyond end
    Found := False;
    Location := IndexType'Succ(Right);
  ELSE
    WHILE (Left <= Right) AND (NOT Success) LOOP

      Middle := IndexType'Val((IndexType'Pos(Left)
                          + IndexType'Pos(Right)) / 2);
      IF Target = KeyOf(List(Middle)) THEN
        Success := True;
      ELSIF Target < KeyOf(List(Middle)) THEN
        Right := IndexType'Pred(Middle);    -- search lower subarray
      ELSE
        Left := IndexType'Succ(Middle);     -- search upper subarray
      END IF;

    END LOOP;

    IF (NOT Success) AND KeyOf(List(Middle)) < Target THEN
      Location := IndexType'Succ(Middle);
    ELSE
      Location := Middle;
    END IF;
```

```
      Found := Success;

   END IF;

END Binary_Search_Generic;
```

We see that it has a number of special cases. If the target key is less than or equal to the first key in the table, or greater than or equal to the last key in the table, it saves time simply to indicate this to the caller and return, rather than running the search to completion.

If, in fact, the search must be run, we proceed as described in Section 3.2. A middle location is computed; if the target is equal to the key in the middle of the table, we are finished. Otherwise, if the target is "less" than the middle key, we continue searching in the lower half of the table; if the target is "greater" than the middle key, we continue in the upper half. "Less" and "greater" are, of course, enclosed in quotation marks because the meanings of these terms really depend on which comparison function is plugged in for `"<"`.

Computing the middle location is a bit more complicated than it was in the earlier version of the algorithm. This is because the present version is generic, so we cannot simply do arithmetic on integer subscripts to find the middle one—it is possible that the index type will be a enumeration type! We must therefore compute the middle location using attributes. Instead of adding the subscripts and dividing by 2, we add and divide their positions in `IndexType`.

Be certain you understand the workings of this algorithm; you might try to hand-trace its operation on an array of your choosing. As was the case in the generic sort of Section 5.2, this generic search is completely independent not only of the array size, but also of its subscript and element types. The procedure tells us not only whether the target is in the table, but also where it would should be placed if it is not already there. We can therefore use a call to this procedure as one step in an insertion or deletion operation.

One flaw of the generality is that there is one situation in which it can fail. Suppose the target is "greater" than the "largest" key in the table. In this case, the search returns a location one greater than `Table'Last`, which will cause `Constraint_Error` to be raised. If the table passed to the search is not a slice but the whole table, this means the table is full and cannot accommodate the new value anyway. It is therefore the responsibility of the client to make sure the table is not full before calling the search, or, if it is, to check itself to see whether the target is "greater" than the last value.

5.4   ADT DESIGN: AN ABSTRACT DATA TYPE FOR SETS

Sets are very important both in mathematics and in computer applications. Given a universe of objects or values, a set S is just a collection of objects belonging to that universe. Some common universes are the integers, the positive integers, the letters of the alphabet, and so on. Sets are so important in programming that some languages, especially Pascal, provide sets as a predefined type. Ada does not have a predefined set type;

in this section we will show an ADT that will emulate Pascal's predefined type, using a generic package.

Often sets are described simply by listing their members between braces, as in the set {*a*, *b*}, taken from the universe of English alphabetic characters. In general, there is no ordering associated with a set, so {*a*, *b*} and {*b*, *a*} usually describe the same set. Two sets are said to be *equal* if they have the same members. A set is said to be *empty* if it has no members. In cases where there is no ordering, it also makes no difference if we name a member twice, so {*a*, *b*, *a*} = {*b*, *a*, *b*} = {*a*, *b*}.

Operations on Sets

What are the important operations associated with sets? Certainly inserting a member in a set and deleting a member from a set are essential; so are testing a set to see whether a given element is a member of it and testing a set to see whether it is empty. The last two operations are *predicate* or *inquiry* selector operations; they return true/false values. The most important dyadic constructor operations are

- The *union* of two sets S and T (usually written as $S \cup T$), which returns the set containing all of S's members and all of T's members

- The *intersection* of S and T ($S \cap T$), which returns the set containing all elements which are members of both S and T

- The difference $S - T$, which returns the set containing all elements which are members of S but not of T

An often-used monadic constructor is the complement $-S$, which returns the set containing all elements in the universe that are not members of S.

We will use "+" and "*" to represent the union and intersection, respectively, because the union and intersection symbols are not part of the normal Ada character set. For example, if the universe is the letters a..k inclusive and S = {a, d, e, g} and T = {b, c, d, e, k}, then

$$S + T = \{a, b, c, d, e, g, k\}$$
$$S * T = \{d, e\}$$
$$S - T = \{a, g\} \text{ and } T - S = \{b, c, k\}$$
$$-S = \{b, c, f, h, i, j, k\}$$

Finally, two more inquiry operations are commonly used:

- The *improper subset* operation ($S \subseteq T$) which returns True if and only if all members of S are also members of T

- The *proper subset* operation ($S \subset T$) which returns True if and only if $S \subseteq T$ and S /= T; that is, at least one member of T is not a member of S.

Because the subset symbols are also missing from the Ada character set, we use ≤ and < for improper and proper subset, respectively. For example $\{b, c\} \le \{a, b, c, d, e\}$ and $\{b, c\} < \{a, b, c, d, e\}$ but is not a subset of $\{c, e\}$. Also, $\{a, b\} \le \{a, b\}$.

Specifying the Generic Set ADT

Mathematically, sets can be infinite (all the integers, for example). In programming applications, however, it is finite sets that are most interesting. Therefore we confine ourselves to representing finite sets—specifically, to sets taken from finite universes of integers or enumeration values. As we shall see, it is easy to use Ada's generic facility to build a package providing a good but more flexible approximation to the predefined set facility of Pascal.

A universe is either an integer subtype or an enumeration type; this means that a universe also happens to be a valid index range for arrays. Choosing a universe, we implement a set as a one-dimensional array of Boolean values, with index range corresponding to that universe. Given a set S represented as an array S, if a given member of the universe is a member of S, we let the corresponding element of S be `True`; otherwise we let that element be `False`. This representation is often called the *characteristic function* or *bit map* of a set, and is an especially compact way to represent a large set. For example, suppose we choose the universe a ..g. Every set over this universe is represented as a Boolean array indexed `'a'..'g'`; the set $S = \{a, d, e, g\}$, specifically, is represented as

a	b	c	d	e	f	g
True	False	False	True	True	False	True

Now let us devise a generic Ada package for this ADT. A framework for the generic part of the specification is

```
GENERIC
  TYPE Universe IS (<>);
PACKAGE Sets_Generic IS
  . . .
END Sets_Generic;
```

The second line specifies a generic parameter that can match any discrete type;— that is, any enumeration type or integer subtype. This is exactly what we need for our finite, discrete universes!

Program 5.15 gives the desired specification, complete with `PRIVATE` part defining the type `Set`. Making sets a `PRIVATE` type allows client programs to copy sets and check them for inequality using the predefined assignment, equality, and inequality operations, but denies clients direct access to the implementation of sets. This leaves the package writer the flexibility to change the implementation of sets without requiring any code changes in client programs.

Program 5.15 Specification for Generic Set Package

```
GENERIC

  TYPE Universe IS (<>); -- any integer or enumeration type

PACKAGE Sets_Generic IS
-----------------------------------------------------------------------
--| Specification for sets over discrete universes
--| Author: Michael B. Feldman, The George Washington University
--| Last Modified: October 1995
-----------------------------------------------------------------------

  TYPE Set IS PRIVATE;
  Phi: CONSTANT Set; -- empty set

  -- constructors

  FUNCTION "+" (S: Set; E: Universe) RETURN Set;
  FUNCTION "-" (S: Set; E: Universe) RETURN Set;
  -- Pre:  S and E are defined
  -- Post: returns S with E inserted or deleted respectively;
  --    "+" has no effect if IsIn(S,E); "-" has none if NOT IsIn(S,E)

  FUNCTION Singleton(E: Universe) RETURN Set;
  FUNCTION "+" (E1, E2: Universe) RETURN Set;
  -- Pre:  E, E1, and E2 are defined
  -- Post: returns a set made from one or two elements

  FUNCTION "+" (S, T : Set) RETURN Set;
  FUNCTION "*" (S, T : Set) RETURN Set;
  FUNCTION "-" (S, T : Set) RETURN Set;
  -- Pre:  S and T are defined
  -- Post: returns the union, intersection, and difference of
  --    S and T, respectively

  FUNCTION "-"  (S : Set) RETURN Set;
  -- Pre:  S is defined
  -- Post: returns the complement of S

  -- selectors
  FUNCTION IsIn (S : Set; E : Universe) RETURN Boolean;
  -- Pre:  S and E are defined
  -- Post: returns True if and only if E is a member of S

  FUNCTION IsEmpty (S : Set) RETURN Boolean;
  -- Pre:  S is defined
  -- Post: returns True if and only if S is empty

  FUNCTION SizeOf (S : Set) RETURN Natural;
  -- Pre:  S is defined
  -- Post: returns the number of members in S

  FUNCTION "<=" (S, T : Set) RETURN Boolean;
  FUNCTION "<"  (S, T : Set) RETURN Boolean;
  -- Pre:  S and T are defined
  -- Post: returns True if and only if S is
  --    an improper or proper subset of T, respectively
PRIVATE
  TYPE SetArray IS ARRAY (Universe) OF Boolean;
  TYPE Set IS RECORD
    Store: SetArray := (OTHERS => False);
  END RECORD;
  Phi: CONSTANT Set := (Store => (OTHERS => False));
END Sets_Generic;
```

Note in the type definition that the Boolean array is stored in a record. This is done to let us initialize all sets by default to the empty set: Recall that Ada allows us to default-initialize only objects of a record type. Note also the constant `Phi`, which we use to represent the empty set. The constant is partially declared at the top of the specification, then completed in the private part, after the full type definition for the private type is given.

The operations to insert and delete a member are shown as operators `"+"` and `"-"`, respectively, so that given a set `S` and an element `E`, the expressions `S + E` and `S - E` are meaningful. We include an additional constructor operator `Singleton`, which creates a singleton set—a set with a single member—from its element parameter, and another `"+"` operator to create a set from two elements. Specifying all these operations as functions makes it easy to create a set with the desired membership. For example, a client program could instantiate `Sets_Generic` as follows:

```
SUBTYPE SmallNatural is NATURAL RANGE 0..15);
PACKAGE NaturalSets IS NEW Sets_Generic(Universe => SmallNatural);
```

and then, having declared a variable

```
S: NaturalSets.Set;
```

could include the odd small naturals in `S` with

```
S := 7 + 3 + 13 + 5 + 1 + 9 + 11 + 15;
```

Implementing the Generic Set ADT

Program 5.16 shows the body of the package `Sets_Generic`. Note that the union, intersection, and difference operators construct their results by looping through the sets, finding element-wise `AND`, `OR`, and `NOT` values. These operations, as well as the `SizeOf` and subset operations, are therefore $O(N)$ operations, where N is the size of the universe. In Exercise 7, you are asked to exploit a nice feature of Ada's Boolean arrays in order to simplify the operators.

Program 5.16 Body of Generic Set Package

```
PACKAGE BODY Sets_Generic IS
-------------------------------------------------------------------------
--| Body of generic sets package
--| Author: Michael B. Feldman, The George Washington University
--| Last Modified: October 1995
-------------------------------------------------------------------------

  -- constructors

  FUNCTION "+"(S: Set; E: Universe) RETURN Set IS
    Result: Set := S;
  BEGIN -- "+"
    Result.Store (E) := True;
    RETURN Result;
  END "+";
```

```
FUNCTION "-" (S: Set; E: Universe) RETURN Set IS
  Result: Set := S;
BEGIN -- "-"
  Result.Store (E) := False;
  RETURN Result;
END "-";

FUNCTION Singleton(E: Universe) RETURN Set IS
BEGIN -- Singleton
  RETURN Phi + E;
END Singleton;

FUNCTION "+" (E1, E2: Universe) RETURN Set IS
BEGIN -- "+"
  RETURN Phi + E1 + E2;
END "+";

FUNCTION "+" (S, T : Set) RETURN Set IS
  Result: Set;
BEGIN -- "+"
  FOR E IN Universe LOOP
    Result.Store(E) := S.Store(E) OR T.Store(E);
  END LOOP;
  RETURN Result;
END "+";

FUNCTION "*" (S, T : Set) RETURN Set IS
  Result: Set;
BEGIN -- "*"
  FOR E IN Universe LOOP
    Result.Store(E) := S.Store(E) AND T.Store(E);
  END LOOP;
  RETURN Result;
END "*";

FUNCTION "-" (S, T : Set) RETURN Set IS
  Result: Set;
BEGIN -- "-"
  FOR E IN Universe LOOP
    Result.Store(E) := S.Store(E) AND NOT T.Store(E);
  END LOOP;
  RETURN Result;
END "-";

FUNCTION "-" (S : Set) RETURN Set IS
  Result: Set;
BEGIN -- "-"
  FOR E IN Universe LOOP
    Result.Store(E) := NOT S.Store(E);
  END LOOP;
  RETURN Result;
END "-";

-- selectors

FUNCTION IsIn (S : Set; E : Universe) RETURN Boolean IS
BEGIN -- IsIn
  RETURN S.Store (E);
END IsIn;

FUNCTION IsEmpty (S : Set) RETURN Boolean IS
BEGIN -- IsEmpty
```

```
      RETURN S = Phi;
   END IsEmpty;

   FUNCTION SizeOf (S : Set) RETURN Natural IS
      Result: Natural := 0;
   BEGIN -- SizeOf
      FOR E IN Universe LOOP
         IF S.Store(E) THEN
            Result := Result + 1;
         END IF;
      END LOOP;
      RETURN Result;
   END SizeOf;

   FUNCTION "<=" (S, T : Set) RETURN Boolean IS
   BEGIN -- "<="
      FOR E IN Universe LOOP
         IF S.Store(E) AND NOT T.Store(E) THEN
            RETURN False;
         END IF;
      END LOOP;
      RETURN True;
   END "<=";

   FUNCTION "<" (S, T : Set) RETURN Boolean IS
   BEGIN -- "<"
      RETURN S /= T AND THEN S <= T;
   END "<";

END Sets_Generic;
```

5.5 APPLICATION: MUSIC MAKERS

Program 5.17 shows an example of how Sets_Generic might be used. An enumeration type Instruments is declared, representing common musical instruments. The generic package is instantiated for these and variables are created representing different kinds of musical ensembles, depending on the instruments usually found in them. The program shows one local procedure DisplayEnsemble by using an instance of Text_IO.Enumeration_IO and iterating through an ensemble to display only the instruments present in that ensemble.

Program 5.17 A Music-Makers Program

```
WITH Ada.Text_IO;
WITH Sets_Generic;
PROCEDURE Music_Makers IS
------------------------------------------------------------------------
--| Example of the use of Sets_Generic, to create musical ensembles
--| Author: Michael B. Feldman, The George Washington University
--| Last Modified: September 1995
------------------------------------------------------------------------

  TYPE Instruments IS
     (Violin, Viola, Cello, BassViol,      -- classical strings
      Piano, Harpsichord, Organ,           -- classical keyboards
```

```
       Clarinet, Saxophone,                -- single-reed woodwinds
       Oboe, Bassoon,                      -- double-reed woodwinds
       Flute, Piccolo,                     -- flutes
       Trumpet, Trombone, FrenchHorn, Tuba, -- brass
       Tympani, Snare, TomTom, BassDrum,   -- drums
       Cymbals, Triangle, Bells, Marimba,  -- percussion
       Guitar, Banjo, Ukelele,             -- folk strings
       Accordion, Keyboard);               -- miscellaneous


  PACKAGE Music_IO IS NEW Ada.Text_IO.Enumeration_IO(Enum =>
Instruments);
  PACKAGE Ensembles IS NEW Sets_Generic (Universe => Instruments);
  USE Ensembles;

  SUBTYPE Ensemble IS Ensembles.Set; -- nickname for this program

  Strings: CONSTANT Ensemble := Violin + Viola + Cello + BassViol;
  Brasses: CONSTANT Ensemble := Trumpet + Trombone + FrenchHorn + Tuba;
  JazzDrums: CONSTANT Ensemble := Snare + TomTom + BassDrum + Cymbals;


  JazzCombo:        Ensemble;
  StringQuartet:    Ensemble;
  PhillyStringBand: Ensemble;
  RockBand:         Ensemble;


  PROCEDURE DisplayEnsemble(Band: Ensemble) IS
  BEGIN
    FOR Instrument IN Instruments LOOP
      IF IsIn(Band, Instrument) THEN
        Music_IO.Put(Instrument);
        Ada.Text_IO.New_Line;
      END IF;
    END LOOP;
    Ada.Text_IO.New_Line;
  END DisplayEnsemble;

BEGIN -- Music_Makers

  JazzCombo := JazzDrums + Guitar + BassViol + Trumpet;
  Ada.Text_IO.Put(Item => "Jazz Combo:");
  Ada.Text_IO.New_Line;
  DisplayEnsemble(Band => JazzCombo);

  PhillyStringBand := Guitar + Ukelele + Banjo + Accordion
    + Saxophone + Snare + BassDrum;
  Ada.Text_IO.Put(Item => "Philly String Band:");
  Ada.Text_IO.New_Line;
  DisplayEnsemble(Band => PhillyStringBand);

  StringQuartet := Strings - BassViol;
  Ada.Text_IO.Put(Item => "String Quartet:");
  Ada.Text_IO.New_Line;
  DisplayEnsemble(Band => StringQuartet);

  RockBand := Guitar + Keyboard + JazzDrums;
  Ada.Text_IO.Put(Item => "Rock Band:");
  Ada.Text_IO.New_Line;
  DisplayEnsemble(Band => RockBand);


END Music_Makers;
```

One of the ensembles in the program, `PhillyStringBand`, reveals the author's Philadelphia upbringing: This city is the home of the String Band, which—as can be seen from the instruments—includes more than strings and has no violins. A large number of String Bands march in Philadelphia's New Year's Day parade; prizes are awarded to the groups that have the most imaginative costumes as well as the best music.

In Exercise 10, you can create some of your favorite musical ensembles. Try creating a brass band and a symphony orchestra. This example highlights one of the difficulties of using sets in the pure mathematical sense: Because duplicate elements do not change the set, we cannot, using this representation, keep track of just how many of each instrument are in a particular ensemble—only the instrument *types* are represented.

5.6 ADT DESIGN: A GENERIC VECTOR PACKAGE

We continue our study of generics by showing how to build a generic version of the `Vectors` package introduced in Section 4.4. Program 5.18 gives the specification for the package.

Program 5.18 Specification for Generic `Vectors` Package

```
GENERIC

  TYPE ValueType IS PRIVATE;
  TYPE IndexType IS (<>);

  WITH FUNCTION "+"(L,R: ValueType) RETURN ValueType;
  WITH FUNCTION "*"(L,R: ValueType) RETURN ValueType;

  Zero: ValueType;

PACKAGE Vectors_Generic IS
-----------------------------------------------------------------------
--| Generic specification for vector arithmetic package
--| Author: Michael B. Feldman, The George Washington University
--| Last Modified: October 1995
-----------------------------------------------------------------------

  TYPE Vector IS ARRAY(IndexType RANGE <>) OF ValueType;

  -- exported exception, raised if two vectors are not conformable
  -- (i.e., have different bounds)

  Bounds_Error : EXCEPTION;

  FUNCTION "+" (K : ValueType; Right : Vector)  RETURN Vector;
  -- Pre: K and Right are defined
  -- Post: returns the sum of the vector and the scalar
  --    Result(i) := K + Right(i)

  FUNCTION "*" (K : ValueType; Right : Vector) RETURN Vector;
  -- Pre: K and Right are defined
  -- Post: returns the product of the vector and the scalar
  --    Result(i) := K * Right(i)
```

```
FUNCTION "*" (Left, Right : Vector) RETURN ValueType;
-- Pre: Left and Right are defined and have the same bounds
-- Post: returns the inner product of Left and Right

FUNCTION "+" (Left, Right : Vector) RETURN Vector;
-- Pre: Left and Right are defined and have the same bounds
-- Post: returns the sum of Left and Right
--    Result(i) := Left(i) + Right(i)

END Vectors_Generic;
```

The specification promises that we will provide actual parameters for the index type and value type; the package itself will create the vector type so that a client program can use it, just like any other type provided by a package. The two WITH FUNCTION lines are necessary because the body of the package adds and multiplies elements—for example, in the dot product function. Finally, the line

```
Zero: ValueType;
```

promises that we will supply a "zero" value for the element type. Because in the inner product routine the Sum variable needs to be set to zero, this parameter is necessary. We cannot simply write

```
Sum := 0.0;
```

as in the nongeneric version: What if ValueType is not Float? Then 0.0 does not exist! Instead, we need to write

```
Sum := Zero;
```

and pass the value of Zero as a generic parameter. You can write the package body as an exercise; it will be similar to the one shown in Program 4.4. A sample compilable instantiation, which will provide vectors of Float values, indexed by Integer ranges, is

```
WITH Vectors_Generic;
PACKAGE FloatVectors IS NEW Vectors_Generic
  (ValueType => Float,
   IndexType => Integer,
   "+" => "+",
   "*" => "*",
   Zero => 0.0);
```

A client program could use this instance by writing the context clause

```
WITH FloatVectors;
```

Defaults: Short Cut for Specifying Generic Subprogram Parameters

Ada provides a "short cut" for specifying generic function and procedure parameters. By analogy with other kinds of default values—for example, the default initialization of fields in a record type—we can assign a default value to a subprogram parameter. Recall that in the specification of Vectors given in Program 5.19, the line

```
WITH FUNCTION "+" (L,R: ValueType) RETURN ValueType;
```

indicates that a function with the correct parameter profile and return type will be provided at instantiation. The client program, instantiating for, say, `Float` values, as in the example just above, must include

```
"+" => "+"
```

in the actual parameter list. We can simplify the client's job a bit by using a default:

```
WITH FUNCTION "+" (L,R: ValueType) RETURN ValueType IS <>;
```

whose rather strange-looking `IS <>` syntax instructs the compiler to do the work of searching among all the visible operations for a function named `"+"` with the correct profile. This allows—but does not require—the instantiating program to omit that parameter from the list of actuals. In the `Vectors` example, if the `"+"` and `"*"` operators both carried this default, the instantiation could be shortened to

```
WITH Vectors_Generic;
PACKAGE FloatVectors IS NEW Vectors_Generic
   (ValueType => Float,
   IndexType => Integer,
   Zero => 0.0);
```

and the compiler would search for matching operators, finding the predefined addition and multiplication for `Float` values.

Now suppose we wished to instantiate for a user-defined value type—`Rational`, for example. We would then include a `WITH` and a `USE`:

```
WITH Rationals;
USE Rationals;
```

and then write

```
WITH Vectors_Generic;
PACKAGE RationalVectors IS NEW Vectors_Generic
   (ValueType => Rational,
   IndexType => Integer,
   Zero => 0/1);
```

The compiler would find three rational operators: the defaulted `"+"` and `"*"` and the rational constructor `"/"` needed to create the value `0/1`.

Finally, remember that the default allows omission of the actual subprogram parameter only if its name matches that of the formal. Suppose we wished to create a package capable of dealing with vectors of Boolean values (similar to the `Sets` representation above; we will also see other applications later in the book). In Boolean algebra, the role of the addition operator is played by `"OR"` and the role of the multiplication operator by `"AND"`. An instantiation of `Vectors` would look like

```
WITH Vectors_Generic;
PACKAGE BitMaps IS NEW Vectors_Generic
   (ValueType => Boolean,
   IndexType => Integer,
   "+" => "OR",
```

```
"*" =" "AND",
Zero => False);
```

and in this case the two operator parameters *must* be supplied, even with the defaults, because `"OR"` has a different name from `"+"`.

Default values for subprograms are handy, especially in the case of infix operators that appear in `Standard` and user-defined mathematical ADTs such as `Rationals` and `Matrices`. As an exercise, you can revise the matrix system introduced in Section 4.5 so that it is generic and can be instantiated for any mathematical type such as `Integer`, `Float`, or `Rational`.

5.7   SUMMARY OF GENERIC SPECIFICATIONS

A generic specification defines a generic procedure, function, or package, for which a corresponding body must also be provided. The list of generic formal type, procedure or function, and object parameters indicates the structure of the parameters to be supplied at instantiation of the generic.

Here are the forms of the generic type parameters we have seen here, as well as their interpretation. There are other generic type parameters, but their discussion is beyond the scope of this book. The form

```
TYPE ValueParameterName IS PRIVATE;
```

which is most commonly used as a value parameter, indicates that any type can be matched at instantiation, including a private type, as long as it is not `LIMITED PRIVATE`. That is, the operations of assignment and equality testing must be defined for the type. The form

```
TYPE IndexParameterName IS (<>);
```

indicates that any discrete type—that is, an integer or enumeration type or subtype—can be matched at instantiation. This form is commonly used to specify the index type of an array type. The form

```
TYPE ArrayParameterName IS
  ARRAY(IndexParameterName RANGE <>) OF ValueParameterName;
```

indicates that any unconstrained array type with the given index and value types can be matched at instantiation.

A generic procedure parameter specification is of the form

```
WITH PROCEDURE ProcedureName(Param1: Type1; Param2: Type...);
```

and a generic function parameter specification is of the form

```
WITH FUNCTION
  FunctionName(Param1: Type1; Param2: Type2...) RETURN Type3;
```

where either of these can be terminated by `IS <>` to provide a default value.

5.8 ADT DESIGN: GENERIC KEYED TABLE HANDLER

The keyed table ADT was introduced in Section 3.4. The ADT discussed there was only sketched out, in order to discuss the performance ("big *O*") of its operations for sorted and unsorted implementations. Section 3.5 introduced an application of the keyed table, namely employee records. That application is limited in that everything is tailored specifically to employee records and some recoding would be necessary to use the database for other kinds of records.

The purpose of this section is to generalize the keyed table so that with a simple instantiation we can use it for many kinds of record structures. Moreover, we will develop the specification for the ADT in a way that facilitates changing the implementation with no effect on the source code for client programs.

After a description in English of the operations of an ADT for a keyed table, we develop a generic package specification and an array implementation. The keyed table is a recurring theme in this book: In subsequent chapters, we will consider at least three additional implementations: the one-way linked list, the binary search tree, and the hash table.

The Generic Package Specification

We wish to specify the keyed table in a way that is, as far as is possible, independent of the record type, the key type, or, indeed, the data structures used for the implementation. In this manner, we give client programs the most flexibility in supplying keys and records, and we give ourselves the most flexibility in determining and changing implementations without affecting any of the statements of the client program.

To provide the desired flexibility to the client, we make the package generic, with the following list of generic formal parameters:

```
GENERIC

   TYPE Element IS PRIVATE;      -- assignment and equality predefined
   TYPE KeyType IS PRIVATE;      -- here too

   Capacity: IN Positive;        -- maximum table size

   -- These generic parameters specify how to
   -- retrieve the key from an element, compare elements
   WITH FUNCTION KeyOf  (Item: Element) RETURN KeyType IS <>;
   WITH FUNCTION "<"    (Key1, Key2: KeyType) RETURN Boolean IS <>;

   -- This parameter specifies what to do with each element during
   -- a traversal of a table;
   WITH PROCEDURE Visit (Item: Element);

PACKAGE Tables_Generic IS
   . . .
      TYPE TableType IS LIMITED PRIVATE;
   . . .
END Tables_Generic;
```

As in the generic binary search, the types `Element` and `KeyType` are specified as `PRIVATE` to allow any types to be supplied as actual parameters as long as assignment and equality are defined for them. The parameter `Capacity` allows the client program to specify the maximum number of elements the table can hold.

We require the client to provide functions `"<"` and `KeyOf`, which serve the same purpose they served in the search case. Finally, the procedure `Visit` is required so that the client program can specify how each element is to be processed during a traversal of the table.

Program 5.19 gives the full specification of the table package.

Program 5.19 Specification for Generic Tables Package

```
GENERIC

  TYPE Element IS PRIVATE;      -- assignment and equality predefined
  TYPE KeyType IS PRIVATE;      -- here too

  Capacity: IN Positive;        -- maximum table size

  -- These generic parameters specify how to
  -- retrieve the key from an element, compare elements
  WITH FUNCTION KeyOf (Item: Element) RETURN KeyType IS <>;
  WITH FUNCTION "<"   (Key1, Key2: KeyType) RETURN Boolean IS <>;

  -- This parameter specifies what to do with each element during
  -- a traversal of a table;
  WITH PROCEDURE Visit (Item: Element);

PACKAGE Tables_Generic IS
-----------------------------------------------------------------------
--| Specification of the abstract data type for a table of
--| element records, each containing a key.
--| This version has type definitions to implement the table as an
--| array. The client cannot see or use these types
--| because Table is LIMITED PRIVATE.
--| Author: Michael B. Feldman, The George Washington University
--| Last Modified: September 1995
-----------------------------------------------------------------------

-- Data Structure

  TYPE TableType IS LIMITED PRIVATE;

-- Exported exceptions

  UninitializedTable: EXCEPTION;
  NoSpaceLeft       : EXCEPTION;

-- Operators

  PROCEDURE InitializeTable (Table : IN OUT TableType);
  -- initializes a Table.
  -- Pre : None
  -- Post: Table is an initialized TableType

  FUNCTION SizeOfTable (Table : TableType) RETURN Natural;
  -- Returns the number of elements in a Table
  -- Pre : Table is an initialized TableType
  -- Post: Returns the number of elements in Table
```

```
   PROCEDURE Search (Table   : TableType;
                     Target  : KeyType;
                     Success : OUT Boolean);
-- Searches a Table for Target.
-- Pre : Table is an initialized TableType
-- Post: Success is True if Target is found; otherwise,
--       Success is False.

   PROCEDURE Insert (Table   : IN OUT TableType;
                     Item    : Element;
                     Success : OUT Boolean);
-- Inserts Item into a Table.
-- Pre : Table and Item are defined; Table is initialized.
-- Post: Success is True if insertion is performed; Success is False
--       if insertion is not performed because there is already
--       an element with the same key as Item.
-- Raises: NoSpaceLeft if there is no space available for Item.

   PROCEDURE Delete (Table   : IN OUT TableType;
                     Target  : KeyType;
                     Success : OUT Boolean);
-- Deletes the element with key Target from a Table.
-- Pre : Table and Target are defined; Table is initialized.
-- Post: Success is True if deletion is performed; Success is False
--       if deletion is not performed because there is no element
--       whose key is Target.

   PROCEDURE Replace (Table   : IN OUT TableType;
                      Item    : Element;
                      Success : OUT Boolean);
-- Replaces the element of a Table with the same key as
-- Item by the contents of Item.
-- Pre : Table and Item are defined; Table is initialized.
-- Post: Success is True if the replacement is performed; Success is
--       False if there is no element with the same key as Item.

   PROCEDURE Retrieve (Table   : TableType;
                       Target  : KeyType;
                       Item    : OUT Element;
                       Success : OUT Boolean);
-- Copies the element whose key is Target into Item.
-- Pre : Table is an initialized TableType.
-- Post: Success is True if the copy is performed; Success is False
--       if there is no element whose key is Target.

   PROCEDURE Traverse (Table : TableType);
-- Repeatedly calls procedure Visit (a generic parameter) to
--   process each element of a Table.
-- Pre : Table is an initialized TableType.
-- Post: Each element is operated on in turn by procedure Visit.

PRIVATE

   SUBTYPE TableIndex IS Positive RANGE 1..Capacity;
   SUBTYPE TableSize  IS Natural  RANGE 0..Capacity;

   TYPE TableData IS ARRAY(TableIndex RANGE <>) OF Element;

   TYPE TableType IS RECORD
     CurrentSize : TableSize := 0;
     Data        : TableData(TableIndex);
   END RECORD;

End Tables_Generic;
```

Note the declaration of a package-defined exception `UninitializedTable`, which will be raised by several of the package operators if the client sends to them a table that was not initialized by a call to `InitializeTable`. Also declared is `NoSpaceLeft`, which is raised if the client attempts to insert a new element into a full table.

We have added the operations `SizeOfTable`, `Search`, and `Replace` to the specification; their postconditions explain their rather obvious purpose. The `PRIVATE` implementation section shows type declarations for an array implementation similar to that of the employee example of Section 3.5. Program 5.20 gives a skeleton for the package body, with stubs for most of the operations. These stubs use the enter and exit messages provided by the package `Debugging_Support`, as introduced in Section 3.5.

Program 5.20 Body of Generic Tables Package

```
WITH Binary_Search_Generic;
WITH Debugging_Support;
PACKAGE BODY Tables_Generic IS
----------------------------------------------------------------------
--| Body of the abstract data type for a table of
--| element records, each element containing a key.
--| Author: Michael B. Feldman, The George Washington University
--| Last Modified: October 1995
----------------------------------------------------------------------

  PROCEDURE Locate IS
    NEW Binary_Search_Generic(
        ElementType => Element,
        KeyType => KeyType,
        KeyOf => KeyOf,
        "<" => "<",
        IndexType => TableIndex,
        ListType => TableData);

  PROCEDURE InitializeTable (Table : IN OUT TableType) IS
  BEGIN -- stub
    Debugging_Support.Enter (Subprogram => "InitializeTable",
      Message => "Under Construction ");
    Debugging_Support.Leave (Subprogram => "InitializeTable ");
   END InitializeTable;

  FUNCTION SizeOfTable(Table: TableType) RETURN Natural IS
  BEGIN -- stub
    Debugging_Support.Enter (Subprogram => "SizeOfTable ",
      Message => "Under Construction ");
    Debugging_Support.Leave (Subprogram => "SizeOfTable ");
    RETURN 0;
  END SizeOfTable;

  PROCEDURE Search (Table   : TableType;
                    Target  : KeyType;
                    Success : OUT Boolean) IS
  BEGIN -- stub
    Debugging_Support.Enter (Subprogram => "Search ",
      Message => "Under Construction ");
    Debugging_Support.Leave (Subprogram => "Search ");
  END Search;
```

```
      PROCEDURE Insert (Table   : IN OUT TableType;
                        Item    : Element;
                        Success : OUT Boolean) IS
   BEGIN -- stub
     Debugging_Support.Enter (Subprogram => "Insert ",
       Message => "Under Construction ");
     Debugging_Support.Leave (Subprogram => "Insert ");
   END Insert;

      PROCEDURE Delete (Table   : IN OUT TableType;
                        Target  : KeyType;
                        Success : OUT Boolean) IS
   BEGIN -- stub
     Debugging_Support.Enter (Subprogram => "Delete ",
       Message => "Under Construction ");
     Debugging_Support.Leave (Subprogram => "Delete ");
   END Delete;

      PROCEDURE Replace  (Table   : IN OUT TableType;
                          Item    : Element;
                          Success : OUT Boolean) IS
   BEGIN -- stub
     Debugging_Support.Enter (Subprogram => "Replace ",
       Message => "Under Construction ");
     Debugging_Support.Leave (Subprogram => "Replace");
   END Replace;

      PROCEDURE Retrieve (Table   : TableType;
                          Target  : KeyType;
                          Item    : OUT Element;
                          Success : OUT Boolean) IS
   BEGIN -- stub
     Debugging_Support.Enter (Subprogram => "Retrieve",
       Message => "Under Construction");
     Debugging_Support.Leave (Subprogram => "Retrieve");
   END Retrieve;

      PROCEDURE Traverse (Table : TableType) IS
   BEGIN -- stub
     Debugging_Support.Enter (Subprogram => "Traverse">,
       Message => "Under Construction");
     Debugging_Support.Leave (Subprogram => "Traverse");
   END Traverse;

END Tables_Generic;
```

This body implements the table as an ordered array; therefore, `Binary_Search_Generic` can be instantiated and used for the basic search operation. The instantiating statement

```
PROCEDURE Locate IS
   NEW Binary_Search_Generic(
        ElementType => Element,
        KeyType => KeyType,
        KeyOf => KeyOf,
        "<" => "<",
        IndexType => TableIndex,
        ListType  => TableData);
```

takes the generic table parameters and "passes them through" to the generic search; make sure you understand how this works. `Locate` can now be called to locate an element in the table, or to discover where it should be placed; this is the critical part of almost all the table operations. You can complete the body, and test it, as an exercise.

Your test program can be a modification of Program 3.15, suitably extended to cover all the operations. In your test program, instantiate `Tables_Generic` as follows:

```
PACKAGE EmployeeTables IS NEW Tables_Generic(
  Capacity => 25,
  Element  => Employees.Employee,
  KeyType  => Employees.NameType,
  KeyOf    => Employees.RetrieveName,
  "<"      => "<",
  Visit    => Employees.IO.Display);
```

Declare some variables in your test program:

```
Company: EmployeeTables.TableType;
OneEmployee: Employees.Employee;
Done: Boolean;
```

Now you can use the various operations:

```
Employees.IO.ReadEmployee(Item => OneEmployee);
EmployeeTables.Insert(T => Company, E => OneEmployee, Success =>  Done);
```

and so on.

You might even want to develop a simple modification of the menu-driven interface `Employee_UI` (Program 3.16) that uses the generic package.

5.9 ADT DESIGN: A GENERIC BACKUP PACKAGE

Our table package provides useful operations for maintaining a table in main memory. How was that table originally placed in main memory? There are several possibiities:

- Write a main program, consisting of a number of `Insert` calls containing "hardwired" data—that is, with the values of the record fields written out in the program. This is a useful practice for testing the package operations, but it is not a very practical method for maintaining the table dynamically.

- Write an interactive program such as `Employee_UI`, to enter the data into the table. This is the most common way to input the data, but requires the data to be entered anew each time the program is run.

- Provide a way to save the entire contents of the table to an external disk file and then restore the table from that file at a later date.

The last approach is the subject of this section. Save-and-restore capabilities are provided with almost every realistic application program. Word processors, data base managers, even game programs, all have commands that enable the user to save work to, and restore work from, external files.

In this section, we use an Ada generic child package to add save and restore operations to the generic table package. Program 5.21 is the specification for this package, which is called `Tables_Generic.Backup`.

Program 5.21 Specification for Generic Backup Package

```
WITH Ada.Text_IO;
GENERIC
  WITH PROCEDURE Get
    (File: IN Ada.Text_IO.File_Type; Item: OUT Element) IS <>;
  WITH PROCEDURE Put
    (File: IN Ada.Text_IO.File_Type; Item: IN Element) IS <>;
PACKAGE Tables_Generic.Backup IS
------------------------------------------------------------------------
--| Generic Child Package for Save and Restore of a Table
--| Author: Michael B. Feldman, The George Washington University
--| Last Modified: January 1996
------------------------------------------------------------------------

  PROCEDURE Save (T: IN TableType; FileName: IN String);
  -- Pre:  T and FileName are defined
  -- Post: The given file is created and the contents of T
  --       are written to the file.

  PROCEDURE Restore (T: OUT TableType; FileName: IN String);
  -- Pre:  T and FileName are defined
  -- Post: T is restored from the given file

END Tables_Generic.Backup;
```

You can see from the comments and postconditions that the `Save` operation takes a table parameter and a string that gives the name of the desired external file. `Save` creates the desired file and then copies the current table contents into that file. `Restore` takes a string as its file parameter, opens that file, and copies the file contents into the table.

`Save` must repeatedly call a `Put` operation that can write a single table element into a file; `Restore` must repeatedly call a `Get` operation that reads a single element from a file. Because the table package is generic and the element type can vary, the backup package must be generic as well and depends upon the client program providing the single-element `Get` and `Put`. This is done, as usual, with generic procedure parameters.

The details of `Save` and `Restore` are shown in the package body, Program 5.22.

Program 5.22 Body of Generic Backup Package

```
WITH Ada.Text_IO;
WITH Ada.Integer_Text_IO;
WITH Debugging_Support;
```

```
PACKAGE BODY Tables_Generic.Backup IS
------------------------------------------------------------------------
--| Body of generic backup/restore. Save simply copies the occupied
--| part of the array into the file, one record per line. The first
--| line of the file gives the number of records, T.CurrentSize.
--| Note that because this is a child package, it can "see" into the
--| private part of the parent and "knows" the structure of a table.
--| Author: Michael B. Feldman, The George Washington University
--| Last Modified: January 1996
------------------------------------------------------------------------

  PROCEDURE Save (T: IN TableType; FileName: IN String) IS
    BackupFile: Ada.Text_IO.File_Type;
  BEGIN -- Save
    Debugging_Support.Enter(Subprogram => "Save");

    Ada.Text_IO.Create(File => BackupFile,
                       Mode => Ada.Text_IO.Out_File,
                       Name => FileName);
    Ada.Integer_Text_IO.Put(File => BackupFile, Item => T.CurrentSize);
    Ada.Text_IO.New_Line(File => BackupFile);

    FOR Count IN 1..T.CurrentSize LOOP
      Put(File => BackupFile, Item => T.Data(Count));
    END LOOP;

    Ada.Text_IO.Close(File => BackupFile);

    Debugging_Support.Leave(Subprogram => "Save");
  END Save;

  PROCEDURE Restore (T: OUT TableType; FileName: IN String) IS
    BackupFile: Ada.Text_IO.File_Type;
    Count: TableSize;
  BEGIN -- Restore
    Debugging_Support.Enter(Subprogram => "Restore");

    Ada.Text_IO.Open (File => BackupFile,
                      Mode => Ada.Text_IO.In_File,
                      Name => FileName);

    Ada.Integer_Text_IO.Get(File => BackupFile, Item => T.CurrentSize);
    Ada.Text_IO.Skip_Line(File => BackupFile);
    FOR Count IN 1..T.CurrentSize LOOP
      Get(File => BackupFile, Item => T.Data(Count));
    END LOOP;

    Ada.Text_IO.Close(File => BackupFile);

    Debugging_Support.Leave(Subprogram => "Restore");
  END Restore;

END Tables_Generic.Backup;
```

As the comments indicate, this backup package is tailored to our table package. The table is represented as an unordered array. Therefore, `Save` can operate by simply looping through the array and writing each element to the file, using the client-provided `Put`. To keep the file in a standard form, each record is written to one line of the file. The number of records is `T.CurrentSize`; this value is written to the file before the records are copied out, so that `Restore` will know how many records to read back.

As with earlier input/output packages we have introduced, this package is written as a child of `Tables_Generic`. As we know, a child package can "see into" the private section of its parent. We wish to allow `Save` and `Restore` to know the details of a table, so they can loop through the table directly and directly reference `T.CurrentSize`. We reiterate that child packages should be used sparingly, because they can violate the `PRIVATE` nature of the data structures. Do not use a child package where a client program or client package is more appropriate.

Program 5.23 demonstrates the workings of the `Save` and `Restore` operations.

Program 5.23 Demonstration of Generic Backup Package

```
WITH Tables_Generic;
WITH Tables_Generic.Backup;
WITH Dates;
WITH Dates.IO;
WITH Debugging_Support;
USE  Debugging_Support;
PROCEDURE Test_Backup IS
------------------------------------------------------------------
--| Demonstration of generic backup/restore package.
--| Author: Michael B. Feldman, The George Washington University
--| Last Modified: January 1996
------------------------------------------------------------------

  -- set up simple name/birthday record
  SUBTYPE NameType IS String(1..10);

  TYPE BirthRecord IS RECORD
    Name: NameType;
    Birthday: Dates.Date;
  END RECORD;

  -- The next two subprograms satisfy the KeyOf and Visit
  -- parameters of Tables_Generic

  FUNCTION KeyOf (Item: BirthRecord) RETURN NameType IS
  BEGIN
    RETURN Item.Name;
  END KeyOf;

  PROCEDURE Put(Item: IN BirthRecord) IS
  BEGIN
    Ada.Text_IO.Put(Item => Item.Name);
    Dates.IO.Put(Item => Item.Birthday);
    Ada.Text_IO.New_Line;
  END Put;

  -- Now we can instantiate Tables_Generic

  PACKAGE BirthdayTables IS
    NEW Tables_Generic
      (Element => BirthRecord,
       KeyType => NameType,
       Capacity => 50,
       Visit => Put);

  -- We need file-oriented Get and Put to satisfy Tables_Generic.Backup
```

```
PROCEDURE Get(File: IN Ada.Text_IO.File_Type; Item: OUT BirthRecord) IS
BEGIN
  Ada.Text_IO.Get(File => File, Item => Item.Name);
  Dates.IO.Get(File => File, Item => Item.Birthday);
  Ada.Text_IO.Skip_Line(File => File);
END Get;

PROCEDURE Put(File: IN Ada.Text_IO.File_Type; Item: IN BirthRecord) IS
BEGIN
  Ada.Text_IO.Put(File => File, Item => Item.Name);
  Dates.IO.Put(File => File, Item => Item.Birthday);
  Ada.Text_IO.New_Line(File => File);
END Put;

-- Now we can instantiate the backup package. Note that we refer to
-- the instance BirthdayTables, not the generic Tables_Generic.

PACKAGE BirthdayBackup IS
  NEW BirthdayTables.Backup;  -- note - instance used, not generic

Friends: BirthdayTables.TableType;

BEGIN -- Test_Backup

  Debugging_Support.SetDebug(WhichWay => On);

  -- The file birthdays.new should be a copy of birthdays.dat

  BirthdayBackup.Restore(T => Friends, FileName => "birthdays.dat");
  BirthdayBackup.Save(T => Friends, FileName => "birthdays.new");

END Test_Backup;
```

A simple birthday record is defined, consisting of a name and a date. `KeyOf` and
`Put` operations are defined and `Tables_Generic` is instantiated:

```
PACKAGE BirthdayTables IS
  NEW Tables_Generic
    (Element => BirthRecord,
     KeyType => NameType,
     Capacity => 50,
     Visit => Put);
```

Next, `Get` and `Put` operations are written to provide the necessary file operations,
and then `Tables_Generic.Backup` is instantiated as follows:

```
PACKAGE BirthdayBackup IS
  NEW BirthdayTables.Backup; -- note - instance used, not generic
```

When instantiating a generic child of a generic parent, Ada requires that the parent
instance—in this case, `BirthdayTables`—and not the parent *generic*—
`Tables_Generic`—be mentioned in the instantiation statement.

How should we test the backup package? We could write a program to create a
table, call `Save` to produce the backup, and so on. A simpler approach is simply to

1. Create a small file using an ordinary editor

2. Use `Restore` to load it into a table

3. Use `Save` to save it back into another file

4. Compare the two files

Program 5.23 assumes that step 1 has been done, then carries out steps 2 and 3. Suppose the initial file `birthdays.dat` has the following contents:

```
4
Benjamin Nov 2 1971
Keith    Oct 21 1977
Michael  Dec 15 1944
Ruth     Jul 8 1947
```

Executing `test_backup` will produce the following result on the screen:

```
>>>>> Entering Restore
>>>>> Leaving Restore
>>>>> Entering Save
>>>>> Leaving Save
```

Finally, the file `birthdays.new` should contain the same contents as the initial file.

5.10 APPLICATION: AIRLINE PASSENGER LIST

Problem

Develop an interactive program for maintaining a list of airline reservations for a particular flight, given a record for each passenger consisting of the passenger's name, class of travel (First, Business, Economy, and Standby), and number of seats reserved by that passenger. We must provide the abilities to add, to change, and to delete a reservation, and to save and restore the passenger list.

Analysis

We must first find a representation for a passenger record, then build a table to hold the reservations, and create a "front end" program with which the user can interact.

Design

A detailed discussion of the design is left as a programming project; we choose now to specify a package implementing passenger records. Given such a package, we can use our generic table manager to maintain the passenger reservation list.

We leave it as an exercise to provide an ADT package for passenger records, with the record represented as a `PRIVATE` type. You can use `Employees` and `Employees.IO` (Programs 3.7 through 3.9) a models for `Passengers` and `Passengers.IO`. Your interactive program can be modeled on `Employee_UI` (Program 3.16); this program will instantiate the generic table handler as follows:

```
PACKAGE FlightLists IS NEW Tables_Generic(
  Capacity    => 50,
  Element     => Passengers.Passenger,
  KeyType     => Passengers.NameType,
  KeyOf       => Passengers.RetrieveName,
  "<"         => "<",
  Visit       => Passengers.IO.Put);
```

5.11 ADT DESIGN: ADTs VERSUS ABSTRACT DATA OBJECTS

In using the generic table package from Section 5.8, each instantiation allows the client program to declare and use an arbitrary number of tables, just by declaring variables of the provided table type. Since in many applications only one table is needed, an alternative design for the table manager is to encapsulate the table type declarations, as well as a *single* table variable, inside the package body. This changes the table handler from an ADT to an *abstract data object (ADO)* design. The operations no longer require a table parameter.

In an ADO design, each instantiation of the package creates a single table, together with its own associated operations. Program 5.23 shows the modified package specification.

Program 5.24 Specification for Generic Table Object Package

```
GENERIC

   TYPE Element IS PRIVATE;      -- assignment and equality predefined
   TYPE KeyType IS PRIVATE;      -- here too

   Capacity: IN Positive;        -- maximum table size

   WITH FUNCTION  KeyOf      (Item: Element) RETURN  KeyType;
   WITH FUNCTION  "<"        (Key1, Key2: KeyType) RETURN Boolean;

   -- This parameter specifies what to do with each element during
   -- a traversal of a table;
   WITH PROCEDURE Visit (Item: Element);

PACKAGE Table_ADO_Generic IS
------------------------------------------------------------------------
--|
--| Specification of the abstract data object for a table of
--| element records, each containing a key.
--|
--| Author: Michael B. Feldman, The George Washington University
--| Last Modified: October 1995
--|
------------------------------------------------------------------------
```

```
-- Exported exceptions

  UninitializedTable: EXCEPTION;
  NoSpaceLeft        : EXCEPTION;

-- Operations

  PROCEDURE InitializeTable;
  -- Pre : None
  -- Post: the Table ADO is initialized

  FUNCTION SizeOfTable RETURN Natural;
  -- Pre : the Table ADO is initialized
  -- Post: Returns the number of elements in the Table ADO

  PROCEDURE Search (Target  : KeyType;
                    Success : OUT Boolean);
  -- Pre : the Table ADO is initialized
  -- Post: Success is True if Target is found; otherwise,
  --       Success is False.

  PROCEDURE Insert (Item    : Element;
                    Success : OUT Boolean);
  -- Pre : Item is defined; the Table ADO is initialized.
  -- Post: Success is True if insertion is performed; Success is False
  --       if insertion is not performed because there is already
  --       an element with the same key as Item.
  -- Raises: NoSpaceLeft if there is no space available for Item.

  PROCEDURE Delete (Target  : KeyType;
                    Success : OUT Boolean);
  -- Pre : Target are defined; Table ADO is initialized.
  -- Post: Success is True if deletion is performed; Success is False
  --       if deletion is not performed because there is no element
  --       whose key is Target.

  PROCEDURE Replace (Item    : Element;
                     Success : OUT Boolean);
  -- Item by the contents of Item.
  -- Pre : Item is defined; Table ADO is initialized.
  -- Post: Success is True if the replacement is performed; Success is
  --       False if there is no element with the same key as Item.

  PROCEDURE Retrieve (Target  : KeyType;
                      Item    : OUT Element;
                      Success : OUT Boolean);
  -- Pre : Table ADO is initialized
  -- Post: Success is True if the copy is performed; Success is False
  --       if there is no element whose key is Target.

  PROCEDURE Traverse;
  -- Repeatedly calls procedure Visit (a generic parameter) to
  --   process each element of the Table ADO.
  -- Pre : Table ADO is initialized
  -- Post: Each element is operated on in turn by procedure Visit.

END Table_ADO_Generic;
```

Note that there is no `TableType` declaration here; this package does not provide a type, but rather encapsulates a single object. The declarations from the `PRIVATE` section of the ADT package are now moved *inside* the ADO package body:

```
WITH Binary_Search_Generic;
PACKAGE BODY Table_ADO_Generic IS

    SUBTYPE TableIndex IS Positive RANGE 1..Capacity;
    SUBTYPE TableSize  IS Natural  RANGE 0..Capacity;

    TYPE TableData IS ARRAY(TableIndex RANGE <>) OF Element;

    TYPE TableType IS RECORD
      CurrentSize : TableSize := 0;
      Data : TableData(TableIndex);
    END RECORD;

    OneTable: TableType;

    . . .

END Table_ADO_Generic;
```

An instantiation, modified from the one in the previous section, might be

```
PACKAGE Flight23 IS NEW Table_ADO_Generic(
  Capacity   => 50,
  Element    => Passengers.Passenger,
  KeyType    => Passengers.NameType,
  KeyOf      => Passengers.RetrieveName,
  "<"        => ""<",
  Visit      => Passengers.IO.Display);
```

A typical operation now looks like this:

```
Flight123.Insert(Item => OnePassenger, Success => Done);
```

We leave it to you to complete the body and modify the passenger-list application accordingly. Also modify the backup package.

The ADO style of design is very effective if only one or two tables will be needed. However, because some compilers copy the object code for the entire generic package body into every instantiation, the ADO style uses a great deal of space if many objects are required. In this case, the ADT style is recommended.

SUMMARY

When writing generic specifications, it is sometimes difficult to figure out exactly which formal parameters to write. We have studied generic type parameters only briefly, and you would be wise to keep your generic specifications simple, following the examples in this chapter. Neglecting to supply a generic procedure or function parameter (such as "+" in the Vectors package) will result in a compilation error if the compiler encounters that procedure or function in the body. We always need to reassure the compiler that an appropriate operation will be supplied at instantiation, and the way to do this is by defining appropriate formal parameters.

Generic definition allows us to create templates, or recipes, for subprograms and packages. These templates allow us to leave such things as parameter types, sizes, and operations unspecified until instantiation time. Once a generic template is compiled, multiple versions of it, called instances, can then be created, each with a single statement. The availability of generic definition and instantiation gives us the ability to build large and powerful libraries of reusable software components with much less effort and with much greater maintainability. In this chapter, we have seen a number of useful generic components for exchanging values, finding the maximum, sorting, vector handling, sets, and keyed tables. Throughout the remainder of this book, ADTs will almost always be presented as generic units.

EXERCISES

1. Given a generic parameter

   ```
   WITH FUNCTION Compare(L,R: ValueType) RETURN Boolean;
   ```

   explain why it is legal to match this with an operator "<" or ">" at instantiation.

2. One generic parameter form we did not discuss in this chapter is

   ```
   TYPE SomeParameterName IS LIMITED PRIVATE;
   ```

   which allows *any* type, even a LIMITED PRIVATE one, to be supplied as a match at instantiation. Suppose we used one of these type forms in a generic package specification. What limitations would this place on the kinds of statements that could appear in the body of the package?

3. Demonstrate `Maximum_Array_Generic` for some interesting instantiations.

4. A useful function, similar to `Maximum_Array_Generic`, is one that finds the *location* of the "maximum" value in an array or slice, rather than the value itself. Write such a function as a generic, then write a generic sort program that uses it.

5. Modify Program 5.13 for the case in which the array to be searched consists simply of `Integer` elements.

6. Modify Program 5.13 for the case in which the array to be searched consists simply of `Rational` elements.

7. Ada provides an interesting feature for working with Boolean arrays: The logical operators `NOT, AND, OR`, and `XOR` (exclusive OR) are predefined for these arrays. This allows us to simplify the operators in the sets package by removing the loops and replacing them by expressions of the form `S.Store AND T.Store`. Modify the package to take advantage of this feature.

8. The feature described in Exercise 7 can also lead to a very nice code optimization. The `PRAGMA` (compiler directive) `Pack`, applied to a Boolean array type, will often allocate space for objects of this type using a single bit per Boolean value. Because many computers have hardware logical instructions that operate on binary words, the compiler can often implement an intersection, for example, using a small number of "word-wise" machine instructions. If your compiler allows you to examine the machine code it produces, and if you can understand machine or assembly language, check to see whether your compiler is indeed taking advantage of the optimization we have just described.

9. Invent some interesting kinds of sets and instantiate and test the generic sets package for these.

10. Modify Program 5.18 to create some musical ensembles that interest you.

11. Implement the body of the generic vectors package. Test for some interesting index and element types.

12. Revise the matrix package of Section 4.5 to make it generic. Instantiate for matrix elements of types `Integer`, `Float`, and `Rational`.

13. Implement and test the body of the generic keyed table package, then test using the employee example of Section 5.8.

14. Improve the generic backup package (Programs 5.21 and 5.22) so that exceptions raised by the file system are handled within the package operations `Save` and `Restore`.

15. Complete the passenger list project outlined in Section 5.10.

16. Do Exercises 13 and 14 using the abstract data object design instead of the ADT design.

CHAPTER 6

Variant and Tagged Record Types

A *variant record* is one with several different possible structures (instead of just one structure, as seen in earlier chapters). The structure of the record is determined, at execution time, by the value of a special field called the *discriminant* field; CASE constructs are used to declare the record type and, often, to process variables of the type.

The examples in this chapter are taken from four areas: employee records, geometric figures, dimensioned quantities for use in programs modeling physical situations, and variable-length strings. Each of the Ada 95-specific topics—support for variable-length strings, and tagged types—is important enough to be discussed in its own section of the chapter.

6.1   ADA STRUCTURES: VARIANT RECORDS

The records we have seen so far are such that all records of a given record type have exactly the same form and structure. However, it is possible and often very useful to define record types that have some fields that are the same for all variables of that type (fixed part) and some fields that may be different (variant part). Such a structure is called a *variant record*.

Consider an application from business information systems. There are three categories of employee in a particular company: One group (professionals) receives a fixed monthly salary, one group (sales) receives a fixed monthly salary plus commissions on their sales, and the third group (clerical) receives an hourly wage and is paid weekly based on number of hours worked.

How shall we represent a pay record for employees? The record type we saw in Section 3.5 is oversimplified; it does not take into account the different categories. We require a record type that can represent any of several structures, depending on the category. This is a perfect application for a variant record type.

A pay record for a given pay period has a *fixed part*, giving the employee's ID and name and the ending date of the pay period, and a *variant part*, giving the pay information according to the pay status. We start with these basic type declarations:

```
SUBTYPE NameRange IS Positive RANGE 1. .20;
SUBTYPE NameType IS String(NameRange);
SUBTYPE IDType IS Positive RANGE 1111. .9999;
SUBTYPE WorkHours IS Float RANGE 0.0. .168.0;
SUBTYPE CommissionPercentage IS Float RANGE 0.00. .0.50;

TYPE PayCategories IS (Unknown, Professional, Sales, Clerical);
```

Given these declarations, here is a declaration of the variant record type:

```
TYPE Employee (PayStatus : PayCategories := Unknown) IS RECORD
  ID          : IDType;
  NameLength  : NameRange;
  Name        : NameType;
  PayPeriod   : Dates.Date;

  CASE PayStatus IS
    WHEN Professional =>
      MonthSalary : Currency.Quantity;
    WHEN Sales =>
      WeekSalary  : Currency.Quantity;
      CommRate    : CommissionPercentage;
      SalesAmount : Currency.Quantity;
    WHEN Clerical =>
      HourlyWage  : Currency.Quantity;
      HoursWorked : WorkHours;
    WHEN Unknown =>
      NULL;
  END CASE;

END RECORD;
```

The line at the beginning of the record declaration,

```
TYPE Employee (PayStatus : PayCategories := Unknown) IS RECORD
```

indicates to the compiler that the record is a *discriminated record* which may have a variant part and that the *discriminant field*, which indicates which of several variants is present, is `PayStatus`. The discriminant is a special field that looks like a parameter of a procedure; indeed, it has many of the aspects of a parameter in that the record is *parametrized*, or varies, according to the value of the discriminant. The reason for having a value `Unknown` used as a default will be explained shortly.

The fixed part of a record always precedes the variant part. The variant part begins with the phrase

```
CASE PayStatus IS
```

and declares the different forms the variant part can have. The NULL case indicates that there is no variant part for PayStatus equal to Unknown. There are three different pay records, each of a different variant.

For each variable of type PayRecord, the compiler will usually allocate sufficient storage space to accommodate the largest of the record variants shown in Figure 6.1. However, *only one of the variants is defined at any given time; this particular variant is determined by the discriminant field value.*

Suppose we declare

```
Jane: Employee(PayStatus => Professional);
```

Then Jane's record will look like the fixed part and variant 2 of the record in Figure 6.1. Because the value of Jane.PayStatus is Professional, only the variant field MonthSalary may be correctly referenced. All other variant fields are undefined. The program fragment

```
Ada.Text_IO.Put("Jane's full name is ");
Ada.Text_IO.Put(Jane.Name(1 .. Jane.NameLength));
Ada.Text_IO.New_Line;
Ada.Text_IO.Put("and her monthly salary is $ ");
Ada.Float_Text_IO.Put(Jane.MonSalary, Fore => 1, Aft => 2, Exp => 0);
Ada.Text_IO.New_Line;
```

displays the lines

```
Jane's full name is Jane Smith
and her monthly salary is $5000.00
```

In Ada, the compiler and run-time system are very careful to check the consistency of the discriminant value with the references to fields in the record. If, at execution time, an attempt is made to access a field that is not defined in the current variant (i.e., the variant determined by

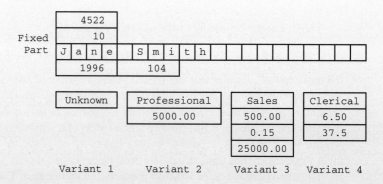

Figure 6.1 Four Variants of a Variant Record

the current discriminant value), `Constraint_Error` is raised. For this reason, a `CASE` statement is often used to process the variant part of a record. By using the discriminant field as the `CASE` selector, we can ensure that only the currently defined variant is manipulated.

Displaying a Variant Record

The fragment in Figure 6.2 displays the data stored in the variant part of a record `CurrentEmp`. The value of `CurrentEmp.PayStatus` determines what information will be displayed.

```
Ada.Text_IO.Put(Item => "Employee ID ");
Ada.Integer_Text_IO.Put(Item => CurrentEmp.ID, Width => 4
Ada.Text_IO.New_Line;
Ada.Text_IO.Put(Item => "Employee Name ");
Ada.Text_IO.Put(Item => CurrentEmp.Name(1..CurrentEmp.NameLength));
Ada.Text_IO.New_Line;
Ada.Text_IO.Put(Item => "Pay Period Ending ");
Dates.Put(Item => CurrentEmp.PayPeriod);
Ada.Text_IO.New_Line;

CASE CurrentEmp.PayStatus IS

  WHEN Unknown =>
    Ada.Text_IO.Put(Item => "Unknown pay status!");
    Ada.Text_IO.New_Line;

  WHEN Professional =>
    Ada.Text_IO.Put("Monthly Salary is $");
    Ada.Float_Text_IO.Put
      (Item=>CurrentEmp.MonthSalary, Fore=>1, Aft=>2, Exp=>0);
    Ada.Text_IO.New_Line;

  WHEN Sales =>
    Ada.Text_IO.Put("Weekly Salary is $ ");
    Ada.Float_Text_IO.Put
      (Item=>CurrentEmp.WeekSalary, Fore=>1, Aft=>2, Exp=>0);
    Ada.Text_IO.New_Line;
    Ada.Text_IO.Put("Commission percent is ");
    My_Flt_IO.Put
      (Item=>CurrentEmp.CommRate, Fore=>1, Aft=>2, Exp=>0);
    Ada.Text_IO.New_Line;
    Ada.Text_IO.Put("Sales this week $");
    Ada.Float_Text_IO.Put
      (Item=>CurrentEmp.SalesAmount, Fore=>1, Aft=>2, Exp=>0);
    Ada.Text_IO.New_Line;

  WHEN Clerical =>
    Ada.Text_IO.Put("Hourly wage is $");
    Ada.Float_Text_IO.Put
      (Item=>CurrentEmp.HourlyWage, Fore=>1, Aft=>2, Exp=>0);
    Ada.Text_IO.New_Line;
    Ada.Text_IO.Put("Hours worked this week ");
    Ada.Float_Text_IO.Put
      (Item=>CurrentEmp.HoursWorked, Fore=>1, Aft=>2, Exp=>0);
    Ada.Text_IO.New_Line;

END CASE;
```

Figure 6.2 Displaying a Variant Record

Declaring Variant Record Types

Consider this rather foolish but illustrative record type:

```
TYPE Face (Bald : Boolean) IS RECORD
  Eyes : Color;
  Height: Inches;
  CASE Bald IS
    WHEN True =>
      WearsWig : Boolean;
    WHEN False =>
      HairColor : Color;
  END CASE;
END RECORD;
```

In both this record and the employee record above, note that the fixed part must be defined first. The CASE values are lists of values of the discriminant field. All field names must be unique. The same field name may not appear in the fixed and variant parts or in two field lists of the variant part. An empty field list (no variant part for that CASE label) is indicated by NULL instead of a field list. As in all CASE forms, all values of the discriminant must be covered by WHEN clauses. Values not covered otherwise can be covered by a WHEN OTHERS clause.

What is the main difference between the two type declarations? In the employee record, the discriminant field is given a default value (in this case, Unknown); in the face record, no default is given. This looks like a simple difference, but in fact it is very important. If a default is omitted from the discriminant declaration, all variables of the type must be *constrained* when they are declared; that is, a value for the discriminant *must* be supplied. If the default is present, unconstrained variables—that is, variables without an explicit discriminant value—may be declared.

Constrained and Unconstrained Variant Records

Ada has very strict rules to guarantee two things:

- The discriminant of a variant record is always defined; that is, it always has *some* value.

- The discriminant value is always consistent with the actual data stored in the record.

The first condition is ensured by requiring that if a default value for the discriminant is *not* present in the record declaration, *all* declarations of variables must supply a value for the discriminant. In the pay status case above, a default of Unknown is supplied; therefore, it is possible to declare a record without a discriminant value, as in

```
CurrentEmp : PayRecord;
```

Supplying a discriminant value is not prohibited, however:

```
AnotherEmp : PayRecord(PayStatus=>Professional);
```

is allowed. In the case of the `Face` record above, it would be a compilation error to declare

```
JohnsFace : Face;
```

and in this case a discriminant value is *required*:

```
JohnsFace : Face(Bald=>False);
```

An *unconstrained* record variable is one that has a default discriminant value while none is supplied in the variable declaration. It is permissible to change the discriminant value of an unconstrained record at execution time, under rules to be specified in the next section. This means that the variable `CurrentEmp` can hold a professional employee at one moment and a sales employee at another. This is a common use of variant records in data processing.

A *constrained* record variable is one whose discriminant value is supplied when the variable is declared. Both `AnotherEmp` and the second `JohnsFace` are constrained. It is *not* permitted to change the discriminant value of a constrained record at execution time; this means that we are "stuck" with the discriminant value. `AnotherEmp` is constrained because we chose to make it so even though the discriminant has a default; `JohnsFace` is constrained because we have no choice, because no default is supplied for `Bald`. `JohnsFace` cannot take into account his losing his hair at a later date.

Storing Values into Variant Records

Ada's rules for variant records may seem cumbersome, but the rules are designed to guarantee that the contents of a variant record are always consistent. Here are the basic rules for storing values into a variant-record variable:

- Any field of the variable may be selected and *read* individually, by a field selector, at any time.

- Any field of the variable may be selected and *changed* individually (by, say, an assignment statement) *except* a discriminant field; if the change is not consistent with the current discriminant value, `Constraint_Error` is raised.

- The discriminant field of a *constrained* record cannot be changed under any circumstances.

- The discriminant field of an *unconstrained* record can be changed, but only if the *entire* record is changed at the same time. There are two ways to do this: Use a record aggregate or copy another record.

A common application of variant records is to read the value of a discriminant from the terminal or from a file, then to create a record variable with that variant. By the rules given above, the value cannot be stored directly into the discriminant. The discriminant value and the other fields of the record must be held in temporary variables and stored *as a unit* into the variant record using an aggregate.

As we have seen, there is often a distinct advantage in supplying a default value for the discriminant. If we do not, all variables of the type must be constrained when they are declared, and much of the flexibility of variant records—especially their ability to change structure at execution time—is lost. As we shall see in Sections 6.2 and 6.3, there is sometimes an advantage in *not* supplying a discriminant—that is, in forcing all variables to be constrained.

Operations on Variant Records

As always in Ada, assignment and equality testing are defined for variant records. However, certain rules apply:

- A variant record value can always be assigned to an *unconstrained* variable of the same record type. This is possible because it is permissible to change the discriminant of an unconstrained variable.

- A variant record value can be assigned to a *constrained* variable of the same record type *only* if the discriminant values match. This restriction follows from the fact that the discriminant value of a constrained variable can *never* be changed.

- Two variant record values can be compared for equality only if the discriminant values agree; otherwise `Constraint_Error` is raised.

Section 3.5 developed an ADT for handling a keyed table of employee records. As an exercise, you can modify that ADT, and the associated interactive client program, to handle the more realistic variant employee records described in the present section.

6.2 ADT DESIGN: GEOMETRIC FIGURES

Requirements

Provide a package to represent, read, and display various geometric figures, including their areas and perimeters.

Analysis

We need to provide, first, a representation scheme for geometric figures, with a useful set of operations, and, second, a means for interactive users to read and display these figures. As in other ADTs we have developed, it is useful to separate these two concerns.

Design

We first develop an abstract data type that allows a client program to construct a geometric figure. The characteristics of a circle are different from those of a rectangle (a square is a rectangle whose width and height are equal), so we use a record with a variant part. In this case, the fixed part of the record will contain its area and perimeter, which are computed automatically as the figure is constructed. Here is the variant type `Figure`:

```
SUBTYPE NonNegFloat IS Float RANGE 0.0 . . Float'Last;
TYPE FigKind IS (Rectangle, Square, Circle);

TYPE Figure (FigShape : FigKind := Rectangle) IS RECORD
  Area : NonNegFloat := 0.0;
  Perimeter : NonNegFloat := 0.0;
  CASE FigShape IS
    WHEN Rect | Square =>
      Width : NonNegFloat := 0.0;
      Height : NonNegFloat := 0.0;
    WHEN Circle =>
      Radius : NonNegFloat := 0.0;
  END CASE;
END RECORD;
```

Implementing the Specification of Geometry

The package specification is presented as Program 6.1.

Program 6.1 Specification for `Geometry` Package

```
PACKAGE Geometry IS
----------------------------------------------------------------------
--| Defines an abstract data type for a geometric figure.
--| Operations include constructors for rectangles, circles,
--| and squares, and selectors for width, height, side,
--| area and perimeter.
--| Author: Michael B. Feldman, The George Washington University
--| Last Modified: September 1995
----------------------------------------------------------------------

   -- Data Types

   SUBTYPE NonNegFloat IS Float RANGE 0.0 . . Float'Last;
   TYPE FigKind IS (Rectangle, Square, Circle);

   TYPE Figure (FigShape : FigKind := Rectangle) IS PRIVATE;

   -- Exported Exception

   ShapeError: EXCEPTION;

   -- Constructor Operations

   FUNCTION MakeRectangle (Width, Height : NonNegFloat) RETURN Figure;
   -- Pre : Width and Height are defined
   -- Post: returns a rectangle
```

```
FUNCTION MakeCircle (Radius : NonNegFloat) RETURN Figure;
-- Pre : Radius is defined
-- Post: returns a circle

FUNCTION MakeSquare (Side : NonNegFloat) RETURN Figure;
-- Pre : Side is defined
-- Post: returns a square


-- selectors
FUNCTION Shape     (OneFig : Figure) RETURN FigKind;
FUNCTION Height    (OneFig : Figure) RETURN NonNegFloat;
FUNCTION Width     (OneFig : Figure) RETURN NonNegFloat;
FUNCTION Radius    (OneFig : Figure) RETURN NonNegFloat;
FUNCTION Side      (OneFig : Figure) RETURN NonNegFloat;
FUNCTION Perimeter (OneFig : Figure) RETURN NonNegFloat;
FUNCTION Area      (OneFig : Figure) RETURN NonNegFloat;
-- Pre   : OneFig is defined.
-- Post  : Returns the appropriate characteristic
-- Raises: ShapeError if the requested characteristic is
--             undefined for the shape of OneFig

PRIVATE

TYPE Figure (FigShape : FigKind := Rectangle) IS RECORD
  Area : NonNegFloat := 0.0;
  Perimeter : NonNegFloat := 0.0;
  CASE FigShape IS
    WHEN Rectangle | Square =>
      Width : NonNegFloat := 0.0;
      Height : NonNegFloat := 0.0;
    WHEN Circle =>
      Radius : NonNegFloat := 0.0;
  END CASE;
END RECORD;

END Geometry;
```

We have defined the data type `Figure` as a `PRIVATE` type. Why? If the client program had access to the details of the record representing the figure, it could, for example, change the `Perimeter` field by simply plugging in a new number. Because the figure would no longer make geometric sense, this action would violate the abstraction. Note the syntax for declaring a `PRIVATE` type with a variant: The discriminant appears first in the partial declaration and later in the complete declaration in the `PRIVATE` part of the specification.

The following design decisions make the data type safe from accidental misuse:

- The data type is declared `PRIVATE` to keep client programs from prying into, and changing, fields of the record such as the area and the perimeter, or changing the length of the side without changing the area and perimeter fields accordingly.

- All fields of the type are initialized to 0.0 by default, so that every variable of the type is automatically well defined (a figure with sides of 0.0 also has area and perimeter of 0.0).

- The area and perimeter are calculated automatically when the figure is constructed, because these are uniquely determined by the other characteristics.

The operations in the package are three constructors, `MakeRectangle`, `MakeCircle`, and `MakeSquare`, which construct the appropriate variant given the relevant characteristics, and a set of selectors, `Shape`, `Width`, `Height`, `Side`, `Radius`, `Area`, and `Perimeter`, which return these characteristics of the figure. Note that even though a square and a rectangle use the same variant, their constructors and selectors are different. Also, we export an exception `ShapeError` to prevent a client from applying an inappropriate selector—for example, finding the radius of a square.

A client program can declare variables of type `Figure` in either constrained or unconstrained form:

```
SomeShape : Figure;
```

can hold, at different moments, a circle, a square, or a rectangle; it is unconstrained. However,

```
BigSquare : Figure (FigShape => Square);
```

can hold only a square, because it is constrained; that is, we plugged a discriminant value into the declaration of the variable and are now "locked into" that value.

Implementing the Package Body

Program 6.2 shows the package body for `Geometry`.

Program 6.2 Body of `Geometry` Package

```
WITH Ada.Numerics; USE Ada.Numerics;
PACKAGE BODY Geometry IS
-----------------------------------------------------------------------
--| Body of abstract data type package for geometric figures.
--| Author: Michael B. Feldman, The George Washington University
--| Last Modified: September 1995
-----------------------------------------------------------------------

-- Body of abstract data type package for geometric figures.

  -- internal functions, not exported to client. ComputePerimeter
  -- and ComputeArea are used to ensure that all figures are
  -- constructed with these attributes automatically inserted.
  -- The exported selectors Perimeter and Area assume that these
  -- fields have been set by the internal functions.

  FUNCTION ComputePerimeter (OneFig : Figure) RETURN NonNegFloat IS
  -- Pre : The discriminant and characteristics of OneFig are defined.
  -- Post: Returns Perimeter of OneFig.

  BEGIN -- ComputePerimeter

    CASE OneFig.FigShape IS
      WHEN Rectangle =>
```

```
        RETURN 2.0 * (OneFig.Width + OneFig.Height);
     WHEN Square =>
        RETURN 4.0 * OneFig.Width;
     WHEN Circle =>
        RETURN 2.0 * Pi * OneFig.Radius;
  END CASE;

END ComputePerimeter;

FUNCTION ComputeArea (OneFig : Figure) RETURN NonNegFloat IS
-- Pre : The discriminant and characteristics of OneFig are defined.
-- Post: Returns Area of OneFig.

BEGIN -- ComputeArea

  CASE OneFig.FigShape IS
     WHEN Rectangle =>
        RETURN OneFig.Width * OneFig.Height;
     WHEN Square =>
        RETURN OneFig.Width ** 2;
     WHEN Circle =>
        RETURN Pi * OneFig.Radius ** 2 ;
  END CASE;

END ComputeArea;

-- Exported Operations

FUNCTION MakeRectangle (Width, Height : NonNegFloat) RETURN Figure IS

  Result : Figure(FigShape => Rectangle);

BEGIN -- MakeRectangle

  Result.Height    := Height;
  Result.Width     := Width;
  Result.Area      := ComputeArea(Result);
  Result.Perimeter := ComputePerimeter(Result);

  RETURN Result;

END MakeRectangle;

FUNCTION MakeCircle (Radius : NonNegFloat) RETURN Figure IS

  Result: Figure (FigShape => Circle);

BEGIN -- MakeCircle

  Result.Radius    := Radius;
  Result.Area      := ComputeArea(Result);
  Result.Perimeter := ComputePerimeter(Result);

  RETURN Result;

END MakeCircle;

FUNCTION MakeSquare (Side : NonNegFloat) RETURN Figure IS

  Result: Figure (FigShape => Square);
```

```
BEGIN -- MakeSquare

  Result.Height    := Side;
  Result.Width     := Side;
  Result.Area      := ComputeArea(Result);
  Result.Perimeter := ComputePerimeter(Result);

  RETURN Result;

END MakeSquare;

FUNCTION Shape (OneFig : Figure) RETURN FigKind IS

BEGIN -- Perimeter
  RETURN OneFig.FigShape;
END Shape;

FUNCTION Perimeter (OneFig : Figure) RETURN NonNegFloat IS

BEGIN -- Perimeter
  RETURN OneFig.Perimeter;
END Perimeter;

FUNCTION Area (OneFig : Figure) RETURN NonNegFloat IS

BEGIN -- Area
  RETURN OneFig.Area;
END Area;

FUNCTION Height (OneFig : Figure) RETURN NonNegFloat IS

BEGIN -- Height
  CASE OneFig.FigShape IS
    WHEN Rectangle | Square =>
      RETURN OneFig.Height;
    WHEN OTHERS =>
      RAISE ShapeError;
  END CASE;
END Height;

FUNCTION Width (OneFig : Figure) RETURN NonNegFloat IS

BEGIN -- Width
  CASE OneFig.FigShape IS
    WHEN Rectangle | Square =>
      RETURN OneFig.Width;
    WHEN OTHERS =>
      RAISE ShapeError;
  END CASE;
END Width;

FUNCTION Side (OneFig : Figure) RETURN NonNegFloat IS

BEGIN -- Side
  CASE OneFig.FigShape IS
    WHEN  Square =>
      RETURN OneFig.Height;
    WHEN OTHERS =>
      RAISE ShapeError;
  END CASE;
END Side;
```

```
FUNCTION Radius (OneFig : Figure) RETURN NonNegFloat IS

BEGIN -- Radius
  CASE OneFig.FigShape IS
    WHEN Circle =>
      RETURN OneFig.Radius;
    WHEN OTHERS =>
      RAISE ShapeError;
  END CASE;
END Radius;

END Geometry;
```

The constructor functions create the appropriate variant of the record from the relevant components, then calculate the area and the perimeter. Local functions `ComputeArea` and `ComputePerimeter` are used to assist. These are not given in the specification. The user can find out the area and perimeter by calling the appropriate selector, whose code is straightforward. Note that even though a square is also a rectangle, we distinguish between them in many of the operations. Note, in many of these operations, how a `CASE` statement is used to control the processing of the variant data.

The Package `Geometry.IO`

Programs 6.3 and 6.4 give the specification and body for a child package `Geometry.IO`. Procedure `Get` reads in the enumeration value denoting the kind of figure, reads the data required for the kind of figure indicated by the discriminant field, and calls the appropriate constructor. This procedure serves as a good example of how to read a variant record from the interactive user. As before, in the `Get` and `Put` procedures, a `CASE` statement controls the processing of the data in the variant part. Note also that in Program 6.4 we have a procedure `RobustGet`, which uses an exception loop to ensure that interactive numeric input is valid and in range.

Program 6.3 Specification for `Geometry.IO` Package

```
PACKAGE Geometry.IO IS
-----------------------------------------------------------------------
--| Child Package: Input/Output for Geometric Figures
--| Author: Michael B. Feldman, The George Washington University
--| Last Modified: September 1995
-----------------------------------------------------------------------

  PROCEDURE Get (Item : OUT Geometry.Figure);
  -- Pre : None
  -- Post: Item  contains a geometric figure.

  PROCEDURE Put (Item : IN Geometry.Figure);
  -- Pre : Item is defined.
  -- Post: Item is displayed.

END Geometry.IO;
```

Program 6.4 Body of `Geometry.IO` **Package**

```
WITH Ada.Float_Text_IO;
WITH Ada.Text_IO;
PACKAGE BODY Geometry.IO IS
-----------------------------------------------------------------------
--| Body of Input/Output Package for Geometric Figures
--| Author: Michael B. Feldman, The George Washington University
--| Last Modified: September 1995
-----------------------------------------------------------------------

  MaxSize: CONSTANT NonNegFloat := 1_000_000.0;

  PACKAGE FigKind_IO IS
    NEW Ada.Text_IO.Enumeration_IO (Enum => FigKind);

  -- Local procedure ReadShape and RobustGet are used only within
  -- the package, therefore not exported.

  PROCEDURE ReadShape (Item : OUT FigKind) IS
  -- Pre:  none
  -- Post: Item contains a figure kind. ReadShape reads robustly.

    TempItem: FigKind;

  BEGIN -- ReadShape

    LOOP
      BEGIN
        Ada.Text_IO.Put
          (Item => "Enter a shape: rectangle, circle, square > ");
        FigKind_IO.Get(Item => TempItem);
        Item := TempItem;
        EXIT;
      EXCEPTION
        WHEN :Ada.Text_IO.Data_Error =>
          Ada.Text_IO.Put
            ("Value not a valid shape. Please try again.");
          Ada.Text_IO.New_Line;
          Ada.Text_IO.Skip_Line;
      END;
    END LOOP;
    -- assert: Item is rect, circle, or square

  END ReadShape;

  PROCEDURE RobustGet (Item : OUT NonNegFloat;
                MinVal : IN NonNegFloat;
                MaxVal : IN NonNegFloat) IS
  -- Pre:  MinVal and MaxVal are defined
  -- Post: MinVal <= Item <= MaxVal

    SUBTYPE TempType IS NonNegFloat RANGE MinVal..MaxVal;
    TempItem : TempType;      -- temporary copy of MinVal
  BEGIN -- RobustGet

    LOOP
      BEGIN          -- exception handler block
        Ada.Text_IO.Put
          (Item => "Enter a floating-point value between ");
        Ada.Float_Text_IO.Put
          (Item => MinVal, Fore=> 1, Aft => 2, Exp => 0);
```

```
        Ada.Text_IO.Put(Item => " and ");
        Ada.Float_Text_IO.Put
          (Item => MaxVal, Fore=> 1, Aft => 2, Exp => 0);
        Ada.Text_IO.Put(Item => " > ");
        Ada.Float_Text_IO.Get(Item => TempItem);
        Item := TempItem;
        EXIT;        -- valid data
      EXCEPTION    -- invalid data
        WHEN Constraint_Error =>
          Ada.Text_IO.Put
            ("Value entered is out of range. Please try again.");
          Ada.Text_IO.New_Line;
          Ada.Text_IO.Skip_Line;
        WHEN Ada.Text_IO.Data_Error =>
          Ada.Text_IO.Put
            ("Value entered not floating point. Please try again.");
          Ada.Text_IO.New_Line;
          Ada.Text_IO.Skip_Line;
      END;          -- exception handler block
    END LOOP;
    -- assert: Item is in the range MinVal to MaxVal

END RobustGet;

PROCEDURE Get (Item : OUT Figure) IS

  Shape  : FigKind;
  Height : NonNegFloat;
  Width  : NonNegFloat;
  Side   : NonNegFloat;
  Radius : NonNegFloat;

BEGIN  -- Get

  -- Read the shape character and define the discriminant
  ReadShape(Shape);

  -- Select the proper variant and read pertinent data
  CASE Shape IS
    WHEN Rectangle =>
      Ada.Text_IO.Put(Item => "Enter width.");
      Ada.Text_IO.New_Line;
      RobustGet(Item => Width, MinVal => 0.0, MaxVal => MaxSize);
      Ada.Text_IO.Put(Item => "Enter height.");
      Ada.Text_IO.New_Line;
      RobustGet(Item => Height, MinVal => 0.0, MaxVal => MaxSize);
      Item := MakeRectangle(Width, Height);

    WHEN Square    =>
      Ada.Text_IO.Put(Item => "Enter length of side.");
      Ada.Text_IO.New_Line;
      RobustGet(Item => Side, MinVal => 0.0, MaxVal => MaxSize);
      Item := MakeSquare(Side);

    WHEN Circle    =>
      Ada.Text_IO.Put(Item => "Enter circle radius.");
      Ada.Text_IO.New_Line;
      RobustGet(Item => Radius, MinVal => 0.0, MaxVal => MaxSize);
      Item := MakeCircle(Radius);

  END CASE;

END Get;
```

```
PROCEDURE Put (Item: IN Figure) IS

BEGIN -- DisplayFigure

  -- Display shape and characteristics
  Ada.Text_IO.Put(Item => "Figure shape: ");
  FigKind_IO.Put(Item => Shape(Item), Width => 1);
  Ada.Text_IO.New_Line;

  CASE Item.FigShape IS
    WHEN Rectangle =>
      Ada.Text_IO.Put(Item => "height = ");
      Ada.Float_Text_IO.Put
        (Item => Height(Item), Fore=>1, Aft=>2, Exp=>0);
      Ada.Text_IO.Put(Item => "; width = ");
      Ada.Float_Text_IO.Put
        (Item => Width(Item), Fore=>1, Aft=>2, Exp=>0);

    WHEN Square =>
      Ada.Text_IO.Put(Item => "side = ");
      Ada.Float_Text_IO.Put
        (Item => Height(Item), Fore=>1, Aft=>2, Exp=>0);

    WHEN Circle =>
      Ada.Text_IO.Put(Item => "radius = ");
      Ada.Float_Text_IO.Put
        (Item => Radius(Item), Fore=>1, Aft=>2, Exp=>0);

  END CASE;

  Ada.Text_IO.Put(Item => "; perimeter = ");
  Ada.Float_Text_IO.Put
    (Item => Perimeter(Item), Fore=>1, Aft=>2, Exp=>0);
  Ada.Text_IO.Put(Item => "; area = ");
  Ada.Float_Text_IO.Put
    (Item => Area(Item), Fore=>1, Aft=>2, Exp=>0);
  Ada.Text_IO.New_Line;

END Put;

END Geometry.IO;
```

Program 6.5 is a brief and straightforward test program for the package.

Program 6.5 Demonstration of `Geometry` Package

```
WITH Ada.Text_IO;
WITH Ada.Integer_Text_IO;
WITH Geometry;
WITH Geometry.IO;
PROCEDURE Test_Geometry IS
------------------------------------------------------------------------
--| Program to test package Geometry
--| Author: Michael B. Feldman, The George Washington University
--| Last Modified: September 1995
------------------------------------------------------------------------

  MyFig : Geometry.Figure;                    -- a figure

BEGIN -- Test_Geometry

  FOR TestTrial IN 1. .3 LOOP
```

```
      Ada.Text_IO.New_Line;
      Ada.Text_IO.Put(Item => "     Trial #");
      Ada.Integer_Text_IO.Put(Item => TestTrial, Width => 1);
      Ada.Text_IO.New_Line;
      Geometry.IO.Get (Item => MyFig);
      Geometry.IO.Put (Item => MyFig);

   END LOOP;

END Test_Geometry;
```

6.3   ADT DESIGN: METRIC SYSTEM

In many science and engineering problems that model situations in the physical world, the *dimensions* of a quantity are important. Vehicles travel *lengths* (distances), moving at certain *velocities*. Objects have *mass*. In the physical world, only certain operations on dimensioned quantities make sense:

- The area of a figure is given by multiplying two lengths.

- Multiplying a velocity by a time gives a distance; multiplying a velocity by another velocity gives no meaningful physical result.

- Adding one velocity to another, or one length to another, is appropriate, but adding a velocity to a length is not physically meaningful.

In writing modeling programs, we do not get much help from our programming languages in making sure that operations on dimensioned quantities make physical sense. Through package `Calendar`, Ada ensures in certain ways that operations on times and elapsed times are meaningful, but that is as far as Ada goes directly. This case study shows how variant records can be used to give a useful representation of dimensioned quantities. Ada's constrained variant records, combined with operator overloading and private types, can be used to great advantage to save a client program from debugging difficulties stemming from mistakes in operations on dimensioned quantities.

Requirements

Develop a means of representing dimensioned quantities so that only physically sensible operations are allowed.

Analysis

We will develop a representation of the metric system's mass, length, and time dimensions. In the physical world, the following rules hold:

- Adding and subtracting dimensioned quantities makes sense only if the two quantities have the same dimensions.

- Multiplying and dividing dimensioned quantities is permitted, but the result of a complex calculation must be a physically meaningful quantity. For example,

```
(Area * area * area) / (area * length)
```

is meaningful because it results in a quantity with volume dimensions.

- Assignment is meaningful only if the dimensions agree on both sides of the assignment.

- Equality and other comparison operations are meaningful only if the dimensions agree; that is, "you can't compare apples and oranges."

Design

We will develop an abstract data type `Metric` for a physical quantity; to do this, we will store the dimensions of the quantity in the three discriminants of a variant record.

Coding the Package Specification

The package specification for `Metric_System` is given in Program 6.6.

Program 6.6 Specification for `Metric_System` Package

```
PACKAGE Metric_System IS
--------------------------------------------------------------------------
--| Specification for Metric System Package
--| Author: Michael B. Feldman, The George Washington University
--| Last Modified: September 1995
--------------------------------------------------------------------------

-- Type definition

  TYPE    Metric(Mass, Length, Time : Integer) IS PRIVATE;

  -- constrained subtypes

  SUBTYPE Scalar    IS Metric(0, 0, 0);

  SUBTYPE Accel     IS Metric(0, 1, -2);
  SUBTYPE Area      IS Metric(0, 2, 0);
  SUBTYPE Length    IS Metric(0, 1, 0);
  SUBTYPE Distance  IS Metric(0, 1, 0);
  SUBTYPE Mass      IS Metric(1, 0, 0);
  SUBTYPE Time      IS Metric(0, 0, 1);
  SUBTYPE Velocity  IS Metric(0, 1, -1);
  SUBTYPE Volume    IS Metric(0, 3, 0);

  -- exported exception

  Dimension_Error : EXCEPTION;

  -- exported unit constants; these will be defined in full below
```

```
Gram       : CONSTANT Metric;
METER      : CONSTANT Metric;
SEC        : CONSTANT Metric;
Square_M   : CONSTANT Metric;
Cubic_M    : CONSTANT Metric;
M_per_Sec  : CONSTANT Metric;
M_per_Sec2 : CONSTANT Metric;

FUNCTION "*" (Left : Float; Right : Metric) RETURN Metric;
-- Pre:  Left and Right are defined
-- Post: constructor: produces a metric quantity from a Float one

FUNCTION Value(Left : Metric) RETURN Float;
-- Pre:  Left is defined
-- Post: selector: returns the Float (dimensionless) part
--    of a metric quantity

FUNCTION "<"  (Left, Right : Metric) RETURN Boolean;
FUNCTION "<=" (Left, Right : Metric) RETURN Boolean;
FUNCTION ">"  (Left, Right : Metric) RETURN Boolean;
FUNCTION ">=" (Left, Right : Metric) RETURN Boolean;
-- Pre:    Left and Right are defined
-- Post:   the usual comparison operations
-- Raises: Dimension_Error if Left and Right
--    have different dimensions

FUNCTION "+" (Right : Metric) RETURN Metric;
FUNCTION "-" (Right : Metric) RETURN Metric;
FUNCTION "abs " (Right : Metric) RETURN Metric;
-- Pre:  Right is defined
-- Post: the usual monadic arithmetic operations;
--    the dimensions of Right are, of course, preserved

FUNCTION "+" (Left, Right : Metric) RETURN Metric;
FUNCTION "-" (Left, Right : Metric) RETURN Metric;
-- Pre:    Left and Right are defined
-- Post:   the usual additive operations are performed on the
--    numeric parts of Left and Right; the dimensions are preserved
-- Raises: Dimension_Error if Left and Right
--    have different dimensions

FUNCTION "*" (Left, Right : Metric) RETURN Metric;
FUNCTION "/" (Left, Right : Metric) RETURN Metric;
-- Pre:    Left and Right are defined
-- Post:   the usual multiplication and division operations
--    are performed on the numeric parts of Left and Right;
--    the dimensions are added pairwise (multiplication)
--    or subtracted pairwise (division)
--    Left and Right need not have the same dimensions.

PRIVATE

  -- A Metric quantity is a 3-discriminant variant record,
  -- with no default values. Each object of the type must
  -- therefore be constrained to a subtype, that is, to a
  -- fixed set of dimensions. This is physically realistic.

  TYPE Metric(Mass, Length, Time : Integer) IS RECORD
    Value : Float := 0.0;
  END RECORD;
```

```
Gram       : CONSTANT Metric := (1, 0,  0, 1.0);
Meter      : CONSTANT Metric := (0, 1,  0, 1.0);
Sec        : CONSTANT Metric := (0, 0,  1, 1.0);
Square_M   : CONSTANT Metric := (0, 2,  0, 1.0);
Cubic_M    : CONSTANT Metric := (0, 3,  0, 1.0);
M_per_Sec  : CONSTANT Metric := (0, 1, -1, 1.0);
M_per_Sec2 : CONSTANT Metric := (0, 1, -2,  1.0);

END Metric_System;
```

Note the way in which the type `Metric` is defined: At the top of the specification, the following lines appear:

```
TYPE    Metric(Mass, Length, Time : Integer) IS PRIVATE;

SUBTYPE Scalar   IS Metric(0, 0, 0);

SUBTYPE Mass     IS Metric(1, 0, 0);
SUBTYPE Length   IS Metric(0, 1, 0);
SUBTYPE Time     IS Metric(0, 0, 1);

SUBTYPE Accel    IS Metric(0, 1, -2);
SUBTYPE Area     IS Metric(0, 2, 0);
SUBTYPE Distance IS Metric(0, 1, 0);
SUBTYPE Velocity IS Metric(0, 1, -1);
SUBTYPE Volume   IS Metric(0, 3, 0);
```

Type `Metric` is a variant record with *three* discriminants for each of the three dimensions. Note that no defaults are given for the discriminants. This is done so that no variable can be unconstrained. It does not make sense for a variable representing length, for example, to change into one representing mass: Physical quantities simply do not change their dimensions.

The type is made `PRIVATE` so that we can precisely exert control over which operations are available and how they operate We have also declared a numbe of subtypes representing some of the more common physical dimensions. In supplying discriminant values, we have made all these subtypes *constrained*. A variable of type `Length` will always represent a length. Note that lengths and distances have the same dimensions, and thus are synonymous.

The discriminant values correspond to the physical dimensions: A length value has dimension length[1] and no mass or time component; a volume value has dimension length $\times$ length $\times$ length, or length[3]; a velocity value has dimensions length/time, or length[1] and time[-1].

Several constants are also partially declared here:

```
Gram       : CONSTANT Metric;
Meter      : CONSTANT Metric;
Sec        : CONSTANT Metric;
Square_M   : CONSTANT Metric;
Cubic_M    : CONSTANT Metric;
M_per_Sec  : CONSTANT Metric;
M_per_Sec2 : CONSTANT Metric;
```

This is done to allow a client program to label numerical values in expressions:

```
Speed: Velocity;

Speed := 35.7 * M_per_Sec;
```

Looking at the PRIVATE part of the specification, we see the completion of the type definition and the constant declarations:

```
PRIVATE

  TYPE Metric(Mass, Length, Time : Integer) IS RECORD
    Value : Float := 0.0;
  END RECORD;

  Gram      : CONSTANT Metric := (1, 0, 0, 1.0);
  METER     : CONSTANT Metric := (0, 1, 0, 1.0);
  SEC       : CONSTANT Metric := (0, 0, 1, 1.0);
  Square_M  : CONSTANT Metric := (0, 2, 0, 1.0);
  Cubic_M   : CONSTANT Metric := (0, 3, 0, 1.0);
  M_per_Sec : CONSTANT Metric := (0, 1, -1, 1.0);
  M_per_Sec2 : CONSTANT Metric := (0, 1, -2, 1.0);
```

The record Metric actually has only a fixed part—a Float value— and no variant part. This is an unusual use of variant records, but it works because of Ada's strict rules about operations on constrained variables. The constants simply give "unit" values for each of the dimensions, so that multiplying them by other values does not change those values.

The constants could not be fully declared above the PRIVATE part because the field structure of the metric type (i.e., its Float value) is not included above. If it were, the type could not be made PRIVATE, but it must be so in order for the entire package to work reliably.

The operations of Metric_System are similar to the ones already available for Float, as given in package Standard. The only operation worthy of note is the first one, which permits values to be given dimensions:

```
FUNCTION "*" (Left : Float; Right : Metric) RETURN Metric;
```

It was this operation that was used above in the assignment to Speed. Finally, an exception Dimension_Error is provided to signal a client program if it attempts a physically meaningless operation, such as adding a length to a time.

Coding the Package Body

Program 6.7 shows the body of the package Metric_System. The operations are repetitive and straightforward, requiring no explanation except to point out the local function SameDimensions, which compares the three dimensions of its two parameters. This function is called by many other operations in the package body.

Program 6.7 Body of Metric_System Package

```
PACKAGE BODY Metric_System IS
-----------------------------------------------------------------------
--| This is the implementation of the package Metric_System.
--| Author: Michael B. Feldman, The George Washington University
--| Last Modified: September 1995
-----------------------------------------------------------------------

  -- local function to check whether its arguments have the same dimensions
```

```
FUNCTION SameDimensions(Left, Right :Metric) RETURN Boolean IS
BEGIN
  RETURN (Left.Length = Right.Length) AND
         (Left.Mass = Right.Mass)      AND
         (Left.Time = Right.Time);
END SameDimensions;

FUNCTION "*" (Left : Float; Right : Metric) RETURN Metric IS
BEGIN
  RETURN (Right.Mass, Right.Length, Right.Time, Left * Right.Value);
END "*";

FUNCTION Value(Left : Metric) RETURN Float IS
BEGIN
  RETURN Left.Value;
END Value;

-- comparison operators

FUNCTION "<" (Left, Right : Metric) RETURN Boolean IS
BEGIN
  IF SameDimensions(Left, Right) THEN
    RETURN Left.Value < Right.Value;
  ELSE
    RAISE Dimension_Error;
  END IF;
END "<";

FUNCTION ">=" (Left, Right : Metric) RETURN Boolean IS
BEGIN
  IF SameDimensions(Left, Right) THEN
    RETURN Left.Value >= Right.Value;
  ELSE
    RAISE Dimension_Error;
  END IF;
END ">=";

FUNCTION ">" (Left, Right : Metric) RETURN Boolean IS
BEGIN
  IF SameDimensions(Left, Right) THEN
    RETURN Left.Value > Right.Value;
  ELSE
    RAISE Dimension_Error;
  END IF;
END ">";

FUNCTION ">=" (Left, Right : Metric) RETURN Boolean IS
BEGIN
  IF SameDimensions(Left, Right) THEN
    RETURN Left.Value >= Right.Value;
  ELSE
    RAISE Dimension_Error;
  END IF;
END ">=";

-- monadic arithmetic operators

FUNCTION "+" (Right : Metric) RETURN Metric IS
BEGIN
  RETURN Right;
END "+";
```

```
FUNCTION "-" (Right : Metric) RETURN Metric IS
BEGIN
   RETURN (Right.Mass, Right.Length, Right.Time, -Right.Value);
END "-";

FUNCTION "ABS " (Right : Metric) RETURN Metric IS
BEGIN
   RETURN (Right.Mass, Right.Length, Right.Time, ABS(Right.Value));
END "ABS ";

-- dyadic arithmetic operators

-- "+" and "-" require two variables of the same subtype,
-- they return a variable of the same subtype passed

FUNCTION "+"(Left, Right : Metric) RETURN Metric IS
BEGIN
   IF SameDimensions(Left, Right) THEN
      RETURN
         (Left.Mass, Left.Length, Left.Time, Left.Value + Right.Value);
   ELSE
      RAISE Dimension_Error;
   END IF;
END "+";

FUNCTION "-" (Left, Right : Metric) RETURN Metric IS
BEGIN
   IF SameDimensions(Left, Right) THEN
      RETURN
         (Left.Mass, Left.Length, Left.Time,  Left.Value - Right.Value);
   ELSE
      RAISE Dimension_Error;
   END IF;
END "-";

-- "*" and "/" require variables of any subtype
-- of Metric.  The subtype of the variable returned depends on
-- the types passed and how the operation combines the units.

FUNCTION "*" (Left, Right : Metric) RETURN Metric IS
BEGIN
   RETURN (Left.Mass + Right.Mass, Left.Length + Right.Length,
           Left.Time + Right.Time, Left.Value * Right.Value);
END "*";

FUNCTION "/" (Left, Right : Metric) RETURN Metric IS
BEGIN
   RETURN (Left.Mass - Right.Mass, Left.Length - Right.Length,
           Left.Time - Right.Time, Left.Value / Right.Value);
END "/";

END Metric_System;
```

Testing the Package

Finally, Program 6.8 shows a short program to test some operators in the package. Notice how the exception blocks are used to report whether an exception was raised without causing the program to terminate. You are encouraged to use this program as a basis for writing your own test programs and applications of Metric_System.

Program 6.8 Using the `Metric_System` Package

```
WITH Ada.Text_IO;
WITH Ada.Float_Text_IO;
WITH Metric_System; USE Metric_System;
PROCEDURE Test_Metric IS
-------------------------------------------------------------------------
--| Test some of the operations of the metric system package
--| Author: Michael B. Feldman, The George Washington University
--| Last Modified: September 1995
-------------------------------------------------------------------------

  V   : Velocity;
  T   : Time;
  D   : Length;
  A   : Area;
  Vol : Volume;

BEGIN

  -- these operations should all work correctly

  V := 23.0 * M_per_Sec;
  T := 3600.0 * Sec;

  D := V * T;

  Ada.Text_IO.Put("Distance = Rate * Time works as advertised ");
  Ada.Text_IO.New_Line;
  Ada.Text_IO.Put("Distance is ");
  Ada.Float_Text_IO.Put
    (Item => Value(D), Fore => 1, Aft => 2, Exp => 0);
  Ada.Text_IO.Put(" meters.");
  Ada.Text_IO.New_Line;
  Ada.Text_IO.New_Line;

  D := 3.0 * Meter;
  A := D * D;

  Ada.Text_IO.Put("Area = Distance * Distance works as advertised ");
  Ada.Text_IO.New_Line;
  Ada.Text_IO.Put("Area is ");
  Ada.Float_Text_IO.Put
    (Item => Value(A), Fore => 1, Aft => 2, Exp => 0);
  Ada.Text_IO.Put(" square meters.");
  Ada.Text_IO.New_Line;
  Ada.Text_IO.New_Line;

  Vol := A * D;

  Ada.Text_IO.Put("Volume = Area * Distance works as advertised ");
  Ada.Text_IO.New_Line;
  Ada.Text_IO.Put(">Volume is ");
  Ada.Float_Text_IO.Put
    (Item => Value(Vol), Fore => 1, Aft => 2, Exp => 0);
  Ada.Text_IO.Put("cubic meters.");
  Ada.Text_IO.New_Line;
  Ada.Text_IO.New_Line;

  D := D + D;

  Ada.Text_IO.Put("Distance = Distance + Distance works as advertised ");
  Ada.Text_IO.New_Line;
  Ada.Text_IO.Put("Distance is ");
```

```
Ada.Float_Text_IO.Put
  (Item => Value(D), Fore => 1, Aft => 2, Exp => 0);
Ada.Text_IO.Put(" meters.");
Ada.Text_IO.New_Line;
Ada.Text_IO.New_Line;

BEGIN -- block for exception handler
  D := D * D;
  Ada.Text_IO.Put
    ("Distance = Distance * Distance worked, but should not ");
  Ada.Text_IO.New_Line;
EXCEPTION
  WHEN Constraint_Error =>
    Ada.Text_IO.Put
      ("Constraint Error Raised on Distance = Distance * Distance ");
    Ada.Text_IO.New_Line;
  WHEN Dimension_Error =>
    Ada.Text_IO.Put
      ("Dimension Error Raised on Distance = Distance * Distance ");
    Ada.Text_IO.New_Line;
END; -- exception block

BEGIN -- block for exception handler
  D := T + D;
  Ada.Text_IO.Put
    ("Distance = Time + Distance worked, but should not ");
  Ada.Text_IO.New_Line;
EXCEPTION
  WHEN Constraint_Error =>
    Ada.Text_IO.Put
      ("Constraint Error Raised on Distance = Time + Distance ");
    Ada.Text_IO.New_Line;
  WHEN Dimension_Error =>
    Ada.Text_IO.Put
      ("Dimension Error Raised on Distance = Time + Distance ");
    Ada.Text_IO.New_Line;
END; -- exception block

END Test_Metric;
```

6.4   ADT DESIGN: VARIABLE-LENGTH STRINGS

As we have seen, Ada has no predefined support for variable-length character strings. The predefined type String is nothing but a character array and needs to be declared with a fixed length. On the other hand, it is common in applications to use string objects with a fixed *maximum* length but a variable *actual* length. If we use only Ada string objects, there is nothing built into Ada to keep track of the number of useful characters that are in the string at any given moment.

Specifying the VStrings Package

We can use Ada's package capability to design and build what we need to support variable-length strings in a way similar to those of other languages like PL/I and Fortran-77. Let us create an ADT VStrings, in which each string variable is declared to have its own fixed maximum or physical length but a variable actual or logical length. Program 6.9 is a package specification for VStrings.

Program 6.9 Specification for Variable-Length String Package

```
PACKAGE VStrings IS
------------------------------------------------------------------------
--| Specification for ADT to handle strings of variable length.
--| Maximum length must be at least 1.
--| Author: Michael B. Feldman, The George Washington University
--| Last Modified: September 1995
------------------------------------------------------------------------

  TYPE    VString(MaxLength: Positive) IS PRIVATE;

  -- exceptions

  StringOverflow   : EXCEPTION;
  EmptyString      : EXCEPTION;
  InvalidArguments : EXCEPTION;


  -- operators

  -- constructors

  FUNCTION MakeVString(S : String; MaxLength: Positive) RETURN VString;
  -- Pre:     S and MaxLength are defined
  -- Post:    returns a VString with S as the Value part,
  --    MaxLength as the MaxLength part and S'Length as the Length part
  -- Raises: StringOverflow if S is longer than MaxLength characters

  FUNCTION MakeVString(C : Character; MaxLength: Positive)
    RETURN VString;
  -- Pre:     C and MaxLength are defined
  -- Post:    returns a VString with C as the Value  part, Length = 1

  FUNCTION EmptyVString(MaxLength: Positive) RETURN VString;
  -- Pre:     MaxLength is defined
  -- Post:    returns a empty VString with the given MaxLength


  -- selectors

  FUNCTION Length(S : VString)    RETURN Natural;
  FUNCTION MaxLength(S : VString) RETURN Positive;
  FUNCTION Value(S : VString)     RETURN String;
  -- Pre:     S is defined
  -- Post:    returns the Length and Value of S, respectively

  FUNCTION Head(S : VString) RETURN Character;
  -- Pre:     S is defined
  -- Post:    returns the first character of S
  -- Raises: EmptyString if S is empty


  -- inquiry

  FUNCTION IsEmpty(S : VString) RETURN Boolean;
  -- Pre: S is defined
  -- Post: returns True if S is empty, False otherwise


  -- concatenation
```

```
FUNCTION "&" (S1, S2 : VString) RETURN VString;
FUNCTION "&" (S1 : VString; C : Character) RETURN VString;
FUNCTION "&" (C : Character; S1 : VString) RETURN VString;
FUNCTION "&" (S1 : VString; S : String) RETURN VString;
FUNCTION "&" S : string; S1 : VString) RETURN VString;
-- Pre:   parameters are defined
-- Post:   each operator returns the concatenation of its arguments;
--   the maximum length of the result is the larger of the two
--   maximum lengths.
-- Raises: StringOverflow if the result would be longer than
--   the longer of the two arguments


-- lexical comparison

FUNCTION "<"  (S1, S2 : VString) RETURN Boolean;
FUNCTION "<=" (S1, S2 : VString) RETURN Boolean;
FUNCTION ">"  (S1, S2 : VString) RETURN Boolean;
FUNCTION ">=" (S1, S2 : VString) RETURN Boolean;
-- Pre: S1 and S2 are defined
-- Post: carries out the desired comparison, returning True or False


-- search

FUNCTION Locate(Sub : VString; Within : VString) RETURN Natural;
FUNCTION Locate(Sub : String;  Within : VString) RETURN Natural;
FUNCTION Locate(C : Character; Within : VString) RETURN Natural;
-- Pre:   Sub, Within. and C are defined
-- Post:   returns the index of the first character of Sub in Within;
--   returns 0 if Sub is not present in Within

FUNCTION Tail(S : VString) RETURN VString;
-- Pre:    S is defined
-- Post: returns a string like S but with the first character removed
-- Raises: EmptyString if S is empty

FUNCTION Slice(S : VString; Start, Finish : Positive) RETURN VString;
-- Pre:    parameters are defined
-- Post:   returns a VString whose value is
--   the substring slice starting at position Start in S.
--   This behaves consistently with Ada's predefined slice.
-- Raises: InvalidParameters if Start or Finish > Length(S).

PRIVATE

  TYPE VString(MaxLength: Positive) IS RECORD
    CurrentLength : Natural := 0;
    StringPart : String(1 .. MaxLength) := (OTHERS => ASCII.NUL);
  END RECORD;

END VStrings;
```

The type VString provided by this package is a PRIVATE type; it is also an interesting kind of variant record type. As before, we know that Ada already gives us assignment and equality operators for such types; any additional operators need to be provided by us in the package. Here is the type definition for VString:

```
TYPE VString (MaxLength: Positive) IS RECORD
  CurrentLength : Index := 0;
  StringPart : String(1. .MaxLength) := (OTHERS => ASCII.NUL);
END RECORD;
```

A diagram of a string `S1` containing John Brown's body is given in Figure 6.3.

In the type definition, we are making use of the ability provided by Ada to initialize fields of a record to a known value. This means that every time a `VString` variable is declared, we can be sure that its current length is set to zero and all its other characters are set to something predictable. It is conventional to use the ASCII character `ASCII.Nul` for this predictable value; this character is used for almost nothing else in programming. (We do not use the "blank" character—which is a different character-set value—for this, so that we can embed blanks in our variable-length strings with no ambiguity.) We make the `VString` type `PRIVATE` so that a client program cannot tinker with the string part of a variable (by, say, adding a character to the end) without adjusting the length field.

A `VString` variable with maximum length 80 is declared as

```
S: VString(MaxLength => 80);
```

or just as

```
S: VString(80);
```

if we are using positional parameter association. The compiler allocates enough space to hold the full 80-character string.

What operations should apply to `VStrings`? First of all, we need a constructor to create a `VString` from a normal Ada string. We call this operation `MakeVString`, and in fact we use overloading to define *two* `MakeVString` operations so that `VStrings` can be made from single characters as well as from strings. Note that we must supply a `MaxLength` parameter to `MakeVString` in both cases. Given a declaration and a statement

```
S : VStrings.VString(80);
T : VStrings.VString(80);
. . .
S := VStrings.MakeVString("Do you like Ada?", 80);
```

the variable `S`, after the assignment, will have a `CurrentLength` value of 16 (the length of the string literal) and a `StringPart` value of the letters in `Do you like Ada?` followed by 64 (80 – 16) `ASCII.Nul` characters.

Note that in an assignment, the following Ada rule still holds: The length of the right side and the length of the left side must match. The advantage of our representation is that even though the physical lengths must match, the actual (meaningful) lengths need not. This gives us the variable-length flexibility we have been seeking, and is consistent with the conventions of other languages as well.

Next, we need selectors so that a client program can get the string length and string value back from a `VString` object. We call these selectors `Length` and `Value`, respectively.

MaxLength	20
CurrentLength	17
StringPart	J o h n B r o w n ' s B o d y Ø Ø Ø

Figure 6.3 A Variable-Length String

Another useful operation on VStrings is concatenation, represented by the infix operator "&". Ada already provides string concatenation; we will use the built-in operations to build our own operation that works with VStrings instead of predefined strings.

The concatenation of two VStrings, S1 and S2, returns a VString containing the useful characters of S1 (not the nulls!) followed by those of S2. The current length of the result is, obviously, the sum of the two current lengths. We choose to make the *maximum* length of the result equal to the *larger* of the two maximum lengths, not the sum of the two. This enables us to declare a number of variables of the same maximum length and use them for concatenations, without any worries about mismatched lengths.

The function call

```
VStrings."&"(
  VStrings.MakeVString("ABC",10),VStrings.MakeVString("DEF ",20))
```

or the simpler form (if USE VStrings appears at the top of the client program)

```
MakeVString("ABC ",10) & MakeVString("DEF ",20)
```

returns a VString with maximum length 20, actual length 6, and value "ABCDEF". Assuming that USE is present, the statement

```
T := S & MakeVString(" I do.");
```

stores in the string part of T the characters

```
Do you like Ada? I do.
```

and a CurrentLength value of 22 (16 + 6). T still has maximum length 80.

For convenience, we define, in fact, *five* overloaded operators for concatenation, all called "&", so that a client program can, without extra calls to MakeVString, concatenate normal Ada strings and characters with VString values.

```
FUNCTION "&" (S1, S2 : VString) RETURN VString;

FUNCTION "&" (S1 : VString; C : Character) RETURN VString;
FUNCTION "&" (C : Character; S1 : VString) RETURN VString;

FUNCTION "&" (S1 : VString; S : String) RETURN VString;
FUNCTION "&" (S : String; S1 : VString) RETURN VString;
```

Recall that the pairs of operations are necessary to ensure that either parameter can appear on the left or the right. The statement

```
T := "I have a question. " & S;
```

returns the VString with string part

```
I have a question. Do you like Ada?
```

and current length 35. As is always the case with overloading, the compiler can discern which operation you mean by looking at its parameters and return type: Here we have a string on the left and a `VString` on the right, so the last of the five operations is selected.

The list of operations includes some comparison operations, which need no explanation except that the comparison assumes "dictionary" or "lexical" order, so that `"BCD" < "BCDE"` (obvious) but also `"BCD" < "CD"` (perhaps less obvious). As it happens, operations similar to these are also predefined for normal Ada strings.

As we know, equality checking is provided by Ada for all types, including `PRIVATE` ones. Does equality work correctly for `VStrings`? The answer is yes: Built-in equality always compares the *entire* data objects. By this principle, Ada states that two `VStrings` are equal if and only if the length fields are equal *and* the string parts are equal. All `MaxLength` positions of the strings are compared! You can appreciate the advantage of preinitializing all characters in a `VString` to something predictable, namely `ASCII.Nul`.

Keep in mind that if the *maximum lengths* of the two strings are not equal, `Constraint_Error` is raised, as will always be the case if equality is applied to two discriminated records with unequal discriminants.

A number of additional operators are in the specification: `Head(S)`, which returns the first character of its `VString` argument, and `Tail(S)`, which returns a `VString` equivalent to `S` with its first character removed. Other useful operations are three `Locate` functions, which search a target `VString` for the presence of another given character, string, or `VString`, returning the position in the target where the substring begins, or 0 if the substring cannot be found in the target. Finally, we have `Slice(S,Start,Finish)`, which returns the `VString` containing the required slice of `S` and a maximum length equal to that of `S`. For example,

```
Locate("BC",MakeVString("ABCDEF"))
```

returns 2,

```
Locate(G',MakeVString("AB"))
```

returns 0 because `'G'` is not in `"AB "`, and

```
Locate("Ada", T)
```

returns 32. The statement

```
S := Slice (T, 10, 17)
```

stores in `S` a `VString` with maximum length 80, actual length 8, and string part `question`.

The Body of `VStrings`

In Program 6.10, we present the body of this package. The various operations make quite heavy use of string slicing; you should study them carefully. Notice also how the exceptions `EmptyString`, `StringOverflow`, and `InvalidArguments` are used to signal a client program that violates an assumption of the package—for example, one that tries to concatenate two 42-character VStrings whose maximum lengths are 80.

Program 6.10 Body of Variable-Length String Package

```
PACKAGE BODY VStrings IS
------------------------------------------------------------------------
--| Body of ADT to handle strings of variable length.
--| Maximum length must be at least 1.
--| Author: Michael B. Feldman, The George Washington University
--| Last Modified: September 1995
------------------------------------------------------------------------

  -- local function
  FUNCTION Maximum(L, R: Positive) RETURN Positive IS
  BEGIN
    IF L > R THEN
      RETURN L;
    ELSE
      RETURN R;
    END IF;
  END Maximum;


  FUNCTION Length(S : VString) RETURN Natural IS
  BEGIN
    RETURN S.CurrentLength;
  END Length;


  FUNCTION MaxLength(S : VString) RETURN Positive IS
  BEGIN
    RETURN S.MaxLength;
  END MaxLength;


  FUNCTION Value(S : VString) RETURN String IS
  BEGIN
    IF S.CurrentLength = 0 THEN
      RETURN "";
    ELSE
      RETURN S.StringPart(1..S.CurrentLength);
    END IF;
  END Value;


  FUNCTION Tail(S : VString) RETURN VString IS
    Result: VString(S.MaxLength);
    CurrLength: Natural;
  BEGIN
    CurrLength := S.CurrentLength;
    IF CurrLength = 0 THEN
      RAISE EmptyString;
    ELSIF CurrLength = 1 THEN
      RETURN Result;             -- other fields default
    ELSE
      Result.CurrentLength := CurrLength - 1;
      Result.StringPart(1..CurrLength-1)
        := S.StringPart(2..CurrLength);
      RETURN Result;
    END IF;
  END Tail;
```

```
FUNCTION Head(S : VString) RETURN Character IS
BEGIN
  IF S.CurrentLength = 0 THEN
    RAISE EmptyString;
  ELSE
    RETURN S.StringPart(1);
  END IF;
END Head;


FUNCTION IsEmpty(S : VString) RETURN Boolean IS
BEGIN
  RETURN S.CurrentLength = 0;
END IsEmpty;


FUNCTION MakeVString(S : String; MaxLength : Positive) RETURN VString IS
  Result: VString(MaxLength);
BEGIN
  IF S'Length > MaxLength THEN
    RAISE StringOverflow;
  ELSE
    Result.CurrentLength := S'Length;
    Result.StringPart(1..S'Length) := S;
  END IF;
  RETURN Result;
END MakeVString;


FUNCTION EmptyVString(MaxLength : Positive) RETURN VString IS
  Result: VString(MaxLength);
BEGIN
  RETURN Result; -- CurrentLength, StringPart both defaulted
END EmptyVString;


FUNCTION MakeVString(C: Character; MaxLength: Positive) RETURN VString IS
  Result: VString(MaxLength);
BEGIN
  Result.CurrentLength := 1;
  Result.StringPart(1) := C;
  RETURN Result;
END MakeVString;


FUNCTION "&" (S1, S2 : VString) RETURN VString IS
  Max: Positive := Maximum(S1.MaxLength, S2.MaxLength);
  CurrLength: Natural;
  Result: VString(Max);
BEGIN
  CurrLength := S1.CurrentLength + S2.CurrentLength;
  IF CurrLength > Max THEN
    RAISE StringOverflow;
  ELSE
    Result.CurrentLength := CurrLength;
    Result.StringPart(1..CurrLength) := Value(S1) & Value(S2);
  END IF;

  RETURN Result;
END "&";

FUNCTION "&" (S1 : VString; C : Character) RETURN VString IS
  Result: VString(S1.MaxLength);
  CurrLength: Natural;
BEGIN
  CurrLength := S1.CurrentLength;
```

```
      IF CurrLength + 1 > S1.MaxLength THEN
        RAISE StringOverflow;
      ELSE
        Result.CurrentLength := CurrLength + 1;
        Result.StringPart(1..CurrLength + 1) := Value(S1) & C;
        RETURN Result;
      END IF;
  END "&";

  FUNCTION "&" (C : Character; S1 : VString) RETURN VString IS
    Result: VString(S1.MaxLength);
    CurrLength: Natural;
  BEGIN
    CurrLength := S1.CurrentLength;
    IF CurrLength + 1 > S1.MaxLength THEN
      RAISE StringOverflow;
    ELSE
      Result.CurrentLength := CurrLength + 1;
      Result.StringPart(1..CurrLength + 1) := C & Value(S1);
      RETURN Result;
    END IF;
  END "&";

  FUNCTION "&" (S1 : VString; S : String) RETURN VString IS
    Max: Positive := S1.MaxLength;
    CurrLength: Natural;
    Result: VString(Max);
  BEGIN
    CurrLength := S1.CurrentLength + S'Length;
    IF CurrLength > Max THEN
      RAISE StringOverflow;
    ELSE
      Result.CurrentLength := CurrLength;
      Result.StringPart(1..CurrLength) := Value(S1) & S;
    END IF;

    RETURN Result;
  END "&";

  FUNCTION "&" (S : String; S1 : VString) RETURN VString IS
    Max: Positive := S1.MaxLength;
    CurrLength: Natural;
    Result: VString(Max);
  BEGIN
    CurrLength := S1.CurrentLength + S'Length;
    IF CurrLength > Max THEN
      RAISE StringOverflow;
    ELSE
      Result.CurrentLength := CurrLength;
      Result.StringPart(1..CurrLength) := S & Value(S1);
    END IF;

    RETURN Result;
  END "&";

  FUNCTION "<=" (S1, S2 : VString) RETURN Boolean IS
  BEGIN
    RETURN Value(S1) <= Value(S2);
  END "<="

  FUNCTION "<" (S1, S2 : VString) RETURN Boolean IS
  BEGIN
    RETURN Value(S1) < Value(S2);
  END "<";
```

```
FUNCTION ">=" (S1, S2 : VString) RETURN Boolean IS
BEGIN
  RETURN Value(S1) >= Value(S2);
END ">=";

FUNCTION ">" (S1, S2 : VString) RETURN Boolean IS
BEGIN
  RETURN Value(S1) > Value(S2);
END ">";

FUNCTION Locate(Sub : String; Within : VString) RETURN Natural IS

  Result  : Natural;
  LSub    : Natural;
  LWithin : Natural;

BEGIN

  LSub := Sub'Length;
  LWithin := Within.CurrentLength;
  Result := 0;
  IF LSub > 0
    AND LWithin > 0
    AND LSub <= LWithin THEN

    FOR Start IN 1..(LWithin - LSub + 1) LOOP
      IF Sub = Within.StringPart(Start..(Start + LSub - 1)) THEN
        Result := Start;
        EXIT;
      END IF;
    END LOOP;
  END IF;

  RETURN Result;

END Locate;

FUNCTION Locate(Sub : VString; Within : VString) RETURN Natural IS
BEGIN
  RETURN Locate(Value(Sub), Within);
END Locate;

FUNCTION Locate(C : Character; Within : VString) RETURN Natural IS

  Temp : String(1..1);

BEGIN

  Temp(1) := C;
  RETURN Locate(Temp, Within);

END Locate;

FUNCTION Slice(S : VString; Start, Finish : Positive) RETURN VString IS
  Result: VString(S.MaxLength);
BEGIN
  IF Start  > Length(S) OR
     Finish > Length(S) THEN
    RAISE InvalidArguments;
  ELSIF Start > Finish THEN
    RETURN Result;                 -- empty; consistent with Ada slice
  ELSE
    Result.CurrentLength := Finish - Start + 1;
    Result.StringPart(1..Result.CurrentLength)
    := S.StringPart(Start. .Finish);
    RETURN Result;
```

```
      END IF;

   END Slice;

END VStrings;
```

It is useful to have the ADT VStrings available; we shall use it several times in this and the remaining chapters. Programs 6.11 and 6.12 give, respectively, the specification and body of VString.IO, which is used for reading and writing VString values.

Program 6.11 Specification for Variable-Length String IO Package

```
WITH Ada.Text_IO;
PACKAGE VStrings.IO IS
------------------------------------------------------------------------
--| input/output for variable-length strings
--| input is done using Ada.Text_IO.Get_Line, so the rules for
--|   this procedure are followed.
--| Author: Michael B. Feldman, The George Washington University
--| Last Modified: September 1995
------------------------------------------------------------------------

   PROCEDURE Get_Line(Item : OUT VString; MaxLength: IN Positive);
   -- Pre:  MaxLength is defined
   -- Post: Item contains the contents of the next line entered
   --    from the keyboard.

   PROCEDURE Get_Line(File: Ada.Text_IO.File_Type;
                      Item: OUT VString; MaxLength: IN Positive);
   -- Pre:  File and MaxLength are defined
   -- Post: Item contains the contents of the next line of the file.

   PROCEDURE Put(File: Ada.Text_IO.File_Type; Item : VString);
   -- Pre:  File and Item are defined
   -- Post: Item is written to the file

   PROCEDURE Put(Item : VString);
   -- Pre:  Item is defined
   -- Post: Item is displayed on the screen.

END VStrings.IO;
```

Program 6.12 Body of Variable-Length String IO Package

```
WITH Ada.Text_IO;
PACKAGE BODY VStrings.IO IS
------------------------------------------------------------------------
--| Body of I/O package for variable-length strings
--| Author: Michael B. Feldman, The George Washington University
--| Last Modified: September 1995
------------------------------------------------------------------------

   PROCEDURE Get_Line(File : Ada.Text_IO.File_Type;
                      Item : OUT VString; MaxLength: IN Positive) IS

     -- reads a VString object from File, using Ada.Text_IO.Get_Line
     -- reading stops if a line terminator is encountered, or if
     -- MaxLength characters have been read.
```

```
      S     : String(1..MaxLength);
      Count : Natural;

   BEGIN

      Ada.Text_IO.Get_Line(File => File, Item => S, Last => Count);
      IF Count > 0 THEN
        Item := MakeVstring(S(1..Count), MaxLength => MaxLength);
      ELSE
        Item := EmptyVstring(MaxLength => MaxLength);
      END IF;

   END Get_Line;

   PROCEDURE Get_Line(Item : OUT VString; MaxLength: IN Positive) IS
   BEGIN
      Get_Line(File => Ada.Text_IO.Standard_Input,
               Item => Item, MaxLength => MaxLength);
   END Get_Line;

   PROCEDURE Put(File: Ada.Text_IO.File_Type; Item : VString) IS
   BEGIN
      Ada.Text_IO.Put(File=>File, Item=>Value(Item));
   END Put;

   PROCEDURE Put(Item : VString) IS
   BEGIN
      Put(File=>Ada.Text_IO.Standard_Output,  Item=>Item);
   END Put;

END VStrings.IO;
```

Program 6.13 shows a test of some of the operations in the package, specifically the file-oriented operations. As an exercise, you can extend this program to test the other operations.

Program 6.13 Using the `VString` Package

```
WITH Ada.Text_IO;
WITH VStrings;
WITH VStrings.IO;
PROCEDURE Test_VStrings IS
-----------------------------------------------------------------------
--| program copies its input file test.dat into its output file
--| test.out, then closes test.out, re-opens it for input,
--| and displays its contents on the screen.
--| Author: Michael B. Feldman, The George Washington University
--| Last Modified: September 1995
-----------------------------------------------------------------------

  MaxLineLength: CONSTANT Positive := 255;

  InData  : Ada.Text_IO.File_Type;
  OutData : Ada.Text_IO.File_Type;
  S       : VStrings.VString(MaxLength => MaxLineLength);
```

```
BEGIN -- Test_VStrings

  Ada.Text_IO.Open
    (File=>InData, Mode=>Ada.Text_IO.In_File, Name=>"test.dat ");
  Ada.Text_IO.Create
    (File=>OutData, Mode=>Ada.Text_IO.Out_File, Name=>"test.out ");

  WHILE NOT Ada.Text_IO.End_of_File(File => InData) LOOP

    VStrings.IO.Get_Line(File => InData,
      Item => S, MaxLength => MaxLineLength);
    VStrings.IO.Put(File => OutData, Item => S);
    Ada.Text_IO.New_Line(File => OutData);

  END LOOP;

  Ada.Text_IO.Close(File => InData);
  Ada.Text_IO.Close(File => OutData);
  Ada.Text_IO.Open
    (File=>InData, Mode=>Ada.Text_IO.In_File,Name=>"test.out");

  WHILE NOT Ada.Text_IO.End_of_File(File => InData) LOOP

    VStrings.IO.Get_Line(File => InData,
      Item => S, MaxLength => MaxLineLength);
    VStrings.IO.Put(Item => S);
    Ada.Text_IO.New_Line;

  END LOOP;

  Ada.Text_IO.Close(File => InData);

EXCEPTION

  WHEN Ada.Text_IO.Name_Error =>
    Ada.Text_IO.Put
      (Item => "File test.dat doesn't exist in this directory!");
    Ada.Text_IO.New_Line;

END Test_V Strings;
```

Why No Default Discriminant Value?

One final question arises from this discussion of VStrings: Why did we not assign a
default value to MaxLength, so that variables could be left unconstrained and therefore "float" in size? Doing so would cause some difficulties because of the way many
Ada compilers allocate space for an unconstrained variable. Some compilers allocate
very little space for such a variable, and therefore must reallocate it dynamically, every
time a variable's size changes. Other compilers avoid the time cost of frequent reallocation by simply allocating the maximum space necessary. For example, if we declared
VString as

```
TYPE VString (MaxLength: Positive := 16) IS RECORD
    CurrentLength : Index := 0;
    StringPart : String(1. .MaxLength) := (OTHERS => ASCII.NUL);
END RECORD;
```

certain compilers would allocate only the 16 characters of the default, reallocating if necessary. However, other compilers, to save the reallocation costs, would try to allocate the largest possible record, so as never to have to reallocate it. How large is this record? Suppose `Positive` is represented in 16 bits. Such compilers would allocate 32767 characters (`Positive'Last`) for each string, even if their actual lengths were only a few characters. You can compute for yourself how much space would be needed if `Positive` were represented in 32 bits!

An alternative is to use some subtype, say 0. .255, as the range of `MaxLength`, instead of `Positive`. The disadvantage here is that the compiler might still allocate 255 characters per string. Also, it would be impossible for us ever to declare a string variable with maximum length greater than 255.

This is a good example of a trade-off situation. There is no perfect solution here, so we choose the one that seems best. Requiring `VString` variables to be constrained is inconvenient because these variables can never float in physical size, but in return we get the ability to declare a variable of *any* reasonable size at all, without concern about exceeding a predetermined maximum. Furthermore, we have a portability advantage in that we know, for all Ada compilers, the sizes of our string variables. There are no surprises here.

6.5 ADA STRUCTURES: STRINGS IN ADA 95

As you know, Ada 83 provides only limited support for strings, as discussed in Section 1.12. This has made it necessary to develop additional packages such as the one just introduced in Section 6.4. Ada 95, on the other hand, provides several standard packages for variable-length strings; these offer a rich collection of operations and make nonstandard packages such as our `VStrings` entirely unnecessary. We include and use `VStrings` in this book because the *implementation* of variable-length strings is an appropriate, and important, subject in a book of this kind.

Covering the Ada 95 string packages here in much detail would go beyond our available space. Instead, we give a summary of the capabilities, referring the reader to Appendix G, in which the specifications and explanations for the character and string facilities are reproduced verbatim from the Ada 95 LRM.

Type `Character`

In Ada 83, the type `Character` is defined in terms of the 128-character ASCII code. In Ada 95, `Character` is given a more international flavor; this type is defined in terms of the Latin-1 character set, which has 256 values and allows for the additional letters used in non-English languages, such as the French à, the German ü, and the Æ used in Scandinavian languages. Since the first 128 characters are the same as those in the familiar ASCII set, the change causes few problems for most work in English.

Package `Ada.Characters.Handling`

This package provides a number of useful functions for classifiying and converting characters—for example,

- `Is_Digit`, `Is_Letter`, `Is_Upper`, and `Is_Lower`, Boolean functions that return `True` if their `Character` parameter falls into the given category

- `To_Upper` and `To_Lower`, which convert the letters in their character or string parameters to uppercase or lowercase.

Packages `Ada.Strings` and `Ada.Strings.Maps`

`Ada.Strings` is brief enough to be reproduced as Figure 6.4. It provides some miscellaneous exceptions and enumeration types for string alignment and string searching.

Ada.Maps provides an interesting set of types and functions used for creating sets of characters and mapping between them. For example, if `M` is of type `Character_Mapping` and `C` is of type `Character`,

```
M := To_Mapping("ABCD", "PQRS");
```

returns in `M` a mapping that maps `'A'` into `'P'`, `'D'` into `'S'`, and so on, and

```
C := Value(M, 'D');
```

returns `'S'` to the variable C.

Packages `Ada.Strings.Fixed`, `Ada.Strings.Bounded`, and `Ada.Strings.Unbounded`

`Ada.Strings.Fixed` provides a large number of search, delete, replace, trim, and other operations on normal Ada fixed-length strings.

```
PACKAGE Ada.Strings IS
  Space       : constant Character      := ' ';
  Wide_Space : constant Wide_Character := ' ';
  Length_Error, Pattern_Error, Index_Error,
    Translation_Error : EXCEPTION;

  TYPE Alignment  IS (Left, Right, Center);
  TYPE Truncation IS (Left, Right, Error);
  TYPE Membership IS (Inside, Outside);
  TYPE Direction  IS (Forward, Backward);

  TYPE Trim_End   IS (Left, Right, Both);

END Ada.Strings;
```

Figure 6.4 Package `Ada.Strings`

`Ada.Strings.Bounded` is a generic package that provides a similar set of operations on bounded strings, which are strings with a given maximum length, similar to our `VString` type in Section 6.4. The package is generic, with a single parameter `Max` to give the maximum length of all strings created by a given instance of the package. For example, consider an instance

```
MaxName: CONSTANT Positive := 30;
PACKAGE Names IS
  NEW Ada.Strings.Bounded.Generic_Bounded_Length(Max => MaxName);
```

A string object, say

```
Name: Names.Bounded_String;
```

can be at most 30 characters long. The package keeps track of the actual length, and is quite similar in behavior to `VStrings`.

Finally, `Ada.Strings.Unbounded` provides similar operations for unbounded strings—that is, strings for which no maximum length is given. The actual length of a string object such as

```
VeryLongString: Ada.Strings.Unbounded.Unbounded_String;
```

can range from 0 to `Positive'Last`. This package is a more elaborate version of the one we will present in Section 7.7, but of course it is standard and is provided with all Ada 95 compilers.

6.6   ADA STRUCTURES: TAGGED TYPES

The variant records we have studied in this chapter provide much expressive power to create complex types with several different parts. However, they have an important limitation: A variant record must be fully defined and compiled, and `CASE` statements are used to control processing its various parts.

Now suppose a new variant must be added. For example, suppose a new category of employee is added to a company. The variant type declaration must be modified to account for the new variant, and all operations on objects of the type must be similarly changed. Further, because the type declaration appeared in a package specification, every client of that package must at least be recompiled, and perhaps even modified. It would be nice if we could somehow extend a type, adding new fields and operations, but without modifying or recompiling existing packages or programs.

Ada 95 and Object-Oriented Programming

Ada 95 provides a facility to extend types, as part of the new Ada 95 capabilities in object-oriented programming (OOP). Recall from Chapter 1 that OOP relies on a number of language features:

- *Encapsulation*, provided very well by Ada 83's packages.

- *Genericity*, provided by Ada 83's generics capability, as we saw in Chapter 5.

- *Inheritance*, through which a new type inherits the properties of an existing one. This is provided in part by Ada 83's derived types and is extended considerably in tagged types, the subject of this section.

- *Polymorphism*, partially supported by Ada 83's procedure and function overloading and extended significantly in Ada 95. We will see examples of what is known as dynamic polymorphism in Chapter 9.

Tagged Types

In Ada 95, a record type can be declared as TAGGED to indicate that it may later be extended by adding additional fields. Each object of a tagged type is given a tag by the compiler; you can think of a tag as analogous to a hidden discriminant. Whereas the programmer writes explicit code to manipulate a discriminant, a tag is manipulated automatically in the executing program.

As an example of a tagged type, consider representing a person by three general characteristics: a name, a gender, and a date of birth. We can declare this as follows:

```
TYPE Person IS TAGGED RECORD
  Name: NameType;
  Gender: Genders;
  BirthDate: Date;
END RECORD;
```

where Genders has been declared as

```
TYPE Genders IS (Female, Male);
```

and the name and birth date fields are, respectively, some string type and a date from our package Dates.

Suppose that Person is declared in a package Persons, together with a number of operations, and some programs are written to use this package. At a later date, we discover a need to represent personnel, or persons working in a company. An employee is a person with a company identifier and a second date indicating when he or she joined the company. Note the "is a" relationship: An employee is a person with additional characteristics. Without tagged types, we would either develop an entire new personnel type or go back and modify our original person type. Using tagged types, we can derive a new type based on the existing one:

```
TYPE Employee IS NEW Person WITH RECORD
  ID: IDRange;
  StartDate: Date;
END RECORD;
```

This declares a new type and reflects the "is a" relationship directly. Each employee now has five fields: the two new ones and the three it *inherited* from the person type.

Furthermore, the new type can be declared in a new package, with a new set of operations, *without disturbing the existing package or any programs that use it*. This technique is called *programming by extension*.

We can carry this further, of course. The payroll department in our company wishes to extend our employee type for payroll purposes, and thus needs three special categories of employees, as we saw in Section 6.1. The new types can be derived from the employee type:

```
TYPE Professional IS NEW Employee WITH RECORD
  MonthSalary : Quantity;
END RECORD;

TYPE Sales IS NEW Employee WITH RECORD
  WeekSalary  : Quantity;
  CommRate    : CommissionPercentage;
END RECORD;

TYPE Clerical IS NEW Employee WITH RECORD
  HourlyWage  : Quantity;
END RECORD;
```

where the `Quantity` values are taken from package `Currency`. In a further refinement of the "is a" relationship, a professional is an employee, which in turn is a person. As before, the new types can be declared and used in one or more new packages, without causing any modification of the older packages or any of their clients.

It is instructive to note that in Ada 83 new types can be derived from ordinary Ada 83 types. The new type has the same structure (set of values) as the original, and the operations of the original type are generally inherited by the new one. Ada 95 adds to this the ability to extend the type.

Converting Among Derived Tagged Types

The five types declared above form a *type hierarchy:*

```
Person
  Employee
    Professional
    Sales
    Clerical
```

Ada 95 allows us to convert explicitly from a lower type to a higher one. If `P` is a `Person`, `E` is an `Employee`, and `R` is a `Professional`, we can write an aggregate

```
R := (Name => "Nancy",
      Gender => Female,
      BirthDate => MakeDate(1950, 10, 21),
      ID => 2345,
      StartDate => MakeDate(1990, 7, 1),
      MonthSalary => 5000.00);
```

and can "up-convert" to P:

```
P := Person(R);
```

which is a familiar conversion construct. In the case of tagged types, the conversion "strips off" the extra fields.

How do we "down-convert?" Since a conversion to a lower type generally adds fields, Ada 95 gives a special aggregate structure for this. If we had

```
P := (Name => "Nancy",
      Gender => Female,
      BirthDate => MakeDate(1950, 10, 21);
```

we could make E by writing

```
E := (P WITH ID => 2345, StartDate => MakeDate(1990, 7, 1));
```

The text following WITH is called an *extension aggregate*. Generally, of course, client programs will not use the aggregate form because types like these will, in general, be PRIVATE. This brings us to the subject of operations on tagged types.

Primitive and Nonprimitive Operations on Tagged Types

The operations on tagged types are rather special. A fundamental Ada 95 idea is the *primitive operation*. Put simply, a primitive operation of a type is either a predefined operator on the type—such as the operators on Integer, for example—or an operation (function, subprogram, or operator) that is declared in the same package specification as the type and has a parameter of that type. Nearly all the operations in the packages so far in this book have been, in Ada 95 terminology, primitive. The term becomes important in the context of tagged types. Each primitive operation of a tagged type T is inherited by all types derived from T; sometimes we desire the inheritance, but sometimes we do not.

We shall explain this in the context of three package specifications, Persons, Personnel, and Payroll, which are shown as Programs 6.14, 6.15, and 6.16, respectively.

Program 6.14 Specification for Persons

```
WITH Dates;
WITH VStrings;
PACKAGE Persons IS
-----------------------------------------------------------------------
--| Specification for Persons. This package provides a root type
--| Person, with the fields Name, Gender, and  BirthDate. Person
--| is a tagged private type, which means that it has all the
--| characteristics of an ordinary private type but also that it
--| can be extended by derivation.
--| Author: Michael B. Feldman, The George Washington University
--| Last Modified: September 1995
-----------------------------------------------------------------------
```

```
TYPE Genders IS (Female, Male);

MaxName: CONSTANT Positive := 30;
SUBTYPE NameType IS VStrings.VString(MaxName);

TYPE Person IS TAGGED PRIVATE;

-- selectors

FUNCTION NameOf  (Whom: Person) RETURN NameType;
FUNCTION GenderOf(Whom: Person) RETURN Genders;
FUNCTION DOBOf   (Whom: Person) RETURN Dates.Date;
-- Pre:  Whom is defined
-- Post: returns the appropriate field value

PROCEDURE Put(Item: IN Person);
-- Pre:  Item is defined
-- Post: Item's fields are displayed

PACKAGE Constructors IS

   -- this inner package is necessary so that MakePerson is not a
   -- "primitive" function, that is, so that it is not inherited
   -- by types derived from Person.

   FUNCTION MakePerson(Name     : String;
                       Gender   : Genders;
                       BirthDate: Dates.Date) RETURN Person;
   -- Pre:  Name, Gender, and BirthDate are defined
   -- Post: returns a Person with the given field values

END Constructors;

PRIVATE

   TYPE Person IS TAGGED RECORD
     Name      : NameType := VStrings.EmptyVString(MaxName);
     Gender    : Genders := Female;
     BirthDate : Dates.Date;
   END RECORD;

END Persons;
```

In Program 6.14, we declare the type `Person`, almost exactly as above, except that here `Person` is a `PRIVATE` type with initialized fields, as in most of our packages. Note that in the visible part of the specification (above the `PRIVATE` line), the declaration

```
TYPE Person IS TAGGED PRIVATE;
```

which is consistent with our understanding of `PRIVATE` declarations, with the addition of `TAGGED`. The package specification further gives four operations in the selector category; this style is familiar to you from packages discussed earlier. However, the constructor operation is declared not here, but rather in an inner package, `Constructors`. Why the unfamiliar structure?

Our intention in writing `Persons` is to allow new types to be derived and extended from `Person`. Consider the type `Employee`, introduced earlier. An employee is a person with additional fields; the type `Employee` inherits all the primitive operations of `Person`; that is, for each primitive `Person` operation, there is a similar one for `Employee`, with a similar parameter profile. Thus, the `Employee` type also has operations `NameOf`, `GenderOf`, and `DOBOf`.

Inheritance is fine for the selectors. For example, a client will certainly wish to find out an employee's name, and an inherited operation just like the `Person` selector is a perfectly good operation to return the name. The constructor is a different story, however, because we need to pass all the field values into it. A person has three fields; an employee has five. If we wrote a person constructor as a primitive operation—for instance, `MakePerson`—it would be inherited by the employee type, so a client could call `MakePerson` with a parameter of type `Employee`. But this would be wrong! The object would be constructed with only three of its fields filled in!

Writing a separate constructor for `Employee` is a useful thing to do, and we shall do it shortly. However, it does not solve our problem, because `MakePerson` would still be available for the client to call.

Because it would be very unsafe and therefore unwise to allow `MakePerson` to be inherited by derived types, we need to take preventive action. There are several ways to do this; here, we handle the problem by realizing that—by Ada's rules of primitive operations—an operation declared in an inner package, such as `Persons.Constructors` in Program 6.14, is *not* primitive and is therefore *not* inherited. Putting the constructor in an inner package puts a small burden on the client programmer, who can write `Persons.NameOf` but must write `Persons.Constructors.MakePerson`. This is a small price to pay for the added safety.

Deriving New Tagged Types

Program 6.15 gives the specification for `Personnel`.

Program 6.15 Specification for Personnel

```
WITH Persons; USE Persons;
WITH Dates; USE Dates;
PACKAGE Personnel IS
------------------------------------------------------------------------
--| Specification for Personnel, which provides a type Employee,
--| a derivative of Persons.Person. Note that the operations on
--| objects of type Persons.Person are inherited by objects of
--| type Employee, so we need selectors only for the new
--| fields! As in the case of Persons, we place the constructor
--| in an inner package.
--| Author: Michael B. Feldman, The George Washington University
--| Last Modified: September 1995
------------------------------------------------------------------------

  TYPE Employee IS NEW Person WITH PRIVATE;
    -- Here is where Employee is derived; the extension fields are
    -- also PRIVATE, so clients cannot access them directly.
```

```
TYPE IDType IS NEW Positive RANGE 1111..9999;

-- selectors

FUNCTION StartOf (Whom: Employee) RETURN Date;
FUNCTION IDOf    (Whom: Employee) RETURN IDType;
  -- Pre:  Whom is defined
  -- Post: return the appropriate field values

PROCEDURE Put(Item: Employee);
  -- Pre:  Item is defined
  -- Post: Item is displayed

PACKAGE Constructors IS

  -- as in Persons, we use an inner package to prevent the
  -- constructor from being inherited by further derivatives
  -- of Employee

  FUNCTION  MakeEmployee(Name     : String;
                         Gender   : Genders;
                         BirthDate: Date;
                         StartDate: Date;
                         ID       : IDType) RETURN Employee;
  -- Pre:  Name, Gender, BirthDate, StateDate, and ID are defined
  -- Post: Whom contains the desired field values

END Constructors;

PRIVATE

  TYPE Employee IS NEW Person WITH RECORD
    ID        : IDType := 1111;
    StartDate : Date;
  END RECORD;

END Personnel;
```

Its structure is similar to that of `Persons`, but note how the type `Employee` is declared:

```
TYPE Employee IS NEW Person WITH PRIVATE;
```

The syntax `WITH PRIVATE` indicates a private extension; it allows `Employee` to be a `PRIVATE` type just as `Person` is. `Personnel` also provides selectors `StartOf` and `IDOf`, and a constructor `MakeEmployee` in an inner package.

The type `Employee` inherits the primitive operations of `Person`: `NameOf`, `GenderOf`, and `DOBOf`. This is fine; employees also have these fields. What about `Put`? `Persons.Put` displays the fields of a person. If `Put` were inherited by `Employee`, it would, of course, display *only* the fields that `Employee` and `Person` have in common, which is not what we desire. We therefore supply another `Put` for the employee type. Because it has a similar parameter profile, the only difference being the substitution of `Employee` for `Person`, this new employee operation is said to *override* the corresponding person operation. The body of `Personnel.Put`, as we will show shortly, displays all five fields of an employee.

Why were we able to override `Person.Put` so simply, without using an inner package? The key is that the two `Put` parameter profiles are so similar. The constructors' parameter profiles are very different from one another, so writing a `MakePerson` in `Personnel`, with a profile appropriate for `Employee`, simply would not have solved that problem.

Program 6.16 gives the specification for `Payroll`, which gives the three pay categories we sketched earlier.

Program 6.16 Specification for `Payroll`

```
WITH Ada.Text_IO;
WITH Ada.Integer_Text_IO;
WITH Ada.Float_Text_IO;
WITH Currency; USE Currency;
WITH Dates; USE Dates;
WITH Persons; USE Persons;
WITH Personnel; USE Personnel;
PACKAGE Payroll IS
-------------------------------------------------------------------
--| Specification for Payroll, a set of payroll categories
--| derived from Personnel. Each type has a primitive operation
--| Put, which overrides the one inherited from Employee.
--| Author: Michael B. Feldman, The George Washington University
--| Last Modified: September 1995
-------------------------------------------------------------------

  SUBTYPE CommissionPercentage IS Float RANGE 0.00..0.50;

  TYPE Professional IS NEW Employee WITH PRIVATE;
  TYPE Sales IS NEW Employee WITH PRIVATE;
  TYPE Clerical IS NEW Employee WITH PRIVATE;

  PROCEDURE Put(Item: Professional);
  PROCEDURE Put(Item: Sales);
  PROCEDURE Put(Item: Clerical);

  PACKAGE Constructors IS

    -- constructors for the three new types
    FUNCTION MakeProfessional(Name       : String;
                              Gender     : Genders;
                              BirthDate  : Date;
                              StartDate  : Date;
                              ID         : IDType;
                              MonthSalary: Quantity)
                              RETURN Professional;

    FUNCTION MakeSales (Name       : String;
                        Gender     : Genders;
                        BirthDate  : Date;
                        StartDate  : Date;
                        ID         : IDType;
                        WeekSalary : Quantity;
                        CommRate   : CommissionPercentage)
                        RETURN Sales;
```

```
    FUNCTION MakeClerical (Name      : String;
                           Gender    : Genders;
                           BirthDate : Date;
                           StartDate : Date;
                           ID        : IDType;
                           HourlyWage: Quantity)
                           RETURN Clerical;

   -- Pre:  All input fields are defined
   -- Post: Returns an initialized value of the respective type

  END Constructors;

PRIVATE

  -- full extensions for the three types

  TYPE Professional IS NEW Employee WITH RECORD
    MonthSalary : Quantity;
  END RECORD;

  TYPE Sales IS NEW Employee WITH RECORD
    WeekSalary  : Quantity;
    CommRate    : CommissionPercentage;
  END RECORD;

  TYPE Clerical IS NEW Employee WITH RECORD
    HourlyWage  : Quantity;
  END RECORD;

END Payroll;
```

The three types are closely related—all are used by the payroll department—so it is sensible to collect them into a single package as we have done here. Note the three derived `PRIVATE` type declarations, the three overriding `Put` operations, and the three constructors in the inner package. We have not included field selectors; we prefer to leave that as an exercise.

Before going on to the package bodies, look at Program 6.17, which illustrates the use of these packages.

Program 6.17 Creating a Company of Employees

```
WITH Ada.Text_IO; USE Ada.Text_IO;
WITH Currency; USE Currency;
WITH Dates; USE Dates;
WITH Persons; USE Persons;
WITH Personnel; USE Personnel;
WITH Payroll; USE Payroll;
PROCEDURE Use_Payroll IS
-------------------------------------------------------------------
--| demonstrates the use of tagged types
--| Author: Michael B. Feldman, The George Washington University
--| Last Modified: September 1995
-------------------------------------------------------------------

  -- demonstrates the use of tagged types

  George: Person;
  Mary  : Employee;
  Martha: Professional;
```

```
      Virginia: Sales;
      Herman: Clerical;

BEGIN -- Use_Payroll

   -- first construct all the people

   George := Persons.Constructors.MakePerson(
            Name      => "George",
            Gender    => Male,
            BirthDate => MakeDate(1971,11,2));

   Mary := Personnel.Constructors.MakeEmployee(
            Name      => "Mary",
            Gender    => Female,
            BirthDate => MakeDate(1950,10,21),
            ID        => 1234,
            StartDate => MakeDate(1989,7,1));

   Martha := Payroll.Constructors.MakeProfessional(
            Name        => "Martha",
            Gender      => Female,
            BirthDate   => MakeDate(1947,7,8),
            ID          => 2222,
            StartDate   => MakeDate(1985,6,6),
            MonthSalary => MakeCurrency(50000.00));

   Virginia := Payroll.Constructors.MakeSales(
            Name       => "Virginia",
            Gender     => Female,
            BirthDate  => MakeDate(1955,2,1),
            ID         => 3456,
            StartDate  => MakeDate(1990,1,1),
            WeekSalary => MakeCurrency(2500.00),
            CommRate   => 0.25);

   Herman := Payroll.Constructors.MakeClerical(
            Name       => "Herman",
            Gender     => Male,
            BirthDate  => MakeDate(1975,5,13),
            ID         => 1557,
            StartDate  => MakeDate(1991,7,1),
            HourlyWage => MakeCurrency(7.50));

   -- Now display them all. Note that each Put is a different
   -- primitive operation.

   Put(Item => George);
   Ada.Text_IO.Put_Line(Item => "------------------------");
   Put(Item => Mary);
   Ada.Text_IO.Put_Line(Item => "------------------------");
   Put(Item => Martha);
   Ada.Text_IO.Put_Line(Item => "------------------------");
   Put(Item => Virginia);
   Ada.Text_IO.Put_Line(Item => "------------------------");
   Put(Item => Herman);
   Ada.Text_IO.Put_Line(Item => "------------------------");

END Use_Payroll;
```

Each of the five variables is of a different type; in each case, the appropriate constructor is called—an Ada compiler would reject an attempt to call an inappropriate one—and the appropriate `Put` is used to display the contents.

Bodies of the Tagged Type Packages

The bodies of `Persons`, `Personnel`, and `Payroll` are given as Programs 6.18, 6.19, and 6.20, respectively. They are quite straightforward, but a few things are worth pointing out.

Program 6.18 Body of `Persons`

```
WITH Ada.Text_IO;
WITH Ada.Integer_Text_IO;
WITH Dates; USE Dates;
WITH VStrings;
WITH VStrings.IO;
PACKAGE BODY Persons IS
------------------------------------------------------------------------
--| Body of Persons package
--| Author: Michael B. Feldman, The George Washington University
--| Last Modified: September 1995
------------------------------------------------------------------------

  PACKAGE Gender_IO IS NEW Ada.Text_IO.Enumeration_IO(Enum => Genders);

  FUNCTION NameOf(Whom: Person) RETURN NameType  IS
  BEGIN
    RETURN Whom.Name;
  END NameOf;

  FUNCTION GenderOf(Whom: Person) RETURN Genders IS
  BEGIN
    RETURN Whom.Gender;
  END GenderOf;

  FUNCTION DOBOf(Whom: Person) RETURN Date IS
  BEGIN
    RETURN Whom.BirthDate;
  END DOBOf;

  PROCEDURE Put(Item: Person) IS
  BEGIN
    Ada.Text_IO.Put(Item => "Name: ");
    VStrings.IO.Put(Item => Item.Name);
    Ada.Text_IO.New_Line;

    Ada.Text_IO.Put(Item => "Gender: ");
    Gender_IO.Put(Item => Item.Gender, Set => Ada.Text_IO.Lower_Case);
    Ada.Text_IO.New_Line;

    Ada.Text_IO.Put(Item => "Birth Date: ");
    Ada.Integer_Text_IO.Put(Item => Month(Item.BirthDate), Width => 1);
    Ada.Text_IO.Put('/');
    Ada.Integer_Text_IO.Put
      (Item=>DayOfMonth(Item.BirthDate),Width=>1);
    Ada.Text_IO.Put('/');
    Ada.Integer_Text_IO.Put
      (Item=>Year(Item.BirthDate) REM 100,Width=>1);
    Ada.Text_IO.New_Line;
  END Put;
```

```
PACKAGE BODY Constructors IS

   FUNCTION MakePerson(Name     : String;
                       Gender   : Genders;
                       BirthDate: Date) RETURN Person IS
     Result: Person;
   BEGIN
     RETURN (Name      => VStrings.MakeVString(Name, MaxName),
             Gender    => Gender,
             BirthDate => BirthDate);
   END MakePerson;

  END Constructors;

END Persons;
```

Program 6.19 Body of `Personnel`

```
WITH Ada.Text_IO;
WITH Ada.Integer_Text_IO;
WITH Persons; USE Persons;
WITH Dates; USE Dates;
PACKAGE BODY Personnel IS
-------------------------------------------------------------------------
--| Body of Personnel package
--| Author: Michael B. Feldman, The George Washington University
--| Last Modified: September 1995
-------------------------------------------------------------------------

  PACKAGE BODY Constructors IS

    FUNCTION  MakeEmployee(Name     : String;
                           Gender   : Genders;
                           BirthDate: Date;
                           StartDate: Date;
                           ID       : IDType) RETURN Employee IS

    BEGIN
      -- note how the Persons constructor is used, with an
      -- aggregate for the Person fields and an
      -- extension aggregate to add in the extra fields.
      RETURN (Persons.Constructors.MakePerson(
        Name           => Name,
        Gender         => Gender,
        BirthDate      => Birthdate)
        WITH StartDate => StartDate, ID => ID);
    END MakeEmployee;

  END Constructors;

FUNCTION StartOf (Whom: Employee) RETURN Date IS
BEGIN
  RETURN Whom.StartDate;
END StartOf;

FUNCTION IDOf (Whom: Employee) RETURN IDType IS
BEGIN
  RETURN Whom.ID;
END IDOf;

PROCEDURE Put(Item: Employee) IS
BEGIN
  -- Note that we can up-convert Employee to Person and
  -- call Persons.Put for the common fields
```

```
        Persons.Put(Item => Persons.Person(Item));

        Ada.Text_IO.Put(Item => "ID Number: ");
        Ada.Integer_Text_IO.Put(Item => Positive(Item.ID), Width => 1);
        Ada.Text_IO.New_Line;

        Ada.Text_IO.Put(Item => "Start Date: ");
        Ada.Integer_Text_IO.Put(Item => Month(Item.StartDate), Width => 1);
        Ada.Text_IO.Put('/');
        Ada.Integer_Text_IO.Put(Item=>DayOfMonth(Item.StartDate),Width=>1);
        Ada.Text_IO.Put('/');
        Ada.Integer_Text_IO.Put(Item=>Year(Item.StartDate) REM 100,Width=>1);
        Ada.Text_IO.New_Line;
    END Put;

END Personnel;
```

Program 6.20 Body of `Payroll`

```
WITH Ada.Text_IO;
WITH Ada.Integer_Text_IO;
WITH Ada.Float_Text_IO;
WITH Currency; USE Currency;
WITH Currency.IO;
WITH Dates; USE Dates;
WITH Personnel; USE Personnel;
PACKAGE BODY Payroll IS
------------------------------------------------------------------------
--| Body of Payroll package
--| Author: Michael B. Feldman, The George Washington University
--| Last Modified: September 1995
------------------------------------------------------------------------

  PACKAGE BODY Constructors IS

    -- constructors for the three new types

    FUNCTION  MakeProfessional (Name      : String;
                               Gender     : Genders;
                               BirthDate  : Date;
                               StartDate  : Date;
                               ID         : IDType;
                               MonthSalary: Quantity)
                               RETURN Professional IS

    BEGIN
      RETURN   (Personnel.Constructors.MakeEmployee(
        Name            => Name,
        Gender          => Gender,
        BirthDate       => Birthdate,
        StartDate       => StartDate,
        ID              => ID)
        WITH MonthSalary => MonthSalary);
    END MakeProfessional;

    FUNCTION MakeSales (Name      : String;
                        Gender    : Genders;
                        BirthDate : Date;
                        StartDate : Date;
```

```
                                  ID          : IDType;
                                  WeekSalary: Quantity;
                                  CommRate   : CommissionPercentage)
                                  RETURN Sales IS
      BEGIN
        RETURN (Personnel.Constructors.MakeEmployee
          (Name            => Name,
           Gender          => Gender,
           BirthDate       => Birthdate,
           StartDate       => StartDate,
           ID              => ID)
           WITH WeekSalary => WeekSalary, CommRate => CommRate);
      END MakeSales;

      FUNCTION MakeClerical (Name       : String;
                             Gender     : Genders;
                             BirthDate  : Date;
                             StartDate  : Date;
                             ID         : IDType;
                             HourlyWage: Quantity)
                             RETURN Clerical IS
      BEGIN
        RETURN  (Personnel.Constructors.MakeEmployee
          (Name            => Name,
           Gender          => Gender,
           BirthDate       => Birthdate,
           StartDate       => StartDate,
           ID              => ID)
           WITH HourlyWage => HourlyWage);
      END MakeClerical;

    END Constructors;

    PROCEDURE Put(Item: Professional) IS
    BEGIN
      Put(Item => Employee(Item));
      Ada.Text_IO.New_Line;

      Ada.Text_IO.Put(Item => "Category: Professional");
      Ada.Text_IO.New_Line;
      Ada.Text_IO.Put(Item => "Monthly Salary: ");
      Currency.IO.Put(Item => Item.MonthSalary);
      Ada.Text_IO.New_Line;
    END Put;

    PROCEDURE Put(Item: Sales) IS
    BEGIN
      Put(Item => Employee(Item));
      Ada.Text_IO.New_Line;

      Ada.Text_IO.Put(Item => "Category: Sales");
      Ada.Text_IO.New_Line;
      Ada.Text_IO.Put(Item => "Weekly Salary: ");
      Currency.IO.Put(Item => Item.WeekSalary);
      Ada.Text_IO.New_Line;
      Ada.Text_IO.Put(Item => "Commission Rate: ");
      Ada.Float_Text_IO.Put(Item => Item.CommRate, Fore=>1,Aft=>2,Exp=>0);
      Ada.Text_IO.New_Line;
    END Put;

    PROCEDURE Put(Item: Clerical) IS
    BEGIN
```

```
      Put(Item => Employee(Item));
      Ada.Text_IO.New_Line;

      Ada.Text_IO.Put(Item => "Category: Clerical ");
      Ada.Text_IO.New_Line;
      Ada.Text_IO.Put(Item => "Hourly Wage: ");
      Currency.IO.Put(Item => Item.HourlyWage);
      Ada.Text_IO.New_Line;
   END Put;

END Payroll;
```

Looking at Program 6.19, in the body of the constructor `MakeEmployee` we "up-convert" the employee to a person, then use `MakePerson` to fill in the person fields. Finally, we use an extension aggregate to fill in the remaining fields. Similarly, in the `Put` procedure, we "up-convert" as before and reuse the `Persons.Put` to display the person fields; then we display the additional employee fields.

Variables of Tagged Types

Throughout this development, we have declared each variable to be of a specific tagged type. This is, in fact, analogous to declaring *constrained* variant variables, as in the earlier sections of this chapter. A plausible question is, then, whether there exists something analogous to *unconstrained* variant types and variables. The answer to the question is yes, but for further details we must wait for Chapter 9. A related question is whether, and how, we can create a "database" or table of tagged records—that is, an array of them. We will return to this important and interesting question in Chapter 9.

SUMMARY

In this chapter, we have introduced variant records. A variant record is one that can have one of several structures, depending on the value of a special field called the discriminant. We used variant records to represent employee records, variable-length strings, and dimensioned metric quantities.

Understanding variant records is not always easy. In defining variant record structures, remember that the only way to allow for changing the variant stored in a variant record variable is to supply a default value for the discriminant. This action makes the variable unconstrained.

In using variant record variables, keep in mind that the value of the discriminant field determines the form of the variant part that is currently defined; attempting to manipulate any other variant will cause either a compilation error or the raising of `Constraint_Error`. It is the programmer's responsibility to ensure that the correct variant is being processed; consequently, a variant record should always be manipulated in a `CASE` statement with the discriminant field used as the `CASE` selector to ensure that the proper variant part is being manipulated.

We also introduced Ada 95 support for strings, as well as some introductory material on tagged types. The latter is a very important capability of Ada 95, because it facilitates object-oriented programming.

EXERCISES

1. Write the variant declaration for Supplies, which consist of either Paper, Ribbon, or Labels. For Paper, the information needed is the number of sheets per box and the size of the paper. For Ribbon, the size, color, and kind (Carbon or Cloth) are needed. For Labels, the size and number per box are needed. For each supply, the cost, the number on hand, and the reorder point must also be stored. Use whatever data types are appropriate for each field.
2. Write the declaration for Vehicle. If the vehicle is a Truck, then BedSize and CabSize are needed. If the vehicle is a Wagon, then third seat or not is needed (Boolean). If the vehicle is a Sedan, then the information needed is TwoDoor or FourDoor. For every vehicle, we need to know whether the transmission is Manual or Automatic; whether it has AirConditioning, PowerSteering, or PowerBrakes (all Boolean); and its gas mileage. Use whatever data types are appropriate for each field.
3. How many bytes of storage are required for each of the variants of PayRecord? You will probably have to check your Ada compiler documentation to determine the storage required by each of the fields comprised by this record.
4. Write a procedure to display a record of type Face as declared in Section 6.1.
5. Revise the employee database program from Chapter 5 so that the variant Employee record is used instead of the simple one.
6. Draw a diagram of a VString with your full name stored in it. Write a call to VStrings.SubString showing how your last name could be retrieved.
7. Extend Program 6.8 to test and demonstrate the remaining operations of VStrings. Make sure you include tests for conditions that will raise exceptions, to be certain that the exceptions are raised properly.
8. Revise the metric system package of Section 6.3 so that the value part of a dimensioned value is a generic parameter. Instantiate the package for Integer, Float, and Rational. (*Hint*: You will be required to provide a generic parameter for each arithmetic and comparison operation on the value type.)
9. Modify the geometric shapes example from Section 6.2, so that the basic shape is a tagged type with perimeter and area fields, and other shapes are derived from the basic one.

CHAPTER 7

Queues and Stacks

Two very common, important, and easy-to-understand structures in computing are the queue and the stack. These are distinguished from each other, and from vectors and lists, by the rules by which their elements are accessed for storage and retrieval.

Recall that in a vector the access is random in the sense that we can store a value at an arbitrary location, or retrieve a value from an arbitrary location, without having to search any other locations. In a list, the access is sequential in that a sequential search must be performed to locate the position of an arbitrary element. However, in stacks and queues we are allowed only a controlled method of access. In queues, this is *First-In, First-Out*, or *FIFO*; in stacks, it is *Last-In, First-Out*, or *LIFO*.

In this chapter you will see ADTs for these two structures and implementation schemes for them. Specifically, you will see how stacks and queues can be constructed using arrays.

An important application of stacks, namely evaluating and translating arithmetic expressions, is shown in this chapter. Two application sections develop an algorithm for translating an expression into reverse Polish notation (RPN) form and a discrete event simulation.

7.1   QUEUES AND STACKS INTRODUCED

The queue is analogous to the waiting line at a supermarket checkout or bank teller's station: customers are served one at a time, in the exact order of their arrival. Because of this first-come, first-served serving strategy, the queue is often called a *First-In, First-*

Out, or *FIFO*, structure. Notice that this means that customers must always go to the end of the line when they arrive, and the server—the checkout clerk or bank teller—serves whoever is first in line. (We assume that all customers are polite and that "breaking in" never occurs.) That customer then leaves the line, and the line moves up. Obviously, it doesn't make sense for the server to try to serve an empty queue.

The stack, on the other hand, finds its intuitive analogy in the spring-loaded tray stackers often found in self-service restaurants. In such a stacker, only the top tray is visible. Only the top tray may be removed; when a new clean tray is placed on top of the stack, all the others are pushed down, and when a tray is removed all the others move up. It doesn't make sense to remove the top tray from an empty stacker.

We shall see that there are a number of computing applications for the stack, which is often called a *Last-In, First-Out*, or *LIFO*, device because, continuing with the restaurant analogy, the last tray put on the stacker is the first one removed.

With this intuitive introduction, let us formalize our consideration of queues and stacks.

7.2   ADT DESIGN: FIFO QUEUES

Let us think of a queue as an abstract entity. It has a head and a tail; at any given time, it has a certain length (the number of items awaiting service); and items arrive on the queue and are removed from it (the actual type of these items obviously depends on the application, so we shall leave it abstract and unspecified).

An item joins the queue only at the tail and leaves the queue only at the head, and only the head item can be examined. Thus, the appropriate set of operations on queues are `MakeEmpty` (reset a queue to the empty condition), `IsEmpty` (test whether a queue is empty), `Enqueue` (put an item on the queue), and `Dequeue` (take an item off the queue). It is convenient to add another operation `First`, which examines the item at the front of the queue without removing it. Accordingly, we will write the `Dequeue` operation so that it just "throws away" the first item. This corresponds with the reality of most queues, in which the object at the front of the queue is first served, then leaves the queue.

Array Implementation of Queues

A first attempt at implementing a queue uses an array with a cursor indicating the tail of the queue. The capacity of the queue is then determined by the length of the array. Initially the tail cursor is set to 1; a new arrival is inserted into the array at the location indicated by the cursor, then the cursor is incremented to indicate the next available location.

What happens when an item is removed from the head of the queue? In a supermarket, when a customer is finished at the checkout, the remaining customers move up one position in the queue. Our implementation works in an exactly analogous manner. The `Enqueue` and `Dequeue` operations in this implementation are shown in Figure 7.1.

In Ada, we can set up this implementation by declaring a type `Queue`, which is a record containing the tail cursor and the queue array as its fields. Program 7.1 gives a

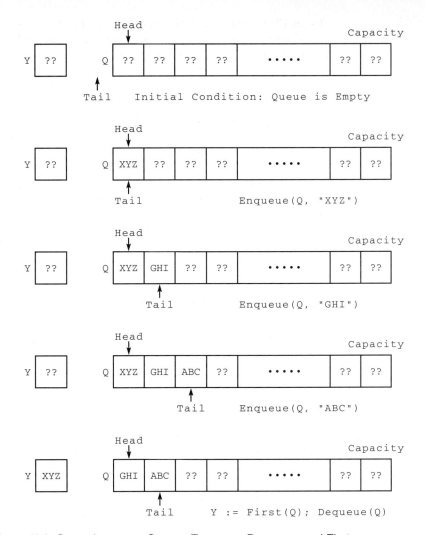

Figure 7.1 Operations on a Queue: Enqueue, Dequeue, and First

generic specification for the queue ADT. The only generic parameter is the element type. We use an unconstrained array type for the queue data; the array is contained in a variant record with a discriminant that gives the queue capacity. There is no default, so the client program must declare each queue variable with a fixed capacity. This is a reasonable requirement.

PROGRAM 7.1 Specification for Generic FIFO Queues Package

```
GENERIC
  TYPE Element IS PRIVATE;
PACKAGE Queues_Generic IS
```

```
--------------------------------------------------------------------
--| Specification for Generic FIFO Queues Package
--| Author: Michael B. Feldman, The George Washington University
--| Last Modified: January 1996
--------------------------------------------------------------------
  -- type definition

  TYPE Queue (Capacity: Positive) IS LIMITED PRIVATE;

  -- exported exceptions

  QueueFull  : EXCEPTION;
  QueueEmpty : EXCEPTION;

  -- constructors

  PROCEDURE MakeEmpty (Q : IN OUT Queue);
  -- Pre:    Q is defined
  -- Post:   Q is empty

  PROCEDURE Enqueue (Q : IN OUT Queue; E : IN Element);
  -- Pre:    Q and E are defined
  -- Post:   Q is returned with E as the top Element
  -- Raises: QueueFull if Q already contains Capacity Elements

  PROCEDURE Dequeue (Q : IN OUT Queue);
  -- Pre:    Q is defined
  -- Post:   Q is returned with the top Element discarded
  -- Raises: QueueEmpty if Q contains no Elements

  -- selector

  FUNCTION First (Q : IN Queue) RETURN Element;
  -- Pre:    Q is defined
  -- Post:   The first Element of Q is returned
  -- Raises: QueueEmpty if Q contains no Elements

  -- inquiry operations

  FUNCTION IsEmpty (Q : IN Queue) RETURN Boolean;
  -- Pre:    Q is defined
  -- Post:   returns True if Q is empty, False otherwise

  FUNCTION IsFull  (Q : IN Queue) RETURN Boolean;
  -- Pre:    Q is defined
  -- Post:   returns True if Q is full, False otherwise
PRIVATE
  TYPE List IS ARRAY (Positive RANGE <>) OF Element;
  TYPE Queue (Capacity: Positive) IS RECORD
    Tail  : Natural := 0;
    Store : List(1..Capacity);
  END RECORD;
END Queues_Generic;
```

The package provides the required queue operations, as well as inquiry functions `IsFull` and `IsEmpty` so that the client program can test for these conditions. Also provided are exceptions `QueueFull` and `QueueEmpty`. An unwitting attempt to remove an item from an empty queue usually indicates a misuse of the queue abstraction; since in this implementation a queue can also become full, we need a way to signal that pragmatic condition as well. In this way, we can guarantee the integrity of the queue ADT.

Why is the queue type `LIMITED PRIVATE`? As before, we do this to prevent a client program from using the predefined := and = operations. In this case, comparing two queues for equality using the predefined operator is not meaningful, because the part of the queue that is not occupied at any given moment contains unpredictable "garbage." We also wish to keep open the option to reimplement the queue using another structure, and we do not wish to require any recoding of the client program.

Program 7.2 shows the body of the queue package; note that the Dequeue operation uses array slicing to move the elements. This may be a single statement in Ada, but in the executable program, the time required to execute the copy is still generally proportional to the number of elements in the queue.

PROGRAM 7.2 Body of Generic Queues Package, Array Implementation

```
PACKAGE BODY Queues_Generic IS
-------------------------------------------------------------------------
--| Body of Generic Queues Package, Array Implementation
--| Author: Michael B. Feldman, The George Washington University
--| Last Modified: January 1996
-------------------------------------------------------------------------
  PROCEDURE MakeEmpty (Q : IN OUT queue) IS
  BEGIN
    Q.Tail := 0;
  END MakeEmpty;

  PROCEDURE Enqueue (Q : IN OUT Queue;
                     E : IN Element) IS
  BEGIN
    IF Q.Tail = Q.Capacity THEN
      RAISE QueueFull;
    ELSE
      Q.Tail           := Q.Tail + 1;
      Q.Store (Q.Tail) := E;
    END IF;
  END Enqueue;

  PROCEDURE Dequeue (Q : IN OUT Queue) IS
  BEGIN
    IF Q.Tail = 0 THEN
      RAISE QueueEmpty;
    ELSE
      Q.Store (1..Q.Tail - 1) := Q.Store (2..Q.Tail); -- slice
      Q.Tail := Q.Tail -1;
    END IF;
  END Dequeue;

  FUNCTION First (Q : IN Queue) RETURN Element IS
  BEGIN
    IF Q.Tail = 0 THEN
      RAISE QueueEmpty;
    ELSE
      RETURN Q.Store (1);
    END IF;
  END First;

  FUNCTION IsEmpty (Q : IN Queue) RETURN Boolean IS
  BEGIN
    RETURN Q.Tail = 0;
  END IsEmpty;

  FUNCTION IsFull (Q : IN Queue) RETURN Boolean IS
  BEGIN
```

```
      RETURN Q.Tail = Q.Capacity;
   END IsFull;

END Queues_Generic;
```

Circular Array Implementation of Queues

The array implementation discussed previously has a major problem associated with it. The `Enqueue` operation is $O(1)$, requiring only a one-position move of the tail cursor. However, because the entire queue is moved up every time an element is removed from the head (as in real-life supermarket queues), this `Dequeue` operation is $O(N)$. Let's see how we can do better.

Instead of requiring the queue to move whenever a `Dequeue` is done, let us "move the cash register" instead. Let's start with the queue in this initial state:

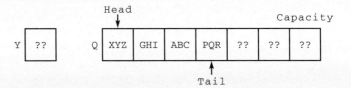

A `Dequeue` operation will then leave the queue as follows:

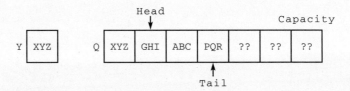

XYZ is still physically present in the array, but logically it has become "garbage." Another `Enqueue` and another `Dequeue` have the following effects on the queue:

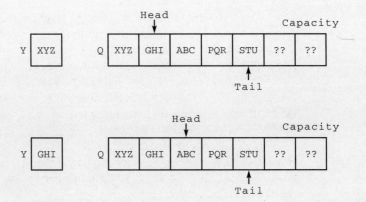

We maintain a cursor to the current head of the queue, and move it ahead one position when an element is removed. Thus, a constant amount of time will be needed to remove an element, since only the head cursor moves, and then only by one position. The new `Dequeue` operation is, therefore, $O(1)$.

This scheme works smoothly until the tail cursor reaches the upper limit of the array. After two more `Enqueue` operations, we have

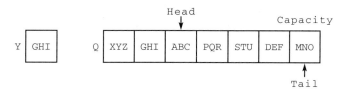

No new elements can be enqueued. Note that the queue is not really full: it has the capacity for seven elements, but we are using only five. The `Dequeue` operations left us with available space; we need only discover how to use it.

One solution is to reorganize the queue whenever the tail cursor reaches the end of the array: Simply copy all the elements currently in the queue—the slice bounded by the `Head` and `Tail` cursors—up to the front of the array. The queue would look like this:

The last two elements are "garbage" now. The reorganization is, of course, $O(N)$, but it is done much less frequently.

A more elegant and "self-regulating" solution that gives $O(1)$ `Enqueue` and `Dequeue` operations is to treat the array as though the last position were "glued" back to the first position. The tail cursor "wraps around," using empty space at the beginning of the array for new arrivals—space that was vacated by previous departures. This "circular" arrangement is depicted in Figure 7.2. The initial condition shows the state of the queue when `Tail` points to the last physical array element; the other two diagrams show the state after an additional `Enqueue` and another `Dequeue`. Note how `Tail` wraps around to element 1 of the array.

We can implement this structure with some modifications to our generic package. We keep track of the number of elements currently in the queue with a `CurrentSize` field in the data structure. Here are the declarations in the modified `PRIVATE` section:

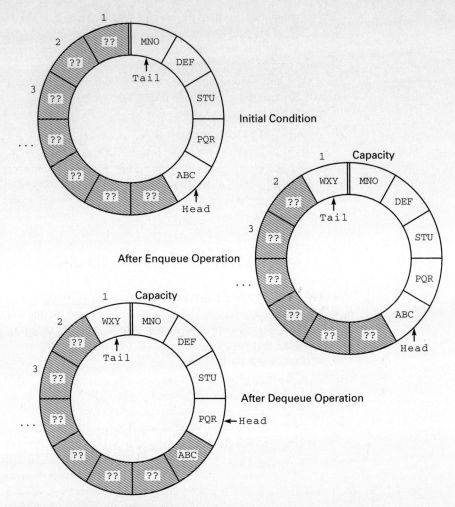

Figure 7.2 A Circular Queue

```
TYPE List IS ARRAY (Positive RANGE <>) OF Element;
TYPE Queue (Capacity: Positive) IS RECORD
  CurrentSize : Natural := 0;
  Head        : Natural := 1;
  Tail        : Natural := 0;
  Store       : List(1..Capacity);
END RECORD;
```

Here are the bodies of `IsFull` and `Enqueue`:

```
FUNCTION IsFull (Q : IN Queue) RETURN Boolean IS
BEGIN
  RETURN Q.CurrentSize = Q.Capacity;
END IsFull;

PROCEDURE Enqueue (Q : IN OUT Queue;
                   E : IN Element) IS
```

```
BEGIN
  IF IsFull(Q) THEN
     RAISE QueueFull;
  ELSE
     Q.CurrentSize := Q.CurrentSize + 1;
     Q.Tail := (Q.Tail REM Q.Capacity) + 1;
     Q.Store (Q.Tail) := E;
  END IF;
END Enqueue;
```

Note how REM is used to effect the wraparound; REM would be used in a similar way to implement Dequeue. Exercise 1 invites you to modify the queue package according to this scheme, completing the other operations yourself. Circular queues are very commonly used in operating systems and real-time systems. They are often called "ring buffers" in those systems.

7.3   ADT DESIGN: PRIORITY QUEUES

The previous section discussed queues whose processing method is strictly FIFO. Another important kind of queue is the *priority queue*. In this structure, each element in the queue has a priority, or level of importance, associated with it. Elements must be processed in order of priority.

There are really two ways to handle priority queues. We can take the priority into account in the Enqueue operation, inserting the new arrival into the queue in priority order, then use the same Dequeue as in the FIFO case. Alternatively, we can use the FIFO Enqueue, then search for and delete the element of highest priority during Dequeue. It is easier to use the first method.

A priority-queue ADT can be implemented analogously to a keyed table: the key is the element's priority. An Enqueue operation is then nothing but an ordered Insert; a Dequeue operation removes the first element, as usual. You can, as Exercise 2, build this ADT by using the implementation of the keyed table as a model.

Later in this book, we will examine another, more commonly used, implementation of a priority queue, namely the heap.

7.4   ADT DESIGN: STACKS

Recall the intuitive explanation of a stack given at the beginning of the chapter. Here we make this intuition more concrete, defining a stack or LIFO device in ADT terms.

An item is inserted in the stack ("pushed") and deleted from it ("popped") only at the top, and only the top item can be examined. So the appropriate operations are MakeEmpty, IsEmpty, Push, and Pop. As in the queue case, we will add an operation Top, which examines the top item, and then write Pop so that it just "throws away" the top item.

Array Implementation of Stacks

Program 7.3 gives a generic package specification.

PROGRAM 7.3 Specification for Generic Stack Package

```
GENERIC

  TYPE Element IS PRIVATE;

PACKAGE Stacks_Generic IS
-------------------------------------------------------------------------
--| Specification for Generic Stacks Package, Array Implementation.
--| Author: Michael B. Feldman, The George Washington University
--| Last Modified: January 1996
-------------------------------------------------------------------------

  -- type definition

  TYPE Stack (Capacity: Positive) IS LIMITED PRIVATE;

  -- exported exceptions

  StackFull  : EXCEPTION;
  StackEmpty : EXCEPTION;

  -- constructors

  PROCEDURE MakeEmpty (S : IN OUT Stack);
  -- Pre:    S is defined
  -- Post:   S is empty

  PROCEDURE Push (S : IN OUT Stack; E : IN Element);
  -- Pre:     S and E are defined
  -- Post:    S is returned with E as the top Element
  -- Raises: StackFull if S already contains Capacity Elements

  PROCEDURE Pop (S : IN OUT Stack);
  -- Pre:    S is defined
  -- Post:   S is returned with the top Element discarded
  -- Raises: StackEmpty if S contains no Elements

  -- selector

  FUNCTION Top (S : IN Stack) RETURN Element;
  -- Pre:    S is defined
  -- Post:   The top Element of S is returned
  -- Raises: StackEmpty if S contains no Elements

  -- inquiry operations

  FUNCTION IsEmpty (S : IN Stack) RETURN Boolean;
  -- Pre:    S is defined
  -- Post:   returns True if S is empty, False otherwise

  FUNCTION IsFull  (S : IN Stack) RETURN Boolean;
  -- Pre:    S is defined
  -- Post:   returns True if S is full, False otherwise

PRIVATE
```

```
TYPE List IS ARRAY (Positive RANGE <>) OF Element;
TYPE Stack (Capacity: Positive) IS RECORD
  Latest : Natural := 0;
  Store  : List(1..Capacity);
END RECORD;

END Stacks_Generic;
```

In the array implementation of a stack, we will consider the stack to be a record consisting of a cursor, `Latest`, pointing to the current stack top, and an array representing the stack itself. Notice that the "top" of the stack really keeps moving toward the "bottom" of the array; this avoids the necessity of moving any other items when a new one arrives. Thus, `Push` and `Pop` operations are $O(1)$, done in fixed time, independent of the current stack depth.

Figure 7.3 illustrates the array structure and a few operations. In Exercise 3, you can complete the stack package body.

7.5 EXPRESSION EVALUATION AND POLISH NOTATION

Consider the sort of lengthy computation often carried out on a hand-held calculator; for instance,

```
(5*2)-(((3+4*7)+8/6)*9)
```

A Brand X calculator allows the user to enter the above expression, parentheses and all; this form is called *parenthesized*, or *infix*, notation. On the other hand, a Brand Y calculator requires the user to convert the expression into what is called *reverse Polish notation (RPN)*, often called *postfix notation*. The corresponding RPN form would be:

```
5 2 * 3 4 7 * + 8 6 / + 9 * -
```

which looks thoroughly unintelligible. Most people seem to prefer the parenthesized form.

Since the calculator is just a special-purpose computer, it follows some algorithm to evaluate (find the final result of) the expression, given in one form or the other. The purpose of this section is to introduce the relationship between a parenthesized or infix expression and RPN. You will see how a stack can be used to evaluate an RPN expression and also how to convert "by hand" from the parenthesized form to the RPN form (which is what the Brand X calculator does internally). Section 7.5 will develop an algorithm for this conversion.

Polish notation got its name from the Polish mathematician Jan Łukasiewicz, who first published it in 1951. Łukasiewicz was more interested in mathematical logic than in computers per se (computers weren't very common in the early 1950s!); his notation was developed as a convenient, parenthesis-free way to represent logic expressions. Today, Polish notation is very widely used in interpreters and compilers as an intermediate representational form for statements (a hand-held calculator is nothing but a kind of interpreter).

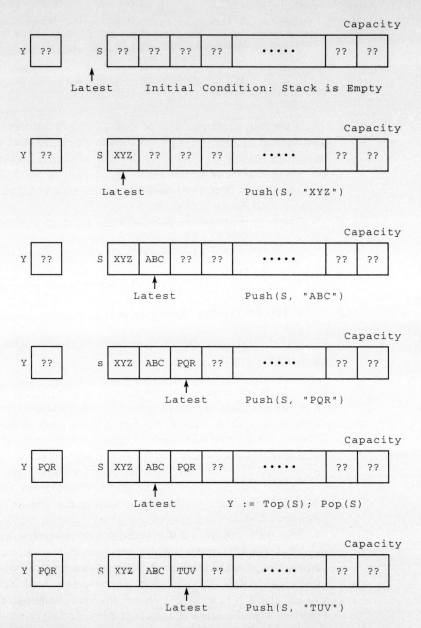

Figure 7.3 Array Implementation of a Stack, with Several Push and Pop Operations

The term *reverse* or *postfix* is used to indicate that an operator follows its operands instead of appearing between them; there is also a *prefix*, or *forward Polish*, notation, in which the operator precedes its operands. The latter form will be considered in an exercise.

```
WITH Stacks_Generic;
PACKAGE Integer_Stacks IS NEW Stacks_Generic (Element => Integer);
```

Infix Expression	RPN Expression
3	3
3+2	3 2 +
(3+2)*4	32+ 4 *
3+(2*4)	3 24* +
(3/5)+(2*4)	35/ 24* +
(3+5)*(2-4)/6	35+ 24- * 6 /
(5*2)-((3+4*7)+8/6)*9	52* 3 47* + 86/ + 9 * -

Figure 7.4 Infix and RPN Expressions

A bit later on, we will consider how to convert an infix expression to its corresponding RPN form. For the moment, examine the examples in Figure 7.4. Brackets are used to indicate the two operands of each operator; they are not part of the RPN. Notice that the numerical quantities in each RPN expression occur in the same order as they do in the original infix form. This is always true.

Evaluating RPN Expressions

We will evaluate an RPN expression using a left-to-right scan. An operator is preceded by its two operands, so in evaluating the expression we need a way to remember what the operands are until we encounter the corresponding operator. This is easy if the expression has only one operator in it (for instance, 3 5 +). We somehow store the first operand, 3, then store the second operand, 5, then, when the operator arrives, we determine that it is indeed + and therefore add the two operands together, obviously getting 8 as the result.

But suppose the RPN has more than one operator. Take the expression 3 5 + 10 * (the equivalent of (3+5)*10, or 80). If we scan the expression left-to-right, we store 3, then store 5, then add them, getting 8 as before. But what do we do with the 8? We need to store it, then store the 10, then discover the * and multiply the 8 by the 10, getting 80.

Evidently we have to save intermediate results as well as input numbers, and then, when we see an operator, apply it to the last two things we stored. The expression 3 5 2 * – (equivalent to 3–(5*2) or –7) makes this even clearer. We need to store the 3, then the 5, then the 2. When the * is scanned, we multiply the last two numbers stored (2 and 5), then store this intermediate result. When the – arrives, we have two operands for it—3 and the intermediate result from the multiplication, 10—so we get –7.

We have been saving values in such a way that the last two values saved become the first two retrieved. This is a perfect application for a stack. Let's represent the RPN expression in the form of a `VString` object using the variable-length string package of Chapter 6, and assume it is well-formed—that is, that it follows the rules given above for forming an RPN expression. For simplicity, we just use single digits to represent numbers. We'll also use the array-stack package from this chapter, instantiated and compiled as follows:

An Ada function is shown in Program 7.4.

PROGRAM 7.4 RPN Expression Evaluator

```
WITH Integer_Stacks; USE Integer_Stacks;
WITH VStrings; USE VStrings;
FUNCTION Evaluate_RPN (X : IN VString) RETURN Integer IS
-- Pre:  X is defined and represents an RPN arithmetic expression
--    of single digits and operators
-- Post: returns the value of the expression.
  ZeroPos   : Integer := Character'Pos ('0');
  C         : Character;
  T         : VString(MaxLength(X)) := X;
  S         : Stack(Capacity => 100);
  Y, Z      : Integer;
BEGIN -- Evaluate_RPN
  IF IsEmpty (T) THEN
    RETURN 0;
  END IF;
  LOOP
    C := Head (T);
    IF C IN '0' .. '9' THEN
      Push (S, Character'POS (C) - ZeroPos); -- convert to integer
    ELSE
      Y := Top (S);
      Pop (S);
      Z := Top (S);
      Pop (S);
      CASE C IS
        WHEN '+' =>
          Push (S, Z + Y);
        WHEN '-' =>
          Push (S, Z - Y);
        WHEN '*' =>
          Push (S, Z * Y);
        WHEN '/' =>
          Push (S, Z / Y);
        WHEN OTHERS =>
          NULL;                 -- skip bad characters, if any
      END CASE;
    END IF;
    T := Tail (T);
    EXIT WHEN IsEmpty (T);
  END LOOP;

  RETURN Top (S);

END Evaluate_RPN;
```

Here's how the algorithm works. We scan the text from left to right, removing the first character as we go, checking to see whether it's a number—we'll use only single numeric digits here for simplicity—or an operator (+, –, *, or /). If it's a numeric digit, we need to convert it to its integer form so we can do arithmetic with it, then push it onto the stack. If it's an operator, we remove the top two items from the stack, do the operation, then push the result back onto the stack.

Assuming we started with a legal RPN expression, when all the characters in it have been exhausted, the final value will be the only value left on top of the stack.

Figure 7.5 shows the evaluation of an RPN expression by this algorithm; you should try the program "by hand" on a number of examples to be sure how it works. Make sure you understand that it works correctly even when the RPN expression is just a single digit.

Converting Manually from Infix to RPN Form

In this section, we'll discuss the notions of *operator associativity* and *operator priority* or *precedence* and develop an informal method for doing the translation "by hand." Section 7.5 will present a program for carrying out the translation.

The program in the preceding section, which emulates a hand-held calculator, works with RPN expressions containing only numeric values. Most other applications need to work with expressions containing variables as well. Thus, we need a more general understanding of an expression. For our purposes, an arithmetic expression is a restricted version of the expressions you are familiar with from whatever programming languages

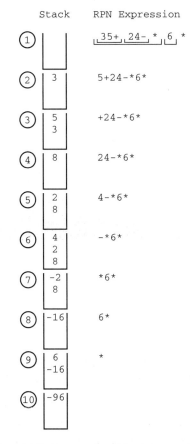

Figure 7.5 Evaluation of an RPN Expression (Each "snapshot" is taken before the leftmost input character is examined.)

Infix Expression	RPN Expression
A	A
A – B	A B –
(A – B) + C	A B – C +
A – (B + C)	A B C + –
(A + B) * (C – D)	A B + C D – *

Figure 7.6 More Infix and RPN Expressions

you have used. An expression consists of identifiers or variable names (limited to single letters for simplicity), numerical constants (limited to one-digit integers for simplicity), the operators +, –, *, and / (which have their familiar meanings), and parentheses.

In the first instance, we consider only fully parenthesized expressions—that is, expressions in which parentheses are always used to indicate the order in which operations are to be performed—and show how these are transformed into RPN form.

An RPN expression is of one of two forms: It is either a single variable or constant, or it is two RPN expressions followed by an operator. The last (rightmost) operator in the RPN form is the "main" operator of the expression—that is, the operator that is performed last as the expression is evaluated, to produce the final result of the evaluation.

To give a few examples, Figure 7.6 shows several infix expressions and their RPN equivalents.

Notice carefully how these are constructed, and make sure that you understand well how (A–B)+C and A–(B+C) give rise to different expressions. In (A–B)+C, the + is the main operation, since it is performed last; in A–(B+C), it is the – that is the main operation. If numerical values were assigned to A, B, and C—say 2, 3, and 4—it is easy to see that the result of evaluating (A–B)+C is 3 and the result of evaluating A–(B+C) is –5. Try (A*B)–(C+(D/E)) and ((A–B)+(C/D))*E to make certain you understand how their RPN forms are produced.

Now we are ready to relax the condition that expressions must be fully parenthesized. We do this by stating some assumptions about the order in which operations will be done. For example, in the expression A–B–C, how do we know whether to evaluate it as though it were (A–B)–C, or as though it were A–(B–C)? Most programming languages use the rule that a sequence of + and – operations, without parentheses, is evaluated left-to-right, so that A–B–C is treated as though it were (A–B)–C and A–B+C is done as though it were (A–B)+C. That's the rule we'll use here. The mathematical term for a rule like this is an *association* or *associativity* rule; our addition and subtraction operators associate left-to-right.

Look at Figure 7.7 and compare the unparenthesized forms with the parenthesized forms and the RPN expressions.

Unparenthesized	Assumed Parenthesized Form	RPN
A + B + C	(A + B) + C	A B + C +
A – B – C	(A – B) – C	A B – C –
W – X + Y	(W – X) + Y	W X – Y +
W + X – Y + Z	((W + X) – Y) + Z	W X + Y – Z +

Figure 7.7 Left-to-Right Associativity of + and –

Unparenthesized	Assumed Parenthesized Form	RPN
A * B * C	(A * B) * C	A B * C *
K / G/ Z	(K / G) / Z	K G / Z /
Q / S * D	(Q / S) * D	Q S / D *
P * D / E * K	((P * D) / E) * K	P D * E / K *

Figure 7.8 Left-to-Right Associativity of * and /

The same associativity rule applies to sequences of * and / operators. These are also evaluated in left-to-right order. So A/B/C is always done as though it were (A/B)/C and A/B*C as though it were (A/B)*C. Figure 7.8 shows a number of expressions involving only * and /, their assumed parenthesized forms, and the corresponding RPN forms.

Left-to-right associativity is not the only possible way. Programming languages with a built-in exponentiation operator, often represented as **, often apply a right-to-left rule for this operator, so that A**B**C is treated like A**(B**C). In an exercise, you will be asked to explain why this rule is chosen. In this section, we are ignoring exponentiation and using only left-to-right associativity.

What happens in the case of expressions where mixtures of all four operators can occur? This is usually handled by assigning *priorities* or *precedences* to the different operators. Usually, + and – have the same priority and * and / have the same priority. For definiteness, let + and – be called *priority 2* operators, and let * and / be called *priority 1* operators. Given two adjacent operators, one of priority 1 and the other of priority 2, the priority 1 operator will be performed first. So the expression A+B*C will be evaluated as though it were parenthesized A+(B*C); A/B–C will be evaluated as though it were parenthesized (A/B)–C. Thus, in the first expression, + is the main operator; in the second it is –. These expressions and their RPN forms are shown in Figure 7.9.

You can now see how to convert, manually, an arbitrary expression, in which parentheses are sometimes used to group subexpressions. Following the two rules given just above, add the necessary parentheses (on paper until you have gained enough experience to do it by inspection), then produce the RPN from the fully parenthesized version.

Let's examine two examples. Consider first A+B–C+D. Since adjacent operators of equal priority are handled left-to-right, we get ((A+B)–C)+D. Now look at A–(B+C)*D. Here, the two adjacent operators of interest are – and * (the + doesn't count because it's inside a subexpression!), and the * is done first because it's priority 1. So this expression is handled as though it were A–((B+C)*D). These RPN forms are shown in Figure 7.10.

Try A–B*C/(D–E) and A*B–(C+D)+E to be sure you've got it.

Unparenthesized	Assumed Parenthesized Form	RPN
A + B * C	A + (B * C)	A B C * +
A * B + C	(A * B) + C	A B * C +
A + B * C + D	A * (B * C) + D	A B C * + D +

Figure 7.9 Operator Priorities

Original	Assumed Parenthesized Form	RPN
A * B − C + D	((A + B) − C) + D	A B + C − D +
A − (B + C) * D	A − ((B + C) * D)	A B C + D * −

Figure 7.10 Parenthesized Expressions

7.6 APPLICATION: AN INFIX-TO-RPN TRANSLATOR PROGRAM

In the preceding section, you learned how to translate an expression manually from infix form to RPN. Here, we will develop a program to do it. Our program will be a function, taking as its input the infix expression and returning the RPN expression as its result.

Consider first an unparenthesized expression with all operators of the same priority and left-to-right associativity. The operators and operands alternate in such an expression; the operands in the RPN appear in the same order as in the original.

Assume that the input and result expressions are represented as VString objects, as in Program 7.4. We scan the input expression from left to right. If the first character we see is an operand, we can immediately output it (concatenate it to the RPN string). If it is an operator, we need to remember it until after we've seen its other operand, which will be when the next operator is scanned. We then output the saved operator and save the new one.

An example of this operation is shown in Figure 7.11; an Ada function is given as Program 7.5.

	RPN	OP	Input Expression
①			A+B−C+D
②	A		−B−C+D
③	A	+	B−C+D
④	AB	+	−C+D
⑤	AB+	−	C+D
⑥	AB+C	−	+D
⑦	AB+C−	+	D
⑧	AB+C−D	+	
⑨	AB+C−D+		

Figure 7.11 Simple Infix-to-RPN Translation

PROGRAM 7.5 Simple Infix-to-RPN Translator

```
WITH VStrings; USE VStrings;
FUNCTION RPN_Simple (X : IN VString) RETURN VString IS
-- Pre:  X is defined and represents an arithmetic expression
--    with single-letter variable names
```

```
-- Post: returns the RPN_Simple of X;
--   no operator priorities are taken into account.
  C      : Character;
  T      : VString(MaxLength(X)) := X;
  Op     : Character := ' ';
  Result : VString(MaxLength(X));   -- empty by default
BEGIN -- RPN_Simple
  IF NOT IsEmpty (T) THEN
    LOOP
      C := Head (T);

      CASE C IS
        WHEN 'A' .. 'Z' | 'a' .. 'z' | '0' .. '9' =>
          Result := Result & C;

        WHEN '+' | '-' | '*' | '/' =>
          IF Op = ' ' THEN              -- first operator seen
            Op := C;
          ELSE
            Result := Result & Op; -- get rid of old op
            Op := C;
          END IF;
        WHEN OTHERS =>
          NULL;                   -- skip bad character
      END CASE;

      T := Tail (T);
      EXIT WHEN IsEmpty (T);
    END LOOP;

    Result := Result & Op;

    RETURN Result;
  END IF;
END RPN_Simple;
```

Taking Operator Priorities into Account

Now assume that operators of different priorities are allowed. Consider the infix
expression A+B*C. Its RPN form is A B C * +. We cannot just output the + when
the B is scanned, because the *, having higher priority, must be done first. So the +
must be remembered longer, and we need to tackle the problem a bit more systematically. The priority of the incoming operator needs to be checked against the priority of
the previous one; if the new operator has higher priority, we need to remember it as
well, until we've scanned its second operand! When its second operand has been
scanned and output, we can output the operator.

   We have, in this case, remembered two operators, and the last one remembered is
the first one output. This suggests that the best way to remember the operators is to put
them in a stack, which, after all, is precisely a LIFO device. This is shown in Figure
7.12, where an example is worked through.

   A modified version of the Infix-to-RPN algorithm that uses priorities is shown
as Program 7.6. The function includes a simple local function for determining the
priority of an operator in the set (+, −, *, /) and uses an instantiation of the stacks
package.

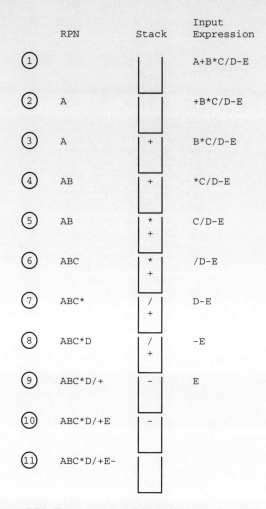

Figure 7.12 Infix-to-RPN Translation with Priorities

PROGRAM 7.6 Infix-to-RPN Translator That Considers Priorities

```
WITH VStrings; USE VStrings;
WITH Character_Stacks; USE Character_Stacks;
FUNCTION RPN_Priorities (X : VString) RETURN VString IS
-- Pre:  X is defined
-- Post: returns a string containing the RPN_Priorities for X;
--   operator priority and association, but no parentheses,
--   are taken into account. Parentheses are simply skipped.
  C        : Character;
  T        : VString(MaxLength(X)) := X;
  S        : Stack(MaxLength(X));
  Result   : VString(MaxLength(X));  -- empty by default

  FUNCTION Priority (Operator : IN character) RETURN integer IS
  BEGIN
    IF Operator = '+' OR Operator = '-' THEN
```

```
            RETURN 1;
      ELSE
            RETURN 2;
      END IF;
    END Priority;

BEGIN

  IF NOT IsEmpty (T) THEN
    LOOP
      C := Head (T);

      CASE C IS
        WHEN 'A' .. 'Z' | 'a' .. 'z' | '0' .. '9' =>
          Result := Result & C;
        WHEN '+' | '-' | '*' | '/' =>
          IF IsEmpty (S) THEN
            Push (S, C);
          ELSIF Priority (Top (S)) < Priority (C) THEN
            Push (S, C);
          ELSE
            LOOP -- clear stack of higher priority operators
              Result := Result & Top (S);
              Pop (S);
              EXIT WHEN IsEmpty (S)
                OR ELSE Priority (Top (S)) < Priority (C);
            END LOOP;
            Push (S, C);
          END IF;
        WHEN OTHERS =>
          NULL;                    -- skip bad characters
      END CASE;

      T := Tail (T);
      EXIT WHEN IsEmpty (T);
    END LOOP;

    WHILE NOT IsEmpty (S) LOOP
      Result := Result & Top (S);
      Pop (S);
    END LOOP;

    RETURN Result;

  END IF;

END RPN_Priorities;
```

In this new algorithm an operator is stacked until one of equal or lower priority comes along; then it is popped and added to the RPN. The new operator is then pushed onto the stack. The process continues until the input is empty, at which time the stack is emptied of all remaining operators. Try the function on a few examples of your own, to make sure you understand its operation.

Taking Parentheses into Account

The final modification accommodates parentheses. The way this is done becomes clear when it is realized that parentheses really override the priority scheme, essentially creating a whole new expression inside. We can change our algorithm to allow parentheses by pushing a left paren onto the stack, which creates a sort of 'false bottom' in the stack. The algorithm progresses as in the previous case, but when a right paren is seen, the stack is emptied as far back as the 'false bottom,' then the 'false bottom' is discarded.

In Figure 7.13, an example is worked; we leave it to you to modify the program as Exercise 6.

7.7   APPLICATION: AN EVENT-DRIVEN SIMULATION

As an example of the application of queues, we consider the simulation of a real-life situation in which people must wait in line for some service. It might be a bank, post office, or supermarket checkout. For definiteness, we choose the last.

A supermarket manager must think carefully about the number of checkout lines that will be open at a given time. Clearly, enough lines must be open to permit a customer to check out in a reasonable amount of time; otherwise, the shopper will find another store with shorter lines. On the other hand, the cashiers must be paid, so the manager doesn't want unnecessary lanes to be open. A computer simulation of the store at different levels of shopping traffic can aid the manager in finding the right number.

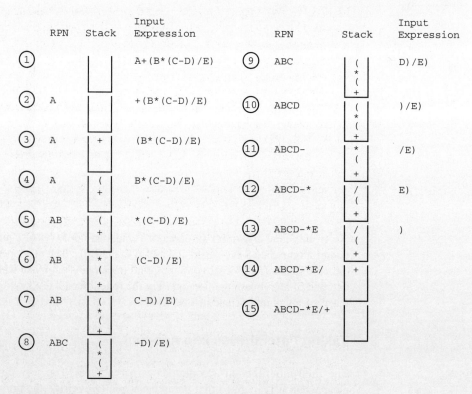

Figure 7.13 Infix-to-RPN Translation with Priorities and Parentheses

In a simulation of this type, we try to model the real-world situation as closely as possible with our program objects and algorithms.

Here is the scenario: A shopper arrives at the checkout area of the store at a certain time of day with a certain number of items in a shopping cart. The shopper finds the shortest line and joins it. For simplicity, we will assume that the shopper cannot see into other shoppers' carts, and that therefore the choice of line is not influenced by how full or empty they are. Another simplifying assumption is that the path to the checkout area is narrow and therefore two shoppers cannot enter it at the same instant. We also assume that no shopper gets tired of waiting and abandons a cart, leaving the store without checking out.

We will represent the time of day as an integer representing the number of time units since the store opened that day, and will assume that each item requires an average of one time unit to ring up and put in a bag. We define *average checkout time* as the sum of the length of time a shopper waits in line and the length of time taken to check out all his or her items. The goal of the simulation is to find, for a given store opening period, and a given group of shoppers and cart loads, the average checkout time as a function of the number of open lines.

To set up the simulation, we provide a set of FIFO queues, each representing one checkout line in the market. We define *departure time* as the time when a customer reaches the front of his or her queue, departs from that queue, and begins to be checked out by the cashier. Thus, the first customer in line is *waiting* to be served; the customer *being* served is thought of as having left the queue. If this seems unrealistic, consider the queueing system in use in many banks, post offices, and airports, where a single queue is processed by many servers. In such a system, the customer leaves the queue to be processed by the next available server. The assumption that a customer leaves the queue just before being served allows the simulation model to be changed easily to accommodate the single-queue scheme just described.

How will our simulation program operate? In a real supermarket, all the people are independent processes needing no external control; in a program, we need a control mechanism. This kind of simulation, in which there are a number of queues all moving at different rates, can be controlled by means of an *event list*, and is called an *event-driven simulation*.

There is no direct supermarket analogy to the event list; it is a special queue containing scheduled arrival and departure events. The event list is not FIFO; the events must be ordered by time. We therefore use a priority queue for the event list; the item with the earliest time is processed with the highest priority.

The event list contains, at any given time, no more than one arrival event, and at most as many departure events as there are open queues. The event list is initialized with the first arrival record, and the simulation proceeds, processing arrival and departure events until the event list is empty.

When an arriving shopper record is read from a file, an *arrival event* is placed on the event list (sorted by time because there may be departure events already scheduled). When the arrival record reaches the front of the event list, it is removed and joins the shortest checkout queue. If it is the only customer in the queue, it can be served immediately; its arrival and departure times are the same and a *departure event*, indicating the scheduled departure time and queue number, is placed on the event list. At this point, another arrival record is read from the file to replace the one just removed from the event list.

When a departure event reaches the front of the event list, we remove the first node from the corresponding queue, say queue *k*. We know its arrival time, its time of departure from the queue, and the time required to process all its purchased items, so we can compute its checkout time and add it to a grand total from which we can, at the end of the simulation, compute the average service time. We can also compute the scheduled departure time for the next customer in queue *k*: Because the next customer begins to be served just as the previous customer finishes, the next customer's departure time is the sum of the current customer's departure time and that customer's processing time. Having computed the scheduled departure time for the customer at the front of queue *k* (the customer waiting to be served), we place the associated depsrture event on the event list.

Program 7.7 shows a sketch of the main program of the simulation, with the necessary declarations.

PROGRAM 7.7 Sketch of Event-Driven Simulation

```
WITH Queues_Circular_Generic;
WITH Queues_Priority_Generic;
PROCEDURE Simulation IS
-------------------------------------------------------------------------
--| Sketch of event-driven simulation
--| Author: Michael B. Feldman, The George Washington University
--| Last Modified: January 1996
-------------------------------------------------------------------------

  NumQueues : CONSTANT Positive := -- number of open checkouts

  TYPE CustomerRecord IS RECORD -- put these records on the queues
    ArrivalTime: Positive;
    NumItems:    Positive;
  END RECORD;

  PACKAGE MarketQueues IS
    NEW Queues_Circular_Generic (Element => CustomerRecord);
  USE MarketQueues;

  TYPE Market IS ARRAY(1..NumQueues) OF Queue;
  Queues: Market;

  TYPE EventType IS (Arrival, Departure);

  TYPE Event (. . .) IS RECORD -- these records go on the event list

                    -- remember that an arrival event holds
       . . .        -- an arrival time and number of items
                    -- and a departure event holds a departure
  END RECORD;        -- time and a queue number

  PACKAGE EventQueues IS
    NEW Queues_Priority_Generic (Element => Event);

  EventList: EventQueue (Capacity => 4);

  PROCEDURE Process_Arrival(ArrivalTime: IN Positive;
                            NumItems:    IN Positive) IS SEPARATE;

  PROCEDURE Process_Departure(DepartureTime: IN Positive;

                              Q: IN OUT Queue) IS SEPARATE;

BEGIN -- main simulation
```

```
-- initialize queues, event list, other variables
-- read ArrivalTime and NumItems from customer file
-- place arrival event on event list

WHILE -- there are still events on the event list LOOP

  -- remove first event from event list
  IF -- this event is an arrival event  THEN
    ProcessArrival( -- pass time, number of items );
  ELSE -- it is a departure event
    ProcessDeparture( -- pass time, which queue );
  END IF;

END LOOP;

-- compute and print average checkout time

END Simulation;
```

The generic ADTs for queues and priority queues are instantiated as needed. To show the two key procedures in the simulation as separate program examples, we have used an Ada feature called *subunits*. A subunit is simply a separate file containing a local procedure or function, or one in a package body. To indicate to the compiler that a given procedure, say, `Process_Arrival`, is moved to a subunit, we put the lines

```
PROCEDURE Process_Arrival(ArrivalTime: IN Positive;
                          NumItems : IN Positive) IS SEPARATE;
```

in the main procedure.

The arrival-processing subunit itself, `ProcessArrival` in this case, is shown as Program 7.8, which begins with the lines

```
SEPARATE(Simulation)
PROCEDURE Process_Arrival(ArrivalTime: IN Positive;
                          NumItems   : IN Positive) IS . . .;
```

Note the syntax: No semicolon appears at the end of the first line, because that line is not a statement by itself; it is just a prefix of the second line.

PROGRAM 7.8 Subunit `Process_Arrival`

```
SEPARATE (Simulation)
PROCEDURE Process_Arrival(ArrivalTime: Positive;
                          NumItems:    Positive)  IS

-- sketch of procedure to process arrival event

BEGIN -- Process_Arrival

  -- find k, index of shortest queue
  -- enqueue ArrivalTime and NumItems on Queues(k)

  IF -- p is the only node on Queues(k) THEN
    -- this customer can be served immediately, so
    -- departure time = arrival time; therefore
```

```
      -- place departure event (from Queues(k))
      -- on event list (ordered by time)
   END IF;

   IF -- customer file is not empty THEN
      -- read ArrivalTime and NumItems from customer file
      -- place arrival event on event list (ordered by time)
   END IF;

END Process_Arrival;
```

Ada subunits are frequently used in large programs in industry, to divide a large package body up into smaller pieces, possibly for assignment to different members of a programming team. We use them here for convenience in the presentation.

Program 7.9, another subunit `Process_Departure`, shows how a departure is processed. Completing the simulation is left as an exercise.

PROGRAM 7.9 Subunit `Process_Departure`

```
SEPARATE (Simulation)
PROCEDURE Process_Departure(DepartureTime : Positive;
                               Q : IN OUT Queue) IS

-- sketch of procedure to process departure from queue k

BEGIN -- Process_Departure

  -- dequeue node from Queues(k); store its info in
  -- ArrivalTime and NumItems

  -- calculate elapsed checkout time
  CheckoutTime := DepartureTime + NumItems - ArrivalTime;

  -- update values which contribute to the average
   TotalCheckoutTime := TotalCheckoutTime + CheckoutTime;
  NumCustomers := NumCustomers + 1;

  IF -- Queues(k) is not empty THEN
    -- compute departure time for next node
    NextDepartureTime := DepartureTime + NumItems;

    -- place departure event (from queue k) on event list
    -- using NextDepartureTime, ordered by time

  END IF;

END Process_Departure;
```

SUMMARY

Stacks and queues are two important data structures with restricted access. The stack is a Last-In, First-Out (LIFO) device; the queue is a First-In, First-Out (FIFO) device. The FIFO and LIFO access methods have many uses in computing applications: Stacks are used in implementing general procedure calling and returning, and in language translation such as in the RPN example given here. Queues turn up in operating systems, and in any number of simulation problems where the physical system being simulated involves waiting lines.

EXERCISES

1. Modify the generic queues package (Programs 7.1 and 7.2) to implement the circular queue scheme described in Section 7.2.

2. Develop and test a generic package for priority queues.

3. In some applications where two stacks are necessary, a bit of space can be saved by using an array representation but allowing the two stacks to share the same array. This is done by having one stack fill from the low-subscript end of the array forward, and the other stack fill from the high-subscript end backward. An exception must be raised if the two stacks "collide" in the middle somewhere. Design and implement a package to handle such a "double stack." (*Note*: Such a double stack is often called a "deque," which is an abbreviation of "double-ended queue." This is odd, because the structure represents two stacks, not a queue of any kind.)

4. In most programming languages that have a built-in exponentiation (**) operator, this operator associates right-to-left; that is, A**B**C is treated as though it were written A**(B**C). Explain why this is a sensible convention.

5. A common parenthesis-free notation is *forward Polish* or *prefix Polish* notation. In this scheme an operator *precedes* its operands, so that, for example, A+B becomes +AB. For the infix expressions of Sections 5.5 and 5.6, find the forward Polish forms.

6. Modify the Infix-to-RPN translator of Section 7.6 so that parenthesized expressions are handled correctly.

7. Modify the Infix-to-RPN translator of Section 7.6 so that the exponentiation operator is allowed and is handled correctly.

8. Write a translator that converts an infix expression to its forward Polish notation (FPN) form.

9. Write a translator that converts an RPN expression to its forward Polish notation (FPN) form.

10. Modify the hand-held-calculator example of Section 7.5 so that the numbers in the input can have more than one digit.

11. Complete the event-driven simulation of Section 7.7.

12. Modify the simulation so that the standard deviation of the average checkout time is computed along with the mean.

13. Many banks, post offices, and airline ticket counters have adopted a scheme in which there is only one waiting line and a customer reaching the front of the line goes to whichever server is available. Change the simulation to support this scheme. For the same set of customer records, are the mean and the standard deviation the same as in the multiqueue scheme?

14. Change the simulation so that instead of having arrivals come from a file created in advance, they are generated by a random number generator. Let the transaction time be uniformly distributed over some reasonable interval; also, let an arrival time occur a random (but reasonable) number of time units after the previous one.

CHAPTER 8

Access Types and Dynamic Data Structures

Dynamic data structures are data structures that expand and contract as a program executes. A dynamic data structure is a collection of elements (called *nodes*) that are generally implemented as records. Whereas an array always contains storage for a fixed number of elements, in a dynamic data structure the programmer can increase or reduce the allocated storage, as elements are added to or deleted from the structure.

Dynamic data structures are extremely flexible. It is relatively easy to add new information by creating a new node and inserting it between two existing nodes. It is also relatively easy to delete a node. In this chapter, we introduce dynamic data structures and a new kind of Ada type, called an *access type*. Access types—often called *pointer types*—are an essential part of using dynamic data structures. We examine interesting applications of dynamic data structures starting in Chapter 8 and continuing through the rest of the book.

8.1 ADA STRUCTURES: ACCESS TYPES AND THE NEW OPERATOR

You know how to use arrays to store collections of data. We know that it is possible for each array element to be a record, and have seen a number of examples of such data structures. One characteristic of data collections is that they can vary considerably in size from

312

one run of a program to the next, or even during a run. In such cases, an array is not the best structure in which to store the records, because the array size is fixed, and therefore must be estimated before the records are read in. If only a few records are present, much space is wasted. Worse, the array cannot expand to hold a number of records greater than its size.

There is a solution to this problem, known as *dynamic data structures* or *linked data structures*. Using dynamic data structures, the programmer can increase or decrease the allocated storage in order to add or delete data items in the collection. In languages, such as Ada, that provide built-in support for linked structures, the compiler associates with an executable program a special storage area, called the *dynamic storage pool*, or sometimes just the *pool*, which it initially leaves unassigned to any program variable. (The storage pool is often called the "heap"; we avoid this term to avoid confusion with the heap data structure introduced in Chapter 11.)

A system module called the *storage allocator* is linked into the program and assumes responsibility for allocating blocks of storage from the pool, and returning extra blocks to the pool, at *execution time*. The pool is like a "storage account" from which a program can "borrow" storage to expand a structure, returning the storage when it is no longer needed. The storage allocator can then use that storage to satisfy another storage request from the program.

A special kind of variable is provided for referencing space allocated dynamically from the pool. In Ada, these are called *access variables*; in other languages, such as Pascal and C, they are referred to as *pointer variables*. Ada allows us to declare *access types*; each access variable is an object of an access type. The values of each access type are called *access values* or, informally, *pointers*. A pointer, or access value, is an abstraction for a hardware address, but often does not have the same form.

Consider a record type called `RecType`, defined as

```
TYPE RecType IS RECORD
. . . fields . . .
END RECORD;
```

the type definition

```
TYPE RecPointer IS ACCESS RecType;
```

gives us the ability to declare access variables of type `RecPointer`—that is, variables that can *designate*, or hold pointers to, things of type `RecType`. For example, the declaration

```
P1, P2, P3: RecPointer;
```

allocates storage for three such variables.

When an access variable is created in Ada, its value is always initialized to a special, unique internal value known as `NULL`. This indicates that the pointer doesn't point to anything (yet). It is important to realize that declaring such variables does not cause any records to be allocated; each variable is given just enough space to hold the address of a record.

How do the records themselves come into being? The Ada operator `NEW` exists to create them. An assignment statement such as

```
P1 := NEW RecType;
```

causes the storage allocator to search the pool, looking for a block of space large enough to hold a record of type `RecType`. When such a block is found, an access value designating (pointing to) this block is stored in the variable `P1`. Figure 8.1 shows diagrammatically how dynamic allocation works. The cloud-like shape represents the pool, arrows represent pointers, and diagonal lines represent `NULL`.

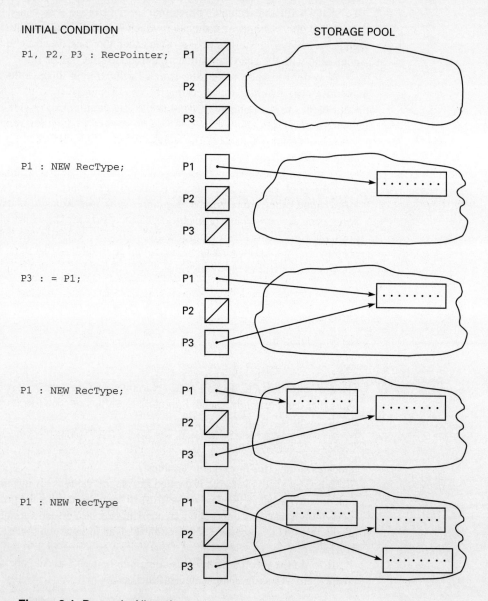

Figure 8.1 Dynamic Allocation

An access variable can acquire a value in only two ways: A value can be delivered by a NEW operation, as above, or it can be copied from another access value. For example,

```
P3 := P1;
```

causes P3 to point to the same record to which P1 points. *An assignment statement to an access variable copies only an access value; it does not copy the designated value*!

If we write

```
P1 := NEW RecType;
```

a second time, then space for another record is found in the pool, its address is stored in P1, and P3 is left pointing to the "old" record. If we write

```
P1 := NEW RecType;
```

a third time, the record previously pointed to by P1 is left with nothing pointing to it, thus making it *inaccessible*. This space, in general, remains allocated and unavailable for other use. This situation is often called, picturesquely, a "storage leak," because the storage "leaks away" and can no longer be used. We will return to this subject later in this chapter.

Creating a Linked Structure

Because we do not know beforehand how many nodes will be needed in a dynamic data structure, we cannot allocate storage for it in the conventional way—that is, through a variable declaration. Instead, we must allocate storage for each individual node as needed and somehow join that node to the rest of the structure.

We can connect two nodes if we include a pointer field in each node. The declarations

```
TYPE ElectricityType IS (DC, AC);

TYPE Node;
TYPE NodePointer IS ACCESS Node;
TYPE Node IS RECORD
   Power : ElectricityType;
   Volts : Natural;
   Next : NodePointer;
END RECORD;
```

identify NodePointer as a pointer type. A pointer variable of type NodePointer points to a record of type Node with three fields: Power, Volts, and Next. The Next field is also of type NodePointer. We can use this field to point to the next node in a dynamic data structure.

Note that the first declaration of Node is *incomplete*; it just mentions the name Node without filling in the details. This device is used to inform the compiler of the existence of the type Node, so that the next type definition can use it. Using an incomplete type definition meets Ada's requirement that types must be defined before they can be used.

Now let us declare some pointer variables:

```
P : NodePointer;
Q : NodePointer;
R : NodePointer;
```

As in the previous example, P, Q, and R are automatically given initial NULL values. The assignment statements

```
P := NEW Node;
Q := NEW Node;
```

allocate storage for two records of type Node, storing their addresses in P and Q. Initially, the Power and Volts fields of these records are undefined; the Next fields of both are initially NULL. Pointer initialization is one of the few cases in Ada in which objects are given initial values at declaration.

In Ada terminology, a nonnull access object *designates* a value. The block of space pointed to by P is P's designated value. We can refer to the designated value of P using the expression P.ALL, and to the Power field of P.ALL by the expression P.ALL.Power. The assignment statements

```
P.ALL.Power := AC;
P.ALL.Volts := 115;
Q.ALL.Power := DC;
Q.ALL.Volts := 12;
```

define the nonlink fields of these nodes, as shown in Figure 8.2. The Next fields are still NULL.

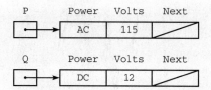

Figure 8.2 Nodes P.ALL and Q.ALL

The .ALL construct is the way Ada represents a *dereferencing* operation, that is, an operation to find that value to which a pointer points. To simplify the syntax necessary to select a field of a designated value, Ada allows us to omit the .ALL part and just select the field directly. Therefore, the following four assignment statements are equivalent to the ones just given. We will use the abbreviated form throughout this chapter. Because P is an access variable, we can read the expression P.Power as "Find the value designated by P and select its Power field."

```
P.Power := AC;
P.Volts := 115;
Q.Power := DC;
Q.Volts := 12;
```

Let us do some more pointer manipulation. The assignment statement

```
R := P;
```

copies the value of pointer variable P into pointer variable R. This means that pointers P and R contain the same access value and, therefore, point to the same node, as shown in Figure 8.3. Here and in later figures, we have left out the cloud symbol for simplicity.

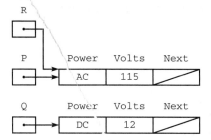

Figure 8.3 Nodes R.ALL/P.ALL and Q.ALL

The pointer assignment statements

```
P := Q;
Q := R;
```

have the effect of exchanging the nodes pointed to by P and Q, as shown in Figure 8.4. The statements

```
Electricity_IO.Put(Item => Q.Power, Width => 4);
Electricity_IO.Put(Item => P.Power, Width => 4);
```

display the Power fields of the records designated by Q and P. For the situation depicted in Figure 8.4, the line

```
AC DC
```

would be displayed. (As usual, Electricity_IO is an instance of Enumeration_IO.)

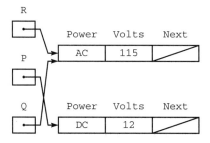

Figure 8.4 Nodes R.ALL/Q.ALL and P.ALL

The statement

```
Q := NEW Node;
```

changes the value of Q to designate a new node, thereby disconnecting Q from its previous node. The new values of pointer variables P, Q, and R are shown in Figure 8.5. The data fields of the new node designated by Q are, of course, initially undefined.

It is important to understand the difference between P and P's designated value. P is an access variable (type NodePointer) and is used to store the address of a data structure of type Node. P can be assigned a new value either by calling NEW or by

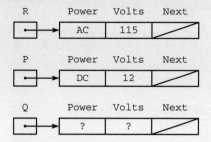

Figure 8.5 Nodes `R.ALL`, `P.ALL` and `Q.ALL`

copying another access value of the same type. `P.ALL` is the name of the record designated by `P` and can be manipulated like any other Ada record. The field selectors `P.Power` and `P.Volts` may be used to reference data (in this case, an enumeration value and an integer) stored in this record.

Connecting Nodes

One purpose of introducing dynamically allocated nodes is to be able to grow data structures of varying size. We can accomplish this by connecting individual nodes. If we look at the nodes allocated in the last section, we see that their `Next` fields are currently `NULL`. Since the link fields are of type `NodePointer`, they can themselves be used to designate values. The assignment statement

```
R.Next := P;
```

copies the value stored in `P` (an access value) into the `Next` field of node `R.ALL`. In this way, nodes `R` and `P` become connected. Similarly, the assignment statement

```
P.Next := Q;
```

copies the access value stored in access variable `Q` into the link field of node `P.ALL`, thereby connecting nodes `P` and `Q`. The situation after execution of these two assignment statements is shown in Figure 8.6.

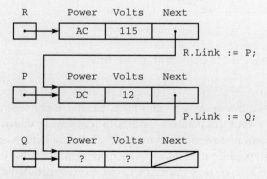

Figure 8.6 Connecting Nodes `R.ALL`, `P.ALL` and `Q.ALL`

The data structure pointed to by R has now grown to form a chain of all three nodes. The first node is referenced by R.ALL. The second node can be referenced by P.ALL or R.Next.ALL, because they both have the same value. Finally, the third node may be referenced by Q.ALL or P.Next.ALL, or even R.Next.Next.ALL.

Summary of Operations on Access Values

Let us summarize the operations available for access values. Access types are actually similar to private types. Given types

```
TYPE Something IS . . . ;
TYPE PointerToSomething IS ACCESS Something;
```

if P1 and P2 are variables of type PointerToSomething and S is a variable of type Something, the available operations are.

- *Allocation*, for example: P1 := NEW Something;

which allocates a block of type Something, returning to P1 an access value designating the new block.

- *Assignment*, for example: P2 := P1;

which copies the access value from P1 to P2.

- *Dereferencing*, for example: S := P1.ALL;

which copies the value designated by P1 into S.

- *Equality/inequality*, for example: IF P1 = P2 THEN . . .

which is true if and only if P1 and P2 are equal.
Make sure you understand the difference between the line above and

```
IF P1.ALL = P2.ALL THEN . . .
```

which compares the designated values.

You may be aware that in some other programming languages, especially C, other operations, for example incrementation and decrementation, are available for pointer values. These operations are *not* available in Ada.

Returning Dynamic Storage to the Pool

In Figure 8.1, we allocated a block of storage from the pool but later caused its pointer to point elsewhere (see the last two diagrams in Figure 8.1). Because no other access value designated it, the block became inaccessible. What happens to an inaccessible block?

In theory, the Ada storage allocator could include a module that automatically keeps track of inaccessible blocks and makes them available to be reallocated. Such a module is often called a *garbage collector*, because it keeps track of discarded memory blocks. Garbage collectors are provided in some languages, especially Lisp and Snobol, but are very rarely included in Ada systems. This is because Ada was designed for use in real-time systems, in which program timing is very important. Garbage collection is a complex process whose time performance can be unpredictable because it depends on how badly fragmented the storage pool is. For this reason, many Ada users prefer not to have a garbage collector and therefore compiler implementers usually do not provide it.

An Ada program that continually allocates blocks, then discards them just by making them inaccessible, could well run out of pool storage at some point in operation. Because an Ada system is unlikely to provide an automatic garbage collector, the programmer is responsible for recycling the garbage. Ada provides a standard operation, `Unchecked_Deallocation`, to return dynamically allocated storage to the pool. This is a generic procedure, with the specification

```
GENERIC
  TYPE Object IS LIMITED PRIVATE;
  TYPE Name IS ACCESS Object;
PROCEDURE Unchecked_Deallocation (X: IN OUT Name);
```

To use this procedure, it must be `WITH`-ed in a context clause, and instantiated using the access type and the designated type as actual parameters. For example,

```
PROCEDURE Dispose IS
  NEW Unchecked_Deallocation (Object => Node, Name => NodePointer);
```

creates an instance for the types used in this section, and the procedure call statement

```
Dispose (X => P);
```

will return `P`'s designated value to the pool. Paraphrasing the Ada standard, we describe this operation as follows:

- After execution of the `Dispose` call, the value of `P` is `NULL`.

- If `P` is already `NULL`, the call has no effect.

- If `P` is not `NULL`, the call indicates that `P.ALL` is no longer needed and may be returned to the pool.

Because we can copy access values, a situation can arise in which more than one access value designates the same block of storage. For this reason, we must be careful when returning storage to the pool. Errors will result if the cells returned are later referenced by another access value that still designates them; indeed, the Ada standard says specifically that the effect of doing so is unpredictable. Suppose `P` designates a node. If we write

```
Q := P;
Dispose(X => P);
```

the cells designated by `P` are returned to the pool and the meaning of `Q.ALL` or `Q.Volts` is unpredictabie. In this situation, a variable such as `Q` is usually called a *dangling pointer*. It is important to make sure that there is no need for a particular record before returning the storage occupied by it. Also, we must be careful when coding not to create dangling pointers; these lead to execution errors that will not always give rise to nice Ada exceptions.

Running Out of Dynamic Storage?

It is possible to exhaust the supply of cells in the pool. If this happens in Ada, the storage allocator raises the predefined exception `Storage_Error`.

Normally, we can assume that there are enough memory cells available in the pool. However, when writing large programs that create sizable dynamic data structures, it is advisable to code an exception handler for `Storage_Error` in the part of the program that does the allocation. Later in this chapter, we will discuss some methods for avoiding unnecessary calls to the allocator.

8.2 DATA STRUCTURES: LINKED LISTS AND THEIR OPERATIONS

A *linked list* is a sequence of list elements, or *nodes*, in which each node is linked, or connected, to the node following it. A linked list with three nodes follows.

Each node in this list has two fields: The first field contains data and the second field is a pointer to the next node. There is a pointer (`Head`) to the first node, or *list head*. The last node always has a `NULL` pointer value, indicated as usual by a diagonal line.

Lists are an important data structure because a list can be modified easily, regardless of how many elements may be in the list. For example, a new node containing the string `"Bye"` can be inserted between the strings `"Boy"` and `"Cat"` by changing only one pointer value (the one from `"Boy"`) and setting the pointer from the new node to point to `"Cat"`:

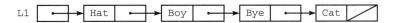

Similarly, it is easy to delete a list element. Only one pointer value has to be changed—the pointer that currently points to the element being deleted. For example, we can delete the string `"Boy"` from the previous linked list by changing the pointer from the node `"Ace"`. The node containing string `"Boy"` is effectively disconnected from the list because there is no longer a pointer to it. The new list consists of the strings `"Hat"`, `"Bye"`, and `"Cat"`.

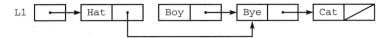

In Section 8.1, we saw how to connect three nodes with pointer fields. The data structure shown in Figure 8.6 could be considered a list of three nodes with pointer variable R as the pointer to its head. Each node has two data fields (Power and Volts) and one pointer field (Next). The pointer value NULL is once again drawn as a diagonal line.

Some Linked-List Operations

This section and those that follow will treat some common list-processing operations and explain how they are implemented using access types and variables. We will start out with a simple package specification, shown in Program 8.1.

Program 8.1 Specification for Linked-List Package

```
PACKAGE Singly_Linked_Lists IS
------------------------------------------------------------------------
--| Specification for simple linked lists with a single pointer
--| Author: Michael B. Feldman, The George Washington University
--| Last Modified: September 1995
------------------------------------------------------------------------

  SUBTYPE WordType IS String(1..3);

  TYPE List IS PRIVATE;

  PROCEDURE AddToFront (L: IN OUT List; Word: IN WordType);
  -- Pre:  Word is defined; L may be empty
  -- Post: Word is inserted at the beginning of L

  PROCEDURE AddToEnd (L: IN OUT List; Word: IN WordType);
  -- Pre:  Word is defined; L may be empty
  -- Post: Word is appended to the end of L

  FUNCTION Copy(L: IN List) RETURN List;
  -- Pre:  L may be empty
  -- Post: returns a complete copy of the list L

  PROCEDURE Traverse(L: IN List);
  -- Pre:  L may be empty
  -- Post: displays the contents of L's Word fields, in the
  --    order in which they appear in L
PRIVATE

  TYPE ListNode;
  TYPE List IS ACCESS ListNode;
  TYPE ListNode IS RECORD
    Word: WordType := "###";
    Next: List;
  END RECORD;

END Singly_Linked_Lists;
```

This package provides a private type List:

```
TYPE List IS PRIVATE;
```

The type declarations in the `PRIVATE` part are as follows:

```
TYPE ListNode;
TYPE List IS ACCESS ListNode;
TYPE ListNode IS RECORD
  Word: WordType := "###";
  Next: List;
END RECORD;
```

The package provides four operations:

* `AddToFront`, which adds a new node to the beginning of a list

* `Traverse`, which displays all the values in the list, in the order in which the nodes occur

* `AddToEnd`, which adds a new value to a list by first storing the value in a node, then connecting this node to the end of the list

* `Copy`, which returns a complete copy of the list

Given a list `L1` as follows:

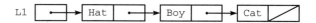

`Traverse` displays

```
Hat . . . Boy . . . Cat . . .
```

and the statement

```
AddToEnd(L1, "Dog");
```

changes `L1` as follows:

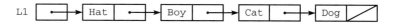

Program 8.2 is an illustration of these linked-list operations.

Program 8.2 A Demonstration of the Linked-List Package

```
WITH Ada.Text_IO; USE Ada.Text_IO;
WITH Singly_Linked_Lists; USE Singly_Linked_Lists;
PROCEDURE Test_Lists IS
---------------------------------------------------------------------
--| Illustrates the singly linked list package operations
--| Author: Michael B. Feldman, The George Washington University
--| Last Modified: September 1995
---------------------------------------------------------------------

  L1: List;
  L2: List;
```

```
BEGIN -- Test_Lists

   -- first test the traverse and copy operations for empty list

   Ada.Text_IO.Put_Line(Item => "--------");
   Traverse(L1);
   Ada.Text_IO.New_Line;
   L2 := Copy(L1);
   Traverse(L2);
   Ada.Text_IO.New_Line;
   Ada.Text_IO.Put_Line(Item => "--------");

   -- add to end of empty list

   AddToEnd(L1, "Hat");
   Traverse(L1);
   Ada.Text_IO.New_Line;
   L2 := Copy(L1);
   Traverse(L2);
   Ada.Text_IO.New_Line;
   Ada.Text_IO.Put_Line(Item => "--------");

   -- add to end of nonempty list

   AddToEnd(L1, "Boy");
   Traverse(L1);
   Ada.Text_IO.New_Line;
   Ada.Text_IO.Put_Line(Item => "--------");

   -- add again to end of nonempty list

   AddToEnd(L1, "Cat");
   Traverse(L1);
   Ada.Text_IO.New_Line;
   Ada.Text_IO.Put_Line(Item => "--------");

   -- add to front of nonempty list and copy result

   AddToFront(L1, "Top");
   Traverse(L1);
   Ada.Text_IO.New_Line;
   L2 := Copy(L1);
   Traverse(L2);
   Ada.Text_IO.New_Line;
   Ada.Text_IO.Put_Line(Item => "--------");

END Test_Lists;
```

If the package were completed and compiled, compiling and executing this program would produce the output

```
--------

--------
Hat...
Hat...
--------
Hat...Boy...
--------
Hat...Boy...Cat...
--------
Top...Hat...Boy...Cat...
Top...Hat...Boy...Cat...
--------
```

Program 8.3 gives the body of the package. In order to show the bodies of the various operations as separate programs, we have again used Ada subunits as in Section 7.7.

Program 8.3 Body of Linked-List Package

```
WITH Ada.Text_IO;
PACKAGE BODY Singly_Linked_Lists IS
-----------------------------------------------------------------------
--| skeleton of package body for singly-linked lists;
--| the operations are provided as subunits of the package.
--| Author: Michael B. Feldman, The George Washington University
--| Last Modified: September 1995
-----------------------------------------------------------------------

  PROCEDURE AddToFront (L: IN OUT List; Word: IN WordType) IS SEPARATE;

  PROCEDURE AddToEnd (L: IN OUT List; Word: IN WordType) IS SEPARATE;

  FUNCTION Copy(L: IN List) RETURN List IS SEPARATE;

  PROCEDURE Traverse(L: IN List) IS SEPARATE;

END Singly_Linked_Lists;
```

We are now ready to examine how the various linked-list operations are implemented. For absolute clarity in this set of program illustrations, we include the explicit dereferencing operations (the .ALLs). Be certain you understand exactly how each operation works before moving to the next.

Program 8.4 shows the implementation of AddToFront. It is simple and straightforward, but one must be very careful, in writing operations like this, to get the order of statements exactly right.

Program 8.4 Implementation of AddToFront

```
SEPARATE (Singly_Linked_Lists)
PROCEDURE AddToFront (L: IN OUT List; Word: IN WordType) IS
-----------------------------------------------------------------------
--| Subunit of singly linked list package
--| Author: Michael B. Feldman, The George Washington University
--| Last Modified: September 1995
-----------------------------------------------------------------------

  Temp: List;

BEGIN -- AddToFront

  Temp := NEW ListNode;
  Temp.ALL.Word := Word;
  Temp.ALL.Next := L;
  L := Temp;

END AddToFront;
```

1. Allocate a new node, returning an access value in Temp.

2. Store the word value in the new node.

3. Copy the access value in L—pointing to the first node in the list, if any—to the Next field of our new node.

4. Copy Temp's value back into L, which makes L point to the new first node.

Suppose we wrote these statements in the wrong order—for instance, we copied Temp to L before copying L to Temp. This would overwrite L's old value, and we would lose access to the entire list!

In writing linked-list operations, one must always ask whether the operation behaves properly if its list parameter is empty. In this case, if L is initially empty, its NULL value is copied into the Next field of the new node, and all is well.

In the next two sections, we implement the remaining three operations, first recursively and then iteratively.

8.3 RECURSIVE IMPLEMENTATIONS OF LINKED-LIST OPERATIONS

Linked lists are sometimes called *recursive data structures*, because each node contains a pointer to a node of the same type, which is a bit like a recursive procedure containing a call to the same procedure. Indeed, linked-list operations can easily be implemented as recursive subprograms.

Traverse

Program 8.5 gives the implementation of Traverse.

Program 8.5 Recursive Implementation of Linked-List Traversal

```
SEPARATE (Singly_Linked_Lists)
PROCEDURE Traverse(L: IN List) IS
-----------------------------------------------------------------------
--| Recursive implementation of Traverse
--| subunit of singly linked list package
--| Author: Michael B. Feldman, The George Washington University
--| Last Modified: September 1995
-----------------------------------------------------------------------

BEGIN -- Traverse

  IF L = NULL THEN
    RETURN;                     -- stopping case
  ELSE
    Ada.Text_IO.Put(Item => L.ALL.Word);
    Ada.Text_IO.Put(Item => "...");

    Traverse(L => L.ALL.Next); -- recursion
  END IF;

END Traverse;
```

Note carefully that like every recursive subprogram, `Traverse` has a stopping case; namely, the end of the list is reached when a `NULL` link is encountered. If the link is not `NULL`, we are not yet at the end of the list, so we display the value in the node, then invoke `Traverse` recursively for a smaller set of the data—that is, the remainder of the list following the first node.

AddToEnd

Program 8.6 shows the recursive implementation of `AddToEnd`.

Program 8.6 Recursive Implementation of `AddToEnd`

```
SEPARATE (Singly_Linked_Lists)
PROCEDURE AddToEnd (L: IN OUT List; Word: IN WordType) IS
--------------------------------------------------------------------------
--| Recursive implementation of AddToEnd
--| subunit of singly linked list package
--| Author: Michael B. Feldman, The George Washington University
--| Last Modified: September 1995
--------------------------------------------------------------------------

BEGIN -- AddToEnd

  IF L = NULL THEN
    L := NEW ListNode'(Word,NULL);   -- stopping case
  ELSE
    AddToEnd(L.ALL.Next, Word);      -- recursive case
  END IF;

END AddToEnd;
```

Note again that it has the required stopping case, namely that its parameter is `NULL`. In this stopping case, the `IN OUT` parameter representing the list is simply made to point to a new list node containing the desired word. The syntax of the line

```
L := NEW ListNode'(Word,NULL);
```

warrants explanation. Here, we are calling `NEW` and plugging in the fields of the newly allocated block with a record aggregate (`Word, NULL`). The apostrophe preceding the aggregate it is required. The construct

```
ListNode'(Word,NULL)
```

is called a *qualified aggregate*.

Returning to Program 8.6, if we are not at the stopping case—that is, not yet at the end of the list—we make a recursive call of `AddToEnd`, which attempts to add the new value to the end of a list that is shorter by one node.

Copy

You might think that `Copy` is a very simple, almost trivial operation. Suppose we implemented `Copy` with the following body:

```
SEPARATE (SinglyLinkedLists)
FUNCTION Copy(L: IN List) RETURN List IS
BEGIN

  RETURN L;

END Copy;
```

Would a client program with the line

```
L2 := Copy(L1);
```

receive a correct result in `L2`? No, indeed! Simply copying the access value in `L1` does *not* copy the list; it only copies the pointer to the beginning of the list! The result would be that `L1` and `L2` would both point to the same node. Now suppose a modification is made to `L1`; for example, a new node is added to its end. Since `L2` points to the same list, changing the list headed by `L1` would also change the list headed by `L2`, because they are exactly the same list.

This is not what "copying" a value usually means in programming. If you copy an array `A` into another one `B` of the same type, `A` and `B` are distinct, and changing a value in `A` does not change `B` at all. In order to get a faithful copy of a list, we must copy the entire list; that is, the word in each node of the original must be copied to a newly allocated node of the result.

Program 8.7 shows a recursive implementation of `Copy`. In the stopping case, the parameter is `NULL` so we just return that value. If the parameter is nonnull, the result of the recursive call is a node whose word value is copied from the original, and whose link is a pointer to a copy of the remainder of the original.

Program 8.7 Recursive Implementation of `Copy`

```
SEPARATE (Singly_Linked_Lists)
FUNCTION Copy(L: IN List) RETURN List IS
-----------------------------------------------------------------------
--| Recursive implementation of Copy
--| subunit of singly linked list package
--| Author: Michael B. Feldman, The George Washington University
--| Last Modified: September 1995
-----------------------------------------------------------------------

BEGIN -- Copy

  IF L = NULL THEN
    RETURN NULL;                   -- stopping case
  ELSE
    RETURN                         -- recursive case
      NEW ListNode'(L.ALL.Word, Copy(L.ALL.Next));
  END IF;

END Copy;
```

If you are having any trouble understanding this, there is nothing more effective than pretending you are the copy function and drawing a picture of the input list and the result list as it is constructed at each level of recursion.

Copying an entire list structure in this manner is often called *deep copying*; similarly, copying only the pointer to the beginning of the list is called *shallow copying*, or, sometimes, *sharing* the list.

8.4 ITERATIVE IMPLEMENTATION OF LINKED-LIST OPERATIONS

Recursively implemented linked-list operations are clean and sometimes even elegantly simple. On the other hand, consider their time and space performance. `Traverse`, for example, requires $O(N)$ time for a list with N nodes. This is to be expected: After all, the list is linear. But the recursive `Traverse` also requires $O(N)$ *space*, because of the N recursive calls. For a long list, the space requirements can add up; for a very long list, they could exhaust the memory available for nested procedure calls. Looking at the recursive implementations of `AddToEnd` and `Copy`, you can see that they too require $O(N)$ time and $O(N)$ space for recursive calls.

Linked-list operations generally require $O(N)$ time, because they usually involve visiting each node once in sequence. That is the nature of linear lists. However, we can eliminate the $O(N)$ space requirement by eliminating the recursive calls. We will develop iterative versions of the list routines; in most real applications of linked lists, iterative operations are used. The price we pay for eliminating the recursion is that the iterative versions are often more complicated, and sometimes more difficult to understand, than their recursive counterparts.

Traverse

Program 8.8 shows an iterative version of `Traverse`.

Program 8.8 Iterative Implementation of Linked-List Traversal

```
SEPARATE (Singly_Linked_Lists)
PROCEDURE Traverse(L: IN List) IS
---------------------------------------------------------------------
--| Iterative implementation of Traverse
--| subunit of singly linked list package
--| Author: Michael B. Feldman, The George Washington University
--| Last Modified: September 1995
---------------------------------------------------------------------

  Current: List;   -- designates each node in turn

BEGIN -- Traverse

  -- initialize loop
  Current := L;

  WHILE Current /= NULL LOOP

    Ada.Text_IO.Put(Item => Current.ALL.Word);
    Ada.Text_IO.Put(Item => ". . .");

    -- be sure to advance the pointer!
    Current := Current.ALL.Next;

  END LOOP;

END Traverse;
```

Iterative list operations generally consist of a main WHILE loop, and, in fact, are generally quite similar to many array algorithms. Every WHILE loop must contain three distinct features:

- *Initialization* that appears before the WHILE

- A *condition*, given in the WHILE statement itself, for continuing the loop

- *Incrementation*, in which some variable is modified to keep the loop moving forward toward completion

These three features are present in Program 8.8: A pointer Current, declared to serve as the loop variable, is initialized by

```
Current := L;
```

which sets Current to point to the beginning of the list. The test to continue the loop is

```
WHILE Current /= NULL LOOP
```

which indicates that the loop continues until the end of the list is reached—that is, until Current becomes null. Finally, the incrementation step is

```
Current := Current.ALL.Next;
```

in which Current is dereferenced and set to the Next value in the designated node. To be certain you understand Traverse, practice tracing its execution. Draw a pointer variable Current and move it down the list during each loop iteration. Practice on the following list:

Make sure it is clear why the output should be

```
Hat...Boy...Cat...Dog...
```

AddToEnd

The iterative AddToEnd is shown as Program 8.9.

Program 8.9 Iterative Implementation of AddToEnd

```
SEPARATE (Singly_Linked_Lists)
PROCEDURE AddToEnd (L: IN OUT List; Word: IN WordType) IS
----------------------------------------------------------------------------
--| Iterative implementation of AddToEnd
--| we must do a linear search to find the end of the list
--| Author: Michael B. Feldman, The George Washington University
--| Last Modified: September 1995
----------------------------------------------------------------------------
```

```
  Current: List;  -- designates each node of input list in turn
BEGIN -- AddToEnd

  IF L = NULL THEN

    L := NEW ListNode'(Word,NULL);

  ELSE

      -- initialize the loop
      Current := L;

      -- search until the end
      WHILE Current.ALL.Next /= NULL LOOP
        Current := Current.ALL.Next;
      END LOOP;

      -- we found the end; Current designates last node
      -- so attach a new node to the node Current designates
      Current.ALL.Next := NEW ListNode'(Word, NULL);

  END IF;

END AddToEnd;
```

Here we need a special case to see whether the head pointer L itself needs to be modified; this will happen only if L is initially empty. Assuming L is nonempty, we have another WHILE loop, with Current initialized (as in Traverse) to the start of the list. In this case, the loop body consists only of the incrementation step, because we are simply searching to find the end of the list.

Note that in Traverse, the loop-continuation condition was

```
WHILE Current /= NULL LOOP
```

but in this case, it is

```
WHILE Current.ALL.Next /= NULL LOOP
```

After this loop is finished, we wish Current's value to be pointing to the last node of the list. This is so that we can connect the new node to the last node's Next field. This is accomplished by the statement

```
Current.ALL.Link := NEW ListNode'(Word, NULL);
```

Once again, you should practice on the list given above. Try tracing AddToEnd to add a new node containing "Art" to the list.

Copy

Finally, Program 8.10 gives an iterative version of Copy.

Program 8.10 Iterative Implementation of Copy

```
SEPARATE (Singly_Linked_Lists)
FUNCTION Copy(L: IN List) RETURN List IS
--------------------------------------------------------------------
--| Iterative implementation of Copy
--| Author: Michael B. Feldman, The George Washington University
--| Last Modified: September 1995
```

```
--------------------------------------------------------------------------
    Result : List;   -- points to head of new list
    NewTail: List;   -- points to tail of new list
    Current: List;   -- points to current node of input list
BEGIN -- Copy

  IF L = NULL THEN
    RETURN Result;
  END IF;

  -- "prime" the algorithm with the first node

  Result := NEW ListNode;
  Result.ALL.Word :=  L.ALL.Word;

  -- initialize loop

  NewTail := Result;
  Current := L.ALL.Next;
  WHILE Current /= NULL LOOP

    -- allocate new node, attach to tail of new list
    NewTail.ALL.Next := NEW ListNode'(Current.ALL.Word, NULL);

    NewTail := NewTail.ALL.Next; -- move Newtail to new node, and
    Current := Current.ALL.Next; -- Current to next node in old list

  END LOOP;

  RETURN Result;

END Copy;
```

Here we need two pointer variables: one, `Current`, to travel down the input list `L`, and the other, `NewTail`, to keep track of the last node of the new list `Result`. Note the statement

```
NewTail.ALL.Link := NEW ListNode'(Current.ALL.Word, NULL);
```

which allocates a new node, copies the `Word` field into it, and connects it to the end of the new list. As before, make sure you understand the workings of this procedure by carefully tracing its execution.

8.5 LINKED LISTS WITH HEAD AND TAIL POINTERS

The operations `AddToFront` and `AddToEnd` are two of the most common and important list operations. We have seen that `AddToFront` is very simple: A node is allocated and a few values copied. Clearly the performance of `AddToFront` does not depend on the length of the list, so its performance is $O(1)$. On the other hand, we have seen in the previous section that `AddToEnd` is $O(N)$, because the entire list is searched in order to find the last node.

We can turn `AddToEnd` into a $O(1)$ operation by making a very simple change to our data structures: Keep track of the last node by building in a pointer to it. All we need to do is change the declarations in the `PRIVATE` part to

```
TYPE ListNode;
TYPE ListPtr IS ACCESS ListNode;
TYPE ListNode IS RECORD
  Word: WordType := "###";
  Next: ListPtr;
END RECORD;

TYPE List IS
  Head: ListPtr;
  Tail: ListPtr;
END RECORD;
```

We introduce a new type `ListPtr`, which serves the role of our former `List` type. We also change our `List` type from a simple pointer into a *header record* containing two pointers, one to the head of the list and one to the tail. This gives a list like

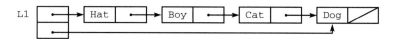

The various operations must be modified to reflect the changed data structures. The key change is to `AddToEnd`, which is shown as Program 8.11. Note that the `WHILE` loop or recursive call is gone; no search is necessary, because we know immediately where the last node is.

Program 8.11 `AddToEnd` with Head and Tail Pointers

```
SEPARATE (Singly_Linked_Lists)
PROCEDURE AddToEnd (L: IN OUT List; Word: IN WordType) IS
-------------------------------------------------------------------
--| AddToEnd using head and tail pointers
--| Author: Michael B. Feldman, The George Washington University
--| Last Modified: September 1995
-------------------------------------------------------------------

-- if we have a pointer to the tail of the list,
-- adding a new node is very easy.

BEGIN -- AddToEnd

  IF L.Head = NULL THEN

    L.Head := NEW ListNode'(Word,NULL);
    L.Tail := L.Head;

  ELSE -- L.Tail points to a node; new node goes after it

    L.Tail.ALL.Next := NEW ListNode'(Word,NULL);
    L.Tail := L.Tail.ALL.Next;

  END IF;

END AddToEnd;
```

This is a very good example of the way a small change to a data structure can result in a large change in performance. Here we have used a bit more space for the extra pointer, but have speeded up an important operation from $O(N)$ to $O(1)$.

We leave it as an exercise to modify the entire package so that the operations are consistent with the two-pointer header record.

8.6 ORDERED INSERTIONS IN LINKED LISTS

A linked list is often used as an implementation for an ordered sequence of elements, which appear in order according to some key. This can be thought of as a linked-list analogy to a sorted array. It is therefore important to understand how to insert a new value into a linked list that is already sorted.

The insertion process has four distinct cases:

Case 1. An inserted node is the first one to be added to an empty list.

Case 2. The inserted node's key is less than those of all others in the list; thus, the node goes at the beginning of a nonempty list.

Case 3. The key is greater than all the others; thus, the node goes at the end of the list.

Case 4. The key lies between two others; thus, the node goes in the middle of the list somewhere.

For the list representation we have been using, these four cases are illustrated in Figure 8.7. A procedure `InsertInOrder` is shown as Program 8.12.

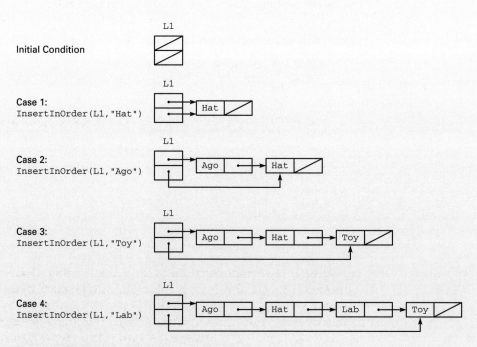

Figure 8.7 Ordered Insertion in Linked List

Program 8.12 Ordered Linked-List Insertion

```
SEPARATE (Singly_Linked_Lists)
PROCEDURE InsertInOrder (L: IN OUT List; Word: IN WordType) IS
----------------------------------------------------------------------
--| Iterative implementation of InsertInOrder
--| if Word already in list, second occurrence must follow first one
--| Author: Michael B. Feldman, The George Washington University
--| Last Modified: September 1995
----------------------------------------------------------------------

  Current:  ListPtr;  -- designates each node of  input list in turn
  Previous: ListPtr;  -- trailer - one node behind Current
  Temp:     ListPtr;  -- holds pointer to newly allocated node

BEGIN -- InsertInOrder

  IF L.Head = NULL THEN                 -- case (1)
    AddToFront (L, Word);

  ELSIF Word < L.Head.ALL.Word THEN     -- case (2)
    AddToFront (L, Word);

  ELSIF Word >= L.Tail.ALL.Word THEN    -- case (3)
    AddToEnd (L, Word);

  ELSE                                  -- case (4)

    -- at this point, we know L is not empty and
    -- first word >= Word < last word

    Temp     := NEW ListNode'(Word, NULL);
    Previous := L.Head;               -- first node
    Current  := Previous.ALL.Next;    -- second node, if any

    WHILE Word >= Current.ALL.Word LOOP

      Previous := Current;
      Current  := Current.ALL.Next;

    END LOOP;

    -- assert: Previous.ALL.Word <= Word > Current.ALL.Word

    -- insert new node between Previous and Current
    Temp.ALL.Next := Current;
    Previous.ALL.Next := Temp;

  END IF;

END InsertInOrder;
```

Notice how the each of the four cases is handled: Only Case 4 requires a search through the list. Note also that two pointers are used to search the list, because the new node is inserted between two others, in this case those designated by `Previous` and `Current`, respectively. Make sure you understand exactly how the procedure operates by tracing its actions on the example cases shown in the figure. This succession of calls to `InsertInOrder` builds and maintains a sorted list.

8.7 DEBUGGING PROGRAMS WITH LINKED LISTS

The three most common errors in writing programs using dynamic structures are dereferencing a null pointer, infinite loops, infinite recursion, and off-by-one problems.

Dereferencing a Null Pointer

When processing linked data structures, make sure that the pointer to the next node is not NULL. If pointer P has the value NULL, the record P.ALL is undefined. Therefore, the condition

```
(P.ALL.ID /= 9999) AND (P /= NULL)
```

will cause Constraint_Error to be raised when P is NULL. You can prevent this by writing the expression using the short-circuit operator AND THEN:

```
(P /= NULL) AND THEN (P.ALL.ID /= 9999)
```

This causes the left side to be evaluated first and evaluates the right side only if the left side is True.

Infinite Loops

A linked-list program can get into an infinite loop in two ways. First, if you write a WHILE loop and forget to write an incrementation step, the loop has no way to progress toward completion. In this case, the program either will appear to "hang," or, possibly, will display the same value over and over.

Second, your program could get stuck in an infinite loop or an infinite recursion while creating a dynamic data structure. If this happens, it is quite possible that the program will keep allocating new blocks and consume all memory cells in the storage pool. If this happens, Storage_Error is raised. For both of these reasons, be especially careful in writing the WHILE condition and the loop incrementation statement. Be certain the loop is always initialized properly and incremented each time through. Also, make sure that your recursive programs will eventually reach a stopping case.

Off-by-One Errors

Off-by-one errors are common in linked-list programs. In traversing a list with K elements, for example, sometimes only the first $K-1$ elements, or the last $K-1$, are displayed. These logic errors will not raise exceptions but will give incorrect results. They are usually caused by careless loop initialization or termination conditions. Note that a program that tries to go one step too far will generally "fall off the end of the list," causing Constraint_Error to be raised upon dereferencing a null pointer.

Some debugging tools allow you to display the value of a pointer variable, but such a value cannot normally be displayed with Text_IO procedures. It is therefore difficult to debug programs that manipulate pointers. You will have to trace the execution of such a program by printing an information field that uniquely identifies the list element being processed instead of the pointer value itself. In doing a trace, drawing a picture of the list as it is built and manipulated is enormously helpful.

When writing driver programs, it is often helpful to create a sample linked structure using the technique shown in Section 8.1. The data and pointer fields of the structure can be defined using assignment statements.

SUMMARY

Access types and dynamic data structures are used to create linked lists, which are extremely important data structures in computing. Linked lists are found in nearly every kind of computer application: Spreadsheet processing, operating system modules, compilers, and many others commonly employ linked lists and other dynamic data structures. Armed with your understanding of simple linked lists, you are now ready to proceed to Chapter 9 and the remaining chapters, in which various applications of dynamic data structures are introduced.

EXERCISES

1. Write a function to return the number of nodes in a singly linked list with head and tail pointers.
2. Write a procedure that attaches one list to the end of another. Note that this procedure destroys the original lists.
3. Write a function that returns the concatenation of two lists L1 and L2—that is, a list containing copies of all the nodes of L1 followed by copies of all the nodes of L2. Note that this function must *not* destroy either L1 or L2.
4. Write a procedure that deletes from an ordered list L the *first* node containing a given word.
5. Write a procedure that deletes from an ordered list L the *last* node containing a given word.
6. Write a procedure `DeleteAll(L:List; K:KeyType)`, that deletes from an ordered list L *all* nodes containing a given word.
7. Write a function that searches a list L with a dummy node, returning a pointer to the first node containng a given word. Do this for both an unordered and an ordered list.
8. Write a function that takes two ordered lists as inputs, then returns a list in which the two input lists are merged. That is, if L1 contains "ABC", "HIJ", and "PQR", and L2 contains "DEF", "HIJ", "MNO", and "STU", the result list contains "ABC", "DEF", "HIJ", "HIJ", "MNO", "PQR", and "STU".
9. Sometimes a list node is declared to have *two* pointers, one to the next node and one to the previous node. Develop a package for such doubly linked lists; write the operations so that advantage is taken of the fact that each node points to its predecessor as well as to its successor. Specifically, how does having the extra pointers simplify operations such as ordered insertion and deletion?
10. Starting with the package for singly linked lists, develop a generic list package that enables a client program to specify the nonlink information—that is, to instantiate with any type for which assignment and equality are defined.

CHAPTER 9

Linked-List Applications

Now that you are familiar with the basics of dynamic data structures, let us look at some applications. After first setting up a generic ADT package for singly linked lists, we will examine unbounded (linked-list) implementations of stacks and queues, a linked-list implementation of the generic keyed table handler, a design for variable-length strings of unbounded length, and sparse vectors and matrices. Along the way, we will consider active iterators, an important ADT design technique. Finally, we will discuss how dynamic memory management can be simulated using arrays, without records, access types, or storage pools.

The Ada 95 sections discuss unbounded strings, general access types (which can designate declared variables as well as dynamically allocated blocks) and composite types—arrays and records—with tagged-type objects as their components.

9.1   ADT DESIGN: A GENERIC ADT FOR SINGLY LINKED LISTS

We now develop an ADT for singly linked lists. Naturally, it is generic; it provides a useful collection of operations on linked lists in such a way that a client program can just instantiate for a given element type. The advantage of providing an ADT is that the client program does not have to deal with implementation details; furthermore, the implementation of the list structure can be changed if desired. Later in the chapter, we will explain how to change the implementation of `Singly_Linked_Lists` so that nodes are stored in an array of nodes instead of in the pool.

Specification of the Generic List ADT

The specification for `Lists_Generic` is given in Program 9.1. Two types are provided: `Position`, which is `PRIVATE` and represents a pointer, and `List`, which is `LIMITED PRIVATE` because the := and = operations are obviously not meaningful for a linked structure.

Program 9.1 Specification of Generic Linked-List Package

```
GENERIC

  TYPE ElementType IS PRIVATE;

PACKAGE Lists_Generic IS
-------------------------------------------------------------------------
--| Generic ADT for singly-linked lists
--| Author: Michael B. Feldman, The George Washington University
--| Last Modified: September 1995
-------------------------------------------------------------------------

  -- exported types

  TYPE Position IS PRIVATE;
  TYPE List IS LIMITED PRIVATE;

  -- exported exceptions

  OutOfSpace: EXCEPTION;   -- raised if no space left for a new node
  PastEnd    : EXCEPTION;   -- raised if a Position is past the end
  PastBegin : EXCEPTION;   -- raised if a Position is before the begin
  EmptyList : EXCEPTION;

  -- basic constructors

  PROCEDURE Initialize(L: IN OUT List);
  -- Pre:  none
  -- Post: L is initialized. If L contained nodes, these are deleted.

  PROCEDURE AddToFront(L: IN OUT List; X: ElementType);
  PROCEDURE AddToRear (L: IN OUT List; X: ElementType);
  -- Pre:  L and X are defined
  -- Post: a node containing X is inserted
  --    at the front or rear of L, respectively

  -- basic selectors
```

```
FUNCTION First (L: List) RETURN Position;
FUNCTION Last  (L: List) RETURN Position;
-- Pre:  L is defined
-- Post: returns the position of the first or last node
--   of L, respectively; return NULL if L is empty

FUNCTION Retrieve (L: IN List; P: IN Position) RETURN ElementType;
-- Pre:    L and P are defined; P designates a node in L
-- Post:   returns the value of the element at position P
-- Raises: EmptyList if L is empty
--         PastBegin if P points before the beginning of L
--         PastEnd   if P points beyond the end of L

-- other constructors

PROCEDURE Insert (L: IN OUT List; X: ElementType; P: Position);
-- Pre:  L, X, and P are defined; P designates a node in L
-- Post: X is inserted into L at position P; equivalent to
--   AddToRear if P is NULL

PROCEDURE Replace (L: IN OUT List; X: ElementType; P: Position);
-- Pre:    L, X, and P are defined; P designates a node in L
-- Post:   X replace the element in L at position P
-- Raises: PastEnd if P is NULL

PROCEDURE Delete (L: IN OUT List; P: Position);
-- Pre:    L and P are defined; P designates a node in L
-- Post:   the node at position P of L is deleted
-- Raises: EmptyList if L is empty
--         PastBegin if P is NULL

PROCEDURE Copy (To: IN OUT List; From: IN List);
-- Pre:  From is defined
-- Post: To is a list whose elements are the same as those
--   of From, in the same order.

-- iterator operations

PROCEDURE GoAhead (L: List; P: IN OUT Position);
-- Pre:    L and P are defined; P designates a node in L
-- Post:   P is advanced to designate the next node of L
-- Raises: EmptyList if L is empty
--         PastEnd   if P points beyond the end of L

PROCEDURE GoBack   (L: List; P: IN OUT Position);
-- Pre:    L and P are defined; P designates a node in L
-- Post:   P is moved to designate the previous node of L
-- Raises: EmptyList if L is empty
--         PastBegin if P points beyond the end of L

-- inquiry operators

FUNCTION  IsEmpty   (L: List) RETURN Boolean;
FUNCTION  IsFirst   (L: List; P: Position) RETURN Boolean;
FUNCTION  IsLast    (L: List; P: Position) RETURN Boolean;
FUNCTION  IsPastEnd (L: List; P: Position) RETURN Boolean;
FUNCTION  IsPastBegin (L: List; P: Position) RETURN Boolean;
-- Pre:    L and P are defined
-- Post:   return True iff the condition is met; False otherwise

PRIVATE

TYPE Node;
TYPE Position IS ACCESS Node;
```

```
TYPE Node IS RECORD
  Info: ElementType;
  Link: Position;
END RECORD;

TYPE List IS RECORD
  Head: Position;
  Tail: Position;
END RECORD;

END Lists_Generic;
```

The operations are grouped as usual into constructors, selectors, and inquiry operations. The postconditions in the specification describe these operations; the descriptions are straightforward and should be easy to understand.

Several of the operations and exceptions merit discussion: The exceptions PastBegin and PastEnd are used to indicate that a pointer (rather, a Position value) has "fallen off" either the beginning or the end of the list. Similarly, the inquiry operations IsPastBegin and IsPastEnd are for the client programs, to test for these conditions. Once again, we are providing inquiry operations for the client and also exceptions to be raised in case the client errs in testing for the conditions. Our package must be as "bulletproof" as possible.

The type declarations given in the PRIVATE part of Program 9.1 should be familiar to you by now. We represent a List as a record with pointers to the beginning and head of the list; these are NULL if the list is empty. A Node is as before; note that the node contains just a field of type Element (the generic parameter) and a pointer to the next node.

Body of the Generic List ADT

Look now at Program 9.2, which gives the body of the package. We first instantiate Unchecked_Deallocation to provide an operation to return nodes to the pool. We will return to this issue shortly.

Program 9.2 Body of Generic Linked-List Package

```
WITH Unchecked_Deallocation;
PACKAGE BODY Lists_Generic IS
-------------------------------------------------------------------------
--| Body of Generic Linked List Package
--| Author: Michael B. Feldman, The George Washington University
--| Last Modified: September 1995
-------------------------------------------------------------------------
  PROCEDURE Dispose IS
    NEW Unchecked_Deallocation(Object => Node, Name => Position);

  FUNCTION Allocate (X: ElementType; P: Position) RETURN Position IS
    Result: Position;
  BEGIN
    Result := NEW Node'(Info => X, Link => P);
    RETURN Result;
  EXCEPTION
    WHEN Storage_Error =>
```

```
      RAISE OutOfSpace;
END Allocate;

PROCEDURE Deallocate (P: IN OUT Position) IS
BEGIN
  Dispose (X => P);
END Deallocate;

PROCEDURE Initialize(L: IN OUT List) IS
  Previous: Position;
  Current : Position;
BEGIN
  IF L.Head /= NULL THEN
    Current := L.Head;
    WHILE Current /= NULL LOOP
      Previous := Current;
      Current := Current.Link;
      Deallocate(Previous);
    END LOOP;
    L := (Head => NULL, Tail => NULL);
  END IF;
END Initialize;

PROCEDURE AddToFront(L: IN OUT List; X: ElementType) IS
BEGIN
  L.Head := Allocate(X, L.Head);
  IF L.Tail = NULL THEN
    L.Tail := L.Head;
  END IF;
END AddToFront;

PROCEDURE AddToRear (L: IN OUT List; X: ElementType) IS
  P: Position;
BEGIN
  P := Allocate(X, NULL);
  IF L.Head = NULL THEN
    L.Head := P;
  ELSE
    L.Tail.Link := P;
  END IF;
  L.Tail := P;
END AddToRear;

FUNCTION IsEmpty (L: List) RETURN Boolean IS
BEGIN
  RETURN L.Head = NULL;
END IsEmpty;

FUNCTION IsFirst (L: List; P: Position) RETURN Boolean IS
BEGIN
  RETURN (L.Head /= NULL) AND (P = L.Head);
END IsFirst;

FUNCTION IsLast (L: List; P: Position) RETURN Boolean IS
BEGIN
  RETURN (L.Tail /= NULL) AND (P = L.Tail);
END IsLast;

FUNCTION IsPastEnd (L: List; P: Position) RETURN Boolean IS
BEGIN
  RETURN P = NULL;
END IsPastEnd;

FUNCTION IsPastBegin (L: List; P: Position) RETURN Boolean IS
BEGIN
```

```
    RETURN P = NULL;
END IsPastBegin;

FUNCTION First (L: List) RETURN Position IS
BEGIN
  RETURN L.Head;
END First;

FUNCTION  Last (L: List) RETURN Position IS
BEGIN
  RETURN L.Tail;
END Last;

FUNCTION Retrieve
  (L: IN List; P: IN Position) RETURN ElementType IS
BEGIN
  IF IsEmpty(L) THEN
    RAISE EmptyList;
  ELSIF IsPastBegin(L, P) THEN
    RAISE PastBegin;
  ELSIF IsPastEnd(L, P) THEN
    RAISE PastEnd;
  ELSE
    RETURN P.Info;
  END IF;
END Retrieve;

PROCEDURE GoAhead (L: List; P: IN OUT Position) IS
BEGIN
  IF IsEmpty(L) THEN
    RAISE EmptyList;
  ELSIF IsPastEnd(L, P) THEN
    RAISE PastEnd;
  ELSE
    P := P.Link;
  END IF;
END GoAhead;

PROCEDURE GoBack (L: List; P: IN OUT Position) IS
  Current: Position;
BEGIN
  IF IsEmpty(L) THEN
     RAISE EmptyList;
  ELSIF IsPastBegin(L, P) THEN
    RAISE PastBegin;
  ELSIF IsFirst(L, P) THEN
    P := NULL;
  ELSE                         -- see whether P is in the list
    Current := L.Head;
    WHILE (Current /= NULL) AND THEN (Current.Link /= P) LOOP
      Current := Current.Link;
    END LOOP;

    IF Current = NULL THEN -- P was not in the list
      RAISE PastEnd;
    ELSE
      P := Current;          -- return predecessor pointer
    END IF;
  END IF;
END GoBack;

PROCEDURE Delete   (L: IN OUT List; P: Position) IS
  Previous: Position;
  Current : Position;
```

```
      BEGIN
        Current := P;
        IF IsEmpty(L) THEN
          RAISE EmptyList;
        ELSIF IsPastBegin(L, Current) THEN
          RAISE PastBegin;
        ELSIF IsFirst(L, Current) THEN   -- must adjust list header
          L.Head := Current.Link;
          IF L.Head = NULL THEN          -- deleted the only node
            L.Tail := NULL;
          END IF;
        ELSE                             -- "normal" situation
          Previous := Current;
          GoBack(L, Previous);
          Previous.Link := Current.Link;
          IF IsLast(L, Current) THEN     -- deleted the last node
            L.Tail := Previous;
          END IF;
        END IF;
        Deallocate(Current);
      END Delete;

      PROCEDURE Insert (L: IN OUT List; X: ElementType; P: Position) IS
      BEGIN
        IF P = NULL THEN
          AddToRear(L, X);
        ELSE
          P.Link := Allocate(X, P.Link);
        END IF;
      END Insert;

      PROCEDURE Replace (L: IN OUT List; X: ElementType; P: Position) IS
      BEGIN
        IF P = NULL THEN
          RAISE PastEnd;
        ELSE
          P.Info := X;
        END IF;
      END Replace;

      PROCEDURE Copy (To: IN OUT List; From: IN List) IS
        Current: Position;
      BEGIN
        Initialize(To);
        Current := First(From);
        WHILE NOT IsPastEnd(From, Current) LOOP
          AddToRear(To, Retrieve(From, Current));
          GoAhead(From, Current);
        END LOOP;
      END Copy;

END Lists_Generic;
```

The first two operations are internal to the package: They are called by other package operations when a node must be allocated or released. We write these as subprograms so that the method of allocation or deallocation can be changed without requiring recoding of other operations.

The next operation is `Initialize`, which makes a list empty. Note that we *cannot* simply set the head and tail pointers to NULL, because that would only disconnect the header from the nodes in the list, leaving them inaccessible! Instead, we must loop through the entire list (in time proportional to the list length!), disconnecting and disposing of each node as we arrive at it. To do this, we need to maintain two pointer variables, `Previous` and `Current`. Be certain you understand *exactly* how this operation works.

The next two operations, `AddToFront` and `AddToRear`, are the basic constructors for adding nodes to the beginning and end of a list. These are similar to the same-named operations in the simple list package of Chapter 8.

The inquiry and selector operations are straightforward; we skip to `GoAhead` and `GoBack`, which move forward and backward in the list, respectively. Going forward is easy; we do need to check to be sure that we *can* go forward—that is, that we are not already off the end. Going backward from a node designated by `P` is not so easy. We need, somehow, to find the predecessor pointer—the pointer in the list that designates the same node that `P` does. In a singly linked list, the only way we can accomplish this is to start at the beginning, moving down the list until we reach a `Link` field equal to `P`. This field will be in some other node; it is the pointer to *that* node that we must return to the calling program. Trace `GoBack` very carefully to persuade yourself that you understand it. What is its "big O"?

The next operation is `Delete`, which disconnects from a list the node designated by a pointer `P`. The only way we can do this is to go back to the node preceding the one we wish to delete; we use `GoBack` for this. Once we find the predecessor node, we connect it to the node *following* the deleted one, then deallocate the deleted node.

Finally we examine `Copy`, which makes a copy of the elements in the list. As in the case of `Initialize`, copying a list is not just a matter of copying the pointers in the header; that would make *both* headers point to the same list. If we changed the contents of one, the contents of the other one would change! This is not a copy! To copy a list `From` to a list `To`, we must start at the beginning of `From`, then move through `From`, copying each node's contents (not its links!) into newly allocated nodes, which are then attached to `To`.

Look closely at `Copy`: We are able to write it purely in terms of the other list operations, with no direct reference to the list implementation. Indeed, strictly speaking, it need not even be a part of the package; a client could write it without knowing the list details. We include `Copy` in the package as a convenience.

Testing the List ADT

Program 9.3 uses most of the operations in the list ADT. It is actually more useful than that; we have included in it a number of local procedures that use the list operations in interesting ways. You can use these procedures as models for writing your own list-handling procedures.

Program 9.3 Demonstration of Generic Linked-List Package

```
WITH Lists_Generic;
WITH Ada.Text_IO;
PROCEDURE Test_Lists_Generic IS
------------------------------------------------------------------------
--| Test program for generic one-way lists
--| illustrates how to use the basic operations of the package
```

```
--| Author: Michael B. Feldman, The George Washington University
--| Last Modified: September 1995
---------------------------------------------------------------------------


  PACKAGE CharLists IS
    NEW Lists_Generic (ElementType => Character);
  USE CharLists;


  C1, C2, C3: List;
  Ch: Character;

  PROCEDURE PrintList(L: List) IS
  -- Pre:  L is defined
  -- Post: displays the (character) contents of L
    Current: Position;
  BEGIN
    Current := First(L);
    WHILE NOT IsPastEnd(L, Current)  LOOP
      Ada.Text_IO.Put(Item => Retrieve(L, Current));
      GoAhead(L, Current);
    END LOOP;
    Ada.Text_IO.Put(Item => '#');
    Ada.Text_IO.New_Line;
  END PrintList;


  PROCEDURE CopyBack (To: IN OUT List; From: IN List) IS
  -- Pre:  From is defined
  -- Post: copies From to To, starting with the last node of
  --    From and moving forward.
    Current: Position;
  BEGIN
    Initialize(To);
    Current := Last(From);
    WHILE NOT IsPastBegin(From, Current) LOOP
      AddToFront(To, Retrieve(From, Current));
      GoBack(From, Current);
    END LOOP;
  END CopyBack;


  PROCEDURE Weave (From: IN OUT List) IS
  -- Pre:  From is defined
  -- Post: inserts a character after each node of L
    Current: Position;
  BEGIN
    Current := Last(From);
    WHILE NOT IsPastBegin(From, Current) LOOP
      Insert(From, '%', Current);
      GoBack(From, Current);
    END LOOP;
  END Weave;


  PROCEDURE Subst (From: IN OUT List) IS
  -- Pre:  From is defined
  -- Post: replaces each character of L by '@'
    Current: Position;
  BEGIN
    Current := Last(From);
    WHILE NOT IsPastBegin(From, Current) LOOP
```

```
            Replace(From, '@', Current);
            GoBack(From, Current);
         END LOOP;
      END Subst;


BEGIN -- Test_Lists_Generic
   AddToFront(C1, 'a');
   PrintList(C1);
   AddToFront(C1, 'b');
   PrintList(C1);
   AddToFront(C1, 'c');
   PrintList(C1);
   AddToFront(C1, 'd');
   PrintList(C1);
   Copy(To => C2, From => C1);
   PrintList(C2);
   Copy(To => C3, From => C1);
   PrintList(C3);
   FOR Count IN 1..2 LOOP
      Delete(C1, First(C1));
      PrintList(C1);
      Ada.Text_IO.Put(Retrieve(C1, Last(C1)));
      Ada.Text_IO.Put('*');
      Delete(C1, Last(C1));
      PrintList(C1);
   END LOOP;
   FOR Count IN 1..2 LOOP
      Delete(C2, First(C2));
      PrintList(C2);
      Ada.Text_IO.Put(Retrieve(C2, Last(C2)));
      Ada.Text_IO.Put('*');
      Delete(C2, Last(C2));
      PrintList(C2);
   END LOOP;
   AddToFront(C1, 'a');
   PrintList(C1);
   AddToFront(C1, 'b');
   PrintList(C1);
   AddToFront(C1, 'c');
   PrintList(C1);
   AddToFront(C1, 'd');
   PrintList(C1);
   Weave(C1);
   PrintList(C1);
   Copy(To => C2, From => C1);
   PrintList(C2);
   Initialize(C1);
   PrintList(C1);
   CopyBack(To => C1, From => C2);
   PrintList(C1);
   FOR Count IN 1..4 LOOP
      Delete(C1, First(C1));
      PrintList(C1);
      Ada.Text_IO.Put(Retrieve(C1, Last(C1)));
      Ada.Text_IO.Put('*');
      Delete(C1, Last(C1));
      PrintList(C1);
   END LOOP;
   Subst(C2);
   PrintList(C2);
END Test_Lists_Generic;
```

9.2 ALLOCATION USING A LIST OF AVAILABLE SPACE (LAVS)

As written in Program 9.2, our `Allocate` and `Deallocate` operations use `NEW` and an instance of `Unchecked_Deallocation` to allocate and release nodes. In fact, there is a better way. Dynamic data structures are used because they can grow and shrink with time; for each node deleted, it is quite likely that another will be allocated. This is especially true in applications where a number of lists of the same type are active at the same time. Some are longer; others are shorter.

Let us use this fact to set up a "recycling system" for deleted nodes. Instead of releasing a node back to the pool, which can be fairly costly in terms of machine instructions, let us recognize that it is likely to be needed later and simply attach it to an extra list that is the package's property and, therefore, is declared within the package body itself. Historically this list was called `LAVS`, for *List of AVailable Space*. Sometimes it is called `FreeList` or a similar name.

Here is a client's list `L1` and the `LAVS`. We assume that, as a result of previous deletions, `LAVS` currently has two nodes in it.

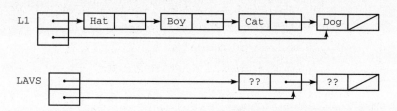

Each time a node is deleted from an active list, we add it to the front or rear of `LAVS`. In our example, deleting `Boy` from `L1` will have these results:

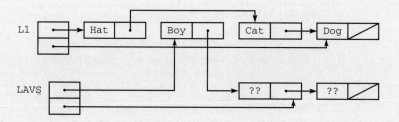

The same physical node is detached from one list (L1) and attached to another (LAVS). Each time a node must be allocated, we first check LAVS to see if there are any "recycled" nodes. If LAVS is not empty, we just disconnect the first node from LAVS and return a pointer designating it. If LAVS is empty, there are "no recycled" nodes and we must call NEW to allocate a new one from the storage pool.

The advantage of the LAVS approach is that it does not depend on the particular deallocation scheme used by the Ada system and uses NEW, which can be expensive in machine instructions, only when absolutely necessary. You can also carry your knowledge of the LAVS scheme to other languages; it is a universally useful method that has been employed almost since the very beginning of computer history.

As an exercise, you can modify the package body, specifically Allocate and Deallocate, so that LAVS is used instead of Unchecked_Deallocation to recycle deleted nodes.

9.3 UNBOUNDED QUEUES AND STACKS

In Chapter 7, we introduced LIFO stacks and FIFO queues, implementing them with array structures. Because an array has a lower bound and an upper bound, and therefore has a fixed number of components, we call them *bounded* implementations. A linked-list implementation, where there is no fixed bound on the size of the stack or queue, is usually called an *unbounded* implementation.

Linked Implementation of Queues

An unbounded queue implementation is very straightforward. We allocate a new list node (using LAVS or not) whenever an item is to be enqueued; we use whatever deallocation mechanism is available to free the node when an item is dequeued. As it happens, we can get all the services we need directly from an instantiation of Lists_Generic: Enqueue is implemented by a call to AddToRear; Dequeue is implemented just by deleting the first node in the list.

Program 9.4 shows the revised package specification for the linked-list implementation; completing the package body is left as an exercise.

Program 9.4 Specification for Generic Queues, Implemented with Linked Lists

```
WITH Lists_Generic;
GENERIC

  TYPE Element IS PRIVATE;

PACKAGE Queues_Generic_List IS
-----------------------------------------------------------------------
--| Specification for Generic Queues, Implemented with Linked Lists
--| Author: Michael B. Feldman, The George Washington University
--| Last Modified: September 1995
-----------------------------------------------------------------------

  -- type definition
```

```
      TYPE Queue (Capacity: Positive) IS LIMITED PRIVATE;

      -- exported exceptions

      QueueFull  : EXCEPTION;
      QueueEmpty : EXCEPTION;

      -- constructors

      PROCEDURE MakeEmpty (Q : IN OUT Queue);
      -- Pre:    Q is defined
      -- Post:   Q is empty

      PROCEDURE Enqueue (Q : IN OUT Queue; E : IN Element);
      -- Pre:     Q and E are defined
      -- Post:    Q is returned with E as the top Element
      -- Raises: QueueFull if Q already contains Capacity Elements

      PROCEDURE Dequeue (Q : IN OUT Queue);
      -- Pre:     Q is defined
      -- Post:    Q is returned with the top Element discarded
      -- Raises: QueueEmpty if Q contains no Elements

      -- selector

      FUNCTION First (Q : IN Queue) RETURN Element;
      -- Pre:     Q is defined
      -- Post:    The first Element of Q is returned
      -- Raises: QueueEmpty if Q contains no Elements

      -- inquiry operations

      FUNCTION IsEmpty (Q : IN Queue) RETURN Boolean;
      -- Pre:     Q is defined
      -- Post:    returns True if Q is empty, False otherwise

      FUNCTION IsFull  (Q : IN Queue) RETURN Boolean;
      -- Pre:     Q is defined
      -- Post:    returns True if Q is full, False otherwise

PRIVATE

   PACKAGE Lists IS
     NEW Lists_Generic(ElementType => Element);

   TYPE Queue (Capacity: Positive) IS RECORD
     Count : Natural := 0;
     Store : Lists.List;
   END RECORD;

END Queues_Generic_List;
```

Linked Implementation of Stacks

An unbounded stack implementation is analogous. Items are both pushed and popped at the head of the list; both operations are thus done in fixed time. Given the specification for stacks (Program 7.5), you should have little difficulty in writing a generic package specification and body for the unbounded implementation of stacks. This is left as an exercise.

9.4   ADT DESIGN: THE KEYED TABLE AS A LINKED LIST

So far in this chapter, we have seen many advantages of using pointer variables and dynamic allocation to implement linked lists. We have repeatedly emphasized the ease with which insertions and deletions can be performed on such a list. Let us therefore reimplement the keyed table first introduced in Section 5.8 as a linked list, using the ADT from Section 9.1 to support us. Program 9.5 shows the specification of `Tables_Generic_List`. Comparing it with Program 5.20 reveals that the two are nearly identical. The only difference is the context clause

```
WITH Lists_Generic;
```

at the top, and a different `PRIVATE` section, as follows:

```
PACKAGE Lists IS
  NEW Lists_Generic (ElementType => Element);

TYPE TableType IS RECORD
  Data : Lists.List;
  NumItems: Natural;
END RECORD;
```

The data field of a table, formerly an array in Program 5.20, is now just a list taken from an instance of `Lists_Generic`. `NumItems` is a count of the number of items in the table, as before.

Program 9.5 Specification for Generic Tables, Implemented with Linked Lists

```
WITH Lists_Generic;
GENERIC

   TYPE Element IS PRIVATE;      -- assignment and equality predefined
   TYPE KeyType IS PRIVATE;      -- here too

   Capacity: IN Positive;        -- maximum table size

   -- These generic parameters specify how to insert a key in an
   -- element, retrieve the key from an element, compare elements
   WITH FUNCTION KeyOf (Item: Element) RETURN KeyType IS <>;
   WITH FUNCTION "<" (Key1, Key2: KeyType) RETURN Boolean IS <>;

   -- This parameter specifies what to do with each element during
   -- a traversal of a table;
   WITH PROCEDURE Visit (Item: Element);

PACKAGE Tables_Generic_List IS
-----------------------------------------------------------------------
--| Specification of the abstract data type for an ordered table of
--| element records, each containing a key.
--| This version has type definitions to implement the table as a
--| singly-linked list. The client cannot see or use these types
--| because Table is LIMITED PRIVATE.
--| Author: Michael B. Feldman, The George Washington University
--| Last Modified: September 1995
-----------------------------------------------------------------------
```

```
-- Data Structure

  TYPE TableType IS LIMITED PRIVATE;

-- Exported exceptions

  UninitializedTable: EXCEPTION;
  NoSpaceLeft       : EXCEPTION;

-- Operators

  PROCEDURE InitializeTable (Table : IN OUT TableType);
  -- initializes a Table.
  -- Pre : None
  -- Post: Table is an initialized TableType

  FUNCTION SizeOfTable (Table : TableType) RETURN Natural;
  -- Returns the number of elements in a Table
  -- Pre : Table is an initialized TableType
  -- Post: Returns the number of elements in Table

  PROCEDURE Search (Table   : TableType;
                    Target  : KeyType;
                    Success : OUT Boolean);
  -- Searches a Table for Target.
  -- Pre : Table is an initialized TableType
  -- Post: Success is True if Target is found; otherwise,
  --       Success is False.

  PROCEDURE Insert (Table   : IN OUT TableType;
                    Item    : Element;
                    Success : OUT Boolean);
  -- Inserts Item into a Table.
  -- Pre : Table and Item are defined; Table is initialized.
  -- Post: Success is True if insertion is performed; Success is False
  --       if insertion is not performed because there is already
  --       an element with the same key as Item.
  -- Raises: NoSpaceLeft if there is no space available for Item.

  PROCEDURE Delete   (Table   : IN OUT TableType;
                      Target  : KeyType;
                      Success : OUT Boolean);
  -- Deletes the element with key Target from a Table.
  -- Pre : Table and Target are defined; Table is initialized.
  -- Post: Success is True if deletion is performed; Success is False
  --       if deletion is not performed because there is no element
  --       whose key is Target.

  PROCEDURE Replace  (Table   : IN OUT TableType;
                      Item    : Element;
                      Success : OUT Boolean);
  -- Replaces the element of a Table with the same key as
  -- Item by the contents of Item.
  -- Pre : Table and Item are defined; Table is initialized.
  -- Post: Success is True if the replacement is performed; Success is
  --       False if there is no element with the same key as Item.

  PROCEDURE Retrieve (Table   : TableType;
                      Target  : KeyType;
                      Item    : OUT Element;
                      Success : OUT Boolean);
  -- Copies the element whose key is Target into Item.
```

```
-- Pre : Table is an initialized TableType.
-- Post: Success is True if the copy is performed; Success is False
--         if there is no element whose key is Target.

PROCEDURE Traverse (Table : TableType);
-- Pre : Table is an initialized TableType.
-- Post: Each element is operated on in turn by procedure Visit.
PRIVATE

  SUBTYPE TableIndex IS Positive RANGE 1..Capacity;
  SUBTYPE TableSize  IS Natural  RANGE 0..Capacity;

  PACKAGE Lists IS
    NEW Lists_Generic(ElementType => Element);

  TYPE TableType IS RECORD
    CurrentSize: TableSize := 0;
    Data: Lists.List;
  END RECORD;

END Tables_Generic_List;
```

Dummy Nodes in an Ordered List

It will simplify the list-processing operations if we assume that an ordered list always begins a *dummy node*.

The dummy node is analogous to a sentinel. The presence of the first dummy node means that we never have to change the value of `Table.Info.Head` when a new node is inserted. In this implementation, an "empty" table is not really empty; it always contains a dummy node, as shown in Figure 9.1. The symbols "?" indicate that we are not concerned with the element value in the dummy node. The statement

```
InitializeTable (MyTable);
```

builds this list with one physical node in it—the dummy—but no actual table elements.

The Package Body

Program 9.6 shows the package body of `Tables_Generic_List`. Note that `InitializeTable` just adds a dummy node to the list header.

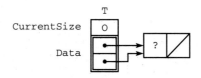

Figure 9.1 Initialized Table T (Note Dummy Node)

Program 9.6 Body of Generic Tables, Implemented with Linked Lists

```
PACKAGE BODY Tables_Generic_List IS
---------------------------------------------------------------------------
--| Implementation of the abstract data type for a table of
--| element records, each containing a key.
--| This implementation uses an instantiation of singly-linked lists.
--| Author: Michael B. Feldman, The George Washington University
--| Last Modified: September 1995
---------------------------------------------------------------------------

  USE Lists;


  PROCEDURE InitializeTable (Table : IN OUT TableType) IS
  -- initialize the table by creating the dummy node
    Dummy: Element;
  BEGIN -- InitializeTable

    Lists.AddToRear (L => Table.Data, X => Dummy);
    Table.CurrentSize := 0;                -- dummy node doesn't count

  END InitializeTable;


  -- local procedure, not exported to client, just used by the others.

  PROCEDURE Locate(Table        : IN OUT TableType;
                   Target       : KeyType;
                   Previous     : OUT Position;
                   Current      : OUT Position;
                   SearchSuccess: OUT Boolean) IS

  --  Attempts to locate a node with key value Target in the
  --  list whose first node is pointed to by Previous.
  --  Pre : Target is defined; L is initialized.
  --  Post: If Target is located, SearchSuccess is set to True;
  --     otherwise, SearchSuccess is set to False.
  --     Previous points to the last list node with key < Target,
  --     Current points to the first one with key >= Target.
  --     We need the Temps because Previous and Current are OUT

    CurrentKey   : KeyType;
    TempPrevious : Position;
    TempCurrent  : Position;       -- keeps track of current node
    Found        : Boolean;

  BEGIN -- Locate

    IF IsEmpty(Table.Data) THEN    -- no dummy nodes!
      RAISE UninitializedTable;    -- unlikely; Locate not user operation
    END IF;

    -- Search for first node with key >= Target.
    -- Start with first actual node.
    Found := False;
    TempCurrent  := First(Table.Data);      -- points to dummy node
    TempPrevious := TempCurrent;

    IF IsLast(Table.Data,TempCurrent) THEN  -- table empty
      Previous := TempPrevious;
      Current  := TempCurrent;
      SearchSuccess := False;
```

```
         RETURN;
      END IF;

      TempPrevious := TempCurrent;
      GoAhead(Table.Data, TempCurrent);   -- to first "real" node

      WHILE NOT IsPastEnd(Table.Data, TempCurrent)
        AND THEN NOT Found LOOP
      -- invariant:
      --   Target > key of each node pointed to by Current so far.
        CurrentKey := KeyOf (Retrieve(Table.Data, TempCurrent));
        IF Target < CurrentKey THEN
          Found := True;
        ELSE
          TempPrevious := TempCurrent;      -- advance Previous
          GoAhead(Table.Data, TempCurrent);
        END IF;
      END LOOP;
      -- assert: Target is located or CurrentKey is larger than Target.

      -- Set Next and flag to indicate search results.
      Previous := TempPrevious;
      Current  := TempCurrent;
      SearchSuccess :=
        (NOT IsPastEnd(Table.Data, TempCurrent))
        AND THEN CurrentKey = Target;

   END Locate;

-- Operators

   FUNCTION SizeOfTable (Table : TableType) RETURN Natural IS
   BEGIN
      RETURN Table.CurrentSize;
   END SizeOfTable;

   PROCEDURE Search (Table   : TableType;
                     Target  : KeyType;
                     Success : OUT Boolean) IS
   BEGIN -- stub
      NULL;
   END Search;

   PROCEDURE Insert (Table   : IN OUT TableType;
                     Item    : Element;
                     Success : OUT Boolean) IS

      Previous      : Position;   -- pointer to node preceding Item
      Current       : Position;   -- pointer to  node following Item
      SearchSuccess : Boolean;    -- search result
      ItemKey       : KeyType;    -- key of record Item

   BEGIN -- Insert

      IF IsEmpty(Table.Data) THEN
        RAISE UninitializedTable;
      END IF;

      -- Validate ItemKey and search for a valid key.
      ItemKey := KeyOf (Item);
        -- Search the list for ItemKey.
      Locate (Table, ItemKey, Previous, Current, SearchSuccess);

      -- Insert if ItemKey is in range and is a new key
```

```
      IF NOT SearchSuccess THEN              -- insert after Previous
        Success := True;                     -- Key is new iff search failed
        Insert(Table.Data, Item, Previous); -- insert right here
        Table.CurrentSize := Table.CurrentSize + 1;
      ELSE
        Success := False;
      END IF;

    END Insert;

    PROCEDURE Delete     (Table   : IN OUT TableType;
                          Target  : KeyType;
                          Success : OUT Boolean) IS
    BEGIN -- stub
      NULL;
    END Delete;

    PROCEDURE Replace    (Table   : IN OUT TableType;
                          Item    : Element;
                          Success : OUT Boolean) IS
    BEGIN -- stub
      NULL;
    END Replace;

    PROCEDURE Retrieve (Table   : TableType;
                        Target  : KeyType;
                        Item    : OUT Element;
                        Success : OUT Boolean) IS
    BEGIN -- stub
      NULL;
    END Retrieve;

    PROCEDURE Traverse (Table : TableType) IS
      Current: Position;
    BEGIN -- Traverse

      IF IsEmpty(Table.Data) THEN
        RAISE UninitializedTable;
      END IF;

      Current := First(Table.Data);
      GoAhead(Table.Data, Current);    -- start at first node after dummy
      WHILE NOT IsPastEnd(Table.Data, Current) LOOP
        Visit (Retrieve(Table.Data, Current));        -- visit node
        GoAhead(Table.Data, Current);
      END LOOP;

    END Traverse;

END Tables_Generic_List;
```

Recall from Chapter 5 that procedure Search is used to determine whether a particular target key is present in the list; it returns a Boolean value to indicate the search result. Search calls procedure Locate—a procedure internal to the package body and not available to clients—to perform the actual search.

Locate is the critical procedure to understand. It returns a pointer to the node containing the target key, and also a pointer to that node's predecessor. In writing Locate, we can take advantage of the fact that the key values are in ascending sequence. Consequently, while searching for the target key, if we reach a list element whose key value is larger than the target key, we know that the target key cannot be present in the list. In this case, the `SearchSuccess` flag is set to `False` but the `Previous` and `Current` pointers are returned anyway. If `SearchSuccess` is `True`, we know the location of both the target and its predecessor; if `SearchSuccess` is `False`, we know where the key would go if it were inserted. In this way, we can use `Locate` as a step not only in `Search`, but in `Insert`, `Delete`, and `Replace` as well. Because `Locate` is so critical to the other operations, you should study it very carefully, drawing a diagram if necessary. Also study the procedure `Insert` to see how it uses `Locate`.

Procedures `Search`, `Delete`, `Retrieve`, and `Replace` are quite similar and are left as an exercise along with function `SizeOfTable`. Finally, procedure `Traverse` traverses the ordered list, visiting each actual node but not the dummy node.

Analysis of Operations on an Ordered List

We have gone to considerable effort to maintain our linked list in ascending order by key value; however, the improvement in search efficiency that results is relatively modest. If we assume that a target key is as likely to be at the front of a list as at the end of the list, then on the average we will have to examine half of the list elements. This is true whether or not the target key is in the list. If a list is not ordered, we will have to examine all of its elements to determine that a key is not in the list, but only half of its elements, on the average, to find a key that *is* in the list. Therefore, list search is an $O(N)$ process for both ordered and unordered lists.

It takes considerably longer to insert an item into an ordered list than into an unordered list. In an unordered list, we can arbitrarily insert a new element at the list head. In an ordered list, we must first search for the appropriate position of the new element before inserting it. The main advantage of using ordered lists occurs when displaying the list contents. An ordered list is always ready to be printed or displayed. If the list is unordered, we must find some way to sort it before we can display it. We shall see later that using a different linked structure—a search tree—can reduce the time required for most table operations to $O(\log_2 N)$.

9.5 APPLICATION: THE AIRLINE PASSENGER LIST AGAIN

In Section 5.9, we used an airline passenger list as an example of the use of a generic table ADT. In the preceding section, we have reimplemented the table ADT using a singly linked list, but we have not changed the public part of the specification. It is therefore very easy to reuse the airline passenger example: Simply recompile and relink everything, this time using the linked-list version of the table ADT. The client program `BuildFlightList` should work exactly as it did before. This serves as a very good example of the benefits of `LIMITED PRIVATE` types and careful package specifications: A data structure can be reimplemented without causing any change at all to client programs.

9.6 ADT DESIGN: PASSIVE AND ACTIVE ITERATORS

The generic table-handler specification introduced in Section 9.4 provides an operation called `Traverse`, which moves through the table, one element at a time, until each element has been "visited" once. Recall that a generic procedure parameter `Visit` must be supplied by the client program; this procedure contains the actual work to be done in visiting each table element.

Formally, `Traverse` operation is an example of a *passive iterator* operation. An `iterator` is any operation that iterates through a data structure one element at a time; we call it *passive* because the client program simply calls it once and "stands back" passively while the iterator roams through the entire table.

Sometimes an application requires iterating through a table but allowing the client program the flexibility to decide just when to proceed to the next element, or indeed to stop the iteration early, before the entire table is processed. Moving through a table in this fashion is called *active iteration*, because the client program is actively involved in the process at every step.

Active Iterator Operations

To be actively involved in the iteration, the client program must execute a loop, using operations provided by the table package for loop initialization, termination, and incrementation and for retrieval of the current element in the traversal. We will call these operations `StartTraversal`, `MoreElements`, `MoveToNextElement`, and `RetrieveCurrentElement`, respectively. If the table being used by the client is called T, and E is a variable of type `Element`, then the basic client-program algorithm is

```
StartTraversal(T);
LOOP
  E := RetrieveCurrentElement(T);

  --process the current element E here

  EXIT WHEN NOT MoreElements(T);
  MoveToNextElement(T);
END LOOP;
```

The details of these operations depend on the way the table is implemented. Suppose, for example, that the table is implemented as a sorted array. We might include, as a field in the record defining the table type, an array index, `WhichElement`, indicating which element of the array is being processed, and another, `CurrentSize`, indicating the current number of elements in the array. In this implementation,

- `StartTraversal` sets `WhichElement` to its initial value at the beginning of the array.

- `MoreElements` returns `True` if and only if `WhichElement` has not reached `NumElements`—that is, has not reached the end of the currently filled part of the array.

- `MoveToNextElement` increments `WhichElement`.

- `RetrieveCurrentElement` returns the value of the current element.

Protecting the Table During an Active Iteration

Given that a traversal is performed element by element and, by definition, must visit each element exactly once, it is not reasonable to change the number of elements during a traversal. Adding an element to the part of the table already visited would probably ruin the iteration; so would deleting an element from that part of the table. Modifying a previously visited element would be equally unwise. On the other hand, modifying the element *currently* being visited might be the very purpose of the iteration.

In the interest of reliability, therefore, during a traversal the table should be locked against certain table operations. This can be done by adding a `Boolean` field—say, `Iterating`—to the table record and exporting an exception from the table package—say, `TableLocked`. The flag is set to `True` at the start of a traversal and to `False` at the end of the traversal. Each of the operations that modifies the table will raise the exception where appropriate.

Because the client cannot be prevented from ending the iteration early—that is, before the entire table has been visited—it is reasonable for the table package to provide an operation `StopTraversal`, which the client can call at any point to end the traversal. This operation unlocks the table.

To support active iteration, we change the type declaration for `TableType` as follows:

```
TYPE Table IS RECORD
  NumItems     : Positive := 0;
  Store        : Lists.List;
  Iterating    : Boolean := False;
  WhichElement: Lists.Position;
END RECORD;
```

We leave it as an exercise to modify the list version of `GenericTables` so that active iteration is supported. Note that, in effect, `Lists_Generic` already supports active iteration over a list, providing the operations `First`, `GoAhead`, `Retrieve`, `IsLast`, and `IsPastEnd`. You can use these to build the iterator operations for `GenericTables`.

9.7 ADT DESIGN: UNBOUNDED VARIABLE-LENGTH STRINGS

In this section, we return to the package for variable-length-string handling that we developed back in Section 6.4. Recall that in that design, a `VString` object consisted of a discriminant giving the maximum length, a string array of that length, and a current-length field. The design is seriously limited for general text-handling work by the fact that every text object must have a specified maximum length and occupies that amount of space. This wastes a lot of space, especially if many of the objects have only a few characters in use.

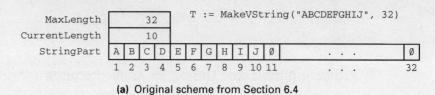

(a) Original scheme from Section 6.4

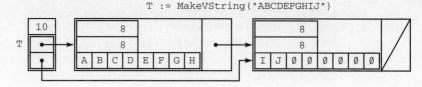

(b) New scheme Using Singly-linked List

Figure 9.2 Bounded and Unbounded Structures for Variable-Length Strings

We can solve this problem with an alternative design, namely letting a `VString` object consist of a linked list of smaller objects, for example with a length of eight characters. If the actual length of the string is not a multiple of eight, some space is wasted at the end, but it is probably much less than in the other design. A comparison showing how a particular ten-character string would be stored in both schemes appears in Figure 9.2. This new style of `VString` need not have a specified maximum length and is essentially unlimited in length; like all dynamic objects, it is limited in practice by the size of the pool, but that is usually quite large.

We can easily reuse the work we did developing `VStrings` in Section 6.4; our new package need only `WITH VStrings`, then define a short subtype—for example,

```
SUBTYPE ShortText IS VString(MaxLength => 8);
```

and use this as the element type with which to instantiate `Lists_Generic`.

Concatenating one `VString` object to another is now a matter of copying the first object to a result list (using the `Copy` already provided in `ListsGeneric`), then copying the second `VString` object, character by character, onto the end of the result. The character-by-character copy is necessary to fill in the empty space at the end of the first list. This makes substring searching and equality checking much easier.

A diagram showing the concatenation of two of these new `VString` objects is given in Figure 9.3; writing this function and completing the package is left as an exercise.

9.8 APPLICATION: SPARSE VECTORS AND MATRICES

Vectors and matrices with a high proportion of zeros—sometimes as high as 95 percent—are common in real-world numerical applications; the number of elements is often very large, sometimes too large to fit in main memory if all elements are stored.

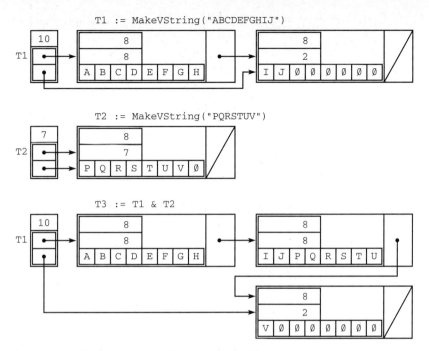

Figure 9.3 Concatenation of Unbounded VStrings

It is thus important to think about how to store such structures economically. The idea is to devise a way to store only those elements that are not zero, in some data structure such that if an element does not appear at all, it is treated as being zero.

Generally, in such applications, the values are constantly changing as a numerical problem is iteratively solved.

We can therefore think of this situation as strongly analogous to our keyed tables. Indeed, we can use a keyed table to represent a sparse vector. A vector element, as discussed in Chapter 4, has a subscript and a value. To represent that vector in a sparse form, we represent a nonzero vector element as a record, using as the key field the subscript (the one the element would have had in an ordinary vector), and the nonzero value as a nonkey field. A ten-element vector V of `Float` values, with only three nonzero values—for example,

```
V := (0.0, 1.5, -3.7, 0.0., 0.0, 0.0, 2.4, 0.0, 0.0, 0.0);
```

will be represented as a keyed table with three pairs inserted, namely <2, 1.5>, <3, -3.7>, and <7, 2.4>.

Sparse Vector Operations

Recall from the discussion in Section 4.6 that two of the operations on vectors are *store an element into a vector with a given subscript* and *retrieve a given element from a vector*. If an array is used to represent an ordinary vector, these operations are just the usual array-element operations. If V is a vector of Float values and X is a Float variable, then *store* and *retrieve* are, respectively, just

```
V(5) := 23.7;
X := V(K);
```

If the vector is represented in some sort of sparse structure, we cannot use ordinary array subscripting. Instead, we write a procedure Store and a function Retrieve so that the two lines above become

```
Store(Vector => V, Subscript => 5, Value => 23.7);
X := Retrieve(Vector => V, Subscript => K);
```

If we use a keyed table, we must be careful to retain only nonzero elements in the table. Therefore, the algorithms for Retrieve and Store are as follows:

To Retrieve a Sparse Vector Element by Subscript:

1. Search the table for an element with the desired subscript.

2. If the search is successful, return the associated value.

3. If the search is unsuccessful, return 0.

To Store a Sparse Vector Element by Subscript:

1. If the element value is 0.0, delete it from the table (recall that our keyed-table Delete just returns a false success flag if the element was not already in the table).

2. If the element value is not 0.0, search the table for an element with the desired subscript.

3. If the search is successful, replace that element with the new element.

4. If the search is unsuccessful, insert the new element.

Given Retrieve and Store, we can sketch out the algorithm for adding two sparse vectors, by analogy with the corresponding algorithm from Section 4.6. Recall that the two vectors must be conformable, so assume that vectors Left and Right both have bounds LowBound and HighBound. The potential number of components—if they were all nonzero—is HighBound-LowBound+1; let us call this number MaxNonZero. The algorithm is

```
FOR Which IN LowBound. .HighBound LOOP
  Store(Vector => Result, Subscript => Which,
    Value => Retrieve(Vector => Left, Subscript => Which) +
            Retrieve(Vector => Right, Subscript => Which));
END LOOP;
```

or, using positional instead of named parameters, the simpler form

```
FOR Which IN LowBound. .HighBound LOOP
  Store(Result, Which,
    Retrieve(Left, Which) + Retrieve(Right, Which));
END LOOP;
```

Let's look at the performance of vector addition using this scheme. Assume that each vector has `ActualNonZero` nonzero components (i.e., the list has `ActualNonZero` nodes). Then each Retrieve operation is O(`ActualNonZero`), since on the average half the list must be searched.

Now, since the vector is defined for `MaxNonZero` components, `MaxNonZero` calls to `Retrieve` must be executed for each of the two vectors, and—in the worst case—`MaxNonZero` insertions must be done. Since each insertion is also O(`ActualNonZero`), the overall addition operation is O(`MaxNonZero * ActualNonZero`)! But vector addition as done in Section 4.6 is O(`MaxNonZero`), since the two arrays are traversed only once. Thus, we have paid a price in time performance in return for the economy of space achieved by storing vectors in sparse form.

Actually, the trade-off is between abstraction and performance: The slow performance came from our unwillingness to let the addition function know the details of a sparse vector. We required the addition algorithm to use calls to `Store` and `Retrieve`, which in turn used table operations. If we are willing to let that function use knowledge of the fact that sparse vectors are stored as lists, we can speed it up considerably. Only one pass through the two lists is required: Since the lists are stored in order on the subscripts, we use a "merge" algorithm, whose effect is illustrated in Figure 9.4.

Begin at the beginning of both vectors `Left` and `Right`. If the subscript of the first node of `Left` is less than that of `Right`, we know the corresponding element of `Right` is zero. So we just copy the element of `Left` onto the end of the sum vector `Result`. Then we find the successor node in `Left` and try again.

On the other hand, if the `Right` subscript is less, we copy the node from `Right` onto the end of the `Result` list, moving to its successor.

If the two subscripts are ever equal, both `Left` and `Right` have nonzero values in that position and we add the values together before adding a node for that subscript onto the end of `Result`.

Eventually, we reach the end of one of the vectors. Suppose we reach `Left`'s end first. At that point, we just copy the rest of `Right` onto `Result`, since all remaining components of `Left` are zero.

Our merge algorithm is somewhat more complicated to code than the earlier version, but it is a lot faster, since its performance is O(`ActualNonZero`) instead of O(`MaxNonZero * ActualNonZero`)! If `MaxNonZero` is much larger than `ActualNonZero`—a good assumption, of course, in the case of sparse vectors—the speedup is really significant.

Implementation of sparse vectors in this fashion, instead of a keyed table, is straightforward given the generic singly linked list package of Section 9.1. This is left as an exercise.

Sparse Matrices

The linked-list implementation of sparse vectors can be extended to two dimensions to handle sparse matrices. Several operations on "normal" matrices represented as arrays were presented in Section 4.5; you should review those operations before continuing here.

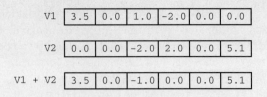

(a) Dense representation using arrays

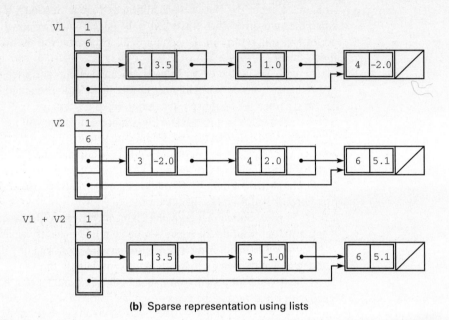

(b) Sparse representation using lists

Figure 9.4 Dense and Sparse Vector Representations

Moving now to a *sparse* matrix situation, to implement the operations as efficiently as we did in the vector case, we will need to be able to scan rows or columns with equal ease. We thus define a node of a sparse matrix as having row and column subscripts and row and column pointers.

The "header" of a sparse matrix contains two arrays, to serve as heads of the respective row and column lists. Each node is thus on two lists, a row list and a column list. To scan a row, we follow its row pointers; to scan a column, we follow its column pointers.

Filling in the details of a package for sparse-matrix arithmetic is left as an exercise. An example of the structure of a sparse matrix is given in Figure 9.5, where both the "normal" and the sparse forms of a 5×5 matrix of integers are shown.

This sparse matrix implementation is often called *cross lists* or *orthogonal lists*. It is a special case of a more general one in which each node has N keys and N pointers; the values may be, for example, information records of some sort. In the general situation, the structure is often called a multilist structure and appears in discussions of database organization.

$$\begin{bmatrix} 1.0 & 2.1 & 0 & 0 & 0 \\ 0 & -3.2 & 0 & 4.5 & 1.1 \\ 0 & 0 & 0 & 2.1 & 0 \\ 5.6 & 0 & -3.0 & 0 & 0 \\ 0 & 0 & -1.3 & 0 & 0 \end{bmatrix}$$

Abstract View

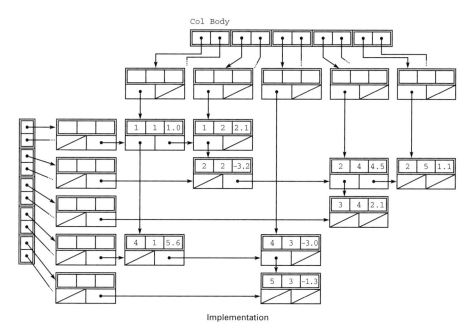

Implementation

Figure 9.5 Sparse Matrix Represented as Cross-List Structure (Tail Pointers Are Omitted to Avoid Clutter)

9.9   SIMULATING DYNAMIC MEMORY MANAGEMENT

Let us use the sparse vector example of Section 9.8 to illustrate how dynamic memory management might be done in a system where no access type or storage pool is available. We will pretend that Ada has no access types and no storage pool; we will go a step further by pretending that Ada has no record types either. This gives a realistic emulation of the data structures actually available in older languages, such as Fortran-77.

We simulate an array of records using *parallel arrays*—that is, a separate one-dimensional array to represent each field. We simulate pointers using subscripts in these parallel arrays. Our basic routines for handling list and vector elements can then easily be recoded to suit the new implementation.

In this example, we assume that the application requires storage of many vectors at one time. Let the vector range be 1. .1000 as before; assume that no more than 500 vector elements will be nonzero at any one time, independent of the number of vectors

```
MaxElements: CONSTANT Integer := 1000;
MaxNonZero:  CONSTANT Integer := 500;

SUBTYPE VectorRange IS Integer RANGE 1. .MaxElements;
SUBTYPE NodePointer IS Integer RANGE 0. .MaxNonZero;
SUBTYPE ValueType   IS Integer; — (or whatever)

Subscripts: ARRAY(1. .MaxNonZero) OF VectorRange;
Values:     ARRAY(1. .MaxNonZero) OF ValueType;
Links:      ARRAY(1. .MaxNonZero) OF NodePointer;

LAVS:       NodePointer;

TYPE SparseVector IS ARRAY(1. .2) OF NodePointer;
```

Figure 9.6 Definitions for Sparse Vectors in Simulated Storage Pool Implementation.

currently active. We now redefine the type `NodePointer` to be an integer link; the null pointer value is represented by 0. Figure 9.6 gives the declarations for a number of structures. Make sure you understand why there are three arrays and why the dimensions and types are what they are! A sparse vector is, now, just a one-dimensional array of two elements—a head "pointer" and a tail "pointer," as shown in the figure.

To handle allocation of nodes in this simulated storage pool, let's declare another vector, called `LAVS`, that will let us know the location of the next available node in the array, and initialize the whole array by calling a routine `StoragePoolInit` that just sets the link of each node to point at the next physical node, so that the entire pool becomes a list of available space. The Ada code for `StoragePoolInit` is given in Figure 9.7; a diagram of the initialized space is shown in Figure 9.8.

This scheme is a miniature version of the `NEW` operation in Ada and its equivalents in other languages. As a new node is required to store a vector value, it is allocated from `LAVS`. If a node is deleted, it is just returned to `LAVS` by adding it to the front of the list. This is really just another example of the approach discussed in Section 7.2, translated to a situation where a "real" `NEW` operation is no longer available.

A number of vectors can be stored in our simulated storage pool and they can grow and shrink as required. The link structure maintains the logical order of each list; all the

```
PROCEDURE StoragePoolInit IS

BEGIN
  LAVS := 1;

  FOR k IN 1 . . MaxNonZero-1 LOOP
     Links(k) := k + 1;
  END LOOP;

  Links(MaxNonZero) := 0;

END StoragePoolInit;
```

Figure 9.7 Storage Pool Initialization for Array-Based Simulated Storage Pool

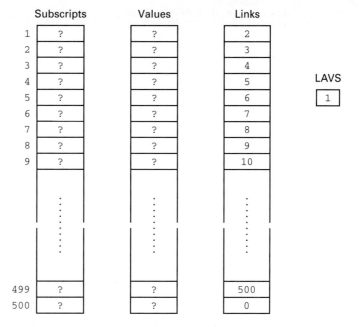

Figure 9.8   Simulated Storage Pool Using Parallel Arrays

lists share the same physical array space. The only time it is necessary to refuse to add a new item to a vector is in the event that all nodes in the list space are simultaneously occupied and allocated to vectors.

The name "cursor" is often given to a pointer that is simulated by a value in an array; the name is just used to distinguish this case from the "real" pointers available in Ada and other such languages.

9.10   ADA STRUCTURES: ADA 95 UNBOUNDED STRINGS

As we have discussed previously, Ada 95 provides a set of packages for dealing with strings. In earlier sections, we discussed fixed-length and bounded strings; here, we mention `Ada.Strings.Unbounded`, which provides a `PRIVATE` type `Unbounded_String`. An object of this type represents a string whose lower bound is 1 and whose upper bound can vary conceptually between 0 and `Natural'Last`. The operations are similar to those for fixed-length strings. The details appear in Appendix G, which contains the full LRM descriptions of the predefined string packages.

The LRM does not, of course, specify an implementation for `Unbounded_String`; this is left to the provider of the package. However, it is typical to implement unbounded strings as linked lists of some sort, similarly to the implementation we described in Section 9.7.

9.11 ADA STRUCTURES: ADA 95 GENERAL ACCESS TYPES

We have seen in Chapters 8 and 9 that access types can acquire values in only two ways: as the result of an allocator (NEW) operation or as a copy of another access value. In particular, there is no direct way to cause an access value to designate a declared variable or constant. This has caused problems in certain applications, and so Ada 95 extends the access-type concept to allow access values to designate variables and constants.

In order to provide a safe pointer construct that minimizes the likelihood of undefined or dangling pointers, Ada 95 now provides two kinds of access types:

- *Pool-specific access types*, which are just the access types of Ada 83, the ones we've been working with in Chapters 8 and 9

- *General access types*, which can designate variables, constants, and dynamically allocated values

Here are three versions of an access type declaration:

```
TYPE IntegerPointer IS ACCESS Integer;
TYPE IntegerPointer IS ACCESS ALL Integer;
TYPE IntegerPointer IS ACCESS CONSTANT Integer;
```

The first declares a familiar access type, which Ada 95 now calls *pool-specific*. It can designate only an Integer value allocated from the pool. The second declares a *general access type* that can designate an integer variable, integer constant, or pool value. The third is a restricted "read-only" form of the second: If P is of this type, it can be dereferenced only to *read* the designated value, not to *write* it. That is, P.ALL is not valid on the left side of an assignment statement. This is analogous to an IN parameter.

Given a general access type of the second kind, can its values point to *any* integer variable or constant? No. In keeping with Ada's general philosophy of explicitness in operations, Ada 95 requires the programmer to indicate explicitly that a variable or constant is intended to be "pointed to." For example, the integer variable X, declared as

```
X :Integer;
```

cannot be designated by an access value, but the variable Y, declared as

```
Y: ALIASED Integer;
```

can indeed be so designated. In everyday English, an *alias* is a nickname, or a name a person uses in addition to his or her given name. (A criminal might use a number of aliases to avoid detection.) In programming, the term "aliased" is a fairly standard one, and means, by analogy, that the variable can be referred to not only by its name but by any number of aliases (access values).

Suppose P is a general access type, as above. How does P acquire a value? Of course, P can still be copied from another access variable, or assigned the result of a NEW, but we are interested in designating *variables*. We can cause P to designate Y, for example, by writing

```
P := Y'Access;
```

The 'Access attribute returns an access value designating Y, or, informally, a pointer to Y.

Program 9.7 illustrates general access types. An array, PromptTable, is made to contain access values that designate strings of different lengths. The four prompts are declared as ALIASED, to allow them to be designated. If we wished the prompts to be CONSTANT strings, the access type would then be written

```
TYPE StringPointer IS ACCESS CONSTANT String;
```

Program 9.7 Illustration of Ada 95 General Access Types

```
WITH Ada.Text_IO;
PROCEDURE General_Access_Types IS
------------------------------------------------------------------------
--| Illustrates general access types
--| Author: Michael B. Feldman, The George Washington University
--| Last Modified: September 1995
------------------------------------------------------------------------

  TYPE StringPointer IS ACCESS ALL String;
  -- ALL makes StringPointer a "general access type" as opposed to
  -- a "pool-specific access type." StringPointer values
  -- can designate declared variables and constants,
  -- as well as dynamically allocated (NEW) values

  Prompt1: ALIASED String := "Enter a command >";
  Prompt2: ALIASED String := "Thank you.";
  Prompt3: ALIASED String := "Invalid; try again.";
  Prompt4: ALIASED String := "Bye now.";
  -- ALIASED means
  --    "able to be designated by a general access value"

  PromptTable: ARRAY (1..4) OF StringPointer :=
    (Prompt1'Access, Prompt2'Access,
     Prompt3'Access, Prompt4'Access);
  -- We fill the array with access values: for example,
  -- Prompt1'Access returns an access value designating Prompt1

BEGIN -- General_Access_Types

  -- display all the prompts in the table
  FOR Which IN PromptTable'Range LOOP
    Ada.Text_IO.Put(Item => PromptTable(Which).ALL); -- dereference
    Ada.Text_IO.New_Line;
  END LOOP;

END General_Access_Types;
```

9.12 HETEROGENEOUS STRUCTURES AND DYNAMIC DISPATCHING

Recall that in Section 6.6 we introduced Ada 95 *tagged types*, which can be extended by deriving new types from them, adding fields and operations as appropriate. We introduced the notion of *primitive operations*, which, for a given tagged type, are those declared in the same place as the type. A primitive operation is *inherited* by a new type derived from the original, but can be *overridden* for the new type, in case the inheritance is not desired.

We used Programs 6.14 through 6.20 to illustrate a hierarchy of tagged types, defining `Person`, `Employee`, `Professional`, `Sales`, and `Clerical`. We declared one variable of each type, `George`, `Mary`, `Martha`, `Virginia`, and `Herman`, demonstrating the appropriate constructors and selectors for each. The time has come to answer two questions left open in Section 6.6:

- How can we declare a variable that can hold a value of *any* type in the hierarchy?

- How can we declare an array each of whose elements can be a value of any type in the hierarchy?

Class-Wide Types

For a tagged type `T`, Ada 95 provides an attribute `T'Class`, which represents the entire type hierarchy for which `T` is the parent. In our example, a variable of type `Person'Class` can hold a value of any of our five types, or indeed of any type derived from any of these in the future. `Person'Class` is known as a *class-wide type*, and the variable is known as a *class-wide variable*.

We are getting closer to answering our questions. However, there is a small 'catch': Ada 95 requires that a class-wide variable be immediately initialized to a specific value of one of the types, and thereafter the variable can change its value but not its type.

This rule is analogous to the rules for constrained variant records. The reason for the rule here is that a tagged type can be extended indefinitely, with an unknown number of derived types, each with an unknown number of extension fields. The compiler cannot know which types might be derived—added to `T'Class`—in the future, so it cannot even guess at the size of a variable of such an unknown type.

This is not very helpful when we contemplate setting up a dynamic table of tagged objects. Suppose we wanted to use a table to represent a company. Since there are different types of employee, each element of the array could be of a different type. Furthermore, these elements could not all be immediately initialized, because we might obtain the employee data interactively or from an external file. Moreover, we might later wish to add new types of employees without having to modify the table structure. Indeed, the possibility of future modifications is exactly what first motivated our use of tagged types.

All this leads us to ask—continuing the analogy with variant records—whether there is a tagged-type analogue to an *unconstrained* variant record (that is, a variable whose type—within a class—can be left initially unspecified and can change over time).

The answer here is yes, but the solution is not quite as simple as that for variant records. The difference is that by the time an unconstrained variant object is declared, the compiler knows all the possible variants, and can therefore know how to arrange for the space to be allocated. In contrast, as we have just seen, a class-wide variable can be declared and the class later extended.

Class-Wide General Access Types and Heterogeneous Arrays

We solve the problem using access types in Program 9.8.

Program 9.8 Creating an Array of Payroll Records

```
WITH Ada.Text_IO; USE Ada.Text_IO;
WITH Currency; USE Currency;
WITH Dates; USE Dates;
WITH Persons; USE Persons;
WITH Personnel; USE Personnel;
WITH Payroll; USE Payroll;
PROCEDURE Payroll_Array IS
---------------------------------------------------------------------
--| demonstrates the use of classwide general access types
--| and dispatching operations
--| Author: Michael B. Feldman, The George Washington University
--| Last Modified: September 1995
---------------------------------------------------------------------

  George  : ALIASED Person;
  Mary    : ALIASED Employee;
  Martha  : ALIASED Professional;
  Virginia: ALIASED Sales;
  Herman  : ALIASED Clerical;
  -- These values can now be designated by general access values

  TYPE PayrollPointer IS ACCESS ALL Person'Class;
  -- a PayrollPointer value can designate a value of type
  -- Person, or of any type derived from Person, such as
  -- Employee, Sales, Professional, or Clerical

  TYPE PayrollArray IS ARRAY (1..5) OF PayrollPointer;
  -- We can put all our employees in an array by designating
  -- them with PayrollPointer values

  Company: PayrollArray;

BEGIN

  -- first construct all the people, as before

  George := Persons.Constructors.MakePerson(
          Name     => "George",
          Gender   => Male,
          BirthDate => MakeDate(1971,11,2));

  Mary := Personnel.Constructors.MakeEmployee(
          Name     => "Mary",
          Gender   => Female,
          BirthDate => MakeDate(1950,10,21),
          ID       => 1234,
          StartDate => MakeDate(1989,7,1));

  Martha := Payroll.Constructors.MakeProfessional(
          Name       => "Martha",
          Gender     => Female,
          BirthDate  => MakeDate(1947,7,8),
          ID         => 2222,
```

```
                    StartDate   => MakeDate(1985,6,6),
                    MonthSalary => MakeCurrency(50000.00));
     Virginia := Payroll.Constructors.MakeSales(
                    Name        => "Virginia",
                    Gender      => Female,
                    BirthDate   => MakeDate(1955,2,1),
                    ID          => 3456,
                    StartDate   => MakeDate(1990,1,1),
                    WeekSalary  => MakeCurrency(2500.00),
                    CommRate    => 0.25);

     Herman := Payroll.Constructors.MakeClerical(
                    Name        => "Herman",
                    Gender      => Male,
                    BirthDate   => MakeDate(1975,5,13),
                    ID          => 1557,
                    StartDate   => MakeDate(1991,7,1),
                    HourlyWage  => MakeCurrency(7.50));

     -- Now put the people into the company; each array element is
     -- a different type!

     Company := (Herman'Access, Martha'Access, Virginia'Access,
                 Mary'Access, George'Access);

     -- Now display them all. Note that each time Put is invoked,
     -- precisely the appropriate Put is "dispatched".

     FOR Which IN Company'Range LOOP
       Put(Company(Which).ALL);
       Ada.Text_IO.Put_Line(Item => "-----------------------");
     END LOOP;

END Payroll_Array;
```

Here our five people are declared as before, but now they are ALIASED. We have further declared a general access type PayrollPointer and an array of values of this type:

```
TYPE PayrollPointer IS ACCESS ALL Person'Class;
TYPE PayrollArray IS ARRAY (1..5) OF PayrollPointer;
```

The access type can designate any type in Person'Class; each array element is a value of that access type. We can now declare a variable

```
Company: PayrollArray;
```

and, after constructing all the people as in Section 6.6, we can put them into the company, using an array aggregate:

```
Company := (Herman'Access, Martha'Access, Virginia'Access,
            Mary'Access, George'Access);
```

The type PayrollArray is an example of the way Ada 95 provides for *heterogeneous arrays*—that is, arrays each of whose values is a different type. Strictly speaking, the values in Company are all just class-wide access values, but each designated values is a different type, so the desired behavior is obtained. Our questions are answered.

Dynamic Dispatching

Given our array of values, we can display the entire company just by looping through the array, dereferencing each pointer to obtain the value to display:

```
FOR Which IN Company'Range LOOP
  Put(Company(Which).ALL);
  Ada.Text_IO.Put_Line(Item => "-----------------------");
END LOOP;
```

There is more to the `Put` in the above loop than meets the eye. Note that each value being displayed is of a *different* type, each of which has its own `Put` as defined in the three packages of Section 6.6. If we had used variant records, we would need a `CASE` to decide which variant to display. Here, the appropriate `Put` is selected, at execution time, automatically. This is called *dynamic dispatching*; it is an extremely important technique in object-oriented programming. The correct `Put` is said to be *dispatched*.

Dispatching is closely related to primitive operations. In our example, `Put` is a primitive operation of `Person`. For `Person` and for each type derived from `Person`, that is, each type in `Person'Class`—`Put` is inherited by default, or, as in our situation, overridden. The five `Puts` have the same name, and parameters differing only by the type within `Person'Class`. The correct `Put` can thus be dispatched.

We note that the values designated by `Company(Which)` could have been placed in `Company` by dynamic allocation instead of by using aliased variables. In fact, the next section shows how to make `Company` fully dynamic.

Heterogeneous Linked Lists

To end our discussion of tagged types and also of linked lists, we show in Program 9.9 a fully dynamic example.

Program 9.9 Creating a Linked List of Payroll Records

```
WITH Ada.Text_IO; USE Ada.Text_IO;
WITH Currency; USE Currency;
WITH Dates; USE Dates;
WITH Persons; USE Persons;
WITH Personnel; USE Personnel;
WITH Payroll; USE Payroll;
WITH Lists_Generic;
PROCEDURE Payroll_List IS
-------------------------------------------------------------------
--| Demonstrates the use of a heterogeneous list.
--| Author: Michael B. Feldman, The George Washington University
--| Last Modified: September 1995
-------------------------------------------------------------------

  TYPE PayrollPointer IS ACCESS ALL Person'Class;
  -- as before, this can designate a Person or anything
  -- derived from Person

  PACKAGE PayrollLists IS NEW Lists_Generic
```

```
          (ElementType => PayrollPointer);
   USE PayrollLists;
   -- The list element type is now a classwide pointer

   Company: List;
   Which  : Position;
   Temp   : PayrollPointer;

BEGIN -- Payroll_List

   -- Construct all the people dynamically, and add each one
   -- to the end of the list as it is constructed. We no longer
   -- need an explicit variable for each person.

   Temp := NEW Person'(Persons.Constructors.MakePerson(
              Name       => "George",
              Gender     => Male,
              BirthDate  => MakeDate(1971,11,2)));
   AddToRear(Company, Temp);

   Temp := NEW Employee'(Personnel.Constructors.MakeEmployee(
              Name       => "Mary",
              Gender     => Female,
              BirthDate  => MakeDate(1950,10,21),
              ID         => 1234,
              StartDate  => MakeDate(1989,7,1)));
   AddToRear(Company, Temp);

   Temp := NEW Professional'(Payroll.Constructors.MakeProfessional(
              Name       => "Martha",
              Gender     => Female,
              BirthDate  => MakeDate(1947,7,8),
              ID         => 2222,
              StartDate  => MakeDate(1985,6,6),
              MonthSalary => MakeCurrency(50000.00)));
   AddToRear(Company, Temp);

   Temp := NEW Sales'(Payroll.Constructors.MakeSales(
              Name       => "Virginia",
              Gender     => Female,
              BirthDate  => MakeDate(1955,2,1),
              ID         => 3456,
              StartDate  => MakeDate(1990,1,1),
              WeekSalary => MakeCurrency(2500.00),
              CommRate   => 0.25));
   AddToRear(Company, Temp);

   Temp := NEW Clerical'(Payroll.Constructors.MakeClerical(
              Name       => "Herman",
              Gender     => Male,
              BirthDate  => MakeDate(1975,5,13),
              ID         => 1557,
              StartDate  => MakeDate(1991,7,1),
              HourlyWage => MakeCurrency(7.50)));
   AddToRear(Company, Temp);

   -- Now we can traverse the list. Note again that Put is a
   -- dispatching operation; the correct Put is dispatched at
   -- execution time.

   Which := First(Company);
   WHILE NOT IsPastEnd(Company, Which) LOOP
      Put(Item => Retrieve(Company,Which).ALL); -- dispatching
      Ada.Text_IO.Put_Line(Item => "------------------------");
```

```
   GoAhead(Company, Which);
  END LOOP;

END Payroll_List;
```

Here we use our generic singly linked list package from Section 9.1, instantiating it for our class-wide access type and declaring a few useful variables:

```
TYPE PayrollPointer IS ACCESS ALL Person'Class;

PACKAGE PayrollLists IS NEW Lists_Generic
  (ElementType => PayrollPointer);
USE PayrollLists;

Company: List;
Which  : Position;
Temp   : PayrollPointer;
```

Note that the element type in each list node is one of our class-wide pointers. We can now use `Temp` as a "holding area" for a dynamically allocated `Professional`, for example, and then add it to the end of our company list:

```
Temp := NEW Professional'(Payroll.Constructors.MakeProfessional)
  Name        => "Martha",
  Gender      => Female,
  BirthDate   => MakeDate(1947,7,8),
  ID          => 2222,
  StartDate   => MakeDate(1985,6,6),
  MonthSalary => MakeCurrency(50000.00)));
AddToRear(Company, Temp);
```

After building a linked list of five persons constructed in this manner, the program traverses the list, using various operations from the linked-list package, and dispatching the appropriate `Put` to display each person:

```
Which := First(Company);
WHILE NOT IsPastEnd(Company, Which) LOOP
  Put(Item => Retrieve(Company,Which).ALL); -- dispatching
  Ada.Text_IO.Put_Line(Item => "--------------------");
  GoAhead(Company, Which);
END LOOP;
```

This presentation has only scratched the surface of Ada 95's facilities for object-oriented programming; a full treatment is beyond the scope of this book. The discussion here should give you an indication of the power of type extension and dynamic dispatching, and perhaps an appreciation of why object-oriented programming has become such a popular technique for building software systems.

No technique is perfect, and there is a price to be paid for inheritance. Large, deep type hierarchies, while very powerful, can also be difficult to work with and maintain, because all the derived types and operations depend very intimately on types and operations that are higher in the hierarchy. A change at the top can cause a "ripple effect" through the hierarchy; this may be an advantage, but the high degree of coupling among types might also have unanticipated effects. There can also be a performance penalty in excessive use of dynamic dispatching. Compare this to the ADT approach used heavily in this book, in which packages and clients depend mostly on other units in their immediate "neighborhoods."

Like any other powerful tool, inheritance must be used with common sense and moderation, and the trade-offs carefully considered. Use it to build hierarchical structures of types that are truly related in some obvious way; avoid the trap of using it solely because it is there.

SUMMARY

This chapter has introduced a number of interesting techniques for using linked lists and several representative applications. With this background in dynamic data structures, you are ready to proceed to the remaining chapters, in which linked structures are used to implement graphs, trees, and hash tables.

EXERCISES

1. Write an algorithm to remove a node (identified by `TargetID`) from an ordered list that does not contain a dummy record at the beginning.
2. Write the necessary procedures to duplicate all elements with a GPA of 3.5 or above in one linked list in another linked list. The original list is ordered by ID number; the new list should be ordered by GPA. Do not remove nodes from the existing list.
3. Write a procedure to delete all males over 25 from an existing linear linked list. Define an appropriate node type with which to instantiate `Lists_Generic`.
4. Complete the procedure stubs in Program 9.6 and test these with a driver program.
5. Use the generic table package shown in Section 9.4 to maintain an airline passenger list. The main program should be menu-driven and should allow its user to display the data for a particular passenger, display the entire list, create a list, insert a node, delete a node, and replace the data for a particular passenger.
6. Modify your employee database system from Chapters 3, 4, and 5 so that the database is represented as an instance of the generic keyed table package from Section 9.4.
7. In specifying the keyed table ADT, the assumption was made that there would be no insertion if the key of a new record was already present in the table. Modify procedure `Insert` from Program 9.8 so that it allows several occurrences of records with the same key. Change `Insert` so that a record with a duplicate key is placed in a position immediately following all other records in the table record with the same key. Discuss various possible meanings for the other table operations under this assumption.
8. Modify `Tables_Generic_List` to support active iterators, as described in Section 9.6.
9. Develop a linked-list representation to store sets. Write the routines necessary to insert and delete integer values from a set. Also write the routines necessary to implement the set operations of difference, intersection, and union. To verify the results, display the contents of the sets before and after each operation.
10. A polynomial may be represented as a linked list in which each node contains the coefficient and exponent of a term of the polynomial. The polynomial $4x^3 + 3x^2 - 5$ would be represented as the following linked list:

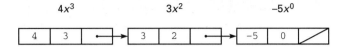

Write an abstract data type for polynomials that has operators for creating a polynomial, reading a polynomial, and adding and subtracting a pair of polynomials.
(*Hint*: To add or subtract two polynomials, traverse both lists. If a particular exponent value is present in either one, it should be present in the result polynomial
unless its coefficient is zero.)

11. Because each student in the university takes a different number of courses, the
registrar has decided to use a linked list to store each student's class schedule and
a table to represent the whole student body. Each table element is a student record,
containing, among other information, the linked list just described.

For example, one student (ID 1111) is taking section 1 of CIS120 for 3
credits and section 2 of HIS001 for 4 credits; a second student (ID 1357) is not
enrolled, and so on. Develop an implementation for this system using the generic-
linked list and keyed-table packages. Write a menu-driven client program so that
the registrar can specify appropriate operations.

12. Develop a linked-list implementation for sparse vectors as discussed in Section 9.8.

13. Develop a cross-list implementation for sparse matrices as discussed in Section 9.8.

CHAPTER 10

Directed Graphs

The *graph* is an important mathematical structure, with wide application in computing problems. While this book is not the place for a really general treatment of the graph, we can introduce the mathematical structure and go from it to a discussion of directed graphs.

A *directed graph* consists of a set of points, or *vertices*, and a set of arcs, or *edges*, which represent connections between the points. We will consider a number of important mathematical properties of directed graphs and look at some implementation methods. These implementations are the *adjacency matrix*, the *adjacency list*, the *weighted adjacency matrix*, and the *state table*.

You will learn two important traversal algorithms for directed graphs. A *traversal* is a "walk" around a graph in a systematic fashion, in such a way that each vertex is officially "touched," or visited, exactly once. The algorithms to be introduced are called *depth-first search* and *breadth-first search*. These algorithms use the generic packages for sets and queues developed in earlier chapters.

The "Application" section of this chapter shows how to build a very simple lexical scanner, representing it as a state table.

One of the most important characteristics of the directed graph is that the *tree*, to be introduced in Chapter 11, is a special case of the graph.

10.1   UNDIRECTED AND DIRECTED GRAPHS

A *graph G* is an ordered pair of sets <*V, E*>, where *V* is a set of *vertices* (which may be thought of as points) and *E* is a set of *edges* (which may be thought of as lines connecting the points). Other authors refer to vertices as *points* or, frequently, *nodes*; they

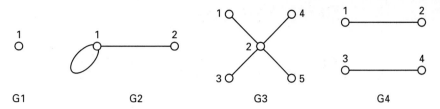

Figure 10.1 Some Undirected Graphs

sometimes refer to edges as *arcs*. An edge is given as a pair $\{m, n\}$, where m and n are in the vertex set *V*. Notice that no direction is given to the edge, so $\{m, n\}$ and $\{n, m\}$ really represent the same edge.

Figure 10.1 shows some undirected graphs. This is all we will do with undirected graphs, since in this book we are interested mainly in directed graphs, or graphs in which the edges have direction.

A *directed graph G* (often abbreviated *digraph*) is a graph $G = <V, E>$. In a digraph an edge is given as an *ordered pair* $<s, d>$, where *s* and *d* are in the vertex set *V*. The vertex *s* is called the *source* vertex; the vertex *d* is called the *destination* vertex. This imposes a certain directionality on the edge; that is why *G* is called a directed graph.

Figure 10.2 shows some directed graphs. Note that in graph *G1*, the edge $<1, 3>$, for example, is not the same as the edge $<3, 1>$, because even though they connect the same pair of vertices, the direction is different.

For convenience later, we will write *sGd* to mean "the edge $<s, d>$ is in the edge set of *G*." If *sGd*, we say that *d is adjacent to s*. The set of all vertices adjacent to *s* is called the *adjacency set* of *s*.

10.2 PROPERTIES OF DIGRAPHS

It is interesting to study a number of properties of digraphs that have important applications. In defining these properties, we will always use *G* to refer to an arbitrary digraph and lowercase letters to refer to vertices in *G*'s vertex set. Also, the abbreviation *iff* will be used—as is common in mathematics—to mean *if and only if*.

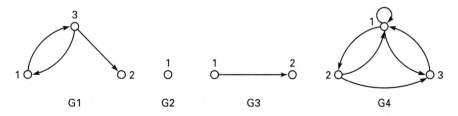

Figure 10.2 Some Directed Graphs

Reflexivity

G is *reflexive* iff *xGx* for all vertices *x* in *V*. If we refer to <*x*, *x*> as a *self-loop*, then *G* is reflexive iff every vertex in *G*'s vertex set has a self-loop.

Irreflexivity

G is *irreflexive* if no vertex has a self-loop. Note that it is quite possible for *G* to be neither reflexive nor irreflexive. This will be true if some vertices, but not all, have self-loops. Be careful not to confuse the assertion "*G* is not reflexive" with the assertion "*G* is irreflexive."

Figure 10.3 shows some digraphs that are reflexive, some that are irreflexive, and some that are neither.

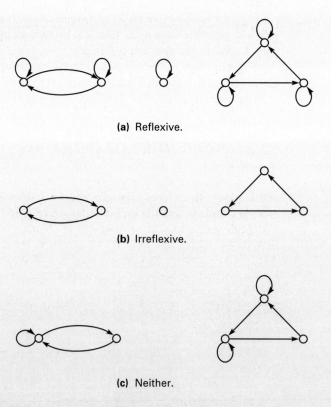

(a) Reflexive.

(b) Irreflexive.

(c) Neither.

Figure 10.3 Reflexivity and Irreflexivity

Symmetry

G is *symmetric* iff for every case where *xGy* it is also true that *yGx*. Note carefully that this does not say that every pair of vertices must be connected by an edge, but only that *if* there is an edge <*x*, *y*>, *then* there must be an edge <*y*, *x*> for *G* to be symmetric. For example, a digraph consisting of a single vertex with no edges is symmetric. Such a digraph is possible because nothing in the definition of a graph requires *E* to be nonempty. You might consider this to be a "pathological" situation, but it does make the point.

Antisymmetry

G is *antisymmetric* iff *xGy* and *yGx* imply *x* = *y*. This is a way of saying that no two distinct vertices have edges in both directions, but that self-loops are permitted. As in the case of reflexivity, be careful with your language: Saying "*G* is not symmetric" is *not* the same as saying "*G* is antisymmetric," since *G* may have some pairs of vertices with edges both ways and some pairs with edges only one way. In this case, *G* is neither symmetric nor antisymmetric. To get pathological again, it is interesting that the digraph with one vertex and no edges is both symmetric and antisymmetric!

Some authors do not permit antisymmetric graphs to have any vertices with self-loops. This would make the definition simpler: We could just say that if we have *xGy*, then we cannot have *yGx*. On the other hand, in that case a reflexive graph could never be antisymmetric—indeed, an antisymmetric graph would necessarily be irreflexive—and this would mix up two properties that we prefer to keep independent.

In Figure 10.4, you can see some symmetric digraphs, some antisymmetric ones, and some that are neither.

Transitivity

G is *transitive* iff for each triple of vertices such that *xGy* and *yGz*, it is true that *xGz*. In other words, if we can get from *x* to *z* by way of *y*, we can get there directly if *G* is transitive. Note again that this does not mean that there must ever be edges <*x*, *y*> and <*y*, *z*>. It says only that if there are, then if *G* is to be transitive there must be an edge <*x*, *z*>. There is also no requirement that *x*, *y*, and *z* be distinct, so that self-loops must be considered in determining transitivity. Is it possible for a digraph to be symmetric and transitive without being reflexive?

Figure 10.5 shows some transitive digraphs and some others that (as it is explained) are not transitive.

Paths

A *path* is a sequence of edges <v_1, v_2>, <v_2, v_3>, . . ., <v_{k-1}, v_k>—that is, a sequence of edges such that the destination of one is the source of the next. The path is *simple* iff all

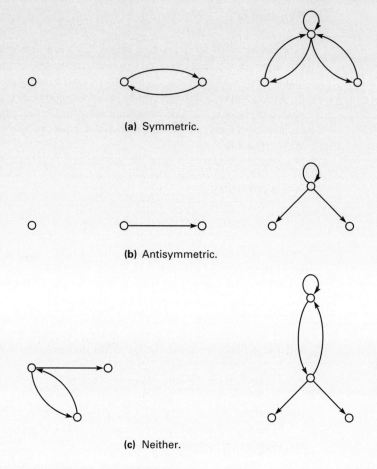

(a) Symmetric.

(b) Antisymmetric.

(c) Neither.

Figure 10.4 Symmetry and Antisymmetry

vertices in the path, except possibly for the first and the last, are distinct. The *length* of the path is the number of edges (not vertices) in it. Thus, a single edge $<x, y>$ is a path of length 1. Note that a self-loop $<x, x>$ is a path of length 1. If there is a path from x to y, we say that y is *reachable* from x.

Cycles

A *cycle* is a path such that the destination of the last edge is the source of the first edge (it gets back to where it started). Note, then, that a self-loop is a cycle of length 1. A digraph is *acyclic* if it has no cycles in it. A *simple cycle* is a simple path that is a cycle.

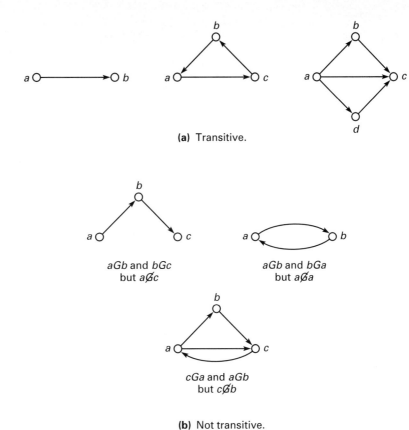

(a) Transitive.

aGb and *bGc*
but *aⱠc*

aGb and *bGa*
but *aⱠa*

cGa and *aGb*
but *cⱠb*

(b) Not transitive.

Figure 10.5 Transitivity

Connectivity

Intuitively, a graph (directed or otherwise) is *connected* iff it is "all one piece." In other words, a digraph is connected iff, treating all edges as though they were two-way, we can find a path from any vertex to any other. The "pieces" of a graph that is in several pieces are called *connected components*.

Strong Connectivity

A digraph *G* is *strongly connected* iff from each vertex there is at least one path (not necessarily of length 1!) to all the other vertices, even if we take directionality into account. Can a strongly connected digraph ever be acyclic?

Strong connectivity differs from connectivity in that in determining strong connectivity, we examine the graph as it is; in determining ordinary connectivity, we ignore the directions on the edges.

Figure 10.6 illustrates connectivity and strong connectivity.

In-Degree and Out-Degree

The *in-degree* of a vertex z in a digraph G is the number of edges that have z as their destination (visually, the number of arrowheads arriving at z). The *out-degree* of a vertex z is the number of edges with z as their source (or the number of arrowtails leaving z). Note that these two properties apply to an individual vertex, not to the graph as a whole.

10.3   IMPLEMENTATIONS OF DIRECTED GRAPHS

In this section, we will look at several of the common ways of implementing directed graphs in programs. These are the adjacency matrix, the adjacency list, the weighted adjacency matrix, and the state graph.

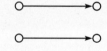

(a) Not connected.

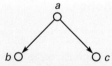

(b) Connected but not strongly connected
(a cannot be reached from b or c).

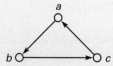

(c) Strongly connected.

Figure 10.6 Connectivity and Strong Connectivity

Adjacency Matrix

The most straightforward way to represent a digraph G with K vertices is by a $K \times K$ Boolean matrix G ', called the *adjacency matrix*, where G'(x, y) is True iff xGy and False otherwise. In this representation, row x of the matrix indicates the adjacency set of vertex x.

In this matrix, it is easy to determine whether y is adjacent to x and this is done in $O(1)$ time, since only a subscript calculation is involved. However, a disadvantage of using this scheme is that even if the graph has few edges, K^2 cells are needed to store it and any algorithm to examine the whole graph, or even read or print it, must be $O(N^2)$. A digraph and its adjacency matrix are given in Figure 10.7.

Adjacency List

In most graphs, the vertices have relatively small adjacency sets, so the adjacency matrix is sparse, and most of its elements are false. For this reason, a variant of the sparse-matrix technique is often used to implement a digraph. This representation is the adjacency list. Each vertex x is a header for a linear list, each cell of which represents a

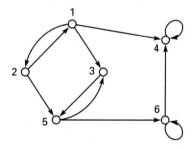

(a) A digraph

	1	2	3	4	5	6
1	F	T	T	T	F	F
2	T	F	F	F	T	F
3	F	F	F	F	T	F
4	F	F	F	T	F	F
5	F	F	T	F	F	T
6	F	F	F	T	F	T

(b) Adjacency matrix for this diagram

Figure 10.7 Adjacency Matrix for a Digraph

destination vertex for edges leaving x. The headers can be stored in an array. This structure is shown in Figure 10.8.

Assuming that Booleans, pointers, and integers identifying vertices all occupy the same number of bytes of storage, when is this scheme more economical than an adjacency matrix? Let L be the average number of cells in a single vertex list. The pointer array requires K cells, each of one storage unit; each list cell requires two storage units and there are $K \times L$ such cells. So the structure requires $K + (2 \times K \times L)$ or $K \times (1 + 2 \times L)$ storage units. To find the crossover point, we set $K^2 = K \times (1 + 2 \times L)$, or $L = (K - 1)/2$.

The assumption we just made—that Booleans, pointers, and vertex identifiers are all the same size—is often wrong. Many programming languages, including Ada, give the programmer a way of implementing an array of Booleans in such a way that each array entry is represented by a single bit. In such a situation, the "dense" matrix (two-dimensional array) can be considerably more economical in its use of space than the "sparse" matrix (list).

We cannot neglect differences in time performance, though. To print the entire adjacency list takes $O(K \times L)$ operations, which is usually much less than $K \times K$. On the other hand, simply determining whether xGy requires $O(L)$ operations (on the average), whereas it was $O(1)$ in the adjacency matrix representation. We have here another clear example of the trade-offs inherent in selecting implementations for abstract objects.

Weighted Adjacency Matrix

The implementations just described give the *structure* of a digraph, but provide no information about its *content*. In many graph applications, vertices or edges are associated with data values of one kind or another. These are often called *weights*. For example, Figure 10.9 contains a digraph with numbers attached to its edges.

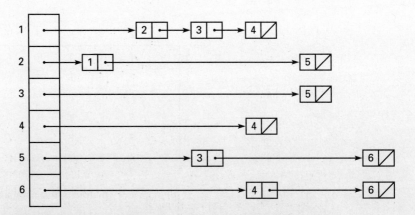

Figure 10.8 Adjacency List Structure for Digraph of Figure 10.7

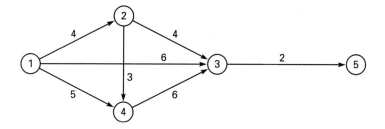

(a) A weighted digraph.

	1	2	3	4	5
1	0	4	6	5	0
2	0	0	4	3	0
3	0	0	0	0	2
4	0	0	6	0	0
5	0	0	0	0	0

(b) Weighted adjacency matrix for this digraph.

Figure 10.9 Weighted Digraph and Weighted Adjacency Matrix

One interpretation of such a number might be the distance between points on a graph representing a road map. Another interpretation might be the time required to perform a certain task in a complex project. Yet another interpretation is the number of flights from city *A* to city *B* in an airline service table such as the Cloud Nine service table of Figure 4.2. Implementing such a weighted graph is a straightforward extension of the adjacency matrix: Each entry of the matrix contains the weight, instead of just a Boolean; entries that correspond to missing edges contain some indication to that effect, for example zero or null.

Weights can also be used in the list implementation: Weights for edges emanating from a given vertex are just stored in the vertices of the corresponding adjacency list.

State Table

A special kind of weighted digraph, the *state graph*, comes from the field of abstract machine theory. It is useful in hardware design and also in building language translators. Section 10.9 will discuss an application of state graphs, but here we limit ourselves to a description of the structure. We will also return to state graphs in Chapter 11.

In most cases, the weights in a weighted digraph can be arbitrary values. In a state graph, however, it is required that the weights be a (usually small) discrete set of values, for example the letters of the alphabet or the numeric characters.

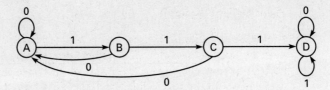

Figure 10.10 A State Graph

The graph is implemented as a two-dimensional array, with a row for each vertex and a column for each *weight*. Each row represents a source vertex; entries in the matrix represent *destination vertices*, not weights as before. For an example, look at the graph in Figure 10.10. The vertices of this state graph are called *A, B, C,* and *D*; the weights are just the digits 0 and 1. The corresponding state table is shown in Figure 10.11.

10.4 GRAPH TRAVERSALS

Some applications of graphs require the graph to be traversed. (As we have mentioned, this means that, starting from some designated vertex, the graph is "walked around" in a systematic way such that every vertex reachable from that starting vertex is officially "touched" or visited, exactly once.) Two frequently-used traversal algorithms are called *depth-first search* (DFS) and *breadth-first search* (BFS).

The DFS algorithm finds all graph vertices reachable from a particular starting vertex, in a way that explores a given path from the starting vertex before starting another path. The search strategy, then, is to probe deeper and deeper along a path; hence, the designation *depth-first*.

The BFS algorithm visits all vertices adjacent to the starting vertex, then visits all vertices adjacent to those vertices, and so on. Since all adjacent vertices are visited before probing farther away, the search is broad rather than deep; hence, the name *breadth-first*.

These algorithms are introduced in this section and programs are given for them.

	0	1
A	A	B
B	A	C
C	A	D
D	D	D

Figure 10.11 A State Table

Depth-First Search

A traversal algorithm requires that each vertex be *officially* visited exactly once. Since a vertex can be adjacent to many other vertices, and since graphs can have cycles, we need a way of keeping track of the vertices that have already been visited. Accordingly, the DFS algorithm uses an auxiliary set, called *Visited*, which is initially empty. A vertex of *G* is added to the set when it is visited. The algorithm is recursive and operates as follows:

Algorithm for DFS

1. Place the designated starting vertex *x* in the set *Visited*.

2. Do whatever application-dependent things need to be done upon visiting a vertex.

3. For each vertex *y* adjacent to *x*, if *y* has not been visited, call DFS recursively with *y* as the starting vertex.

   This algorithm pursues a given path until a previously visited vertex is reached, then returns to the original vertex and pursues another path. If it terminates with the entire vertex set in *Visited*, all vertices were reachable from the given starting vertex.

   Figure 10.12 shows an example of DFS in action.

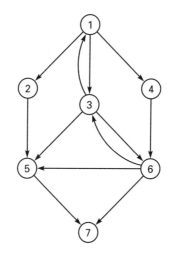

(a) A directed graph.

```
starting at 1 : 1-2-5-7-3-6-4
starting at 2 : 2-5-7
(graph isn't strongly connected, so only
    three nodes are visited!)
starting at 3 : 3-1-2-5-7-4-6
```

(b) Some depth-first searches of the digraph.

Figure 10.12 Depth-First Search on a Graph

Breadth-First Search

In BFS, we start from a vertex x and first visit all vertices adjacent to x. Then all vertices adjacent to those vertices are visited, and so on. We use a queue to keep track of vertices we have visited but whose adjacent vertices we haven't yet visited. The same set *Visited* is used to keep a record of visited vertices.

Algorithm for BFS

1. Make the queue Q empty.

2. Place the designated starting vertex x in the set *Visited*.

3. Enqueue x on Q.

4. Do whatever application-dependent things need to be done upon visiting a vertex.

5. Repeat Steps 6 and 7 until Q is empty:

   6. Dequeue a value y from Q.

   7. FOR each vertex z adjacent to y, LOOP

      IF z is not in *Visited* THEN

        Place z in *Visited*

        Do the application-dependent task for z

        Enqueue z on Q

      END IF

   END LOOP

Figure 10.13 shows examples of BFS.

10.5   A GENERIC ADT FOR DIRECTED GRAPHS

Program 10.1 gives the specification for a generic package for directed graphs, using the adjacency matrix representation. Note that the vertex set is permitted to be any discrete (integer or enumeration) type and that the adjacency matrix is doubly indexed by the vertex set used as a generic parameter.

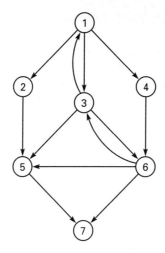

(a) A directed graph.

```
starting at 1 : 1-2-3-4-5-6-7
starting at 3 : 3-1-5-6-2-4-7
```

(b) Some breadth-first searches of the digraph.

Figure 10.13 Breadth-First Search on a Graph

Program 10.1 Specification for Generic Digraphs Package

```
GENERIC

  TYPE Vertices IS (<>);

PACKAGE Digraphs_Generic IS
---------------------------------------------------------------------
--| Specification for unweighted digraphs with discrete vertex sets
--| Author: Michael B. Feldman, The George Washington University
--| Last Modified: January 1996
---------------------------------------------------------------------

  TYPE Digraph IS LIMITED PRIVATE;

  -- constructors

  PROCEDURE InitializeGraph (G: IN OUT Digraph);
  -- Pre:  none
  -- Post: G has no edges

  PROCEDURE AddEdge
    (G: IN OUT Digraph; Source, Destination: IN Vertices);
  PROCEDURE DeleteEdge
    (G: IN OUT Digraph; Source, Destination: IN Vertices);
  -- Pre:  G, Source, and Destination are defined
  -- Post: returns G with the edge <Source, Destination> added or
  --       deleted respectively; AddEdge has no effect if the edge is
  --       already in G; DeleteEdge has no effect if edge is not in G
```

```
FUNCTION IsEmpty (G: Digraph) RETURN Boolean;
-- Pre:  G is defined
-- Post: returns True if and only if G has no edges

FUNCTION NumberOfEdges (G: Digraph) RETURN Natural;
-- Pre:  G is defined
-- Post: returns the number of edges in G

FUNCTION IsAdjacent (G: Digraph; Source, Destination: Vertices)
  RETURN Boolean;
-- Pre:  G, Source, and Destination are defined
-- Post: returns True if and only if
--       G has an edge <Source, Destination>

PROCEDURE DisplayGraph(G: Digraph);
-- Pre:  G is defined
-- Post: displays G in matrix form using T or F
--       for presence or absence of edge

GENERIC
  WITH PROCEDURE Visit(V: Vertices);
PROCEDURE Traverse_BFS (G: IN Digraph; Start: Vertices);
-- Pre:  G and V are defined
-- Post: performs breadth-first traversal of G starting at vertex V

GENERIC
  WITH PROCEDURE Visit(V: Vertices);
PROCEDURE Traverse_DFS (G: IN Digraph; Start: Vertices);
-- Pre:  G and V are defined
-- Post: performs depth-first traversal of G starting at vertex V

PRIVATE

TYPE AdjacencyMatrix IS ARRAY (Vertices, Vertices) OF Boolean;
TYPE Digraph IS RECORD
  Store: AdjacencyMatrix := (Others => (OTHERS => False));
END RECORD;

END Digraphs_Generic;
```

The two traversal operations warrant attention because they are themselves generic. Making a traversal operation generic allows it to be specialized to the kind of operation performed as each vertex is visited; instead of making `Visit` a generic parameter of the package, we make it a parameter of the traversals, so that several different instances of a traversal, each with its own `Visit`, can be created for the same instance of the overall package.

Program 10.2 gives the body of this package, with the traversal operations shown as subunits. The traversals use the generic packages for sets (Programs 5.15 and 5.16) and queues (Programs 7.1 and 7.2); the package body therefore contains the following instantiations:

```
PACKAGE VertexSets IS NEW Sets_Generic (Universe => Vertices);
USE VertexSets;

PACKAGE VertexQueues IS NEW Queues_Generic (Element => Vertices);
USE VertexQueues;
```

Program 10.2 Body of Generic Digraphs Package

```
WITH Sets_Generic;
WITH Queues_Generic;
WITH Text_IO;
PACKAGE BODY Digraphs_Generic IS
------------------------------------------------------------------------
--| Body for unweighted digraphs with discrete vertex sets
--| Author: Michael B. Feldman, The George Washington University
--| Last Modified: January 1996
------------------------------------------------------------------------
  PACKAGE VertexSets IS
    NEW Sets_Generic(Universe => Vertices);
  USE VertexSets;
  PACKAGE VertexQueues IS
    NEW Queues_Generic(Element => Vertices);
  USE VertexQueues;

  -- constructors

  PROCEDURE InitializeGraph (G: IN OUT Digraph) IS
  BEGIN
    G.Store := (OTHERS => (OTHERS => False));
  END InitializeGraph;

  PROCEDURE AddEdge
    (G: IN OUT Digraph; Source, Destination: IN Vertices) IS
  BEGIN
    G.Store(Source, Destination) := True;
  END AddEdge;

PROCEDURE DeleteEdge
    (G: IN OUT Digraph; Source, Destination: IN Vertices) IS
  BEGIN
    G.Store(Source, Destination) := False;
  END DeleteEdge;

  FUNCTION IsEmpty (G: Digraph) RETURN Boolean IS
  BEGIN
    FOR Row IN Vertices LOOP
      FOR Column IN Vertices LOOP
        IF G.Store(Row, Column) THEN
          RETURN False;
        END IF;
      END LOOP;
    END LOOP;
    RETURN True;
  END IsEmpty;

  FUNCTION NumberOfEdges (G: Digraph) RETURN Natural IS
    Total: Natural := 0;
  BEGIN
    FOR Row IN Vertices LOOP
      FOR Column IN Vertices LOOP
        IF G.Store(Row, Column) THEN
          Total := Total + 1;
        END IF;
      END LOOP;
    END LOOP;
    RETURN Total;
  END NumberOfEdges;
```

```
FUNCTION IsAdjacent (G: Digraph; Source, Destination: Vertices)
  RETURN Boolean
 IS
BEGIN
  RETURN G.Store(Source, Destination);
END IsAdjacent;

PROCEDURE DisplayGraph(G: Digraph) IS
BEGIN
  FOR Row IN Vertices LOOP
    FOR Column IN Vertices LOOP
      IF G.Store(Row, Column) THEN
        Text_IO.Put (Item => "T");
      ELSE
        Text_IO.Put (Item => "F");
      END IF;
    END LOOP;
    Text_IO.New_Line;
  END LOOP;
END DisplayGraph;

 PROCEDURE Traverse_BFS (G: IN Digraph; Start: Vertices) IS SEPARATE;

 PROCEDURE Traverse_DFS (G: IN Digraph; Start: Vertices) IS SEPARATE;
END Digraphs_Generic;
```

Program 10.3 shows the procedure `Traverse_DFS`; note that the set `Visited` is declared as an object of type `VertexSets`, and that `Traverse_DFS` contains an inner procedure `DepthFirst`. The inner procedure is called recursively; the set `Visited` is modified by each recursive call. We could have avoided the inner procedure by making `Visited` an IN OUT parameter of `Traverse_DFS`; we chose not to give the user responsibility for declaring and passing this set. In some applications, the client might wish to have access to this set after the traversal; you can make the necessary modifications to provide this.

Program 10.3 Depth-First Search Procedure

```
SEPARATE (Digraphs_Generic)
PROCEDURE Traverse_DFS (G: IN Digraph; Start: Vertices) IS
------------------------------------------------------------------------
--| Depth_First_Search, subunit of Digraphs_Generic
--| Author: Michael B. Feldman, The George Washington University
--| Last Modified: January 1996
------------------------------------------------------------------------

  Visited: VertexSets.Set;

  PROCEDURE DepthFirst (Start: Vertices) IS
  BEGIN
    Visit (Start);
    Visited := Visited + Start;
    FOR Destination IN Vertices LOOP
      IF IsAdjacent (G, Start, Destination) AND NOT
           IsIn (Visited, Destination) THEN
        DepthFirst (Start => Destination);
      END IF;
    END LOOP;
  END DepthFirst;
```

```
BEGIN
  DepthFirst(Start => Start);
END Traverse_DFS;
```

Program 10.4 gives the procedure `Traverse_BFS`. The queue `Q` is "sized" according to the number of vertices in the graph; clearly it can never contain more elements than there are vertices, because a vertex is added to the queue if and only if it has not been visited. Because the vertex set can be an enumeration type, we calculate the queue capacity by doing arithmetic on the positions of the first and last values of the vertex set.

Program 10.4 Breadth-First Search Procedure

```
SEPARATE (Digraphs_Generic)
PROCEDURE Traverse_BFS (G: IN Digraph; Start: Vertices) IS
-----------------------------------------------------------------------
--| Breadth_First_Search procedure, subunit of Digraphs_Generic
--| Author: Michael B. Feldman, The George Washington University
--| Last Modified: January 1996
-----------------------------------------------------------------------

  Visited   :       VertexSets.Set;
  Source, Dest : Vertices;
  Q    :            VertexQueues.Queue(Capacity =>
                        Vertices'Pos(Vertices'Last)
                     - Vertices'Pos(Vertices'First)
                     + 1);

BEGIN -- Traverse_BFS
  Visit (Start);
  Visited := Visited + Start;
  Enqueue (Q, start);
  WHILE NOT IsEmpty (Q) LOOP
    Source := First (Q);
    Dequeue (Q);
    FOR Dest IN Vertices LOOP
      IF IsAdjacent (G, Source, Dest) AND NOT IsIn (Visited, Dest) THEN
        Visit (Dest);
        Visited := Visited + Dest;
        Enqueue (Q, Dest);
      END IF;
    END LOOP;
  END LOOP;

END Traverse_BFS;
```

10.6   APPLICATION: A SIMPLE LEXICAL SCANNER

An Ada identifier consists of a letter followed by zero or more letters, digits, and underscore characters. In this section, we describe a program or algorithm capable of deciding whether an arbitrary string of characters is a valid Ada identifier. The program is a simple *lexical scanner*; lexical scanners are used for the initial phase of a language translation, for checking the validity of commands in an interactive system, and for other, similar applications.

_	invalid	(starts with _)
L	valid	
L5	valid	
5	invalid	(starts with a digit)
L	valid	
_L	invalid	(starts with _)
LL5L	valid	
L___5	valid	
L@5L	invalid	(contains @)
5LLL	invalid	(starts with a digit)

Figure 10.14 Valid and Invalid Words in a Language over a Limited Alphabet

We represent the scanner by a state graph. In this graph, one vertex is designated as the *start state* and two other vertices are designated as the *accepting* and *rejecting* states. A vertex that is a source is called a *current state*; a vertex that is a destination is called a *next state*. A weight is used to represent each possible character in the string.

The state graph operates as a little computer: It is started in its start state, "reads" the first character of the string, then moves to the next state corresponding to the character just seen. The next state thus becomes a current state. The machine reads another character, moves to a new state, and so on. If the machine is in its accepting state when the input string is empty, the string was a valid identifier; if it is in its rejecting state, the string had an invalid character in it.

To keep this example simple, we use a very small alphabet for our identifiers. The only letter allowed is L; the only digit is 5. Underscore characters are permitted; all illegal characters are represented by @. These are the only characters that ever appear in a string. A valid identifier must begin with a letter. Figure 10.14 gives a number of legal and illegal identifiers in this limited alphabet.

Figure 10.15 shows the state graph for this machine; Figure 10.16 gives a diagram of the state table.

In Figure 10.17 are shown some Ada type definitions and a variable for the state table implementation. Note the use of enumeration types to list the states (the vertex set of the graph) and the input alphabet (discrete set of weights).

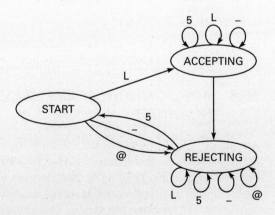

Figure 10.15 State Graph for Simple Scanner

	L	5	–	@
START	ACCEPTING	REJECTING	REJECTING	REJECTING
ACCEPTING	ACCEPTING	ACCEPTING	ACCEPTING	REJECTING
REJECTING	REJECTING	REJECTING	REJECTING	REJECTING

Figure 10.16 State Table for Simple Scanner

```
TYPE State IS (Start, Accepting, Rejecting);
TYPE InputClass IS (Letter, Digit, Underscore, Illegal);
TYPE StateTable IS ARRAY (State, InputClass) OF State;

SimpleID: StateTable :=
  ((Accepting, Rejecting, Rejecting, Rejecting),
   (Accepting, Accepting, Accepting, Rejecting),
   (Rejecting, Rejecting, Rejecting, Rejecting));
```

Figure 10.17 Type Definitions and a State Table

To make this data structure work as a machine, we need a program to "run" it. We'll write this as an Ada function `Valid_Ident`, which accepts a `VString` object, starts the state graph in its start state, then reads characters, returning a Boolean that indicates whether the input string was a valid identifier. Formally, a machine like this is called a *finite state machine*; in this case, the finite-state machine keeps running until its input string is empty; if it ever gets to the rejecting state, it keeps reading characters and cycling in that state until the input is empty. This program is shown in Program 10.5.

Program 10.5 A Simple Lexical Scanner

```
WITH VStrings; USE VStrings;
FUNCTION Valid_Ident (T : IN VString) RETURN Boolean IS
-----------------------------------------------------------------------
--| Simple Lexical Scanner to Determine Validity of an Identifier
--| Author: Michael B. Feldman, The George Washington University
--| Last Modified: January 1996
-----------------------------------------------------------------------
  TYPE State IS (Start, Accepting, Rejecting);
  TYPE InputClass IS (Letter, Digit, Underscore, Illegal);
  TYPE StateTable IS ARRAY (State, InputClass) OF State;
  SimpleID : StateTable :=
    ((Accepting, Rejecting, Rejecting, Rejecting),
     (Accepting,  Accepting, Accepting, Rejecting),
     (Rejecting,  Rejecting, Rejecting, Rejecting));
  S            : VString(MaxLength(T));
  C            : Character;
  Class        : InputClass;
  CurrentState : State;
```

```
BEGIN -- Valid_Ident
  S := T;
  CurrentState := Start;

  IF IsEmpty (S) THEN
    RETURN False;
  END IF;

  LOOP
    C := Head (S);

    IF C = 'L' THEN
      Class := Letter;
    ELSIF C = '5' THEN
      Class := Digit;
    ELSIF C = '_' THEN
      Class := Underscore;
    ELSE
      Class := Illegal;
    END IF;

    CurrentState := SimpleID (CurrentState, Class);

    S := Tail (S);
    EXIT WHEN IsEmpty (S);

  END LOOP;

  RETURN (CurrentState = Accepting);
END Valid_Ident;
```

We will return to the lexical scanner idea in Chapter 11, where we introduce a finite-state machine for scanning English text in order to build a cross-reference generator.

SUMMARY

Graphs have many uses: They are used to show relationships between elements in a set, for example, orderings or precedences, sequencing of activities in a project, sequences of characters in a string, and others. This book cannot treat graphs in a completely general way; graph theory and application is an entire mathematical discipline in itself. However, we have presented a number of important concepts of directed graphs: mathematical properties such as reflexivity, symmetry, transitivity, connectedness; traversals such as depth-first and breadth-first search; and a bit of application.

We are now ready to proceed to the study of *trees*, which are directed graphs with certain special properties. Chapters 11 and 12 consider trees at length.

EXERCISES

1. One interpretation of a digraph is a *relation* on a set. The vertices in the graph represent elements of the set; an edge from vertex *x* to vertex *y* means "*x* is related to *y*." A relation is called an *equivalence relation* if it is reflexive, transitive, and symmetric. Clearly a relation has these properties iff its digraph representation

does. Write a function to determine whether a graph G, implemented as an adjacency matrix, represents an equivalence relation.

2. A relation is called a *partial ordering* if it is reflexive, transitive, and antisymmetric. Using the graph interpretation from the preceding problem, write a function to determine whether a graph G represents a partial ordering.

3. Given a digraph with vertex set $\{A, B, C, D\}$ and edge set $\{<A, A>, <A, B>, <A, D>, <B, B>, <C, B>, <C, D>, <D, C>\}$, draw the graph and its adjacency matrix and adjacency list forms.

4. For the digraph specified in the preceding problem, indicate whether or not the graph has each of the following properties: reflexive, irreflexive, symmetric, antisymmetric, transitive, connected, strongly connected, acyclic. For each property the graph *does not* have, make a list of the *minimum* number of changes necessary to give the graph that property.

5. For the digraph specified above, find the depth-first and breadth-first searches starting with each of the four vertices.

6. Repeat the preceding three problems for the digraph with vertex set $\{A, B, C, D\}$ and edge set $\{<A, B>, <A, C>, <B, B>, <B, C>, <C, C>, <C, A>, <C, C>, <C, D>\}$.

7. Given a graph G represented by its unweighted adjacency matrix M, consider the matrix product of M with itself (the square of M) obtained by using *or* and *and* as the addition and multiplication operators in the matrix product. Calling this matrix MM, show that $MM(r, c)$ = True iff there is a path of length 2 or less from vertex r to vertex c.

8. Starting from the previous problem, show that in the matrix representing the pth power of M, a True entry in the rth row and cth column indicates that there is a path of length p or less from vertex r to vertex c of the matrix M.

9. Reimplement the generic digraph package so that it is possible to represent *weighted* digraphs. In this case, three generic parameters are needed: one for the vertex set, one for the vertex weights, and one for the edge weights. Be sure to take into account the need to indicate the absence of an edge; this can be some special value of the weight.

10. Construct a generic weighted digraph package that uses a sparse-matrix implementation for the graph.

CHAPTER 11

Binary Trees

A tree is a special case of a directed graph, with many applications in computing. More formally, a *tree* is just a connected digraph such that exactly one vertex (called the *root*) has an in-degree of 0 and all other vertices have an in-degree of 1. The consequence of this definition is that starting from the root, there is exactly one path to each of the other vertices. This makes a tree useful for representing hierarchical relationships.

This chapter focuses mainly on the important special case of the *binary tree*, in which no vertex has more than two outgoing edges. Two important applications of binary trees are the *expression tree*, which is used in translating or interpreting programming language statements; the other is the *binary search tree*, or BST, which is yet another implementation of a dynamic table.

An important concept in the study of trees is the *traversal*. As in directed graphs and other structures, a traversal is an algorithm for "walking around" the tree so that all its vertices are visited exactly once in some systematic sequence. There are many possible traversals; we shall study three of them. All are written as recursive algorithms.

There are three applications in this chapter. The first shows how to construct a parser for simple arithmetic expressions, the second gives a reimplementation of the generic table-handler package as a binary search tree, and the third shows how an indexing or cross-reference program can be constructed using a binary search tree.

Chapter 12 presents some useful, more advanced material on trees, based on the foundation presented in this chapter.

11.1 TREES

A tree is a special case of a directed graph whose main application is expressing purely hierarchical relationships of some kind. For example, Figure 11.1 shows the basic structure of a hypothetical company, with a single president, a few vice-presidents, some managers, and some workers.

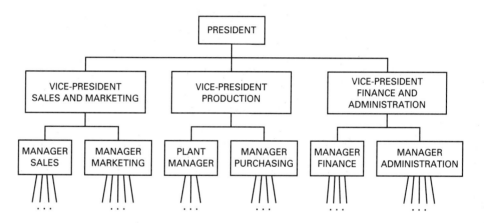

Figure 11.1 Hypothetical Corporate Structure

Figure 11.2 shows a family tree, representing three generations of descendants of one person.

Figure 11.3 illustrates the operator-operand relationship in a programming language assignment statement.

The common characteristics of all these examples are that there is a single vertex—the *root*—that can be identified as the "top" of the tree and that from the root to any other vertex in the tree there is *exactly one path*. Formally, a tree has these properties:

1. A tree is a *connected digraph*.

2. A tree has exactly one vertex with in-degree = 0. This vertex is called the *root*.

3. In a tree, all vertices except the root have in-degree = 1.

Notice that the definition says nothing about out-degree. In a general tree, there is no restriction on the out-degree of a vertex, nor indeed on whether the vertex set must

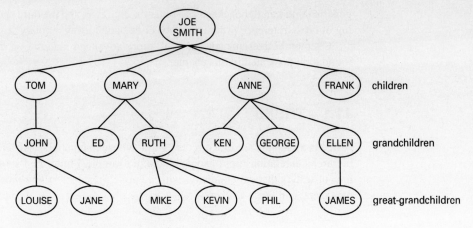

Figure 11.2 Descendants of Joe Smith

$$x := Y+Z-(A*B)/W)+G$$

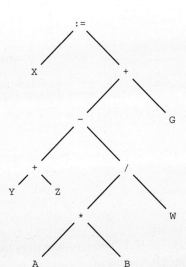

Figure 11.3 Operator-Operand Relationships in an Arithmetic Assignment
Statement

even be finite. In most of the important applications, however, the tree has a finite number of vertices, so there is necessarily a subset of the vertex set with out-degree = 0. These vertices are at the "bottom" of the tree; we call them *leaves* or sometimes *terminal* vertices. The remaining vertices are called *interior* or sometimes *nonterminal* vertices. In this book, you can assume that all trees are finite.

Look at Figure 11.4 and make sure you understand why the structures in Figure 11.4a are trees and those in Figure 11.4b are not.

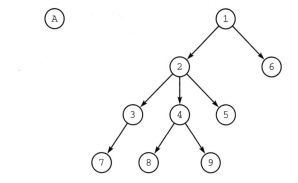

(a) These digraphs are trees.

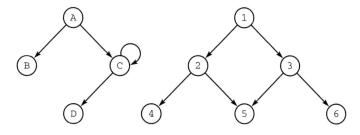

(b) These digraphs are not trees.

Figure 11.4 Some Trees and Some Digraphs That Are Not Trees

Because a tree is a digraph, it makes sense to consider which graph properties pertain to trees. Because a vertex of a tree has at most one edge leading to it, all trees have certain graph properties and lack others. For instance, because there is *at most* one path from any vertex to any other vertex, and because there is *exactly* one path from the root to any leaf, a tree is necessarily antisymmetric and irreflexive; we leave consideration of other graph properties as an exercise.

From the way we have defined trees, the vertex at the destination end of an edge for which the root is the source is itself the root of a tree. We shall call this structure a *subtree*. Note that a single vertex, by itself, is a tree.

The *depth* of a tree is defined to be the length of the longest of the paths from the root to the various leaves. The *level* of a vertex is the length of the path (remember, there is only one path!) from the root to that vertex. The level of the root itself is then 0. Figure 11.5 shows some trees and indicates their depths.

Drawing some terminology from genealogical (family) trees, we will refer to the destination vertices of a vertex as its *children*, and to a vertex from which one or more children grow as the *parent* of those children. Children of the same parent are referred to as *siblings*, and all vertices reachable from a given vertex are called that vertex's *descendants*. Also, note that a child of any vertex is itself the root of a tree. That tree is called a subtree of the parent.

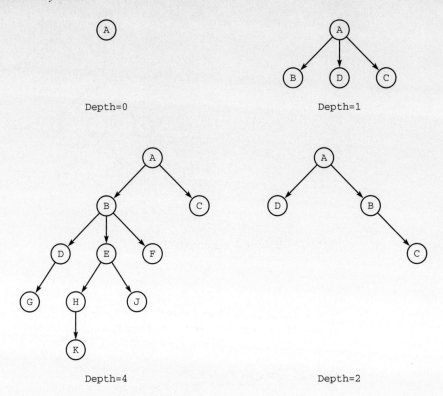

Figure 11.5 Some Trees and Their Depths

Despite the genealogical terminology, the analogy with family trees is imperfect, though, because whereas humans and most animals have precisely two parents, a vertex in our type of trees has precisely *one* parent!

In applications of trees in computing, there is often information associated with each of the vertices of a tree. Obviously, the nature and interpretation of this information depend on the application; we will refer to it generically by a number of names—for example, *label*, *data*, *value*, or *key*.

In general, we do not bother to draw the arrowheads on the edges of a tree, but write the root at the top and "grow" the tree in a downward direction on the page. Thus, it is obvious which direction is meant. Also, it is sometimes convenient to omit the circle indicating a vertex, simply writing the data instead, as in Figure 11.6.

We will return to the subject of general trees in Chapter 12; for now, let us limit our attention to the special and useful case of *binary trees*.

11.2 PROPERTIES OF BINARY TREES

A *binary tree* is a tree all of whose vertices have out-degree ≤ 2. Furthermore, the subtrees of a binary tree are *ordered* in the sense that there is a *left* child and a *right* child. If a vertex has only one child, it must be clearly identified as left or right. The two trees

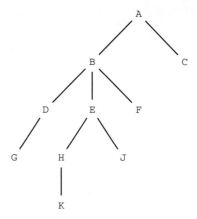

Figure 11.6 Simplified Tree Notation

shown in Figure 11.7a are different binary trees; so are the two trees in Figure 11.7b. Here are two important properties of binary trees.

Strictly Binary

T is a *strictly binary tree* iff each of its vertices has out-degree = 0 or out-degree = 2. Vertices with out-degree = 1 are not allowed in strictly binary trees.

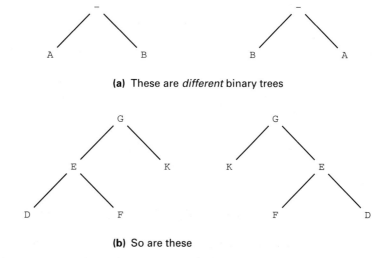

(a) These are *different* binary trees

(b) So are these

Figure 11.7 Binary Trees Have Ordered Children

Balanced

Intuitively, a binary tree is *balanced* if it is not "heavy" on either side. There are several alternative balance conditions, each with its areas of application. For our purposes here, we will say that T is a balanced (sometimes called *height-balanced*) binary tree iff for each vertex v in T, the depths of v's right and left subtrees differ by at most one. If one subtree is null, the other subtree must either be null or be a leaf.

It is important to understand that for a tree to be balanced, the property must hold for every vertex in the tree, not just its root. For all the trees in Figure 11.8, make sure you know why each is either balanced or not balanced.

The definition of balance can also be stated recursively:

1. A binary tree consisting of a single vertex is balanced.

2. A vertex with a single subtree is balanced iff that subtree is a leaf.

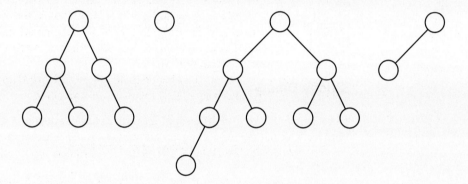

(a) These binary trees are height-balanced.

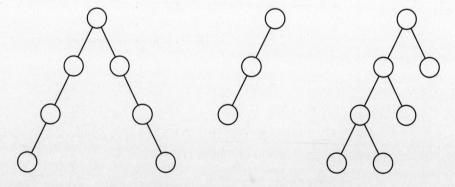

(b) These binary trees are not height-balanced.

Figure 11.8 Balanced (or Height-Balanced) Binary Trees

3. A binary tree is balanced iff its left and right subtrees are balanced and their depths differ by at most 1.

Balance is an important property of binary search trees.

11.3   IMPLEMENTING BINARY TREES

Since a binary tree is really a digraph, we could implement it using one of the graph representations. However, it is usually better to make use of our knowledge that a binary tree has right and left subtrees and create a more specialized structure.

Accordingly, we represent each vertex as a linked node—that is, a record with an information field, a pointer to the left subtree, and a pointer to the right subtree. Thus, a tree can be built as a linked structure using either dynamic storage allocation, if such a feature is available in the coding language, or cursor allocation otherwise.

In Figure 11.9, we show some Ada type definitions for these vertices and pointers (using, of course, the built-in pointer and allocation facilities of the language).

A sequence of statements declaring and manipulating vertices is given in Figure 11.10, along with diagrams showing the results of each operation. For simplicity, we have used single characters to represent `InfoType`. Also recall that in Ada, pointer fields are initialized by default to `NULL`.

Generally, we will avoid drawing boxes to represent the vertices and simply use the more abstract diagrams, as in all the other previous examples.

11.4   TRAVERSALS OF BINARY TREES

Many applications require traversing a tree in a particular way so that all the vertices are visited in a certain order. Three traversal algorithms are particularly useful in dealing with binary trees. These are sometimes called *preorder*, *inorder*, and *postorder*, but different authors occasionally disagree on what these three terms should mean. To avoid any confusion, we will call these algorithms by names that are more descriptive once they are understood, namely `Traverse_NLR`, `Traverse_LNR`, and

```
TYPE InfoType IS ...;    -- some type

TYPE BinaryTreeNode;

TYPE Tree IS ACCESS BinaryTreeNode;

TYPE BinaryTreeNode IS RECORD
  Info: InfoType;
  Left: Tree;
  Right:Tree;
END;
```

Figure 11.9 Type Definitions for Binary Tree Node

Statement	Resulting Structure

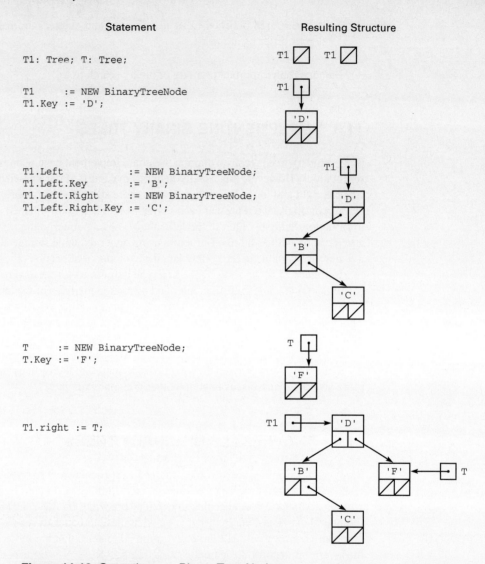

```
T1: Tree; T: Tree;
```

```
T1       := NEW BinaryTreeNode
T1.Key := 'D';
```

```
T1.Left             := NEW BinaryTreeNode;
T1.Left.Key         := 'B';
T1.Left.Right       := NEW BinaryTreeNode;
T1.Left.Right.Key := 'C';
```

```
T       := NEW BinaryTreeNode;
T.Key := 'F';
```

```
T1.right := T;
```

Figure 11.10 Operations on Binary Tree Nodes

Traverse_LRN, respectively. In these names, L stands for "left subtree," R stands for "right subtree," and N stands for "node." The order of the letters indicates the traversal order. For example, in Traverse_NLR, a node is visited, then its left subtree is traversed, then its right subtree is traversed; in Traverse_LNR, the left subtree is traversed before the node is visited, then the right subtree is traversed.

How do these algorithms work? Since a binary tree is recursively defined (every subtree of a binary tree is a binary tree), a traversal defined for a tree is also defined for any subtree. We can thus write the three traversal algorithms recursively, as shown in Figure 11.11. In each one, the details of the Visit operation are deferred, because precisely what Visit should accomplish is application-dependent.

```
PROCEDURE Traverse_NLR(T: Tree) IS

BEGIN
  IF T = NULL THEN
    RETURN;
  ELSE
    Visit(T);
    Traverse_NLR(T.left);
    Traverse_NLR(T.right);
  END IF;
END Traverse_NLR;

PROCEDURE Traverse_LNR(T: Tree) IS

BEGIN
  IF T = NULL THEN
    RETURN;
  ELSE
    Traverse_LNR(T.left);
    Visit(T);
    Traverse_LNR(T.right);
  END IF;
END Traverse_LNR;

PROCEDURE Traverse_LRN(T: Tree) IS

BEGIN
  IF T = NULL THEN
    RETURN;
  ELSE
    Traverse_LRN(T.left);
    Traverse_LRN(T.right);
    Visit(T);
  END IF;
END Traverse_LRN;
```

Figure 11.11 Recursive Tree Traversals

The three parts of Figure 11.12 show the steps in performing these three traversals for the given tree.

11.5 EXPRESSION TREES

One common application of binary trees is in interpreters or compilers for programming languages, where the statements of a source program are converted into trees so that the structure of the statements is apparent. As a simple case of this type, we will consider expression trees, which are transformations of arithmetic expressions into binary trees.

We will use, for simplicity, the same restricted expressions that we used in Chapter 7 in the discussion of stacks and RPN. Recall that an expression consists of single-letter identifiers or variable names, one-digit integer constants, the four arithmetic operators +, −, *, and /, and parentheses.

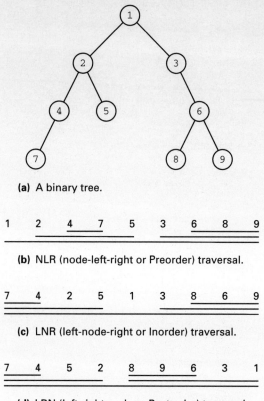

(a) A binary tree.

| 1 | 2 | 4 | 7 | 5 | 3 | 6 | 8 | 9 |

(b) NLR (node-left-right or Preorder) traversal.

| 7 | 4 | 2 | 5 | 1 | 3 | 8 | 6 | 9 |

(c) LNR (left-node-right or Inorder) traversal.

| 7 | 4 | 5 | 2 | 8 | 9 | 6 | 3 | 1 |

(d) LRN (left-right-node or Postorder) traversal.

Figure 11.12 Three Traversals of a Binary Tree

Constructing Expression Trees

The next section shows how to construct a scanner or parser program that can construct an expression tree for these simple expressions. For now, let us just see how to construct an expression tree manually. The general idea is very similar to the way we constructed an RPN expression from an infix one.

We consider first only fully parenthesized expressions. An expression tree always has an operator at its root and identifiers or constants at its leaves. (The exception is an expression consisting only of a single identifier or constant; here, there is just one vertex, both root and leaf.) The root operator is the "main" operator of the expression—that is, the operator that is performed *last* as the expression is evaluated. Interior vertices are the operators of subexpressions.

To give a few examples, Figure 11.13 shows the expression trees for A, A-B, (A-B)+C, A-(B+C), and (A+B)*(C-D). Notice carefully how these trees are constructed and make sure you understand well how (A-B)+C and A-(B+C) give

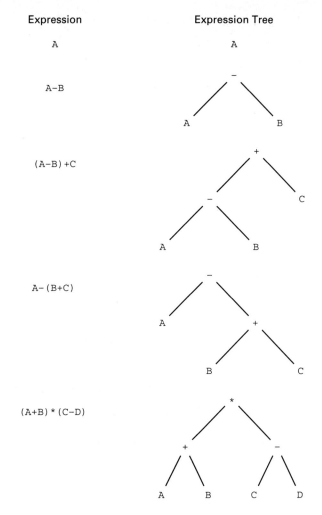

Expression	Expression Tree

Figure 11.13 Some Expression Trees

rise to *different* trees. In `(A–B)+C`, the + is the main operation, since it is performed last; in `A–(B+C)`, it is the – that is the main operation.

Try building expression trees from `(A*B)–(C+(D/E))` and `((A–B)+(C/D))*E` to make sure you understand how these trees are produced.

As we did in Chapter 7, let us now relax the condition that expressions must be fully parenthesized. We use the association and priority rules developed in Chapter 7: + and – are priority 2 operators, * and / are priority 1 operators, and adjacent operators of equal priority associate left-to-right. The expression `A+B*C` will be treated as though it were parenthesized `A+(B*C)`; `A/B–C` will be evaluated as though it were parenthesized `(A/B)–C`. So in the first expression the main operator is + and in the second it is –. Their expression trees are as shown in Figure 11.14.

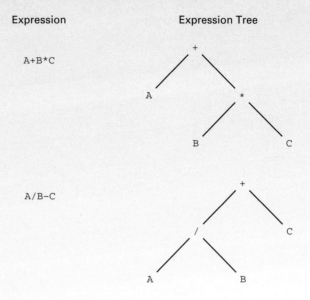

Expression   Expression Tree

A+B*C

A/B-C

Figure 11.14 More Expression Trees

Using the left-to-right rule in the case of equal-priority operators, A-B-C is treated as though it were written (A-B)-C and A/B*C is treated as though it were written (A/B)*C.

As we did in Chapter 7, let's look at expressions containing a mixture of parentheses and operators of both priorities. Consider first A+B-C+D. Since adjacent operators of equal priority are handled left-to-right, we treat it as though it were ((A+B)-C)+D. Now look at A-(B+C)*D. As before, the two operators of interest are - and * (the + doesn't count because it's inside a subexpression) and the * is done first because its priority is 1. So this expression is handled as though it were A-((B+C)*D). These trees are shown in Figure 11.15. Try A-B*C/(D-E) and A*B-(C+D)+E.

Traversing Expression Trees

The three parts of Figure 11.16 show the three traversals Traverse_NLR, Traverse_LNR, and Traverse_LRN performed on the given expression trees. It is interesting that Traverse_NLR produces the forward Polish, or prefix, form of the original expression, and Traverse_LRN produces the RPN form.

What about Traverse_LNR? This traversal turns out not to be terribly useful for expression trees, since it produces an infix form of the expression *with the parentheses removed*. Thus, it can lead to ambiguities, since, for example, the expressions (A-(B-C)) and ((A-B)-C), which clearly have different expression trees, have the same Traverse_LNR infix form, namely A-B-C. Indeed, if numerical values were substituted for A, B, and C, the two original expressions would evaluate to different results, only one of which would result from evaluating the infix form.

Expression   Expression Tree

A+B−C+D

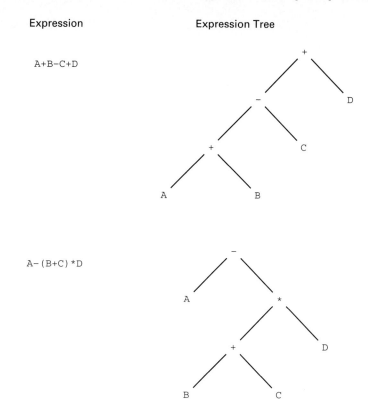

A−(B+C)*D

Figure 11.15 Still More Expression Trees

Note that no similar ambiguities arise in the prefix and postfix cases. Even though `Traverse_LNR` is not very useful for expression trees, we will see in the next section that it does have a very useful application.

You have seen that there is an intimate relationship between an infix expression, its tree, and its forward and reverse Polish forms. In compiler applications, some form of the expression tree is often used as a convenient intermediate internal representation of a program. An expression tree is a structure that can easily be manipulated by a program and can even be restructured to optimize the object-program instructions that are generated.

11.6   APPLICATION: BUILDING AN EXPRESSION TREE

In Section 7.6, a function was developed to translate an arithmetic expression to its RPN form. It turns out that the algorithm to produce the expression tree is very similar, and the decision process for pushing and popping operators on and off the stack is exactly the same.

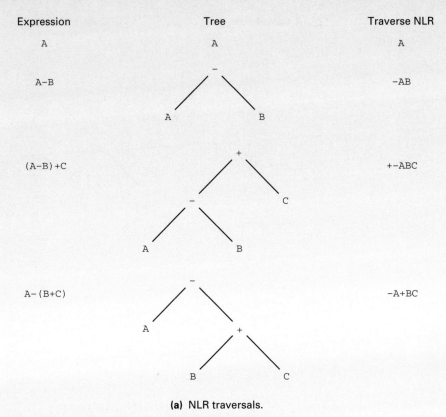

(a) NLR traversals.

Figure 11.16 Traversals of Expression Trees

There is a difference, though. In the previous case, when an operand (letter or number) was scanned, it was immediately output (concatenated to the RPN string). Similarly, an operator that was popped from the stack was immediately output.

In this situation, we need to retain those operands and operators, connecting them together in a tree. We do this by maintaining a separate stack for intermediate tree results, letting items in the stack be pointers to subtrees instead of just characters. Our operator stack is also converted to hold pointers to tree nodes; an operator is placed in such a node before being pushed.

At the end of the algorithm, a pointer to the root of the resultant tree is left on top of the node stack. Figure 11.17 shows the conversion of an expression to a tree. All the details of the nodes are illustrated.

An Ada function for the translator is given as Program 11.1. This function needs the following type definitions:

```
TYPE TreeNode;
TYPE Tree IS ACCESS TreeNode;
TYPE TreeNode IS RECORD
   Info: Character;
   Left: Tree;
   Right: Tree;
END RECORD;
```

Expression	Tree	Traverse LNR

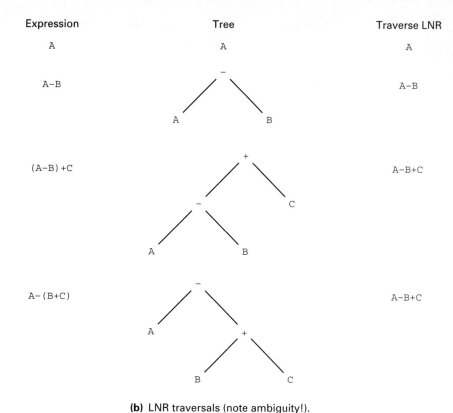

(b) LNR traversals (note ambiguity!).

Figure 11.16 (*Continued*)

and the following instantiation of the generic stacks package:

```
PACKAGE TreeStacks IS NEW Stacks_Generic (Element => Tree);
USE TreeStacks;
```

Program 11.1 Expression-to-Tree Translator

```
FUNCTION Exp_to_Tree (X : VString) RETURN Tree IS
-------------------------------------------------------------------
--| Function to Convert Infix Expression to Expression Tree
--| Author: Michael B. Feldman, The George Washington University
--| Last Modified: January 1996
-------------------------------------------------------------------
   C         : Character;
   T         : VString(MaxLength(X)) := X;
   OpStack   : Stack(Capacity => Length(T));
   NodeStack : Stack(Capacity => Length(T));
   Temp      : Tree := NULL;

PROCEDURE PopConnectPush IS
BEGIN
   Temp := Top (OpStack);
```

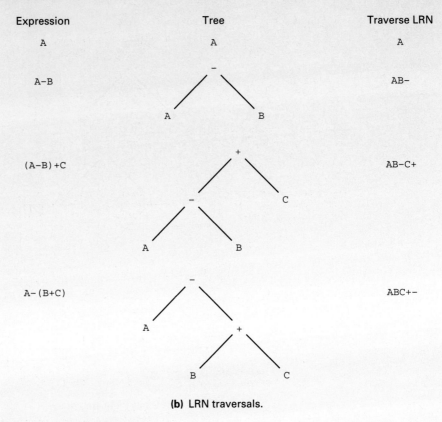

Expression	Tree	Traverse LRN
A	A	A
A–B		AB–
(A–B)+C		AB–C+
A–(B+C)		ABC+–

(b) LRN traversals.

Figure 11.16 (*Continued*)

```
      Pop (OpStack);
      Temp.Right := Top (NodeStack);
      Pop (NodeStack);
      Temp.left := Top (NodeStack);
      Pop (NodeStack);
      Push (NodeStack, Temp);
   END PopConnectPush;

BEGIN -- Exp_to_Tree
   IF IsEmpty (T) THEN
      RETURN NULL;
   END IF;
   LOOP
      C := Head (T);

      CASE C IS
         WHEN 'A' . . 'Z' | 'a' . . 'z' | '0' . . '9' =>
            Push (NodeStack, MakeNode (C));

         WHEN '+' | '-' | '*' | '/' =>
            IF IsEmpty (OpStack) THEN
               Push (OpStack, MakeNode (C));
            ELSIF Top (OpStack).Info = '(' THEN
```

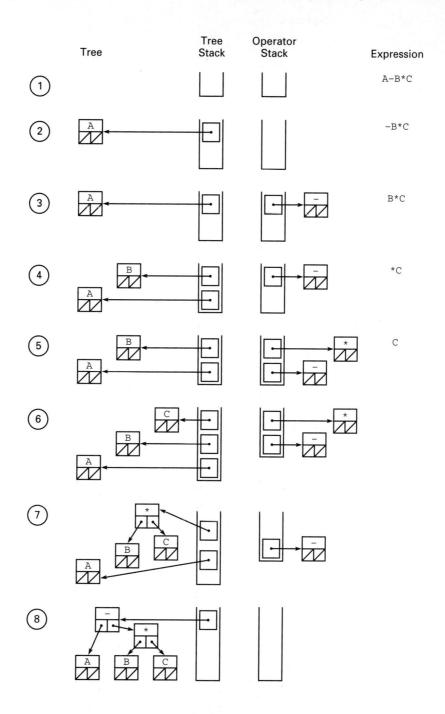

Figure 11.17 Translation of Infix Expression to Tree

```
                Push (OpStack, MakeNode (C));
            ELSIF Priority (Top (OpStack).Info) < Priority (C) THEN
              Push (OpStack, MakeNode (C));
            ELSE
              LOOP -- clear stack of higher priority operators
                PopConnectPush;
                EXIT WHEN IsEmpty (OpStack)
                  OR ELSE Top (OpStack).Info = '('
                  OR ELSE Priority (Top (OpStack).Info) < Priority (C);
              END LOOP;
              Push (OpStack, MakeNode (C));
            END IF;

          WHEN '(' =>
            Push (OpStack, MakeNode (C));

          WHEN ')' =>
            WHILE Top (OpStack).Info /= '(' LOOP
              PopConnectPush;
            END LOOP;
            Pop (OpStack); -- throw away the '('

          WHEN OTHERS =>
            NULL;
        END CASE;

      T := Tail (T);
      EXIT WHEN IsEmpty (T);
    END LOOP;

    WHILE NOT IsEmpty (OpStack) LOOP
      PopConnectPush;
    END LOOP;

    RETURN Top (NodeStack);

END Exp_to_Tree;
```

Note the declarations in Program 11.1, specifically the two stacks `OpStack` and `NodeStack`. The translator uses a local procedure, `PopConnectPush`, which pops an operator node from the operator stack, pops the two top nodes from the node stack, connects the operator node as the root of the new tree, then pushes this node back onto the node stack. This procedure is really the difference between the expression-to-RPN translator and this expression-to-tree translator.

The similarity of these two algorithms illustrates once again the intimacy of the relationship of infix expressions, trees, and Polish notation.

11.7 BINARY SEARCH TREES (BSTS)

Another useful application of binary trees is in the implementation of efficient insertions and deletions in tables with dynamically varying entries. We define a binary search tree (BST) as a binary tree with the property that the value of the key at any vertex is greater than all values in that vertex's left subtree and less than or equal to all values in that vertex's right subtree. We can state this property recursively as follows:

1. A leaf vertex is a BST.

2. A vertex is the root of a BST if its key value is greater than that of its left child and less than or equal to that of its right child, and if both of its children are either null or the roots of BSTs.

Figure 11.18 shows some trees that are BSTs and some that are not. As usual, make sure you can distinguish between them.

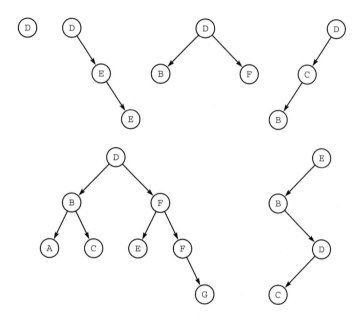

(a) These trees are BSTs.

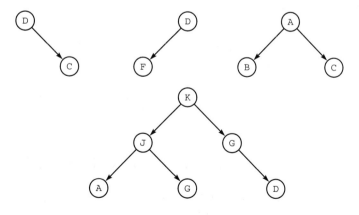

(b) These trees are not BSTs.

Figure 11.18 Binary Search Trees

Operations on Binary Search Trees

Program 11.2 shows a specification for a generic package implementing these operations. The generic parameters will be familiar to you from earlier examples.

Program 11.2 Specification for Generic Binary Search Tree Package

```
GENERIC

    TYPE Element IS PRIVATE;    -- assignment and equality predefined
    TYPE KeyType IS PRIVATE;    -- here too

    -- These generic parameters specify how to
    -- retrieve the key from an element, compare elements
    WITH FUNCTION KeyOf (Item: Element) RETURN KeyType IS <>;
    WITH FUNCTION "<" (Key1, Key2: KeyType) RETURN Boolean IS <>;

PACKAGE Binary_Search_Trees_Generic IS
------------------------------------------------------------------------
--| Specification for Generic Binary Search Tree Package
--| Author: Michael B. Feldman, The George Washington University
--| Last Modified: January 1996
------------------------------------------------------------------------

    TYPE Tree IS LIMITED PRIVATE;

    NotFound: EXCEPTION;

    PROCEDURE Initialize (T: IN OUT Tree);
    -- Pre: none
    -- Post: T is an empty tree

    PROCEDURE Insert (T : IN OUT Tree; E : Element);
    -- Pre:  T and E are defined
    -- Post: T is returned with E stored in a node in
    --       its proper place in T. If E is already in the tree,
    --       Insert has no effect.

    FUNCTION Search (T: Tree; K : KeyType) RETURN Tree;
    -- Pre:    T and K are defined
    -- Post:   if T has an node with an element E that contains K,
    --            returns a pointer to E's location;
    -- Raises: NotFound if no such E is in T

    FUNCTION Retrieve (T: Tree) RETURN Element;
    -- Pre:    T is defined
    -- Post:   returns the element stored at the node designated by T
    -- Raises: NotFound if T is NULL

    PROCEDURE Delete (T : IN OUT Tree; K : IN KeyType);
    -- Pre:    T and K are defined
    -- Post:   If T has a node that contains K, T is returned
```

```
   --           with that node deleted
   -- Raises: NotFound if E is not in the tree.

   GENERIC
     WITH PROCEDURE Visit (E : Element);
   PROCEDURE Traverse_LNR (T : Tree);
   -- Pre:  T is defined
   -- Post: T is traversed in left-node-right order

PRIVATE

   TYPE BinaryTreeNode;
   TYPE Tree IS ACCESS BinaryTreeNode;
   TYPE BinaryTreeNode IS RECORD
     Info : Element;
     Left : Tree := NULL;
     Right : Tree := NULL;
   END RECORD;

END Binary_Search_Trees_Generic;
```

Program 11.3 shows a simple test of some of the operations. The output of this program is

```
K
CK
CKL
CKLV
CDKLV
CDKV
CDKQV
CDQV
CQV
CQ
C
```

Program 11.3 Simple Test of Generic Binary Search Tree Package

```
WITH Ada.Text_IO;
WITH Binary_Search_Trees_Generic;
PROCEDURE Test_BST IS
-----------------------------------------------------------------------
--| Simple test of generic binary search tree package
--| Author: Michael B. Feldman, The George Washington University
--| Last Modified: January 1996
-----------------------------------------------------------------------

   FUNCTION KeyOf(C: Character) RETURN Character IS
   BEGIN
     RETURN C;
   END KeyOf;

   PACKAGE Trees IS NEW Binary_Search_Trees_Generic
     (Element => Character, KeyType => Character); USE Trees;
   PROCEDURE PrintTree IS
     NEW Trees.Traverse_LNR(Visit => Ada.Text_IO.Put);

   Tree1: Tree;
   C: Character;

BEGIN -- Test_BST

   Initialize(Tree1);
```

```
      Insert(Tree1, 'K');
      PrintTree(Tree1);
      Ada.Text_IO.New_Line;

      Insert(Tree1, 'C');
      PrintTree(Tree1);
      Ada.Text_IO.New_Line;

      Insert(Tree1, 'L');
      PrintTree(Tree1);
      Ada.Text_IO.New_Line;

      Insert(Tree1, 'V');
      PrintTree(Tree1);
      Ada.Text_IO.New_Line;

      Insert(Tree1, 'D');
      PrintTree(Tree1);
      Ada.Text_IO.New_Line;

      Delete(Tree1, 'L');
      PrintTree(Tree1);
      Ada.Text_IO.New_Line;

      Insert(Tree1, 'Q');
      PrintTree(Tree1);
      Ada.Text_IO.New_Line;

      Delete(Tree1, 'K');
      PrintTree(Tree1);
      Ada.Text_IO.New_Line;

      Delete(Tree1, 'D');
      PrintTree(Tree1);
      Ada.Text_IO.New_Line;

      Delete(Tree1, 'V');
      PrintTree(Tree1);
      Ada.Text_IO.New_Line;

      Delete(Tree1, 'Q');
      PrintTree(Tree1);
      Ada.Text_IO.New_Line;

END Test_BST;
```

Program 11.4 shows the body of the BST package, with several of the operations shown as subunits. We will discuss the operations one by one.

Program 11.4 Body of Generic Binary Search Tree Package

```
PACKAGE BODY Binary_Search_Trees_Generic IS
------------------------------------------------------------------------
--| Body of Generic Binary Search Tree Package
--| Author: Michael B. Feldman, The George Washington University
--| Last Modified: January 1996
------------------------------------------------------------------------
```

```
      -- local operations, not exported

   FUNCTION MakeNode (E : Element) RETURN Tree IS
   -- Pre: E is defined
   -- Post: returns a pointer to a tree node containing E.
     Result: Tree;
   BEGIN
     Result := NEW BinaryTreeNode;
     Result.Info := E;
     RETURN Result;
   END MakeNode;

   PROCEDURE ConnectLeft (T : IN OUT Tree; E : Element) IS
   -- Pre:  T and E are defined; T.Left = NULL
   -- Post: creates a node containing E and connects it to
   --    the left subtree of T
   BEGIN
     T.Left := MakeNode (E);
   END ConnectLeft;

   PROCEDURE ConnectRight (T : IN OUT Tree; E : Element) IS
   -- Pre:  T and E are defined; T.Right = NULL
   -- Post: creates a node containing E and connects it to
   --    the right subtree of T
   BEGIN
     T.Right := MakeNode (E);
   END ConnectRight;

   PROCEDURE Initialize (T: IN OUT Tree) IS
   BEGIN
     T := NULL;
   END Initialize;

   FUNCTION Retrieve (T: Tree) RETURN Element IS
   BEGIN
     IF T = NULL THEN
       RAISE NotFound;
     ELSE
       RETURN T.Info;
     END IF;
   END Retrieve;

   FUNCTION Search (T: Tree; K : KeyType) RETURN Tree IS SEPARATE;

   PROCEDURE Insert (T : IN OUT Tree; E : Element) IS SEPARATE;

   FUNCTION FindSmallest (T : Tree) RETURN Tree IS SEPARATE;

   PROCEDURE Delete (T : IN OUT Tree; K : IN KeyType) IS SEPARATE;

   PROCEDURE Traverse_LNR (T : Tree) IS SEPARATE;

END Binary_Search_Trees_Generic;
```

The package body in Program 11.4 shows three auxiliary routines that are needed by the `Insert` operation. Two of these procedures, `ConnectLeft` and `ConnectRight`, are responsible for connecting a leaf node, created by the function `MakeNode`, as the left or right child of its parent respectively.

Initialize

The initialization procedure in Program 11.4 just sets the root node to NULL, making all the nodes in the tree inaccessible. This policy is not a particularly good one, because it causes storage leaks. We leave it as an exercise to modify Initialize so that it deallocates all the nodes in the tree.

Retrieve

The retrieve function in Program 11.4 simply returns the information part of the node to its calling program.

Search

By the definition of a BST, at any given node, key values in that node's left subtree are less than the node's key value; key values in the node's right subtree are greater or equal. Therefore, trying to locate an item in a binary search tree is analogous to performing a binary search on an array that has already been sorted. To find a particular item, we compare its key (the target key) to the key of the root node. If the target key is less than the root key, we can eliminate the right subtree and search only the left subtree, thereby cutting the number of nodes to be searched in half. For this reason, the binary tree search is an $O(\log_2 N)$ algorithm.

A recursive function for searching a binary tree is given as the subunit in Program 11.5. From this algorithm, it is easy to see how the binary search tree got its name: It can be seen as a binary tree used for searching (binary (search tree)) or as a tree that implements binary search ((binary search) tree).

Program 11.5 BST Search Operation

```
SEPARATE (Binary_Search_Trees_Generic)
FUNCTION Search (T: Tree; K : KeyType) RETURN Tree IS
-----------------------------------------------------------------------
--| BST Search Operation, subunit of Binary_Search_Trees_Generic
--| Author: Michael B. Feldman, The George Washington University
--| Last Modified: January 1996
-----------------------------------------------------------------------

BEGIN -- Search

  IF T = NULL THEN            -- not in tree
    RAISE NotFound;
  ELSIF K < KeyOf(T.Info) THEN    -- search left subtree
    RETURN Search(T.Left, K);
  ELSIF KeyOf(T.Info) < K THEN    -- search right subtree
    RETURN Search(T.Right, K);
  ELSE                        -- found it!
    RETURN T;
  END IF;

END Search;
```

Traverse_LNR

We have mentioned that the LNR or inorder traversal of a binary tree has an interesting use. A BST has the property that an LNR traversal will visit the vertices in the order of their key values. This can be readily understood by realizing that every key in the root's left subtree is necessarily less than the root key (otherwise it wouldn't be a BST!), so visiting all the nodes in the left subtree prior to visiting the root will visit smaller keys. Similarly, visiting vertices in the right subtree after visiting the root will visit the root before visiting any keys greater than or equal to the root. This operation is shown in Program 11.6.

Program 11.6 BST Traverse Operation

```
SEPARATE (Binary_Search_Trees_Generic)
PROCEDURE Traverse_LNR (T : Tree) IS
-----------------------------------------------------------------
--| Binary Search Tree Traverse Operation, subunit of
--| Binary_Search_Trees_Generic
--| Author: Michael B. Feldman, The George Washington University
--| Last Modified: January 1996
-----------------------------------------------------------------
BEGIN -- Traverse_LNR

  IF T = NULL THEN
    RETURN;
  ELSE
    Traverse_LNR (T.Left);
    Visit (T.Info);
    Traverse_LNR (T.Right);
  END IF;

END Traverse_LNR;
```

Since LNR traversal is recursive and the left and right subtrees of the root are themselves BSTs, the vertices must be visited in sorted order. This is illustrated in Figure 11.19.

Insert

Since BSTs are recursively defined, we can discover a very natural recursive algorithm for inserting a new key in the tree. Assuming first that the tree is not empty, we just test the key against the root key. If it is less, we insert it in the left subtree; if it is equal or greater, we insert it in the right subtree. Eventually, after several recursive calls, we will reach a point where the subtree into which the new key is to be inserted is empty. At this point, we just create a new node for it and link it to the appropriate pointer in the parent node.

How shall we handle the case where a "duplicate key" is encountered—that is, where a given key is seen for the second time? The action to be taken is application-dependent: Sometimes duplicate keys are not allowed, in which case Insert should raise an exception. In the present example, Insert simply does nothing. Another approach might be to treat the second occurrence of a key as though it were greater than

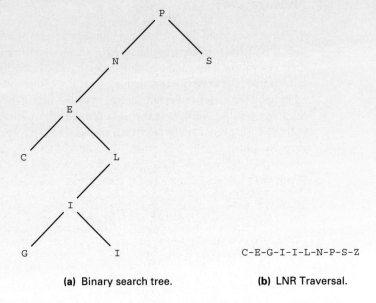

(a) Binary search tree.   **(b)** LNR Traversal.

Figure 11.19 LNR Traversal of a Binary Search Tree

the original; this forces the second occurrence into the right subtree. This strategy gives what is known as a *stable sort*, in which equal keys appear in the LNR traversal in precisely the order in which they arrived.

The BST insertion operation is shown as a subunit in Program 11.7.

Program 11.7 BST Insertion Operation

```
SEPARATE (Binary_Search_Trees_Generic)
PROCEDURE Insert (T : IN OUT Tree; E : IN Element) IS
-------------------------------------------------------------------
--| BST Insert Operation, subunit of Binary_Search_Trees_Generic
--| Author: Michael B. Feldman, The George Washington University
--| Last Modified: January 1996
-------------------------------------------------------------------
BEGIN -- Insert

  IF T = NULL THEN
    T := MakeNode (E);
  ELSIF KeyOf(E) < KeyOf(T.Info) THEN
    IF T.Left = NULL THEN
      ConnectLeft (T, E);
    ELSE
      Insert (T.Left, E);
    END IF;
  ELSIF KeyOf(T.Info) < KeyOf(E) THEN
    IF T.Right = NULL THEN
      ConnectRight (T, E);
    ELSE
      Insert (T.Right, E);
    END IF;
```

```
      ELSE
        Insert(T.Right, E);
      END IF;

  END Insert;
```

What is the time performance of `Insert`? Suppose the BST is balanced. Then if there are K vertices in the tree, the number of levels will be (approximately) log K, and finding the right place for a new arrival will take (approximately) log K comparisons.

But will the BST be balanced? There is no guarantee whatever that it will be, because this property depends on the order of arrival of the new keys.

How bad can it get? Suppose that the keys arrive *in sequential order*—for example, sorted ascending. Then each new arrival will necessarily be greater than the previous one, and will thus go into the right subtree. No arrival ever goes into a left subtree! Thus, the tree will be badly deformed: It will look like a linear list! So adding a new arrival will be a *linear* function of the number of keys already there, instead of a *logarithmic* one. Figure 11.20 shows this worst-case situation.

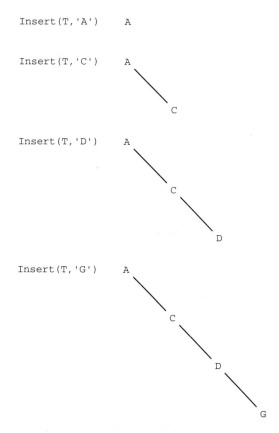

Figure 11.20 A Worst-Case Situation for BST Insertion

The best-case performance of `Insert`, then, is logarithmic; the worst-case one is linear; the average case will be somewhere in between. In practice, BSTs are not useful for applications in which there is a high probability that the incoming data items are already sorted. In situations where the data is reasonably "mixed up," the average performance is acceptable.

As it happens, algorithms exist for balancing BSTs. A balanced BST is sometimes called an AVL tree, after Adel'son-Vel'skii and Landis. The algorithm they discovered is interesting but rather complicated; its discussion is deferred until the next chapter.

Delete

We are studying BSTs in part because they are useful for storing dynamically varying sets of records. Thus, records are deleted as well as added. Deletions need to be done, of course, in such a way that the BST property of the remaining tree is preserved.

Assuming that deletion of a vertex from a BST always takes the form "delete the record containing a given key," what is the algorithm? If the desired vertex is a leaf, we have an easy problem: Just cut it off the tree. Otherwise, it has subtrees and we need to rearrange the subtrees so that the BST property is not disturbed. If only one subtree is present, we can just delete the vertex by making its parent point to whichever child is there. If both subtrees are present, we replace the vertex by its LNR, or inorder, successor. Formally, we have:

To delete a node from a BST:

1. Locate the desired vertex by a search; call it *t*.

2. If *t* is a leaf, disconnect it from its parent (set the pointer in the parent's node equal to null).

3. If *t* has a left child but no right child, remove *t* from the tree by making *t*'s parent point to *t*'s left child.

4. If *t* has a right child but no left child, remove *t* from the tree by making *t*'s parent point to *t*'s right child.

5. Otherwise, find *t*'s LNR successor, which is the node in *t*'s right subtree with the smallest key. Copy this node's information into *t*; delete the node.

In Figure 11.21, you will see some deletions from a BST that illustrate each case above.

To arrive at a procedure for `Delete`, consider the last case in the algorithm shown above. To handle that case, we write an auxiliary procedure `FindSmallest(T)`, which finds the node in a tree `T` with the smallest key, just by moving recursively down to the left from the given node. Program 11.8 shows this auxiliary function; Program 11.9 shows the overall deletion procedure. This procedure depends on the fact that the tree is an IN OUT parameter; make sure you understand how it works. You might find it helpful to draw pictures of the process.

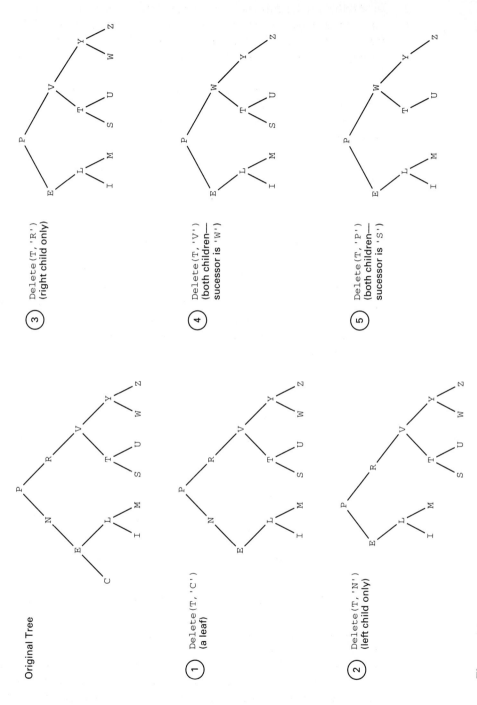

Figure 11.21 Deletion from a Binary Search Tree

Program 11.8 Find Smallest Key in a BST

```
SEPARATE (Binary_Search_Trees_Generic)
FUNCTION FindSmallest (T : Tree) RETURN Tree IS
-------------------------------------------------------------------------
--| Find Smallest Key in Binary Search Tree
--| Author: Michael B. Feldman, The George Washington University
--| Last Modified: January 1996
-------------------------------------------------------------------------
-- Pre: T is defined
-- Post: returns a pointer to the node of T containing the
--   "smallest" value, namely the leaf at the far left side
--   of the tree.

BEGIN -- FindSmallest

  IF T = NULL THEN
    RETURN NULL;
  ELSIF T.Left = NULL THEN
    RETURN T;
  ELSE
    RETURN FindSmallest(T.Left);
  END IF;

END FindSmallest;
```

Program 11.9 BST Deletion Operation

```
SEPARATE (Binary_Search_Trees_Generic)
PROCEDURE Delete (T : IN OUT Tree; K : IN KeyType) IS
-------------------------------------------------------------------------
--| BST Delete Operation, subunit of Binary_Search_Trees_Generic
--| Author: Michael B. Feldman, The George Washington University
--| Last Modified: January 1996
-------------------------------------------------------------------------
  Temp: Tree;
BEGIN -- Delete

  IF T = NULL THEN
    RAISE NotFound;
  END IF;

  IF K < KeyOf(T.Info) THEN             -- check left subtree
    Delete (T.Left, K);
  ELSIF KeyOf(T.Info) < K THEN          -- check right subtree
    Delete (T.Right, K);
  ELSE                                  -- delete this node
    IF T.Left = NULL AND T.Right = NULL THEN
      T := NULL;                        -- T is a leaf; delete it
    ELSIF T.Right = NULL THEN           -- replace T by its predecessor
      T := T.Left;
    ELSIF T.Left = NULL THEN            -- replace T by its successor
      T := T.Right;
    ELSE                                -- both children there
      Temp := FindSmallest(T.Right);
      T.Info := Temp.Info;
      Delete(T.Right, KeyOf(T.Info));
    END IF;
  END IF;

END Delete;
```

There are really two possible deletion algorithms; we could just as well have used *t*'s in order *predecessor*, the node in its *left* subtree with the *largest* key. Finding an algorithm for this is left as an exercise.

Notice that a deletion clearly affects the tree's balance. Experimental results have shown that in a practical BST, with many insertions and deletions, all coming in random order, the tree's balance is best maintained by *alternating* successor and predecessor deletions. In an exercise, you can write such a deletion operation.

11.8   ADT DESIGN: THE KEYED TABLE AS A BST

Recall that in Sections 5.8 and 9.4, we implemented the keyed table using an array and a linear linked list, respectively. We show in Program 11.10 the specification of a version of the table package using a BST as a storage structure. This package uses the generic BST package from Programs 11.2 and 11.4; we leave it as an exercise to complete the body of the table package, and to retest using the passenger list example first developed in Section 5.9.

Program 11.10 Implementing the Keyed Table as a BST

```
WITH Binary_Search_Trees_Generic;
GENERIC

  TYPE Element IS PRIVATE;     -- assignment and equality predefined
  TYPE KeyType IS PRIVATE;     -- here too

  Capacity: IN Positive;       -- maximum table size

  -- These generic parameters specify how to
  -- retrieve the key from an element, compare elements
  WITH FUNCTION KeyOf (Item: Element) RETURN KeyType IS <>;
  WITH FUNCTION "<"   (Key1, Key2: KeyType) RETURN Boolean IS <>;

  -- This parameter specifies what to do with each element during
  -- a traversal of a table;
  WITH PROCEDURE Visit (Item: Element);

PACKAGE Tables_Generic_BST IS
----------------------------------------------------------------------
--| Specification of the abstract data type for an ordered table of
--| element records, each containing a key.
--| This version has type definitions to implement the table as a
--| binary search tree. The client cannot see or use these types
--| because Table is LIMITED PRIVATE.
--| Author: Michael B. Feldman, The George Washington University
--| Last Modified: January 1996
----------------------------------------------------------------------

-- Data Structure

  TYPE TableType IS LIMITED PRIVATE;

-- Exported exceptions

  UninitializedTable: EXCEPTION;
  NoSpaceLeft       : EXCEPTION;

-- Operators
```

```
PROCEDURE InitializeTable (Table : IN OUT TableType);
-- initializes a Table.
-- Pre : None
-- Post: Table is an initialized TableType

FUNCTION SizeOfTable (Table : TableType) RETURN Natural;
-- Returns the number of elements in a Table
-- Pre : Table is an initialized TableType
-- Post: Returns the number of elements in Table

PROCEDURE Search (Table   : TableType;
                  Target  : KeyType;
                  Success : OUT Boolean);
-- Searches a Table for Target.
-- Pre : Table is an initialized TableType
-- Post: Success is True if Target is found; otherwise,
--       Success is False.

PROCEDURE Insert (Table   : IN OUT TableType;
                  Item    : Element;
                  Success : OUT Boolean);
-- Inserts Item into a Table.
-- Pre : Table and Item are defined; Table is initialized.
-- Post: Success is True if insertion is performed; Success is False
--       if insertion is not performed because there is already
--       an element with the same key as Item.
-- Raises: NoSpaceLeft if there is no space available for Item.

PROCEDURE Delete (Table   : IN OUT TableType;
                  Target  : KeyType;
                  Success : OUT Boolean);
-- Deletes the element with key Target from a Table.
-- Pre : Table and Target are defined; Table is initialized.
-- Post: Success is True if deletion is performed; Success is False
--       if deletion is not performed because there is no element
--       whose key is Target.

PROCEDURE Replace (Table   : IN OUT TableType;
                   Item    : Element;
                   Success : OUT Boolean);
-- Replaces the element of a Table with the same key as
-- Item by the contents of Item.
-- Pre : Table and Item are defined; Table is initialized.
-- Post: Success is True if the replacement is performed; Success is
--       False if there is no element with the same key as Item.

PROCEDURE Retrieve (Table   : TableType;
                    Target  : KeyType;
                    Item    : OUT Element;
                    Success : OUT Boolean);
-- Copies the element whose key is Target into Item.
-- Pre : Table is an initialized TableType.
-- Post: Success is True if the copy is performed; Success is False
--     if there is no element whose key is Target.

PROCEDURE Traverse (Table : TableType);
-- Repeatedly calls procedure Visit (a generic parameter) to
--  process each element of a Table.
-- Pre : Table is an initialized TableType.
-- Post: Each element is operated on in turn by procedure Visit.

PRIVATE

  PACKAGE Trees IS NEW
    Binary_Search_Trees_Generic
      (Element => Element, KeyType => KeyType);
```

```
   TYPE TableType IS RECORD
     Data   : Trees.Tree;
     NumItems: Natural;
   END RECORD;

END Tables_Generic_BST;
```

In developing the original specification for `Tables_Generic` (Section 5.8), we wrote very general and fundamental operations on keyed tables and took care not to allow client programs direct access to details of our table representation. We argued there that making the table type `LIMITED PRIVATE` gave us the flexibility to choose our implementation. In Section 9.4, we saw how the table implementation could be changed to a linked list. Here the careful ADT design pays off again: We can change to a search tree implementation by changing only the package body, with very little change to the package specification. More important, the identical client programs can be used with no change at all!

Saving and Restoring a BST Table

It is convenient to provide clients of our table package with a version of the generic backup package first introduced in Section 5.9. How shall we save a BST to a disk file? With the array and linked-list table implementations, we could do a simple traversal because both structures are linear. In the case of a BST, we must consider what sort of traversal would be best.

Suppose we simply called `Traverse_LNR` to copy the tree to a disk file, using a file-oriented element `Put` as our `Visit` procedure. This would result in a file containing all the elements in the tree, but it would be disastrous from a performance point of view. As we know, `Traverse_LNR` is designed specifically to visit the nodes in order by key. The file would thus contain the records in key order. Assuming we implemented `Restore` as a series of `Insert` operations, this would result in a worst-case, linear BST!

The solution is to implement `Save` as a traversal that preserves the structure of the actual tree, writing the records to disk so that reading them back in and inserting them will produce a tree whose shape is the same as that of the original one. As it happens, `Traverse_NLR` will do exactly this. As an exercise, you can show that this is the case and implement a generic table backup child package tailored to the BST implementation.

11.9   APPLICATION: A CROSS-REFERENCE GENERATOR

A *cross-reference generator* is an example of an indexing program. Two common applications come from the fields of programming and text analysis.

```
1 We wish to point out the difference
2 between the terms "data type", "abstract
3 data type", and "data structure."

Cross Reference Listing for xreftest.dat

We                       1
abstract                 2
and                      3
between                  2
data                     2      3      3
difference               1
out                      1
point                    1
structure                3
terms                    2
the                      1      2
to                       1
type                     2      3
wish                     1
```

Figure 11.22 A Cross-Reference Listing

A programmer uses a cross-reference listing of a program to help debug that program. The cross-reference listing indicates, for each identifier in the program, the statements in which that identifier appears. A person analyzing text in a natural language uses a cross-reference listing of that text (this kind of cross-reference listing is sometimes called a concordance) to indicate how frequently and in which lines each important word occurs. For example, centuries ago—long before computers, in any case—a number of monks in England produced a concordance of the entire Bible, all by hand, of course!

An example of a cross-reference listing, for a small sample of English text, appears in Figure 11.22.

A cross-reference generator, whatever its application, consists of two parts. One part is some kind of dynamic table handler to hold the words read from the text, and all their references, in some efficient way. The other part is some kind of *scanner*, or parser, that knows the specifics of the language being analyzed and therefore how to distinguish a meaningful word from other things.

In our case, the scanner and table packages are called `EngLexer` and `Trees_Xref_Generic`, respectively; their specifications appear as Programs 11.11 and 11.12. The scanner provides a `VString` subtype `WordType`, and a procedure `GetWord` to read text from the input file and return the next word it finds; `GetWord` also indicates end-of-line and reports end-of-file at the right time. The table handler provides `Insert`, to put a word and its line number into the table, and `Display`, to display the table after all text is read.

Program 11.11 Specification for Cross-Reference Trees

```
GENERIC

  TYPE KeyType        IS PRIVATE;
  TYPE NonKeyInfoType IS PRIVATE;
```

```
   WITH FUNCTION "<" (Left, Right : KeyType) RETURN Boolean;
   WITH PROCEDURE DisplayKey (K : IN KeyType);
   WITH PROCEDURE DisplayRef (N : IN NonKeyInfoType);

PACKAGE Trees_Xref_Generic IS
-------------------------------------------------------------------------
--| Soecification for Cross-Reference-Tree Package
--| Author: Michael B. Feldman, The George Washington University
--| Last Modified: January 1996
-------------------------------------------------------------------------

   TYPE Tree IS LIMITED PRIVATE;

   PROCEDURE Insert (T : IN OUT Tree;
                     K : KeyType;
                     N : NonKeyInfoType);
   -- Pre:  T, K, N are defined
   -- Post: T is returned with K and N stored in a node in
   --       its proper place in T.

   PROCEDURE Display (T : Tree);
   -- Pre: T is defined
   -- Post: The contents of T are displayed in key order

PRIVATE

   TYPE BinaryTreeNode;
   TYPE Tree IS ACCESS BinaryTreeNode;

END Trees_Xref_Generic;
```

Program 11.12 Specification for English Lexical Scanner

```
WITH Ada.Text_IO, VStrings;
PACKAGE English_Lexer IS
-----------------------------------------------------------------------
--| Simple English Lexical Scanner
--| Author: Michael B. Feldman, The George Washington University
--| Last Modified: January 1996
-----------------------------------------------------------------------

   MaxWordSize : CONSTANT Positive := 20;
   SUBTYPE WordType IS VStrings.VString(MaxLength => MaxWordSize);

   PROCEDURE GetWord (F  : IN Ada.Text_IO.File_Type;
               Word    : OUT WordType;
               Success: OUT Boolean;
               EOL     : OUT Boolean;
               EOF     : OUT Boolean);
   -- Pre:  F is defined
   -- Post: reads the next simple English word from F, returning
   --   it in Word. Success is True if and only if Word is non-empty.
   --   EOL is True if and only if the end of the current line was
   --   reached; EOF is true if and cnly if end of file was reached.

END English_Lexer;
```

The main program of the cross-reference generator is shown as Program 11.13.

Program 11.13 Main Program for English Cross-Referencer

```
WITH Ada.Text_IO;
WITH Ada.Integer_Text_IO;
WITH Trees_Xref_Generic;
WITH English_Lexer;
WITH VStrings, VStrings.IO;
PROCEDURE English_Xref IS
-----------------------------------------------------------------------
--| Cross-Reference Builder for Simple English
--| Author: Michael B. Feldman, The George Washington University
--| Last Modified: January 1996
-----------------------------------------------------------------------

  PROCEDURE DisplayKey(Item : IN English_Lexer.WordType);    -- forward
  PROCEDURE DisplayRef(Item : IN Positive);             -- forward


  PACKAGE XrefTrees IS
    NEW Trees_Xref_Generic (KeyType => English_Lexer.WordType,
                            NonKeyInfoType => Positive,
                            "<" => VStrings."<",
                            DisplayKey => DisplayKey,
                            DisplayRef => DisplayRef);


  FileName : VStrings.VString(80);
  F        : Ada.Text_IO.File_Type;
  T        : XrefTrees.Tree;
  LineNumber : Positive := 1;
  ThisWord   : English_Lexer.WordType;
  EOF    : Boolean := False;
  EOL    : Boolean := False;
  Success: Boolean;

  PROCEDURE DisplayKey(Item : IN English_Lexer.WordType) IS
  BEGIN
    Ada.Text_IO.New_Line;
    VStrings.IO.Put(Item => Item);
    Ada.Text_IO.Set_Col(Ada.Text_IO.Positive_Count(22) );
  END DisplayKey;


  PROCEDURE DisplayRef(Item : IN Positive) IS
  BEGIN
    Ada.Integer_Text_IO.Put(Item => Item, Width => 4);
  END DisplayRef;

BEGIN -- English_Xref

  Ada.Text_IO.Put_Line ("Please enter name of data file");
  VStrings.IO.Get_Line(FileName, 80);
  Ada.Text_IO.Open(F, Ada.Text_IO.In_File, VStrings.Value(FileName));
  Ada.Text_IO.New_Line;
  Ada.Integer_Text_IO.Put(Item => LineNumber, Width => 4);
  Ada.Text_IO.Put(Item => ' ');
  LOOP
    English_Lexer.GetWord (F, ThisWord, Success, EOL, EOF);
    IF Success THEN
      XRefTrees.Insert (T, ThisWord, LineNumber);
    END IF;
```

```
      IF EOL THEN
        LineNumber := LineNumber + 1;
        Ada.Text_IO.New_Line;
        Ada.Integer_Text_IO.Put(Item => LineNumber, Width => 4);
        Ada.Text_IO.Put(Item =>  ' ');
      END IF;
      EXIT WHEN EOF;
    END LOOP;

    Ada.Text_IO.New_Line(Spacing => 2);
    Ada.Text_IO.Put ("Cross Reference Listing for ");
    VStrings.IO.Put (FileName);
    Ada.Text_IO.New_Line;
    XrefTrees.Display(T);

END English_Xref;
```

The tree package is instantiated for `VString` words and `Positive` line numbers. The main loop of this program is very simple: `EngLexer.GetWord` is called repeatedly, and if `GetWord` returns a nonempty word, that word and the current line number are put into the table with a call to `XRefTrees.Insert`. When the input file is exhausted, `XRefTrees.Display` is called to print out the cross-reference listing. Notice how all the details of the scanning and table handling are encapsulated in the respective bodies.

The Body of the Table Handler

Let us look first at the requirements for the table handler. We assume that the distinct words in the text or program are few enough in number that the table can be constructed in main memory. The input text will be scanned, the cross-reference built, then the results reported once. Also, we do not know either precisely how many different words will arrive or how many references each will have. Furthermore, words and references are only added, never deleted. These facts argue for a table structure whose `Insert` is efficient. The `Display` operation is not worrisome, since it is performed only once per run, and `Delete` is never done at all.

Unless the total number of words is very large, the BST structure is a useful solution. Since people don't often write either programs or essays with the words in alphabetical order, the chances of getting a badly unbalanced tree are slim. Each `Insert` performs in roughly $O(\log N)$ time.

A first attempt to build a BST package would carry a node for each word and reference (line number): The word would be the key and the reference would be the non-key information. A moment's thought reveals that this is wasteful of space, since we really need only one copy of each word. Let's put all the references to a given word in a one-way list, then use the value part of the tree vertex as the list header. A diagram for this is shown in Figure 11.23.

The body of the tree package is shown as Program 11.14. The declarations at the top indicate that our generic singly linked list package is instantiated, and the BST node contains two fields in addition to the pointers: the `Key` field, which contains a word, and the `Refs` field, containing the list of line numbers.

```
1 We wish to point out the difference
2 between the terms "data type," "abstract
3 data type," and "data structure."
```

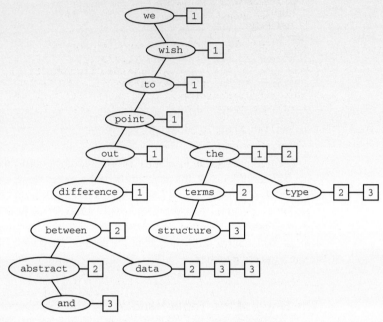

Figure 11.23 A Cross-Reference Tree for English Text

Program 11.14 Body of Cross-Reference Tree Package

```
WITH Lists_Generic;
PACKAGE BODY Trees_Xref_Generic IS
------------------------------------------------------------------------
--| Body of generic cross-reference tree package
--| Author: Michael B. Feldman, The George Washington University
--| Last Modified: January 1996
------------------------------------------------------------------------

  PACKAGE XrefLists IS
    NEW Lists_Generic (ElementType => NonKeyInfoType);
  USE XrefLists;
  TYPE BinaryTreeNode IS RECORD
    Key   : KeyType;
    Refs  : List;
    Left  : Tree;
    Right : Tree;
  END RECORD;

  -- procedure definitions, not exported

  FUNCTION MakeNode (K : IN KeyType;
                     V : IN NonKeyInfoType) RETURN Tree IS
  -- Pre:  K and V are defined
  -- Post: returns a pointer to a tree node, with K in
  --    the key field and V in the first node of a reference list
```

```
    Result : Tree;
BEGIN
   Result    := NEW BinaryTreeNode;
   Result.Key := K;
   AddToRear(Result.Refs, V);
   RETURN Result;
END MakeNode;

PROCEDURE ConnectLeft (T : IN OUT tree;
                       K : KeyType;
                       V : NonKeyInfoType) IS
-- Pre:  T, K, and V are defined; T.Left is NULL
-- Post: creates a tree node using MakeNode, then attaches
--    this new node to the left subtree of T
BEGIN
   T.Left := MakeNode (K, V);
END ConnectLeft;

PROCEDURE ConnectRight (T : IN OUT tree;
                        K : KeyType;
                        V : NonKeyInfoType) IS
-- Pre:  T, K, and V are defined; T.Right is NULL
-- Post: creates a tree node using MakeNode, then attaches
--    this new node to the right subtree of T
BEGIN
   T.Right := MakeNode (K, V);
END ConnectRight;

PROCEDURE ProcessDuplicate (T : IN OUT tree;
                            K : IN KeyType;
                            V : IN NonKeyInfoType) IS
-- Pre:  T, K, and V are defined
-- Post: attaches V to the end of the reference list headed at T
BEGIN
   AddToRear (T.Refs, V);
END ProcessDuplicate;

PROCEDURE Insert (T : IN OUT tree;
                  K : KeyType;
                  N : NonKeyInfoType) IS
BEGIN

   IF T = NULL THEN
     T := MakeNode (K, N);

   ELSIF K < T.key THEN
     IF T.left = NULL THEN
       ConnectLeft (T, K, N);
     ELSE
       Insert (T.left, K, N);
     END IF;

   ELSIF T.Key < K THEN
     IF T.right = NULL THEN
       ConnectRight (T, K, N);
     ELSE
       Insert (T.right, K, N);
     END IF;

   ELSE
     ProcessDuplicate (T, K, N);
   END IF;
END Insert;
```

```
PROCEDURE VisitTree (T : Tree) IS
-- Pre:  T is defined
-- Post: traverses the list of references headed at T
  Current: Position;
BEGIN
  DisplayKey (T.Key);
  Current := First(T.Refs);
  WHILE NOT IsPastEnd(T.Refs, Current) LOOP
    DisplayRef (Retrieve(T.Refs, Current));
    GoAhead (T.Refs, Current);
  END LOOP;
END VisitTree;

PROCEDURE Display (T : tree) IS
BEGIN
  IF T = NULL THEN
    RETURN;
  ELSE
    Display (T.Left);
    VisitTree (T);
    Display (T.Right);
  END IF;
END Display;

END Trees_Xref_Generic;
```

How does `Insert` work? The first time a given word is seen, `Insert` sets up a tree node for it and then creates the reference list with the current line number in the first node of the list. For subsequent references to the same word, an auxiliary procedure `ProcessDuplicate` just calls `AddToRear` to add this reference to the end of the list.

`Display`, just a variation of `Traverse_LNR`, calls an auxiliary routine `VisitTree`, which prints the word in the tree node and then traverses the reference list, printing out line numbers as it goes.

The Scanner as a Finite-State Machine

Developing scanners for languages is a science in itself; a general treatment is beyond the scope of this book. For this example, we'll simplify the scanner by relying on some key assumptions about the text to be scanned. We assume that the text is English, that uppercase and lowercase letters are treated separately, and that numeric characters are treated just like letters, so dates, phone numbers, and so on, will be indexed along with normal words. Punctuation is not to be indexed; there is no embedded punctuation, such as an apostrophe or a hyphen. A word is never broken across two lines. In the exercises, you have the chance to relax some of these assumptions.

Our scanner can be implemented using an important structure which generalizes nicely to many other scanning applications, namely the *finite-state machine*. Figure 11.24 shows a simple diagram for this structure, which was introduced in Chapter 10 as a state graph, or transition graph. The circles represent *states* of the machine. The arrows represent *transitions* from one state to another. An arrow is labeled to indicate two things: The left part is the *input class* of the character just scanned and the right part is an *action* to be taken just before the machine moves to its new state.

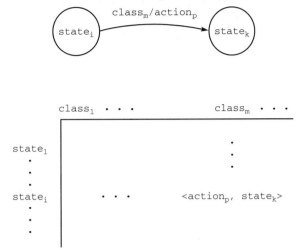

Figure 11.24 Graph and Table Notations for Finite-State Machine

Figure 11.25 gives the state graph for our simple English scanner. It begins in its Start state and continues to cycle in that state until it sees a letter. If a carriage return is seen, the scanner updates the line counter and returns to the Start state (we need to account for the possibility of a line's containing all blanks or all punctuation).

Once a letter is seen (remember, digits count as letters!), the machine executes an action called StartWord, which initializes a string in which to store the word, stores the letter in this string, and transfers to a state called Build.

While in the Build state, the machine reads characters, adding the letters it finds on to the word string using an action called AddLetter. When a nonletter character

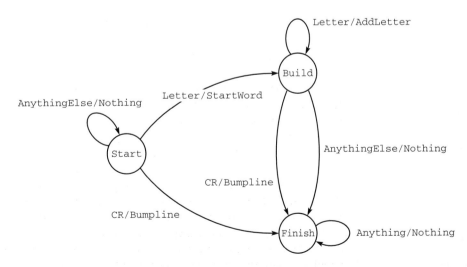

Figure 11.25 State Graph for Scanner for Simple English

is seen, the word is complete and the machine transfers to its Finish state. If the non-letter was a carriage return, the line counter is incremented.

How is the finite-state machine implemented? This is all shown in the package body, Program 11.15. The state names, input classes, and actions are written as enumeration types. The transition graph is implemented as a two-dimensional array, which uses the states as its row subscripts and classes of inputs as its column subscripts. Each entry in the array is itself a record, containing an action field and a new-state field.

Program 11.15 Body of Lexical Scanner for Simple English

```
WITH Ada.Text_IO, VStrings;
USE Ada.Text_IO, VStrings;
PACKAGE BODY English_Lexer IS
-------------------------------------------------------------------------
--| Body of English Lexical Scanner
--| Author: Michael B. Feldman, The George Washington University
--| Last Modified: January 1996
-------------------------------------------------------------------------

  TYPE State IS (Start, Build, Finish);
  TYPE InputClass IS (Letter, CR, AnythingElse);
  TYPE Action IS (Nothing, StartWord, BumpLine, AddLetter);

  TYPE LexicalEntry IS RECORD
    NewState   : State;
    ThisAction : Action;
  END RECORD;

  TYPE FSM_Table IS ARRAY (State, InputClass) OF LexicalEntry;

  FUNCTION Classify (Ch: Character) RETURN InputClass IS
  BEGIN
    CASE Ch IS
      WHEN 'A'..'Z' | 'a'..'z' | '0'..'9' =>
        RETURN Letter;
      WHEN OTHERS =>
        RETURN AnythingElse;
    END CASE;
  END Classify;

  PROCEDURE GetWord (F      : IN File_Type;
                     Word   : OUT WordType;
                     Success: OUT Boolean;
                     EOL    : OUT Boolean;
                     EOF    : OUT Boolean) IS

    Char         : character;
    ThisClass    : InputClass;
    PresentState : State;
    ThisEntry    : LexicalEntry;
    NewAction    : Action;
    TempWord     : WordType;

    --   Lexical table for simplified English text.

    EnglishText : CONSTANT FSM_Table :=

    ( --   entries for current state = Start,       current input =
          ((Build, StartWord),                             -- Letter
```

```
                   (Finish, BumpLine),                -- CR
                   (Start,  Nothing)),                 -- AnythingElse

         --   entries for current state = Build,   current input =
              ((Build,  AddLetter),                    -- Letter
               (Finish, BumpLine),                     -- CR
               (Finish, Nothing)),                     -- AnythingElse

         --   entries for current state = Finish,  current input =
              ((Finish, Nothing),                      -- Letter
               (Finish, Nothing),                      -- CR
               (Finish, Nothing)));                    -- AnythingElse

       --   End of lexical table for simple English

   BEGIN --- body of GetWord

     EOL := false;
     EOF := false;
     PresentState := Start;

     LOOP

       IF PresentState = Finish THEN
         EXIT;
       END IF;

       IF End_of_File (F) THEN
         EOF := true;
         EXIT;
       ELSIF End_of_Line (F) THEN
         Skip_Line (F);
         ThisClass := CR;
       ELSE
         Get (F, Char);
         Put(Char);
         ThisClass := Classify (Char);
       END IF;

       NewAction := EnglishText (PresentState, ThisClass).ThisAction;

       CASE NewAction IS
         WHEN Nothing =>
           NULL;
         WHEN StartWord =>
           TempWord := TempWord & Char;
         WHEN AddLetter =>
           TempWord := TempWord & Char;
         WHEN BumpLine =>
           EOL := true;
       END CASE;

       PresentState := EnglishText (PresentState, ThisClass).NewState;

     END LOOP;

     Word    := TempWord;
     Success := NOT VStrings.IsEmpty(Word);

   END GetWord;

END English_Lexer;
```

The procedure GetWord is the "machine" that actually moves around the state graph. It reads a character, classifies it, determines the action to be taken by looking in the array using its current state and input class as subscripts, executes the action, then goes to its new state. If the new state is `Finish`, the procedure returns to its caller.

This design example has shown the advantages of separating the independent functions of scanning and table handling into manageable pieces; it has also illustrated the clarity with which structures such as tables can be written using enumeration types. A number of the exercises invite the reader to develop various modifications to this design.

11.10 SUBPROGRAM POINTERS AND TABLE-DRIVEN PROGRAMMING

In this section, we introduce an alternative design for the lexical scanner, using *table-driven programming*.

In certain kinds of programs, such as numerical applications or graphic user interfaces, it is useful to be able to select dynamically which of a number of functions or procedures is to be called, depending upon circumstances in the program or its environment. This is typically done by providing a type whose values represent names of subprograms. The programmer can then

1. declare a variable of that type;

2. store in that variable the name of a subprogram;

3. execute precisely the subprogram whose name is in that variable.

Some capabilities for this are provided in other languages, in particular Fortran, Pascal, and C; Ada 83 does not include such facilities.

Of course, in Ada 83 we can select among several subprograms using an `IF` or `CASE` structure, but the selection, and the subprograms to be called, are predetermined at compilation time and cannot be changed without modifying and re-compiling the program.

Ada 95 Subprogram Pointers

This is a situation analogous to the variant record case we examined in Section 6.6, in which the Ada 95 solution was to provide tagged types. Recall further that in Section 9.11, we introduced general access types and used them to designate tagged objects. The Ada 95 solution to provide dynamic selection of subprograms is to allow the declaration of access types that designate subprograms. For example,

```
TYPE IntegerProcPointer IS ACCESS PROCEDURE (Item: IN Integer);
```

declares a type whose value can designate a procedure with a single `IN` parameter of type `Integer`, and

```
TYPE FloatFuncPointer IS
  ACCESS FUNCTION (Left, Right: Float) RETURN Float;
```

declares a type whose values designate functions with `Float` parameters and return types. Suppose we had a function `Maximum`, such as

```
FUNCTION Maximum (X, Y: Float) RETURN Float IS
BEGIN
  IF X > Y THEN
    RETURN X;
  ELSE
    RETURN Y;
  END IF;
END Maximum;
```

and variables

```
F             : Float;
WhichFunction: FloatFuncPointer;
```

then, using the `'Access` attribute as we did in Section 9.11, we could set this variable to designate `Maximum`:

```
WhichFunction := Maximum'Access;
```

and, finally, call whichever function is designated by this variable:

```
F := WhichFunction.ALL(3.5, -27.4);
```

which, in this case, calls `Maximum`.

Consistent with Ada's commitment to type safety, a subprogram access type declares only a specific parameter profile—`IntegerProcPointer` designates procedures with a single `IN` parameter of type `Integer`—and a variable of the type can then designate *only* subprograms with that profile. For example, suppose a variable of type `IntegerProcPointer` were assigned a value `P'Access`, where `P` is a procedure that expects two `Integer` parameters instead of one. The mismatch between the calling program's expectation and the subprogram's behavior would be unpredictable, causing either an incorrect result or even an unexpected program termination. For this reason, Ada 95 enforces the argument profile rule very strictly.

Another Design for the Lexical Scanner

As an example of how subprogram access types can be used, we consider an illustration of what is often called *table-driven programming*—namely, programming in which a table contains references to subprograms, which are executed as the table is traversed in some manner.

In our case, we revise the lexical scanner of Section 11.9 so that in the finite-state machine transition table, the action fields are no longer enumeration values but actual pointers to action procedures. This structure is often used in table-driven language scanners such as those found in compilers.

The revised scanner is shown in Program 11.16.

Program 11.16 An Alternative Body for the Lexical Scanner

```
WITH Ada.Text_IO, VStrings;
USE Ada.Text_IO, VStrings;
PACKAGE BODY English_Lexer IS
--------------------------------------------------------------------------
```

```
--| Ada 95 version of lexical scanner for simple English.
--| This version uses procedure pointers for the actions
--| of the finite-state machine. The FSM executes the actions
--| directly instead of using a CASE statement.
--| Author: Michael B. Feldman, The George Washington University
--| Last Modified: January 1996
-------------------------------------------------------------------------

  TYPE State IS (Start, Build, Finish);
  TYPE InputClass IS (Letter, CR, AnythingElse);

  -- Ada 95 feature: access-to-procedure type
  TYPE Action IS ACCESS PROCEDURE;

  TYPE LexicalEntry IS RECORD
    NewState   : State;
    ThisAction : Action;
  END RECORD;

  TYPE FSM_Table IS ARRAY (State, InputClass) OF LexicalEntry;

  FUNCTION Classify (Ch: Character) RETURN InputClass IS
  BEGIN
    CASE Ch IS
      WHEN 'A'..'Z' | 'a'..'z' | '0'..'9' =>
        RETURN Letter;
      WHEN OTHERS =>
        RETURN AnythingElse;
    END CASE;
  END Classify;

  PROCEDURE GetWord (F       : IN File_Type;
                     Word    : OUT WordType;
                     Success: OUT Boolean;
                     EOL     : OUT Boolean;
                     EOF     : OUT Boolean) IS

    Char         : character;
    ThisClass    : InputClass;
    PresentState : State;
    ThisEntry    : LexicalEntry;
    NewAction    : Action;
    TempWord     : WordType;

    -- Action procedures — will be designated in the lexical table,
    -- then dereferenced to dispatch the appropriate action

    PROCEDURE Nothing IS
    BEGIN
      NULL;
    END Nothing;

    PROCEDURE StartWord IS
    BEGIN
      TempWord := TempWord & Char;
    END StartWord;

    PROCEDURE AddLetter IS
    BEGIN
      TempWord := TempWord & Char;
    END AddLetter;

    PROCEDURE BumpLine IS
    BEGIN
```

```
      EOL := True;
   END BumpLine;

   -- Lexical table for simplified English text.
   -- Note values like StartWord'Access, etc., in the action fields

   EnglishText : CONSTANT FSM_Table :=

   (  --    entries for current state = Start,        current input =

             ((Build, StartWord'Access),                 -- Letter
              (Finish, BumpLine'Access),                 -- CR
              (Start, Nothing'Access)),                  -- AnythingElse

       --    entries for current state = Build,        current input =

             ((Build, AddLetter'Access),                 --  Letter
              (Finish, BumpLine'Access),                 --  CR
              (Finish, Nothing'Access)),                 --  AnythingElse

       --    entries for current state = Finish,       current input =

             ((Finish, Nothing'Access),                  --  Letter
              (Finish, Nothing'Access),                  --  CR
              (Finish, Nothing'Access)));                --  AnythingElse

   --    End of lexical table for simple English

BEGIN --- body of GetWord

   EOL := false;
   EOF := false;
   PresentState := Start;

   LOOP

     IF PresentState = Finish THEN
        EXIT;
     END IF;

     IF End_of_File (F) THEN
        EOF := true;
        EXIT;
     ELSIF End_of_Line (F) THEN
        Skip_Line (F);
        ThisClass := CR;
     ELSE
        Get (F, Char);
        Put(Char);
        ThisClass := Classify (Char);
     END IF;

     -- Dereference the appropriate action, which causes it to
     -- be dispatched (called).
     EnglishText (PresentState, ThisClass).ThisAction.ALL;

     -- Just get new state from the table.
     PresentState := EnglishText(PresentState,ThisClass).NewState;
   END LOOP;

Word     := TempWord;
Success := NOT VStrings.IsEmpty(Word);
```

```
  END GetWord;

END English_Lexer;
```

Note that within the exported procedure `GetWord`, we declare four small parameterless procedures: `Nothing`, `StartWord`, `AddLetter`, and `BumpLine`. For example, `AddLetter` is

```
PROCEDURE AddLetter IS
BEGIN
  TempWord := TempWord & Char;
END AddLetter;
```

These procedures correspond exactly to the actions specified in the state graph of Figure 11.25, and the FSM table `EnglishText` now contains actions such as `AddLetter'Access`. Instead of the `CASE` statement we used to select an action in Program 11.10, here we dispatch an action directly from the table:

```
EnglishText (PresentState, ThisClass).ThisAction.ALL;
```

which executes the action procedure designated by the pointer in that spot in the table. This greatly simplifies the main loop of the scanner.

SUMMARY

This chapter has presented a number of definitions pertaining to trees. Binary trees were emphasized, and the two applications covered in detail were expression trees and binary search trees (BSTs).

An important part of this chapter has been the traversal of a binary tree—that is, visiting each node of the tree in some specified order. The usefulness of three of these traversal schemes—the NLR, LNR, and LRN algorithms—has been considered in detail, and you have seen the close connection between trees and expressions in infix or Polish form.

Finally, we presented a design for a cross-reference generator, using a finite-state machine (FSM) to scan an input file and a BST to store the words and line numbers. Finally, we showed how to use procedure pointers to implement a table-driven program.

EXERCISES

1. Given a connected diagraph represented by its adjacency matrix G, write a Boolean function `IsTree(G)` that returns `True` iff G represents a tree. (*Hint*: Review the definition of a tree!)
2. Given a connected digraph represented by its adjacency matrix G, write a Boolean function `IsBinaryTree(G)` that returns `True` iff G represents a binary tree. (*Hint*: You can use the results of Exercise 1 to simplify your work.)
3. Given a connected digraph represented by its adjacency matrix G, write a boolean

function `IsStrictlyBinaryTree(G)` that returns `True` iff G represents a strictly binary tree. Which properties of digraphs must all trees have? Which properties does no tree have?

4. Given a binary tree T, write a boolean function `IsBalanced(T)` which returns `True` iff T is height-balanced, `False` otherwise. (*Hint*: Think recursively.)

5. Given a binary tree T, write a function `Depth(T)` that returns the depth of the tree. (*Hint*: Think recursively.)

6. In a binary tree T, each leaf vertex can be reached by only one path from the root. Write a function `MinPathLength(T)` that returns the length of the shortest of all such paths. (*Hint*: Think recursively.)

7. Modify the `Initialize` and `Delete` operations of Program 11.4 so that no storage leaks occur when these operations are performed. This can be done in one of two ways: Use `Unchecked_Deallocation` to return nodes to the storage pool, or use a LAVS (list of available space; review Section 9.2) to build a list of deleted nodes.

8. Write a procedure implementing a BST `Delete` operation in which, if the element to be deleted possesses both children, it is replaced by its LNR predecessor instead of its successor.

9. Write a BST `Delete` operation in which successive deletions are done alternately by the successor and predecessor methods.

10. Show that if in the BST backup package, `Save` is implemented using `Traverse_NLR`, implementing `Restore` as a series of `Insert` operations will produce a tree shaped like the original saved one. Implement this child package for `Tables_Generic_BST`.

11. Develop a procedure implementing the `Delete` operation for a cross-reference tree. Be careful: This depends on whether all references associated with a key are to be deleted, or only one.

12. A limitation of the scanner in Section 11.9 is that it is case-sensitive—that is, the words *we* and *We* would be indexed separately. This is not usually desirable in a concordance. Modify the scanner so that no distinction is made between the cases of the letters of a word. (*Hint*: Change the input classes to distinguish the case, and change the scanner table actions so that an uppercase letter is converted to lowercase before adding it onto the current word.)

13. Further modify the scanner of Section 11.9 so that words containing digits are skipped instead of inserted into the cross-reference tree.

CHAPTER 12

Advanced Tree Concepts

In this chapter, we will present some more advanced examples of the use of tree structures. We first show how a binary search tree can be *threaded* to facilitate nonrecursive operations on it. Next, we consider another binary tree structure, called the *heap*, and show its use for representing priority queues. The next example is the *digital search tree*, an application of a tree in which a node has a number of children that is potentially large and highly variable.

Finally, we show two very important extensions of the binary search tree (BST). The *AVL tree* is a BST that is maintained in a balanced state every time an insertion or deletion is performed. The B-tree is a generalization of the AVL tree and is used frequently in structuring large files on secondary storage devices. A B-tree node of order K can hold up to K keys and $K + 1$ pointers.

12.1   THREADED BINARY SEARCH TREES

The recursive algorithms for tree insertion and traversal operations are elegant and not difficult to understand. However, it is sometimes useful to have iterative algorithms available, for two main reasons:

1.   Recursion requires extra storage and time for all those subprogram calls.

2.   Recursive traversal algorithms can provide only passive iteration; it is not possible to separate a recursive traversal into the parts needed to support active iteration.

450

In this section, we show a technique called *threading*. Threading is a modification to the data structure of a tree to support iterative operations. We illustrate threading for the case of a BST. It is equally applicable to expression trees; the details are left as an exercise.

Threading is a very simple idea: As we build a BST, we utilize empty pointer fields to contain pointers helping us move up the tree as well as down. A thread, if it exists, points to the LNR successor of a node—that is, to the next node to be visited during a `Traverse_LNR` operation. Figure 12.1 shows several threaded BSTs with the threads represented by dashed lines. Such a tree is sometimes called *right in-threaded*, because it contains threads to facilitate its right inorder traversal.

Where are the threads stored? If a node has a nonempty right child, its LNR successor is below it, somewhere in the right subtree. Otherwise, its LNR successor is above it in the tree. Because a node has a thread only if it has no right child, it is common practice to store the thread in the right-child field of a node with a null right child, using a flag to indicate that it is a thread that points upward and not an ordinary downward pointer. We add to each vertex a Boolean field called `Thread`, which is True if a thread is stored in the right child field and False otherwise. Figure 12.2 gives the modified type definitions.

Now let us give a modified `Traverse_LNR` procedure. Essentially, the procedure just moves all the way down the left side of the tree to find the first vertex to be visited, follows the threads back up until a vertex with a right child is encountered, then starts back down that child's left subtree. This procedure is shown as Program 12.1, a subunit of a generic package `BST_Threaded_Generic`. The full package is not included here and is left as an exercise. Note that `Traverse_LNR` is nonrecursive.

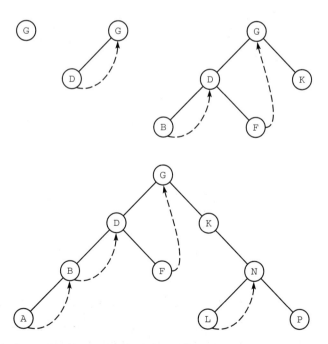

Figure 12.1 Some Threaded Binary Search Trees

```
TYPE BinaryTreeNode;
TYPE Tree IS ACCESS BinaryTreeNode;
TYPE BinaryTreeNode IS RECORD
  Info   : ElementType;
  Left   : Tree;
  Right  : Tree;
  Thread : Boolean := False;
END RECORD;
```

Figure 12.2 Type Definitions for Threaded Binary Tree Node

Program 12.1 Nonrecursive `Traverse_LNR` for Threaded BST

```
SEPARATE (BST_Threaded_Generic)
PROCEDURE Traverse_LNR (T: Tree) IS
------------------------------------------------------------------------
--| Nonrecursive Traverse_LNR for Threaded BST
--| Author: Michael B. Feldman, The George Washington University
--| Last Modified: January 1996
------------------------------------------------------------------------

  Current : Tree;
  Previous: Tree;

BEGIN -- Traverse_LNR

  Current := T;

  LOOP
    Previous := NULL;

    -- down left branch to bottom
    WHILE Current /= NULL LOOP
      Previous := Current;
      Current := Current.Left;
    END LOOP;

    IF Previous /= NULL THEN
      Visit(Previous.Info);
      Current := Previous.Right;

      -- now back up following threads
      WHILE Previous.Thread LOOP
        Visit (Current.Info);
        Previous := Current;
        Current := Previous.Right;
      END LOOP;
    END IF;

    EXIT WHEN Previous = NULL;

  END LOOP;

END Traverse_LNR;
```

Finally, we develop a nonrecursive `Insert` procedure that threads the tree as it goes along. When a node is inserted as the left child of another node, its parent is its LNR successor. When a node is inserted as the right child of another node, it becomes its parent's LNR successor; the LNR successor of the new vertex is the parent's former LNR successor. Figure 12.3 gives several examples of how new vertices are added. The new procedure is shown as Program 12.2.

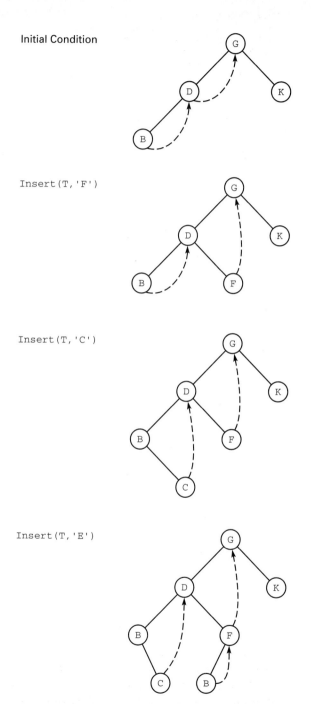

Figure 12.3 Inserting in a Threaded BST

Program 12.2 Nonrecursive `Insert` for Threaded BST

```
SEPARATE (BST_Threaded_Generic)
PROCEDURE Insert (T : IN OUT Tree; E : ElementType) IS
-------------------------------------------------------------------------
--| Nonrecursive Insert procedure for Threaded BST
--| Author: Michael B. Feldman, The George Washington University
--| Last Modified: January 1996
-------------------------------------------------------------------------

  Current: Tree;
  Temp : Tree;

  FUNCTION MakeNode(E: ElementType) RETURN Tree IS
    Result: Tree;
  BEGIN
    Result := NEW BinaryTreeNode;
    Result.Info := E;
    RETURN Result;
  END MakeNode;

BEGIN -- Insert

  IF T = NULL THEN
    T := MakeNode (E);
    RETURN;
  END IF;
  Current := T;
  LOOP
    IF E < Current.Info THEN
      IF Current.Left = NULL THEN    -- Connect to left subtree
        Current.Left := MakeNode (E);
        Current.Left.Thread := True;
        Current.Left.Right := Current;
        EXIT;
      ELSE
        Current := Current.Left;
      END IF;

    ELSE                            -- Equal treated as greater
      IF Current.Right = NULL OR Current.Thread THEN
        Current.Thread := False;
        Temp := MakeNode (E);        -- Connect to right subtree
        IF Current.Right /= NULL THEN
          Temp.Thread := True;
          Temp.Right := Current.Right;
        END IF;
        Current.Right := Temp;
        EXIT;
      ELSE
        Current := Current.Right;
      END IF;
    END IF;

  END LOOP;

END Insert;
```

Completing a package for right in-threaded BSTs is left as an exercise.

12.2 HEAPS

A heap is a rather special binary tree. One of its main virtues is that it can be stored as a simple array without the use of pointer fields. This makes the heap an important structure in implementing priority queues, as we shall see in this section, and in sorting, as we shall see in Chapter 14. First we need a few key definitions.

Complete Binary Trees

T is a *complete binary tree of depth K* iff each vertex at level *K* is a leaf and each vertex whose level is less than *K* has nonempty left and right children. So a complete binary tree has all its leaves at the same level and every nonleaf vertex has both children present. Notice that a complete binary tree of depth *K* always has exactly $2^{(K+1)} - 1$ vertices: A tree consisting of a single vertex has depth 0; a complete binary tree of depth 1 has three vertices; one of depth 2 has seven vertices; and so on.

Viewed another way, a complete binary tree of *N* vertices has depth equal to $\log_2(N + 1) - 1$.

Almost-Complete Binary Trees

T is an *almost-complete binary tree (ACBT) of depth K* iff it either is complete, or fails to be complete only because some of its leaves are at the right-hand end of level $K - 1$. This has the effect of concentrating all the level-*K* leaves at the left end of the level and all the level-$(K - 1)$ leaves at the right end. The three parts of Figure 12.4 show complete and almost-complete binary trees and some trees with neither property.

An ACBT is useful because an ordinary array may be viewed as an implementation of an ACBT. The first element of the array is considered to be the root of the tree; the second and third elements are the children of the root; and so on. If we number the vertices of an ACBT, starting at the root and proceeding level by level and left to right within a level, these numbers correspond to the subscripts of the array, as indicated in Figure 12.5.

This representation is extremely convenient, because we can represent an ACBT without using any pointers. In fact, given the array subscript `Current` of a vertex in an ACBT, we can *calculate* the subscript of its parent as `Current/2` (integer division!) and calculate the subscripts of `Current`'s left and right child as `2*Current` and `2*Current+1`, respectively.

ACBTs become useful when we turn our view around and notice that we can view a partially filled array as an ACBT, then move up and down the tree by the above-described calculations. The practicality of this will be apparent in the next section.

A note on terminology: Some authors use the term *full binary tree* for a tree we call *complete*; those authors use the term *complete* for a tree we call *almost complete*.

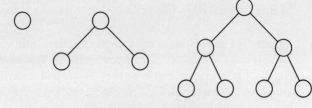

(a) These binary trees are complete

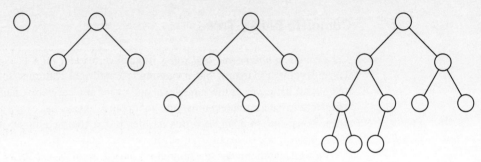

(b) These binary trees are almost complete.
(note: a complete tree is almost complete).

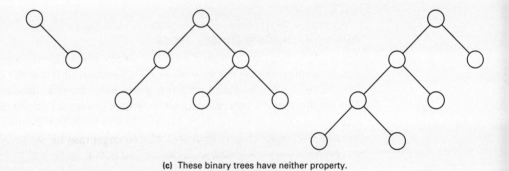

(c) These binary trees have neither property.

Figure 12.4 Complete and Almost-Complete Binary Trees

Heaps and Their Operations

A *heap* is an ACBT in which the key at every node is greater than or equal to the keys of its children. Note that a leaf is a heap by this definition. Note also that a heap is very different from a binary search tree. In a BST, the value of a parent lies between the values of its children, whereas in a heap the parent's value cannot be smaller than its children's values. There is also no requirement that a left child must be smaller than a right child.

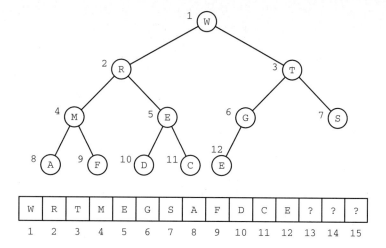

W	R	T	M	E	G	S	A	F	D	C	E	?	?	?
1	2	3	4	5	6	7	8	9	10	11	12	13	14	15

Figure 12.5 An Array, Viewed as an Almost-Complete Binary Tree (The tree would be complete if elements 13, 14, and 15 were present.)

One more definition will allow us to proceed. An *almost-heap* is an ACBT that fails to be a heap only because its root key may be smaller than one or both of its children's keys. Figure 12.6 shows some heaps; Figure 12.7 shows some almost-heaps.

Creating a Heap

Let us show first how to extend an existing heap by adding a new value to it. This is shown in Figure 12.8.

Taking the heap from Figure 12.8a as an example, let us add a key 13 to it. Let us temporarily position this new value in the next available leaf in the heap (note that because a heap is an ACBT, this position is always known!). Now, in order to maintain the heap property, the new arrival must be no larger than its parent. If it is, we are finished. Otherwise, we exchange the new arrival with its parent.

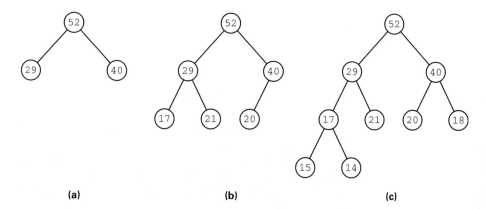

(a)   (b)   (c)

Figure 12.6 Some Heaps

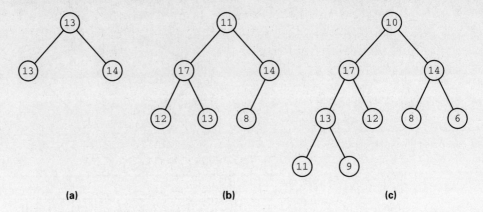

Figure 12.7 Some Almost-Heaps

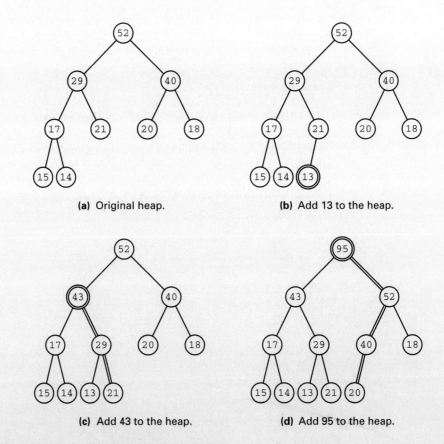

Figure 12.8 Adding New Keys to a Heap

This has the effect of moving the new arrival one level up in the heap. Notice that the subtree consisting of the new arrival and its children must still be a heap. But the new arrival may still be greater than its new parent. So we just continue the exchange process, moving the new arrival up in the heap until it is no greater than its parent. Convince yourself that we maintain the heap property throughout. Figure 12.8b shows our heap with 13 added. As it happens, 13 is added as a leaf.

Let us now add key 43 to the heap. Notice in Figure 12.8c how the other nodes are displaced in order to preserve the heap property. Similarly, adding 95 to the heap entails putting the 95 at the root, as shown in Figure 12.8d.

Let us refer to this algorithm as `ExtendHeap`.

Converting an Almost-Heap to a Heap

Let us look at the almost-heap from Figure 12.7c and consider how to convert it into a heap. We need first to exchange the root with the larger of its two children— which, of course, imposes the heap property with respect to the other branch. We now have the former root located one level down, and possibly smaller than its children. So we exchange again with the larger child, and continue this process until the former root key finds its proper place (i.e., no smaller than either of its children). Since only the root was out of place to begin with, the process leaves us with a heap. The steps in this process are shown in Figure 12.9. We refer to this algorithm as `AlmostHeapToHeap`.

Performance of Heap Operations

In `ExtendHeap`, a new element starts at the lowest level of an ACBT, moving up one level at a time until it reaches its proper place. Since it may be required to move all the way to the root, the maximum number of moves is logarithmically related to the number of existing vertices, so `ExtendHeap` is $O(\log N)$. Similarly, in an `AlmostHeapToHeap` operation, a value starts at the root and moves downward until it reaches its proper place. Since it may need to move all the way down, `AlmostHeapToHeap` is also $O(\log N)$.

A Heap Package

Program 12.3 shows the specification of a generic heap package.

Program 12.3 Specification for Generic Heap Package

```
GENERIC
  TYPE KeyType IS PRIVATE;
  TYPE ElementType IS PRIVATE;
  TYPE IndexType IS RANGE <>; -- integer subscripts
  TYPE ListType IS ARRAY (IndexType RANGE <>) OF ElementType;
  WITH FUNCTION KeyOf (Element: ElementType) RETURN KeyType IS <>;
  WITH FUNCTION "<"(Left, Right: KeyType) RETURN Boolean IS <>;
```

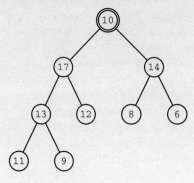

(a) Original almost-heap.

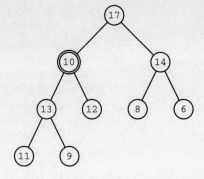

(b) 17 is 10's larger child, so exchange 10, 17.

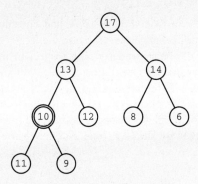

(c) Now 13 is 10's larger child, so exchange 10, 13.

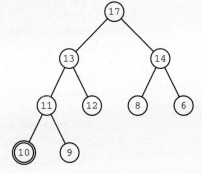

(d) Now 11 is 10's larger child, so exchange 10, 11; we have a heap!

Figure 12.9 Converting an Almost-Heap to a Heap

```
PACKAGE Heaps_Generic IS
------------------------------------------------------------------------
--| Specification for Generic Heaps Package
--| Author: Michael B. Feldman, The George Washington University
--| Last Modified: January 1996
------------------------------------------------------------------------

   PROCEDURE ExtendHeap(List: IN OUT ListType);
   -- Pre: List(List'First..List'Last-1) is a heap such that
   --    List(List'First) is the "largest" element.
   -- Post: extends heap by adding List(List'Last) to it.

   PROCEDURE AlmostHeapToHeap(List: IN OUT ListType);
   -- Pre: List(List'First..List'Last) is an "almost heap",
   --    that is, it would be a heap except that List(List'First) may be
   --    "smaller" than one or both of its children
   -- Post: List(List'First..List'Last) is a heap

END Heaps_Generic;
```

This package is designed to be used in heap applications in which it is desirable for the client program to create an array directly and manipulate its array; we therefore do not provide a heap type, but require the client to pass us the array type as a generic parameter.

The specification calls for two operations, `ExtendHeap` and `AlmostHeap` `ToHeap`; details of these are given in the pre- and post-conditions. Program 12.4 shows the body of this package, with the two operations given in detail.

Program 12.4 Body of Generic Heap Package

```
WITH Swap_Generic;
PACKAGE BODY Heaps_Generic IS
------------------------------------------------------------------------
--| Body of Generic Heaps Package
--| Author: Michael B. Feldman, The George Washington University
--| Last Modified: January 1996
------------------------------------------------------------------------

  PROCEDURE Exchange IS NEW Swap_Generic(ValueType => ElementType);
  FUNCTION ">="(Left, Right: KeyType) RETURN Boolean IS
  BEGIN
    RETURN NOT (Left < Right);
  END ">=";

  PROCEDURE ExtendHeap(List: IN OUT ListType) IS
    Top : CONSTANT Integer := Integer(List'First);

    Child : Integer;
    Parent : Integer;
    IChild : IndexType; -- to satisfy type compatibility rules
    IParent: IndexType;

  BEGIN -- ExtendHeap

    IF List'First = List'Last THEN -- heap has only one element
      RETURN;
    END IF;

    Child := Integer(List'Last);
    Parent := Child / 2;

    WHILE (Parent >= Top) LOOP
      IParent := IndexType(Parent);
      IChild := IndexType(Child);
      EXIT WHEN KeyOf(List(IParent)) >= KeyOf(List(IChild));

      Exchange(List(IChild),List(IParent));
      Child := Parent;
      Parent:= Parent / 2;

    END LOOP;

  END ExtendHeap;

  PROCEDURE AlmostHeapToHeap(List: IN OUT ListType) IS
    Bottom   : CONSTANT Integer:= Integer(List'Last);
    Parent   : Integer;
    Child    : Integer;
    IParent: IndexType; -- for type compatibility
    IChild : IndexType;
    Placed   : Boolean := False;

  BEGIN -- AlmostHeapToHeap
    IF List'First = List'Last THEN -- only one element
      RETURN;
    END IF;
```

```
      Parent := Integer(List'First);
      Child := Integer(List'First) + 1;

      WHILE (Child <= Bottom) AND NOT Placed LOOP

        IChild := IndexType(Child);
        IParent := IndexType(Parent);

        IF Child+1 <= Bottom THEN -- Parent has 2 Children

          IF KeyOf(List(IParent)) >= KeyOf(List(IChild))
            AND KeyOf(List(IParent)) >= KeyOf(List(IChild + 1)) THEN
            Placed := True;

          ELSIF KeyOf(List(IChild+1)) < KeyOf(List(IndexType(Child))) THEN
            Exchange(List(IParent),List(IChild));
            Parent := Child; --left Child was larger
            Child := 2 * Parent;

          ELSE
            Exchange(List(IParent),List(IChild+1));
            Parent := Child+1; --right Child was larger
            Child := 2 * Parent;
            END IF;

        ELSE -- Parent has only one Child
          IF KeyOf(List(IParent)) < KeyOf(List(IChild)) THEN
            Exchange(List(IParent),List(IChild));
        END IF;

          Placed := True;

        END IF;

      END LOOP;

    END AlmostHeapToHeap;

END Heaps_Generic;
```

Several aspects of these operations are noteworthy. First, notice the halving and doubling of array subscripts in these subprograms. Second, in these operations, we have declared variables of two types: `IndexType` and `Integer`. For example, the declarations

```
Top     : CONSTANT Integer := Integer(List'First);
Bottom  : Integer;
Parent  : Integer;
Child   : Integer;
IParent : IndexType;
IChild  : IndexType;
```

appear in `ExtendHeap`. We do this to satisfy Ada's type compatibility rules. The basic WHILE loop to move a new arrival up the tree to its proper home is given by

```
Child := List'Last;
Parent := Child / 2;
WHILE (Parent >= Top) LOOP
  EXIT WHEN KeyOf(List(Parent)) >= KeyOf(List(Child));

  Exchange(List(Child),List(Parent));
  Child := Parent;
  Parent:= Parent / 2;

END LOOP;
```

This would be fine if we could count on subscripts of type `Integer`, but we cannot, because we want the array index type to be any integer type or subtype. On the other hand, we cannot use `IndexType` exclusively either, because the statement

```
Parent:= Parent / 2;
```

may cause `Constraint_Error` to be raised. To see this, note that the `WHILE` loop termination condition is `Parent < Top`. However, `Top` is `List'First`, so `Parent` cannot be less than `Top` unless it is out of range! To allow the temporary out-of-range condition, we let `Parent` and `Child` be of type `Integer`. However, now we cannot use these to subscript the array, whose subscript type must be `IndexType`. Therefore, we declare `IParent` and `IChild`. Under Ada's type-conversion rules, we can convert between the two integer-valued types as necessary. The final loop is

```
Child := Integer(List'Last);
Parent := Child / 2;
WHILE (Parent >= Top) LOOP
  IParent := IndexType(Parent);
  IChild := IndexType(Child);

  EXIT WHEN KeyOf(List(IParent)) >= KeyOf(List(IChild));

  Exchange(List(IChild),List(IParent));
  Child := Parent;
  Parent:= Parent / 2;
END LOOP;
```

Study this procedures `ExtendHeap` and `AlmostHeapToHeap` carefully; draw the array views of the heaps in Figures 12.8 and 12.9 and trace the actions of the operations on them.

The next section shows how a priority queue can be represented as a heap; in Chapter 14, we will consider how to use a heap as a part of a popular sorting algorithm.

12.3 APPLICATION: THE PRIORITY QUEUE AS A HEAP

Recall from Section 7.3 that a *priority queue* is a queue in which elements are enqueued and dequeued according to some priority scheme. Priority queues have many applications; a common one is the queueing system used in a multiuser operating system.

Assuming that each arriving element has a key field indicating its priority, we could imagine implementing a priority queue as a circular array with a difference. An element is inserted (enqueued) according to its priority; a dequeue operation is just like that of a FIFO queue—the head element is removed and the queue adjusted. The performance of an enqueue operation is clearly linear; that of a dequeue operation is clearly constant.

An implementation using a linked list would use as an enqueue operation the ordered-list insertion algorithm from Section 8.6; a dequeue operation would simply remove the first element. Performance here is similar to that in the array implementation.

One particularly clever implementation of a priority queue uses a heap. Since a heap is just an array viewed differently, no more space is necessary than that required for a normal array queue. An enqueue operation is implemented as an `ExtendHeap`: The new element is added to the end of the array, then moved up the heap until its priority (key) is greater than its children's priorities. In a dequeue operation, the first element of the array is removed (it is obviously the one with the largest key!), then the last element is moved to the first position. This leaves, precisely, an almost-heap. A call of `AlmostHeapToHeap` moves it into its proper place.

As we discovered in Section 12.2, both of these operations are logarithmic. Comparing this implementation of priority queues with the others discussed above, we have traded one constant-time operation and one linear operation for two logarithmic ones. In cases where the queue is likely to grow long, the trade-off is advantageous.

Programs 12.5 and 12.6 show the specification and the body, respectively, of a priority queue package using a heap implementation.

Program 12.5 Specification for Generic Priority Queue Package

```
GENERIC

  TYPE KeyType IS PRIVATE;
  TYPE ElementType IS PRIVATE;
  WITH FUNCTION KeyOf (Element: ElementType) RETURN KeyType IS <>;
  WITH FUNCTION "<" (Left, Right: KeyType) RETURN Boolean IS <>;

PACKAGE Queues_Generic_Priority IS
-----------------------------------------------------------------------
--| Generic package for Priority Queues
--| "<" is used as the means of assigning priority;
--| "<" means lower priority
--| Author: Michael B. Feldman, The George Washington University
--| Last Modified: January 1996
-----------------------------------------------------------------------

  -- type definition

  TYPE Queue (Capacity: Positive) IS LIMITED PRIVATE;

  -- exported exceptions

  QueueFull  : EXCEPTION;
  QueueEmpty : EXCEPTION;

  -- constructors

  PROCEDURE MakeEmpty (Q : IN OUT Queue);
  -- Pre:   Q is defined
  -- Post:  Q is empty

  PROCEDURE Enqueue (Q : IN OUT Queue; E : IN ElementType);
  -- Pre:   Q and E are defined
  -- Post:  Q is returned with E inserted in its proper
  -- position according to Smaller: the largest Element is at
  -- the head of the queue.
  -- Raises:QueueFull if Q already contains Capacity Elements

  PROCEDURE Dequeue (Q : IN OUT Queue);
  -- Pre:   Q is defined
  -- Post:  Q is returned with the first Element discarded
  -- Raises:QueueEmpty if Q contains no Elements
```

```
   -- selector

   FUNCTION First (Q : IN Queue) RETURN ElementType;
   -- Pre:   Q is defined
   -- Post:  The first Element of Q is returned
   -- Raises:QueueEmpty if Q contains no Elements

   -- inquiry operations

   FUNCTION IsEmpty (Q : IN Queue) RETURN Boolean;
   -- Pre:   Q is defined
   -- Post:  returns True if Q is empty, False otherwise

   --FUNCTION IsFull (Q : IN Queue) RETURN Boolean;
   -- Pre:   Q is defined
   -- Post:  returns True if Q is full, False otherwise

PRIVATE

   TYPE List IS ARRAY (Positive RANGE <>) OF ElementType;
   TYPE Queue (Capacity: Positive) IS RECORD
     CurrentSize: Natural := 0;
     Store   : List(1..Capacity);
   END RECORD;

END Queues_Generic_Priority;
```

Program 12.6 Body of Generic Priority Queue Package

```
WITH Heaps_Generic;
PACKAGE BODY Queues_Generic_Priority IS
-------------------------------------------------------------------------
--| Body of Generic Priority Queue Package
--| Author: Michael B. Feldman, The George Washington University
--| Last Modified: January 1996
-------------------------------------------------------------------------

   -- instantiate generic heap package for these conditions
   PACKAGE Heaps IS
     NEW Heaps_Generic(ElementType => ElementType,
                       KeyType => KeyType,
                       IndexType => Positive,
                       ListType => List);

   PROCEDURE MakeEmpty (Q : IN OUT Queue) IS
   BEGIN
     Q.CurrentSize := 0;
   END MakeEmpty;

   PROCEDURE Enqueue (Q : IN OUT Queue; E : IN ElementType) IS
   BEGIN
     F IsFull(Q) THEN
       RAISE QueueFull;
     ELSE
       -- put new item at end of heap, then filter it up.
       Q.CurrentSize := Q.CurrentSize + 1;
       Q.Store (Q.CurrentSize) := E;
       Heaps.ExtendHeap(Q.Store(1..Q.CurrentSize));
     END IF;
   END Enqueue;
```

```
PROCEDURE Dequeue (Q : IN OUT Queue) IS
BEGIN
  IF IsEmpty (Q) THEN
    RAISE QueueEmpty;
  ELSE
    -- overwrite first item with last item,
    -- then decrease heap size by 1 and filter down
    Q.Store(1) := Q.Store(Q.CurrentSize);
    Q.CurrentSize := Q.CurrentSize - 1;
    Heaps.AlmostHeapToHeap(Q.Store(1..Q.CurrentSize));
  END IF;
END Dequeue;

FUNCTION First (Q : IN Queue) RETURN ElementType IS
BEGIN
  IF IsEmpty(Q) THEN
    RAISE QueueEmpty;
  ELSE
    RETURN Q.Store (1);
  END IF;
END First;

FUNCTION IsEmpty (Q : IN Queue) RETURN Boolean IS
BEGIN
  RETURN Q.CurrentSize = 0;
END IsEmpty;

FUNCTION IsFull (Q : IN Queue) RETURN Boolean IS
BEGIN
  RETURN Q.CurrentSize = Q.Capacity;
END IsFull;

END Queues_Generic_Priority;
```

12.4   DIGITAL SEARCH TREES

Consider the problem of designing a program to check whether the words in a report are spelled correctly. This is usually solved by creating a dictionary of all those words likely to be used in the report. Then the report is scanned, word by word, and all words not appearing in the dictionary are reported to the user as possible spelling errors. A word will be reported if it is misspelled, but also if it is a valid word that just isn't in the dictionary.

Theoretically, any kind of table can be used to represent the dictionary: an ordered array or a balanced BST, for example. The difficulty is that for real-world dictionaries, the amount of space required would be enormous, since in the usual tables each word would have to be stored in full.

The digital search tree provides a solution: Only a single character is stored in each node. There are as many separate trees as there are possible first letters (such a collection of trees is usually called a forest); each tree has a different first letter at its root. The children of the root contain the second letters of all the words with the given first letter; the children of a given second-letter node contain the third letters of words with the given second letter, and so on.

A search for a word in such a forest then involves starting with its first letter and trying, letter by letter, to find a path through the appropriate tree. If one is found, the word is valid; otherwise, it is reported.

Figure 12.10 shows a diagram of a pair of digital search trees for some words beginning with C and D. Notice that we have added a special character # to indicate "end of word," so that, for example, the word DEE (not a valid English word) would not be erroneously reported as correct by going part-way down the path for DEER.

CAN, CANE, CON, CONE, COP, COPE, CURE, CURT, CUT, CUTE, CUTS

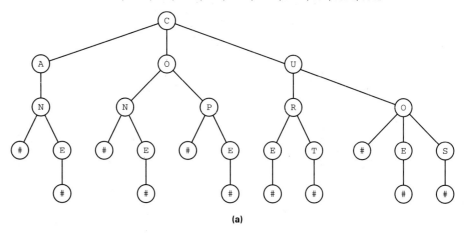

(a)

DEBT, DEBTOR, DEEP, DEEPLY, DO, DON, DONATE, DONE

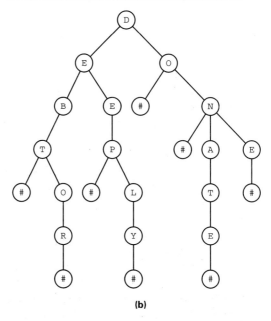

(b)

Figure 12.10 Two Digital Search Trees

If we can find an appropriate implementation of this tree, great storage savings can be achieved; indeed, this savings can make it feasible to build a dictionary that can be loaded into primary memory in its entirety, thus avoiding time-consuming disk accesses.

A possible implementation is to represent a node by an array of 27 pointers, one for each letter and the end-of-word character, so a parent can have up to 27 children. This has the advantage of letting us determine in constant time whether, say, the letter s in a given node has a child for the letter q: We just check to see whether the pointer for q in the s node is null or not. On the other hand, this implementation uses space very inefficiently, since such arrays will normally be sparse—whatever the language of the dictionary, many letter combinations do not appear. A given letter, at a given "level" of the words being indexed, will have only a few successors.

A better approach is to represent the children of a given parent as an ordered linear list, as shown in Figure 12.11.

Now each node has only two pointers: one to its leftmost child, the other to its immediate right sibling. The trees in the forest are all connected at the top level to an artificial "super-root," representing "beginning of word" (we can use the same artificial "end of word" # here). A part of the dictionary used in the preceding figure is shown in this form in Figure 12.12.

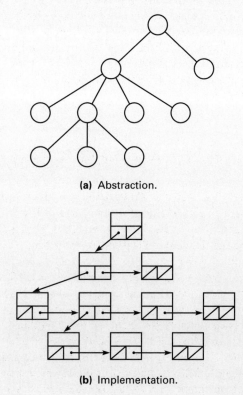

(a) Abstraction.

(b) Implementation.

Figure 12.11 Left Child/Right Sibling Implementation of a General Tree

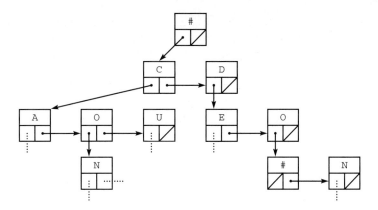

Figure 12.12 Digital Search Tree Implementation

In using this technique, we have traded space for time. Determining whether a certain letter has another given letter as a child requires a linear search through the child list. On the other hand, the child lists are likely to be short for this type of application. You can write an appropriate package for the digital search tree as an exercise; another exercise examines the space and time requirements.

The use of a linked list to represent the siblings is not limited to the spelling-checker application; it is a common implementation structure for general trees. Sometimes each node carries a pointer back up to its parent as well. As an exercise, you can consider how to represent a family tree, such as that of Figure 11.2, in this fashion.

12.5   AVL BALANCED BINARY SEARCH TREES

We discovered in Section 11.7 that the binary search tree can be an efficient data structure. BST insert, search, and delete operations are, for randomly distributed input data, approximately $O(\log N)$, because in this average case, the tree remains relatively balanced and therefore the number of levels is roughly the log of the number of nodes.

We also saw in Section 11.7 that the BST has a very undesirable worst case: If the input data happen to arrive in approximately sorted order (either upward or downward), the BST operations degenerate from $O(\log N)$ to $O(N)$, which, for a tree with many nodes in it, is a very large difference indeed.

Adelson-Velskii and Landis published, in 1962, a very interesting insertion algorithm to guard against this performance degradation. Though conceptually simple, this algorithm is a bit involved in detail, so we give it an extensive treatment here. The goal of the algorithm is to maintain the tree constantly in a height-balanced state, adjusting it with each insertion as necessary.

The AVL Algorithm

Recall that a tree is balanced iff, at every node, the heights of that node's subtrees differ by at most 1. The AVL algorithm operates during an insertion. The height of each node is tracked using an extra field in each node that carries its height. Program 12.7 shows a function that returns the height of a node, or –1 if its argument is a null pointer. This function and the other procedures we will show in this section are assumed to be subunits of a package `AVL_Trees_Generic`.

Program 12.7 Returning the Height of a Node

```
SEPARATE (AVL_Trees_Generic)
FUNCTION Height (T: Tree) RETURN Integer IS
-----------------------------------------------------------------------
--| Returns the height of a node in an AVL tree
--| Author: Michael B. Feldman, The George Washington University
--| Last Modified: January 1996
-----------------------------------------------------------------------

BEGIN
  IF T = NULL THEN
    RETURN -1;
  ELSE
    RETURN T.Height;
  END IF;
END Height;
```

Every time an insertion is performed, the height field is adjusted and the subtree in question is reshaped if the latest insertion disturbs the balance at any node. We illustrate the method using a series of examples. See the code of Program 12.8 to understand how it is related to the illustrations. You should draw a picture of the pointer manipulations.

Program 12.8 Right Rotation in an AVL Tree

```
SEPARATE (AVL_Trees_Generic)
PROCEDURE Rotate_R (T: IN OUT Tree) IS
-----------------------------------------------------------------------
--| Right rotation of a node in an AVL tree
--| Author: Michael B. Feldman, The George Washington University
--| Last Modified: January 1996
-----------------------------------------------------------------------
  Temp: Tree := T.Right;

BEGIN -- Rotate_R

  T.Right := Temp.Left;
  Temp.Left := T;
  T.Height := Max(Height(T.Right),Height(T.Left)) + 1;
  Temp.Height := Max(Height(Temp.Right), T.Height) + 1;
  T := Temp;

END Rotate_R;
```

Consider the BST consisting only of the node A, as shown in Fig. 12.13. This is clearly balanced: its two (nonexistent) subtrees are of equal height. The two subtrees are null. It is convenient to think of a null tree's height as -1; this gives the node A a height of 0. Let us identify a node by the letter stored in its info field, and represent its height by $h(\ldots)$ so that $h(A) = 0$.

Figure 12.13 A Balanced BST

Inserting C in the tree, in normal BST fashion (Figure 12.14), results in $h(C) = 0$ and $h(A) = 1$. A's two subtrees differ in height by 1 (its left subtree still has height -1), so the tree is still balanced.

Figure 12.14 The Tree Is Still Balanced

Now insert E. Its normal place in a BST is in C's right subtree (Fig. 12.15a), but this unbalances the tree rooted at A: $h(A.left) = -1$ but $h(A.right) = 1$. We adjust the tree by "pulling up" C to make it the root, letting A drop into the left subtree (Figure 12.15b). This is called a *right rotation* because the unbalance is caused by adding a node to the right child of a right child. Note that now $h(C) = 1$ and $h(A) = 0$.

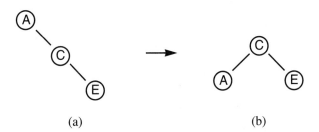

(a)   (b)

Figure 12.15 A Right-Subtree Rotation

We call this a right rotation because inserting a node in the *right* subtree caused the imbalance. The rotation is in a counterclockwise direction. We now insert G (Figure 12.16). This does not disturb the balance.

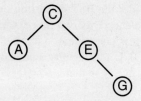

Figure 12.16 Still Balanced; No Rotation Needed

Inserting *I*, however (Figure 12.17), unbalances the subtree rooted at *E*, so we do a right (counterclockwise) rotation of that subtree.

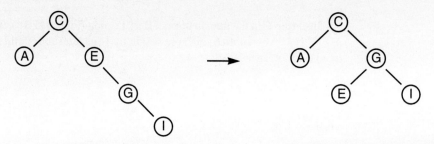

Figure 12.17 Another Right-Subtree Rotation

Now we insert *K* (Figure 12.18). In this case, the subtree rooted at *G* is still balanced, but the one rooted at *C* is not—its left subtree, rooted at *A*, is two levels shallower than its right subtree, rooted at *G*. Again we do a right rotation to move *G* to the root, but this time note that *G* itself has a left subtree, which, in a larger tree, could contain more than one node. This subtree—all of whose key values lie between *C* and *G* (why?)—is moved below *C*.

Note in this case that we did not discover the imbalance at the lowest possible level, but farther up in the tree. This is an important consideration in the algorithm we will develop shortly.

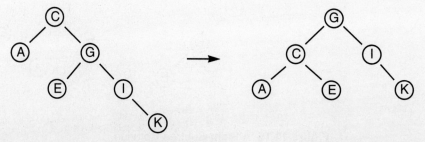

Figure 12.18 Another Right-Subtree Rotation

Inserting *M* in the tree (Figure 12.19) produces a right rotation of the subtree rooted at *I*. Inserting *Z* (Figure 12.20) requires no rotation.

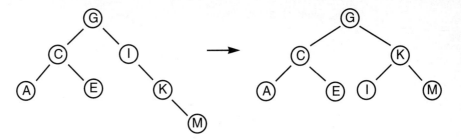

Figure 12.19 Still Another Right-Subtree Rotation

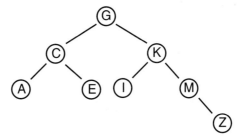

Figure 12.20 No Rotation Needed

We now insert *X* in the tree (Figure 12.21). This causes an unbalance in the subtree rooted at *M*. This is a bit different from the previous cases, because *X* is inserted into a node's *left* subtree (the one rooted at *Z*). We handle this by a *double rotation*. First we rotate the subtree rooted at *Z clockwise*, producing the *M-X-Z* subtree similar to previous cases. This is shown in the middle diagram in the figure and is a mirror image of the counterclockwise rotations in previous cases. Now rotating the subtree rooted at *M*, as we did before, completes the rebalancing.

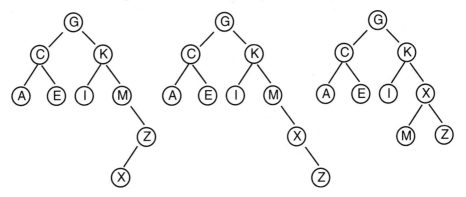

Figure 12.21 Double Rotation: First Left Subtree, Then Right

This double rotation is called a *left-right rotation*. It was necessitated by inserting a node in the *left* subtree of a *right* subtree. First the left subtree (*Z-X* in this case) is rotated clockwise, then its parent—in this case, the right subtree *M-X-Z*—is rotated counterclockwise. Procedures implementing left and left-right rotations are shown as Programs 12.9 and 12.10, respectively.

Program 12.9 Left Rotation in an AVL Tree

```
SEPARATE (AVL_Trees_Generic)
PROCEDURE Rotate_L (T: IN OUT Tree) IS
--------------------------------------------------------------------------
--| Left Rotation in an AVL Tree
--| Author: Michael B. Feldman, The George Washington University
--| Last Modified: January 1996
--------------------------------------------------------------------------

  Temp: Tree := T.Left;
BEGIN
  T.Left := Temp.Right;
  Temp.Right := T;
  T.Height := Max(Height(T.Left),Height(T.Right)) + 1;
  Temp.Height := Max(Height(Temp.Left), T.Height) + 1;
  T := Temp;
END Rotate_L;
```

Program 12.10 Left-Right Rotation in an AVL Tree

```
SEPARATE (AVL_Trees_Generic)
PROCEDURE Rotate_LR(T: IN OUT Tree) IS
--------------------------------------------------------------------------
--| Left-Right Rotation in an AVL Tree
--| Author: Michael B. Feldman, The George Washington University
--| Last Modified: January 1996
--------------------------------------------------------------------------

BEGIN
  Rotate_L(T.Right);
  Rotate_R(T);
END Rotate_LR;
```

Continuing with the example, we insert *V* (Figure 12.22). The imbalance is discovered not at *X*, but at *K*. *V* was inserted in the left subtree (*M*) of a right subtree (*X*). Again

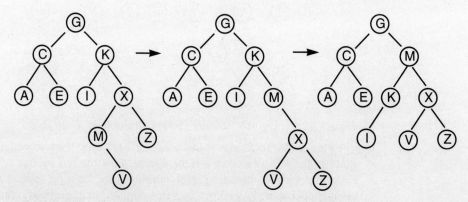

Figure 12.22 Another Left-Subtree-Then-Right-Subtree Rotation

we do a left-right rotation, first rotating K's right subtree clockwise, then rotating K counterclockwise.

Inserting U in the tree (Figure 12.23) causes an imbalance that is discovered only when we get all the way to G. The addition was to G's right subtree, so we do a right rotation. Note that, as in the rotation of Fig. 12.18, M's left subtree becomes G's right subtree.

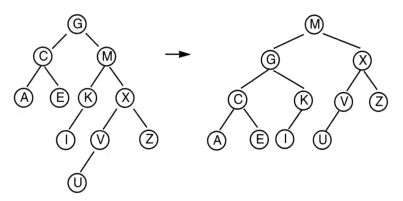

Figure 12.23 A Right-Subtree Rotation

Several more insertions complete this lengthy example. Inserting T (Figure 12.24) causes imbalance to the subtree rooted at V; the insertion was in a left subtree, so a *left rotation*—a clockwise one—corrects the situation.

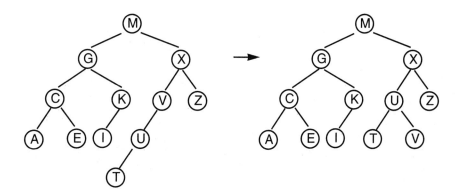

Figure 12.24 A Left-Subtree Rotation

Inserting R (Figure 12.25) causes an imbalance in the subtree rooted at X, so we do a left rotation, which also moves U's left subtree into X's left subtree.

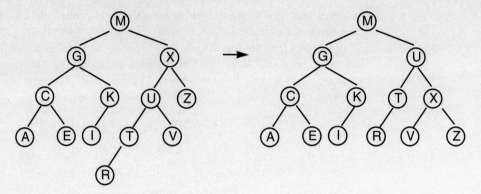

Figure 12.25 Another Left-Subtree Rotation

Inserting *P* causes another left rotation (Figure 12.26); inserting *Q* (Figure 12.27) leaves the tree balanced.

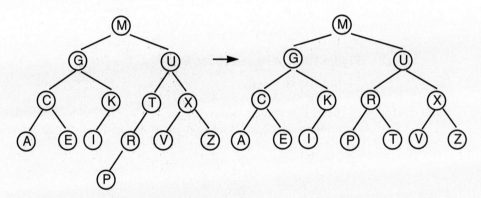

Figure 12.26 Still Another Left-Subtree Rotation

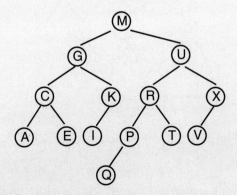

Figure 12.27 No Rotation Needed

We have shown three small rotation procedures; you can write the fourth, `Rotate_RL`, as an exercise. Let us now develop the overall AVL insertion operation. This is shown in Program 12.11.

Program 12.11 Insertion in an AVL Tree

```
SEPARATE (AVL_Trees_Generic)
PROCEDURE Insert (T : IN OUT Tree; E : ElementType) IS
------------------------------------------------------------------------
--| Insertion in an AVL Tree
--| Author: Michael B. Feldman, The George Washington University
--| Last Modified: January 1996
------------------------------------------------------------------------

BEGIN -- Insert

  IF T = NULL THEN
    T := MakeNode (E);

  ELSIF E < T.Info THEN
    IF T.Left = NULL THEN
      ConnectLeft(T,E);
    ELSE
      Insert (T.Left, E);
    END IF;

    -- now rotate from this level, if necessary
    IF Height(T.Left) — Height(T.Right) = 2 THEN
      IF E < T.Left.Info THEN
        Rotate_L(T);
      ELSE
        Rotate_RL(T);
      END IF;
    ELSE
      T.Height := Max(Height(T.Left), Height(T.Right)) + 1;
    END IF;

  ELSIF T.Info < E THEN
    IF T.Right = NULL THEN
      ConnectRight(T,E);
    ELSE
      Insert (T.Right, E);
    END IF;

    -- now rotate from this level, if necessary
    IF Height(T.Right) — Height(T.Left) = 2 THEN
      IF T.Right.Info < E THEN
        Rotate_R(T);
      ELSE
        Rotate_LR(T);
      END IF;
    ELSE
      T.Height := Max(Height(T.Left), Height(T.Right)) + 1;
    END IF;

  END IF;

END Insert;
```

The recursive AVL insertion procedure is similar to a normal BST insertion, but after a recursive insertion call, the balance must be checked. If the recursive insertion was into the left subtree of a node T, we check to see if $h(\texttt{T.Left}) - h(\texttt{T.Right})$ is now 2 (it can never be greater than 2). If so, the tree is out of balance and either a left rotation or a left-right double rotation is invoked. If the insertion was into the right subtree, the action is mirror-imaged. Finally, the height of the current node T must be adjusted; it is 1 plus the larger of the two subtree heights.

The maximum is computed by calling a function `Max`; this function should be part of the package body and can be just an instantiation of `Maximum_Generic` (Programs 5.4 and 5.5).

Because the insertion operation is recursive, the height is adjusted at each level as the recursive call to lower levels is completed. This ensures that the tree is rebalanced at just the point where the imbalance occurs.

As an exercise, you can complete the AVL tree package.

Lazy Deletion

Physical deletion from an AVL tree is complicated and in fact is often unnecessary. In many applications, deletions occur much less frequently than insertions, so it is convenient to use "lazy deletion." In this method, the node structure is modified to contain a Boolean flag `Deleted` to indicate when a node is *logically* deleted. This flag is set by the delete operation; other operations are changed to pretend that the "deleted" node is no longer there.

One final word on AVL trees. Since the purpose of the AVL algorithm is to maintain the balanced structure of a BST, it is helpful to have a debugging tool that allows us to observe this structure directly. As we mentioned in Chapter 11 in the context of the generic backup package, calling `Traverse_LNR` will not really show us the tree structure, but calling `Traverse_NLR` will do so.

12.6   B-TREES

The B-tree is a generalization of the balanced BST (or AVL tree), frequently used as a basis for structuring large files on external devices such as disks.

The BST can obviously be generalized to allow the nodes of the tree to be stored on disk instead of in memory: all that is involved is to use a disk input/output package that permits addressing individual records on disk, then letting node pointers represent disk-record addresses rather than main-memory locations.

For a BST large enough to provoke consideration of storing it externally, this scheme could use too many disk accesses, and disk accesses are slow because of the time required to search for a given record on the device. A balanced BST with N nodes, however stored, requires $O(\log N)$ record accesses in the worst case. For really large files, 10, 20, or 30 disk operations to carry out a search are just too many.

(a) B-tree node, order 2.

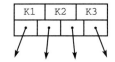

(b) B-tree node, order 3.

Figure 12.28 B-Tree Nodes

On the other hand, if the entire tree is large enough to justify disk storage, we do not usually need more than a few records at a time in main memory, so these records can be rather large. Disk storage is relatively inexpensive as well, and the time for retrieving a large record from disk is about the same as the time for retrieving a small one, since most of the time is used to find the record, not to transfer it to main memory.

This all gives rise to the idea of a *B-tree of order K*, in which each node is of *fixed size*, capable of holding K keys and $K + 1$ child pointers, as shown in Figure 12.28. A balanced BST is a special case: a B-tree of order 1. Another special case, the B-tree of order two, often goes by the name *2–3 tree*.

The keys in a given node are ordered. Looking at the diagram in the figure, we construct the tree so that the two pointers surrounding a given key point to subtrees in such a way that the BST property is preserved! All the values in a given key's left subtree are less than that key; the values in its right subtree are greater than it but less than the adjacent key. A 2–3 tree, or B-tree of order 2, is shown in Figure 12.29b; its corresponding balanced BST is shown in Figure 12.29a for comparison.

Note the difference in the depths of the two trees. In this particular case, the depths differ by only 1, but notice that there is still a good bit of "extra capacity" for keys in the 2–3 tree, which can be filled before more levels are added. Generally speaking, we maintain the balance in a B-tree by requiring that a node must always be at least half full. Combining a number of keys into each node leads to a "flatter" tree, and thus to fewer disk accesses.

For completeness, we should add that B-tree nodes don't usually carry the entire record around, since that would require more space per node, much of it unused. The tree is used as a directory structure: Along with the K keys, the actual disk addresses of the corresponding records are often stored; addresses take a lot less space than full records!

Detailed implementation of the B-tree structure is left for the exercises.

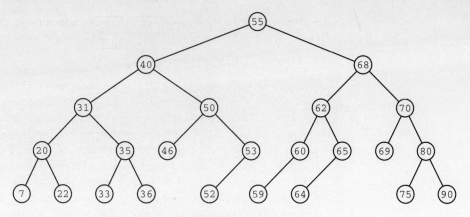

(a) A balanced BST (or AVL tree).

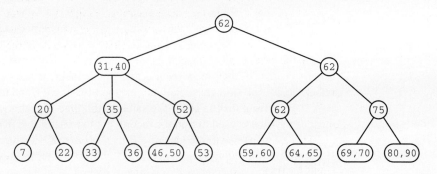

(b) A 2-3 tree (or B-tree of order 2) for the same data.

Figure 12.29 Balanced BST Compared with B-Tree

SUMMARY

This chapter has illustrated some important advanced applications of trees: threaded binary trees, heaps, digital search trees, AVL trees, and B-trees.

This chapter is the last one in which data structures per se are presented. The next two chapters will take up two important applications, namely hash tables and sorting arrays. In these chapters, much use is made of all the structures we have used until now; there is also serious emphasis on performance issues.

EXERCISES

1. Develop a nonrecursive `Search` operation for a threaded BST.
2. Develop a nonrecursive `Delete` operation for a threaded BST.
3. Develop a procedure implementing the `Traverse` operation for a digital search tree.

4. Develop a procedure implementing the `Insert` operation for a digital search tree.

5. Develop a procedure implementing the `Delete` operation for a digital search tree.

6. An interesting application of the digital search tree is the implementation of a multidimensional array. One of the difficulties with row- and column-major implementations is that the storage mapping functions contain multiplications, which may be rather slow to execute. Instead, use a digital search tree that has as many levels as the array has dimensions. For example, an array dimensioned (1..10, 1..5, 1..8) has three levels. The root has ten children; each child points to a vertex with five children; each of these points to a one-dimensional, eight-element array. Storing and retrieving values becomes a matter of following pointers instead of doing a subscript calculation. Design a package implementing such a scheme.

7. Another interesting digital search tree application is in code translators. As one example, consider Morse Code, developed by Samuel F. B. Morse when he developed the telegraph system in the 1840s. This code, which is still used occasionally in telegraphy and radio communications, assigns to each alphabet character a code consisting of "dots" and "dashes." These are transmitted via telegraph or radio as short and long pulses. Here is a version of the code, now called the International Morse Code:

```
A   · —
B   — · · ·
C   — · — ·
D   — · ·
E   ·
F   · · — ·
G   — — ·
H   · · · ·
I   · ·
J   · — — —
K   — · —
L   · — · ·
M   — —
N   — ·
O   — — —
P   · — — ·
Q   — — · —
R   · — ·
S   · · ·
T   —
U   · · —
V   · · · —
W   · — —
X   — · · —
Y   — · — —
Z   — — · ·
```

The human telegrapher transmits a message by closing a hand-operated switch called a telegraph key, sending dots and dashes as short and long pulses, and leaving a brief interval between letters. It is interesting that the code makes efficient use of the telegrapher, in that the length of each letter's code is inversely proportional to the frequency of that letter's occurrence in typical message texts. For example, *E* and *T* have the shortest codes; *J, Q*, and *Y* have the longest ones.

The programming exercise is to use a digital search tree to represent the Morse Code translator—that is, when a letter in Morse arrives, to use the tree to discover which letter the code represents. Use the # symbol to indicate the end of a letter, so that the famous SOS international distress call would be represented as

$\cdots$ # $---$ # $\cdots$ #

Write a program that uses this search tree to decode an entire incoming Morse message.

8. Complete the implementation of the AVL tree package. Use lazy deletion to implement the `Delete` operation.

9. Write a package implementing the abstract table operations for a 2–3 tree.

CHAPTER 13

Hash Table Methods

We now take up again the problem of updating and searching for items in a table, implemented as an array, whose contents vary dynamically, with a mixture of insertions, searches, and deletions. After a reconsideration of the issues and time performance associated with our old friends linear search and binary search, we wll develop the idea of a *hash table*, or *scatter storage*, method. This is a table scheme in which updates, searches, and deletions are done, ideally, in constant time. As we shall see, in actuality the performance of these operations can be made to approximate constant time, but rarely to achieve it exactly.

In a hash table scheme, we identify a record by its key field and assume that there are many more possible key values than there are storage positions in the table. We then seek a mathematical function called a *hash function*, or *key-to-address transformation*, which produces a table address when supplied with a key.

Since there are many more possible key values than addresses, this is a many-to-one function, in which many different key values can lead to the same table address. Since we do not know which keys will actually arrive for placement in the table, it is possible that two keys with the same address actually will arrive. Two or more keys with the same hash address are called *synonyms* of each other; an arrival of a second key after its synonym has already been placed in the table is called a *collision*, or sometimes a *hash clash*.

There are many different hash functions. In fact, there are a number of *classes* of hash functions; the details depend on the structure and distribution of the keys. Designing a hash table involves two essential parts: finding a hash function that minimizes the likelihood of collisions and finding an appropriate scheme for resolving the collisions that do occur.

13.1 SEQUENTIAL AND BINARY SEARCH REVISITED

Let us go back to the table-searching strategies we considered in Chapter 3. Remember that these are grouped into two main strategies: sequential (or linear) and binary (or logarithmic).

In the sequential case, the items in the array, which we always assume have a key part and a value part, are maintained in unordered form. The `Insert` operation depends upon simply keeping track of the location of the next "empty" position in the array, then inserting a new arrival just by placing it in that position. On the other hand, the `Search` and `Delete` operations require looking sequentially through the array, item by item, until either the desired item is found or the end of the array is reached.

In the binary case, we store the table elements in order, sorted by their keys. `Insert` then requires a logarithmic operation (finding the correct position), followed by a linear one (moving the elements to make room for the new one). For tables that are large enough for us to care about performance, the linear component dominates. `Search` is purely logarithmic; `Delete` is similar to `Insert`.

Figure 13.1 repeats the table of Figure 3.17, giving the "big *O*s" of these operations for the two implementations. In the next section, we introduce the notion of a hash table, where insert, search, and delete operations are carried out in approximately *constant* time.

13.2 THE HASH TABLE

In most applications, the set of possible keys *K* is much larger than the table we wish to maintain. Suppose you have about 100 friends whose phone numbers you wish to keep in your list, and you want to retrieve a friend's number according to, say, the first four letters of his or her name. Since you keep making new friends and you don't know in advance what their names will be, you have to assume a large number of possible four-letter combinations. There are 26^4, or 456,976, four-letter combinations in the English alphabet. Of course, not every combination shows up in people's names—*QQQQ* would be very unlikely, for instance—but the realistic number is still quite large.

Another example is a university with 10,000 students, in which each student is assigned, say, a six-digit number on first arriving at the school. There are one million possible numbers, but only about 10,000 students at any given time. A teacher keeping a list of students in a given course may be dealing with only 100 or so of those. Of

	Implementation 1 Unordered	Implementation 2 Ordered
Initialize Table	$O(1)$	$O(1)$
Insert	$O(1)$	$O(N)$
Search	$O(N)$	$O(\log N)$
Delete	$O(N)$	$O(N)$
Traverse	$O(N \log N)$	$O(N)$

Figure 13.1 Comparative Performance of Table Operations for Linear and Binary Strategies

course, since the numbers are assigned purely sequentially, the group of numbers in use will tend to drift over time, so that at a given moment all currently registered students have numbers with a leftmost digit of, say, 3 or 4. But this still leaves 200,000 possible keys for a table of only 100 or so students.

Yet a third example is the symbol table used by a compiler or assembler to keep track of the machine addresses it allocates to program variables or identifiers. The keys are the identifiers; the values are the assigned addresses. The number of possible identifiers is huge: Programming languages allow identifier names to be very long. In practice, of course, a given program will have only a few dozen variables or so, but obviously the compiler writer cannot predict which ones a programmer will choose.

In the *hash table*, or *scatter storage*, technique, the entries are scattered around the table in an approximately uniform fashion. This involves designing a mathematical transformation, called the *hash function*, or *key-to-address transformation*, which accepts a key as its input and returns a table address (array subscript) as its result. Such a function is usually designated $h(k)$, where k represents a key. A pictorial representation of this is shown in Figure 13.2.

In the next section, you will be introduced to a number of these transformations; for the moment, realize that a typical transformation might be simply to take the first few digits or the last few digits of the key, or to multiply the key by some number and select the middle few digits of the result. The point is that these computations generally have constant performance, since arithmetic operations generally don't depend on the value of their arguments and therefore are independent of the number of items in the table and usually of the table size as well. Given a well-chosen transformation, a table address can be delivered in $O(1)$ time.

If, for a given key structure and desired table size, we can invent a good $h(k)$, then the `Insert` operation consists simply of passing the key of an arriving item through this "transformer" to get a table address, usually called the *hash address* or *hash code*, then storing the item there (in constant time, of course!).

`Search` works in similar fashion, passing the key whose value is sought through $h(k)$, then looking in that table location. Similarly, `Delete` just removes the item to be deleted by finding its location and marking that location as available.

All this would work wonderfully—and with guaranteed $O(1)$ performance—were it not for the fact that there are usually many more possible keys than there are locations in the table, and we don't know just which keys will arrive. Therefore, the $h(k)$ function *cannot*, in general, be one-to-one, and hence will deliver the same table address for many different keys. Thus, potentially, many items will compete for the same table location.

As mentioned in the introduction to this chapter, we denote by *synonyms* the set of keys for which a given $h(k)$ will deliver the same hash address. An entire set of synonyms is, mathematically, an equivalence class. A situation in which a given table loca-

Figure 13.2 A Key-to-Address Transformer

tion is occupied by one item, and then one of its synonyms arrives, is called a *collision* or *hash clash*. Designing a good hash table depends upon finding good solutions to the following two problems:

1. Find an *h(k)* that will minimize the number of collisions by spreading arriving records around the table as evenly and uniformly as possible.

2. Since any *h(k)* must be many-to-one, and therefore collisions are inevitable, find a good way of resolving them.

One meaning of the verb to *hash* is to *chop*. The term *hash function* derives from our desire to "chop up" or "hash together" the characters or digits of the key to get a high degree of randomness in the hash code. The next two sections of this chapter introduce, respectively, a number of different kinds of *h(k)* functions and some methods of resolving collisions.

A word about one operation we haven't mentioned: `Traverse`. The items in a hash table are, by definition, scattered around the table in no particular order. Moreover, in any good hashing scheme, they're not even stored in contiguous locations. So `Traverse` is a rather expensive operation involving a sort. This is, of course, not much worse than `Traverse` for an unordered array, but it's worth pointing out.

13.3   CHOOSING A HASH FUNCTION

In this section, we will introduce three classes of *h(k)* functions: *truncation, division*, and *partitioning* or *folding*. There is no one "best" hash function in general. The choice of a particular *h(k)* depends heavily on the structure of the keys, the degree of unpredictability, and the amount of extra table space the designer is willing to tolerate in the interest of achieving a fast search. The only generalizations to be made are that certain hash functions can turn out to be disastrous, and that in the end the best way to know whether a hash function is effective is to try it in practice on real data.

Truncation

By *truncation*, we mean just taking the first few or the last few characters or digits of the key as the hash code. We cannot do this naively: in some cases the method will work acceptably; in other cases it can be disastrous.

Consider a student ID consisting of six decimal digits, as described above. The school assigns these numbers on a first-come first-served basis, so of the million possible numbers, only a fairly dense subset will be in active use at a given time. For example, at the author's university at one point, almost all active student IDs had a high-order digit of 4 or 5.

Now take the three high-order digits of the ID as a hash code into a 1000-item table. Almost all codes will begin with 4 or 5, and thus only about 200 of the 1000 pos-

sible codes from 000 to 999 will actually be generated by this code. Frequent collisions are guaranteed by the fact that arriving items are really competing for only 20
percent of the available positions! On the other hand, taking the low-order three digits
is much better, since at least any of the 1000 combinations has an equal likelihood of
occurrence.

This example shows one of the criteria of a good *h(k)*: It must at least be capable of
generating the full range of table addresses! Taking the first three digits of the student
ID is *obviously* wrong because it is so extreme; other key sets can have biases that are
less obvious but just as damaging. It is important, then, in designing an *h(k)*, to study
the set of keys thoroughly to determine what bias there might be and then to design a
function that will minimize the effect of the bias.

How, exactly, do we write such a hashing function? Suppose that the six-digit student ID is represented as a numeric string. It is easy to find the last three digits: Just take
the corresponding string slice. Now we need to produce an integer value to use in subscripting the array: Just use the attribute function `Integer'Value`, which takes a
numeric string as input and returns the corresponding integer value. If the string does
not represent a valid integer literal, `Constraint_Error` is raised.

Program 13.1 shows a function that behaves as described here.

Program 13.1 A Truncation Hashing Function

```
FUNCTION Hash_Truncation (K: String) RETURN Natural IS
-------------------------------------------------------------------------
--| Truncation Hash Function
--| Author: Michael B. Feldman, The George Washington University
--| Last Modified: February 1996
-------------------------------------------------------------------------

  Last3: String(1..3);

BEGIN -- Hash_Truncation

  Last3 := K (K'Last - 2 .. K'Last);
  RETURN Integer'Value (Last3);

END Hash_Truncation;
```

Program 13.2 is designed to test the hash function. We use an instance of
`Ada.Numeric.Discrete_Random` (details of this package can be found in
Appendix F) to generate 100 random keys in the range 111111..999999, passing each
key in turn to `Hash_Truncation`, and displaying the key and the hash value.

Program 13.2 A Test Program for Hash_Truncation

```
WITH Ada.Text_IO;
WITH Ada.Integer_Text_IO;
WITH Ada.Numerics.Discrete_Random;
WITH Hash_Truncation;
PROCEDURE Random_Numbers IS
-------------------------------------------------------------------------
--| Generates 100 random hash codes in the range 0..999
--| Keys are in the range 111111..999999
```

```
--| Uses the random number generator from Ada.Numerics
--| Author: Michael B. Feldman, The George Washington University
--| Last Modified: February 1996
-----------------------------------------------------------------------

  SUBTYPE KeyRange IS Positive RANGE 111111..999999;
  SUBTYPE HashRange IS Natural RANGE 0..999;

  RandomKey: KeyRange;
  KeyString: String(1..7); -- to hold string form of key
  HashValue: HashRange;

  PACKAGE RandomKeys IS NEW Ada.Numerics.Discrete_Random
    (Result_Subtype => KeyRange);

  G: RandomKeys.Generator;

BEGIN -- Random_Numbers

  RandomKeys.Reset (Gen => G);  -- starts G from time of day clock

  FOR Row IN 1..20 LOOP           -- displays 20 rows of 5 pairs <k, h(k)>

    FOR Num IN 1..5 LOOP

      RandomKey := RandomKeys.Random(Gen => G); -- integer
      KeyString := Integer'Image(RandomKey);  -- to string
      HashValue := Hash_Truncation(K => KeyString);

      Ada.Text_IO.Put(Item => KeyString);
      Ada.Integer_Text_IO.Put(Item => HashValue, Width => 4);
      Ada.Text_IO.Put(Item => "   ");

    END LOOP;

    Ada.Text_IO.New_Line;

  END LOOP;

END Random_Numbers;
```

Figure 13.3 shows the output from a run of this program. Running the program several times should produce different sets of output, because the program resets the random-number generator using the time-of-day clock. Note that in this 100-number sample, there are very few collisions.

Division

An alternative to truncation, which works reasonably well given a hardware implementation of fixed-point division, is dividing the key by the size of the table, which we will call `Capacity`, then taking the remainder as the hash code. It can be shown that the best policy here is to choose a prime number as `Capacity`—that is, to make the table size a prime number. You can consider why this is so in an exercise.

```
174350 350    920057  57   945642 642   598215 215   119983 983
673725 725    347498 498   264258 258   246691 691   423448 448
904650 650    179293 293   552868 868   834003   3   749919 919
648213 213    876455 455   155758 758   670787 787   560695 695
242749 749    643613 613   293895 895   125730 730   876408 408
196635 635    797344 344   589509 509   404378 378   139008   8
698515 515    369633 633   902006   6   847367 367   505989 989
555697 697    316996 996   523991 991   166753 753   426048  48
737952 952    623089  89   559033  33   933953 953   576389 389
608330 330    396168 168   565459 459   539608 608   157467 467
502455 455    363858 858   893914 914   453368 368   595841 841
726192 192    795610 610   480360 360   406990 990   757176 176
471946 946    572864 864   413413 413   301621 621   711119 119
431493 493    918663 663   510301 301   841887 887   581708 708
264228 228    580890 890   478330 330   956139 139   172564 564
250656 656    579179 179   484324 324   813403 403   535971 971
516782 782    183404 404   547244 244   526124 124   687010  10
512905 905    598373 373   864146 146   365730 730   629069  69
506912 912    288563 563   946359 359   283420 420   835999 999
877175 175    775353 353   349589 589   478999 999   825968 968
```

Figure 13.3 Output from a Run of `Random_Numbers`

Program 13.3 shows a function that implements a division method. Note again that we assume the key is a numeric string.

Program 13.3 A Division Hashing Function (Keys are Numeric)

```
FUNCTION Hash_Division_Integer
  (K: String; Capacity: Positive) RETURN Natural IS
-----------------------------------------------------------------------
--| Division_Integer Hash Function
--| Assumes K is a numeric string
--| Author: Michael B. Feldman, The George Washington University
--| Last Modified: February 1996
-----------------------------------------------------------------------

BEGIN -- Hash_Division_Integer

  RETURN Integer'Value (K) REM Capacity;

END Hash_Division_Integer;
```

Suppose Ada did not provide the `Integer'Value` function. We could convert the numeric string to an integer digit by digit. Look at Program 13.4, which finds the integer value in this manner. We just loop through the digits, starting with the high-order position. In each iteration, we multiply the previous result by 10, which shifts it one decimal digit to the left, and add the value

```
Result + (Character'Pos(K(Count)) - Zero_pos)
```

where

```
Zero_pos : Natural := Character'Pos('0');
```

to the sum. This is a very well-known algorithm for converting a numeric string to an integer value; indeed, `Integer'Value` itself is probably implemented by a very similar algorithm.

Program 13.4 A Division Hashing Function (Does Not Use `Integer'Value`)

```
FUNCTION Hash_Division_Integer_2
   (K: String; Capacity: Positive) RETURN Natural IS
-------------------------------------------------------------------
--| Division_Integer Hash Function
--| Assumes K is a numeric string;
--| pretends Integer'Value did not exist.
--| Author: Michael B. Feldman, The George Washington University
--| Last Modified: February 1996
-------------------------------------------------------------------

  Result: Natural := 0;
  Zero_pos : Natural := Character'Pos('0');

BEGIN -- Hash_Division_Integer_2

  FOR Count IN K'Range LOOP
    Result := 10 * Result + (Character'Pos(K(Count)) - Zero_pos);
  END LOOP;

  RETURN Result REM Capacity;

END Hash_Division_Integer_2;
```

Now suppose the keys are not necessarily numeric. For example, in programming languages, the identifiers begin with a letter and contain letters and digits (and, in Ada, underscores as well). In cases such as this, it is common to find the sum of the relative ASCII positions of the characters and then take the remainder, as in the preceding example.

Program 13.5 shows such a hash function; it assumes that the keys are strings of lowercase letters.

Program 13.5 Another Division Hashing Function (Keys Are Lowercase Letter Strings)

```
FUNCTION Hash_Division_Letter
   (K: String; Capacity: Positive) RETURN Natural IS
-------------------------------------------------------------------
--| Division_Letter Hash Function
--| Assumes K is a string of lowercase letters;
--| hash just sums the relative positions of the letters.
--| Author: Michael B. Feldman, The George Washington University
--| Last Modified: February 1996
-------------------------------------------------------------------

  Result: Natural := 0;
  a_pos : CONSTANT Natural := Character'Pos('a');

BEGIN -- Hash_Division_Letter

  FOR Count IN K'Range LOOP
    Result := Result + (Character'Pos(K(Count)) - a_pos);
  END LOOP;

  RETURN Result REM Capacity;

END Hash_Division_Letter;
```

This algorithm is acceptable for small hash tables, but fails for large ones. Suppose that no key is longer than six letters. This means that the largest key is zzzzzz, so the largest hash code is 6×25 (the relative position of z), or 150. If a table is larger than 151 positions (0. .150), no matter how large it is, this algorithm will use only the first 150 positions. This is not a very good "spread" of hash values!

Program 13.6 finds 100 random values using the hash function above. The random key strings are produced using two instances of Ada.Numerics.Discrete_Random— one generates random string lengths in the range 1. .6; the other generates random letters.

Program 13.6 A Test Program for Hash_Division_Letter

```
WITH Ada.Text_IO;
WITH Ada.Integer_Text_IO;
WITH Ada.Numerics.Discrete_Random;
WITH Hash_Division_Letter;
PROCEDURE Random_Strings IS
------------------------------------------------------------------------
--| Generates 100 random hash codes in the range 0. .997
--| Keys are in the range a . . zzzzzz
--| Uses the random number generator from Ada.Numerics
--| Author: Michael B. Feldman, The George Washington University
--| Last Modified: February 1996
------------------------------------------------------------------------

  SUBTYPE LengthRange IS Positive RANGE 1. .6;
  SUBTYPE LetterRange IS Character RANGE 'a'. .'z';
  SUBTYPE HashRange IS Natural RANGE 0. .996;

  KeyString: String(1. .6); -- to hold string form of key
  HashValue: HashRange;
  KeyLength: LengthRange;

  PACKAGE RandomLength IS NEW Ada.Numerics.Discrete_Random
    (Result_Subtype => LengthRange);

  G1: RandomLength.Generator;

  PACKAGE RandomLetter IS NEW Ada.Numerics.Discrete_Random
    (Result_Subtype => LetterRange);

  G2: RandomLetter.Generator;

BEGIN -- Random_Strings

  RandomLength.Reset (Gen => G1);  -- starts G from time of day clock
  RandomLetter.Reset (Gen => G2);  -- starts G from time of day clock

  FOR Row IN 1. .20 LOOP     -- displays 20 rows of 5 pairs <k, h(k)>

    FOR Num IN 1. .5 LOOP

      KeyString := "      ";
      KeyLength := RandomLength.Random(Gen => G1); -- length

      FOR Count IN 1. .KeyLength LOOP
        KeyString(Count) := RandomLetter.Random(Gen => G2);
      END LOOP;
```

```
      HashValue := Hash_Division_Letter (KeyString(1..KeyLength), 997);

      Ada.Text_IO.Put(Item => KeyString);
      Ada.Integer_Text_IO.Put(Item => HashValue, Width => 4);
      Ada.Text_IO.Put(Item => "    ");

    END LOOP;

    Ada.Text_IO.New_Line;

  END LOOP;

END Random_Strings;
```

The output from a run of this program is shown in Figure 13.4. Note that even though we are trying to use a 1000-element table, no hash value is larger than 150!

We can improve the distribution of hash values in the table by using an algorithm similar to that in Program 13.4. Instead of finding a decimal integer from a numeric string, we treat the letter string as though it represented a base-26 number, then convert that number to decimal. To do this, we multiply by 26 instead of by 10.

Program 13.7 Improved Division Hashing Function (Keys are Lowercase Letter Strings)

```
FUNCTION Hash_Division_Letter_2
  (K: String; Capacity: Positive) RETURN Natural IS
-----------------------------------------------------------------------
--| Division_Letter_2 Hash Function
--| Assumes K is a string of lowercase letters; treats key as a base
--| 26 number and converts to decimal.
--| Author: Michael B. Feldman, The George Washington University
--| Last Modified: February 1996
-----------------------------------------------------------------------

  Result: Natural := 0;
  a_pos : Natural := Character'Pos('a');

BEGIN -- Hash_Division_Letter_2

  FOR Count IN K'Range LOOP
    Result := 26 * Result + (Character'Pos(K(Count)) - a_pos);
  END LOOP;

  RETURN Result REM Capacity;

END Hash_Division_Letter_2;
```

The program `Random_Strings` (Program 13.6), modified to use this new hash function, produced the output shown in Figure 13.5 in a sample run. Note the far better distribution of hash values.

Folding, or Partitioning

The folding, or partitioning, method is another way of ensuring a good randomizing of the digits of the key. The key is partitioned, or divided into several pieces; then the pieces are operated on together in some way—typically by adding them together—and

ij	17	euro	55	f	5	hsyzpp	104	blxwdy	84
lrkq	54	usjyvt	111	vfz	51	fgwr	50	kh	17
z	25	wlax	56	wrlkjd	72	exlzn	76	glmtag	54
e	4	itdl	41	lv	32	s	18	yboc	41
mhpq	50	j	9	houjp	65	tsqeyk	91	xz	48
kyoemv	85	yk	34	z	25	jodu	46	y	24
ufrv	63	pgsyu	83	zw	47	wls	51	vpjvz	91
vusg	65	cg	8	psmtrc	83	sylbt	73	ascoh	41
z	25	owc	38	u	20	byv	46	lulz	67
px	38	snqdk	60	gumta	57	jfkt	43	j	9
mjckb	34	ugfvmp	79	cjnekv	59	zxnffp	86	mbj	22
q	16	nigc	29	btcrj	48	wocfm	55	erm	33
d	3	bacznl	52	sxjxi	81	u	20	ey	28
eog	24	fuq	41	negspp	71	wepk	51	hfzs	55
zypzqt	124	pd	18	s	18	xcxe	52	xr	40
icrzqr	85	gy	30	aduxo	60	f	5	r	17
vduobe	63	vl	32	xurrk	87	bupxzb	85	cm	14
vkcieq	61	erhyv	73	cdy	29	qfyn	58	yb	25
kndxv	70	kuuuad	73	f	5	plqqps	91	arh	24
uvgkht	83	ycek	40	eh	11	nsqqzx	111	uknlt	73

Figure 13.4 Output from a Run of `Random_Strings`

then taking the necessary number of digits of the result as the hash code. Two different ways of doing this are shown in Figure 13.6.

How can we implement the folding algorithm? Suppose the key is represented as a six-digit numeric string. The appropriate string slices are converted to integer values, then these values are summed to find the hash value. Implementing a hash function using the folding method is left as an exercise.

Having discussed a number of methods for arriving at a hash code for each arriving item, let's move on to look at some steps we can take to resolve collisions when they occur.

nmhg	499	eegav	9	ig	214	rb	443	f	5
xztqk	106	um	532	pers	605	y	24	f	5
box	66	fd	133	sr	485	kbimx	897	dcnixs	301
ddef	30	f	5	qk	426	ws	590	efvpib	849
w	22	kxmc	198	scywn	435	rmzju	718	ickql	274
iohn	717	o	14	eraj	51	li	294	q	16
imysg	103	uuqv	575	egyjo	697	xps	4	fsgtst	100
jedxth	533	v	21	mglw	921	bxhs	423	ewli	725
kymzhy	402	euqv	513	pc	392	u	20	cs	70
bpfdo	266	wtrvss	887	iqov	265	xkfc	376	sa	468
xsob	35	rs	460	hym	383	qmd	164	ssgbk	741
io	222	pp	405	pxdvro	566	junfrc	178	pkving	396
zoefw	444	jyu	746	roahhb	10	mux	679	nlgk	798
px	413	hjgtkj	974	ys	642	gwk	650	hclmk	495
ld	289	evr	276	jshtti	253	gu	176	idfua	605
rpco	925	vevp	480	l	11	hpmm	895	snftdw	981
zllkj	421	pg	396	twn	468	dw	100	j	9
byyj	535	jsypnq	84	vtqj	514	nyik	665	li	294
yc	626	ljojks	744	t	19	ud	523	pjfdp	408

Figure 13.5 Output from a Second Run of `Random_Strings`

K=510324

(a) A key.

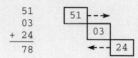

for a 1000-element table,h(k)=078

(b) Folding method 1: "slide" left and right sections.

for a 1000-element table,h(k)=060

(c) Folding method 2: "fold" left and right sections.

Figure 13.6 The Folding Method

13.4 RESOLVING COLLISIONS IN HASH TABLES

If a collision arises in attempting to place an item in the table, we need to search in a systematic and repeatable fashion for an alternative position. This is called *probing*; and several different methods exist for doing it. They all depend upon selecting an *increment* function, which we shall denote *inc(i)*, which takes a hash address (not a key) *i* and produces another hash address. If that position is occupied, we take that hash address and pass it again through the increment function, and so on until we find an open position. With luck and good choices of *h(k)* and *inc(i)*, we should be able to do this, in most cases, with only a few additional probes, so we still have approximately $O(1)$ performance.

Finding an unoccupied position in the table depends upon our being able to tell that the position is empty. The two most common ways of doing this are as follows:

- The `InitializeTable` operation initializes all the positions of the table with some value we can use to indicate "unoccupied."

- Each table position contains a flag or code indicating "unoccupied."

You will see shortly that we need to make a distinction between currently "unoccupied" and "never occupied," so whatever indicator we use will need three states, not two.

Program 13.8 adapts the generic table specification of Program 5.15.

Program 13.8 Generic Table Handler, Hash Table Implementation

```
GENERIC

  TYPE Element IS PRIVATE;      -- assignment and equality predefined
  TYPE KeyType IS RANGE <>;     -- must be an integer-valued type!

  Capacity: IN Positive;        -- maximum table size

  -- These generic parameters specify how to
  -- retrieve the key from an element, compare elements
  WITH FUNCTION KeyOf (Item: Element) RETURN KeyType IS <>;

  -- WITH FUNCTION "<" (Key1, Key2: KeyType) RETURN Boolean IS <>;
  -- This no longer must be a parameter; we know the key is integer

  -- This parameter specifies what to do with each element during
  -- a traversal of a table;
  WITH PROCEDURE Visit (Item: Element);

PACKAGE Tables_Generic_Hash IS
-----------------------------------------------------------------------
--| Specification of the abstract data type for an ordered table of
--| element records, each containing a key.
--| This version has type definitions to implement the table as a
--| hash table. The client cannot see or use these types
--| because Table is LIMITED PRIVATE.
--| Author: Michael B. Feldman, The George Washington University
--| Last Modified: February 1996
-----------------------------------------------------------------------

-- Data Structure

  TYPE TableType IS LIMITED PRIVATE;

-- Exported exceptions

  UninitializedTable: EXCEPTION;
  NoSpaceLeft        : EXCEPTION;

-- Operators

  PROCEDURE InitializeTable (Table : IN OUT TableType);
  -- Pre : None
  -- Post: Table is an initialized TableType

  FUNCTION SizeOfTable (Table : TableType) RETURN Natural;
  -- Pre : Table is an initialized TableType
  -- Post: Returns the number of elements in Table

  PROCEDURE Search (Table   : TableType;
                    Target  : KeyType;
                    Success : OUT Boolean);
  -- Pre : Table is an initialized TableType
  -- Post: Success is True if Target is found; otherwise,
  --       Success is False.

  PROCEDURE Insert (Table : IN OUT TableType;
                    Item : Element;
                    Success : OUT Boolean);
```

```
--   Pre : Table and Item are defined; Table is initialized.
--   Post: Success is True if insertion is performed; Success is False
--         if insertion is not performed because there is already
--         an element with the same key as Item.
--   Raises: NoSpaceLeft if there is no space available for Item.

     PROCEDURE Delete (Table   : IN OUT TableType;
                       Target  : KeyType;
                       Success : OUT Boolean);
--   Pre : Table and Target are defined; Table is initialized.
--   Post: Success is True if deletion is performed; Success is False
--         if deletion is not performed because there is no element
--         whose key is Target.

     PROCEDURE Replace (Table   : IN OUT TableType;
                        Item    : Element;
                        Success : OUT Boolean);
--   Pre : Table and Item are defined; Table is initialized.
--   Post: Success is True if the replacement is performed; Success is
--         False if there is no element with the same key as Item.

     PROCEDURE Retrieve (Table   : TableType;
                         Target  : KeyType;
                         Item    : OUT Element;
                         Success : OUT Boolean);
--   Pre : Table is an initialized TableType.
--   Post: Success is True if the copy is performed; Success is False
--         if there is no element whose key is Target.

     PROCEDURE Traverse (Table : TableType);
--   Pre : Table is an initialized TableType.
--   Post: Each element is operated on in turn by procedure Visit.

PRIVATE

   SUBTYPE TableIndex IS Positive RANGE 1. .Capacity;
   SUBTYPE TableSize  IS Natural  RANGE 0. .Capacity;

   TYPE OccupancyIndicator IS
     (NeverOccupied, FormerlyOccupied, CurrentlyOccupied);

   TYPE ElementRecord IS RECORD
     Info    : Element;
     Occupied: OccupancyIndicator;
   END RECORD;

   TYPE TableData IS ARRAY(TableIndex RANGE <>) OF ElementRecord;

   TYPE TableType IS RECORD
     CurrentSize : TableSize := 0;
     Data        : TableData(TableIndex);
   END RECORD;

END Tables_Generic_Hash;
```

This specification differs from Program 5.15 in two respects. First, note the presence of an occupancy indicator in each table element. Second, we have changed two of the generic parameters. KeyType can no longer be an arbitrary type, because we

would then have no knowledge of how to find a hash value. We therefore declare
`KeyType` as

```
TYPE KeyType IS RANGE <>;
```

which indicates that any integer-valued type or subtype can be a key type. Also, we
have eliminated the `"<"` function as a generic parameter. Because we (and the compiler) know the type is integer-valued, we (and the compiler) can rely on the predefined
`"<"` for integers.

The framework for the body, which implements a hash table, is given in Program
13.9.

Program 13.9 Body of Generic Table Handler, Hash Table Implementation

```
PACKAGE BODY Tables_Generic_Hash IS
-----------------------------------------------------------------------
--| Body of Generic Hash Table Package
--| Author: Michael B. Feldman, The George Washington University
--| Last Modified: February 1996
-----------------------------------------------------------------------

  -- these two functions are not exported to the user

  FUNCTION Hash(K: KeyType) RETURN TableIndex IS
  BEGIN -- stub
    RETURN TableIndex'First;
  END Hash;

  FUNCTION Increment(I: TableIndex) RETURN TableIndex IS
  BEGIN -- stub
    RETURN TableIndex'First;
  END Increment;

  FUNCTION Available(T: TableType; Probe: TableIndex) RETURN Boolean IS
  BEGIN
    RETURN T.Data(Probe).Occupied /= CurrentlyOccupied;
  END Available;

  FUNCTION NeverOccupied
    (T: TableType; Probe: TableIndex) RETURN Boolean IS
  BEGIN
    RETURN T.Data(Probe).Occupied = NeverOccupied;
  END NeverOccupied;

  -- exported operations

  PROCEDURE Search (Table   : TableType;
                    Target  : KeyType;
                    Success : OUT Boolean) IS

    ProperHome: TableIndex;
    Probe      : TableIndex;
    TempKey    : KeyType;

  BEGIN -- Search
    ProperHome := Hash(Target);
    Probe := ProperHome;
```

```
      LOOP
        TempKey := KeyOf(Table.Data(Probe).Info);
        IF TempKey = Target THEN
          Success := True;
          EXIT;
        ELSIF NeverOccupied(Table, Probe) THEN
          Success := False;
          EXIT;
        ELSE
          Probe := Increment(Probe);
          IF Probe = ProperHome THEN
            Success := False;
            EXIT;
          END IF;
        END IF;
      END LOOP;

   END Search;

   PROCEDURE Insert (Table   : IN OUT TableType;
                     Item    : Element;
                     Success : OUT Boolean) IS

     ProperHome: TableIndex;
     Probe     : TableIndex;
     Target    : KeyType;

   BEGIN -- Insert
     Target := KeyOf (Item);
     ProperHome := Hash(Target);
     Probe := ProperHome;
     LOOP
       EXIT WHEN Available(Table, Probe);
       Probe := Increment(Probe);
       IF Probe = ProperHome THEN
         RAISE NoSpaceLeft;
       END IF;
     END LOOP;
     Table.Data(Probe) :=
       (Info => Item, Occupied => CurrentlyOccupied);
   END Insert;

   PROCEDURE InitializeTable (Table : IN OUT TableType) IS
   BEGIN -- stub
     NULL;
   END InitializeTable;

   FUNCTION SizeOfTable (Table : TableType) RETURN Natural IS
   BEGIN -- stub
     RETURN 0;
   END SizeOfTable;

   PROCEDURE Delete (Table   : IN OUT TableType;
                     Target  : KeyType;
                     Success : OUT Boolean) IS

   BEGIN -- stub
     NULL;
   END Delete;

   PROCEDURE Replace (Table   : IN OUT TableType;
                      Item    : Element;
                      Success : OUT Boolean) IS
```

```
    BEGIN -- stub
      NULL;
    END Replace;

    PROCEDURE Retrieve (Table   : TableType;
                        Target  : KeyType;
                        Item    : OUT Element;
                        Success : OUT Boolean) IS

    BEGIN -- stub
      NULL;
    END Retrieve;

    PROCEDURE Traverse (Table : TableType) IS
    BEGIN -- stub
      NULL;
    END Traverse;

END Tables_Generic_Hash;
```

The hash and increment functions are not given in detail; one could choose any of the hash methods described above, and any of the increment methods shown below. `Insert` and `Search` operations are shown, as are the two functions `Available` and `NeverOccupied`, which hide the details of the occupancy indicator. The rest of the operations are left as stubs for you to complete as an exercise.

An alternative design is to allow the key type to be arbitrary, but to add the hash function as a generic parameter. The disadvantage of this approach, of course, is that it requires the client to supply the hash function. In our other table implementations, we took care of all the details and did not bother the client with them.

This kind of hash table scheme is often called *closed hashing*, because all items are stored in the same table, which is of fixed size. In the next section you will see other schemes, called *open hashing* and *bucket hashing*.

Linear Probing

In linear probing, we let the increment function be

$$inc(i) := (i + 1) \, \texttt{REM Capacity}$$

That is, we just add 1 to the hash address and "wrap around" if we reach the end of the table. If that position is occupied, we add 1 again, continuing to search linearly for an open position. As long as there is "enough" extra space in the table and it doesn't become too densely filled, we should be able to find a position in a reasonable number of tries.

Now let's see how `Search` and `Delete` work in such a scheme. Intuitively, we should just apply the same sequence of $h(k)$ followed by as many calls to $inc(i)$ as we need, checking the key of every item we find along the way until we arrive at the right one. A problem arises when we ask how we know that we've searched long enough. The simple answer—stop when we reach an "open" position—just isn't enough.

Consider the example in Figure 13.7.

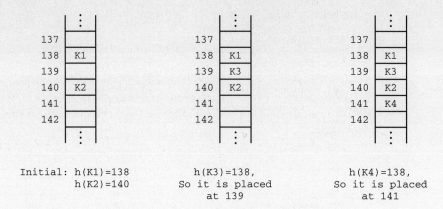

Figure 13.7 Linear Probing and the Clustering Problem

Suppose keys *K1* and *K2* are successfully placed in their "own" positions—that is, just after being transformed by *h(k)*. Now suppose *K3*, a synonym of *K1*, arrives. By linear probing, it will be placed adjacent to *K1*. *K4*, another synonym of *K1*, arrives and, of course, is placed just beyond *K2*. At this point a search for any of the items will succeed.

Now suppose we need to delete *K3*. No problem yet: *K1* is in the "official" position for *K3*, so we try the next position, find *K3*, then mark the position as "open." Now comes trouble: Let's try to search for *K4*! We'll stop at the position formerly occupied by *K3* and think *K4* isn't there!

The problem arises because we haven't distinguished between two meanings of "open": "never occupied" and "formerly occupied." We really need three, not two, states for the status indicator. One state indicates "never occupied," another indicates "formerly occupied," and the third indicates "currently occupied." We use "never occupied" as an indicator that we can stop looking in a `Search` or `Delete` operation: Finding a "never occupied" position indicates that the target item isn't in the table. In an `Insert` operation, either the "never occupied" or the "formerly occupied" state can be used to place the arriving item.

Clearly, linear probing will result in a situation called "clustering," in which a group of synonyms will all be placed adjacently and mixed together with some "official" occupants. As the table system runs, these clusters will inevitably grow larger and larger, making the `Insert`, `Search`, and `Delete` operations run progressively more slowly.

NonLinear Probing

Other probing methods have been proposed and analyzed, to reduce clustering and thus speed up the average search performance. One way is to keep track of the number of probes, then give the increment function two arguments: the value of the previous hash address and the number of probes carried out thus far to place the current item. So instead of

$$inc(i) := (i + 1) \text{ REM Capacity}$$

we get

$$inc(i, p) := (i + p) \text{ REM Capacity}$$

where p is the number of probes. The first increment will be one position away; the next probe will move two positions from the last, the next probe three positions, and so on. This scheme tends to put more space between successive synonyms and thus reduces clustering.

Another method is the so-called *quadratic hashing* method, where

$$inc(i, p) := (i + ap + bp^2) \text{ REM Capacity}$$

where a and b are constants, usually +1 or –1. You can show in an exercise that this method spreads items out over the table and will cover exactly half the table before repeating. There is little clustering, because—as you can show in the exercise—if one search starts at location $i1$ and continues over $i2, i3, i4, \ldots, iN$, then another search that starts at, say, $i2$ will not touch any of the locations $i3, i4, \ldots, iN$.

Still another method is to use a pseudo-random number generator as an increment function. This will eliminate clustering, but may be a slower computation than those previously described.

All these methods assume that successive synonyms are placed in the same closed or fixed-size table. In the next section we discuss another strategy, called bucket hashing or chained hashing.

Bucket Hashing

The bucket hashing method establishes a *bucket*, or separate storage area, for all members of a given synonym (equivalence) class. Then $h(k)$ is used just to determine in which bucket the new arrival belongs.

The most common way to do this is to use a linear-list structure for the buckets. In this case, the original table contains not records but list headers; each arriving entry goes into its appropriate list. An illustration of this appears in Figure 13.8.

This method has the obvious disadvantage of requiring extra space for the lists, but that is offset by the fact that the list nodes can be allocated dynamically (given a programming language with that feature) and thus the space not used is shared with other program structures. Furthermore, the amount of space allocated to the original table can be reduced.

There is a time/space trade-off operating here: if the number of buckets is B, then the average list length is `T.CurrentSize/B` (assuming a decently random $h(k)$). The linear search to find an item in the list is obviously $O(`T.CurrentSize/B`)$, so a larger B results in a shorter search.

A minute's thought reveals that the bucket method is really a miniaturization of the other sequential table-handling strategies. The bucket idea just cuts down the length of the sequential searches by reducing the list length from `T.CurrentSize` to (an average of) `T.CurrentSize/B`.

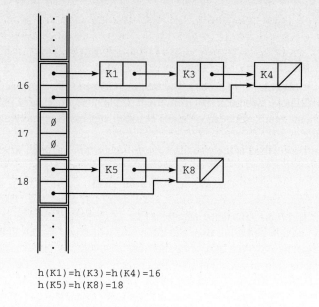

```
h(K1)=h(K3)=h(K4)=16
h(K5)=h(K8)=18
```

Figure 13.8 Bucket Hashing

Ordered Hashing

In an application where it frequently happens that a search operation frequently reports "The item is not in the table"—we call this an *unsuccessful search*—and the unsuccessful search is not immediately followed by an insertion of that item, we can cut down the time for an unsuccessful search by inserting synonyms into a bucket in an ordered sequence, say in ascending order. Thus, an unsuccessful search takes the same time as a successful one, because the search can stop when an item with a key greater than the target is found. Of course, this strategy also increases the time for an insertion, because a new arrival cannot just be placed at the end of a bucket.

Note that this ordering can also be used in a closed-hashing scheme (the details are left to an exercise). Remember that it is only worth the trouble where there are frequent unsuccessful searches that are not followed by insertions. For example, it is useless in compiler symbol-table applications, in which an unsuccessful search is almost always followed by an insertion!

13.5 HYBRID SEARCH STRATEGIES

There is no law requiring an application to use only a single search strategy. Often several methods can be combined, perhaps in earlier and later stages of the application's task.

A good example of this is a translator—compiler or assembler—symbol table. When the translator makes an early pass over the source program, the main goal is to discover the first appearance of an identifier or program variable, so that an object-program address can be assigned to it. A fast `Insert` operation is then of interest: Unsuccessful searches are always followed by insertions; successful searches (the identifier is already in the table!) are not interesting at all.

In the code-generation pass of the translation, each time an identifier is discovered in the source program its address must be looked up in the symbol table. Therefore, a fast search is most desirable; insertions don't occur after the table has been built, and deletions never occur at all in this application!

Some translator designers use different table structures for these two passes. For example, a binary search tree or bucket hash table is used for the scanning pass, because neither the number of identifiers nor their spelling is known before the source program is scanned, and in most language a tremendous number of possible identifiers exists. The BST insertion will probably perform in a time reasonably close to $O(\log N)$ because programmers rarely, if ever, declare or use their identifiers in alphabetical order. Both the BST and bucket hash methods handle dynamic space allocation with ease.

On the other hand, once that pass is completed, the table contents are fixed and only search operations are ever done. Therefore compiler designers sometimes reorganize the symbol table between passes, sorting it and storing it in an ordered array, so that the search operation—ordinary binary search—is guaranteed to perform in $O(\log N)$ time.

Working out the details of this hybrid structure is left to an exercise.

SUMMARY

Our goal has been to establish a method for maintaining a dynamic table such that the performance of the `Insert`, `Search`, and `Delete` operations approximates $O(1)$ or constant time. We have seen that by constructing an appropriate hash function $h(k)$, just a mathematical transformation of the key, the "official" position of an item can certainly be calculated in $O(1)$ time.

Unfortunately, hash functions are inherently many-to-one, with many different keys—synonyms—all yielding the same hash address. Therefore, the problem is really twofold: Find an $h(k)$ that minimizes the likelihood of these coincidences or collisions, then find a good way of resolving those collisions that do occur.

The truncation, division, and partitioning methods are all commonly used as hash functions. There is no mechanical way to decide on a best $h(k)$, but two important considerations arc (1) the uniformity with which $h(k)$ spreads the items around the table and (2) speed of calculation.

The two most common ways of resolving collisions are the closed method and the open, or bucket, method. In the closed method, when the "official" position of an arriving item is already occupied, a search ensues that probes for the first open position by using an increment function $inc(i)$, then places the arriving item there. Several different increment functions are possible—for example, linear, quadratic, and random. Each of these methods has its strengths and weaknesses regarding uniform spread and speed; what they have in common is a sequential search, whose linear performance damages the ability to place or search for an item in constant time. So in practice, our goal of $O(1)$ performance is achieved only approximately.

In the open, or bucket, collision-resolution method, items in the same synonym class are all placed in a bucket, typically a linear list. Though detailed implementations vary and small optimizations are possible, a linear search is usually involved in at least one of the operations.

EXERCISES

1. In designing a hash table where $h(k)$ is a division-method function, show why it is best that the divisor, and therefore the table size, be a prime number.

2. A certain computer does all its arithmetic and array subscripting in *binary-coded decimal*, not the usual binary integers. A word in this machine consists of eight decimal digits; characters are coded as two decimal digits, according to the following code:

character	code
0–9	00 through 09
A–I	11 through 19
J–R	21 through 29
S–Z	32 through 39

   Now consider this hash-coding problem. There is a table of 100 items, indexed by two-digit decimal subscripts. The key part of each item is a four-letter sequence. A hashing method is proposed in which $h(k)$ is computed by dividing the key by 10 (integer division!), then taking the rightmost two digits of the result. Find $h(k)$ for each of the keys MARY, JACK, WILL, and MACK. Is this a good hashing method? Why or why not?

3. Implement a hash function using the folding method.

4. Suggest strategies for implementing the `Traverse` operation for a hash table. Don't forget that `Traverse` must print out the table in sorted order by key.

5. Show that the quadratic method of collision resolution eliminates clustering and covers exactly one half the table before repeating.

6. Reimplement the generic table handler using a hash table. Design your own hash function and incrementation scheme.

7. Design a symbol-table scheme for a high-level or assembler language with which you are familiar, using a bucket hash method for the scanning pass of the translator and an ordered array for the code-generation pass. Show how you will reorganize the table between passes.

CHAPTER 14

Internal Sorting Methods

Sorting, or putting a list of records in sequence, is an important part of all aspects of computing. To take a somewhat extreme example, one data processing installation with which the author is familiar conducted a survey of its applications that were being run on a multi-million-dollar large-mainframe computer. It turned out that somewhere near 50 percent of the central-processor machine cycles were absorbed just in sorting!

In smaller-scale situations, putting a list in order is often a part of a larger program, and so it is important to understand how to develop sort procedures that will work correctly and speedily to carry out this function.

Also, the technology of sorting is well understood and many different and varied algorithms exist. Therefore, comparative study of sorting algorithms gives useful experience in predicting run-time performance.

In Section 5.2, we introduced a generic array-sorting procedure. In this chapter, we formalize the earlier discussion with a comparative study of various sorting algorithms. We assume that the number of records is small enough for all of them to fit simultaneously into main memory. We call this *internal sorting*. For each of the algorithms we consider, we will study briefly how each one performs, in "big *O*" terms. Most algorithms are $O(N^2)$ or $O(N \log N)$, but there are some exceptions.

14.1 INTRODUCTION

In this discussion, we will focus on sorting an array of data. It is, strictly speaking, not necessary to limit ourselves in this manner, but doing so will help us compare the algorithms more easily. Suppose we are given an array A(1..N) of records, each record containing its key field. (In the simplest case, the record consists only of the key.) That array is said to be *upward sorted*, or *sorted in ascending order*, if for every index I from 1 to N it is true that A(I) <= A(I+1). If, on the other hand, for each I, A(I) >= A(I+1), the array is said to be *downward sorted*, or *sorted in descending order*.

A *sort algorithm* (or *sort procedure*) will, given A in some original state (sorted or unsorted), produce a sorted array. For simplicity, we will limit our discussion to ascending sorts, and so "sorted" will mean "upward sorted." As we saw in Programs 5.9 through 5.11, using generic sort procedures makes the extension to descending sorts simple and straightforward.

An *internal sort* is one that assumes that the array is of sufficiently small size that all records can fit into main memory at one time. An *external sort* is one that assumes the number of records is so large that some of them must reside on external storage (tape or disk) at any given instant. External sorting is beyond the scope of this book.

Given an array A, we say that a record R1 *precedes* a record R2 if R1 is located at A(I), R2 is located at A(J), and I < J. A sort is said to be *stable* if for any pair of records R1 and R2 such that R1 precedes R2 and KeyOf(R1) = KeyOf(R2) in the unsorted array, R1 precedes R2 in the sorted array. In other words, a stable sort preserves the relative positions of records with equal keys.

An *in situ sort* is one in which the unsorted and sorted arrays occupy the same space, possibly with the use of a small amount of auxiliary working storage to carry out the sort. In other words, no copy of the array is needed for an *in situ* sort.

In this chapter, we present various internal sorting methods and consider their performance. Each of these algorithms is designed to operate on an array of arbitrary size, whose contents are initially in arbitrary order. Accordingly, in predicting their performance, we can make no assumptions about the initial ordering of the records. We will, though, try to find the *best-case*, *average-case*, and *worst-case* performance wherever possible. Decades of work on sorting theory and practice have established that most internal sorts are of growth rate $O(N^2)$ or $O(N \log(N))$.

The simplest and most straightforward sort methods are those with growth rate $O(N^2)$. These methods are easy to understand and require little additional memory; they also have relatively small time-per-operation characteristics. For occasional sorting of reasonably small arrays, the payoff of these methods in simplicity and ease of debugging is often worth the price of quadratic performance.

We first present four $O(N^2)$ sorts: *simple selection, delayed selection, bubble sort*, and *linear insertion*. We then give three sort algorithms with performance $O(N \log N)$: *merge sort, heap sort*, and *quick sort*. You will notice immediately that in each of the three a price is paid for the improved "big O" performance, either in extra space required or in increased complexity of the algorithm, or in both.

Finally, three interesting additional sort algorithms are presented. These are *shell sort, quadratic selection sort*, and *radix sort*.

All these sort algorithms show clearly that there are time-space and time-complexity tradeoffs that just cannot be avoided.

14.2 *O(N²)* SORTS: SIMPLE SELECTION SORT

Our first sort is intuitively very easy to understand. Given the array A(1..N) to be sorted, we *select* the smallest element in the array and place it in the first position, then select the second smallest and place it in the second position, and so on. This is done, say, for the first position by comparing KeyOf(A(1)) with KeyOf(A(2)) and exchanging them if KeyOf(A(2)) is smaller. We then compare (the possibly new) KeyOf(A(1)) with KeyOf(A(3)), exchanging them if necessary, and so on until KeyOf(A(1)) and KeyOf(A(N)) are compared. It should be clear to you that this procedure will guarantee that the smallest element ends up in the first position.

This being the case, we can forget about A(1) and do the same thing with A(2) through A(N), which will bring the second smallest element to the second position. If we call each scan of the partial array a pass, then we will finally execute a pass such that A(N-1) and A(N) find their proper places, and the array will be sorted. The sort process is illustrated in Figure 14.1.

The specification of a generic procedure is shown in Program 14.1. As in many previous examples, the generic specification allows the element and key types to be any types for which assignment and equality are predefined, and requires the client to provide comparison and key-extraction (KeyOf) functions. Furthermore, in this specification—as in all the sorts presented in this chapter—the array index type can be any integer type or subtype.

```
25 12        12            12           12
57           57 48 37 25   25           25
48           48 57         57 48 37 33   33
37           37 48         48 57         57 48 37
12 25        25 37         37 48         48 57
92           92            92            92
86           86            86            86
33           33            33 37         37 48

First Pass   Second Pass   Third Pass    Fourth Pass
```

Figure 14.1 Simple Selection Sort

Program 14.1 Specification of Simple Selection Sort

```
GENERIC

  TYPE KeyType IS PRIVATE;
  TYPE ElementType IS PRIVATE;
  TYPE IndexType IS RANGE <>;    -- integer subscripts
  TYPE ListType IS ARRAY (IndexType RANGE <>) OF ElementType;
  WITH FUNCTION KeyOf (Element: ElementType) RETURN KeyType IS <>;
  WITH FUNCTION "<" (Left, Right: KeyType) RETURN Boolean IS <>;

PROCEDURE Sort_SimpleSelection_Generic(List: IN OUT ListType);
------------------------------------------------------------------------
--| Pre: The procedure has been instantiated and List is defined
--| Post: The contents of List are in order defined by "<"
--| Author: Michael B. Feldman, The George Washington University
--| Last Modified: January 1996
------------------------------------------------------------------------
```

The body appears in Program 14.2. This procedure, like many in this chapter, uses an instantiation of the generic swap procedure that was given as Programs 5.1 and 5.2. We will not provide test programs for these sorts, but refer you instead to Program 5.11 as a starting point.

Program 14.2 Body of Simple Selection Sort

```
WITH Swap_Generic;
PROCEDURE Sort_SimpleSelection_Generic(List: IN OUT ListType) IS
------------------------------------------------------------------------
--| Procedure body for Sort_SimpleSelection_Generic
--| Author: Michael B. Feldman, The George Washington University
--| Last Modified: January 1996
------------------------------------------------------------------------

  PROCEDURE Exchange IS NEW Swap_Generic(ValueType => ElementType);

BEGIN -- Sort_SimpleSelection_Generic

  FOR PositionToFill IN List'First. .List'Last - 1 LOOP

    -- Store in List(PositionToFill) the "smallest" element remaining
    -- in the subarray List(PositionToFill + 1. .List'Last)

    FOR ItemToCompare IN PositionToFill + 1. .List'Last LOOP
      IF KeyOf(List(ItemToCompare)) < KeyOf(List(PositionToFill)) THEN
        Exchange(List(PositionToFill), List(ItemToCompare));
      END IF;
    END LOOP;

  END LOOP;

END Sort_SimpleSelection_Generic;
```

What is the time performance of this algorithm? The structure of this program is a double loop with a decision inside. We accommodate the decision, as outlined in Chapter 3, by assuming that the slower leg is always executed. So we assume that an exchange is done every time a comparison is done. The first pass requires $N-1$ operations, the second $N-2$ operations, and so on. The N-1st pass requires one operation.

Thus the total number of operations is $(N-1)+(N-2)+\ldots+1$ or $N \times (N-1)/2$, as you will remember from Chapter 3. Multiplying out, we get $(N \times N/2) - N/2$, and so the algorithm is $O(N^2)$, since the squared term will dominate the linear term for nontrivial N (even for $N = 10$, we are off by only 10 percent).

Our assumption that an exchange is done for each comparison corresponds to worst-case conditions, in which the original array is sorted downward. If the original array is sorted upward, no exchanges at all will be done. The actual execution time, then, will be faster, but the growth rate will still be proportional to the square of the array size.

14.3   *O(N²)* SORTS: DELAYED SELECTION SORT

We can speed up the selection sort a bit if we try to reduce the number of exchanges that are made, under less-than-best-case conditions. We do this by delaying any exchange until the end of the pass. Instead of, for example, exchanging `A(1)` and `A(2)` if `A(2)` is smaller, we note in an auxiliary variable `IndexOfMin` that `A(2)` is the smallest element we've seen in this pass, by setting this variable to 2. This is the location that we test against `A(3)`, keeping track of which is smaller. At the end of the first pass, this variable will clearly have the location of the smallest key. We then exchange that record with the one at `A(1)`.

Since in this improved algorithm we perform at most one exchange per pass, the overall running time will generally be faster even though it is still an $O(N^2)$ algorithm. Programs 14.3 and 14.4 show the generic procedure for this algorithm.

Program 14.3 Specification of Delayed Selection Sort

```
GENERIC

  TYPE KeyType IS PRIVATE;
  TYPE ElementType IS PRIVATE;
  TYPE IndexType IS RANGE <>;    -- integer subscripts
  TYPE ListType IS ARRAY (IndexType RANGE <>) OF ElementType;
  WITH FUNCTION KeyOf (Element: ElementType) RETURN KeyType IS <>;
  WITH FUNCTION "<"(Left, Right: KeyType) RETURN Boolean IS <>;

PROCEDURE Sort_DelayedSelection_Generic(List: IN OUT ListType);
-------------------------------------------------------------------
--| Pre: The procedure has been instantiated and List is defined
--| Post: The contents of List are in order defined by "<"
--| Author: Michael B. Feldman, The George Washington University
--| Last Modified: January 1996
-------------------------------------------------------------------
```

Program 14.4 Body of Delayed Selection Sort

```
WITH Swap_Generic;
PROCEDURE Sort_DelayedSelection_Generic(List: IN OUT ListType) IS
-------------------------------------------------------------------
--| Body of generic Delayed Selection Sort
--| Author: Michael B. Feldman, The George Washington University
--| Last Modified: January 1996
-------------------------------------------------------------------
```

```
PROCEDURE Exchange IS NEW Swap_Generic(ValueType => ElementType);

IndexOfMin: IndexType;

BEGIN -- Sort_DelayedSelection_Generic

  FOR PositionToFill IN List'First. .List'Last - 1 LOOP

    IndexOfMin := PositionToFill;

    FOR ItemToCompare IN PositionToFill + 1. .List'Last LOOP
      IF KeyOf(List(ItemToCompare)) < KeyOf(List(IndexOfMin)) THEN
        IndexOfMin := ItemToCompare;
      END IF;
    END LOOP;

    Exchange(List(PositionToFill), List(IndexOfMin));

  END LOOP;

END Sort_DelayedSelection_Generic;
```

14.4 $O(N^2)$ SORTS: BUBBLE SORT

Bubble sort is another simple sort with $O(N^2)$ worst-case performance. In this algorithm we compare the keys of adjacent elements, exchanging if necessary. We begin with KeyOf(A(1)) and KeyOf(A(2)), then KeyOf(A(2)) and KeyOf(A(3)), and so on. At the end of the first pass, as shown in Figure 14.2, the "heaviest" element will have "sunk" to the bottom, one location at a time.

```
25              25              25
57 48           48 37           37 12
48 57 37        37 48 12        12 37
37 57 12        12 48           48
12 57           57              57 33
92 86           86 33           33 57
86 92 33        33 86           86
33 92           92              92

First Pass      Second Pass     Third Pass


25 12           12              12
12 25           25              25
37              37 33           33
48 33           33 37           37
33 48           48              48
57              57              57
86              86              86
92              92              92

Fourth Pass     Fifth Pass      Sixth Pass (Sorted!)
```

Figure 14.2 Bubble Sort

Continuing as in the first two sorts above, we then start a second pass that runs through A(1) to A(N-1), sinking the second heaviest element down to the next-to-last position. As before, we will, after *N*-1 passes, have a sorted array.

At first glance, this looks no better than the simple selection sort. But there is a way to improve it that can make a difference. Since only adjacent elements are ever compared, if we ever make a complete pass in which no exchanges are necessary, we know that the array is sorted. Indeed, if the array is received in sorted order, only one pass is necessary to make that determination, so the best-case performance is *O(N)*!

What we need to do, then, is maintain a Boolean variable, AnotherPassNeeded, which is initialized to false at the start of each pass, then set to true whenever an exchange is made. If AnotherPassNeeded is false at the end of a pass, we can stop the sort. A generic procedure for this is given in Programs 14.5 and 14.6. Once again, we allow the index type to be any integer type or subtype.

Program 14.5 Specification for Bubble Sort

```
GENERIC

  TYPE KeyType IS PRIVATE;
  TYPE ElementType IS PRIVATE;
  TYPE IndexType IS RANGE <>;   -- integer subscripts
  TYPE ListType IS ARRAY (IndexType RANGE <>) OF ElementType;
  WITH FUNCTION KeyOf (Element: ElementType) RETURN KeyType IS <>;
  WITH FUNCTION "<"(Left, Right: KeyType) RETURN Boolean IS <>;

PROCEDURE Sort_Bubble_Generic(List: IN OUT ListType);
-----------------------------------------------------------------------
--| Pre: The procedure has been instantiated and List is defined
--| Post: The contents of List are in order defined by "<"
--| Author: Michael B. Feldman, The George Washington University
--| Last Modified: January 1996
-----------------------------------------------------------------------
```

Program 14.6 Body of Bubble Sort

```
WITH Swap_Generic;
PROCEDURE Sort_Bubble_Generic(List: IN OUT ListType) IS
-----------------------------------------------------------------------
--| Body of generic Bubble Sort Procedure
--| Author: Michael B. Feldman, The George Washington University
--| Last Modified: January 1996
-----------------------------------------------------------------------

  PROCEDURE Exchange IS NEW Swap_Generic(ValueType => ElementType);

  AnotherPassNeeded: Boolean := True;
  CurrentBottom: IndexType := List'Last;

BEGIN -- Sort_Bubble_Generic

  WHILE AnotherPassNeeded LOOP

    AnotherPassNeeded := False;

    FOR Current IN List'First . . CurrentBottom - 1 LOOP
      IF KeyOf(List(Current + 1)) < KeyOf(List(Current)) THEN
```

```
            Exchange(List(Current), List(Current + 1));
            AnotherPassNeeded := True;
         END IF;
      END LOOP;

   END LOOP;

END Sort_Bubble_Generic;
```

We have seen that bubble sort has a running time of $O(N)$ in the best case and $O(N^2)$ in the worst case (where the array is originally in reverse order). In general, of course, it will lie somewhere in between.

You may be wondering why this algorithm is called *bubble* sort. Taking a close look at the process, you can see that a pass can just as easily be run "upside down," comparing first, say, A(N) and A(N-1), so that "light" elements "bubble up," instead of "heavy" ones "sinking down." We chose the algorithm the way we did to make it more intuitively comparable with the selection sort.

What factors determine how many passes will be required? It turns out that the most important factor is the fact that even though a "heavy" element can move all the way from top to bottom in one pass, a "light" one moves up only one position at a time! So the number of passes is determined by the number of positions in the longest upward trip. For this reason, the overall performance of bubble sort can often be improved by running alternate passes in opposite directions, so that a "light" element that moved only one position in a given pass will get to move much farther in the next pass. You are asked in an exercise to write a program for this algorithm, which is sometimes called *shaker sort*.

14.5 $O(N^2)$ SORTS: LINEAR INSERTION SORT

Linear insertion is yet another simple sort with $O(N^2)$ running time. This method is very similar to what one does in preparing to play a game of cards, when one receives cards one at a time and orders them in the hand. As each new card arrives, the player scans his hand, right-to-left, searching for the correct place for the new arrival, then inserts the arrival in that place.

In a programming context, let us assume that an *N*-element array A exists, with $K < N$ elements in ascending order already in the first K locations. Here is an algorithm to put a new arrival in its place.

To Place a New Arrival:

1. Insert the new arrival at A(K+1).

2. Repeat Step 3 as long as the new arrival's key is less than the key of the element immediately above it in the array.

3. Exchange the new arrival with the element immediately above it.

To sort N new arrivals, then, we begin by inserting the first arrival in A(1), then looping $N - 1$ times through the above algorithm.

```
    25                  25                  25                  25
   (57)◄── "new         57                  48                  37
    48      arrival"   (48)                 57                  48
    37                  37                  57                  57
    12                  12                 (37)                (12)
    92                  92                  12                  92
    86                  86                  92                  86
    33                  33                  86                  86
                                            33                  37

 Original array     57 inserted         48 inserted         37 inserted


    12                  12                  12                  12
    25                  25                  25                  25
    37                  37                  37                  33
    48                  48                  48                  37
    57                  57                  57                  48
   (92)                 92                  86                  57
    86                 (86)                 92                  86
    33                  33                 (33)                 92

 12 inserted        92 inserted         86 inserted         33 inserted
```

Figure 14.3 Linear Insertion Sort

The preceding has assumed that there are "arrivals." Where do they arrive from? We can make this an in situ sort by having the new arrivals simply come from the array itself. Since the first K arrivals are sorted into the first K locations of the array, the K+1st will fit in somewhere in the first K+1 locations. In other words, the unsorted array "shrinks" from N elements down to none as the sorted one grows from no elements to N, and we can use the same physical space for both arrays, "back to back." This is shown in Figure 14.3.

We have mentioned that this sort has $O(N^2)$ running time. To see this, consider how many comparisons need to be made to place the K+1st "arrival." If we assume that all original orderings are equally probable, then on the average $K/2$ comparisons will be necessary to find the proper place for the K+1st element. Furthermore, an average of $K/2$ moves will be required to make space.

To sort the whole array, then, involves a number of operations characterized by a series that will sum once again to $(N - 1) \times N/2$, giving us $O(N^2)$. Programs 14.7 and 14.8 provide a generic procedure.

Program 14.7 Specification for Linear Insertion Sort

```
GENERIC

  TYPE KeyType IS PRIVATE;
  TYPE ElementType IS PRIVATE;
  TYPE IndexType IS RANGE <>;    -- integer subscripts
  TYPE ListType IS ARRAY (IndexType RANGE <>) OF ElementType;
  WITH FUNCTION KeyOf  (Element: ElementType) RETURN KeyType IS <>;
  WITH FUNCTION "<" (Left, Right: KeyType) RETURN Boolean IS <>;
```

```
PROCEDURE Sort_LinearInsertion_Generic(List: IN OUT ListType);
------------------------------------------------------------------------
--| Pre: The procedure has been instantiated and List is defined
--| Post: The contents of List are in order defined by "<"
--| Author: Michael B. Feldman, The George Washington University
--| Last Modified: January 1996
------------------------------------------------------------------------
```

Program 14.8 Body of Linear Insertion Sort

```
WITH Swap_Generic;
PROCEDURE Sort_LinearInsertion_Generic(List: IN OUT ListType) IS
------------------------------------------------------------------------
--| Body of generic Linear Insertion Sort
--| Author: Michael B. Feldman, The George Washington University
--| Last Modified: January 1996
------------------------------------------------------------------------

  PROCEDURE Exchange IS NEW Swap_Generic(ValueType => ElementType);

  Top:       IndexType := List'First;
  Bottom:    IndexType := List'Last;
  Position:  IndexType;

BEGIN -- Sort_LinearInsertion_Generic

    FOR CurrentBottom IN Top+1. .Bottom LOOP
      Position := CurrentBottom;

      WHILE Position /= Top
        AND THEN KeyOf(List(Position)) < KeyOf(List(Position-1)) LOOP

        Exchange(List(Position), List(Position - 1));
        Position := Position - 1;
      END LOOP;

    END LOOP;

END Sort_LinearInsertion_Generic;
```

14.6 *O*(*N* LOG *N*) SORTS: MERGE SORT

In Chapter 3, we gave a sketch of a recursive algorithm to sort a list by merging. In this section we will develop a nonrecursive version of merge sort, which sorts an array with performance $O(N \log N)$. The price paid for the improved performance is that a second copy of the array is needed.

Consider the general algorithm for merging two sorted lists L1 and L2 to create a third list L3. (These are not necessarily linked lists; we are thinking abstractly here.) The sparse-vector addition algorithm shown in Section 9.8 is a special case of this.

The algorithm proceeds by comparing the key of the first element in L1 with the key of the first element in L2. The element with the smaller key is removed from its list and placed at the end of L3. (If the keys are equal, act as though L1 had the smaller one). At this stage, one of the lists has been shortened by one element.

Now compare the two first elements again, removing the one with the smaller key and attaching it to L3. If we continue this process, eventually either L1 or L2 becomes empty. The remaining elements in the nonempty list are then just removed and copied to L3. Each list is traversed exactly once, and every element is copied exactly once, so the performance of the merge is directly proportional to the total number of elements in the two lists.

Several illustrations of the merge algorithm are given in Figure 14.4. We now need to consider how to use this merge to create a merge sort.

In any sort, we are given an unsorted array of N elements. Let us think of this array as a collection of N sorted lists, each with one element in it. For simplicity, let's assume that N is exactly a power of 2; we'll remove this limitation later.

Now create a "blank" array to use as a result array. Go through the original array, merging each pair of elements into this result array. So elements 1 and 2 are merged into positions 1 and 2 of the result, and so on. When we are all finished, the result array will contain $N/2$ sorted lists, each with two elements.

Copy the result array back to the original, then merge, from the original array, each pair of lists of length 2 into the result. This will give $N/4$ lists of length 4. Again, copy the result array back, and continue merging and copying longer and longer lists, until two lists of length $N/2$ are left in the original array. Merge these into the result array, which is then sorted! This process is illustrated in Figure 14.5.

To see the performance of this algorithm, note that each merge pass performs exactly $2N$ operations—each element is merged once, then copied back once. If N is a

L1	L2	L3=Merge(L1,L2)
3	4	3
5		4
9		5
		9

L1	L2	L3=Merge(L1,L2)
13	2	2
	5	5
	10	10
		13

L1	L2	L3=Merge(L1,L2)
2	1	1
4	3	3
8	6	4
10	11	6
13	15	8
		10
		11
		13
		15

Figure 14.4 Several Examples of Merging

Initially List Length=1	After 1st pass List Length=2	After 2nd pass List Length=4	After 3rd pass List Length=8	Finally List Length=16
23	14	−1	−1	−9
14	23	0	0	−3
0	−1	14	3	−1
−1	0	23	4	0
3	3	3	7	1
4	4	4	8	2
8	7	7	14	3
7	8	8	23	4
19	12	−3	−9	7
12	19	1	−3	8
1	−3	12	1	10
−3	1	19	2	12
10	−9	−9	10	14
−9	10	2	12	15
2	2	10	15	19
15	15	15	19	23

Figure 14.5 Merge Sort

power of 2, there are log N passes, so the growth rate of the whole algorithm is $O(N \log N)$. If N is not a power of 2, the number of passes is the logarithm of the next higher power of 2. You can show this in an exercise.

Program 14.9 gives the specification for merge sort. We have added an extra generic parameter,

```
WITH PROCEDURE Put(List: ListType); -- for debugging
```

just as a debugging aid. In debugging a sort algorithm, it is helpful to be able to display the contents of the array at various times during the sort process. Because the key, element, and array types can vary from instantiation to instantiation, we cannot simply include a display routine in the body of the sort; the client must supply a procedure with knowledge of the array details.

Program 14.9 Specification for Merge Sort

```
GENERIC

  TYPE KeyType IS PRIVATE;
  TYPE ElementType IS PRIVATE;
  TYPE IndexType IS RANGE <>;   -- integer subscripts
  TYPE ListType IS ARRAY (IndexType RANGE <>) OF ElementType;
  WITH FUNCTION KeyOf  (Element: ElementType) RETURN KeyType IS <>;
  WITH FUNCTION "<" (Left, Right: KeyType) RETURN Boolean IS <>;


  WITH PROCEDURE Put(List: ListType); -- for debugging
PROCEDURE Sort_Merge_Generic(List: IN OUT ListType);
-----------------------------------------------------------------------
--| Pre: The procedure has been instantiated and List is defined
--| Post: The contents of List are in order defined by "<"
--| Author: Michael B. Feldman, The George Washington University
--| Last Modified: January 1996
-----------------------------------------------------------------------
```

Program 14.10 shows the body of this sort procedure. Here we have used variables whose type is `Integer`, to make the algorithm independent of the actual index type. In particular, because the algorithm depends on `WHILE` loop conditions for termination, the loop control variables can go temporarily out of the array's subscript range. An example of this is

```
WHILE Left <= Max LOOP
```

where

```
Max : CONSTANT Integer := Integer(List'Last);
```

`Left`'s value is `Max+1` at the end of the last iteration, to cause the loop to terminate. If we declared `Left` as having type `IndexType`, this temporary out-of-range condition would cause `Constraint_Error` to be raised. To prevent this, we use `Integer` variables. Because these are incompatible with the actual index type of the array, we must then use type conversion for our subscript references. An example is

```
List(IndexType(M)) := TempArray(IndexType(Right));
```

in which the subscript variables are converted to `IndexType`. This conversion is carried out at compilation time, to satisfy Ada's type-compatibility rules, and normally imposes no execution-time overhead.

Program 14.10 Body of Nonrecursive Merge Sort

```
WITH Swap_Generic;
PROCEDURE Sort_Merge_Generic(List: IN OUT ListType) IS
-------------------------------------------------------------------------
--| Body of generic Merge Sort
--| Author: Michael B. Feldman, The George Washington University
--| Last Modified: January 1996
-------------------------------------------------------------------------

  PROCEDURE Exchange IS NEW Swap_Generic(ValueType => ElementType);

  TempArray        : ListType(List'Range);
  Max              : CONSTANT Integer := Integer(List'Last);
  CurrentLength    : Integer;  -- Length of subarrays
  M                : Integer;  -- Position in Result
  Left, TopLeft    : Integer;  -- Position and end of Left
  Right, TopRight  : Integer;  -- Position and end of Right

BEGIN
  CurrentLength := 1;
  WHILE CurrentLength < Max LOOP -- New phase

    TempArray := List;
    Left := Integer(List'First);
    M := Integer(List'First);

    WHILE Left <= Max LOOP -- Find pair of subarrays

      IF Left + CurrentLength <= Max THEN
        TopLeft := Left + CurrentLength;
      ELSE
        TopLeft := Max + 1;
```

```
        END IF;
        Right := TopLeft;

        IF Right + CurrentLength <= Max THEN
          TopRight := Right + CurrentLength;
        ELSE
          TopRight := Max + 1;
        END IF;


        -- Go until one subarray runs out
        WHILE Left < TopLeft AND Right < TopRight LOOP

          IF KeyOf(TempArray(IndexType(Left)))
            < KeyOf(TempArray(IndexType(Right))) THEN
            List(IndexType(M)) := TempArray(IndexType(Left));
            Left := Left + 1;

          ELSE
            List(IndexType(M)) := TempArray(IndexType(Right));
            Right := Right + 1;
          END IF;
          M := M + 1;

        END LOOP;

        -- Now "copy tail" of whichever subarray remains
        WHILE Left < TopLeft LOOP
          List(IndexType(M)) := TempArray(IndexType(Left));
          Left := Left + 1;
          M := M + 1;
        END LOOP;

        WHILE Right < TopRight LOOP
          List(IndexType(M)) := TempArray(IndexType(Right));
          Right := Right + 1;
          M := M + 1;
        END LOOP;

        Left := TopRight;   -- Next pair of subarrays
      END LOOP;


      -- Now double size of subarrays
      -- and go back for next phase

      Put (List);  -- for debugging; display array at end of each phase

      CurrentLength := 2 * CurrentLength;
    END LOOP;

END Sort_Merge_Generic;
```

Notice that near the end of the procedure, the `Put` procedure is called. This call causes the array to be displayed at the end of each sort phase.

It is convenient to include such a `Put` parameter as part of the generic specification, while the procedure is in the debugging stage; once the program is fully debugged, you should remove this "extra" parameter from the specification and the body.

The merge sort algorithm can be speeded up by avoiding the extra copying of the temporary array back to the original. This is done by alternating the "original" and "temporary" arrays, using a flag to keep track of which array is which. We leave the development of a program for this as an exercise.

14.7 *O(N LOG N)* SORTS: HEAP SORT

Heap sort is an important *N* log *N* algorithm for internal sorting. It is an unusual method in that no space penalty is exacted for the good performance: indeed, it is an *in situ* sort.

Recall the discussion of heaps in Section 12.2. There we developed the algorithms `ExtendHeap`, which adds a new value to an existing heap, and `AlmostHeapToHeap`, which moves a value down an existing heap until it finds its proper position.

In Section 12.2, we represented a heap as an array, or—to look at it another way— we viewed an array as a heap. Given an unsorted array to sort, we can view our unsorted array as a heap and use heap operations to sort it. To do this, we first turn the unsorted array A into a heap, by calling `ExtendHeap` repeatedly, using increasing slices of the array each time. The first time, we add `A(1)` to an empty heap, then we add `A(2)` to the heap consisting of the slice `A(1. .1)`, then we add `A(3)` to the slice `A(1. .2)`, and so on until we have added all values to the heap.

This application of `ExtendHeap` is slightly different from its use as an `Enqueue` operation for a priority queue, as in Section 12.3. There, we supposed that each new value to be enqueued was newly arrived; here, all the values are in the array right from the start. The `ExtendHeap` algorithm works just as well in both cases. Figure 14.6

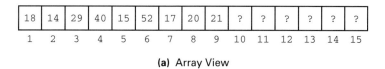

(a) Array View

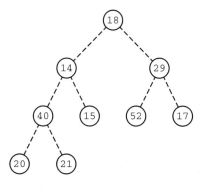

(b) ACBT View

Figure 14.6 An Unsorted Array

shows an unsorted array and its ACBT view; Figure 14.7 shows the same array after some of its elements have been added to the heap; Figure 14.8 shows the final heap. Be sure you understand how the heap was built; practice the sequence of ExtendHeap operations on an array of your own.

Once we have turned our unsorted array into a heap by repeatedly calling ExtendHeap, we can sort the array. Note that the largest element in the original list is now *necessarily* at the root of the heap. Now take this largest key and exchange it with the key in the rightmost position of the lowest level of the heap. This puts the largest value in its final position in the sorted array. If we then (conceptually) cut this leaf off the tree, what are we left with? If the original heap had *N* nodes, we are left with an almost-heap of *N* − 1 nodes (remember, we are ignoring the rightmost lowest leaf).

Now we convert the almost-heap to a heap (of *N* − 1 nodes), by just calling AlmostHeapToHeap. It is clear that the second-largest key in the original list is now at the root. Exchange it with the rightmost lowest leaf of the (*N* − 1-node) heap. Conceptually cut this leaf off, producing an *N* − 2-node almost-heap. Convert it to a heap, then continue the process until all *N* keys have been removed from the heap and swapped into their final positions. At this point, the heap is empty and the array is sorted! This is illustrated in Figure 14.9.

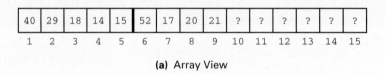

(a) Array View

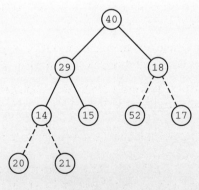

(b) ACBT View

Figure 14.7 Array after First Five Elements Have Been Added to the Heap

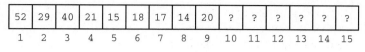

(a) Array View

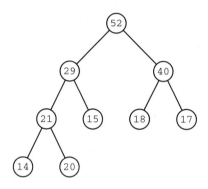

(b) ACBT View

Figure 14.8 Array, Fully Converted to Heap

The heap sort algorithm can be summarized as follows:

Heap Sort:

1. `A(1)` is a heap trivially.

2. Make a heap of the entire array by adding the values in `A(2)` through `A(N)` in turn. The heap "grows" in the left end of the array; the values yet to be added dwindle in the right end.

3. Remembering that the rightmost lowest key is now at `A(N)`, exchange it with `A(1)` and convert this almost-heap `A(1..N-1)` into a heap.

4. Continue the process in (3) by exchanging `A(N-1)` with `A(1)`, converting to a heap, and so on.

The heap is now dwindling in the left end of the array and the sorted list is growing in the right end.

Programs 14.11 and 14.12 show a generic procedure for heap sort. This procedure uses the generic heap package given in Programs 12.3 and 12.4; note that, given the procedures `ExtendHeap` and `AlmostHeapToHeap`, the heap sort procedure is quite brief.

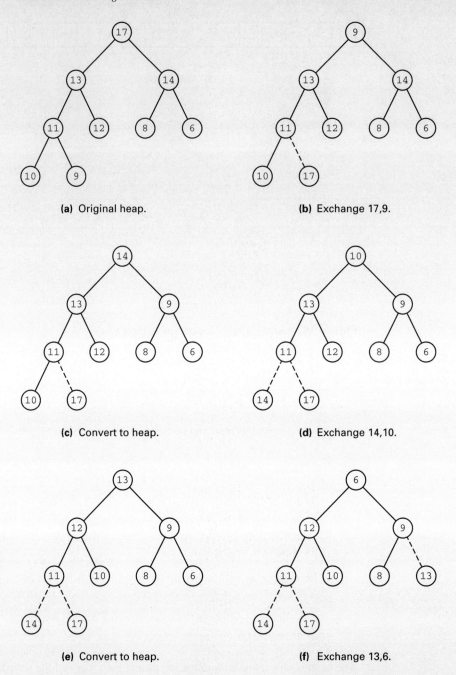

(a) Original heap.

(b) Exchange 17,9.

(c) Convert to heap.

(d) Exchange 14,10.

(e) Convert to heap.

(f) Exchange 13,6.

Figure 14.9 Sorting with a Heap

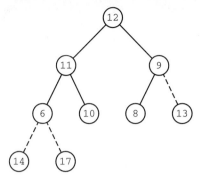

(g) Convert to heap.

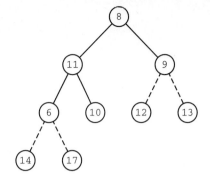

(h) Exchange 12,8.

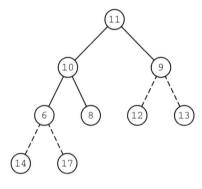

(i) Convert to heap.

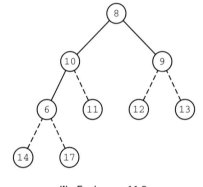

(j) Exchange 11,8.

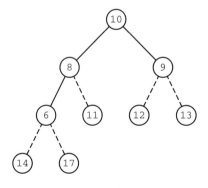

(k) Convert to heap.

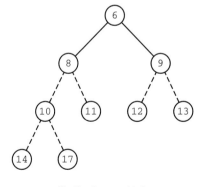

(l) Exchange 10,6.

Figure 14.9 *(continued)*

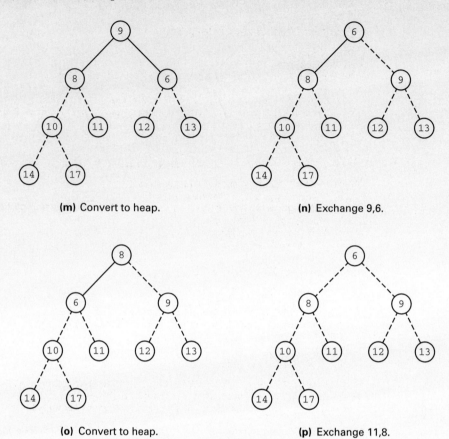

(m) Convert to heap.

(n) Exchange 9,6.

(o) Convert to heap.

(p) Exchange 11,8.

Figure 14.9 *(continued)*

Program 14.11 Specification for Heap Sort

```
GENERIC

  TYPE KeyType IS PRIVATE;
  TYPE ElementType IS PRIVATE;
  TYPE IndexType IS RANGE <>;  -- integer subscripts
  TYPE ListType IS ARRAY (IndexType RANGE <>) OF ElementType;
  WITH FUNCTION KeyOf (Element: ElementType) RETURN KeyType IS <>;
  WITH FUNCTION "<" (Left, Right: KeyType) RETURN Boolean IS <>;

PROCEDURE Sort_Heap_Generic(List: IN OUT ListType);
------------------------------------------------------------------------
--| Pre: The procedure has been instantiated and List is defined
--| Post: The contents of List are in order defined by "<"
--| Author: Michael B. Feldman, The George Washington University
--| Last Modified: January 1996
------------------------------------------------------------------------
```

Program 14.12 Body of Heap Sort

```
WITH Heaps_Generic;
WITH Swap_Generic;
PROCEDURE Sort_Heap_Generic(List: IN OUT ListType) IS
--------------------------------------------------------------------
--| Body of Generic Heap Sort Procedure
--| Author: Michael B. Feldman, The George Washington University
--| Last Modified: January 1996
--------------------------------------------------------------------

  PROCEDURE Exchange IS NEW Swap_Generic(ValueType => ElementType);

  PACKAGE Heaps IS NEW Heaps_Generic
    (ElementType => ElementType,
     IndexType => IndexType,
     ListType => ListType,
     KeyType => KeyType);
  USE Heaps;

BEGIN -- Sort_Heap_Generic

  -- first build a heap

  FOR WhichElement IN List'First. .List'Last LOOP
    ExtendHeap(List(List'First. .WhichElement));
  END LOOP;


  -- now sort the heap

  FOR WhichElement IN REVERSE List'First. .List'Last LOOP
    Exchange(List(List'First),List(WhichElement));
    AlmostHeapToHeap(List(List'First. .WhichElement-1));
  END LOOP;

END Sort_Heap_Generic;
```

What is the performance of heap sort? We can estimate it conservatively by noting that since the tree we are using is—by definition—balanced, its depth is equal to log $N - 1$, where N is the number of nodes rounded up to the next higher power of 2. To build the heap, we call ExtendHeap approximately N times. Since ExtendHeap is a log N operation, building the heap is, conservatively, $O(N \log N)$. In fact, it is faster than that, for two reasons: first, an element may not have to travel all the way up the heap; second, because the number of levels in the heap grows as the heap grows, even the maximum travel for most elements is less than log N. A similar argument can be made for the N calls of AlmostHeapToHeap. Estimating conservatively, then, heap sort has two phases, each $O(N \log N)$, so the overall algorithm is $O(N \log N)$.

Suppose the original array is already sorted. Since all the larger elements are at the right-hand end of the array, they are at the bottom of the tree to be turned into a heap. Thus elements will have farther to move into their "heap" positions if the array is sorted or nearly so. Ironically, then, heap sort's worst-case performance is for a sorted array. On the other hand, heap sort's best-case performance is achieved when the original array is sorted *downward*, because in that case it is already a heap!

Heap Sort is interesting partly because it can be made to run with a relatively small time per operation. Because parents and children are calculated by dividing and multiplying by 2, respectively, finding the parent or a child of a node can be implemented as a single-bit shift in assembly language or in a high-level language in which the compiler implements a division or multiplication by 2 as a single shift.

14.8 *O(N* LOG *N)* SORTS: QUICK SORT

Quick sort is one sorting method that has been shown by much experimenting to perform well in the average case: On the average quick sort requires $O(N \log N)$, even though its worst-case performance is $O(N^2)$.

Quick sort is often called *partition sort*. It is in fact a recursive method, in which the unsorted array is first rearranged so that there is some record, somewhere in the middle of the array, whose key is greater than all keys to its left and less than or equal to all keys to its right.

Once this "middle" record (which is probably not really in the middle of the array) is found, the same method can be applied again to sort the section of the array to its left, then to sort the section of array to its right.

This algorithm is thus another example of a "divide and conquer" method, in which a structure is divided into two pieces by some criterion, then the two pieces are attacked separately. Each piece is then subdivided, and so on, until the whole structure is processed.

Philosophically this method is in the same category with binary search, and with the binary search tree methods we have seen earlier.

The Quick Sort Algorithm

The idea is to take a guess at a "median" or "middle" value, one an element in the array such that half the other elements are less than, and the other half greater than, the median. It would be a true median if exactly half the elements were greater, half less, and we could partition into equal-sized pieces. In general, we won't guess correctly, but whichever value we guess will clearly let us partition the array into two pieces—generally of unequal size—such that one piece has all the smaller elements and the other piece has all the larger ones.

How shall we take a guess? Since we're not assuming any prior ordering in the array, any element has as good a chance of being the median as any other. So we might just as well take the first element in the array. In fact, we'll be a little more clever than that; since the first few elements in the array could all be the same value, we'll choose the leftmost distinct element. Since our guessed "median" really isn't a median, because in general it doesn't fall in the middle of the array, it's conventional to call it a *pivot* instead.

Now, having found the location of the pivot, how do we partition? The idea is to start two *cursors* moving: one will move rightward from the left end of the array, the other leftward from the right end. The rightward-moving cursor (which we'll call "up") will keep moving as long as the elements it scans are less than the pivot; the leftward-moving one (which we'll call "down") will keep moving as long as the elements it scans are greater than the pivot.

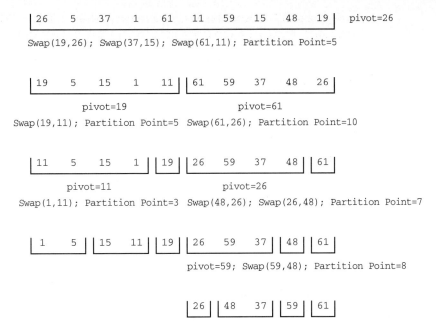

Figure 14.10 Quick Sort

If the "up" cursor finds a value greater than the pivot and the "down" cursor finds one less than the pivot, those two values are exchanged. Then the cursors are started again from those points.

Eventually, the two cursors will meet. At the point where they meet, all values to the left are guaranteed to be less than the pivot and all values to the right are guaranteed to be greater than the pivot. We call that meeting point the *partition point*.

Now we can write a procedure Quick, which first finds a pivot, then finds the partition point for that pivot. At that stage, the array is partitioned into a section with smaller values on the left and a section with larger values on the right. But the two sections are not yet sorted. On the other hand, we can sort them by calling Quick recursively, first to sort the left section, then to sort the right section.

All that remains is to write a "driver" called QuickSort, which just calls Quick with the entire initial array as input. In Figure 14.10, you can see the various phases of the process as applied to a 10-element array.

The entire procedure is shown in Programs 14.13 and 14.14.

Program 14.13 Specification for Quick Sort

```
GENERIC

   TYPE KeyType IS PRIVATE;
   TYPE ElementType IS PRIVATE;
   TYPE IndexType IS RANGE <>;   -- integer subscripts
   TYPE ListType IS ARRAY (IndexType RANGE <>) OF ElementType;
   WITH FUNCTION KeyOf (Element: ElementType) RETURN KeyType IS <>;
   WITH FUNCTION "<" (Left, Right: KeyType) RETURN Boolean IS <>;
```

```
PROCEDURE Sort_Quick_Generic(List: IN OUT ListType);
--------------------------------------------------------------------------
--| Pre:  The procedure has been instantiated and List is defined
--| Post: The contents of List are in order defined by "<"
--| Author: Michael B. Feldman, The George Washington University
--| Last Modified: January 1996
--------------------------------------------------------------------------
```

Program 14.14 Body of Quick Sort

```
WITH Swap_Generic;
PROCEDURE Sort_Quick_Generic(List: IN OUT ListType) IS
--------------------------------------------------------------------------
--| Body of generic Quick Sort Procedure
--| Author: Michael B. Feldman, The George Washington University
--| Last Modified: January 1996
--------------------------------------------------------------------------

   -- main procedure, which calls recursive procedure
   -- Quick to do the sorting.

   PROCEDURE Exchange IS NEW Swap_Generic (ValueType => ElementType);

   FUNCTION "<="(Left, Right: KeyType) RETURN Boolean IS
   BEGIN
     RETURN (Left < Right) OR (Left = Right);
   END "<=";

   PROCEDURE Partition (List : IN OUT ListType;
             PivIndex : OUT IndexType) IS
   -- Partitions the array slice List with bounds List'First and
   -- List'Last into two subarrays.
   -- Pre : List is defined and T'First <= T'Last.
   -- Post: PivIndex is defined such that all values less than or equal
   --    to List(PivIndex) have subscripts < PivIndex; all values
   --    greater than List(PivIndex) have subscripts > PivIndex.

     Pivot : ElementType;      -- the pivot value
     Up    : IndexType;        -- pointer to values > Pivot
     Down  : IndexType;        -- pointer to values <= Pivot

   BEGIN  -- Partition

     Pivot := List(List'First);  -- define leftmost element as the pivot

     -- Find and exchange values that are out of place.
     Up := List'First;    -- set Up to point to leftmost element
     Down := List'Last;    -- set Down to point to rightmost element

     LOOP
       -- Move Up to the next value larger than Pivot.
       WHILE (KeyOf(List(Up)) <= KeyOf(Pivot)) AND (Up < List'Last) LOOP
         Up := Up + 1;
       END LOOP;
       -- assertion: List(Up) > Pivot or Up is equal to List'Last

       -- Move Down to the next value less than or equal to Pivot.
       WHILE (KeyOf(Pivot) < KeyOf(List(Down)))
```

```
      AND (Down > List'First) LOOP
        Down := Down - 1;
      END LOOP;
      -- assertion: List(Down) <= Pivot


      -- Exchange out of order values.
      IF Up < Down THEN
        Exchange (List(Up), List(Down));
      END IF;


      EXIT WHEN Up >= Down;           -- until Up meets or passes Down
    END LOOP;
    -- Assertion: values <= Pivot have subscripts <= Down and
    --   values > Pivot have subscripts > Down


    -- Put pivot value where it belongs and define PivIndex.
    Exchange (List(List'First), List(Down));
    PivIndex := Down;

END Partition;

PROCEDURE Quick(List: IN OUT ListType) IS
-- Recursive procedure to sort the array slice List with
-- bounds List'First and List'Last.
-- Pre : array List is defined and List'First <= List'Last
-- Post: List is sorted.

  PivIndex : IndexType;          -- subscript of pivot value
                                 -- returned by Partition

BEGIN -- Quick

  IF List'First < List'Last THEN
    -- Split into two subarrays separated by value at PivIndex
    Partition (List, PivIndex);
    -- sort the two subarrays
    IF PivIndex > List'First THEN
      Quick (List(List'First..PivIndex - 1));
    END IF;
    IF PivIndex < List'Last THEN
      Quick (List(PivIndex + 1..List'Last));
    END IF;
  END IF;

  Put(List);

END Quick;

BEGIN -- Sort_Quick_Generic

  Quick(List => List);

END Sort_Quick_Generic;
```

Quick Sort performs, for the average case, in $O(N \log N)$ time. Interestingly, its worst case, which approaches $O(N^2)$, occurs when the original array is already sorted. In that situation, every attempt to partition the array results in a left subarray of length 1 and all the rest of the elements in the right subarray.

In practical applications of Quick Sort, to save some of the overhead of recursive calls, the recursive procedure is not called for small subarrays, say, of four or less.

Instead, a simple N^2 sort such as linear insertion is used to sort these. We leave it as an exercise to implement quick sort in this fashion.

14.9 OTHER SORTS: SHELL SORT

The quite popular Shell sort (named for its inventor, D. Shell) can be viewed as a modification of either the bubble sort or the linear insertion sort. In both of these sorts, an element moves toward its proper place only one "slot" at a time. The distance each element moves determines the overall running time; Shell sort tries to reduce this time by first putting the array in rough order. The algorithm does this by comparing elements that are separated from each other rather than immediately adjacent ones. This is done by choosing a *distance* and sorting subfiles, each of which is made up of elements separated from each other by that distance. For instance, suppose the distance—call it d—is 3 and the total length of the array is 15. Then, as in the second column of Figure 14.11, we first use linear insertion to sort the subarray {A(1), A(4), A(7), A(10), A(13)}, then the subarray {A(2), A(5), A(8), A(11), A(14)}, followed by {A(3), A(6), A(9), A(12), A(15)}. This constitutes one phase.

Having put all these subarrays in mutual order—which moves small elements nearer the top and large elements nearer the bottom in larger steps than normal linear insertion—we reduce the distance. Each phase reduces the distance until, eventually, $d = 1$ and we sort the entire array by a final phase of linear insertion. By now each element needs to move only a very short distance to reach its home.

There is no general agreement in the literature on how best to choose the distances. Shell originally chose $d_1 = N/2$ and $d_{k+1} = d_k/2$ (integer division, of course!). Other authors advocate choosing a set of mutually prime distances. For simplicity, we choose the for-

	Initially d=5	After 1st Pass d=3	After 2nd Pass d=2	After 2nd Pass d=2	Finally d=2
1	23	1	-9	-9	-9
2	14	-3	-3	-3	-3
3	0	0	-1	-1	-1
4	-1	-9	1	0	0
5	3	2	2	2	1
6	4	4	0	1	2
7	8	8	3	3	3
8	7	7	7	7	4
9	19	-1	4	4	7
10	12	3	8	8	8
11	1	23	19	10	10
12	-3	14	12	12	12
13	10	10	10	14	14
14	-9	19	23	23	19
15	2	12	14	19	23

Figure 14.11 Shell Sort

mer method. Programs 14.15 and 14.16 show the generic procedure. Note in the body that the algorithm for each phase (each value of `Distance`) is very similar to linear insertion.

Program 14.15 Specification for Shell Sort

```
GENERIC

  TYPE KeyType IS PRIVATE;
  TYPE ElementType IS PRIVATE;
  TYPE IndexType IS RANGE <>;  -- integer subscripts
  TYPE ListType IS ARRAY (IndexType RANGE <>) OF ElementType;
  WITH FUNCTION KeyOf  (Element: ElementType) RETURN KeyType IS <>;
  WITH FUNCTION "<" (Left, Right: KeyType) RETURN Boolean IS <>;


PROCEDURE Sort_Shell_Generic(List: IN OUT ListType);
-----------------------------------------------------------------------
--| Pre: The procedure has been instantiated and List is defined
--| Post: The contents of List are in order defined by "<"
--| Author: Michael B. Feldman, The George Washington University
--| Last Modified: January 1996
-----------------------------------------------------------------------
```

Program 14.16 Body of Shell Sort

```
WITH Swap_Generic;
PROCEDURE Sort_Shell_Generic(List: IN OUT ListType) IS
-----------------------------------------------------------------------
--| Body of generic Shell Sort
--| Author: Michael B. Feldman, The George Washington University
--| Last Modified: January 1996
-----------------------------------------------------------------------

  PROCEDURE Exchange IS NEW Swap_Generic(ValueType => ElementType);

  NewArrival: ElementType;
  Top:         IndexType := List'First;
  Bottom:      IndexType := List'Last;
  Position:    IndexType;
  Distance:    IndexType;
  IntegerDistance:     Integer;

BEGIN

  IntegerDistance := Integer(Bottom/2);
  WHILE IntegerDistance > 0 LOOP

    Distance := IndexType(IntegerDistance);

    FOR CurrentBottom IN Top+Distance..Bottom LOOP
      Position := CurrentBottom;

      WHILE Position >= Top + Distance AND THEN
        KeyOf(List(Position)) < KeyOf(List(Position - Distance)) LOOP

        Exchange(List(Position), List(Position - Distance));
        Position := Position - Distance;
      END LOOP;

    END LOOP;
```

```
        IntegerDistance := IntegerDistance / 2;

    END LOOP;

END Sort_Shell_Generic;
```

The performance of the Shell sort is in the neighborhood of $O(N \sqrt{N})$; the analysis is beyond the scope of this book.

14.10   OTHER SORTS: QUADRATIC SELECTION SORT

An interesting sort algorithm trades a penalty in space for a payoff in running time, where the running time is $O(N \sqrt{N})$. Let $\sqrt{N}$ be denoted by M. The unsorted array is divided up into segments of M (rounded up to the nearest integer, of course) and copied into a square M-by-M array. Call this array A'. The algorithm then proceeds as follows:

Quadratic Selection Sort:

1. By comparing and swapping as in the delayed selection sort, get the smallest element in each row of A' into the first position of that row.

2. Find the smallest element in the first column of A', then output it to the sorted array.

3. Replace that element in A' with the smallest element in the row from which it came, then "compress" the row by replacing the element just removed with the current last element in the row.

4. Continue the process until all rows are empty. The original array is then sorted.

An example of this algorithm in action is shown in Figure 14.12; writing a procedure for it is suggested as an exercise.

What is the running time of quadratic selection? Since when we first create A', each row has at most M elements, and there are M rows, initializing the first column as in step 1 takes at most $M \times M = N$ operations. Step 2 takes $M - 1$ operations; step 3 takes a variable number, but surely no more than $M - 1$. But we carry out steps 2 and 3 once for each element in the original array, or N times. So we have the sum of an $O(N)$ term and an $O(N \times M)$ term; for nontrivial N the second term dominates, and thus the overall algorithm is $O(N \times M) = O(N \times \sqrt{N})$.

14.11   OTHER SORTS: RADIX SORT

This sort is probably best explained in terms of electromechanical punched-card sorting machines. These machines were widely used during the 1930s, 1940s, and 1950s, before computers became widespread; their popularity declined through the 1960s

| 26 | 5 | 37 | 1 | 61 | 11 | 59 | 15 | 48 | 19 | 0 | −3 | 7 |

(a) Orginal unsorted array

26	61	48	7
5	11	19	
37	59	0	
1	15	−3	

(b) Initial square array made from the array above.

7	61	48	26
5	11	19	
0	59	37	
−3	15	1	

(c) Row minima located and placed at heads of rows.

7	61	48	26
5	11	19	
0	59	37	
1	15		

Result Array −3

7	61	48	26
5	11	19	
37	59		
1	15		

−3 0

7	61	48	26
5	11	19	
37	59		
1	15		

−3 0 1

(d) A few steps of the algorithm (the reader can complete it).

Figure 14.12 Quadratic Selection Sort

and 1970s, and they are hardly to be found anymore. The author recalls having to operate such a machine for several consecutive weeks as part of a summer job he held in 1965.

A punched card, as you probably know, has 80 data positions or columns, each with 12 rows. Ten of these rows are numbered 0 through 9. Each position can hold one character of data. If we assume for simplicity that all the data is numeric, then each character is one of the digits 0 through 9, and a digit in a given column is encoded by a single punch in the appropriate row of that column. A numerical value—a sequence of numeric digits—is encoded by a single punch in each of several consecutive columns. Figure 14.13 shows a section of a punched card with a six-digit number punched into it in positions 5 through 10.

The card sorter has 13 bins or pockets, each capable of holding several hundred cards, and an equally large input hopper. The machine operates on one column at a time.

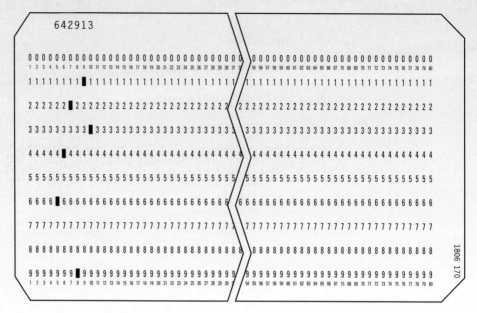

Figure 14.13 A Punched Card

The operator sets an indicator to the desired column, loads the input hopper with a face-up stack of cards, then presses the start button. The machine, with much noise and furious movement of cards, places each card in the bin corresponding to the row in which a punch appears in the chosen column. The thirteenth bin collects those cards with no punch at all in the chosen column. Figure 14.14 shows a diagram of the machine.

How is such a machine used to sort a deck of cards on an entire key? The deck must be run through the card sorter once for each digit of the key! Here is a sketch of an algorithm:

Card Sorter Algorithm:

1. Set column indicator to rightmost (low-order) column of key to be sorted.

2. Place deck, face up, in input hopper.

3. Start sorter; wait until input hopper is empty (the machine stops by itself).

4. Remove the decks of cards from each bin, making one deck with the contents of bin 0 on top and the contents of bin 9 on the bottom.

5. If all columns have not yet been processed, move column indicator one position to the left and repeat steps 2 through 5.

In Figure 14.15, we illustrate this sort for an eight-card deck to be sorted on a three-digit key. Be sure you understand why the sort must begin with the rightmost digit and move to the left, and why it won't work the other way around.

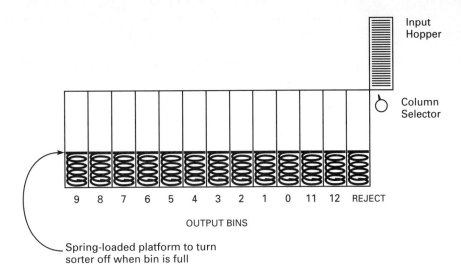

Figure 14.14 Electromechanical Punched-Card Sorter

This sort algorithm can be adapted to operate on a computer, and works rather well if we realize that the keys are represented as binary sequences (like everything else on most computers!). If the keys are unsigned binary integers, or character strings, we can just treat the keys as bit sequences. We just use two "bins," generally arrays, and sort bit by bit, from the rightmost bit to the leftmost. This sort is called radix sort because the number of bins is determined by the radix, or base, of the digits being sorted.

What is the performance of this algorithm? The number of passes is determined, clearly, by the number of bits in the key. For a fixed-size key, the number of passes is fixed. Each pass examines each record exactly once, so the total number of operations is a constant (the number of passes) times the number of records (N); in other words, this sort has growth rate $O(N)$. It is not very widely used because of the extra space required for the bins and because the usually large number of passes means that the $O(N)$ growth rate may well be dominated by the very large constant of proportionality.

SUMMARY

In this chapter, you have seen a number of sorting methods, along with performance estimation discussions. You should be equipped to make a sensible choice of a method for whatever sorting problem faces you.

Clearly, if you only need to sort a small list, the best method is the one that's easiest for you to write, since in that case your time is more expensive than the computer's. On the other hand, if you have a large list to sort, particularly as part of an application that will be run frequently, it pays to think the problem through and choose wisely, because the computer time used in the sort will no longer be negligible.

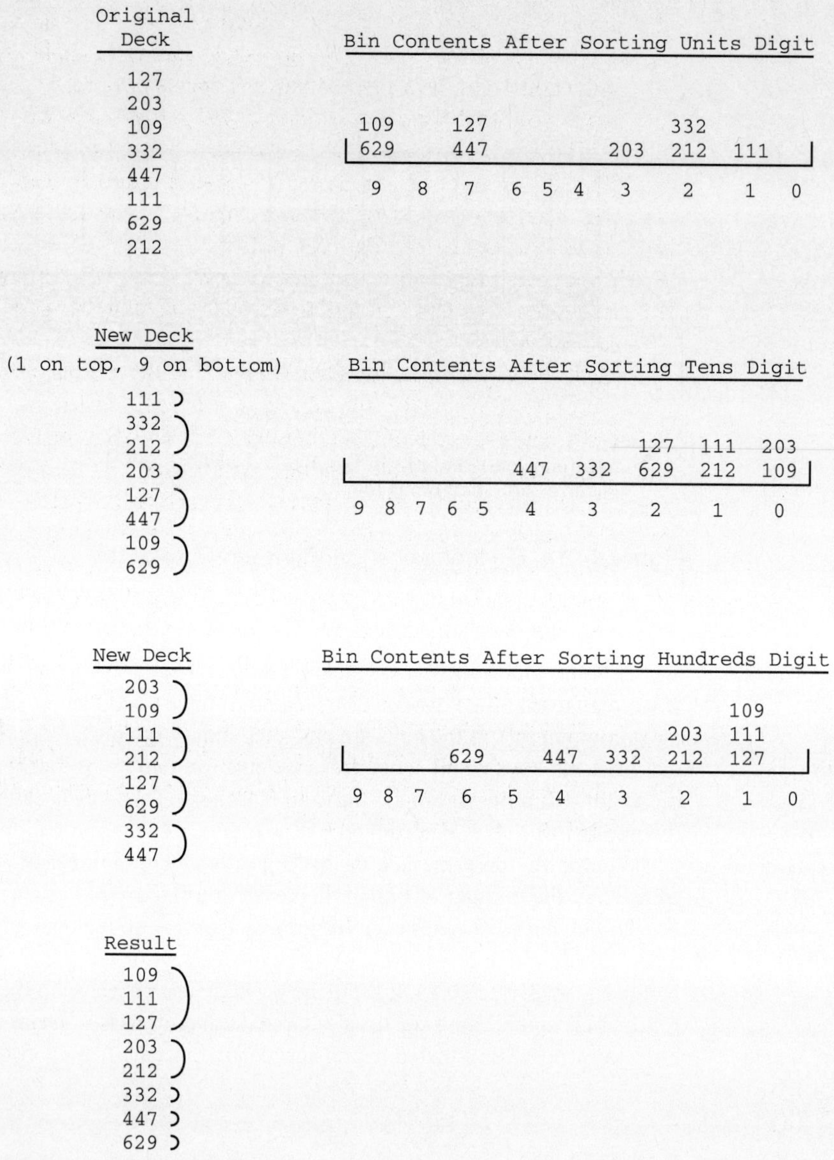

```
        Original
          Deck                Bin Contents After Sorting Units Digit
          ─────
          127
          203
          109          109     127                   332
          332         ┌629     447            203    212    111┐
          447          9   8   7   6   5   4   3     2     1    0
          111
          629
          212
```

```
        New Deck
  (1 on top, 9 on bottom)     Bin Contents After Sorting Tens Digit
          ─────────
          111 )
          332 )
          212 )                              127    111    203
          203 )                 447    332   629    212    109
          127 )        ┌                                        ┐
          447 )         9   8   7   6   5   4     3      2      1      0
          109 )
          629 )
```

```
        New Deck               Bin Contents After Sorting Hundreds Digit
        ────────
          203 )                                           109
          109 )                                    203    111
          111 )                 629    447   332   212    127
          212 )        ┌                                        ┐
          127 )         9   8   7   6   5   4   3     2     1     0
          629 )
          332 )
          447 )
```

```
        Result
        ──────
          109 )
          111 )
          127 )
          203 )
          212 )
          332 )
          447 )
          629 )
```

Figure 14.15 Radix Sort

EXERCISES

1. Examine the bubble sort procedure presented in Section 14.4. Define *trip length* as the number of upward moves an element in the array must make on its way to its final position. Show that the number of passes required by the bubble sort algorithm depends on the maximum of all the trip lengths in the array.

2. In the bubble sort algorithm of Section 14.4, we begin at the top of the array and move elements downward. Write a procedure for a bubble sort in which we start at the bottom of the array and move elements upward.

3. In the modified bubble sort often called *shaker sort*, we run successive passes alternately in the upward and downward directions. Write a procedure for this sort. Why does this method sometimes offer improved performance?

4. Calculate the number of passes in the merge sort when the number of elements in the array is not exactly a power of 2.

5. Write a modified merge sort procedure in which it is not necessary to recopy the array after each pass. *Hint*: Do this by "switching" alternately the input and output arrays.

6. Modify the quick sort procedure of Section 14.8 so that a simple sort such as linear insertion is used to sort subarrays of length 4 or less.

7. Write a procedure implementing the quadratic selection sort of Section 14.10.

8. Write a procedure implementing a decimal radix sort, assuming that the keys are all the same length and are represented as strings of digits.

9. Write a procedure implementing a binary radix sort, as suggested in Section 14.11. Note that since only two bins are required, only one additional array is needed because the array can be filled from both ends: all "0" elements inserted from the top of the array, all "1" elements from the bottom.

10. Design an experiment to do some measurements on a group of sort algorithms. Use a version of CPUClock (Programs 3.17 through 3.19) appropriate for your computer. Test the various sort procedures on arrays of length 4 to length 1024, doubling the array size each time (i.e., 4, 8, 16, . . . , 1024). Try best, worst, and random cases. How do the actual running times compare with the theoretical ones predicted by "big *O*" analysis?

CHAPTER 15

Introduction to Concurrent Programming

Each program we have seen so far has been a *sequential*, or *single-threaded*, one; that is, it has consisted of a series of steps that are executed in sequence, one after the other. In this chapter, we introduce the idea of a *concurrent*, or *multithreaded*, program, one in which several things can happen—or at least appear to happen—simultaneously.

Concurrent actions are really part of most interesting programs. For example, a time-shared operating system must deal with a number of human users working simultaneously at their terminals. Further, many real-time applications, especially those controlling physical processes, are composed of concurrent program segments, each responsible for its own physical subsystem. Finally, the world is concurrent, filled with people doing different things all at the same time, and a program that would model that world is best seen as comprising concurrent program segments.

This chapter introduces you to the fascinating field of *concurrent programming*, which is the writing of concurrent programs. Ada provides an especially rich and interesting set of structures for concurrent programming; this chapter presents some of these structures. In particular, we introduce Ada *task types* and *protected types*. A task object is an active program, carrying on its activities independently of other tasks and interacting with others only when necessary. A protected object is passive; its purpose is to encapsulate a data structure and provide services to tasks on request, allowing many tasks to view the structure simultaneously but authorizing only one task at a time to modify the structure.

15.1   WHAT IS CONCURRENT PROGRAMMING?

Much of the programming world involves concurrent applications. Here are some examples from operating systems, real-time systems, and simulation.

Operating Systems

When you and your colleagues all log in at terminals connected to the same time-sharing system, each of you works separately, but you are all using the same computer. Each of you has the feeling that the computer is working only on your task, yet many of you are working simultaneously. How is this seeming paradox possible?

The illusion that you are alone on the time-shared computer is caused by a combination of fast computers and clever programming. Suppose you are using the computer to edit a program or read electronic mail. You read and type at human speed. A very fast typist can enter 100 words per minute, or—at an average of six characters per word—about 10 characters per second. In the tenth of a second between two of your keystrokes, a modern computer can execute hundreds of thousands of machine instructions. If those "extra" machine instructions could be put to productive use, the computer would have plenty of time between your keystrokes to service other human users. It is not unusual for a modern time-shared computer to handle 100 or more simultaneous users, each working at human speed.

Managing all those instructions and users is part of the responsibility of a modern operating system. An operating system is, as you know by now, just a sophisticated program; in fact, it is a *concurrent* program, capable of managing many devices and human users to give the illusion of simultaneity.

Some time-shared computers consist of a single CPU; others consist of a set of identical CPUs. With more than one CPU, programs can be executed *in parallel*—that is, literally at the same time. With a single CPU, no real parallel execution is possible, but that one CPU can be shared in such a way that many programs *seem* to be executing in parallel. Concurrent programming is the creation of programs that consist of segments that have the potential for parallel execution; depending upon the actual number of CPUs available, execution of a concurrent program may be literally parallel, entirely time-shared, or some combination of the two.

Real-Time Systems

Many computer systems exist to control physical systems of one kind or another. Examples abound in medical technology, manufacturing and robotics, and transportation. In the latter domain, real-time computer programs control modern automotive fuel systems, aircraft such as the Boeing 777, and railroads such as the Channel Tunnel between France and England and the subway system in Washington, DC. These are, of necessity, concurrent programs: They must manage a number of electronic devices simultaneously; these devices, in turn, are connected to physical machines such as an automobile's fuel injection system or a railroad's "turnout" (a movable section of track that allows a train to enter one or the other of two rail lines).

Modeling and Simulation

Concurrent programming is useful in modeling or simulating physical systems, even if those systems are not directly controlled by a computer. For example, the waiting and service times in a bank, supermarket, or other service organization can be studied by writing a program in which each customer and each server—bank teller, supermarket checker, airline reservation clerk—is represented by its own program segment, which interacts with the other segments.

Similarly, a subway system can be modeled by a program in which each train, station, turnout, and block (section of track that is permitted to hold at most one train) is represented by a program segment. The flow of simulated customers in the bank, or of simulated trains in the subway, can be controlled or varied at will.

Simulation is an important tool in optimizing physical systems—for example, choosing the most effective number of open checkout lines in a supermarket or the frequency and maximum speed of trains in a subway. Studying the computer model provides information and insight into the behavior of the physical system if the former is a faithful representation of the latter; concurrent programming provides a natural way of assigning program segments to represent physical objects and therefore aids greatly in developing good simulations.

Ada is one of only a few programming languages—and the only popular one—to provide built-in structures for concurrent programming. In this chapter, we use a series of examples to present a few of the basic Ada structures and end with two simulations: one of a bank and the other of a group of philosophers in a Chinese restaurant.

Ada Structures for Concurrent Programming

In concurrent programming, an execution of a program segment is called a *process*. For example, when, logged into a time-sharing system, you invoke the electronic mail program, a process is created. The mail program itself is just a file on disk; when it is loaded into memory and executed, that execution is a process. If you and several friends all log in at the same time and invoke the e-mail program, several copies of that program are executing simultaneously on the same computer. One *program* has given rise to multiple simultaneous *processes*. Ada's term for *process* is *task*; Ada provides *task types* to allow the creation of multiple processes, which Ada calls *task objects*, resulting from a single program declaration.

Generally, your incoming e-mail is stored in a system file called the electronic mailbox, or just the mailbox. Suppose you are reading your mail when a friend sends you a message. The new message must be added to your mailbox file; your reading must be momentarily suspended while the file is modified (you may not notice the temporary suspension, but it happens anyway). Now suppose that two incoming messages arrive at the same time. Not only must your reading be suspended, but something in the mail software must update your mailbox one message at a time. If this protection were not provided—if two messages could update the mailbox literally at the same time—the mailbox would become hopelessly garbled and therefore useless.

The e-mail situation is an example of a *readers-writers problem*, a category of computing problems in which multiple readers of, and multiple writers to, a data structure must be prevented from interfering with one another. The prevention technique is called *mutual exclusion*; update actions on the data structure are handled one at a time while other actions are excluded. Ada's *protected types* provide mutual exclusion; we can declare a protected type, and variables of that type, with read operations (called *protected functions*) and update operations (*protected procedures*), which Ada guarantees it will execute correctly. Specifically, multiple calls to a protected procedure are executed one at a time.

Section 15.2 introduces task types and task objects; Section 15.3 introduces protected types and protected objects.

15.2   ADA STRUCTURES: TASK TYPES AND TASK OBJECTS

An Ada task is an interesting structure. It has aspects of a package, of a procedure, and of a data structure, but is really none of these; it is something different altogether:

- Like a package, a task has a specification and a body. Unlike a package, it must be declared in an enclosing structure, not put in a separate file and compiled separately.

- Like a procedure, a task has a declaration section and a sequence of executable statements. However, it is not called like a procedure; rather, it starts executing implicitly, automatically, as part of its enclosing block.

- Like a data structure, it has a type and is brought into existence by declaring a variable of the type. Indeed, like a variant record, it can have one or more discriminants.

Program 15.1 illustrates these aspects of tasks.

Program 15.1 A Task within a Main Program

```
WITH Ada.Text_IO;
PROCEDURE One_Task IS

------------------------------------------------------------------------
--| Show the declaration of a simple task type and one
--| variable of that type.
--| Author: Michael B. Feldman, The George Washington University
--| Last Modified: December 1995
------------------------------------------------------------------------
```

```
-- A task type has a specification
TASK TYPE SimpleTask (Message: Character);

-- A task type has a body
TASK BODY SimpleTask IS

BEGIN -- SimpleTask

  FOR Count IN 1..10 LOOP
    Ada.Text_IO.Put(Item => "Hello from Task " & Message);
    Ada.Text_IO.New_Line;
  END LOOP;

END SimpleTask;

Task_A: SimpleTask(Message => 'A');

BEGIN -- One_Task

-- Unlike procedures, tasks are not "called" but are activated
-- automatically.

-- Task_A will start executing as soon as control reaches this
-- point, just after the BEGIN but before any of the main program's
-- statements are executed.

NULL;

END One_Task;
```

A sample run of this program would look like this:

```
Hello from Task A
Hello from Task A
Hello from Task A
Hello from Task A
Hello from Task A
Hello from Task A
Hello from Task A
Hello from Task A
Hello from Task A
Hello from Task A
```

First note the overall structure of the program. A task type, `SimpleTask`, is declared with a discriminant, `Message`. This task specification is followed by a task body in which the message is displayed 10 times. Next, `Task_A` is declared as a task variable, usually called a task object, with a discriminant value of `'A'`.

Reaching the main `BEGIN` of this program, we discover that the program has no executable statements, just a `NULL` statement to satisfy the rule that a procedure must have at least one statement. Yet the sample run shows the task actually displaying `Hello from Task A` 10 times. The task was never called from the main program, but it executed anyway.

In fact, the task began its execution just after the main `BEGIN` was reached. In Ada, this is called "task activation": All tasks declared in a given block are activated just after the `BEGIN` of that block. Here, there is only one task, `Task_A`.

Multiple Task Objects of the Same Type

Program 15.2 shows the declaration of two task objects, `Task_A` and `Task_B`. Further, the task type is modified to allow two discriminants, the message and the number of times the message is to be displayed. Here, a discriminant acts like a parameter of the task, but it is not a fully general parameter; like a variant-record discriminant, it must be of a discrete—integer or enumeration—type. A string, for example, cannot be used as a task discriminant.

Program 15.2 Two Tasks within a Main Program

```
WITH Ada.Text_IO;
PROCEDURE Two_Tasks IS
-------------------------------------------------------------------------
--| Show the declaration of a simple task type and two
--| variables of that type.
--| Author: Michael B. Feldman, The George Washington University
--| Last Modified: December 1995
-------------------------------------------------------------------------
  -- A task type has a specification
  TASK TYPE SimpleTask (Message: Character; HowMany: Positive);

  -- A task type has a body
  TASK BODY SimpleTask IS

  BEGIN -- SimpleTask

    FOR Count IN 1..HowMany LOOP
      Ada.Text_IO.Put(Item => "Hello from Task " & Message);
      Ada.Text_IO.New_Line;
    END LOOP;

  END SimpleTask;

  -- Now we declare two variables of the type
  Task_A: SimpleTask(Message => 'A', HowMany => 5);
  Task_B: SimpleTask(Message => 'B', HowMany => 7);

BEGIN -- Two_Tasks

-- Task_A and Task_B will both start executing as soon as control
-- reaches this point, again before any of the main program's
-- statements are executed. The Ada standard does not specify
-- which task will start first.

  NULL;

END Two_Tasks;
```

This time, the program execution might look like this:

```
Hello from Task B
Hello from Task B
Hello from Task B
Hello from Task B
Hello from Task B
Hello from Task B
Hello from Task B
```

```
Hello from Task A
Hello from Task A
Hello from Task A
Hello from Task A
Hello from Task A
```

As in Program 15.1, `Task_A` and `Task_B` are activated just after the main `BEGIN`. Now there are two tasks. In which order are they activated? The Ada standard does not specify this, leaving it up to the compiler implementer instead. In a short while, we will see how to control the order in which tasks start their work.

Looking at the sample run from Program 15.2, we see that `Task_B` evidently started—and completed—its work before `Task_A` even started its own work. This tells us first that the compiler we used activated `Task_B` first, and also that, once scheduled for the CPU, `Task_B` was allowed to continue executing until it completed its run. This seems odd: The tasks do not really execute as though they were running in parallel; there is, apparently, no time-sharing. If there were, we would expect `Task_A` and `Task_B` output to be interleaved in some fashion.

In fact, the Ada standard allows, but does not require, *time-slicing*. Time-slicing, implemented in the run-time support software, supports "parallel" execution by giving each task a slice, usually called a *quantum*, which is a certain amount of time on the CPU. At the end of the quantum, the run-time system steps in and gives the CPU to another task, allowing it a quantum, and so on, in "round-robin" fashion.

Cooperating Tasks

If Program 15.2 were compiled for a computer with several processors, in theory `Task_A` and `Task_B` could have been executed—truly in parallel—on separate CPUs, and no time-slicing would be needed. With a single CPU, we'd like to emulate the parallel operation, ensuring concurrent execution of a set of tasks even if the Ada run-time system does not time-slice.

To get "parallel" behavior portably, using one CPU or many, with or without time-slicing, we code the tasks in a style called *cooperative multitasking*; that is, we design each task so that it periodically "goes to sleep," giving up its turn on the CPU so that another task can execute for a while.

Program 15.3 shows how this is done, using a `DELAY` statement in each iteration of the task body's `FOR` loop. The `DELAY` causes the task to suspend its execution, or "sleep." Now while `Task_A` is "sleeping," `Task_B` can be executing, and so on. The cooperating nature of the two tasks is easily seen in the sample output.

Program 15.3 Using `DELAY` to Achieve Cooperation

```
WITH Ada.Text_IO;
PROCEDURE Two_Cooperating_Tasks IS
-------------------------------------------------------------------------
--| Show the declaration of a simple task type and two
--| variables of that type. The tasks use DELAYs to cooperate.
--| The DELAY causes another task to get a turn in the CPU.
```

```
--| Author: Michael B. Feldman, The George Washington University
--| Last Modified: December 1995
-----------------------------------------------------------------------

  -- A task type has a specification
  TASK TYPE SimpleTask (Message: Character; HowMany: Positive);

  -- A task type has a body
  TASK BODY SimpleTask IS

  BEGIN -- SimpleTask

    FOR Count IN 1..HowMany LOOP
      Ada.Text_IO.Put(Item => "Hello from Task " & Message);
      Ada.Text_IO.New_Line;
      DELAY 0.1;                -- lets another task have the CPU
    END LOOP;

  END SimpleTask;

  -- Now we declare two variables of the type
  Task_A: SimpleTask(Message => 'A', HowMany => 5);
  Task_B: SimpleTask(Message => 'B', HowMany => 7);

BEGIN -- Two_Cooperating_Tasks

-- Task_A and Task_B will both start executing as soon as control
-- reaches this point, again before any of the main program's
-- statements are executed. The Ada standard does not specify
-- which task will start first.

  NULL;

END Two_Cooperating_Tasks;
```

This time, the execution output is interleaved.

```
Hello from Task B
Hello from Task A
Hello from Task B
Hello from Task A
Hello from Task B
Hello from Task A
Hello from Task B
Hello from Task A
Hello from Task B
Hello from Task A
Hello from Task B
Hello from Task B
```

Controlling the Starting Order of Tasks

We know that the Ada standard does not specify an order of activation for multiple tasks in the same program. Each compiler can use a different order; indeed, a compiler is—theoretically—free to use a different starting order each time the program is run, though practical compilers rarely, if ever, take advantage of this freedom.

Although we cannot control the actual activation order of tasks, we can gain control of the order in which these tasks start to do their work by using a so-called "start button." This is a special case of a *task entry*, which is a point in a task at which it can *synchronize* with other tasks. This is illustrated in Program 15.4.

Program 15.4 Using "Start Buttons" to Control Tasks' Starting Order

```
WITH Ada.Text_IO;
PROCEDURE Start_Buttons IS

------------------------------------------------------------------------
--| Show the declaration of a simple task type and three
--| variables of that type. The tasks use DELAYs to cooperate.
--| "Start button" entries are used to to control starting order.
--| Author: Michael B. Feldman, The George Washington University
--| Last Modified: December 1995
------------------------------------------------------------------------

  TASK TYPE SimpleTask (Message: Character; HowMany: Positive) IS

    -- This specification provides a "start button" entry.
    ENTRY StartRunning;

  END SimpleTask;

  TASK BODY SimpleTask IS

  BEGIN -- SimpleTask

    -- The task will "block" at the ACCEPT, waiting for the "button"
    -- to be "pushed" (called from another task, Main in this case).
    ACCEPT StartRunning;

    FOR Count IN 1..HowMany LOOP
      Ada.Text_IO.Put(Item => "Hello from Task " & Message);
      Ada.Text_IO.New_Line;
      DELAY 0.1;               -- lets another task have the CPU
    END LOOP;

  END SimpleTask;

  -- Now we declare three variables of the type
  Task_A: SimpleTask(Message => 'A', HowMany => 5);
  Task_B: SimpleTask(Message => 'B', HowMany => 7);
  Task_C: SimpleTask(Message => 'C', HowMany => 4);

BEGIN -- Start_Buttons

-- Tasks will all start executing as soon as control
-- reaches this point, but each will block on its ACCEPT
-- until the entry is called. In this way we control the starting
-- order of the tasks.

  Task_B.StartRunning;
  Task_A.StartRunning;
  Task_C.StartRunning;

END Start_Buttons;
```

The execution output is

```
Hello from Task B
Hello from Task A
Hello from Task C
Hello from Task B
Hello from Task A
Hello from Task C
Hello from Task B
Hello from Task A
Hello from Task C
Hello from Task B
Hello from Task A
Hello from Task C
Hello from Task B
Hello from Task A
Hello from Task B
Hello from Task B
```

In this program, the task specification is expanded to include an entry specification:

```
ENTRY StartRunning;
```

This is, syntactically, similar to the subprogram specifications that usually appear in package specifications. The task body includes, immediately after its BEGIN, the corresponding line

```
ACCEPT StartRunning;
```

According to the rules of Ada, a `SimpleTask` object, upon reaching an ACCEPT statement, must *wait* at that statement until the corresponding entry is called by another task. In Program 15.4, then, each task—Task_A, Task_B, and Task_C—is activated just after the main program's BEGIN, but—before it starts any work—each reaches its respective ACCEPT and must wait there (in this simple case, possibly forever) until the entry is called.

How is the entry called? In our first three examples, the main program had nothing to do. In this case, its job is to "press the start buttons" of the three tasks, with the entry call statements

```
Task_B.StartRunning;
Task_A.StartRunning;
Task_C.StartRunning;
```

These statements are syntactically similar to procedure calls. The first statement "presses the start button" of `Task_B`. Since `Task_B` was waiting for the button to be pressed, it accepts the call and proceeds with its work.

The main program is apparently executing—in this case, pressing the start buttons—"in parallel" with the three tasks. In fact, this is true. In a program with multiple tasks, the Ada run-time system treats the main program as a task as well.

A task body can contain code that is much more interesting than what we have seen. Ada provides the SELECT statement to give a programmer much flexibility in coding task bodies. For example, using the SELECT,

- The ACCEPT statement can be written to "time out" if a call is not received within a given time interval.

- The task can be made to terminate—end its execution—if the call is never received.

- The task specification can provide a number of entries and its body can be made to respond to whichever of a set of different entry calls occurs first, then loop around and respond again.

The SELECT construct is one of the most interesting in all of programming. We will return to it a bit later, in Section 15.4, when we introduce a bank simulation.

In this section, we have seen the basics of task types and objects. We will now introduce protected types and objects.

15.3 ADA STRUCTURES: PROTECTED TYPES AND PROTECTED OBJECTS

In Section 15.1, we discussed mutual exclusion, using the example of an e-mail reader. Here we look at an analogous, but simpler, situation. Suppose we have a three-task program like Program 15.4, but we want each task to write its output in its own area of the screen. The desired output is

```
Hello from Task A        Hello from Task B        Hello from Task C
Hello from Task A        Hello from Task B        Hello from Task C
Hello from Task A        Hello from Task B        Hello from Task C
Hello from Task A        Hello from Task B        Hello from Task C
Hello from Task A        Hello from Task B
                         Hello from Task B
                         Hello from Task B
```

This simple example is representative of multiwindow programs. We modify the task specification to read

```
TASK TYPE SimpleTask (Message: Character;
                      HowMany: Screen.Depth;
                      Column : Screen.Width) IS . . .
```

adding a third discriminant, Column, to indicate which screen column each task should use for the first character of its repeated message. Further, we modify the main loop of the task body as follows:

```
FOR Count IN 1..HowMany LOOP
  Screen.MoveCursor(Row => Count, Column => Column);
  Ada.Text_IO.Put(Item => "Hello from Task " & Message);
  DELAY 0.5;              --lets another task have the CPU
END LOOP;
```

That is, the task positions the screen cursor in the proper column before writing the message. Program 15.5 shows the full program.

Program 15.5 Several Tasks Using the Screen

```
WITH Ada.Text_IO;
WITH Screen;
PROCEDURE Columns IS
```

```
  ------------------------------------------------------------------
--| Shows tasks writing into their respective columns on the
--| screen. This will not always work correctly, because if the
--| tasks are time-sliced, one task may lose the CPU before
--| sending its entire "message" to the screen. This may result
--| in strange "garbage" on the screen.
--| Author: Michael B. Feldman, The George Washington University
--| Last Modified: December 1995
  ------------------------------------------------------------------

   TASK TYPE SimpleTask (Message: Character;
                         HowMany: Screen.Depth;
                         Column :  Screen.Width) IS
     -- This specification provides a "start button" entry.
     ENTRY StartRunning;

   END SimpleTask;

   TASK BODY SimpleTask IS

   BEGIN -- SimpleTask

     -- Each task will write its message in its own column
     ACCEPT StartRunning;

     FOR Count IN 1..HowMany LOOP
       Screen.MoveCursor(Row => Count, Column => Column);
       Ada.Text_IO.Put(Item => "Hello from Task " & Message);
       DELAY 0.5;               -- lets another task have the CPU
     END LOOP;

   END SimpleTask;

   -- Now we declare three variables of the type
   Task_A: SimpleTask(Message => 'A', HowMany => 5, Column => 1);
   Task_B: SimpleTask(Message => 'B', HowMany => 7, Column => 26);
   Task_C: SimpleTask(Message => 'C', HowMany => 4, Column => 51);

BEGIN -- Columns

  Screen.ClearScreen;
  Task_B.StartRunning;
  Task_A.StartRunning;
  Task_C.StartRunning;

END Columns;
```

Here is the execution output:

```
Hello from Task A        Hello from Task B        Hello from Task C
                                                  2Hello from Task C;
                                                  26f[2;1fHello
from Task AHello from Task B               [[3;1fHello from Task A3;
                                                  26fHello
from Task BHello from Task C4;4;1fHello from Task A51fHello from Task
C26fHello
from Task B5;526;f1fHello from Task BHello from Task A
                                 Hello from Task B
                                 Hello from Task B
```

The output from running this program is not exactly what we intended! Instead of the desired neat columns, we got messages displayed in seemingly random locations, interspersed with apparent "garbage" like

```
C;26f[2;1f
```

What happened here? To understand this, recall the body of `Screen.Move Cursor` (Program 2.16):

```
PROCEDURE MoveCursor (Column : Width; Row : Depth) IS
BEGIN
  Ada.Text_IO.Put (Item => ASCII.ESC);
  Ada.Text_IO.Put ("[");
  Ada.Integer_Text_IO.Put (Item => Row, Width => 1);
  Ada.Text_IO.Put (Item => ';');
  Ada.Integer_Text_IO.Put (Item => Column, Width => 1);
  Ada.Text_IO.Put (Item => 'f');
END MoveCursor;
```

Positioning the cursor requires an instruction, up to eight characters in length, to the ANSI terminal software: the `ESC` character, then `'['`, followed by a possibly two-digit `Row`, then `';'`, then a possibly two-digit `Column` value, and finally `'F'`. Once it receives the entire instruction, the terminal actually moves the cursor on the screen.

Suppose the `MoveCursor` call is issued from within a task, as in the present example. Suppose further that in this case the Ada run-time system *does* provide time-slicing to produce "parallel" behavior by multiple tasks. It is quite possible that the task's quantum will expire after only some of the eight characters have been sent to the terminal, and then another task will attempt to write something to the terminal. In this case, the terminal never recognized the first instruction, because it received only part of it, so instead of obeying the instruction, it just displays the characters. The "garbage" string above, `C;26f[2;1f`, consists of pieces from several different intended instructions.

This problem arose because a task was interrupted in mid-instruction and then another task was allowed to begin its own screen instruction. This is called a *race condition*, because two tasks are, effectively, in a race to write to the screen, with unpredictable results. It is actually a readers-writers problem: Multiple tasks are interfering with each other's attempts to write to the screen.

To prevent this problem from ruining our columnar output, we must *protect* the screen so that—whether or not we have time-slicing—a task is allowed to finish an entire display operation before another task can begin one. We do this in Ada with a protected type, as shown in Program 15.6.

Program 15.6 Using a Protected Type to Ensure Completion of a Screen Action

```
WITH Ada.Text_IO;
WITH Screen;
PROCEDURE Protect_Screen IS
----------------------------------------------------------------------
--| Shows tasks writing into their respective columns on the
--| screen. This time we use a protected type, whose procedure
--| can be executed by only one task at a time.
--| Author: Michael B. Feldman, The George Washington University
--| Last Modified: December 1995
----------------------------------------------------------------------
```

```
PROTECTED TYPE ScreenManagerType IS

-- If multiple calls of Write are made simultaneously, each is
-- executed in its entirety before the next is begun.
-- The Ada standard does not specify an order of execution.

  PROCEDURE Write (Item:   IN String;
                   Row:    IN Screen.Depth;
                   Column: IN Screen.Width);

END ScreenManagerType;

PROTECTED BODY ScreenManagerType IS

  PROCEDURE Write (Item:   IN String;
                   Row:    IN Screen.Depth;
                   Column: IN Screen.Width) IS
  BEGIN -- Write

    Screen.MoveCursor(Row => Row, Column => Column);
    Ada.Text_IO.Put(Item => Item);

  END Write;

END ScreenManagerType;

Manager: ScreenManagerType;

TASK TYPE SimpleTask (Message: Character;
                      HowMany: Screen.Depth;
                      Column:  Screen.Width) IS

  -- This specification provides a "start button" entry.
  ENTRY StartRunning;

END SimpleTask;

TASK BODY SimpleTask IS

BEGIN -- SimpleTask

  -- Each task will write its message in its own column
  -- Now the task locks the screen before moving the cursor,
  -- unlocking it when writing is completed.

  ACCEPT StartRunning;

  FOR Count IN 1..HowMany LOOP

    -- No need to lock the screen explicitly; just call the
    -- protected procedure.
    Manager.Write(Row => Count, Column => Column,
                  Item => "Hello from Task " & Message);

    DELAY 0.5;               -- lets another task have the CPU
  END LOOP;

END SimpleTask;

-- Now we declare three variables of the type
Task_A: SimpleTask(Message => 'A', HowMany => 5, Column => 1);
Task_B: SimpleTask(Message => 'B', HowMany => 7, Column => 26);
Task_C: SimpleTask(Message => 'C', HowMany => 4, Column => 51);
```

```
BEGIN -- Protect_Screen

  Screen.ClearScreen;
  Task_B.StartRunning;
  Task_A.StartRunning;
  Task_C.StartRunning;

END Protect_Screen;
```

In this program, we declare a type

```
PROTECTED TYPE ScreenManagerType IS

  PROCEDURE Write (Item: IN String;
                   Row: IN Screen.Depth;
                   Column: IN Screen.Width);

END ScreenManagerType;

Manager: ScreenManagerType;
```

An object of this type—in this case, `Manager`—provides a procedure `Write` to which all the parameters of the desired screen operation are passed: the string to be written, the row, and the column. Any task wishing to write to the screen must do so by passing these parameters to the screen manager. The `SimpleTask` body now contains the call

```
Manager.Write(Row => Count, Column => Column,
              Item => "Hello from Task " & Message);
```

as required. The body of the protected type is

```
PROTECTED BODY ScreenManagerType IS

  PROCEDURE Write (Item:   IN String;
                   Row:    IN Screen.Depth;
                   Column: IN Screen.Width) IS
  BEGIN -- Write

    Screen.MoveCursor(Row => Row, Column => Column);
    Ada.Text_IO.Put(Item => Item);

  END Write;

END ScreenManagerType;
```

and the `Write` procedure encapsulates the `MoveCursor` and `Put` operations. `Write` is a *protected procedure*.

What is the difference between this protected write procedure and an ordinary procedure? Ada guarantees that each call of a protected procedure will complete before another call can be started. Even if several tasks are running, trading control of the CPU among them, a task will not be allowed to start a protected procedure call if another call of the same procedure, or any other procedure of the same protected object, is still incomplete. In our case, this provides the necessary mutual exclusion for the screen.

Protected types can provide functions and entries in addition to procedures. Protected functions allow multiple tasks to examine a data structure simultaneously but not to modify the data structure. Protected entries have some of the properties of both task entries and protected procedures. A detailed discussion of these is beyond our scope here.

15.4   DATA STRUCTURES: THE TASK AS A DATA STRUCTURE

We mentioned earlier in this chapter that a task has characteristics resembling those of a procedure, of a package, and of a data structure. We have seen examples of the first two; we will now consider the third.

So far, we have declared task types and task variables. In Program 15.7, we declare an array of tasks, with the declaration

```
Family: ARRAY (1..3) OF SimpleTask;
```

Program 15.7 Creating an Array of Tasks

```
WITH Ada.Text_IO;
WITH Screen;
PROCEDURE Task_Array IS
-----------------------------------------------------------------
--| Shows tasks writing into their respective columns on the
--| screen. This time we use a protected type, whose procedure
--| can be executed by only one task at a time.
--| The task objects are stored in an array, and receive their
--| configuration parameters through "start buttons" rather than
--| discriminants.
--| Author: Michael B. Feldman, The George Washington University
--| Last Modified: December 1995
-----------------------------------------------------------------

  PROTECTED TYPE ScreenManagerType IS

  -- If multiple calls of Write are made simultaneously, each is
  -- executed in its entirety before the next is begun.
  -- The Ada standard does not specify an order of execution.

    PROCEDURE Write (Item:   IN String;
                     Row:    IN Screen.Depth;
                     Column: IN Screen.Width);

  END ScreenManagerType;

  PROTECTED BODY ScreenManagerType IS

    PROCEDURE Write (Item:   IN String;
                     Row:    IN Screen.Depth;
                     Column: IN Screen.Width) IS
    BEGIN -- Write

      Screen.MoveCursor(Row => Row, Column => Column);
      Ada.Text_IO.Put(Item => Item);

    END Write;
```

```
      END ScreenManagerType;

   Manager: ScreenManagerType;

   TASK TYPE SimpleTask IS

      -- Task receives its parameters through a start-button entry
      -- instead of discriminants This is more flexible..
      ENTRY StartRunning (Message: Character;
                          HowMany: Screen.Depth;
                          Column:  Screen.Width);

   END SimpleTask;

   TASK BODY SimpleTask IS

      MyMessage: Character;
      MyCount  : Screen.Depth;
      MyColumn : Screen.Width;

   BEGIN -- SimpleTask

      -- Each task will write its message in its own column
      -- Now the task locks the screen before moving the cursor,
      -- unlocking it when writing is completed.

      ACCEPT StartRunning (Message: Character;
                           HowMany: Screen.Depth;
                           Column:  Screen.Width) DO
        MyMessage := Message;
        MyCount   := HowMany;
        MyColumn  := Column;

      END StartRunning;

      FOR Count IN 1..MyCount LOOP

         -- No need to lock the screen explicitly; just call the
         -- protected procedure.
         Manager.Write(Row => Count, Column => MyColumn,
                       Item => "Hello from Task " & MyMessage);

         DELAY 0.5;              -- lets another task have the CPU
      END LOOP;

   END SimpleTask;

   Family: ARRAY (1..3) OF SimpleTask;
   Char  : CONSTANT Character := 'A';

BEGIN -- Task_Array;

   Screen.ClearScreen;
   FOR Which IN Family'Range LOOP
      Family(Which).StartRunning
         (Message => Character'Val(Character'Pos(Char) + Which),
          HowMany => 3 * Which,
          Column  => 3 + (24 * (Which - 1)));
   END LOOP;

END Task_Array;
```

This program creates three task objects, just as declaring an array of three integers would create three integer objects. We refer to the task objects with array subscripts, as in an ordinary array. In this case, each task has a "start button" entry

```
ENTRY StartRunning (Message: Character;
                    HowMany: Screen.Depth;
                    Column : Screen.Width);
```

and we call each task's respective entry in the loop

```
FOR Which IN Family'Range LOOP
  Family(Which).StartRunning
    (Message => Character'Val(Character'Pos(Char) + Which),
     HowMany => 3 * Which,
     Column => 3 + (24 * (Which - 1)));
END LOOP;
```

In this program, we have passed each task's parameters in the "start button" instead of using the discriminants of earlier examples.

It is also possible to declare a task as a field of a record. Finally, it is possible to declare an access type such as

```
TYPE TaskPointer IS ACCESS SimpleTask;
```

Then, given a variable

```
Task_1: TaskPointer;
```

we can allocate a task dynamically, like any other dynamic data structure:

```
Task_1 := NEW SimpleTask;
```

The task starts running when it is allocated; we can call its entry with a statement such as

```
Task_1.ALL.StartRunning(Message =>'Z', HowMany => 10, Column => 20);
```

or, more concisely,

```
Task_1.StartRunning(Message =>'Z', HowMany => 10, Column => 20);
```

Further examples of tasks as record fields, and of dynamically allocated tasks, are beyond the scope of this book.

Because a task type is a *type*, it makes sense to ask how it is related to the overall Ada type system. Specifically, which operations are available for task types? The answer is that task types are similar to `LIMITED PRIVATE` types—no operations at all are predefined for them. Task objects can be declared, but the only operations are those provided by entries. In particular, assignment and equality test are *not* available.

Having introduced the basics of task types and protected types through a series of simple examples, we now proceed to two extended aplications: a bank simulation and the Dining Philosophers.

15.5 APPLICATION: SIMULATION OF A BANK

One interesting application of concurrent programming is simulating the behavior of a physical system or a real-life situation. For example, it is relatively straightforward to simulate a customer/server environment such as a bank. The objects in our model of a bank are:

- The *bank* itself

- A set of *customers*, who visit the bank periodically to open accounts, deposit money, and withdraw money

- A set of *tellers*, the bank employees who are responsible for interacting with the customers

- The *database*, a file of account information to which the tellers have access

We will model the bank using a main program for the bank and packages for the database, tellers, and customers. The dependencies are shown in Figure 15.1; the bank and the three packages are shown in the middle column; to the right and the left are other packages that provide services to them. As in other dependency diagrams, an arrow from one unit to a second unit means that the second is a client of the first. CPUClock refers to the package introduced in Programs 3.17 and 3.18; Random refers to Ada.Numerics.Discrete_Random (details in Appendix F). We will shortly introduce Types and Reporter.

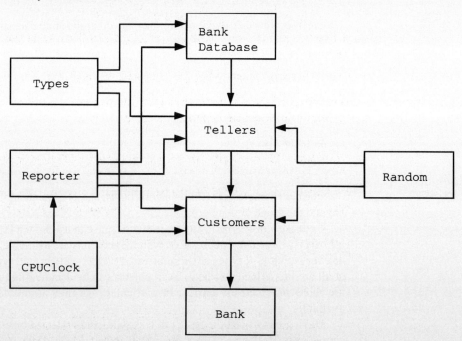

Figure 15.1 Package Dependencies for Bank Simulation

Executing the main program simulates a time period in the life of the bank. Here is a sample of the line-by-line output from the simulation after it has been running for a while:

```
T = 11 Account 3 depositing 398 with Teller C
T = 11   Teller B: Acct 1 - Balance is 0
T = 11 Account 1 will return after 2 sec
T = 13 Account 1 withdrawing 179 with Teller B
T = 13   Teller B: Transaction will take 6 sec
T = 15 Account 2 checking balance with Teller A
T = 15    Teller A: Transaction will take 7 sec
T = 15    Teller C: Acct 5 - Balance is 0
T = 15    Teller C: Transaction will take 1 sec
T = 15 Account 5 alive.
T = 15 Account 5 will return after 5 sec
T = 16    Teller C: Acct 3 - Balance is 398
T = 16 Account 3 will return after 6 sec
T = 17 Account 4 withdrawing 816 with Teller C
T = 17    Teller C: Transaction will take 1 sec
T = 18    Teller C: Acct 4 - InsufficientFunds
T = 18 Account 4 will return after 9 sec
```

Each line of the output begins with a "time stamp"—for example, T = 15—that gives the number of seconds that elapsed since the start of the run. The line

```
T = 11 Account 1 will return after 2 sec
```

indicates that Customer 1 has completed a transaction, and will come back for another one after 2 seconds have elapsed. The line

```
T = 13 Account 1 withdrawing 179 with Teller B
```

indicates that Customer 1 communicates to Teller B its desire to withdraw $179. The line

```
T = 13 Teller B: Transaction will take 6 sec
```

indicates that Teller B expects this transaction to take 6 seconds. We will see shortly how these times and amounts are generated.

The Bank Main Program and the Package Specifications

First we examine Program 15.8, the main program Bank. This program has nothing to do but cause the Customers and Tellers packages to be elaborated (by the WITH clauses).

Program 15.8 Body of the Bank Main Program

```
WITH Customers; USE Customers;
WITH Tellers; USE Tellers;
PROCEDURE Bank IS
-----------------------------------------------------------------
--| Main program for bank simulation; it does nothing but cause
--| the customers and tellers to come into existence.
--| Author: Michael B. Feldman, The George Washington University
--| Last Modified: January 1996
-----------------------------------------------------------------
```

```
BEGIN -- Bank

  NULL;

END Bank;
```

Next, we look at the various package specifications. Program 15.9 provides a set of types that are used by all the other packages.

Program 15.9 Some Types Needed by the Bank Simulation

```
PACKAGE Types IS
------------------------------------------------------------------------
--| Types package for the bank simulation. This contains only public
--| declarations, and therefore needs no package body.
--| Author: Michael B. Feldman, The George Washington University
--| Last Modified: January 1996
------------------------------------------------------------------------

    -- These 2 constants can be altered to change
    --  the behavior of the simulation
    SUBTYPE TellerRange IS Character RANGE 'A'..'C';
    NumberOfCustomers : CONSTANT Integer := 5;

    -- These 2 ranges can be altered to change
    --  the behavior of the simulation
    SUBTYPE TransactionTimeRange IS Integer RANGE 1 .. 7;
    SUBTYPE TimeBetweenVisitsRange IS Integer RANGE 1 .. 11;

    -- Global types
    SUBTYPE Money IS Integer RANGE 0 .. Integer'LAST;
    TYPE Status IS (OK, InsufficientFunds, BadCustId);
    SUBTYPE CustId IS Integer RANGE 0 .. NumberOfCustomers;

END Types;
```

How shall we model the customers? We declare a task type `Customer`; each task object represents one human customer. This task type has no entries because the customer objects are created at the start of the run, but do not need to be called. They simply live out their lives, occasionally making transactions at the bank. The customer type, and an array of customers, are defined in Program 15.10.

Program 15.10 Specification of the Customer Package

```
WITH Types; USE Types;
PACKAGE Customers IS
------------------------------------------------------------------------
--| Customer package for bank siumulation. Each customer is
--| a task object.
--| Author: Michael B. Feldman, The George Washington University
--| Last Modified: January 1996
------------------------------------------------------------------------

    TASK TYPE Customer IS  -- Requestor task type, no entries
    END Customer;

    CustomerGroup : ARRAY (1 .. NumberOfCustomers) OF Customer;

END Customers;
```

Program 15.11 shows the specification for `Tellers`.

Program 15.11 Specification of the Teller Package

```
WITH Types; USE Types;
PACKAGE Tellers IS
-----------------------------------------------------------------------
--| Teller package for bank siumulation
--| Author: Michael B. Feldman, The George Washington University
--| Last Modified: January 1996
-----------------------------------------------------------------------
  TASK TYPE Teller (TellerID: TellerRange) IS
    -- Entries to do simple transactions and return status
    ENTRY NewAcct (ID   : OUT CustID;
                   Stat: OUT Status);
    ENTRY Deposit (ID   : CustID;
                   Val  : IN Money;
                   Stat: OUT Status);
    ENTRY Withdraw (ID   : CustID;
                    Val  : IN Money;
                    Stat: OUT Status);
    ENTRY Balance (ID   : CustID;
                   Stat: OUT Status);
  END Teller;

  -- declare tellers and give them "names"
  A: ALIASED Teller(TellerID => 'A');
  B: ALIASED Teller(TellerID => 'B');
  C: ALIASED Teller(TellerID => 'C');

  TYPE TellerPointer IS ACCESS ALL Teller;

  -- a bank full of tellers
  TellerGroup : ARRAY (TellerRange) OF TellerPointer :=
    (A'Access, B'Access, C'Access);

END Tellers;
```

Here we have declared the task type `Teller` with a discriminant to initialize the teller's "name."

Each teller object has four entries that customers can call:

- `NewAcct` opens a new account for a customer.

- `Deposit` processes a customer's deposit transaction.

- `Withdraw` processes a customer's withdrawal transaction.

- `Balance` allows a customer to view its account balance.

Each operation returns a status code to the customer; the codes—OK, `InsufficientFunds`, and `BadCustId`—are defined in `Types`.

Because each teller object needs a different value of the discriminant (each teller needs a unique name), an array of tellers is heterogeneous. We cannot simply declare an array of tellers, but must instead declare an array of *pointers* to tellers, and initialize this array with pointers to the three teller objects. This is similar to the technique used in Program 9.8.

Program 15.12 gives the specification for `Database`. The database manager provides operations documented by the postconditions. It is a protected object, which provides mutual exclusion in case several tellers make concurrent calls of the database operations.

Program 15.12 Specification of the Database Package

```
WITH Types; USE Types;
PACKAGE Database IS
-------------------------------------------------------------------------
--| Maintains bank's internal data about open accounts and balances
--| Author: Michael B. Feldman, The George Washington University
--| Last Modified: January 1996
-------------------------------------------------------------------------

  PROTECTED Manager IS

    -- All these procedures are protected, so only one call at a time
    -- will be executed, even if the calls arrive concurrently.

    PROCEDURE EnterCustID (ID : OUT CustID; Stat  : OUT Status);
    -- Pre:  None
    -- Post: ID is the next available customer ID; Stat is OK.

    PROCEDURE Deposit (ID : IN CustID; Amount : IN Money;
                       NewBalance : OUT Money; Stat : OUT Status);
    -- Pre:  ID and Amount are defined
    -- Post: If ID is valid, NewBalance is the resulting balance
    --       and Stat is OK; otherwise, Stat is BadCustID.

    PROCEDURE Withdraw (ID : IN CustID; Amount : IN Money;
                        NewBalance : OUT Money; Stat : OUT Status);
    -- Pre:  ID and Amount are defined
    -- Post: If ID is valid and NewBalance would be nonnegative,
    --       Stat is OK and NewBalance is returned.
    --       If ID is invalid, Stat is BadCustID; if NewBalance
    --       would be negative, Stat is InsufficientFunds

    PROCEDURE Balance (ID : IN CustID; Amount : OUT Money;
                       Stat : OUT Status);
    -- Pre:  ID is defined
    -- Post: If ID is invalid, Stat is BadCustID; otherwise,
    --       Stat is OK and Amount is current balance
  END Manager;

END Database;
```

Finally, we turn to the specification for `Reporter`, shown in Program 15.13. The protected object `ScreenManager` provides an operation `Put`, which is protected, so only one call at a time can be executed.

Program 15.13 Specification of the Reporter Package

```
PACKAGE Reporter IS
-------------------------------------------------------------------------
--| Reporter package for bank simulation; Put is protected
--| Author: Michael B. Feldman, The George Washington University
--| Last Modified: January 1996
-------------------------------------------------------------------------
```

```
   PROTECTED ScreenManager IS

     PROCEDURE Put(Message: IN String);

   END ScreenManager;

END Reporter;
```

The Package Bodies in the Bank Simulation

We now turn to the bodies of the various packages. First look at `Reporter`, in Program 15.14. The `Put` procedure uses `CPUClock` to produce a "time stamp" that indicates the number of seconds elapsed since the start of the simulation. Note that this package body has its own executable statement part, following the `BEGIN`. The statement there is executed once, when `Reporter` is elaborated at the start of the program execution. The `Flush` statement is in `Put` because Ada input/output is usually buffered, and "flushing" (emptying) the buffer ensures that screen output appears as soon as possible after it is generated.

Program 15.14 Body of the Reporter Package

```
WITH Ada.Text_IO;
WITH CPUClock; USE CPUClock;
PACKAGE BODY Reporter IS

-----------------------------------------------------------------------
--| Body of Reporter - a simple screen protector
--| Author: Michael B. Feldman, The George Washington University
--| Last Modified: January 1996
-----------------------------------------------------------------------

   PROTECTED BODY ScreenManager IS

     PROCEDURE Put(Message: IN String) IS
     BEGIN -- Put
       Ada.Text_IO.Put("T =" & Integer'Image(Integer(CPUTime))
                        & " " & Message);
       Ada.Text_IO.New_Line;
       Ada.Text_IO.Flush;
     END Put;

   END ScreenManager;

BEGIN -- Reporter

   -- These two lines are executed once, when the package is elaborated.
   ResetCPUTime;

END Reporter;
```

Let us look next at the body of `Customers`. Each customer task opens an account, then executes a main loop that waits a random amount of time before beginning a transaction, then constructs a transaction from a random teller, a random transaction type, and a random amount of money. The customer then calls the appropriate entry of the selected teller. This requires four random number generators—instances of Ada.Numerics.Discrete_Random—each with its own range of random quantities.

Program 15.15 Body of the Customer Package

```
WITH Reporter; USE Reporter;
WITH Ada.Numerics.Discrete_Random;
WITH Tellers; USE Tellers;
WITH Types; USE Types;
PACKAGE BODY Customers IS
---------------------------------------------------------------------------
--| Body of customer package. Each customer executes ten random
--| transactions with random tellers before terminating.
--| Author: Michael B. Feldman, The George Washington University
--| Last Modified: January 1996
---------------------------------------------------------------------------

  TYPE Transactions IS (Deposit, Withdraw, Balance);

  PACKAGE RandomTransactions IS
    NEW Ada.Numerics.Discrete_Random (Transactions);

  PACKAGE RandomTellers IS
    NEW Ada.Numerics.Discrete_Random (TellerRange);

  SUBTYPE MoneyRange IS Money RANGE 1 .. 999;
  PACKAGE RandomAmounts IS
    NEW Ada.Numerics.Discrete_Random (MoneyRange);

  PACKAGE RandomTimesBetweenVisits IS
    NEW Ada.Numerics.Discrete_Random (TimeBetweenVisitsRange);

  TASK BODY Customer IS

    -- Local variables
    ID               : CustID;
    Amount           : Money;
    Stat             : Status;
    WaitTime         : TimeBetweenVisitsRange;
    Teller           : TellerRange;
    Transaction      : Transactions;
    NumTransactions  : CONSTANT Integer := 10;

    T: RandomTransactions.Generator;
    R: RandomTellers.Generator;
    A: RandomAmounts.Generator;
    V: RandomTimesBetweenVisits.Generator;

  BEGIN -- Customer

    RandomTransactions.Reset(T);
    RandomTellers.Reset(R);
    RandomAmounts.Reset(A);
    RandomTimesBetweenVisits.Reset(V);

    Teller := RandomTellers.Random(R);
    TellerGroup(Teller).NewAcct(ID, Stat); -- Get new cust id
    ScreenManager.Put ("Account" & Integer'Image(ID) & " alive.");

    FOR I IN 1 .. NumTransactions LOOP

      WaitTime := RandomTimesBetweenVisits.Random(V);
      ScreenManager.Put("Account" & Integer'Image(ID)
```

```
          & " will return after" & Integer'Image(WaitTime)
          & " sec");
        DELAY Duration (WaitTime);

        Teller := RandomTellers.Random(R);
        Transaction := RandomTransactions.Random(T);
        Amount := RandomAmounts.Random(A);

        CASE Transaction IS -- Pick random transaction
          WHEN Deposit =>
            ScreenManager.Put("Account" & Integer'Image(ID)
              & " depositing" & Integer'Image(Amount)
              & " with Teller " & Teller);
            TellerGroup (Teller).Deposit (ID, Amount, Stat);
          WHEN Withdraw =>
            ScreenManager.Put("Account" & Integer'Image(ID)
              & " withdrawing" & Integer'Image(Amount)
              & " with Teller " & Teller);
            TellerGroup (Teller).Withdraw (ID, Amount, Stat);
          WHEN Balance =>
            ScreenManager.Put("Account" & Integer'Image(ID)
              & " checking balance"
              & " with Teller " & Teller);
            TellerGroup (Teller).Balance (ID, Stat);
        END CASE;
      END LOOP;
      ScreenManager.Put("Account" & Integer'Image(ID) & " closed.");
    END Customer;

END Customers;
```

Program 15.16 shows the body of `Database`. This is very straightforward; the protected object `Manager` performs operations on the array `Accounts`. Each account is represented by a record that contains a flag (which is set when the account is opened) and shows the current balance. The four operations of the database manager are all protected: Only one at a time can be executed even if there are simultaneous calls from multiple tasks.

Program 15.16 Body of the Database Package

```
WITH Reporter; USE Reporter;
WITH Types; USE Types;
PACKAGE BODY Database IS
-----------------------------------------------------------------------
--| Body of database package. The protected procedures ensure that
--| only one call at a time is exexuted.
--| Author: Michael B. Feldman, The George Washington University
--| Last Modified: January 1996
-----------------------------------------------------------------------

  TYPE AccountRecord IS RECORD
    Valid: Boolean := False;
    Balance: Money := 0;
  END RECORD;

  TYPE AccountType IS ARRAY (CustID) OF AccountRecord;

  Next: CustID;
  Accounts: AccountType;
```

```
PROTECTED BODY Manager IS

  PROCEDURE EnterCustID (ID: OUT CustID; Stat: OUT Status) IS
  BEGIN
    Next := Next + 1;
    ID := Next;
    Accounts(ID).Valid := True;
    Stat := OK;

  END EnterCustID;

  PROCEDURE Deposit (ID: CustID; Amount: IN Money;
                 NewBalance: OUT Money; Stat: OUT Status) IS
  BEGIN
    IF NOT Accounts(ID).Valid THEN
      Stat := BadCustID;
    ELSE
      Accounts(ID).Balance := Accounts(ID).Balance + Amount;
      NewBalance := Accounts(ID).Balance;
      Stat := OK;
    END IF;
  END Deposit;

  PROCEDURE Withdraw (ID: CustID; Amount  IN Money;
                 NewBalance: OUT Money; Stat: OUT Status) IS
  BEGIN
    IF NOT Accounts(ID).Valid THEN
      Stat := BadCustID;
    ELSIF Accounts(ID).Balance - Amount <= 0 THEN
      Stat := InsufficientFunds;
    ELSE
      Accounts(ID).Balance := Accounts(ID).Balance + Amount;
      NewBalance := Accounts(ID).Balance;
      Stat := OK;
    END IF;
  END Withdraw;

  PROCEDURE Balance (ID: CustID; Amount: OUT Money;
                    Stat: OUT Status) IS
  BEGIN
    IF NOT Accounts(ID).Valid THEN
      Stat := BadCustID;
    ELSE
      Amount := Accounts(ID).Balance;
      Stat := OK;
    END IF;
  END Balance;

END Manager;

END Database;
```

Finally, Program 15.17 shows the body of `Tellers`. The `Teller` task body contains two auxiliary procedures: `SimulateWait` selects a random length of time and then waits that long. This simulates the varying length of time taken by a transaction in an actual bank. `ReportResult` just assembles a message and sends it to `Reporter`; the message contents depend on the status code returned by the transaction.

Program 15.17 Body of the Tellers Package

```ada
WITH Reporter; USE Reporter;
WITH Types; USE Types;
WITH Database; USE Database;
WITH Ada.Numerics.Discrete_Random;
PACKAGE BODY Tellers IS
------------------------------------------------------------------------
--| Body of teller package. A teller object just waits a random
--| length of time (to simulate the time of a transaction), then
--| waits for a customer to ask for a transaction.
--| Author: Michael B. Feldman, The George Washington University
--| Last Modified: January 1996
------------------------------------------------------------------------

  PACKAGE RandomTransactionTimes IS
    NEW Ada.Numerics.Discrete_Random (TransactionTimeRange);
  T: RandomTransactionTimes.Generator;

  TASK BODY Teller IS

    NewBalance     : Money;
    Del            : Integer;
    Stat           : Status;

    PROCEDURE SimulateWait IS
      WaitTime: TransactionTimeRange
        := RandomTransactionTimes.Random(T);
    BEGIN
      ScreenManager.Put
        ("  Teller " & TellerID & ": Transaction will take"
        & Integer'Image(WaitTime) & " sec");
      DELAY Duration(WaitTime);
    END SimulateWait;

    PROCEDURE ReportResult (Stat: Status; TellID: TellerRange;
                            ID: CustID; NewBalance: Money) IS
    BEGIN
      CASE Stat IS
        WHEN OK =>
          ScreenManager.Put("  Teller " & TellerID
            & ": Acct"  & Integer'Image(ID)
            & " - Balance is" & Integer'Image(NewBalance));
        WHEN BadCustID =>
          ScreenManager.Put("  Teller " & TellerID
            & ": Acct"  & Integer'Image(ID)
            & " - Invalid Account Number");
        WHEN InsufficientFunds =>
          ScreenManager.Put("  Teller " & TellerID
            & ": Acct"  & Integer'Image(ID)
            & " - InsufficientFunds");
      END CASE;
    END ReportResult;

  BEGIN -- Teller
    RandomTransactionTimes.Reset(T); -- seed random sequence
    ScreenManager.Put("  Teller  " & TellerID  & " - at your service");
    LOOP
      SELECT -- Wait for any transaction request
        ACCEPT NewAcct(Id : OUT CustId; Stat: OUT Status) DO
          SimulateWait;
          Database.Manager.EnterCustID(Id, Stat);
          NewBalance := 0;
```

```
                    ReportResult (Stat, TellerID, ID, NewBalance);
                  END NewAcct;
            OR
              ACCEPT Deposit (Id: CustId; Val: IN Money; Stat: OUT Status) DO
                SimulateWait;
                Database.Manager.Deposit (Id, Val, NewBalance, Stat);
                ReportResult (Stat, TellerID, ID, NewBalance);
              END Deposit;
            OR
              ACCEPT Withdraw (Id: CustId; Val: IN Money; Stat: OUT Status) DO
                SimulateWait;
                Database.Manager.Withdraw (Id, Val, NewBalance, Stat);
                ReportResult (Stat, TellerID, ID, NewBalance);
              END Withdraw;
            OR
              ACCEPT Balance (Id: CustId; Stat: OUT Status) DO
                SimulateWait;
                Database.Manager.Balance (Id, NewBalance, Stat);
                ReportResult (Stat, TellerID, ID, NewBalance);
              END Balance;
            OR
              TERMINATE; -- if no more customers
            END SELECT;
        END LOOP;

    END Teller;

END Tellers;
```

The SELECT Statement

The teller task body also introduces a very interesting new Ada statement type, the
SELECT statement. Figure 15.2 gives a flowchart-like depiction of the statement

```
LOOP
  SELECT -- Wait for any transaction request
    ACCEPT NewAcct(Id : OUT CustId; Stat: OUT Status) DO
    . . .
    END NewAcct;
  OR
    ACCEPT Deposit (Id: CustId; Val: IN Money; Stat: OUT Status) DO
    . . .
    END Deposit;
  OR
    ACCEPT Withdraw (Id: CustId; Val: IN Money; Stat: OUT Status) DO
    . . .
    END Withdraw;
  OR
    ACCEPT Balance (Id: CustId; Stat: OUT Status) DO
    . . .
    END Balance;
  OR
    TERMINATE; -- if no more customers
  END SELECT;
END LOOP;
```

The diagram shows that the teller processes *one* transaction at each iteration of the
loop. The Ada run-time system provides each entry with a FIFO queue; entry calls are

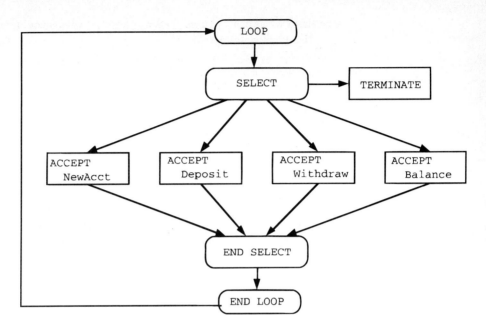

Figure 15.2 A Loop with a SELECT Statement

placed in the queues in the order of their arrival. Now consider several cases, assuming the teller has just arrived at the SELECT statement:

1. *The bank is quiet; no customers are calling entries.* In this case, the teller waits at the SELECT until a customer entry call arrives, accepts that call, and executes the statements within that DO-END block. The DO-END block is called a *rendezvous*; as in a real bank, the customer waits while the transaction is processed. After executing the rendezvous code, the teller loops around to the SELECT again and the customer goes about its other business.

2. *Several customers have called the same entry of the same teller.* In this case, the teller accepts the first call. The teller can accept only the *first* call because the queue is FIFO. The entry call is dequeued, the teller loops around to the SELECT, and the customer proceeds with other matters.

3. *Calls are waiting at the heads of more than one entry queue.* In this case, the teller chooses one of these callers and proceeds as in case 2. The mechanism for choosing a caller is not specified by the Ada standard and, therefore, depends on the specific Ada run-time system. To give just two possibilities, the choice can rotate among the queue heads—one queue per iteration—or it can be random.

The fifth SELECT alternative, TERMINATE, is provided to allow the teller to terminate when there is no more activity on any of its entry queues. Termination conditions are rather complicated to explain for the full generality of Ada tasks; this is a subject beyond the scope of this book. Here we simply say that the teller will select the TERMINATE alternative, leave its apparently infinite loop, and quit when there is nothing left for it to do.

This example has shown the use of tasks to simulate real-life situations. The next, and last, section introduces a more humorous example, which has served for more than 20 years as a vehicle for studying problems of resource allocation and deadlock.

15.6 APPLICATION: THE DINING PHILOSOPHERS

Imagine a group of five brilliant philosophers who lead very sheltered lives: Each has nothing to do but think deep thoughts, stopping occasionally to eat a meal. Their plates are automatically refilled from an infinite supply of delicious Chinese food. However, like most philosophers, these thinkers must interrupt their simple lives to solve an especially difficult problem: They sit around a circular table and only five chopsticks—made of titanium and therefore unbreakable—are provided, one chopstick between each pair of plates. Figure 15.3 depicts the philosophers and their dining table.

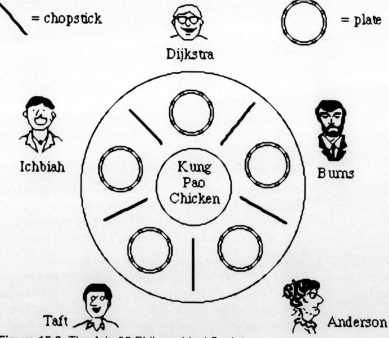

Figure 15.3 The Ada 95 Philosophical Society

It has become traditional to name the philosophers for major contributors to the field. Our philosophers are (counterclockwise from the top of the cartoon)

- Edsger Dijkstra, the Dutch computer science professor who first described the Dining Philosophers in 1971

- Jean Ichbiah, the French software engineer who led the original Ada design team beginning in the late 1970s

- Tucker Taft, the American software engineer who led the Ada 9X design team and whose work resulted in the Ada 95 standard

- Christine Anderson, the American aerospace engineer who managed the Ada 95 design project for the U.S. government

- Alan Burns, the British professor who has written very wisely and well about concurrency in Ada

How should the philosophers behave? To eat, a philosopher must pick up the chopsticks to his or her immediate left and right. The problem is caused by the circularity of the table: Each left chopstick is also another philosopher's right chopstick. Suppose each philosopher first grabs his or her left-hand chopstick and refuses to put it down while waiting for the right-hand chopstick. In this case, nobody will get to eat and all the philosophers will die of hunger. This state of affairs—each philosopher waiting indefinitely for his or her right-hand neighbor to act—is called *deadlock*, or, sometimes, *deadly embrace*. We will discuss some deadlock-avoiding philosopher algorithms a bit later.

Modeling the Philosophers

Let us model the philosophical society with an Ada program. As with the bank simulation, a small excerpt from the program's execution looks like this:

```
T = 3      Jean Ichbiah      Eating meal 1 for 3 seconds.
T = 6      Jean Ichbiah       Yum-yum (burp)
T = 6      Chris Anderson    Second chopstick 3
T = 6      Jean Ichbiah       Thinking 6 seconds.
T = 6      Chris Anderson    Eating meal 1 for 3 seconds.
T = 9      Tucker Taft       First chopstick 4
T = 9      Tucker Taft        Second chopstick 5
T = 9      Tucker Taft        Eating meal 2 for 10 seconds.
T = 9      Chris Anderson    Yum-yum (burp)
T = 9      Chris Anderson     Thinking 5 seconds.
T = 9   Edsger Dijkstra    Second chopstick 2
T = 9   Edsger Dijkstra    Eating meal 1 for 5 seconds.
```

Figure 15.4 shows the various units of the program and the dependencies among them.

Program 15.18 is the specification for `Society`, a types package similar to the one in the bank example. As you can see, it just provides a subtype to index the philosophers and a set of philosopher names in string form.

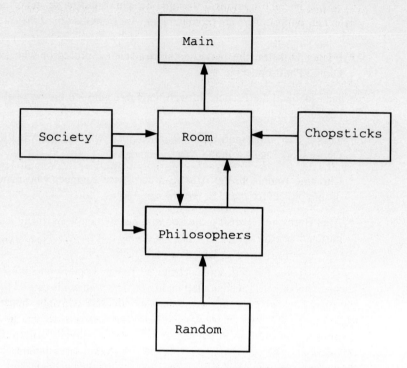

Figure 15.4 Package Dependencies for Dining Philosophers

Program 15.18 The Society Package

```
PACKAGE Society IS
----------------------------------------------------------------------
--| Dining Philosophers - Ada 95 edition
--| Society gives unique ID's to people, and registers their names
--| Author: Michael B. Feldman, The George Washington University
--| Last Modified: January 1996
----------------------------------------------------------------------

  SUBTYPE Unique_DNA_Codes IS Positive RANGE 1..5;

  Name_Register : ARRAY(Unique_DNA_Codes) OF String(1..18) :=

      ("Edsger Dijkstra    ",
       "Alan Burns         ",
       "Chris Anderson     ",
       "Tucker Taft        ",
       "Jean Ichbiah       ");

END Society;
```

Next, we examine Program 15.19, the main program. As you can see, it consists only of an entry call,

```
Room.Maitre_D.Start_Serving;
```

which presses the "start button" of the maître d', or manager, of the dining room. We will see the details of Room shortly.

Program 15.19 The Diners Main Program

```
WITH Ada.Text_IO;
WITH Room;
PROCEDURE Diners IS
-------------------------------------------------------------------------
--| Dining Philosophers - Ada 95 edition
--| This is the main program, responsible only for telling the
--| Maitre_D to get busy.
--| Author: Michael B. Feldman, The George Washington University
--| Last Modified: January 1996
-------------------------------------------------------------------------

BEGIN -- Diners

  Ada.Text_IO.New_Line;      -- artifice to flush output buffer
  Room.Maitre_D.Start_Serving;

END Diners;
```

Program 15.20 shows the specification of the philosophers package. Each philosopher is a task object with a discriminant to assign its name and a "start button" to cause it to begin its lifetime of eating and thinking. The "start button" parameters Chopstick1 and Chopstick2 are used to assign chopsticks to the philosophers; each philosopher will always pick up Chopstick1 first, then Chopstick2. In this way, the task that presses the "start button" can determine each philospher's eating algorithm.

Philosophers exist only to eat and think, not to communicate with the outside world. However, to allow us to observe their behavior, each philosopher reports his or her current state to the maître d', who will broadcast a running account of the happenings in the dining room. To make this possible, this package also provides an enumeration type States:

```
TYPE States IS (Breathing, Thinking, Eating, Done_Eating,
                Got_One_Stick, Got_Other_Stick, Dying);
```

Program 15.20 Philosopher Specification

```
WITH Society;
PACKAGE Phil IS

-------------------------------------------------------------------------
--| Dining Philosophers - Ada 95 edition
--| Philosopher is an Ada 95 task type with discriminant
--| Author: Michael B. Feldman, The George Washington University
--| Last Modified: January 1996

-------------------------------------------------------------------------

  TASK TYPE Philosopher (My_ID : Society.Unique_DNA_Codes) IS

    ENTRY Start_Eating (Chopstick1 : IN Positive;
                        Chopstick2 : IN Positive);
```

```
END Philosopher;

TYPE States IS (Breathing, Thinking, Eating, Done_Eating,
                Got_One_Stick, Got_Other_Stick, Dying);

END Phil;
```

The dining room specification is given in Program 15.21. This is where the set of chopsticks, an array of type `Chop.Stick`, is defined. `Maitre_D` is a task, with a "start button," as mentioned above, and a second entry, `Report_State`, that is called by the various philosophers.

Program 15.21 Room Specification

```
WITH Chop;
WITH Phil;
WITH Society;
PACKAGE Room IS
-------------------------------------------------------------------------
--| Dining Philosophers - Ada 95 edition
--| Room.Maitre_D IS responsible for assigning seats at the
--|   table, "left" and "right" chopsticks, and for reporting
--|   interesting events to the outside world.
--| Author: Michael B. Feldman, The George Washington University
--| Last Modified: January 1996
-------------------------------------------------------------------------

   Table_Size : CONSTANT := 5;
   SUBTYPE Table_Type IS Positive RANGE 1 .. Table_Size;

   Sticks : ARRAY (Table_Type) OF Chop.Stick;

   TASK Maitre_D IS
     ENTRY Start_Serving;
     ENTRY Report_State (Which_Phil : IN Society.Unique_DNA_Codes;
                         State      : IN Phil.States;
                         How_Long   : IN Natural := 0;
                         Which_Meal : IN Natural := 0);
   END Maitre_D;

END Room;
```

We have not yet shown a specification for chopsticks; we will come back to this after looking at the philosopher and room package bodies.

Implementing the Philosophers and the Dining Room

The body of the philosopher package is shown in Program 15.22. As in the bank customer case, each philosopher task draws random numbers to simulate its eating and thinking times. The start-button parameters `Chopstick1` and `Chopstick2` are saved in the variables `First_Grab` and `Second_Grab`, respectively. The basic philosopher algorithm is

```
FOR Meal IN Life_Time LOOP

  Room.Sticks (First_Grab).Pick_Up;
  Room.Sticks (Second_Grab).Pick_Up;
```

```
Meal_Time := Meal_Length.Random(M);
DELAY Duration (Meal_Time);

Room.Sticks (First_Grab).Put_Down;
Room.Sticks (Second_Grab).Put_Down;

Think_Time := Think_Length.Random(T);
DELAY Duration (Think_Time);

END LOOP;
```

The code in Program 15.22 is slightly more elaborate, to allow the philosopher to report its current state to the maître d'.

Program 15.22 Philosopher Body

```
WITH Society;
WITH Room;
WITH Ada.Numerics.Discrete_Random;
PACKAGE BODY Phil IS
------------------------------------------------------------------------
--| Dining Philosophers - Ada 95 edition
--| Philosopher is an Ada 95 task type with discriminant.
--| Chopsticks are assigned by a higher authority, which
--|   can vary the assignments to show different algorithms.
--| Philosopher always grabs First_Grab, then Second_Grab.
--| Philosopher is oblivious to outside world, but needs to
--|   communicate its life-cycle events to the Maitre_D.
--| Author: Michael B. Feldman, The George Washington University
--| Last Modified: January 1996
------------------------------------------------------------------------
  SUBTYPE Think_Times IS Positive RANGE 1..8;
  PACKAGE Think_Length IS
    new Ada.Numerics.Discrete_Random (Result_Subtype => Think_Times);

  SUBTYPE Meal_Times IS Positive RANGE 1..10;
  PACKAGE Meal_Length IS
    new Ada.Numerics.Discrete_Random (Result_Subtype => Meal_Times);

  TASK BODY Philosopher IS  -- My_ID is discriminant

    SUBTYPE Life_Time IS Positive RANGE 1..5;

    Who_Am_I    : Society.Unique_DNA_Codes := My_ID; -- discrim
    First_Grab  : Positive;
    Second_Grab : Positive;
    Meal_Time   : Meal_Times;
    Think_Time  : Think_Times;
    T           : Think_Length.Generator;
    M           : Meal_Length.Generator;

  BEGIN

    Think_Length.Reset(T);
    Meal_Length.Reset(M);

      -- get assigned the first and second chopsticks here

    ACCEPT Start_Eating (Chopstick1 : IN Positive;
                         Chopstick2 : IN Positive) do

      First_Grab  := Chopstick1;
      Second_Grab := Chopstick2;
    END Start_Eating;
```

```
      Room.Maitre_D.Report_State (Who_Am_I, Breathing);

      FOR Meal IN Life_Time LOOP

         Room.Sticks (First_Grab).Pick_Up;
         Room.Maitre_D.Report_State
           (Who_Am_I, Got_One_Stick, First_Grab);

         Room.Sticks (Second_Grab).Pick_Up;
         Room.Maitre_D.Report_State
           (Who_Am_I, Got_Other_Stick, Second_Grab);

         Meal_Time := Meal_Length.Random(M);
         Room.Maitre_D.Report_State Who_Am_I, Eating, Meal_Time, Meal);

         DELAY Duration (Meal_Time);

         Room.Maitre_D.Report_State (Who_Am_I, Done_Eating);

         Room.Sticks (First_Grab).Put_Down;
         Room.Sticks (Second_Grab).Put_Down;
         Think_Time := Think_Length.Random(T);
         Room.Maitre_D.Report_State (Who_Am_I, Thinking, Think_Time);
         DELAY Duration (Think_Time);

      END LOOP;

      Room.Maitre_D.Report_State (Who_Am_I, Dying);

   END Philosopher;

END Phil;
```

Program 15.23 shows the body of the dining room package. As with the bank tellers, the philosophers are declared as ALIASED variables, each with its own discriminant value. The maître d' task has the job of assigning seats and chopsticks to philosophers. Seats are assigned by the statement

```
Phils :=
  (Dijkstra'Access,
   Anderson'Access,
   Taft'Access,
   Ichbiah'Access,
   Burns'Access);
```

Chopsticks are assigned by pressing the "start buttons" as follows:

```
Phils (1).Start_Eating (1, 2);
Phils (3).Start_Eating (3, 4);
Phils (2).Start_Eating (2, 3);
Phils (5).Start_Eating (1, 5);
Phils (4).Start_Eating (4, 5);
```

The peculiar order of starting the tasks is just to ensure that the action starts early; note that philosophers 1 and 3 can begin eating immediately. Philosophers 1, 2, 3, and 4 are told to grab their left chopsticks first, but philosopher 5 (Burns) is told to grab its right chopstick first. This ensures that the situation in which all the philosophers hold only their left chopsticks cannot occur. The circularity is broken and there is no deadlock.

Program 15.23 Room Body

```
WITH Ada.Text_IO;
WITH Chop;
WITH Phil;
WITH Society;
WITH Calendar;
PRAGMA Elaborate (Phil);
PACKAGE BODY Room IS
-------------------------------------------------------------------------
--| Dining Philosophers, Ada 95 edition
--| A line-oriented version of the Room package
--| Author: Michael B. Feldman, The George Washington University
--| Last Modified: January 1996
-------------------------------------------------------------------------

  -- philosophers sign into dining room, giving Maitre_D their DNA code

  Dijkstra  : ALIASED Phil.Philosopher (My_ID => 1);
  Burns     : ALIASED Phil.Philosopher (My_ID => 2);
  Anderson  : ALIASED Phil.Philosopher (My_ID => 3);
  Ichbiah   : ALIASED Phil.Philosopher (My_ID => 4);
  Taft      : ALIASED Phil.Philosopher (My_ID => 5);

  TYPE Philosopher_Ptr IS ACCESS ALL Phil.Philosopher;
  Phils : ARRAY (Table_Type) OF Philosopher_Ptr;

  TASK BODY Maitre_D IS

    T          : Natural;
    Start_Time : Calendar.Time;
    Blanks : CONSTANT String := "      ";

  BEGIN

    ACCEPT Start_Serving;
    Ada.Text_IO.New_Line;
    Ada.Text_IO.Put_Line
      ("Ada 95 Philosophical Society is Open for Business!");

    Start_Time := Calendar.Clock;

    -- now Maitre_D assigns phils to seats at the table

    Phils :=
      (Dijkstra'Access,
       Anderson'Access,
       Taft'Access,
       Ichbiah'Access,
       Burns'Access);

    -- and assigns them their chopsticks.

    Phils (1).Start_Eating (1, 2);
    Phils (3).Start_Eating (3, 4);
    Phils (2).Start_Eating (2, 3);
    Phils (5).Start_Eating (1, 5);
    Phils (4).Start_Eating (4, 5);

    LOOP
      SELECT
        ACCEPT Report_State (Which_Phil : IN Society.Unique_DNA_Codes;
                             State      : IN Phil.States;
                             How_Long   : IN Natural := 0;
                             Which_Meal : IN Natural := 0) do

            T := Natural (Calendar."-" (Calendar.Clock, Start_Time));
```

```
            CASE State IS

               WHEN Phil.Breathing =>
                  Ada.Text_IO.Put_Line ("T =" & Integer'Image (T) & " "
                        & Blanks(1..Which_Phil)
                        & Society.Name_Register(Which_Phil)
                        & "Breathing");
               WHEN Phil.Thinking =>
                  Ada.Text_IO.Put_Line ("T =" & Integer'Image (T) & " "
                        & Blanks(1..Which_Phil)
                        & Society.Name_Register(Which_Phil)
                        & "Thinking"
                        & Integer'Image (How_Long) & " seconds.");
               WHEN Phil.Eating =>
                  Ada.Text_IO.Put_Line ("T =" & Integer'Image (T) & " "
                        & Blanks(1..Which_Phil)
                        & Society.Name_Register(Which_Phil)
                        & "Eating meal"
                        & Integer'Image (Which_Meal)
                        & " for"
                        & Integer'Image (How_Long) & " seconds.");
               WHEN Phil.Done_Eating =>
                  Ada.Text_IO.Put_Line ("T =" & Integer'Image (T) & " "
                        & Blanks(1..Which_Phil)
                        & Society.Name_Register(Which_Phil)
                        & "Yum-yum (burp)");
               WHEN Phil.Got_One_Stick =>
                  Ada.Text_IO.Put_Line ("T =" & Integer'Image (T) & " "
                        & Blanks(1..Which_Phil)
                        & Society.Name_Register(Which_Phil)
                        & "First chopstick"
                        & Integer'Image (How_Long));
               WHEN Phil.Got_Other_Stick =>
                  Ada.Text_IO.Put_Line ("T =" & Integer'Image (T) & " "
                        & Blanks(1..Which_Phil)
                        & Society.Name_Register(Which_Phil)
                        & "Second chopstick"
                        & Integer'Image (How_Long));
               WHEN Phil.Dying =>
                  Ada.Text_IO.Put_Line ("T =" & Integer'Image (T) & " "
                        & Blanks(1..Which_Phil)
                        & Society.Name_Register(Which_Phil)
                        & "Croak");

            END CASE; - State

            Ada.Text_IO.Flush;

         END Report_State;

      OR
         TERMINATE;
      END SELECT;

   END LOOP;

 END Maitre_D;
END Room;
```

Having assigned seats and chopsticks, bringing the philosophers to life, the maître d' enters its main loop, which is just to wait for a philosopher to report a state, use a CASE statement to determine which state was reported, and display an appropriate message on the screen.

The Chopsticks Package

We have left the chopstick package for last because it introduces some new material about protected types. Program 15.24 shows the specification for the chopsticks package. A chopstick is a protected object with a data structure of its own, declared in its PRIVATE section. The Boolean flag In_Use reflects the fact that a chopstick cannot be picked up while it is in use by another philosopher. Also, the Pick_Up operation is specified as an entry, rather than a protected procedure as in earlier examples.

Program 15.24 Chopstick Specification

```
PACKAGE Chop IS
-----------------------------------------------------------------------
--| Dining Philosophers - Ada 95 edition
--| Each chopstick is an Ada 95 protected object
--| Author: Michael B. Feldman, The George Washington University
--| Last Modified: January 1996
-----------------------------------------------------------------------
  PROTECTED TYPE Stick IS
    ENTRY Pick_Up;
    PROCEDURE Put_Down;
  PRIVATE
    In_Use: Boolean := False;
  END Stick;

END Chop;
```

Program 15.25 gives the body of the chopsticks package. The chopstick's protected procedure Put_Down sets the flag In_Use to False. The entry Pick_Up behaves like a protected procedure, but with one important difference: The entry body—which sets In_Use to True—is executed only when it makes sense to do so, namely when the chopstick is not in use. The clause

```
WHEN NOT In_Use
```

is called a *barrier condition*, and serves to ensure that a chopstick can be held by at most one philosopher.

Program 15.25 Chopstick Body

```
PACKAGE BODY Chop IS
-----------------------------------------------------------------------
--| Chopstick Body
--| Author: Michael B. Feldman, The George Washington University
--| Last Modified: January 1996
-----------------------------------------------------------------------
  PROTECTED BODY Stick IS

    ENTRY Pick_Up WHEN NOT In_Use IS
    BEGIN
      In_Use := True;
    END PIck_Up;
```

```
      PROCEDURE Put_Down IS
      BEGIN
        In_Use := False;
      END Put_Down;

  END Stick;

END Chop;
```

A More Interesting Philosophers Display

As a final example, consider Figure 15.5. Here each philosopher is given its own window, in which its activity is displayed. Such a screen display would give an animated depiction of the philosophers as shown in Figure 15.3. Because all input/output activity in the philosophical society is carried out by the maître d', this window-oriented display can be achieved by modifying *only* the body of Room so that the maître d'' task uses operations from the windows package of Programs 2.19 and 2.20. We leave this interesting modification as an exercise.

As we pointed out at the beginning of this chapter, a single chapter in a book of this kind cannot really do justice to a topic as rich and interesting as concurrent programming. Our intention here has been to introduce you to the subject through some brief examples and two longer simulations. We hope this chapter has stimulated your interest in pursuing concurrency, and Ada's concurrency facilities in particular, through further reading and projects.

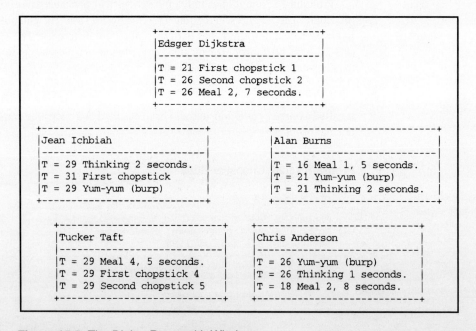

Figure 15.5 The Dining Room with Windows

EXERCISES

1. Investigate whether your Ada implementation supports time-slicing and, if it does, whether time-slicing can be turned on and off at will. Experiment with doing so, using Program 15.2 as a test program.

2. Experiment with using different starting orders in Program 15.4. Is there any difference in the behavior?

3. In the bank example, each teller has four entries and, therefore, four distinct queues. This is not very realistic; in a real bank, a teller has only one queue and processes whichever transaction is at the head of that queue. Modify the tellers package, and other units as necessary, so that each teller task has a single entry with an additional parameter to indicate the nature of the transaction. Use an enumeration type to represent the transaction types.

4. In the dining philosophers example, modify the body of the `Room` package (Program 15.23) so that the maître d' task uses operations from the `Windows` package (Programs 2.19 and 2.20) to display each philosopher's activity in a window as shown in Figure 15.5. *Hint*: The maître d' should open all the windows before bringing the philosophers to life.

Bibliography

This resource list is far from exhaustive and, of course, reflects the subjective judgments of the author. It is divided into four sections: key World Wide Web resources on Ada, other books on Ada 95, other books on algorithms and data structures, and important original and survey papers. The last category is highly selective, focusing on early and often obscure papers that first introduced important topics covered in this book, and a few surveys with extensive bibliographies of their own.

WORLD-WIDE WEB RESOURCES ON ADA

Public Ada Library (PAL). A comprehensive collection of freely available Ada documents, compilers, tutorials, and source code libraries.

`http://wuarchive.wustl.edu/languages/ada/pal2.html`

Home of the Brave Ada Programmers. A World Wide Web page for anyone interested in Ada. Contains links to the other Internet sites. `http://lglwww.epfl.ch/Ada/`

Ada Information Clearinghouse. The "official" U.S. Government-sponsored Ada site. A good place to look for Ada manuals and other documents. Most of this site is copied to the PAL, but this one is less crowded. `http://sw-eng.falls-church.va.us`

ACM Special Interest Group on Ada (SIGAda). The major professional organization for those interested in Ada. This is a membership organization, with very attractive rates for students. `http://info.acm.org/sigada`

SELECTED BOOKS DESCRIBING AND USING ADA 95

Barnes, J. G. P. [1995]: *Programming In Ada 95*. Addison-Wesley. (ISBN 0-201-87700-7) The latest in a series of very popular texts covering the Ada language. Barnes covers the whole language well and very readably, with a fine sense of humor.

Burns, A., and A. Wellings [1995]: *Concurrency in Ada*. Cambridge University Press. (ISBN 0-521-41471-7) A readable and very complete text on concurrent programming and real-time systems in Ada 95.

Cohen, N. [1996]: *Ada as a Second Language*, 2d ed. McGraw-Hill. (ISBN 0-07-011607-5) An encyclopedic work, over 1100 pages long. The first edition received excellent reviews for its thoroughness and complete examples; this new edition, focusing on Ada 95, will also be well received.

Feldman, M. B., and E. B. Koffman [1996]: *Ada 95: Problem Solving and Program Design*. Addison-Wesley. (ISBN 0-201-87009-6.) A text that introduces Ada 95 to readers with no previous programming experience in any language.

Intermetrics, Inc. [1995]. *Ada 95 Reference Manual (RM)*. The official description of the Ada 95 standard. It may be difficult to find in paper form, but is readily available electronically from the Internet sites, in plain text, hypertext, and PostScript forms.

Intermetrics, Inc. [1995]. *Ada 95 Rationale*. A companion volume to the *RM*, this very interesting book explains the "why" behind the Ada 95 design. Contains very useful examples. Also available most easily through the Internet.

Naiditch, David J. [1995]: *Rendezvous with Ada 95*. John Wiley and Sons. (ISBN 0-471-01276-9) A very readable, often humorous, survey of Ada 95.

Rosen, J-P. [1995] *Méthodes de Génie Logiciel avec Ada 95* (Software Engineering Methods with Ada 95) (in French). InterEditions, Paris. (ISBN 2-7296-0569-X) Introduces Ada 95 in the context of several important software engineering methodologies.

Smith, M. A. [1996]: *Object-Oriented Software in Ada 95*. International Thomson Computer Press. (ISBN 1-85032-185-X) For those interested in pursuing object-oriented programming with Ada 95, this book can serve as an excellent followup to the present work.

SELECTED BOOKS ON ALGORITHMS AND DATA STRUCTURES

Baase, S. [1988]: *Computer Algorithms, Second Edition*. Addison-Wesley. ISBN 0-201-06035-3.

Knuth, D.E. [1973]: *Fundamental Algorithms*, 2d ed. Addison-Wesley, Reading, Massachusetts. ISBN 0-201-03809-9.

Knuth, D.E. [1973]: *Sorting and Searching*. Addison-Wesley, Reading, Massachusetts. (ISBN 0-201-03803-X) The best collection of sorting and searching algorithms ever published. More than 20 years old and still timely.

Lukasiewicz, J. [1951]: *Aristotle's Syllogistic from the Standpoint of Modern Formal Logic*. Clarendon Press, England. Introduces "Polish" notation.

Sedgewick, R. [1988]: *Algorithms*, 2d ed. Addison-Wesley (ISBN 0-201-06673-4) A wonderful collection of algorithms in Pascal notation.

Weiss, M.A. [1993]: *Data Structures and Algorithms in Ada*. Benjamin/Cummings. (ISBN 0-8053-9055-3) An excellent book for further reading in algorithms and data structures. Uses Ada as its language of discourse.

Wirth, N. [1976]: *Algorithms + Data Structures = Programs*. Prentice-Hall. An early and very influential text.

IMPORTANT ORIGINAL AND SURVEY ARTICLES

Adelson-Velskii, G. M., and E. M. Landis [1962]: "An Algorithm for the Organization of Information," *Dokl. Akad. Nauk SSSR, Mathemat.*, **146**:2, pp. 263–266. Introduces AVL trees.

Bauer, F. L., and K. Samelson [1960]: "Sequential Formula Translation," *Communications of the ACM*, **2**:2, pp. 76–83. Translating with a stack.

Cardelli, L., and P. Wegner [1985]: "On Understanding Types, Data Abstraction, and Polymorphism," *ACM Computing Surveys*, **17**:4, pp. 471–522. An important early survey on object-oriented programming.

Dijkstra, E. W. [1971]: "Hierarchical Ordering of Sequential Processes," *Acta Informatica* **1**, 115–138. Introduces the Dining Philosophers.

Dijkstra, E. W. [1975]: "Guarded Commands, Nondeterminacy, and Formal Derivation of Programs," *Communications of the ACM* **18**, 8, pp. 453–457. Introduces much of the theory used in the Ada SELECT statement.

Guttag, J. V., E. Horowitz, and D. R. Musser [1978]: "Abstract Data Types and Software Validation," *Communications of the ACM*, **21**:12, pp. 1048–1064. One of the early papers on ADTs.

Hoare, C. A. R. [1962]: "Quicksort," *Computer Journal*, **5**:1, pp. 10–15.

Hoare, C. A. R. [1974]: "Monitors: An Operating System Structuring Concept," *Communications of the ACM* **17**:10, pp. 549–557. Introduces much of the theory behind Ada's protected types.

Hoare, C. A. R. [1978]: "Communicating Sequential Processes." *Communications of the ACM* **21**:8 (1978), pp 666–677. Introduces much of the theory behind rendezvous.

Liskov, B. H., and S. N. Zilles [1975]: "Specification Techniques for Data Abstractions," *IEEE Transactions on Software Engineering.*, **SE-1**:1, pp. 7–18. Another early ADT paper, in the first issue of this journal.

Liskov, B. H., and S. N. Zilles [1977]: "Abstraction Mechanisms in CLU," *Communications of the ACM*, **20**:8, pp. 564–576. Specification vs. implementation.

Martin, W. [1971]: "Sorting," *Computing Surveys*, **3** (4):147.

Maurer, W. D. [1968]: "An Improved Hash Code for Scatter Storage," *Communications of the ACM*, **11**:1. Introduces quadratic hashing.

Maurer, W. D., and T. Lewis [1975]: "Hash Table Methods," *Computing Surveys*, **7**:1, pp. 5–19. Excellent survey article on hash tables.

Nievergelt, J. [1974]: "Binary Search Trees and File Organization," *Computing Surveys*, **6**:3, pp. 195–207.

Perlis, A., and C. Thornton [1960]: "Symbol Manipulation by Threaded Lists," *Communications of the ACM*, **3**:4, pp. 195–204. Threading binary trees.

Shell, D. L. [1959]: "A High-Speed Sorting Procedure," *Communications of the ACM*, **2**:7, pp. 30–32. Shell sort.

Shell, D. L. [1971]: "Optimizing the Polyphase Sort," *Communications of the ACM*, **14**:11, pp. 713–719.

Singleton, R. C. [1969]: "Algorithm 347: An Algorithm for Sorting with Minimal Storage," *Communications of the ACM*, **12**:3, pp. 185–187. Quicksort.

Stroustrup, B. [1982]: "Classes: An Abstract Data Type Facility for the C Language," *SIGPLAN Notices*, **17**:1, pp. 354–356. A very early article on what became C++.

Williams, J. W. J. [1964]: "Algorithm 232 (Heapsort)," *Communications of the ACM*, **7**:6, pp. 347–348.

APPENDIX A

The Ada Character Set, Delimiters, and Reserved Words

This appendix is adapted from the *Ada 95 Reference Manual*, Sections 2.1, 2.2, and 2.9.

THE ADA CHARACTER SET

The Ada 95 standard uses the ISO 8859-1 (Latin-1) character set. This character set includes the usual letters A–Z, but also a number of additional characters to provide for the additional letters used in non-English languages. For example, French uses accented letters like é and à; German has letters using the umlaut such as ü, the Scandinavian languages have dipthongs such as æ, and so forth. For the purposes of this book, we use just the 26 letters of English; if you are in another country and wish to use its additional letters, you can find out locally how to do so on your computer or terminal. The following characters have been used in constructing the programs in this book:

1. Uppercase letters:

    A B C D E F G H I J K L M N O P Q R S T U V W X Y Z

2. Lowercase letters:

    a b c d e f g h i j k l m n o p q r s t u v w x y z

3. Digits:

    0 1 2 3 4 5 6 7 8 9

4. Special characters:

    " # & ' ( ) * + , – . / : ; < = > _ |

5. The space character

   Format effectors are the characters called horizontal tabulation, vertical tabulation, carriage return, line feed, and form feed.
   The characters included in each of the remaining categories of graphic characters are defined as follows:

6. Other special characters

```
! $ % ? @ [ \ ] ^ ` { } ~
```

The following names are used when referring to special characters (4.) and other special characters (6.):

symbol	name	symbol	name
"	quotation	>	greater than
#	sharp	_	underline
&	ampersand	|	vertical bar
'	apostrophe, tick	!	exclamation mark
(	left parenthesis	$	dollar
)	right parenthesis	%	percent
*	star, multiply	?	question mark
+	plus	@	commercial at
,	comma	[	left square bracket
−	hyphen, minus	\	back-slash
.	dot, point, period	]	right square bracket
/	slash, divide	^	circumflex
:	colon	`	grave accent
;	semicolon	{	left brace
<	less than	}	right brace
=	equal	~	tilde

DELIMITERS

A *delimiter* is either one of the following special characters:

```
& ' ( ) * + , - . / : ; < = > |
```

or one of the following *compound delimiters*, each composed of two adjacent special characters:

```
=>   ..   **   :=   /=   >=   <=   <<   >>   <>
```

The following names are used when referring to compound delimiters:

Delimiter	Name
=>	arrow
..	double dot
**	double star, exponentiate
:=	assignment (read as "becomes")
/=	inequality (read as "not equal")
>=	greater than or equal
<=	less than or equal
<<	left label bracket
>>	right label bracket
<>	box

RESERVED WORDS

The identifiers listed below are called *reserved words* and are reserved for special significance in the Ada language. In this book, the reserved words always appear in uppercase.

ABORT	ELSE	NEW	RETURN
ABS	ELSIF	NOT	REVERSE
ABSTRACT	END	NULL	
ACCEPT	ENTRY		SELECT
ACCESS	EXCEPTION		SEPARATE
ALIASED	EXIT	OF	SUBTYPE
ALL		OR	
AND	FOR	OTHERS	TAGGED
ARRAY	FUNCTION	OUT	TASK
AT			TERMINATE
	GENERIC	PACKAGE	THEN
BEGIN	GOTO	PRAGMA	TYPE
BODY		PRIVATE	
	IF	PROCEDURE	
CASE	IN	PROTECTED	UNTIL
CONSTANT	IS		USE
		RAISE	
DECLARE		RANGE	WHEN
DELAY	LIMITED	RECORD	WHILE
DELTA	LOOP	REM	WITH
DIGITS		RENAMES	
DO	MOD	REQUEUE	XOR

A reserved word must not be used as a declared identifier.

APPENDIX B

Ada 95 Syntax Rules

This Appendix is adapted from Annex P of the *Ada 95 Reference Manual*.

The syntactic form of an Ada program is described by means of a context-free notation called Extended Backus-Naur Form or EBNF. EBNF describes a language in terms of a set of *syntax rules* of the form X ::= Y (read "X is defined as Y"), where X is always a single *syntactic category* or *nonterminal* and Y can be one or more symbols.

Lowercase words, some containing embedded underlines, are used to denote non-terminals; for example,

```
case_statement
```

Reserved words are given in the Ada standard in lowercase, but appear here in uppercase for consistency with the text; for example,

```
ARRAY
```

Square brackets enclose optional items; the two following rules are equivalent.

```
return_statement ::= RETURN [expression];
return_statement ::= RETURN; | RETURN expression;
```

Curly brackets enclose a repeated item. The item may appear zero or more times; the two following rules are equivalent.

```
term ::= factor {multiplying_operator factor}
term ::= factor | term multiplying_operator factor
```

A vertical line separates alternative items unless it occurs immediately after an opening curly bracket, in which case it stands for itself:

```
constraint ::= scalar_constraint | composite_constraint
discrete_choice_list ::= discrete_choice {| discrete_choice}
```

We have organized the syntax rules in strict alphabetical order by the left side of the rule. In tracing a syntax error in a student program, the reader will probably wish to begin with the nonterminal compilation_unit.

```
abort_statement ::= ABORT task_name {, task_name};

abortable_part ::= sequence_of_statements

abstract_subprogram_declaration ::=
   subprogram_specification IS ABSTRACT;

accept_alternative ::=
   accept_statement [sequence_of_statements]
```

```
accept_statement ::=
   ACCEPT entry_direct_name [(entry_index)] parameter_profile DO
     handled_sequence_of_statements
   END [entry_identifier]];

access_definition ::= ACCESS subtype_mark

access_type_definition ::=
   access_to_object_definition
 | access_to_subprogram_definition

access_to_object_definition ::=
   ACCESS [general_access_modifier] subtype_indication

access_to_subprogram_definition ::=
   ACCESS [PROTECTED] PROCEDURE parameter_profile
 | ACCESS [PROTECTED] FUNCTION  parameter_and_result_profile

actual_parameter_part ::=
   (parameter_association {, parameter_association})

aggregate ::= record_aggregate | extension_aggregate | array_aggregate

allocator ::=
   NEW subtype_indication | NEW qualified_expression

ancestor_part ::= expression | subtype_mark

array_aggregate ::=
   positional_array_aggregate | named_array_aggregate

array_component_association ::=
   discrete_choice_list => expression

array_type_definition ::=
   unconstrained_array_definition | constrained_array_definition

assignment_statement ::=
   variable_name := expression;

asynchronous_select ::=
   SELECT
     triggering_alternative
   THEN ABORT
     abortable_part
   END SELECT;

at_clause ::= FOR direct_name USE AT expression;

attribute_definition_clause ::=
   FOR local_name'attribute_designator USE expression;
 | FOR local_name'attribute_designator USE name;

attribute_designator ::=
   identifier[(static_expression)]
 | Access | Delta | Digits

attribute_reference ::= prefix'attribute_designator

base ::= numeral
```

```
based_literal ::=
   base # based_numeral [.based_numeral] # [exponent]

based_numeral ::=
   extended_digit {[underline] extended_digit}

basic_declaration ::=
   type_declaration                | subtype_declaration
 | object_declaration              | number_declaration
 | subprogram_declaration          | abstract_subprogram_declaration
 | package_declaration             | renaming_declaration
 | exception_declaration           | generic_declaration
 | generic_instantiation

basic_declarative_item ::=
   basic_declaration | representation_clause | use_clause

binary_adding_operator ::=  +  | -  | &

block_statement ::=
   [block_statement_identifier:]
      [DECLARE
          declarative_part]
       BEGIN
          handled_sequence_of_statements
       END [block_identifier];

body ::= proper_body | body_stub

body_stub ::=
   subprogram_body_stub | package_body_stub
 | task_body_stub       | protected_body_stub

case_statement ::=
   CASE expression IS
      case_statement_alternative
     {case_statement_alternative}
   END CASE;

case_statement_alternative ::=
   WHEN discrete_choice_list =>
      sequence_of_statements

character ::=
   graphic_character | format_effector | other_control_function

character_literal ::= 'graphic_character'

choice_parameter_specification ::= defining_identifier

code_statement ::= qualified_expression;

compilation ::= {compilation_unit}

compilation_unit ::=
   context_clause library_item
 | context_clause subunit

component_choice_list ::=
   component_selector_name {| component_selector_name}
 | OTHERS
```

```
component_clause ::=
   component_local_name AT position RANGE first_bit .. last_bit;

component_definition ::= [ALIASED] subtype_indication

component_item ::= component_declaration | representation_clause

component_list ::=
   component_item {component_item}
 | {component_item} variant_part
 | NULL;

composite_constraint ::=
   index_constraint | discriminant_constraint

compound_statement ::=
   if_statement           | case_statement
 | loop_statement         | block_statement
 | accept_statement       | select_statement

condition ::= boolean_expression

conditional_entry_call ::=
   SELECT
     entry_call_alternative
   ELSE
     sequence_of_statements
   END SELECT;

constrained_array_definition ::=
   ARRAY (discrete_subtype_definition {, discrete_subtype_definition})
   OF component_definition

constraint ::= scalar_constraint | composite_constraint

context_clause ::= {context_item}

context_item ::= with_clause | use_clause

decimal_fixed_point_definition ::=
   DELTA static_expression
   DIGITS static_expression [real_range_specification]

decimal_literal ::= numeral [.numeral] [exponent]

declarative_item ::=
   basic_declarative_item | body

declarative_part ::= {declarative_item}

default_expression ::= expression

default_name ::= name

defining_character_literal ::= character_literal

defining_designator ::=
   defining_program_unit_name | defining_operator_symbol

defining_identifier ::= identifier
```

```
defining_identifier_list ::=
   defining_identifier {, defining_identifier}

defining_operator_symbol ::= operator_symbol

defining_program_unit_name ::= [parent_unit_name . ]defining_identifier

delay_alternative ::=
   delay_statement [sequence_of_statements]

delay_relative_statement ::= DELAY delay_expression;

delay_statement ::= delay_until_statement | delay_relative_statement

delay_until_statement ::= DELAY UNTIL delay_expression;

delta_constraint ::= DELTA static_expression [range_constraint]

derived_type_definition ::=
   [ABSTRACT] NEW parent_subtype_indication [record_extension_part]

designator ::= [parent_unit_name . ]identifier | operator_symbol

digits_constraint ::=
   digits static_expression [range_constraint]

direct_name ::= identifier | operator_symbol

discrete_choice ::= expression | discrete_range | OTHERS

discrete_choice_list ::= discrete_choice {| discrete_choice}

discrete_range ::= discrete_subtype_indication | range

discrete_subtype_definition ::= discrete_subtype_indication | range

discriminant_association ::=
   [discriminant_selector_name
   {| discriminant_selector_name} =>] expression

discriminant_constraint ::=
   (discriminant_association {,  discriminant_association})

discriminant_part ::=
   unknown_discriminant_part | known_discriminant_part

discriminant_specification ::=
   defining_identifier_list : subtype_mark [:= default_expression]
 | defining_identifier_list : access_definition [:= default_expression]

entry_barrier ::= WHEN condition

entry_body ::=
   ENTRY defining_identifier entry_body_formal_part entry_barrier IS
     declarative_part
   BEGIN
     handled_sequence_of_statements
   END [entry_identifier];

entry_body_formal_part ::=
   [(entry_index_specification)] parameter_profile
```

```
entry_call_alternative ::=
   entry_call_statement [sequence_of_statements]

entry_call_statement ::= entry_name [actual_parameter_part];

entry_declaration ::=
   ENTRY defining_identifier
   [(discrete_subtype_definition)] parameter_profile;

entry_index ::= expression

entry_index_specification ::=
   FOR defining_identifier IN discrete_subtype_definition

enumeration_aggregate ::= array_aggregate

enumeration_literal_specification ::=
   defining_identifier | defining_character_literal

enumeration_representation_clause ::=
   FOR first_subtype_local_name USE enumeration_aggregate;

enumeration_type_definition ::=
   (enumeration_literal_specification
   {, enumeration_literal_specification})

exception_declaration ::= defining_identifier_list : EXCEPTION;

exception_choice ::= exception_name | OTHERS

exception_handler ::=
   WHEN [choice_parameter_specification:] exception_choice
   {| exception_choice} =>
     sequence_of_statements

exception_renaming_declaration ::=
   defining_identifier : EXCEPTION RENAMES exception_name;

exit_statement ::=
   EXIT [loop_name] [WHEN condition];

explicit_actual_parameter ::= expression | variable_name

explicit_dereference ::= name.ALL

explicit_generic_actual_parameter ::=
   expression | variable_name
 | subprogram_name | entry_name
 | subtype_mark | package_instance_name

exponent ::= E [+] numeral | E - numeral

expression ::=
   relation {AND relation} | relation {AND THEN relation}
 | relation {OR relation}  | relation {OR ELSE relation}
 | relation {XOR relation}

extension_aggregate ::=
   (ancestor_part with record_component_association_list)

factor ::= primary [** primary] | ABS primary | NOT primary
```

```
first_bit ::= static_simple_expression

fixed_point_definition ::=
    ordinary_fixed_point_definition | decimal_fixed_point_definition

floating_point_definition ::=
    DIGITS static_expression [real_range_specification]

formal_access_type_definition ::= access_type_definition

formal_array_type_definition ::= array_type_definition

formal_decimal_fixed_point_definition ::= DELTA <> DIGITS <>

formal_derived_type_definition ::=
    [ABSTRACT] NEW subtype_mark [WITH PRIVATE]

formal_discrete_type_definition ::= (<>)

formal_floating_point_definition ::= DIGITS <>

formal_modular_type_definition ::= MOD <>

formal_object_declaration ::=
    defining_identifier_list :
    mode subtype_mark [:= default_expression];

formal_ordinary_fixed_point_definition ::= DELTA <>

formal_package_actual_part ::=
    (<>) | [generic_actual_part]

formal_package_declaration ::=
    WITH package defining_identifier
    IS NEW generic_package_name formal_package_actual_part;

formal_part ::=
    (parameter_specification {; parameter_specification})

formal_private_type_definition ::=
    [[ABSTRACT] TAGGED] [LIMITED] PRIVATE

formal_signed_integer_type_definition ::= RANGE <>

formal_subprogram_declaration ::=

    WITH subprogram_specification [IS subprogram_default];

formal_type_declaration ::=
    TYPE defining_identifier[discriminant_part]
        IS formal_type_definition;

formal_type_definition ::=
    formal_private_type_definition
  | formal_derived_type_definition
  | formal_discrete_type_definition
  | formal_signed_integer_type_definition
  | formal_modular_type_definition
  | formal_floating_point_definition
  | formal_ordinary_fixed_point_definition
  | formal_decimal_fixed_point_definition
```

```
  | formal_array_type_definition
  | formal_access_type_definition

format_effector???

full_type_declaration ::=
   TYPE defining_identifier [known_discriminant_part]
      IS type_definition;
  | task_type_declaration
  | protected_type_declaration

function_call ::=
   function_name
  | function_prefix actual_parameter_part

general_access_modifier ::= ALL | CONSTANT

generic_actual_part ::=
   (generic_association {, generic_association})

generic_association ::=
   [generic_formal_parameter_selector_name =>]
   explicit_generic_actual_parameter

generic_declaration ::=
   generic_subprogram_declaration | generic_package_declaration

generic_formal_parameter_declaration ::=
   formal_object_declaration
  | formal_type_declaration
  | formal_subprogram_declaration
  | formal_package_declaration

generic_formal_part ::=
   generic {generic_formal_parameter_declaration | use_clause}

generic_instantiation ::=
   PACKAGE defining_program_unit_name IS
         NEW generic_package_name [generic_actual_part];
  | PROCEDURE defining_program_unit_name IS
         NEW generic_procedure_name [generic_actual_part];
  | FUNCTION defining_designator IS
         NEW generic_function_name [generic_actual_part];

generic_package_declaration ::=
   generic_formal_part package_specification;

generic_renaming_declaration ::=
   GENERIC PACKAGE defining_program_unit_name
         RENAMES generic_package_name;
  | GENERIC PROCEDURE defining_program_unit_name
         RENAMES generic_procedure_name;
  | GENERIC FUNCTION defining_program_unit_name
         RENAMES generic_function_name;

generic_subprogram_declaration ::=
   generic_formal_part subprogram_specification;

goto_statement ::= GOTO label_name;

graphic_character ::=
   identifier_letter | digit | space_character | special_character
```

```
guard ::= WHEN condition =>

handled_sequence_of_statements ::=
    sequence_of_statements
   [EXCEPTION
      exception_handler
     {exception_handler}]

identifier ::=
    identifier_letter {[underline] letter_or_digit}

if_statement ::=
    IF condition THEN
       sequence_of_statements
    {ELSIF condition THEN
       sequence_of_statements}
    [ELSE
       sequence_of_statements]
    END IF;

implicit_dereference ::= name

incomplete_type_declaration ::=
    TYPE defining_identifier [discriminant_part];

index_constraint ::=  (discrete_range {, discrete_range})

index_subtype_definition ::= subtype_mark range <>

indexed_component ::= prefix(expression {, expression})

integer_type_definition ::=
    signed_integer_type_definition | modular_type_definition

iteration_scheme ::= WHILE condition
 | FOR loop_parameter_specification

known_discriminant_part ::=
    (discriminant_specification {; discriminant_specification})

label ::= <<label_statement_identifier>>

last_bit ::= static_simple_expression

letter_or_digit ::= identifier_letter | digit

library_item ::= [PRIVATE] library_unit_declaration
 | library_unit_body
 | [private] library_unit_renaming_declaration

library_unit_body ::= subprogram_body | package_body

library_unit_declaration ::=
    subprogram_declaration | package_declaration
 | generic_declaration   | generic_instantiation

library_unit_renaming_declaration ::=
    package_renaming_declaration
 | generic_renaming_declaration
 | subprogram_renaming_declaration
```

```
local_name ::= direct_name
  | direct_name'attribute_designator
  | library_unit_name

loop_parameter_specification ::=
    defining_identifier IN [REVERSE] discrete_subtype_definition

loop_statement ::=
    [loop_statement_identifier:]
      [iteration_scheme] LOOP
        sequence_of_statements
      END LOOP [loop_identifier];

mod_clause ::= AT MOD static_expression;

mode ::= [IN] | IN OUT | OUT

modular_type_definition ::= MOD static_expression

multiplying_operator ::=  *  | /   | MOD | REM

name ::=
    direct_name            | explicit_dereference
  | indexed_component       | slice
  | selected_component      | attribute_reference
  | type_conversion         | function_call
  | character_literal

named_array_aggregate ::=
    (array_component_association {, array_component_association})

null_statement ::= NULL;

number_declaration ::=
    defining_identifier_list : CONSTANT := static_expression;

numeral ::= digit {[underline] digit}

numeric_literal ::= decimal_literal | based_literal

object_declaration ::=
    defining_identifier_list :
      [ALIASED] [CONSTANT] subtype_indication [:= expression];
  | defining_identifier_list :
      [ALIASED] [CONSTANT] array_type_definition [:= expression];
  | single_task_declaration
  | single_protected_declaration

object_renaming_declaration ::=
    defining_identifier : subtype_mark RENAMES object_name;

operator_symbol ::= string_literal

ordinary_fixed_point_definition ::=
    DELTA static_expression real_range_specification

other_control_function???

package_body ::=
    PACKAGE BODY defining_program_unit_name IS
      declarative_part
```

```
    [BEGIN
       handled_sequence_of_statements]
    END [[parent_unit_name.]identifier];

package_body_stub ::= PACKAGE BODY  defining_identifier IS SEPARATE;

package_declaration ::= package_specification;

package_renaming_declaration ::=
    PACKAGE defining_program_unit_name RENAMES package_name;

package_specification ::=
    PACKAGE defining_program_unit_name IS
      {basic_declarative_item}
    [PRIVATE
      {basic_declarative_item}]
    END [[parent_unit_name.]identifier]

parameter_and_result_profile ::= [formal_part] RETURN subtype_mark

parameter_association ::=
    [formal_parameter_selector_name =>] explicit_actual_parameter

parameter_profile ::= [formal_part]

parameter_specification ::=
    defining_identifier_list :
        mode subtype_mark [:= default_expression]
  | defining_identifier_list :
        access_definition [:= default_expression]

parent_unit_name ::= name

position ::= static_expression

positional_array_aggregate ::=
    (expression, expression {, expression})
  | (expression {, expression}, OTHERS => expression)

pragma ::= PRAGMA identifier
    [(pragma_argument_association {, pragma_argument_association})];

prefix ::= name | implicit_dereference

primary ::=
    numeric_literal | NULL | string_literal | aggregate
  | name | qualified_expression | allocator | (expression)

private_extension_declaration ::=
    TYPE defining_identifier [discriminant_part] IS
        [ABSTRACT] NEW ancestor_subtype_indication  WITH PRIVATE;

private_type_declaration ::=
    TYPE defining_identifier [discriminant_part]
        IS [[ABSTRACT] TAGGED] [LIMITED] PRIVATE;

procedure_call_statement ::=
    procedure_name;
  | procedure_prefix actual_parameter_part;

proper_body ::=
    subprogram_body | package_body | task_body | protected_body
```

```
protected_body ::=
   PROTECTED BODY defining_identifier IS
     { protected_operation_item }
   END [protected_identifier];

protected_body_stub ::= PROTECTED BODY defining_identifier IS SEPARATE;

protected_definition ::=
     { protected_operation_declaration }
   [ PRIVATE
     { protected_element_declaration } ]
   END [protected_identifier]

protected_element_declaration ::=
   protected_operation_declaration | component_declaration

protected_operation_declaration ::= subprogram_declaration
 | entry_declaration
 | representation_clause

protected_operation_item ::= subprogram_declaration
 | subprogram_body
 | entry_body
 | representation_clause

protected_type_declaration ::=
   PROTECTED TYPE defining_identifier [known_discriminant_part]
     IS protected_definition;

qualified_expression ::=
   subtype_mark'(expression) | subtype_mark'aggregate

raise_statement ::= RAISE [exception_name];

range ::= RANGE | simple_expression .. simple_expression

range_attribute_designator ::= Range[(static_expression)]

range_attribute_reference ::= prefix'range_attribute_designator

range_constraint ::=  RANGE range

real_range_specification ::=
   RANGE static_simple_expression .. static_simple_expression

real_type_definition ::=
   floating_point_definition | fixed_point_definition

record_aggregate ::= (record_component_association_list)

record_component_association ::=
   [ component_choice_list => ] expression

record_component_association_list ::=
   record_component_association {, record_component_association}
 | NULL RECORD

record_definition ::=
   RECORD
      component_list
   END RECORD
 | NULL RECORD
```

```
record_extension_part ::= WITH record_definition

record_representation_clause ::=
    FOR first_subtype_local_name USE
        RECORD [mod_clause]
          {component_clause}
        END RECORD;

record_type_definition ::=
    [[ABSTRACT] TAGGED] [LIMITED] record_definition

relation ::=
    simple_expression [relational_operator simple_expression]
  | simple_expression [NOT] IN range
  | simple_expression [NOT] IN subtype_mark

relational_operator ::=  =  | /=  | <   | <= | > | >=

renaming_declaration ::=
    object_renaming_declaration
  | exception_renaming_declaration
  | package_renaming_declaration
  | subprogram_renaming_declaration
  | generic_renaming_declaration

representation_clause ::= attribute_definition_clause
    | enumeration_representation_clause
    | record_representation_clause
    | at_clause

requeue_statement ::= REQUEUE entry_name [WITH ABORT];

return_statement ::= RETURN [expression];

scalar_constraint ::=
    range_constraint | digits_constraint | delta_constraint

select_alternative ::=
    accept_alternative
  | delay_alternative
  | terminate_alternative

select_statement ::=
    selective_accept
  | timed_entry_call
  | conditional_entry_call
  | asynchronous_select

selected_component ::= prefix . selector_name

selective_accept ::=
    SELECT
      [guard]
      select_alternative
    { OR
      [guard]
      select_alternative }
    [ ELSE
      sequence_of_statements ]
    END SELECT;
```

```
selector_name ::= identifier | character_literal | operator_symbol

sequence_of_statements ::= statement {statement}

signed_integer_type_definition ::=
   RANGE static_simple_expression . . static_simple_expression

simple_expression ::=
   [unary_adding_operator] term {binary_adding_operator term}

simple_statement ::= null_statement
 | assignment_statement     | exit_statement
 | goto_statement           | procedure_call_statement
 | return_statement         | entry_call_statement
 | requeue_statement        | delay_statement
 | abort_statement          | raise_statement
 | code_statement

single_protected_declaration ::=
   PROTECTED defining_identifier IS protected_definition;

single_task_declaration ::=
   TASK defining_identifier [IS task_definition];

slice ::= prefix(discrete_range)

space_character???

special_character???

statement ::=
   {label} simple_statement | {label} compound_statement

statement_identifier ::= direct_name

string_element ::= "" | non_quotation_mark_graphic_character

string_literal ::= "{string_element}"

subprogram_body ::=
   subprogram_specification IS
      declarative_part
   BEGIN
      handled_sequence_of_statements
   END [designator];

subprogram_body_stub ::= subprogram_specification IS SEPARATE;

subprogram_declaration ::= subprogram_specification;

subprogram_default ::= default_name | <>

subprogram_renaming_declaration ::=
   subprogram_specification RENAMES  callable_entity_name;

subprogram_specification ::=
   PROCEDURE defining_program_unit_name parameter_profile
 | FUNCTION defining_designator parameter_and_result_profile

subtype_declaration ::=
   SUBTYPE defining_identifier IS subtype_indication;
```

```
subtype_indication ::=  subtype_mark [constraint]

subtype_mark ::= subtype_name

subunit ::= SEPARATE (parent_unit_name) proper_body

task_body ::=
   TASK BODY defining_identifier IS
      declarative_part
   BEGIN
      handled_sequence_of_statements
   END [task_identifier];

task_body_stub ::= TASK BODY defining_identifier IS SEPARATE;

task_definition ::=
      {task_item}
   [ PRIVATE
      {task_item}]
   END [task_identifier]

task_item ::= entry_declaration | representation_clause

task_type_declaration ::=
   TASK TYPE defining_identifier [known_discriminant_part]
      [IS task_definition];

term ::= factor {multiplying_operator factor}

terminate_alternative ::= TERMINATE;

timed_entry_call ::=
   SELECT
      entry_call_alternative
   OR
      delay_alternative
   END SELECT;

triggering_alternative ::=
      triggering_statement [sequence_of_statements]

triggering_statement ::= entry_call_statement | delay_statement

type_conversion ::=
      subtype_mark(expression)
   | subtype_mark(name)

type_declaration ::=  full_type_declaration
   | incomplete_type_declaration
   | private_type_declaration
   | private_extension_declaration

type_definition ::=
      enumeration_type_definition | integer_type_definition
   | real_type_definition       | array_type_definition
   | record_type_definition     | access_type_definition
   | derived_type_definition

unary_adding_operator ::=  +  | -
```

```
unconstrained_array_definition ::=
   ARRAY(index_subtype_definition
  {, index_subtype_definition}) OF component_definition

unknown_discriminant_part ::= (<>)

use_clause ::= use_package_clause | use_type_clause

use_package_clause ::= USE package_name {, package_name};

use_type_clause ::= USE TYPE subtype_mark {, subtype_mark};

variant ::=
   WHEN discrete_choice_list =>
     component_list

variant_part ::=
   CASE discriminant_direct_name IS
      variant
     {variant}
   END CASE;

with_clause ::= WITH library_unit_name {, library_unit_name};
```

APPENDIX C

The Package Standard—Ada's Predefined Environment

This appendix, adapted from the *Ada 95 Reference Manual*, Section A.1, outlines the specification of the package Standard containing all predefined identifiers in the language. The corresponding package body is not specified by the language.

The operators that are predefined for the types declared in the package Standard are given in comments because they are implicitly declared. Italics are used for pseudonames of anonymous types (such as *root_real*) and for undefined information (such as *implementation-defined*).

```
PACKAGE Standard is
  PRAGMA Pure(Standard);

  TYPE Boolean IS (False, True);

  -- The predefined relational operators for this type are as follows:

  -- FUNCTION "="   (Left, Right : Boolean) RETURN Boolean;
  -- FUNCTION "/="  (Left, Right : Boolean) RETURN Boolean;
  -- FUNCTION "<"   (Left, Right : Boolean) RETURN Boolean;
  -- FUNCTION "<="  (Left, Right : Boolean) RETURN Boolean;
  -- FUNCTION ">"   (Left, Right : Boolean) RETURN Boolean;
  -- FUNCTION ">="  (Left, Right : Boolean) RETURN Boolean;

  -- The predefined logical operators and the predefined logical
  -- negation operator are as follows:

  -- FUNCTION "AND" (Left, Right : Boolean) RETURN Boolean;
  -- FUNCTION "OR" (Left, Right : Boolean) RETURN Boolean;
  -- FUNCTION "XOR" (Left, Right : Boolean) RETURN Boolean;

  -- FUNCTION "NOT" (Right : Boolean) RETURN  Boolean;

  -- The integer type root_integer is predefined.
  -- The corresponding universal type is universal_integer.

  TYPE Integer IS RANGE implementation-defined;

  SUBTYPE Natural  IS Integer RANGE  0 .. Integer'Last;

  SUBTYPE Positive IS Integer RANGE  1 .. Integer'Last;

  -- The predefined operators for type Integer are as follows:
```

```
-- FUNCTION "="  (Left, Right : Integer) RETURN Boolean;
-- FUNCTION "/=" (Left, Right : Integer) RETURN Boolean;
-- FUNCTION "<"  (Left, Right : Integer) RETURN Boolean;
-- FUNCTION "<=" (Left, Right : Integer) RETURN Boolean;
-- FUNCTION ">"  (Left, Right : Integer) RETURN Boolean;
-- FUNCTION ">=" (Left, Right : Integer) RETURN Boolean;

-- FUNCTION "+"   (Right : Integer) RETURN Integer;
-- FUNCTION "-"   (Right : Integer) RETURN Integer;
-- FUNCTION "ABS" (Right : Integer) RETURN Integer;

-- FUNCTION "+"   (Left, Right : Integer) RETURN Integer;
-- FUNCTION "-"   (Left, Right : Integer) RETURN Integer;
-- FUNCTION "*"   (Left, Right : Integer) RETURN Integer;
-- FUNCTION "/"   (Left, Right : Integer) RETURN Integer;
-- FUNCTION "REM" (Left, Right : Integer) RETURN Integer;
-- FUNCTION "MOD" (Left, Right : Integer) RETURN Integer;

-- FUNCTION "**"  (Left : Integer; Right : Natural) RETURN Integer;

-- The specification of each operator for the type
-- root_integer, or for any additional predefined integer
-- type, is obtained by replacing Integer by the name of the type
-- in the specification of the corresponding operator of the type
-- Integer. The right operand of the exponentiation operator
-- remains as subtype Natural.

-- The floating point type root_real is predefined.
-- The corresponding universal type is universal_real.

TYPE Float IS DIGITS implementation-defined;

-- The predefined operators for this type are as follows:

-- FUNCTION "="  (Left, Right : Float) RETURN Boolean;
-- FUNCTION "/=" (Left, Right : Float) RETURN Boolean;
-- FUNCTION "<"  (Left, Right : Float) RETURN Boolean;
-- FUNCTION "<=" (Left, Right : Float) RETURN Boolean;
-- FUNCTION ">"  (Left, Right : Float) RETURN Boolean;
-- FUNCTION ">=" (Left, Right : Float) RETURN Boolean;

-- FUNCTION "+"   (Right : Float) RETURN Float;
-- FUNCTION "-"   (Right : Float) RETURN Float;
-- FUNCTION "ABS" (Right : Float) RETURN Float;

-- FUNCTION "+"   (Left, Right : Float) RETURN Float;
-- FUNCTION "-"   (Left, Right : Float) RETURN Float;
-- FUNCTION "*"   (Left, Right : Float) RETURN Float;
-- FUNCTION "/"   (Left, Right : Float) RETURN Float;

-- FUNCTION "**"  (Left : Float; Right : Integer) RETURN Float;

-- The specification of each operator for the type root_real, or
-- for any  additional predefined floating point type, is
-- obtained by replacing Float by the name of the type in the
-- specification of the corresponding operator of the type Float.

-- In  addition, the following operators are predefined for the
-- root numeric types:

FUNCTION "*" (Left : root_integer; Right : root_real)
  RETURN root_real;
```

```
FUNCTION "*" (Left : root_real;   Right : root_integer)
  RETURN root_real;

FUNCTION "/" (Left : root_real;   Right : root_integer)
  RETURN root_real;

-- The type universal_fixed is predefined.
-- The only multiplying operators defined between
-- fixed point types are

FUNCTION "*" (Left : universal_fixed; Right : universal_fixed)
  RETURN universal_fixed;

FUNCTION "/" (Left : universal_fixed; Right : universal_fixed)
  RETURN universal_fixed;

-- The declaration of type Character is based on the standard ISO
-- 8859-1 character set.

-- There are no character literals corresponding to the positions
-- for control characters.
-- They are indicated in italics in this definition.

TYPE Character IS

 (nul,  soh,  stx,  etx,    eot,  enq,  ack,  bel,
  bs,   ht,   lf,   vt,     ff,   cr,   so,   si,

  dle,  dc1,  dc2,  dc3,    dc4,  nak,  syn,  etb,
  can,  em,   sub,  esc,    fs,   gs,   rs,   us,

  ' ',  '!',  '"',  '#',    '$',  '%',  '&',  ''',
  '(',  ')',  '*',  '+',    ',',  '-',  '.',  '/',

  '0',  '1',  '2',  '3',    '4',  '5',  '6',  '7',
  '8',  '9',  ':',  ';',    '<',  '=',  '>',  '?',

  '@',  'A',  'B',  'C',    'D',  'E',  'F',  'G',
  'H',  'I',  'J',  'K',    'L',  'M',  'N',  'O',

  'P',  'Q',  'R',  'S',    'T',  'U',  'V',  'W',
  'X',  'Y',  'Z',  '[',    '\',  ']',  '^',  '_',

  '`',  'a',  'b',  'c',    'd',  'e',  'f',  'g',
  'h',  'i',  'j',  'k',    'l',  'm',  'n',  'o',

  'p',  'q',  'r',  's',    't',  'u',  'v',  'w',
  'x',  'y',  'z',  '{',    '|',  '}',  '~',  del,

  reserved_128,    reserved_129, bph,  nbh,
  reserved_132,    nel,   ssa,  esa,

  hts,  htj,  vts,  pld,    plu,  ri,   ss2,  ss3,

  dcs,  pu1,  pu2,  sts,    cch,  mw,   spa,  epa,

  sos, reserved_153, sci, csi,
  st,   osc,  pm,   apc,

  . . . );
```

```
-- The predefined operators for the type Character are the same as
-- for any enumeration type.

-- The declaration of type Wide_Character is based on the standard
-- ISO 10646 BMP character set.
-- The first 256 positions have the same contents as type
-- Character.

TYPE Wide_Character IS (nul, soh . . . FFFE,  FFFF);

PACKAGE ASCII IS . . . END ASCII;  --Obsolescent; see J.

-- Predefined string types:

TYPE String IS ARRAY(Positive RANGE <>) OF Character;
  PRAGMA Pack(String);

-- The predefined operators for this type are as follows:

--FUNCTION "="  (Left, Right: String) RETURN Boolean;
--FUNCTION "/=" (Left, Right: String) RETURN Boolean;
--FUNCTION "<"  (Left, Right: String) RETURN Boolean;
--FUNCTION "<=" (Left, Right: String) RETURN Boolean;
--FUNCTION ">"  (Left, Right: String) RETURN Boolean;
--FUNCTION ">=" (Left, Right: String) RETURN Boolean;

--FUNCTION "&" (Left: String;    Right: String)    RETURN String;
--FUNCTION "&" (Left: Character; Right: String)    RETURN String;
--FUNCTION "&" (Left: String;    Right: Character) RETURN String;
--FUNCTION "&" (Left: Character; Right: Character) RETURN String;

TYPE Wide_String IS ARRAY(Positive RANGE <>) OF Wide_Character;
  PRAGMA Pack(Wide_String);

-- The predefined operators for this type correspond to
-- those for String

TYPE Duration IS
  DELTA implementation-defined RANGE implementation-defined;

-- The predefined operators for the type Duration are the same
-- as for any fixed point type.

-- The predefined exceptions:

Constraint_Error: EXCEPTION;
Program_Error  : EXCEPTION;
Storage_Error  : EXCEPTION;
Tasking_Error  : EXCEPTION;

END Standard;
```

APPENDIX D

Specification of the Package `Ada.Text_IO`

This appendix, adapted from the *Ada 95 Reference Manual*, Section A.10.1, gives the specification for `Ada.Text_IO`. Note that the numeric sub-packages `Integer_IO` and `Float_IO` are given here as generic. The standard also provides for the preinstantiated packages `Ada.Integer_Text_IO` and `Ada.Float_Text_IO` as we have used them in this book. These last two packages are part of the standard libraries and do not need to be created or compiled by the user.

Explanations of the most common input/output exceptions are given in Appendix H, along with the other exceptions likely to be encountered by a student.

```
WITH Ada.IO_Exceptions;
PACKAGE Ada.Text_IO IS

  TYPE File_Type IS LIMITED PRIVATE;

  TYPE File_Mode IS (In_File, Out_File, Append_File);

  TYPE Count IS RANGE  0 .. implementation-defined;
  SUBTYPE Positive_Count IS Count RANGE  1 .. Count'Last;
  Unbounded : CONSTANT Count :=  ; -- line and page length

  SUBTYPE Field       IS Integer RANGE  0 .. implementation-defined;
  SUBTYPE Number_Base IS Integer RANGE  2 .. 16;

  TYPE Type_Set IS (Lower_Case, Upper_Case);

  -- File Management

  PROCEDURE Create (File : IN out File_Type;
                    Mode : IN File_Mode := Out_File;
                    Name : IN String    := "";
                    Form : IN String    := "");

   PROCEDURE Open  (File : IN out File_Type;
                    Mode : IN File_Mode;
                    Name : IN String;
                    Form : IN String := "");

  PROCEDURE Close  (File : IN out File_Type);
  PROCEDURE Delete (File : IN out File_Type);
  PROCEDURE Reset  (File : IN out File_Type; Mode : IN File_Mode);
  PROCEDURE Reset  (File : IN out File_Type);

  FUNCTION  Mode   (File : IN File_Type) RETURN File_Mode;
  FUNCTION  Name   (File : IN File_Type) RETURN String;
  FUNCTION  Form   (File : IN File_Type) RETURN String;
```

```
FUNCTION  Is_Open(File : IN File_Type) RETURN Boolean;

-- Control of default input and output files

PROCEDURE Set_Input (File : IN File_Type);
PROCEDURE Set_Output(File : IN File_Type);
PROCEDURE Set_Error (File : IN File_Type);

FUNCTION Standard_Input  RETURN File_Type;
FUNCTION Standard_Output RETURN File_Type;
FUNCTION Standard_Error  RETURN File_Type;

FUNCTION Current_Input   RETURN File_Type;
FUNCTION Current_Output  RETURN File_Type;
FUNCTION Current_Error   RETURN File_Type;

TYPE File_Access IS ACCESS CONSTANT File_Type;

FUNCTION Standard_Input  RETURN File_Access;
FUNCTION Standard_Output RETURN File_Access;
FUNCTION Standard_Error  RETURN File_Access;

FUNCTION Current_Input   RETURN File_Access;
FUNCTION Current_Output  RETURN File_Access;
FUNCTION Current_Error   RETURN File_Access;

  --Buffer control
PROCEDURE Flush (File : IN OUT File_Type);
PROCEDURE Flush;

-- Specification of line and page lengths

PROCEDURE Set_Line_Length(File : IN File_Type; To : IN Count);
PROCEDURE Set_Line_Length(To   : IN Count);

PROCEDURE Set_Page_Length(File : IN File_Type; To : IN Count);
PROCEDURE Set_Page_Length(To   : IN Count);

FUNCTION  Line_Length(File : IN File_Type) RETURN Count;
FUNCTION  Line_Length RETURN Count;

FUNCTION  Page_Length(File : IN File_Type) RETURN Count;
FUNCTION  Page_Length RETURN Count;

-- Column, Line, and Page Control

PROCEDURE New_Line   (File    : IN File_Type;
                      Spacing : IN Positive_Count := 1);
PROCEDURE New_Line   (Spacing : IN Positive_Count := 1);

PROCEDURE Skip_Line  (File    : IN File_Type;
                      Spacing : IN Positive_Count := 1);
PROCEDURE Skip_Line  (Spacing : IN Positive_Count := 1);

FUNCTION  End_Of_Line(File : IN File_Type) RETURN Boolean;
FUNCTION  End_Of_Line RETURN Boolean;

PROCEDURE New_Page   (File : IN File_Type);
PROCEDURE New_Page;

PROCEDURE Skip_Page  (File : IN File_Type);
PROCEDURE Skip_Page;
```

```
FUNCTION  End_Of_Page(File : IN File_Type) RETURN Boolean;
FUNCTION  End_Of_Page RETURN Boolean;

FUNCTION  End_Of_File(File : IN File_Type) RETURN Boolean;
FUNCTION  End_Of_File RETURN Boolean;

PROCEDURE Set_Col (File : IN File_Type; To : IN Positive_Count);
PROCEDURE Set_Col (To    : IN Positive_Count);

PROCEDURE Set_Line(File : IN File_Type; To : IN Positive_Count);
PROCEDURE Set_Line(To    : IN Positive_Count);

FUNCTION Col (File : IN File_Type) RETURN Positive_Count;
FUNCTION Col  RETURN Positive_Count;

FUNCTION Line(File : IN File_Type) RETURN Positive_Count;
FUNCTION Line RETURN Positive_Count;

FUNCTION Page(File : IN File_Type) RETURN Positive_Count;
FUNCTION Page RETURN Positive_Count;

-- Character Input-Output

PROCEDURE Get(File : IN File_Type; Item : OUT Character);
PROCEDURE Get(Item : OUT Character);

PROCEDURE Put(File : IN File_Type; Item : IN Character);
PROCEDURE Put(Item : IN Character);

PROCEDURE Look_Ahead (File        : IN File_Type;
                      Item        : OUTCharacter;
                      End_Of_Line : OUT Boolean);
PROCEDURE Look_Ahead (Item        : OUT Character;
                      End_Of_Line : OUT Boolean);

PROCEDURE Get_Immediate(File      : IN File_Type;
                        Item      : OUT Character);
PROCEDURE Get_Immediate(Item      : OUT Character);

PROCEDURE Get_Immediate(File      : IN File_Type;
                        Item      : OUT Character;
                        Available : OUT Boolean);
PROCEDURE Get_Immediate(Item      : OUT Character;
                        Available : OUT Boolean);

-- String Input-Output

PROCEDURE Get(File : IN File_Type; Item : OUT String);
PROCEDURE Get(Item : OUT String);

PROCEDURE Put(File : IN File_Type; Item : IN String);
PROCEDURE Put(Item : IN String);

PROCEDURE Get_Line(File : IN File_Type;
                   Item : OUT String;
                   Last : OUT Natural);
PROCEDURE Get_Line(Item : OUT String; Last : OUT Natural);

PROCEDURE Put_Line(File : IN File_Type; Item : IN String);
PROCEDURE Put_Line(Item : IN String);

  -- Generic packages for Input-Output of Integer Types
```

```
GENERIC
   TYPE Num IS RANGE <>;
PACKAGE Integer_IO IS

   Default_Width : Field := Num'Width;
   Default_Base  : Number_Base := 10;

   PROCEDURE Get(File  : IN  File_Type;
                 Item  : OUT Num;
                 Width : IN Field := 0);
   PROCEDURE Get(Item  : OUT Num;
                 Width : IN  Field := 0);

   PROCEDURE Put(File  : IN File_Type;
                 Item  : IN Num;
                 Width : IN Field := Default_Width;
                 Base  : IN Number_Base := Default_Base);
   PROCEDURE Put(Item  : IN Num;
                 Width : IN Field := Default_Width;
                 Base  : IN Number_Base := Default_Base);
   PROCEDURE Get(From : IN  String;
                 Item : OUT Num;
                 Last : OUT Positive);
   PROCEDURE Put(To   : OUT String;
                 Item : IN Num;
                 Base : IN Number_Base := Default_Base);

END Integer_IO;

GENERIC
   TYPE Num IS mod <>;
PACKAGE Modular_IO IS

   Default_Width : Field := Num'Width;
   Default_Base  : Number_Base := 10;

   PROCEDURE Get(File  : IN  File_Type;
                 Item  : OUT Num;
                 Width : IN Field := 0);
   PROCEDURE Get(Item  : OUT Num;
                 Width : IN Field := 0);

   PROCEDURE Put(File  : IN File_Type;
                 Item  : IN Num;
                 Width : IN Field := Default_Width;
                 Base  : IN Number_Base := Default_Base);
   PROCEDURE Put(Item  : IN Num;
                 Width : IN Field := Default_Width;
                 Base  : IN Number_Base := Default_Base);
   PROCEDURE Get(From : IN  String;
                 Item : OUT Num;
                 Last : OUT Positive);
   PROCEDURE Put(To   : OUT String;
                 Item : IN Num;
                 Base : IN Number_Base := Default_Base);

END Modular_IO;
-- Generic PACKAGEs for Input-Output of Real Types

GENERIC
   TYPE Num IS digits <>;
PACKAGE Float_IO IS
```

```
      Default_Fore: Field := 2;
      Default_Aft : Field := Num'Digits-1 ;
      Default_Exp : Field := 3;

      PROCEDURE Get(File  : IN  File_Type;
                    Item  : OUT Num;
                    Width : IN  Field := 0);
      PROCEDURE Get(Item  : OUT Num;
                    Width : IN  Field := 0);

      PROCEDURE Put(File : IN File_Type;
                    Item : IN Num;
                    Fore : IN Field := Default_Fore;
                    Aft  : IN Field := Default_Aft;
                    Exp  : IN Field := Default_Exp);
      PROCEDURE Put(Item : IN Num;
                    Fore : IN Field := Default_Fore;
                    Aft  : IN Field := Default_Aft;
                    Exp  : IN Field := Default_Exp);

      PROCEDURE Get(From : IN String;
                    Item : OUT Num;
                    Last : OUT Positive);
      PROCEDURE Put(To   : OUT String;
                    Item : IN Num;
                    Aft  : IN Field := Default_Aft;
                    Exp  : IN Field := Default_Exp);
   END Float_IO;

GENERIC
   TYPE Num IS delta <>;
PACKAGE Fixed_IO IS

   Default_Fore: Field := Num'Fore;
   Default_Aft : Field := Num'Aft;
   Default_Exp : Field := 0;

   PROCEDURE Get(File  : IN  File_Type;
                 Item  : OUT Num;
                 Width : IN  Field := 0);
   PROCEDURE Get(Item  : OUT Num;
                 Width : IN  Field := 0);

   PROCEDURE Put(File : IN File_Type;
                 Item : IN Num;
                 Fore : IN Field := Default_Fore;
                 Aft  : IN Field := Default_Aft;
                 Exp  : IN Field := Default_Exp);
   PROCEDURE Put(Item : IN Num;
                 Fore : IN Field := Default_Fore;
                 Aft  : IN Field := Default_Aft;
                 Exp  : IN Field := Default_Exp);

   PROCEDURE Get(From : IN  String;
                 Item : OUT Num;
                 Last : OUT Positive);
   PROCEDURE Put(To   : OUT String;
                 Item : IN Num;
                 Aft  : IN Field := Default_Aft;
                 Exp  : IN Field := Default_Exp);
END Fixed_IO;
```

```
GENERIC
   TYPE Num IS DELTA <> DIGITS <>;
PACKAGE Decimal_IO IS

   Default_Fore : Field := Num'Fore;
   Default_Aft  : Field := Num'Aft;
   Default_Exp  : Field := 0;

   PROCEDURE Get(File  : IN  File_Type;
                 Item  : OUT Num;
                 Width : IN  Field := 0);
   PROCEDURE Get(Item  : OUT Num;
                 Width : IN  Field := 0);

   PROCEDURE Put(File : IN File_Type;
                 Item : IN Num;
                 Fore : IN Field := Default_Fore;
                 Aft  : IN Field := Default_Aft;
                 Exp  : IN Field := Default_Exp);
   PROCEDURE Put(Item : IN Num;
                 Fore : IN Field := Default_Fore;
                 Aft  : IN Field := Default_Aft;
                 Exp  : IN Field := Default_Exp);

   PROCEDURE Get(From : IN  String;
                 Item : OUT Num;
                 Last : OUT Positive);
   PROCEDURE Put(To   : OUT String;
                 Item : IN Num;
                 Aft  : IN Field := Default_Aft;
                 Exp  : IN Field := Default_Exp);
END Decimal_IO;

-- Generic package for Input-Output of Enumeration Types

GENERIC
   TYPE Enum IS (<>);
PACKAGE Enumeration_IO IS

   Default_Width   : Field := 0;
   Default_Setting : Type_Set := Upper_Case;

   PROCEDURE Get(File  : IN  File_Type;
                 Item  : OUT Enum);
   PROCEDURE Get(Item  : OUT Enum);

   PROCEDURE Put(File : IN File_Type;
                 Item : IN Enum;
                 Width : IN Field    := Default_Width;
                 Set   : IN Type_Set := Default_Setting);
   PROCEDURE Put(Item : IN Enum;
                 Width : IN Field    := Default_Width;
                 Set   : IN Type_Set := Default_Setting);

   PROCEDURE Get(From : IN  String;
                 Item : OUT Enum;
                 Last : OUT Positive);
   PROCEDURE Put(To   : OUT String;
                 Item : IN Enum;
                 Set  : IN Type_Set := Default_Setting);
END Enumeration_IO;
```

```
   -- Exceptions

 Status_Error : EXCEPTION RENAMES IO_Exceptions.Status_Error;
 Mode_Error   : EXCEPTION RENAMES IO_Exceptions.Mode_Error;
 Name_Error   : EXCEPTION RENAMES IO_Exceptions.Name_Error;
 Use_Error    : EXCEPTION RENAMES IO_Exceptions.Use_Error;
 Device_Error : EXCEPTION RENAMES IO_Exceptions.Device_Error;
 End_Error    : EXCEPTION RENAMES IO_Exceptions.End_Error;
 Data_Error   : EXCEPTION RENAMES IO_Exceptions.Data_Error;
 Layout_Error : EXCEPTION RENAMES IO_Exceptions.Layout_Error;

PRIVATE
 . . . -- not specified by the language
END Ada.Text_IO;
```

APPENDIX E

Specification of the Package
`Ada.Calendar`

This appendix, adapted from the *Ada 95 Reference Manual*, Section 9.6, gives the specification for the package `Ada.Calendar`.

```
PACKAGE Ada.Calendar IS

  TYPE Time IS PRIVATE;

  SUBTYPE Year_Number  IS Integer  RANGE 1901 .. 2099;
  SUBTYPE Month_Number IS Integer  RANGE 1 .. 12;
  SUBTYPE Day_Number   IS Integer  RANGE 1 .. 31;
  SUBTYPE Day_Duration IS Duration RANGE 0.0 .. 86_400;

  FUNCTION Time_Of (Year : Year_Number;
                    Month  : Month_Number;
                    Day    : Day_Number;
                    Seconds: Day_Duration:=0.0) RETURN Time;

  FUNCTION Year  (Date : Time)  RETURN Year_Number;
  FUNCTION Month (Date : Time)  RETURN Month_Number;
  FUNCTION Day   (Date : Time)  RETURN Day_Number;
  FUNCTION Seconds (Date : Time) RETURN Day_Duration;

  PROCEDURE Split (Date: IN  Time;
                   Year     : OUT Year_Number;
                   Month    : OUT Month_Number;
                   Day      : OUT Day_Number;
                   Seconds  : OUT Day_Duration);

  FUNCTION Clock RETURN Time;

  FUNCTION "<"  (Left, Right : Time)      RETURN Boolean;
  FUNCTION "<=" (Left, Right : Time)      RETURN Boolean;
  FUNCTION ">"  (Left, Right : Time)      RETURN Boolean;
  FUNCTION ">=" (Left, Right : Time)      RETURN Boolean;

  FUNCTION "+" (Left : Time;     Right : Duration) RETURN Time;
  FUNCTION "+" (Left : Duration; Right : Time)     RETURN Time;
  FUNCTION "-" (Left : Time;     Right : Duration) RETURN Time;
  FUNCTION "-" (Left : Time;     Right : Time)     RETURN Duration;
  Time_Error : EXCEPTION;

PRIVATE

  -- not specified by the language

END Ada.Calendar;
```

APPENDIX F

Specifications of the Ada Math Libraries

This appendix, adapted from the *Ada 95 Reference Manual*, Sections A.5.1 and A.5.2, gives the specifications for the packages Ada.Numerics, Ada.Numerics. Elementary_Functions, and Ada.Numerics.Float_Random, and the generic package Ada.Numerics.Discrete_Random.

```
PACKAGE Ada.Numerics IS

  Argument_Error : EXCEPTION;
  Pi : CONSTANT :=
    3.14159_26535_89793_23846_26433_83279_50288_41971_69399_37511;
  e  : CONSTANT :=
    2.71828_18284_59045_23536_02874_71352_66249_77572_47093_69996;

END Ada.Numerics;

PACKAGE Ada.Numerics.Elementary_Functions IS

  FUNCTION Sqrt     (X            : Float)        RETURN Float;
  FUNCTION Log      (X            : Float)        RETURN Float;
  FUNCTION Log      (X, Base      : Float)        RETURN Float;
  FUNCTION Exp      (X            : Float)        RETURN Float;
  FUNCTION "**"     (Left, Right  : Float)        RETURN Float;

  FUNCTION Sin      (X            : Float)        RETURN Float;
  FUNCTION Sin      (X, Cycle     : Float)        RETURN Float;
  FUNCTION Cos      (X            : Float)        RETURN Float;
  FUNCTION Cos      (X, Cycle     : Float)        RETURN Float;
  FUNCTION Tan      (X            : Float)        RETURN Float;
  FUNCTION Tan      (X, Cycle     : Float)        RETURN Float;
  FUNCTION Cot      (X            : Float)        RETURN Float;
  FUNCTION Cot      (X, Cycle     : Float)        RETURN Float;

  FUNCTION Arcsin   (X            : Float)        RETURN Float;
  FUNCTION Arcsin   (X, Cycle     : Float)        RETURN Float;
  FUNCTION Arccos   (X            : Float)        RETURN Float;
  FUNCTION Arccos   (X, Cycle     : Float)        RETURN Float;
  FUNCTION Arctan   (Y            : Float;
                     X            : Float := 1.0) RETURN Float;
  FUNCTION Arctan   (Y            : Float;
                     X            : Float := 1.0;
                     Cycle        : Float)        RETURN Float;
  FUNCTION Arccot   (X            : Float;
                     Y            : Float := 1.0) RETURN Float;
  FUNCTION Arccot   (X            : Float;
                     Y            : Float := 1.0;
                     Cycle        : Float)        RETURN Float;
```

```
FUNCTION Sinh    (X            : Float)        RETURN Float;
FUNCTION Cosh    (X            : Float)        RETURN Float;
FUNCTION Tanh    (X            : Float)        RETURN Float;
FUNCTION Coth    (X            : Float)        RETURN Float;
FUNCTION Arcsinh (X            : Float)        RETURN Float;
FUNCTION Arccosh (X            : Float)        RETURN Float;
FUNCTION Arctanh (X            : Float)        RETURN Float;
FUNCTION Arccoth (X            : Float)        RETURN Float;

END Ada.Numerics.Elementary_Functions;

PACKAGE Ada.Numerics.Float_Random IS

   -- Basic facilities

   TYPE Generator IS limited private;
   SUBTYPE Uniformly_Distributed IS Float RANGE 0.0 .. 1.0;
   FUNCTION Random (Gen : Generator) RETURN Uniformly_Distributed;

   PROCEDURE Reset (Gen        : IN Generator;
                    Initiator  : IN Integer);
   PROCEDURE Reset (Gen        : IN Generator);

   -- Advanced facilities

   TYPE State IS private;

   PROCEDURE Save  (Gen        : IN  Generator;
                    To_State   : OUT State);
   PROCEDURE Reset (Gen        : IN  Generator;
                    From_State : IN  State);

   Max_Image_Width : constant := implementation-defined integer value;

   FUNCTION Image (Of_State    : State)  RETURN String;
   FUNCTION Value (Coded_State : String) RETURN State;

PRIVATE
   . . . -- not specified by the language
END Ada.Numerics.Float_Random;

GENERIC
  TYPE Result_SubTYPE IS (<>);
  PACKAGE Ada.Numerics.Discrete_Random IS

   -- Basic facilities

   TYPE Generator IS limited private;

   FUNCTION Random (Gen : Generator) RETURN Result_SubTYPE;

   PROCEDURE Reset (Gen        : IN Generator;
                    Initiator  : IN Integer);
   PROCEDURE Reset (Gen        : IN Generator);

   -- Advanced facilities

   TYPE State IS private;

   PROCEDURE Save  (Gen        : IN  Generator;
                    To_State   : OUT State);
```

```
PROCEDURE Reset (Gen        : IN  Generator;
                 From_State : IN  State);

Max_Image_Width : constant := implementation-defined integer value;

FUNCTION Image (Of_State    : State)  RETURN String;
FUNCTION Value (Coded_State : String) RETURN State;

PRIVATE
   . . . -- not specified by the language
END Ada.Numerics.Discrete_Random;
```

APPENDIX G

Specification of the Ada String Libraries Used in this Book

This appendix, adapted from the *Ada 95 Reference Manual*, Section A.3, gives the specifications for the packages Ada.Characters.Handling, Ada.Strings, Ada.Strings.Maps, and Ada.Strings.Fixed. Not shown are Ada.Strings.Bounded and Ada.Strings.Unbounded, which have functionality similar to Ada.Strings.Fixed.

```
PACKAGE Ada.Characters.Handling IS
  PRAGMA Preelaborate(Handling);

    --Character classification  FUNCTIONs

  FUNCTION Is_Control          (Item : IN Character) RETURN Boolean;
  FUNCTION Is_Graphic          (Item : IN Character) RETURN Boolean;
  FUNCTION Is_Letter           (Item : IN Character) RETURN Boolean;
  FUNCTION Is_Lower            (Item : IN Character) RETURN Boolean;
  FUNCTION Is_Upper            (Item : IN Character) RETURN Boolean;
  FUNCTION Is_Basic            (Item : IN Character) RETURN Boolean;
  FUNCTION Is_Digit            (Item : IN Character) RETURN Boolean;
  FUNCTION Is_Decimal_Digit    (Item : IN Character) RETURN Boolean
    RENAMES Is_Digit;
  FUNCTION Is_Hexadecimal_Digit (Item : IN Character) RETURN Boolean;
  FUNCTION Is_Alphanumeric     (Item : IN Character) RETURN Boolean;
  FUNCTION Is_Special          (Item : IN Character) RETURN Boolean;

    --Conversion functions for Character and String

  FUNCTION To_Lower (Item : IN Character) RETURN Character;
  FUNCTION To_Upper (Item : IN Character) RETURN Character;
  FUNCTION To_Basic (Item : IN Character) RETURN  Character;

  FUNCTION To_Lower (Item : IN String) RETURN String;
  FUNCTION To_Upper (Item : IN String) RETURN String;
  FUNCTION To_Basic (Item : IN String) RETURN String;

    --Classifications of and conversions between
    --Character and ISO_646

SUBTYPE ISO_646 IS
  Character RANGE Character'Val(0) .. Character'Val(127);
```

```
    FUNCTION Is_ISO_646 (Item : IN Character) RETURN Boolean;
    FUNCTION Is_ISO_646 (Item : IN String)    RETURN Boolean;

    FUNCTION To_ISO_646 (Item       : IN Character;
                         Substitute : IN ISO_646 := ' ')

     RETURN ISO_646;

    FUNCTION To_ISO_646 (Item       : IN String;
                         Substitute : IN ISO_646 := ' ')

     RETURN String;

      -- Classifications of and conversions between
      -- Wide_Character and Character.

    FUNCTION Is_Character (Item : IN Wide_Character) RETURN Boolean;
    FUNCTION Is_String    (Item : IN Wide_String)    RETURN Boolean;

    FUNCTION To_Character (Item       : IN Wide_Character;
                           Substitute : IN Character := ' ')
     RETURN Character;

    FUNCTION To_String    (Item       : IN Wide_String;
                           Substitute : IN Character := ' ')
     RETURN String;

    FUNCTION To_Wide_Character (Item : IN Character)
      RETURN Wide_Character;

    FUNCTION To_Wide_String    (Item : IN String)  RETURN Wide_String;

END Ada.Characters.Handling;


PACKAGE Ada.Strings IS
  PRAGMA Pure(Strings);

  Space      : constant Character      := ' ';
  Wide_Space : constant Wide_Character := ' ';

  Length_Error, Pattern_Error, Index_Error, Translation_Error :
    EXCEPTION;

  TYPE Alignment  IS (Left, Right, Center);
  TYPE Truncation IS (Left, Right, Error);
  TYPE Membership IS (Inside, Outside);
  TYPE Direction  IS (Forward, Backward);
  TYPE Trim_End   IS (Left, Right, Both);

END Ada.Strings;


PACKAGE Ada.Strings.Maps IS
  PRAGMA Preelaborate(Maps);

  -- Representation for a set of character values:
  TYPE Character_Set IS private;

  Null_Set : constant Character_Set;
```

```
TYPE Character_Range IS
  RECORD
     Low  : Character;
     High : Character;
  END RECORD;
-- Represents Character RANGE Low. .High

TYPE Character_Ranges IS array (Positive RANGE <>) OF Character_Range;

FUNCTION To_Set    (Ranges : IN  Character_Ranges)
  RETURN Character_Set;

FUNCTION To_Set    (Span   : IN  Character_Range)
  RETURN Character_Set;

FUNCTION To_Ranges (Set    : IN  Character_Set)
  RETURN Character_Ranges;

 FUNCTION "="   (Left, Right : IN Character_Set) RETURN Boolean;

FUNCTION "NOT" (Right : IN Character_Set)
  RETURN Character_Set;
FUNCTION "AND" (Left, Right : IN Character_Set)
  RETURN Character_Set;
FUNCTION "OR"  (Left, Right : IN Character_Set)
  RETURN Character_Set;
FUNCTION "XOR" (Left, Right : IN Character_Set)
  RETURN Character_Set;
FUNCTION "-"   (Left, Right : IN Character_Set)
  RETURN Character_Set;

FUNCTION Is_In (Element : IN Character;
                Set     : IN Character_Set)
  RETURN Boolean;

 FUNCTION Is_Subset (Elements : IN Character_Set;
                     Set      : IN Character_Set)
   RETURN Boolean;

 FUNCTION "<=" (Left  : IN Character_Set;
                Right : IN Character_Set)
   RETURN Boolean RENAMES Is_Subset;

-- Alternative representation for a set of character values:
SUBTYPE Character_Sequence IS String;

FUNCTION To_Set (Sequence  : IN Character_Sequence)
  RETURN Character_Set;
FUNCTION To_Set (Singleton : IN Character) RETURN Character_Set;

FUNCTION To_Sequence (Set  : IN Character_Set)
  RETURN Character_Sequence;

-- Representation for a character to character mapping:
TYPE Character_Mapping IS PRIVATE;

FUNCTION Value (Map     : IN Character_Mapping;
                Element : IN Character)
  RETURN Character;

Identity : constant Character_Mapping;
```

```
   FUNCTION To_Mapping (From, To : IN Character_Sequence)
     RETURN Character_Mapping;

   FUNCTION To_Domain (Map : IN Character_Mapping)
     RETURN Character_Sequence;
   FUNCTION To_Range  (Map : IN Character_Mapping)
     RETURN Character_Sequence;

   TYPE Character_Mapping_Function IS
      ACCESS  FUNCTION (From : IN Character) RETURN Character;

PRIVATE
   . . . -- not specified by the language
END Ada.Strings.Maps;

WITH Ada.Strings.Maps;
PACKAGE Ada.Strings.Fixed IS
  PRAGMA Preelaborate(Fixed);

-- "Copy" PROCEDURE for strings of possibly different lengths

   PROCEDURE Move (Source  : IN  String;
                   Target  : OUT String;
                   Drop    : IN  Truncation := Error;
                   Justify : IN  Alignment  := Left;
                   Pad     : IN  Character  := Space);

-- Search subprograms

   FUNCTION Index (Source  : IN String;
                   Pattern : IN String;
                   Going   : IN Direction := Forward;
                   Mapping : IN Maps.Character_Mapping
                              := Maps.Identity)
     RETURN Natural;

   FUNCTION Index (Source  : IN String;
                   Pattern : IN String;
                   Going   : IN Direction := Forward;
                   Mapping : IN Maps.Character_Mapping_Function)
     RETURN Natural;

   FUNCTION Index (Source : IN String;
                   Set    : IN Maps.Character_Set;
                   Test   : IN Membership := Inside;
                   Going  : IN Direction  := Forward)
     RETURN Natural;

   FUNCTION Index_Non_Blank (Source : IN String;
                             Going  : IN Direction := Forward)
     RETURN Natural;

   FUNCTION Count (Source  : IN String;
                   Pattern : IN String;
                   Mapping : IN Maps.Character_Mapping
                              := Maps.Identity)
     RETURN Natural;

   FUNCTION Count (Source  : IN String;
                   Pattern : IN String;
                   Mapping : IN Maps.Character_Mapping_Function)
     RETURN Natural;
```

```
FUNCTION Count (Source    : IN String;
                Set       : IN Maps.Character_Set)
   RETURN Natural;

PROCEDURE Find_Token (Source : IN String;
                      Set    : IN Maps.Character_Set;
                      Test   : IN Membership;
                      First  : OUT Positive;
                      Last   : OUT Natural);

   -- String translation subprograms

FUNCTION Translate (Source  : IN String;
                    Mapping : IN Maps.Character_Mapping)
   RETURN String;

PROCEDURE Translate (Source  : IN out String;
                     Mapping : IN Maps.Character_Mapping);

FUNCTION Translate (Source  : IN String;
                    Mapping : IN Maps.Character_Mapping_Function)
   RETURN String;

PROCEDURE Translate (Source  : IN out String;
                     Mapping : IN Maps.Character_Mapping_Function);

   -- String transformation subprograms

FUNCTION Replace_Slice (Source  : IN String;
                        Low     : IN Positive;
                        High    : IN Natural;
                        By      : IN String)
   RETURN String;

PROCEDURE Replace_Slice (Source  : IN out String;
                         Low     : IN Positive;
                         High    : IN Natural;
                         By      : IN String;
                         Drop    : IN Truncation := Error;
                         Justify : IN Alignment  := Left;
                         Pad     : IN Character   := Space);

FUNCTION Insert (Source   : IN String;
                 Before   : IN Positive;
                 New_Item : IN String)
   RETURN String;

PROCEDURE Insert (Source   : IN out String;
                  Before   : IN Positive;
                  New_Item : IN String;
                  Drop     : IN Truncation := Error);

FUNCTION Overwrite (Source   : IN String;
                    Position : IN Positive;
                    New_Item : IN String)
   RETURN String;

PROCEDURE Overwrite (Source   : IN out String;
                     Position : IN Positive;
                     New_Item : IN String;
                     Drop     : IN Truncation := Right);
```

```
      FUNCTION Delete (Source  : IN String;
                       From     : IN Positive;
                       Through : IN Natural)
          RETURN String;

      PROCEDURE Delete (Source  : IN out String;
                        From     : IN Positive;
                        Through : IN Natural;
                        Justify : IN Alignment := Left;
                        Pad      : IN Character := Space);

--String selector subprograms

      FUNCTION Trim (Source : IN String;
                     Side   : IN Trim_End)

          RETURN String;

      PROCEDURE Trim (Source  : IN out String;
                      Side     : IN Trim_End;
                      Justify : IN Alignment := Left;
                      Pad      : IN Character := Space);

      FUNCTION Trim (Source : IN String;
                     Left   : IN Maps.Character_Set;
                     Right  : IN Maps.Character_Set)
          RETURN String;

      PROCEDURE Trim (Source  : IN out String;
                      Left     : IN Maps.Character_Set;
                      Right    : IN Maps.Character_Set;
                      Justify : IN Alignment := Strings.Left;
                      Pad      : IN Character := Space);

      FUNCTION Head (Source : IN String;
                     Count  : IN Natural;
                     Pad    : IN Character := Space)
          RETURN String;

      PROCEDURE Head (Source  : IN out String;
                      Count    : IN Natural;
                      Justify : IN Alignment := Left;
                      Pad      : IN Character := Space);

      FUNCTION Tail (Source : IN String;
                     Count  : IN Natural;
                     Pad    : IN Character := Space)
          RETURN String;

      PROCEDURE Tail (Source  : IN out String;
                      Count    : IN Natural;
                      Justify : IN Alignment := Left;
                      Pad      : IN Character := Space);

      --String constructor  FUNCTIONs

      FUNCTION "*" (Left  : IN Natural;
                    Right : IN Character) RETURN String;

      FUNCTION "*" (Left  : IN Natural;
                    Right : IN String) RETURN String;

END Ada.Strings.Fixed;
```

APPENDIX H

Summary of Ada Execution-Time Exceptions

This appendix summarizes the predefined Ada exceptions. Ada distinguishes exceptions defined in the language from those defined in standard packages. The summary should help students to write exception handlers and to interpret run-time messages that report unhandled exceptions propagated out of a main program.

EXCEPTIONS DEFINED IN THE LANGUAGE

The following exceptions are predefined in the Ada language:

- `Constraint_Error` is raised if an attempt is made to store a value in a variable that is out of range for that variable—that is, out of the range of the variable's type or subtype. It will also be raised if an attempt is made to dereference a null access value (pointer), or to copy a string or similar array into another of a different size, or to copy a variant record object into another that is constrained to a different value of the discriminant.

- `Program_Error` is raised in a number of situations unlikely to arise in courses that use this book. For example, WITH-ing a number of packages may cause an attempted call of a subprogram whose body has not yet been elaborated. This occurrence is rare in student projects with simple package dependencies, but arises occasionally in industry.

- `Storage_Error` is raised if the storage pool is exhausted by dynamic allocation, typically in an infinite loop in whose body a NEW call is executed. The exception is also raised if the run-time stack is exhausted by subprogram calls—for example, by an infinite recursion.

- `Tasking_Error` is raised if two concurrent Ada tasks are unable to communicate.

EXCEPTION DEFINED IN `ADA.CALENDAR`

One exception is defined in the package `Ada.Calendar`:

• `Ada.Calendar.Time_Error` is raised if the actual parameters in a call of `Ada.Calendar.Time_Of` do not form a valid date, or if subtracting two values of type `Ada.Calendar.Time` results in a value that lies outside the range of the predefined type `Duration`.

EXCEPTION DEFINED IN `ADA.NUMERICS`

One exception is defined in the package `Ada.Numerics`:

• The `Argument_Error` exception is raised by a subprogram in a child unit of `Ada.Numerics` to signal that one or more of the actual subprogram parameters are outside the domain of the corresponding mathematical function.

EXCEPTIONS DEFINED IN `ADA.TEXT_IO`

The following exceptions can be raised by `Ada.Text_IO` operations:

• `Ada.Text_IO.Status_Error` is raised by an attempt to operate on a file that is not open, and by an attempt to open a file that is already open.

• `Ada.Text_IO.Mode_Error` is raised by an attempt to read from, or to test for the end of, a file whose current mode is `Out_File`, and also by an attempt to write to a file whose current mode is `In_File`. This exception is also raised by specifying a file whose current mode is `Out_File` in a call of `Set_Input`, `Skip_Line`, `End_Of_Line`, `Skip_Page`, or `End_Of_Page`, or by specifying a file whose current mode is `In_File` in a call of `Set_Output`, `Set_Line_Length`, `Set_Page_Length`, `Line_Length`, `Page_Length`, `New_Line`, or `New_Page`.

• `Ada.Text_IO.Name_Error` is raised by a call of `Create` or `Open` if the string given for the parameter `Name` does not allow the identification of an external file. For example, this exception is raised if the string is improper, or, alternatively, if either no external file or more than one external file corresponds to the string. In student programs, this exception is often raised if the *case* of the file name given in the procedure call does not agree with the case of the name in the student's directory. This is especially common in UNIX, in which file names are case-sensitive.

• `Ada.Text_IO.Use_Error` is raised if an operation is attempted that is not possible for reasons that depend on characteristics of the external file. For example, this exception is raised by the procedure `Create` if, among other circumstances, the given mode is `Out_File` but the form specifies an input-only device, or the parameter `Form` specifies invalid access rights, or an external file with the given name already exists and overwriting is not allowed.

- `Ada.Text_IO.Device_Error` is raised if an input-output operation cannot be completed because of a malfunction of the underlying system. This should rarely occur in a student program.

- `Ada.Text_IO.End_Error` is raised by an attempt to skip (read past) the end of a file. In student programs, this may happen if the file terminator is immediately preceded by a line terminator. In this case, a solution is to include a handler for this exception in the file input section of the program. Sometimes inserting a `Ada.Text_IO.Skip_Line` call in the file input loop will work as well.

- `Ada.Text_IO.Data_Error` is raised by a procedure `Get` if the input character sequence fails to satisfy the required syntax or if the value input does not belong to the range of the required type or subtype. Common causes are entering an integer or character literal where a `Float` literal is required, and entering an invalid enumeration literal.

- `Ada.Text_IO.Layout_Error` is raised by `Col`, `Line`, or `Page` if the value returned exceeds `Count'Last`. The exception `Layout_Error` is also raised on output by an attempt to set column or line numbers in excess of specified maximum line or page lengths, respectively (excluding the unbounded cases). It is also raised by an attempt to `Put` too many characters to a string.

APPENDIX I

Ada Hints for Pascal Users

Ada is a language that is, in many respects, similar to Pascal. However, it is not a "superset" of Pascal. The statement syntax is slightly different (simpler, in the opinion of many) and many familiar Pascal features are implemented somewhat differently. As a learning aid to those experienced in Pascal but new to Ada, this appendix summarizes areas in which the languages differ enough to cause some difficulty in the form of compilation errors.

The most important difference between Ada and Pascal is that the strong Ada standard, coupled with the compiler validation process, ensures that the same Ada language is accepted by all compilers. Syntactic extensions, such as those found in most useful Pascal systems, do not occur in Ada. On the other hand, the Ada language defined by the standard covers nearly all the features of the Pascal extensions.

DECLARATIONS AND DECLARATION ORDER

The Pascal standard requires a rigid declaration order (constants, types, variables, subprograms) that is relaxed by some implementations. Ada declaration order is somewhat more flexible. The Ada standard refers to "basic declarative items" and "later declarative items." Among the former are declarations of constants, types, and variables; among the latter are functions and procedures. (Other declarations are beyond the scope of this book.) In the declarative part of a program or subprogram, basic declarative items can be freely intermixed—with the understanding, of course, that everything must be declared before it is referenced. All basic items must precede all later items; put simply, subprogram declarations must follow the others.

In Pascal, the words TYPE, CONST, and VAR appear only once in a declarative section. In Ada, each type or subtype declaration must be opened by TYPE or SUBTYPE, respectively. A constant is declared as, for example,

```
FirstLetter: CONSTANT Character := 'A';
```

and the reserved word VAR is not used at all; a variable is simply declared as, for example,

```
Sum : Integer;
```

A record type declaration must be closed by END RECORD.

CONTROL STRUCTURES

All control structures are fully bracketed in Ada, including `IF-END IF`, `LOOP-END LOOP`, `CASE-END CASE`. Further, a semicolon terminates a statement; it does not separate statements, as in Pascal. This yields a syntax that is easier to use correctly than Pascal's. For example, the Pascal statement

```
IF X < Y THEN
  A := B;
```

is written in Ada as

```
IF X < Y THEN
  A := B;
END IF;
```

and the Pascal statement

```
IF X < Y THEN
  BEGIN
    A := B;
    Z := X
  END
ELSE
  BEGIN
    A := X;
    Z := B
  END;
```

is written in Ada as

```
IF X < Y THEN
  A := B;
  Z := X;
ELSE
  A := X;
  Z := B;
END IF;
```

   The fully bracketed syntax ensures that a "dangling `ELSE`" cannot be written.
   `FOR` loop control variables are declared implicitly; this is the only exception to the rule that everything must be explicitly declared. A `FOR` counter is local to the loop body. Declaring the loop counter as a variable, as in Pascal, does no real harm, but it declares a different variable, which is then hidden by the actual loop counter and therefore is not visible in the loop body.
   `FOR` loop ranges are often stated as type or subtype names, as in

```
FOR Count IN IndexRange LOOP
```

   Ada has no `REPEAT` loop structure; instead, use `LOOP-END LOOP` with an `EXIT WHEN` clause at the bottom of the loop.
   The choice variable in a `CASE` statement must be of a discrete (integer or enumeration) type; the various `CASE` choices must cover, in a nonoverlapping fashion, all possible values of the choice variable.

TYPES AND DATA STRUCTURES

Two-dimensional arrays are *not* arrays of arrays. Therefore, A(J)(K) is *not* the same as A(J,K): The former indeed refers to an array of arrays, the latter to a two-dimensional array. One reason these are different structures in Ada is that the standard does *not* specify the storage mapping (row- or column-major) for multidimensional arrays. This allows a clever implementer to use a nonlinear mapping, for example. In practice, most current Ada compilers use a row-major mapping, in keeping with Pascal and C rules.

The type of a record field must always be a type name; it cannot be an anonymous type such as ARRAY or RECORD. To build hierarchical record types, build the lower-level ones first, then use their names as fields in the higher-level ones.

There is nothing in Ada that corresponds to Pascal's WITH. All record and array references must always be fully qualified.

Variant records are much more tightly controlled in Ada than in Pascal. It is not possible to write a *free union*, or variant record without a discriminant (tag field). In Pascal and C, free unions are frequently used to evade type checking, but cannot be used for this purpose in Ada. (Ada has a generic function called Unchecked_Conversion that indeed is used to evade type checking, but its use is beyond the scope of this book).

There is no SET type in Ada. A package giving the equivalent functionality is presented in full as Programs 5.15 and 5.16.

TYPE AND SUBTYPE COMPATIBILITY

This matter is discussed at length throughout the book. The most important thing to remember is that Ada uses named type equivalence, not structural equivalence. For example, given the declarations

```
A, B: ARRAY(1..10) OF Float;
C   : ARRAY(1..10) OF Float;
```

the array assignment statements

```
A := B;
C := B;
```

are both invalid, because each of the three arrays has a different anonymous type, assigned by the compiler. (Some Pascal compilers would allow the first assignment.) To allow the array assignments, one must give a type name:

```
TYPE List IS ARRAY(1..10) OF Float;
A, B: List;
C: List;
```

Both assignments are now valid. The Pascal style of using anonymous types is not used in this book, and we recommend not using it.

SUBPROGRAM PARAMETERS

Ada's parameter modes `IN`, `OUT`, and `IN OUT` are only roughly equivalent to the value and `VAR` parameters of Pascal.

Within the body of a subprogram, `IN` parameters can only be read, never written. The main difference between `OUT` and `IN OUT` parameters is that the current value of an actual `IN OUT` parameter is passed to the procedure, whereas, in general, the value of an actual `OUT` parameter is not passed, and can therefore be assumed to be undefined until given a value by the subprogram. Functions cannot have `OUT` or `IN OUT` parameters.

No efficiency is gained by passing as `IN OUT` an array to be used as an `IN` parameter. This is common in Pascal, where large arrays are usually passed as `VAR` parameters. Pascal requires `VAR` parameters to be passed by reference and value parameters to be copied. The rules in Ada are different: Scalar parameters are always passed by value/result, whatever their mode. Ada permits composite (array and record) parameters to be passed by value/result, but compilers almost never do this, especially if the composites are large. Practical compilers pass arrays and large records by reference even if they are `IN`; since `IN` parameters cannot be written, there is no danger of changing their values in the calling program.

In the case of scalar `OUT` and `IN OUT` parameters, the values are copied back to the calling program at *normal* completion of the procedure call. That is, if the procedure call completes by propagating an exception to the caller, the parameter values are not copied back and therefore the caller still has the original values.

The input/output statements in Ada are ordinary procedure calls, which means that only a single integer, float, character, string, or enumeration value can be read or displayed with each call of `Get` or `Put`. One cannot supply an arbitrary number of parameters to input/output statements, as one would do in Pascal. Doing so will surely result in compilation errors of the form "unmatched procedure call" when the compiler searches for a `Get` or `Put` whose expected parameters match the supplied ones.

PACKAGES AND THEIR RELATION TO UNITS

Units are not part of the ISO Pascal standard, but are provided by many extended Pascal systems, including Borland's Turbo and Symantec's Think series. Units are a rough equivalent of Ada packages, with two important differences:

- Whereas a unit interface is generally a part of the same file as the corresponding body, an Ada package should normally be divided into separate files for the specification and the body. Some compilers require this separation. Separation is, in any case, highly recommended, because in Ada, recompiling a package *specification* usually forces recompilation of all clients of that package, whereas recompiling a package *body* does not.

- Pascal systems provide no direct equivalent to an Ada `PRIVATE` type.

THE USE OF IS AND THE SEMICOLON

Endless grief awaits Ada users who confuse the use of the semicolon with the use of
IS; with some compilers, this leads to long sequences of propagation error messages.
The worst offense is using a semicolon instead of IS in a subprogram declaration, as
one would do in Pascal.

```
PROCEDURE DoSomething(X : Integer); ---- <---- this means TROUBLE!

  -- declarations

BEGIN

  -- statements

END DoSomething;
```

The problem is that it is *legal* to use the semicolon, but the meaning is not what you
expect. The line

```
PROCEDURE DoSomething(X : Integer);
```

is not a declaration, but a procedure *specification*, similar to a Pascal FORWARD specification. Confusing the semicolon with the IS is therefore almost guaranteed to lead to
a large number of propagation errors from the compiler: Since the Ada parser treats the
statement as a specification, it is confused by the declarations and BEGIN-END block
that follow, which seem to be out of context and not well-formed. IS is precisely the
way that Ada knows a procedure *body* is expected next; the user forgets this at his or
her peril.

Subprogram specifications appear as a part of package specifications, and can also
be useful in contexts where a Pascal FORWARD would be written. In the latter case, the
first line of the body must be *identical* to the specification, except for replacing the
semicolon with IS. This is different from Pascal, where the parameter list is not
repeated.

APPENDIX J

Timing an Ada Program on a Time-Sharing System

Section 3.6 presents some ideas for measuring the execution time of an Ada program or part of a program. That section points out that `Ada.Calendar.Clock` returns the actual time of day, not the CPU time of the program. On a single-user personal computer, the result of subtracting one time-of-day value from another is a close approximation to the elapsed CPU time. However, on a time-sharing system the difference between two time-of-day values may not even roughly approximate the CPU time, because the user's program may be getting only small slices of time along with many other user programs.

Unfortunately, Ada provides no standard CPU-time service analogous to `Ada.Calendar.Clock`. It is, therefore, necessary to call an operating system (OS) service to get the CPU time. The form and structure of the system service varies from one OS to another, and differences can be found even among the various dialects of UNIX. This appendix shows a single example of a CPU time function, which has been tested under Sun/Solaris and seems to be similar to that of other UNIX versions. Check your local OS manuals for further details.

THE CPUCLOCK PACKAGE REVISITED

Programs 3.17 and 3.18 presented a CPU timing package suitable for use on single-user personal computers. For convenience, the specification and body are repeated here as Programs J.1 and J.2, respectively.

Program J.1 Specification for CPU Timing Package (Repeated from Program 3.17)

```
PACKAGE CPUClock IS

  ------------------------------------------------------------------
  --| Specification for a package to do CPU timing of algorithms
  --| Author: Michael B. Feldman, The George Washington University
  --| Last Modified: October 1995
  ------------------------------------------------------------------

  SUBTYPE CPUSecond IS Float RANGE 0.0 .. Float'Last;
  -- We make CPUSecond a Float type so the usual operations are available

  PROCEDURE ResetCPUTime;
  -- Pre:  none
  -- Post: resets a CPU timer
```

```
FUNCTION CPUTime RETURN CPUSecond;
-- Pre:  none
-- Post: returns the number of CPUSeconds since the last reset

END CPUClock;
```

Program J.2 Body of CPU Timing Package, Personal Computer Version

```
WITH Ada.Calendar; USE Ada.Calendar;
PACKAGE BODY CPUClock IS
-------------------------------------------------------------------------
--| This body is compatible with Ada compilers whose output
--| runs on single-user IBM-PC-family and Apple Macintosh computers
--| Author: Michael B. Feldman, The George Washington University
--| Last Modified: October 1995
-------------------------------------------------------------------------

  SavedTime : Ada.Calendar.Time;

  PROCEDURE ResetCPUTime IS
  BEGIN
    SavedTime := Ada.Calendar.Clock;
  END ResetCPUTime;

  FUNCTION CPUTime RETURN CPUSecond IS
  BEGIN
    RETURN CPUSecond (Ada.Calendar."-"(Ada.Calendar.Clock,SavedTime));
  END CPUTime;

BEGIN -- initialization of package

  -- this statement is executed once, when the package is elaborated,
  -- i.e., just before its client program starts executing

  ResetCPUTime;

END CPUClock;
```

Section 3.6 points out that the package *specification* is portable; using the package with a time-sharing system entails rewriting the *body* to suit the requirements of the local OS.

Program J.3 repeats the test program from Program 3.19, which should be usable without change on a time-sharing system.

Program J.3 Test of CPU Timing Package

```
WITH Ada.Text_IO;
WITH CPUClock;
USE TYPE CPUClock.CPUSecond;
WITH Ada.Integer_Text_IO;
WITH Ada.Float_Text_IO;
PROCEDURE TestClok IS
-------------------------------------------------------------------
--| An example program to show how the CPUClock operations
--| can be used
--| Author: Michael B. Feldman, The George Washington University
--| Last Modified: October 1995
-------------------------------------------------------------------
```

```
      TrialTime        : CPUClock.CPUSecond;   -- CPU time for each trial
      TotalTime        : CPUClock.CPUSecond;   -- total time for all trials
      NumberOfTrials   : CONSTANT Integer := 10;
      NumberOfCycles   : CONSTANT Integer := 5;

      Maxindex         : CONSTANT Integer := 50;
      A                : ARRAY (1 .. Maxindex, 1 .. Maxindex) OF Integer;

BEGIN -- TestClok

   TotalTime := 0.0;

   FOR Trial IN 1 .. NumberOfTrials LOOP

      CPUClock.ResetCPUTime;

      -- this loop runs each trial a number of times before
      -- reading the clock, which allows the time to build up to
      -- a more easily measured value
      FOR Cycle IN 1 .. NumberOfCycles LOOP

         -- this pair of loops is really the algorithm being timed;
         -- for MaxIndex = 50 we are doing 2,500 multiplications
         FOR Row IN 1 .. Maxindex LOOP
           FOR Col IN 1 .. Maxindex LOOP
             A (Row, Col) := Row * Col;
           END LOOP;
         END LOOP;

      END LOOP;

      -- read clock; accumulate total time
      TrialTime := CPUClock.CPUTime;
      TotalTime := TotalTime + TrialTime;
      -- display results for this trial
      Ada.Text_IO.Put(Item => "Trial ");
      Ada.Integer_Text_IO.Put(Item => Trial, Width => 1);
      Ada.Text_IO.Put (Item => " time used ");
      Ada.Float_Text_IO.Put
        (Item => TrialTime, Fore => 1, Aft => 2, Exp => 0);
      Ada.Text_IO.Put (Item => " seconds; total time so far ");
      Ada.Float_Text_IO.Put
        (Item => TotalTime, Fore => 1, Aft => 2, Exp => 0);
      Ada.Text_IO.Put(Item => " seconds.");
      Ada.Text_IO.New_Line;
      Ada.Text_IO.New_Line;

   END LOOP;

END TestClok;
```

A UNIX VERSION OF THE CPUCLOCK BODY

Program J.4 shows a package body suitable for Sun/Solaris (the version of UNIX delivered by Sun Microsystems).

Program J.4 Body of CPU Timing Package, Solaris Version

```
PACKAGE BODY CPUClock IS
-------------------------------------------------------------------------
--| Body of CPUClock, suitable for Sun/Solaris.
--| Other Unix systems may be similar but not identical.
--| Author: Michael B. Feldman, The George Washington University
--| Last Modified: January 1996
-------------------------------------------------------------------------
  FUNCTION unixtime RETURN Integer;
  PRAGMA Import (Convention => C, Entity => unixtime);
  -- We are writing a little C function to get the time from Unix,
  -- and importing it into this Ada package.

  Saved_Time: Integer;

  FUNCTION CPUTime RETURN CPUSecond IS
  BEGIN
    RETURN CPUSecond (unixtime - Saved_Time) / 60.0;
    -- The division by 60 is because UNIX is reporting the time in
    -- 60th's of a second.
  END CPUTime;

  PROCEDURE ResetCPUTime IS
  BEGIN
    Saved_Time := unixtime;
  END ResetCPUTime;
BEGIN -- initialization of package
  ResetCPUTime;
END CPUClock;
```

Comparing the two package bodies reveals much similarity between them; the difference in the UNIX version is that `ResetCPUTime` and `CPUTime` both call a small routine written in C, `unixtime`. The specification of this function is an ordinary Ada function specification:

```
FUNCTION unixtime RETURN Integer;
```

Instead of supplying an Ada body for this function, we indicate to the Ada compiler that the body is written in C and will be "imported" into the Ada program at link time:

```
PRAGMA Import (Convention => C, Entity => unixtime);
```

The function `unixtime` delivers the elapsed CPU time in units of 1/60 second. To meet the requirements of our package specification for a `Float` value in seconds, we divide by 60.0.

Finally, Program J.5 shows our small C routine. The details will be obvious to a programmer with some C experience; if you have none, the comments may be helpful. In any case, you may be able to use this function directly without understanding its details.

Program J.5 C Function to Retrieve CPU Time from UNIX

```
#include <sys/types.h>
#include <sys/times.h>
/*-------------------------------------------------------------------*/
/*| C function to report UNIX user-program execution time;          */
/*| returns time from program start to call time in units of 1/60 sec */
```

```
/*| This works with Sun/Solaris. Not all UNIX versions have the same  */
/*| CPU time calls; check your local UNIX manuals.                     */
/*| Author: Michael B. Feldman, The George Washington University       */
/*| Last Modified: February 1996                                       */
/*-------------------------------------------------------------------*/

int unixtime()   /* C function returning an integer value */
{
  struct tms TimeReading;          /* tms declared in sys/times.h   */

  times(&TimeReading);             /* times declared in sys/times.h */
  return(TimeReading.tms_utime);   /* returning the user time field */
                                   /* in 60ths of a second          */
}
```

As an example of putting this all together, consider the UNIX commands to compile and link everything using the GNAT compiler on Solaris. First, we compile the C function, which we assume is in the file `unixtime.c`:

```
gcc -c unixtime.c
```

which produces an object file `unixtime.o`. We then compile the specification and body of the Ada package, stored as `cpuclock.ads` and `cpuclock.adb`, respectively:

```
gcc -c cpuclock.ads
gcc -c cpuclock.adb
```

The package and C interface function are now compiled and ready to be used repeatedly. We now compile `testclok.adb`, the test program:

```
gcc -c testclok.adb
```

and then bind and link as follows:

```
gnatbl testclok.ali unixtime.o
```

which creates an executable `testclok`. Including `unixtime.o` on the command line is essential; it informs the linker that the C object file must be linked in with the overall program.

In this brief appendix, we have only scratched the surface of the interesting subject of multilanguage programming. In particular, this is sometimes necessary in order to have access to operating system services that are not directly provided by Ada.

Index